Basic Statistical Formulae

Descriptive Statistics

Variance (s^2)

$$s^2 = \frac{\Sigma X^2 - (\Sigma X)^2/N}{N - 1}$$

Standard deviation (s)

$$s = \sqrt{s^2}$$

Hinge Location

$$\frac{(\text{Median Location} + 1)}{2}$$

General Formula for z Score

$$\frac{\text{Score} - \text{Mean}}{\text{Std. Deviation}} \quad \text{or} \quad \frac{\text{Statistic} - \text{Parameter}}{\text{Std. Error of Statistic}}$$

z Score for an Observation

$$z = \frac{X - \bar{X}}{s}$$

Tests on Sample Means

Standard Error of the Mean ($s_{\bar{x}}$)

$$\frac{s_X}{\sqrt{N}}$$

z for $\bar{X}$ Given σ

$$z = \frac{(\bar{X} - \mu)}{\sigma_{\bar{X}}}$$

t for One Sample

$$t = \frac{\bar{X} - \mu}{s_{\bar{X}}} = \frac{\bar{X} - \mu}{\dfrac{s}{\sqrt{N}}}$$

Confidence Interval on μ

$$\text{CI} = \bar{X} \pm t_{.05}(s_{\bar{x}})$$

t for Two Related Samples

$$t = \bar{D}/s_{\bar{D}} = \frac{\bar{D}}{s_D/\sqrt{N}}$$

t for Two Independent Samples (Unpooled)

$$t = \frac{\bar{X}_1 - \bar{X}_2}{s_{\bar{x}_1 - \bar{x}_2}} = \frac{\bar{X}_1 - \bar{X}_2}{\sqrt{\dfrac{s_1^2}{N_1} + \dfrac{s_2^2}{N_2}}}$$

Pooled Variance (s_p^2)

$$s_p^2 = \frac{(N_1 - 1)s_1^2 + (N_2 - 1)s_2^2}{N_1 + N_2 - 2}$$

t for Two Independent Samples (Pooled)

$$t = \frac{\bar{X}_1 - \bar{X}_2}{s_{\bar{x}_1 - \bar{x}_2}} = \frac{\bar{X}_1 - \bar{X}_2}{\sqrt{\dfrac{s_p^2}{N_1} + \dfrac{s_p^2}{N_2}}}$$

Confidence Interval on $\mu_1 - \mu_2$

$$\text{CI} = (\bar{X}_1 - \bar{X}_2) \pm t_{.05}(s_{\bar{x}_1 - \bar{x}_2})$$

To Shawn,
Best of
luck...
Terra '97

FUNDAMENTAL STATISTICS
FOR THE
BEHAVIORAL SCIENCES

FUNDAMENTAL STATISTICS
FOR THE
BEHAVIORAL SCIENCES
THIRD EDITION

David C. Howell
Department of Psychology
UNIVERSITY OF VERMONT

DUXBURY PRESS
An Imprint of Wadsworth Publishing Company
Belmont, California

This book is dedicated to my father and the memory of my mother.

Duxbury Press

An Imprint of Wadsworth Publishing Company
A division of Wadsworth, Inc.

Editor: CURT HINRICHS
Editorial Assistant: MICHELLE O'DONNELL
Production: BOOKS BY DESIGN, INC.
Design: BOOKS BY DESIGN, INC.
Print Buyer: BARBARA BRITTON
Copy Editor: NANCY CAMPBELL WIRTES
Technical Illustrator: TECH GRAPHICS, INC.
Cover: BOOKS BY DESIGN, INC.
Cover Photograph: GRANT FAINT, © THE IMAGE BANK
Compositor: G & S TYPESETTERS, INC.
Printer: R. R. DONNELLEY & SONS, INC.

 This book is printed on acid-free recycled paper.

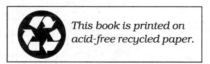

International Thomson Publishing
The trademark ITP is used under license.

© 1995 by Wadsworth, Inc. All rights reserved. No part of this book may be reproduced, stored in a retrieval system, or transcribed, in any form or by any means, without the prior written permission of the publisher, Wadsworth Publishing Company, Belmont, California 94002.

Printed in the United States of America
1 2 3 4 5 6 7 8 9 10—99 98 97 96 95

Library of Congress Cataloging-in-Publication Data
Howell, David C.
    Fundamental statistics for the behavioral sciences / David C.
  Howell. — 3rd ed.
      p.   cm.
    Includes bibliographical references and index.
    ISBN 0-534-23976-5
    1. Social sciences—Statistical methods.   2. Psychometrics.
  I. Title.
  HA29.H78   1995
    519.5—dc20   94-15870

Brief Contents

Contents

*Optional: This chapter may be omitted by an instructor with no loss in continuity.

Preface

Why Statistics?

Those of us who teach in this area hate to admit it, but statistics is seldom listed as the most sought after course on campus. You are probably enrolled because the faculty made this a required course. Under these conditions you have a right to ask "why?" and there are at least two good answers to that question. The traditional answer is that we want our students to learn a specific set of skills about data analysis (including formulae and procedures) so that they can understand the experimental literature and conduct analyses on their own data. The broader answer, and one that applies to perhaps a larger number of students, is that some more general facility with numbers and data in general is an important skill that has life-long and career-related value. Most of us, and not only those who do experimental work, frequently come across numerical data as part of our job, and some broad understanding of how to deal with those data is an important and marketable skill. It is my experience that students who have taken a course in statistics, even if they forget every technique they ever learned, have an understanding of numerical data that puts them ahead of their colleagues. And in a world increasingly dominated by quantitative data, that skill is more and more in demand. Many of my former students have told me that they were assigned an important task because they were the only one in their office who wasn't afraid of data.

Statistics is not really about numbers; it is about understanding our world. Certainly an important activity for statisticians is to answer such questions as whether cocaine taken in a novel context has more of an effect than cocaine taken in a familiar context. But let's not forget that what we are talking about here is drug addiction or the effect of the environment on learning and memory. The results of our experiment have a life beyond the somewhat limited world of the cognitive or social scientist. And let's also remember that the numbers that most people see do not relate to tightly controlled experiments, but to the implications of a traffic study for the development of a shopping center, the density of residential housing and its impact on the local school budget, and a marketing survey for a new product. All of these examples involve many of the basic statistical concepts covered in this book.

Why This Text?

Enough preaching on the value of a course in statistics. Presumably your instructor was convinced before he or she started reading, and I hope that students have become at least a bit more open minded. But the question remains, why should you use this book instead of another of the many available texts?

Part of the answer comes down to the matter of style. I have deliberately set out to make this book both interesting and useful for students and instructors. It is written in an informal style, every example is put in the context of an investigation that one might reasonably conduct, and almost all of the examples are taken from the published literature. It does not make much sense to ask people to learn a series of statistical procedures without supplying examples of situations in which those techniques would actually be applied.

This text is designed for an introductory statistics course in psychology, education, and other behavioral sciences. It does not presuppose a background in mathematics beyond high school algebra, and it emphasizes the logic of statistical procecures rather than their derivation.

Over the past ten years the world of data analysis has changed dramatically. Where we once sat down with a calculator and entered data by hand to solve formulae, we are now much more likely to use a statistical package running on a desktop computer. As the mechanics of doing statistics have changed, so too must our approach to teaching statistical procedures. While we cannot, and should not, forego all reference to formulae and computations, it is time that we relaxed our emphasis on them. And by relaxing the emphasis on computation, we free up the time to increase the emphasis on interpretation. That is what this book tries to do. It moves away from simply declaring group differences to be significant or not significant toward an explanation of what such differences mean relative to the purpose behind the experiment. **I like to think of it as moving toward an analysis of data and away from an analysis of numbers. It becomes less important to concentrate on whether there is a difference between two groups than to understand what that difference means.**

Unique Features

Several features of this book set it apart from other books written for the same audience. One of these was just noted: the use of examples from the research literature. I have attempted to choose studies that address problems of interest to students. Examples include the effect of context on heroin overdose, the relationship between daily stress and psychological symptoms, variables influencing course evaluations, the effect of early parental death on children's feelings of vulnerability, and variables controlling memory changes as a function of age. I want students to have some involvement in the questions being asked, and I want to illustrate that statistical analyses involve more than just applying a few equations.

A second feature of the book is the use of examples of computer analyses of data, for which hand-calculated solutions also appear. In most chapters a section is devoted to an example based on one of the major data analysis computer packages. The purpose of the example is to familiarize the student with the form of computer printouts and the kinds of information they contain. Each example also includes the particular program that generated the output, and those who wish may use these as templates for designing their own solutions. (I am not trying to teach students how to use Minitab or SPSS, but students will see similarities with results given here and any other statistical package.)

Data files for all of the examples and exercises used in the text are available on disk included in the **Instructors Resource Manual.** Tentatively, the data will also be available through an anonymous FTP (please contact your local Wadsworth representative or the author for further information). These files are formatted in ASCII, so they can be read by virtually any statistical program. The availability of these files makes it easy for students and instructors to incorporate any statistical package with the text.

For those interested in integrating a student version of a commercial statistical software, the publisher makes available **StataQuest** at a nominal price when purchased with the **Student Handbook.** StataQuest, from the developers of Stata, is a menu-driven, high-resolution graphical software giving students state-of-the-art capabilities at an incredibly low price. It is available in DOS and Macintosh versions.

In addition to the Answers to Selected Exercises in the back of this book, a **Student Handbook** is available for sale to students showing solutions for approximately half the exercises. These solutions include hints on how to approach the problem, comments on the purpose of the exercise and what it is intended to illustrate, and/or a statement on how to interpret the result. In addition, a tutorial showing how to use StataQuest for all the basic analyses in this book and instructions for conducting advanced research is included.

A third feature of this book is a more extensive than normal use of techniques generally included under the heading of exploratory data analysis (EDA). The intent was not to write a textbook of EDA techniques—only stem-and-leaf displays and boxplots are developed in any depth—but to emphasize the usefulness of those procedures in all data analyses. Thus, for example, the Minitab analysis in Figure 14.3 (page 259) includes stem-and-leaf displays and a check for outliers, skewed distributions, and so on. Exploratory data analysis allows you to take nearly any jumbled set of numbers and quickly put them in a form that you and others can understand. That is the first step toward making sense of the world around you.

New to This Edition

This book differs in several ways from the first two editions. I have benefited greatly from the feedback from instructors who have used earlier editions. Not only has that feedback been gratifying in terms of what people like about the book, but it has pointed out important areas that could be made clearer. One of the most important suggestions that I received was for the inclusion of a final worked example at the end of each chapter. The purpose of this example is to show the student each step that must be gone through to solve a problem in a logical and orderly manner. A second change is the inclusion of a greater number of tables and figures, especially in the early chapters, to supplement or elaborate the presentation in a visual way. Graphs are an ideal way to visualize what the data tell us.

The book includes over 350 homework exercises and answers to half of them. Approximately half of these exercises involve direct calculation, and the others require students to think about the whole process of data analysis. A number of homework problems have been added to the book, with a particular emphasis on problems that require students to think about the material. In addition, the last chapter includes a set of examples of actual research studies for which students are asked to decide upon the appropriate method of analysis. This is an area in which many people have difficulty, and these exercises are intended to help overcome this difficulty.

Finally, a greater effort has been made to involve students in the process of learning. Most of us have a tendency to nod our way through a text, assuming that because we have read the material we have understood it. I have tried in small ways to make you stop and think occasionally by asking simple questions such as "What do you think the results of this experiment will look like?" or "How does this relate to things you already know?" We aren't talking here about major educational innovation—most good teachers do the same things in class—but merely simple things to engage the reader. If you are a student, it will help your understanding considerably if you stop and think for just a few seconds. If you are the instructor, these questions can help you start some interesting discussions.

Organization and Coverage

This section is meant primarily for instructors, because frequent reference is made to terms that students cannot yet be expected to know. Students may wish to skip to the next section.

- The first seven chapters of the book are devoted to standard descriptive statistics, including ways of displaying data, measures of central tendency and variability, the normal distribution, and those aspects of probability that are directly applicable to what follows.

- Chapter 8 on hypothesis testing and sampling distributions serves as a nontechnical introduction to inferential statistics. That chapter was specifically designed to allow students to examine the underlying logic of hypothesis testing without simultaneously being concerned with learning a set of formulae and the intricacies of a statistical test.

- Chapters 9, 10, and 11 deal with correlation and regression, including, at the request of past users, a new chapter on multiple regression.

- Chapters 12–14 are devoted to tests on means, primarily t tests.

- Chapter 15 is concerned with power and its calculation and serves as an easily understood and practical approach to that topic.

- Chapters 16–18 are concerned with the analysis of variance. I have included material on simple repeated-measures designs, but have stopped short of covering mixed designs. These chapters include consideration of basic multiple comparison procedures by way of the Scheffé test and

Fisher's protected t, which not only is an easily understood statistic but has also been shown to be well behaved, under limited conditions, with respect to both power and error rates. At the request of several users of the earlier editions, I have included treatment of the Bonferroni test, which does a very commendable job of controlling error rates, while not sacrificing much in the way of power when used judiciously. Also included are measures of magnitude of effect, a fairly extensive coverage of interactions, and procedures for testing simple effects.

- Chapter 19 deals with the chi-square test, although that material could very easily be covered at an earlier point if desired.
- Chapter 20 covers the most prominent distribution-free tests.
- Chapter 21 offers the student practice in deciding upon the most appropriate statistical procedure for use with a given experimental design.

Not every course would be expected to cover all of these chapters, and several (most notably multiple regression, power, and distribution-free statistical methods) can be omitted or reordered without disrupting the flow of the material. (I cover chi-square early in the course, but it is late in the text on the advice of reviewers.)

Because students often have trouble as a result of having forgotten basic mathematical operations, a review of basic arithmetic is included in Appendix A. Appendix C contains a large data set that is addressed by numerous homework examples throughout the book.

I Am Alive and Well and Living on the Internet!

One of the important changes that is taking place in and outside of education is the Internet. The Internet makes it possible for most people with a computer account to communicate simply by typing a message and entering the "send" command. I welcome responses and questions from students and instructors alike, and will try to answer every message—though I ask that students not ask me how to do their homework assignments. I am also establishing a mailing list of interested people and will make available to that list additional examples, data sets, exercises, and, if necessary, corrections to the text. You can join that list or send me comments and questions simply by sending a mail message to **David.Howell@uvm.edu.**

Acknowledgments

Many people have played an important role in the development of this book. My editor, Curt Hinrichs, was extremely supportive of this revision, offering numerous suggestions for my consideration. Nancy Benjamin, at Books By Design, did an excellent job overseeing the editing of the manuscript and was always supportive on those few occasions when I insisted that quaint spellings were better than the ones Webster's likes. A number of reviewers made many, many helpful suggestions in earlier editions, especially Dr. Drake Bradley

(Bates College), Dr. Maureen Powers (Vanderbilt University), and Dr. Dominic Zerbolio (University of Missouri–St. Louis). For this edition Dr. Eryl Bassett (University of Kent at Canterbury), Dr. Eleanor Willemsen (Santa Clara University), Dr. Jose M. Cortina (Michigan State University), Dr. Edward Johnson (University of North Carolina), Dr. David J. Mostofsky (Boston University), and Dr. Pamela Zappardino (University of Rhode Island) gave extensive and thoughtful feedback. Dr. Karl Wuensch (East Carolina University) filled pages with suggestions and disagreements, and deserves special recognition, as does Dr. Kathleen Bloom (University of Waterloo).

I owe thanks to my colleagues at the University of Vermont and at the University of Bristol, England, where part of a sabbatical leave was devoted to completing the first edition of the book. My wife, Cathy, offered criticism and suggestions on many parts of the first two editions, and insisted, much to my chagrin, that variety is not the spice of life when it comes to statistical notation. Most of all, however, I owe a debt to all of my students who have helped me over the years to see where problems lie and how they can best be approached. Their encouragement has been invaluable. Finally, I want to thank the Biometrika trustees for permission to reproduce the table of Wilcoxon's W statistic.

David C. Howell
Burlington, Vermont
July 1994
Internet: David.Howell@uvm.edu

1

INTRODUCTION

In the past, when I was asked at parties and other social situations what I did for a living, I would answer that I was a psychologist. After several years of receiving the remarks and weird looks that this admission produced, I finally changed tactics and started telling people that I teach statistics—an answer that is also perfectly true. That answer solved one problem—people no longer look at me with blatant suspicion—but it created another. Now either they assume that I am a walking encyclopedia of "useless" facts (such as the number of metric tons of steel shipped last year from the European Community) or they tell me how successful they were in avoiding ever taking a statistics course—not a very tactful remark to someone who teaches that subject.

Let's begin by asking what the field of statistics is all about. After all, you are about to invest a semester in studying statistical methods, so it might be handy to know what you are studying. The word *statistics* is used in at least three different ways. As used in the title of this book, *statistics* refers to a set of procedures and rules for reducing large masses of data to manageable proportions and for allowing us to draw conclusions from those data. That is essentially what this book is all about.

A second, and very common, meaning of the term is expressed by such statements as "statistics show that the number of people applying for unemployment benefits has fallen for the third month in a row." In this case the word *statistics* is used in place of the much better word *data*. For our purposes the word *statistics* will never be used in this sense.

A third meaning of the term is in reference to the result of some arithmetic or algebraic manipulations applied to data. Thus the mean (average) of a set of numbers is a statistic. This perfectly legitimate usage of the word *statistics* will occur repeatedly throughout this book.

We thus have two proper uses of the term: (1) a set of procedures and rules and (2) the outcome of the application of those rules and procedures to samples of data. You should be able to tell from the context which of the two meanings is intended.

There is one other way of looking at the field that people don't usually think of when they see the word *statistics*. That term usually elicits some level of math phobia among many students, but mathematics and mathematical manipulation do not need to, and often don't, play a leading role in the lives of people who work with statistics. (Indeed, one of the best writers of books and articles on statistical issues for psychologists has suggested that he has been so successful in explaining concepts to others because his knowledge of mathematical statistics is woefully inadequate.) Certainly you can't understand any statistical text without learning a few formulae and understanding many more. But the level of mathematics that is required is not great. You learned more than enough in high school. Those who are still concerned should spend a few minutes going over Appendix A, "Arithmetic Review."

The more important issue is learning how to use statistical methods and procedures to tie the results of some experiment to the hypothesis that led to that experiment. In revising this book I have made a major effort to remove as much mathematical material as possible when that material would not contribute significantly to your understanding of data analysis. In its place, however, I am asking you to think a bit more about the logic of what you are doing. I don't mean just the logic of a hypothesis test. I mean the logic behind the way you approach a problem. It doesn't do any good to be able to ask if two groups have different means (averages) if a difference in means has nothing to say about the real question you hoped to ask. One reviewer whose work I respect has complained that I am trying to teach critical thinking skills along with statistics. The reviewer is right, and I enthusiastically plead guilty. You will never be asked to derive a formula, but you will be asked to think. I leave it to you to decide which skill is harder.

Another concern that some students have, and I may have contributed to that concern in the preceding paragraph, is the belief that the only reason to take a course in statistics is to be able to analyze the results of experimental research. Certainly your instructor hopes many of you will use statistical procedures for that purpose, but those procedures and, more important, the way of thinking that goes with them have a life beyond standard experimental research. Much of the material we will cover here will be applicable to whatever you do when you finish college. People who work for large corporations or small family-owned businesses have to work with data. People who serve on a town planning commission have to be able to ask how various changes in the town plan will lead to changes in residential and business development, how those changes will in turn lead to changes in school populations and therefore the level of school budgets, and on and on. Those people may not need to run an analysis of variance (Chapters 16 through 18), though some acquaintance with regression models (Chapters 9 and 10) may be helpful, but the logical approach to data required in the analysis of variance is equally required when dealing with town planning.

A course in statistics is not something you take because it is required and then promptly forget. If taught well, a knowledge of statistics is a job skill you can use (and market). That is largely why I have tried to downplay the mathematical foundations of the field. Those foundations are important, but they are not what will stay with you and be important later. Being able to think through the logic and the interpretation of an experiment or a set of data is an important skill that will stay with you; being able to derive the elements of a regression equation is not. That is why most of the examples used in this book relate to work that people actually do. Work like that requires thought. It may be easier to understand an example that starts out, "Suppose we had three groups labeled A, B, and C" than it is to understand an actual experiment. But the former is boring and doesn't teach you much. A real-life example is more interesting and has more to offer.

1.1 The Importance of Context

Drug use and abuse is a major problem in our society, and heroin addicts die every day from overdoses. Psychologists should have something to contribute to understanding the problem of drug overdoses, and, in fact, they do. I will take the time to describe an important line of research in this area, because a study that derives from that line of research can be used to illustrate a number of important concepts in this chapter and the next.

Morphine is a drug commonly used to alleviate pain, but repeated administrations of morphine lead to morphine tolerance, in which a fixed dose has less and less of an effect (pain reduction) over time. A common experimental task demonstrating morphine tolerance involves placing a mouse on a warm surface. When the heat becomes too uncomfortable, the mouse will lick its paws, and the latency of the paw-lick is used as a measure of the mouse's sensitivity to pain. Mice injected with morphine are less sensitive to pain and show longer paw-lick latencies than noninjected mice. The development of morphine tolerance is indicated by a progressive shortening of paw-lick latencies (indicating increased sensitivity) with repeated morphine injections.

A psychologist at McMaster University, Shepard Siegel, hypothesized that tolerance develops because the cues associated with the context in which morphine is administered (room, cage, and surroundings) come to elicit in the mouse a learned compensatory mechanism that counteracts the effect of the drug. It is as if the mouse had learned to turn off the brain receptors through which morphine worked, making the morphine less effective. As this compensatory mechanism develops over a series of trials, an animal requires larger and larger doses of morphine to have the same pain-killing effect. But suppose you give that larger dose of morphine in an entirely different context. Because the context is different, the animal doesn't compensate for the morphine because it doesn't recognize that the drug is coming. Without the counterbalancing effects, the animal should now feel the full effect of that larger dose of the drug. In that case, it should take a long time for the animal to feel the need to lick its paws, because it has received the larger dose of morphine required by the increased tolerance without the compensating mechanism elicited by the context.

But what do mice on a warm surface have to do with drug overdose? First, heroin is a derivative of morphine. Second, heroin addicts show clear tolerance effects with repeated use and, as a result, often increase the amount of each injection. By Siegel's theory, they are protected from the dangerous effects of the large (and to you and me, lethal) dose of heroin by the learned compensatory mechanism. But if they take what has come to be their standard dose in a entirely new setting, they would not benefit from that protective compensatory mechanism, and what had previously been a safe dose could now be fatal. In fact, Siegel found that a great many drug overdose cases occur when an individual injects heroin in a novel environment. Novelty, to a heroin user, can be deadly!

If Siegel is right, his theory has important implications for the problem of drug overdose. One test of Siegel's theory, which is a simplification of studies he actually ran, is to take two groups of mice who have developed tolerance to morphine and whose standard dosage has been increased above normal levels. One group is tested in the same environment in which they previously have received the drug. The second group is treated exactly the same, except that they are tested in an entirely new environment. If Siegel is correct, the animals tested in the new environment will show a much greater pain threshold (the morphine will have more of an effect) than the animals injected in their usual environment.

1.2 Basic Terminology

Our example of drug tolerance illustrates a number of important statistical concepts. It also will form a useful example in later chapters of this book. Be sure you understand what the experiment demonstrates. What events in your own life or the lives of people around you illustrate the phenomenon of tolerance? What effect has tolerance had on behavior as you (or they) developed tolerance? Can you think of an example where the physical context in which a behavior occurs influences the behavior?

Statistical procedures can be separated into roughly two overlapping areas: descriptive statistics and inferential statistics. The first several chapters of this book will cover descriptive statistics, and the remaining chapters will examine inferential statistics. We will use the simplified version of Siegel's morphine study to illustrate the differences between these two terms.

Descriptive Statistics

Whenever your purpose is merely to *describe* a set of data, you are employing descriptive statistics. A statement about the average length of time it takes a normal mouse to lick its paw when placed on a warm surface would be a descriptive statistic, as would be the time it takes a morphine-injected mouse to do the same thing. Similarly, the amount of change in the latency of paw-licks once morphine has been administered and the variability of change among mice would be other descriptive statistics. Here we are simply reporting measures that describe average latency scores or their variability. Examples from other situations might include an examination of dieting scores on the Eating Restraint Scale, crime rates as reported by the Department of Justice, and certain summary information concerning examination grades in a particular course. Notice that in each of these examples we are just describing what the data have to say about some phenomenon.

Inferential Statistics

All of us at some time or another have been guilty of making unreasonable generalizations on the basis of limited data. If, for example, one mouse showed shorter latencies the second time it received morphine than it did the first, we might try to claim clear evidence of morphine tolerance, even though with no morphine tolerance there would be a 50:50 chance that the second trial's latency would be shorter than that of the first. Or you might hear or read that tall people tend to be more graceful than short people and conclude that that is true because you once had a very tall roommate who was particularly graceful. You conveniently forget about the 6'4" klutz down the hall who couldn't even put on his pants standing up without tripping over them. Similarly, the man who says that girls develop motor skills earlier than boys because his daughter walked at 10 months and his son didn't walk until 14 months is guilty of the same kind of error: generalizing from single (or too limited) observations.

Small samples or single observations may be fine when we want to study something that has very little variability. If we want to know how many legs a cow has, we can find a cow and count its legs. We don't need a whole herd—one will do. However, when what we want to measure varies from one individual to another, such as the length of cows' tails or the change in response latencies with morphine injections in different contexts, we can't get by with only one cow or one mouse. However, neither can we make an unlimited number of observations. If we want to know whether morphine injected in a new context has a greater effect, how long a typical cow's tail is, or when girls usually start to walk, we must look at more than one mouse, one cow, or one girl, but we cannot possibly look at all of them. We must do something in between—we must draw a *sample* from a *population*.

Population
Complete set of events in which you are interested.

Sample
Set of actual observations. Subset of the population.

Statistics
Numerical values summarizing sample data.

Parameters
Numerical values summarizing population data.

Random sample
A sample in which each member of the population has an equal chance of inclusion.

Populations, Samples, Parameters, and Statistics A **population** can be defined as the *entire* collection of events in which you are interested (e.g., the scores of all morphine-injected mice, the lengths of the tails of all the cows in the country, the ages at which every girl first began to walk). Thus if we were interested in the stress levels of all adolescent Americans, then the collection of *all* adolescent Americans' stress scores would form a population, in this case a population of more than 50 million numbers. If, on the other hand, we were interested only in the stress scores of the sophomore class in Fairfax, Vermont (a town of approximately 1800 inhabitants), the population would contain about 60 numbers and could be obtained quite easily in its entirety. If we were interested in paw-lick latencies of mice, we could always run another mouse. In this sense the population of scores theoretically would be infinite. (Mathematicians prefer the word *uncountable*, but *infinite* will do.)

The point is that a population can range from a relatively small set of numbers, which is easily collected, to an infinitely large set of numbers, which can never be completely collected. Unfortunately for us, the populations in which we are interested are usually quite large. The practical consequence is that we can seldom, if ever, collect data on entire populations. Instead, we are forced to draw a **sample** of observations from a population and to use that sample to infer something about the characteristics of the population.

When we draw a sample of observations, we normally compute numerical values (such as averages) that summarize the data in that sample. When such values are based on the sample, they are called **statistics**. The corresponding values in the population (e.g., population averages) are called **parameters**. The major purpose of inferential statistics is to draw inferences about parameters (characteristics of populations) from statistics (characteristics of samples).[1]

Assuming that a sample is a truly **random sample**, meaning that each and every element of the population has an equal chance of being included in the sample, not only can we estimate parameters of the population, but we also

---

[1] The word *inference* as used by statisticians means very much what it means in normal English usage—a conclusion based on logical reasoning. If three-fourths of the people at a picnic suddenly fall ill, I am likely to draw the (possibly incorrect) inference that something is wrong with the food. Similarly, if the average social sensitivity score of a random sample of fifth-grade children is very low, I am likely to draw the inference that fifth graders in general have much to learn about social sensitivity. Statistical inference is generally more precise than everyday inference, but the basic idea is the same.

can have a very good idea of the accuracy of our estimates. To the extent that a sample is not a random sample, our estimates may be meaningless, because the sample may not accurately reflect the entire population.

Let's clear up one point that tends to confuse many people. The problem is that one person's sample might be another person's population. For example, if I were to conduct a study into the effectiveness of this book as a teaching instrument, the scores of one class on an exam might be considered by me to be a sample, though a nonrandom one, of the population of scores for all students who are or might be using this book. The class instructor, on the other hand, cares only about her own students and would regard the same set of scores as a population. In turn, someone interested in the teaching of statistics might regard my population (the scores of everyone using this book) as a nonrandom sample from a larger population (the scores of everyone using *any* textbook in statistics). Thus the definition of a population depends on what you are interested in studying. Notice also that when we speak about populations, we speak about populations of *scores*, not populations of *people* or *things*.

The fact that I have used nonrandom samples here to make a point should not lead the reader to think that randomness is not important. On the contrary, it is the cornerstone of most statistical procedures. As a matter of fact, one could define the relevant population as the collection of numbers from which the sample has been randomly drawn.

Inference We previously defined inferential statistics as the branch of statistics that deals with inferring characteristics of populations from characteristics of samples. This statement is inadequate by itself, because it leaves the reader with the impression that all we care about is determining population parameters such as the average paw-lick latency of mice under the influence of morphine. There are, of course, times when we care about actual population parameters. For example, we often read about the incredible number of hours per day the average child spends in front of a television set. But if that were all there were to inferential statistics, it would be a pretty dreary subject, and the strange looks I get at parties when I admit to teaching statistics would be justified.

In our example of morphine tolerance in mice, we don't really care what the average paw-lick latency of mice is. But we do care whether the average paw-lick latency of morphine-injected mice tested in a novel context is greater or less than the average paw-lick latency of morphine-injected mice tested in the same context in which they had received previous injections. Thus, in many cases inferential statistics is a tool used to estimate parameters of two or more populations, mainly for the purpose of finding if those parameters are different.

Notice that in the previous paragraph it was the population parameters, not the sample statistics, that I cared about. It is a pretty good bet that if I took two different *samples* of mice and tested them, one sample mean (average) would be larger than another. (It's hard to believe that they would come out absolutely equal.) But the real question is whether the sample mean of the mice tested in a novel context is sufficiently longer than the sample mean of mice tested in the same context to lead me to conclude that the corresponding population means are also different.

And don't lose sight of the fact that we really don't care very much about drug addiction in mice. What we do care about is heroin addicts. But we probably wouldn't be very popular if we gave heroin addicts overdoses in novel settings to see what would happen. So we have to make a second inferential leap. We have to make the *statistical* inference from the sample of mice to a population of mice, and then we have to make the *logical* inference from mice to heroin addicts. Both inferences are critical if we want to learn anything useful to reduce the incidence of heroin overdose.

1.3 Selection Among Statistical Procedures

Decision tree
Graphical representation of decisions involved in the choice of statistical procedures.

As we have just seen, there is an important distinction between descriptive statistics and inferential statistics. The first part of this book will be concerned with descriptive statistics because we must describe a set of data before we can use it to draw inferences. When we come to inferential statistics, however, we need to make several additional distinctions to help us focus the choice of an appropriate statistical procedure. On the inside front cover of this book is what is known as a **decision tree**, a device used for selecting among the available statistical procedures to be presented in this book. This decision tree not only represents a rough outline of the organization of the latter part of the text, it also points up some fundamental issues that we should address at the outset. In considering these issues, keep in mind that at this time we are not concerned with which statistical test is used for which purpose. That will come later. Rather, we are concerned with the kinds of questions that come into play when we try to do anything statistically with data, whether we are talking about descriptive or inferential procedures. These issues are listed at the various branching points of the tree. I will discuss the first three of these briefly now and leave the rest to a more appropriate time.

Types of Data

Measurement data (Quantitative data)
Data obtained by measuring objects or events.

Categorical data (Frequency data) (Count data)
Data representing counts or number of observations in each category.

Numerical data generally come in two kinds; there are measurement data and categorical data. By **measurement data** (sometimes called **quantitative data**) we mean the result of any sort of measurement, for example, a score on a measure of stress, a person's weight, the speed at which a person can read this page, or an individual's score on a scale of authoritarianism. In each case some sort of instrument (in its broadest sense) has been used to measure something.

Categorical data (also known as **frequency data** or **count data**) consist of statements such as, "Fifty-eight students reported coming from a one-parent family, while 132 reported coming from two-parent families" or "There were 238 votes for the new curriculum and 118 against it." Here we are counting things, and our data consist of totals or frequencies for each category (hence the name categorical data). Several hundred faculty members might vote on a proposed curriculum, but the results (data) would consist of only two numbers—the number of votes for and the number of votes against the proposal. Measurement data, on the other hand, might measure the paw-lick latencies of dozens of mice, one latency for each mouse.

Sometimes we can measure the same general variable to produce either measurement data or categorical data. Thus, in our experiment we could obtain a latency score for each mouse (measurement data), or we could classify the mice as showing long, medium, or short latencies and then count the number in each category (categorical data).

The two kinds of data are treated in two quite different ways. In Chapter 19 we will examine categorical data to see how we can determine whether there are reliable differences among the numbers of students living under three different levels of stress. In Chapters 9 and 10, 12 through 14, 16 through 18, and 20 we are going to be concerned chiefly with measurement data. But in using measurement data we have to make a second distinction, not in terms of the type of data, but in terms of whether we are concerned with examining differences between groups of subjects or with studying the relationship between variables.

Differences versus Relationships

Most statistical questions fall into two overlapping categories, differences and relationships. For example, one experimenter might be interested primarily in whether there is a difference between smokers and nonsmokers in terms of their performance on a given task. A second experimenter might be interested in whether there is a relationship between the number of cigarettes smoked per day and the scores on that same task. Or we could be interested in whether pain sensitivity increases with the number of previous morphine injections (a relationship) or whether there is a difference in pain sensitivity between those who have had previous injections of morphine and those who have not. Although questions of differences and relationships obviously overlap, they are treated by what appear, on the surface, to be quite different methods. Chapters 12 through 14 and 16 through 18 will be concerned primarily with those cases in which we ask if there are differences between two or more groups, while Chapters 9 through 11 will deal with cases in which we are interested in examining relationships between two or more variables. These seemingly different statistical techniques turn out to be basically the same fundamental procedure, although they ask somewhat different questions and phrase their answers in distinctly different ways.

Number of Groups or Variables

As you will see in subsequent chapters, an obvious distinction between statistical techniques concerns the number of groups or the number of variables to which they apply. For example, you will see that what is generally referred to as an independent *t* test is restricted to the case of data from two groups of subjects. The analysis of variance, on the other hand, is applicable to any number of groups, not just two. The third decision in our tree, then, concerns the number of groups or variables involved.

The three decisions we have been discussing (type of data, differences versus relationships, and number of groups or variables) are fundamental to the way we look at data and the statistical procedures we use to help us interpret those data. One further criterion that some textbooks use for creating categories of tests and ways of describing and manipulating data involves the scale of measurement that applies to the data. We will discuss this topic further in the next chapter, since it is an important concept with which any student should be familiar.

1.4 Using Computers

In the not too distant past, most statistical analyses were done on calculators, and textbooks were written accordingly. Methods have changed, and most calculations are now done by computers, either large mainframes or, more likely, desktop microcomputers. (In fact, the distinction between mainframes and microcomputers is quickly becoming blurred.)

This book, particularly this edition, attempts to deal with the increased availability of computers by incorporating them into the discussion. The level of computer involvement increases as the book proceeds and as computations become more laborious. It is not necessary that you work the problems on a computer (and many students won't), but I have used computer printouts in almost every chapter to give you a sense of what the results would look like. For the simpler procedures, the calculational formulae are important in defining the concept. For example, the formula for a standard deviation or a t test defines and makes meaningful what a standard deviation or a t test actually is. In those cases hand calculation is emphasized even though examples of computer solutions also are given. Later in the book, when we discuss multiple regression for example, the formulae become less informative. The formula for deriving regression coefficients with five predictors would not be expected to add anything to your understanding of the material. In that case I have omitted the formula completely and relied on computer solutions for the answers.

Many statistical software packages currently are available to the researcher or student conducting statistical analyses. A few years ago we would have classified such software as mainframe packages or microcomputer packages, but now we are less likely to make that distinction. Almost all the major mainframe packages are now available for microcomputers, doing virtually the same analyses. The most important large statistical packages, which will carry out nearly every analysis that statisticians have invented, are the BMDP series, Minitab®, SAS®, SPSS™, and SYSTAT. These are highly reliable and relatively easy-to-use packages, and one or more of them generally are available in any college or university computing center. All have complete microcomputer versions. Many examples of their use are scattered throughout this book. Each package has its own set of supporters, but they are all excellent. Choosing among them hinges on subtle differences.

In addition to the "heavyweight" packages, many smaller programs are available for microcomputers, especially for computers running the MS-DOS[2] or Macintosh operating system. The smaller packages often are easier to use, more interactive, faster running, and less expensive. Although such packages may not perform as many different statistical procedures, they run most procedures and are extremely useful in exploring a data set, testing hypotheses, and generally helping you understand your data. Such programs include the student versions of SYSTAT (known as MYSTAT), StataQuest, and JMP (known as JMP-IN), and Minitab (known as STAT101). All but JMP (and JMP-IN) are available for both MS-DOS and Macintosh computers. JMP is available only for the Macintosh. StataQuest is available with this book.

A number of statistical graphics packages produce excellent graphs, some of which appear in this book. Graphs are extremely useful for getting a feel for the data, as you will see in the next chapter. Most of these packages are expensive, but they often are available on college and university computer systems and frequently can be found at greatly reduced prices or with good academic discounts. An excellent combined graphics and statistical analysis package with an inexpensive student edition is EXECUSTAT.

An important aspect of computer packages used for statistical analyses is the way instructions are passed to the program. In the days of mainframe computers, instructions almost always were passed via "command-line statements." For example, one line might contain the name of the procedure to be used, the next line might contain the list of the variables to be included, and so forth. That structure has largely been carried over into statistical packages running under MS-DOS, although there are exceptions. There is a great deal to be said in favor of such an approach. On the other hand, programs written for the Macintosh and Windows™ use "pull-down menus." Here you generally use a mouse (although keyboard equivalents often exist) to choose the analysis, select the variables, specify which variables are independent variables, and so on. This system generally is easier to learn, though it may not be as convenient if you are manipulating large masses of data.

Where possible in this book I have shown command-line statements if they exist. First of all, they apply to a higher percentage of users. Second, there is no simple way of specifying pull-down commands that would mean anything to people using a different statistical package. Third, it is usually relatively easy to translate a command-line instruction into the appropriate pull-down steps. I would be surprised if this created any serious problems for students using pull-down menus, which are sufficiently self-explanatory. I do not expect, through this book, to teach anyone to use any specific statistical package. That is much too large a task. I do, however, want you to have some appreciation of

---

[2]The MS-DOS operating system generally refers to computers that are labeled "IBM compatible," whether they were manufactured by IBM or by one of that company's many high-quality competitors.

what a computer printout looks like for any given problem and how it is to be read, whether or not you have access to that particular package. Where feasible I include the relevant commands to those programs for the benefit of students who can make use of them.

1.5 Summary

In this chapter we examined the two major branches of statistics, descriptive and inferential. We then covered the distinction between populations and samples and defined the concept of a random sample. Finally we dealt with several dimensions along which various statistical procedures could be distinguished. The point to keep in mind, above all else, is that there is a huge difference between statistics and mathematics. They both use numbers and formulae, but statistics does not need to be seen as a mathematical science.

Some important terms in this chapter are:

- Population
- Sample
- Statistics
- Parameters

- Random sample
- Decision tree
- Measurement data
- Categorical data

1.6 Exercises

1.1 To better understand the morphine example that we have been using, think of an example in your own life in which you can see the role played by tolerance. How would you go about testing to see whether context plays a role?

1.2 In testing the effects of context in the example you developed in Exercise 1.1, to what would the words "population" and "sample" refer?

1.3 Think of an example in everyday life where context affects behavior.

1.4 Under what conditions would the entire student body of your college or university be considered a population? Under

what conditions would it be considered a sample?

1.5 If the student body of your college or university were to be considered a sample, as in Exercise 1.4, would it be a random or a nonrandom sample? Why?

1.6 Why would choosing names from a local telephone book not produce a random sample of the residents of that city? Who would be underrepresented and who would be overrepresented?

1.7 Can you suggest ways by which we might be able to produce a random (or more nearly random) sample of people from a small city?

1.8 Even before you began this course you were probably aware of some sample statistics. Name two.

1.9 Give an example of a study in which we would be interested in estimating the average score of a population.

1.10 Give an example of a study in which we don't care about the actual numerical value of a population average, but in which we would want to know whether the average of one population is greater than the average of a different population.

1.11 Give three examples of categorical data.

1.12 Give three examples of measurement data.

1.13 Give an example in which the thing we are studying could be either a measurement or a categorical variable.

1.14 Give two examples of studies in which our primary interest is in looking at relationships between variables.

1.15 Give two examples of studies in which our primary interest is in looking at group differences.

1.16 How might you redesign our study of morphine tolerance to involve three groups of mice to provide more information on the question at hand?

2

BASIC CONCEPTS

2.1 Scales of Measurement	**2.3 Random Sampling**
2.2 Variables	**2.4 Notation**

In the preceding chapter we dealt with a number of statistical terms (e.g., parameter, statistic, population, sample, and random sample) that are fundamental to understanding the statistical analysis of data. In this chapter we will consider some additional concepts that you need. We will start with the concepts of measurement and measurement scales, because in statistics everything we do begins with the measurement of whatever it is we want to study.

Measurement is frequently defined as the assignment of numbers to objects, where the words *numbers* and *objects* are interpreted loosely. When, for example, we use paw-lick latency as a measure of pain sensitivity, we are measuring sensitivity by assigning a number (a score) to an object (a mouse) to assess the sensitivity of that mouse. Similarly, when we use a test of authoritarianism

Measurement
The assignment of
numbers to objects.

(e.g., the Adorno Authoritarianism Scale) to obtain an authoritarianism score for a person, we are measuring that characteristic by assigning a number (a score) to an object (a person). Depending on what we are measuring and how we measure it, the numbers we obtain may have different properties, and those different properties of numbers often are discussed under the specific topic of scales of measurement.

2.1 Scales of Measurement

Scales of measurement
Characteristics of
relations among
numbers assigned
to objects.

Scales of measurement is a topic that some writers think is crucial and others think is irrelevant. Although this book tends to side with the latter group, it is important that you have some familiarity with the general issue. (You do not have to agree with something to think that it is worth studying. After all, evangelists claim to know a great deal about sin.) An additional benefit of this discussion is that you will begin to realize that statistics as a subject is not merely a cut-and-dried set of facts but rather a set of facts put together with a variety of interpretations and opinions.

Probably the foremost leader of those who see scales of measurement as crucially important to the choice of statistical procedures was S. S. Stevens.[1] Basically, Stevens defined four types of scales: nominal, ordinal, interval, and ratio. These scales are distinguished on the basis of the relationships assumed to exist between objects having different scale values. Later scales in this series have all the properties of earlier scales and additional properties as well.

Nominal Scales

Nominal scale
Numbers used only
to distinguish among
objects.

In a sense a **nominal scale** is not really a scale at all, because it does not scale items along any dimension, but rather labels items. The classic example of a nominal scale is the set of numbers assigned to football players. Frequently these numbers have no meaning whatsoever other than as convenient labels that distinguish the players from one another. We could just as easily use letters or pictures of animals. In fact, gender is a nominal scale that uses words (male and female) in place of numbers. Nominal scales generally are used for the purpose of *classification*. Categorical data, which we discussed briefly in Chapter 1, are measured on a nominal scale, because we merely assign category labels (e.g., Male or Female, Same context group or Different context group) to observations. Quantitative (measurement) data are measured on the other three types of scales.

---

[1] Chapter 1 in Stevens's *Handbook of Experimental Psychology* (1951) is an excellent reference for anyone who wants to go further into the substantial mathematical issues underlying his position.

Ordinal Scales

Ordinal scale
Numbers used only to place objects in order.

The simplest true scale is an **ordinal scale**, which orders people, objects, or events along some continuum. An example of an ordinal scale might be the class standings of people graduating from high school. Here the scale tells us which person in the class had the highest average, which had the second-highest average, and so on. Another example would be the Holmes and Rahe (1967) scale of life stress. Using this scale you simply count up (sometimes with differential weightings) the number of changes (marriage, moving, new job, etc.) in the past six months of a person's life. A person with a score of 20 is presumed to have experienced more stress than someone with a score of 15, who is presumed to have experienced more stress than someone with a score of 10. Thus, we order people, in terms of stress, by the changes in their lives.

Notice that these two examples differ in the numbers that are assigned. In the first case we assigned the ranks 1, 2, 3, . . . , whereas in the second case the scores represented the number of changes rather than ranks. Both are examples of ordinal scales, however, because no information is given about the differences between points on the scale. This is an important characteristic of ordinal scales. We do not assume, for example, that the difference between 10 and 15 life changes represents the same increase in stress as the difference between 15 and 20 life changes. Distinctions of that sort must be left to the next type of scale.

Interval Scales

Interval scale
Scale on which equal intervals between objects represent equal differences—differences are meaningful.

An **interval scale** is a scale of measurement about which we can speak legitimately of differences between scale points. A common example is the Fahrenheit scale of temperature, in which a 10-point difference has the same meaning anywhere along the scale. Thus, the difference in temperature between $10°F$ and $20°F$ is the same as the difference between $80°F$ and $90°F$. Notice that this scale also satisfies the properties of the two preceding scales. What we do not have with an interval scale, however, is the ability to speak meaningfully about ratios. Thus, we cannot say, for example, that $40°F$ is one-half as hot as $80°F$ or twice as hot as $20°F$, because the zero point on the scale is arbitrary. For example, $20°F$ and $40°F$ correspond to $-7°$ and $4°$ on the Celsius scale, respectively, and the two sets of ratios are obviously quite different and arbitrary. The Kelvin scale of temperature *is* a ratio scale, but few of us would ever think of using it.

The measurement of pain sensitivity is a good example of something that is probably measured on an interval scale. It seems reasonable to assume that a difference of 10 seconds in paw-lick latency may represent the same difference in sensitivity across most, but not all, of the scale. And notice that I said that our measure can *probably* be taken as an interval measure. This is another way of suggesting that it is rare that you would find a true and unambiguous example of any particular kind of scale. I can think of several reasons why I might argue that paw-lick latencies are not absolutely interval scales, but I would be willing to go along with considering them to be that for purposes of discussion. (I might have considerable reluctance about the calling the scale interval at its extremes, but in our experiment we would not work with a surface that is extremely hot or one that is at room temperature.)

I would be very reluctant, however, to suggest that an animal that takes 25 seconds to lick its paw is *twice* as sensitive as one that takes 50 seconds. To be able to make those types of statements (statements about ratios) we need to go beyond the interval scale to the ratio scale.

Ratio Scales

Ratio scale
A scale with a true zero point—ratios are meaningful.

A **ratio scale** is one that has a true zero point. Notice that the zero point must be a *true* zero point, and not an arbitrary one, such as 0°F or 0°C. A true zero point is the point that corresponds to the absence of the thing being measured. (Because 0°F and 0°C do not represent the absence of temperature, they are not true zero points. However, 0° Kelvin is taken as a true zero point, because it represents, at least in theory, the absence of molecular motion, and thus heat.) Examples of ratio scales are the common physical ones of length, volume, time, and so on. With these scales not only do we have the properties of the preceding scales, but we also can speak about ratios. We can say that in physical terms 10 seconds in twice as long as 5 seconds, 100 lbs is one-third as heavy as 300 lbs, and so on.

One might think that the kind of scale with which we are working would be obvious to everyone who thought about it. Unfortunately, especially with the kinds of measures that we collect in the social sciences, this is rarely the case. Consider for a moment the temperature of the room you are in right now. I just told you that temperature, measured in degrees Celsius or Fahrenheit, is a clear case of an interval scale. Well, it is and it isn't. There is no doubt that to a physicist the difference between 62° and 64° is exactly the same as the difference between 72° and 74°. But if we are measuring temperature as an index of comfort rather than as an index of molecular activity, the same numbers no longer form an interval scale. To a person sitting in a room at 62°F, a jump to 64°F would be distinctly noticeable and probably welcome. The same cannot be said about the difference in room temperature between 72°F and 74°F. This points up the important fact that it is the underlying variable being measured (e.g., comfort), not the numbers themselves, that define the scale.

Because there is usually no unanimous agreement concerning the scale of measurement employed, it's up to you, as an individual user of statistical procedures, to make the best decision you can concerning the nature of the data. All that can be asked of you is that you think about the problem carefully before coming to a decision and not simply assume that the standard answer is necessarily the best answer.

The Role of Measurement Scales

The statement was made earlier that there is a difference of opinion as to the importance assigned to scales of measurement. Some authors have ignored the problem totally, while others have organized whole textbooks around the different scales. It seems to me that the central issue is the absolute necessity of separating in our minds the numbers we collect from the objects or events to which they refer. If one subject in a memory study recalled 20 items and another subject recalled 10 items, the number of words recalled was twice as large for the first subject. However, we might not be willing to say that the first subject remembered twice as much about the material studied.

A similar argument was made for the example of room temperature, where the scale (interval or ordinal) depended on whether we were interested in measuring some physical attribute of temperature or its effect on people. A difference of 2°F is the same *physically* anywhere along the scale, but a difference of 2°F when a room is already warm may not *feel* as large as a difference of 2°F when a room is relatively cool. In other words, we have an interval scale of the physical units, but no more than an ordinal scale of comfort. (In fact it gets worse, because where molecular activity continues to increase as temperature increases, comfort at first rises as the temperature rises, levels off briefly, and then starts to fall. In other words, the relationship is shaped like an inverted U.

Because statistical tests use numbers without considering the objects or events to which those numbers refer, we can carry out standard mathematical operations (addition, multiplication, etc.) regardless of the nature of the underlying scale. An excellent and highly recommended reference on this point is an entertaining paper by Lord (1953) entitled "The Statistical Treatment of Football Numbers." Lord argues that you can treat these numbers in any way you like, since "the numbers do not remember where they came from."

The problem comes when it is time to interpret the results of some form of statistical manipulation. At that point we must ask if the statistical results bear any meaningful relationship to the objects or events in question. Here we are no longer dealing with a statistical issue, but with a methodological one. No statistical procedure can tell us whether the fact that one group received higher grades than another on a history examination reveals anything about group differences in knowledge of the subject matter. (Perhaps they received specific coaching on how to take multiple choice exams.) Moreover, to be satisfied because the examination provides grades that form a ratio scale of correct items (50 correct items is twice as many as 25 correct items) is to lose sight of the fact that we set out to measure knowledge of history, which may not increase in any orderly way with increases in scores. Statistical tests can be applied only to the numbers we obtain, and the validity of statements about the objects or events that we think we are measuring hinges primarily on our knowledge of those objects or events, not on the scale of measurement. We do our best to ensure that our measures bear as close a relationship as possible to what we want to measure, but our results are ultimately only the numbers we obtain and our faith in the *relationship* between those numbers and the underlying objects or events.

To return for a moment to the problem of heroin overdose, notice that in addressing this problem we have had to move several steps away from the heroin addict sticking a needle in his arm under a bridge. Because we can't use actual addicts we have used mice. We assume that pain tolerance under morphine is a good analogue to the tolerance we see in drug addicts, and it probably is. But then to measure pain tolerance we measure changes in sensitivity to pain, and to measure sensitivity we measure paw-lick latency. And finally, to measure changes in sensitivity, we measure changes in paw-lick latencies. All these assumptions are reasonable, but they are assumptions nonetheless. When we worry about the scale of measurement, we need to think about the relationships among these steps. That does not mean that paw-lick latency needs to be an interval measure of heroin tolerance in addicts—that wouldn't make any sense. But it does mean that we need to think about the whole system and not just one of its parts.

2.2 Variables

Variables
Properties of objects that can take on different values.

Discrete variables
Variables that take on a small set of possible values.

Continuous variables
Variables that take on *any* value.

Independent variables
Those variables controlled by the experimenter.

Dependent variables
The variable being measured. The data or score.

Properties of objects or events that can take on different values are referred to as **variables**. Hair color, for example, is a variable because it is a property of an object (hair) that can take on different values (brown, yellow, red, etc.). Properties such as height, length, and speed are variables for the same reason. We can further discriminate between **discrete variables** (such as gender, marital status, and the number of television sets in a private home), in which the variable can take on only a relatively few possible values, and **continuous variables** (such as speed, paw-lick latency, length of a cow's tail, and so on), in which the variable could assume—at least in theory—any value between the lowest and highest points on the scale. (Note that nominal variables cannot be continuous.) As you will see later in this book, the distinction between discrete and continuous variables plays an important role in some of our procedures.

In statistics we also distinguish between different kinds of variables in an additional way. We speak of **independent variables** (those that are manipulated by the experimenter) and **dependent variables** (those that are not under the experimenter's control—the data).[2] In psychological research the experimenter is interested in measuring the effects of independent variables on dependent variables. Common examples of independent variables in psychology are schedules of reinforcement, forms of therapy, placement of stimulating electrodes, methods of treatment, and the distance of the stimulus from the observer. Common examples of dependent variables are running speeds, scores on a test, and number of aggressive behaviors. Basically what the study is all about is the independent variable, and the results of the study (the data) are measurements of the dependent variable. For example, a psychologist may measure the number of aggressive behaviors in depressed and nondepressed adolescents. Here the state of depression is the independent variable, and the number of aggressive acts is the dependent variable. Independent variables

---

[2]Some readers have pointed out that some independent variables are not "manipulated" by the experimenter. For example, we cannot manipulate the subject's gender or, generally, the school that he or she attends. However, we do manipulate those variables in the sense that we *choose* which schools to compare or to compare males and females. In that sense we do manipulate the independent variable, that is, it is under our control.

can be either qualitative (e.g., a comparison of three different forms of psycho-therapy) or quantitative (performance following one, three, or five units of caffeine), while dependent variables are generally—but certainly not always—quantitative.[3] What are the independent and dependent variables in our study of morphine tolerance in mice?

2.3 Random Sampling

In Chapter 1 a sample was said to be a random sample if each and every element of the population has an equal chance of being included in the sample. I further stated that the concept of a random sample is fundamental to the process of using statistics calculated on a sample to infer the values of parameters of a population. It should be obvious that we would be foolish to try to estimate the average level of sexual activity of all high school students on the basis of data on a group of ninth graders who happen to have a study hall at the same time. We would all agree (I hope) that the data would underestimate the average value that would have been obtained from a truly random sample of the entire population of high school students.

There are a number of ways of obtaining random samples from fairly small populations. We could assign every person a number and then use a table of random numbers to select the numbers of those who will be included in our sample. Or, if we would be satisfied with a nearly random sample, we could put names in a hat and draw blindly. The point is that every score in the population should have an equal chance of being included.

It is often helpful to have a table of random numbers to use for drawing random samples, assigning subjects to groups, and other tasks. Such a table can be found in Appendix D (Table D.9). This table is a list of uniform random numbers. The adjective *uniform* is used to indicate that every number is equally (uniformly) likely to occur. (For example, if you counted the occurrences of the digits 1, 5, and 8 in this table, you would find that they all occur about equally often.)

Table D.9 is quite easy to use. For example, if you wanted to draw random numbers between 0 and 9, you would simply close your eyes and put your finger on the table. You would then read down the column (after opening your eyes), recording the digits as they come. When you came to the bottom of the column, you would go to the next column and continue the process until you had as many numbers as you needed. If you wanted numbers between 0 and 99, you would do the same thing, except that you would read off pairs of digits. If you wanted random numbers between 1 and 65, you again would read off pairs of digits, but ignore 00 or any number between 66 and 99.

If, instead of collecting a set of random data, you wanted to use the random-number table to assign subjects to two treatment groups, you could

---

[3]Hint: The next time you come across the independent/dependent-variable distinction on a test, just remember that *dependent* and *data* both start with a *d*. You can figure out the rest from there.

start at any place in the table and assign a subject to Group I if the random number was odd and to Group II if it was even. Common-sense extrapolations of this procedure will allow you to randomly assign subjects to any number of groups.

With large populations most standard techniques for ensuring randomness are no longer appropriate. We cannot put the names of all U.S. women between 21 and 30 in a hat (even a very big hat). Nor could we assign all U.S. women a number and then choose women by matching numbers against a random-number table. Such a procedure would be totally impractical. Unless we have substantial resources, about the best we can do is to eliminate as many potential sources of bias as possible (e.g., don't estimate level of sexual behavior solely on the basis of a sample of people who visit Planned Parenthood), restrict our conclusions on the basis of those sources of bias that we could not feasibly control (e.g., acknowledge that the data came only from people who were willing to complete our questionnaire), and then hope a lot. Any biases that remain will limit the degree to which the results can be generalized to the population as a whole. A large body of literature is concerned with sampling methods designed to ensure representative samples, but such methods are beyond the scope of this book.

2.4 Notation

Any discussion of statistical techniques requires a notational system for expressing mathematical operations. It is thus surprising that no standard notational system has been adopted. Although there have been several attempts to formulate a general policy, the fact remains that no two textbooks use exactly the same notation.

The notational systems that we do have range from the very complex to the very simple. The more complex systems gain precision at the loss of easy intelligibility, while the simpler systems gain intelligibility at the loss of some precision. Because the loss of precision is usually trivial when compared with the gain in comprehension, this book will use an extremely simple system of notation.

Notation for Variables

The general rule for our purposes is that a variable as a whole will be represented by an uppercase letter, usually X or Y. An individual value of that variable will be represented by the letter and a subscript. Suppose, for example, that we have the following five scores on the length of time (in seconds) that third-grade children can sit absolutely still:

45   42   35   23   52

This set of scores will be referred to as X. The first number of this set (45) can be referred to as X_1, the second (42) as X_2, and so on. To refer to a single score without specifying which one, we will refer to X_i, where i can take on any value between 1 and 5. The use of subscripts is essential to precise description of statistical procedures. In practice, however, the use of subscripts is often more of a distraction than an aid. In this book subscripts will generally be omitted where the meaning is clear without them.

Summation Notation

Sigma (Σ)
Symbol indicating summation.

One of the most common symbols in statistics is the uppercase Greek letter **sigma (Σ)**, the standard notation for summation, which is readily translated as "add up, or sum, what follows." Thus, ΣX_i is read "Sum the X_i's." To be perfectly correct, the notation for summing all N values of X is

$$\sum_{i=1}^{N} X_i$$

which translates to, "Sum all the X_i's from $i = 1$ to $i = N$." There is seldom any need in practice to specify what is to be done in such detail. In most cases in this book all subscripts will be dropped, and the notation for the sum of the X_i will be simply ΣX.

Several extensions of the simple case of ΣX must be noted and thoroughly understood. One of these is ΣX^2, which is read, "Sum the squared values of X" (i.e., $45^2 + 42^2 + 35^2 + 23^2 + 52^2$). Another common expression is ΣXY, which means, "Sum the products of the corresponding values of X and Y." The use of these terms is illustrated in the following example.

Imagine a simple experiment in which we record the number of life events (major and minor) in an adolescent's life and a measure of behavior problems. For the sake of our example, we will use only five subjects. The data and simple summation operations on them are illustrated in Table 2.1. Some of these operations have been discussed already; others will be discussed in the next few chapters. Examination of Table 2.1 reveals another set of operations involving parentheses, such as $(\Sigma X)^2$. *The general rule that always applies is to perform operations within parentheses before performing operations outside parentheses.* Thus, for $(\Sigma X)^2$ we would sum the values of X and *then* square the result, as opposed to ΣX^2, in which we would square the X's *before* we sum. You should confirm that ΣX^2 is not equal to ($\neq$) $(\Sigma X)^2$ by using simple numbers such as 2, 3, and 4.

A thorough understanding of notation is essential if you are to learn even the most elementary statistical techniques. Demonstration of the following rules of summation is left to you, since their application can be illustrated with very simple examples.

1. $\Sigma(X - Y) = \Sigma X - \Sigma Y$.

2. $\Sigma CX = C\Sigma X$. The notation ΣCX means to multiply every value of X by the **constant** C and then sum the results. A constant is any number that does not change its value in a given situation (as opposed to a variable, which does). Constants are most often represented by the letters C and k, but other symbols may be used.

Constant
A number that does not change in value in a given situation.

Table 2.1

**Illustration
of Operations
Involving
Summation
Notation**

	Life Events	Behavior Problems				
	X	Y	X²	Y²	X – Y	XY
	10	3	100	9	7	30
	15	4	225	16	11	60
	12	1	144	1	11	12
	9	1	81	1	8	9
	10	3	100	9	7	30
Sum	56	12	650	36	44	141

$$\Sigma X = (10 + 15 + 12 + 9 + 10) = 56$$
$$\Sigma Y = (3 + 4 + 1 + 1 + 3) = 12$$
$$\Sigma X^2 = (10^2 + 15^2 + 12^2 + 9^2 + 10^2) = 650$$
$$\Sigma Y^2 = (3^2 + 4^2 + 1^2 + 1^2 + 3^2) = 36$$
$$\Sigma(X - Y) = (7 + 11 + 11 + 8 + 7) = 44$$
$$\Sigma XY = (10)(3) + (15)(4) + (12)(1) + (9)(1) + (10)(3) = 141$$
$$(\Sigma X)^2 = 56^2 - 3136$$
$$(\Sigma Y)^2 = 12^2 = 144$$
$$(\Sigma(X - Y))^2 = 44^2 = 1936$$
$$(\Sigma X)(\Sigma Y) = (56)(12) = 672$$

3. $\Sigma(X + C) = \Sigma X + NC$. N represents the number of items that are being summed.

2.5 Summary

In this chapter we examined briefly the concept of measurement and considered four different levels, or scales, of measurement. We also discussed variables, the different types of variables, and the system of notation that will be
used throughout this book. At this point you have the basic terminology you
will need to begin looking at data.

Some important terms in this chapter are:

- Measurement
- Scales of measurement
- Nominal scale
- Ordinal scale
- Interval scale
- Ratio scale

- Variables
- Discrete variables
- Continuous variables
- Independent variables
- Dependent variables
- Constant

2.6 Exercises

2.1 Give one example of each kind of scale of measurement.

2.2 Give an example of a scale that might be said to use a ratio scale for some purposes and an interval or ordinal scale for other purposes.

2.3 We trained rats to run a straight-alley maze for food reinforcement. All of a sudden one of the rats lay down and went to sleep half-way through the maze. What does this say about the scale of measurement when speed is used as an index of learning?

2.4 What does Exercise 2.3 say about speed used as an index of motivation?

2.5 Give two examples of independent variables and two examples of dependent variables.

2.6 Write a sentence describing the morphine tolerance experiment in terms of an independent variable and a dependent variable.

2.7 Give three examples of continuous variables.

2.8 Give three examples of discrete variables.

2.9 Suppose that in a hypothetical experiment Harris, Peabody, and Smith (1997) rated 10 Europeans and 10 North Americans on a 12-point scale of musicality. The data for the Europeans are:

10 8 9 5 10 11 7 8 2 7

Using X to represent this variable,

(a) What are X_3, X_5, and X_8?

(b) Calculate ΣX.

(c) Write the summation notation for (b) in its most complex form.

2.10 With reference to Exercise 2.9, the data for the North Americans are:

9 9 5 3 8 4 6 6 5 2

Using Y for this variable,

(a) What are Y_1 and Y_{10}?

(b) Calculate ΣY.

2.11 Using the data from Exercise 2.9,

(a) Calculate $(\Sigma X)^2$ and ΣX^2.

(b) Calculate $\Sigma X / N$, where $N =$ the number of scores.

(c) What do you call what you just calculated?

2.12 Using the data from Exercise 2.10,

(a) Calculate $(\Sigma Y)^2$ and ΣY^2.

(b) Given the answers to (a), calculate

$$\frac{\Sigma Y^2 - \dfrac{(\Sigma Y)^2}{N}}{N - 1}$$

(c) Calculate the square root of the answer to (b).

(d) What are the units of measurement for (b) and (c)? (You will come across these calculations again in Chapter 6.)

2.13 Using the data from Exercises 2.9 and 2.10,

(a) Calculate ΣXY.

(b) Calculate $\Sigma X \Sigma Y$.

(c) Calculate

$$\frac{\Sigma XY - \dfrac{\Sigma X \Sigma Y}{N}}{N - 1}$$

(You will come across these calculations again in Chapter 9. Very few of the calculations in this book will be any more complex than this one.)

2.14 Use the previous data to show that

   (a) $\Sigma(X + Y) = \Sigma X + \Sigma Y$

   (b) $\Sigma XY \neq \Sigma X \Sigma Y$

   (c) $\Sigma CX = C\Sigma X$

   (d) $\Sigma X^2 \neq (\Sigma X)^2$

2.15 Make up five data points and use the third rule of summation to show what happens to the total if you add 10 points to every person's score.

2.16 I have been (correctly) criticized for using "the number of hairs on a goat" as an example of a continuous variable in an earlier edition of this book. Why is this really a discrete variable?

2.17 Can an ordinal variable be measured on a continuous scale?

2.18 I have argued that paw-lick latencies can reasonably be taken to be an interval scale of pain sensitivity in mice. Suppose that someone else felt that the square root of paw-lick latency was more appropriate. How might we decide between these two competing measures?

$$\frac{231 - \frac{672}{N}}{N-1}$$

3

DISPLAYING DATA

A collection of raw data, taken by itself, is no more exciting or informative than junk mail before election day. Whether you have neatly arranged the data in rows on a data collection form or scribbled them on the back of an out-of-date announcement you tore from the bulletin board, a collection of numbers is still just a collection of numbers. To be interpretable, they first must be organized in some sort of logical order.

How do human beings process information that is stored in their short-term memory? If I asked you to tell me if the number "6" was included as one of a set of five digits that you just saw presented on a screen, do you use *sequential processing* to search your short-term memory of the screen and say "Nope, it wasn't the first one; nope, it wasn't the second," and so on? Or do you use *parallel processing* to compare the digit "6" with your memory of all the previous digits at the same time? Obviously in this case the latter approach would be faster and more efficient, but human beings don't always do things in the fastest and most efficient manner. How do *you* think that you do it? How do you search back through your memory and identify the person who just walked in as Jennifer? Do you compare her one at a time with all the women her age whom you have met, or do you make comparisons in parallel? (This second example uses long-term memory rather than short-term memory, but the questions are analogous.)

In 1966 Sternberg ran a simple but important study that examined how people recall data from short-term memory. On a screen in front of the subject, he presented a *comparison* set of one, three, or five digits. Shortly after each presentation he flashed a single test digit on the screen and required the subject to push one button (the positive button) if the test digit had been included in the comparison set or another button (the negative button) if the test digit had not been part of the comparison set. For example, the two stimuli might look like this:

Comparison	2	7	4	8	1
Test			5		

(Remember, the two stimuli were presented sequentially, not simultaneously.) Since the numeral "5" was not part of the comparison set, the subject should have responded by pressing the negative button. Sternberg then measured the time, in 100ths of a second, that the subject took to respond. This process was repeated over many randomly organized trials. Because Sternberg was interested in how people process information, he was interested in how reaction times varied as a function of the number of digits in the comparison set and as a function of whether the test digit was a positive or negative instance for that set. (If you make comparisons sequentially, the time to make a decision should increase as the number of digits in the comparison set increases. If you make comparisons in parallel, the number of digits in the comparison set shouldn't matter.)

Although Sternberg's primary aim was to compare data for the different conditions, we can gain an immediate impression of our data by taking the full set of reaction times, regardless of the stimulus condition. We will come back and compare the different conditions later. The data in Table 3.1 were collected in an experiment similar to Sternberg's but with only one subject—myself. No correction of responses was allowed, and the data presented here come only from correct trials.

3.1 Plotting Data

As you can see, there are simply too many numbers in Table 3.1 for us to be able to interpret them at a glance. One of the simplest methods to reorganize data to make them more intelligible is to plot them in some sort of graphical

Table 3.1

Reaction Time Data from Letter Identification Experiment

Comparison Stimuli*	Reaction Times, in 100ths of a Second
1Y	40 41 47 38 40 37 38 47 45 61 54 67 49 43 52 39 46 47 45 43 39 49 50 44 53 46 64 51 40 41 44 48 50 42 90 51 55 60 47 45 41 42 72 36 43 94 45 51 46 52
1N	52 45 74 56 53 59 43 46 51 40 48 47 57 54 44 56 47 62 44 53 48 50 58 52 57 66 49 59 56 71 76 54 71 104 44 67 45 79 46 57 58 47 73 67 46 57 52 61 72 104
3Y	73 83 55 59 51 65 61 64 63 86 42 65 62 62 51 62 72 55 58 46 67 56 52 46 62 51 51 61 60 75 53 59 56 50 43 58 67 52 56 80 53 72 62 59 47 62 53 52 46 60
3N	73 47 63 63 56 66 72 58 60 69 74 51 49 69 51 60 52 72 58 74 59 63 60 66 59 61 50 67 63 61 80 63 60 64 64 57 59 58 59 60 62 63 67 78 61 52 51 56 95 54
5Y	39 65 53 46 78 60 71 58 87 77 62 94 81 46 49 62 55 59 88 56 77 67 79 54 83 75 67 60 65 62 62 62 60 58 67 48 51 67 98 64 57 67 55 55 66 60 57 54 78 69
5N	66 53 61 74 76 69 82 56 66 63 69 76 71 65 67 67 55 65 58 64 65 81 69 69 63 68 70 80 68 63 74 61 85 125 59 61 74 76 62 83 58 72 65 61 95 58 64 66 66 72

*1, 3, and 5 refer to the number of digits in the comparison stimuli, and Y and N refer to whether the test digit was included in the comparison (Y) or was not (N).

form. There are several common ways in which data can be represented graphically. Some of these methods are frequency distributions, histograms, and stem-and-leaf displays, which we will discuss in turn.

Frequency Distributions

Frequency distribution
A distribution in which the values of the dependent variable are tabled or plotted against their frequency of occurrence.

As a first step, we can make a **frequency distribution** of the data as a way of organizing them in some sort of logical order. For our example of reaction times, we would count the number of times that each possible reaction time occurred. For example, the subject responded in 50/100 of a second five times and in 51/100 of a second twelve times. On one occasion he became confused and took 1.25 seconds (125/100 of a second) to respond. The frequency distribution for these data is presented in Table 3.2, which reports how often each time occurred, and in Figure 3.1, on which the data are plotted so they can be seen graphically.

From the distribution shown in Table 3.2 and graphically in Figure 3.1, it is clear that there is a wide distribution of reaction times, with times as low as 36/100 of a second and as high as 125/100 of a second. The data tend to cluster around about 60/100, with most of the scores between 40/100 and

Table 3.2

Frequency Distribution of Reaction Times

Reaction Time, in 100ths of a Second	Frequency	Reaction Time, in 100ths of a Second	Frequency
36	1	71	4
37	1	72	8
38	2	73	3
39	3	74	6
40	4	75	2
41	3	76	4
42	3	77	2
43	5	78	3
44	5	79	2
45	6	80	3
46	11	81	2
47	9	82	1
48	4	83	3
49	5	84	0
50	5	85	1
51	12	86	1
52	10	87	1
53	8	88	1
54	6	89	0
55	7	90	1
56	10	91	0
57	7	92	0
58	12	93	0
59	11	94	2
60	12	95	2
61	11	96	0
62	14	97	0
63	10	98	1
64	7	99	0
65	8	. . .	. . .
66	8	. . .	. . .
67	14	104	2
68	2	. . .	. . .
69	7	125	1
70	1		

Figure 3.1

**Plot of Reaction
Times Against
Frequency**

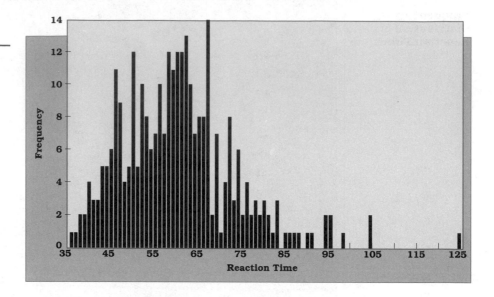

90/100. This tendency was not apparent from the unorganized data shown in Table 3.1.

3.2 Histograms

In the preceding discussion of frequency distributions, I plotted the frequency of the individual values of reaction time. But when we are dealing with a variable, such as this one, that has many different values, each individual value often occurs with low frequency, and there is often substantial fluctuation of the frequencies in adjacent intervals. Notice, for example, that there are fourteen 67s, but only two 68s. In situations such as this it makes more sense to group adjacent values together into a **histogram**. Doing so obscures some of the random "noise" that is not likely to be meaningful, but preserves important trends in the data. We might, for example, group the data into blocks of 5/100 of a second, combining the frequencies for all outcomes between 35 and 39, between 40 and 44, and so on. An example of such a distribution is shown in Table 3.3.

In Table 3.3 I have reported the upper and lower boundaries of the intervals as whole integers, for the simple reason that it makes the table easier to read. However, you should realize that the true limits of the interval (known as the real lower limit and the real upper limit) are decimal values that fall halfway between the top of one interval and the bottom of the next. The **real lower limit** of an interval is the smallest value that would be classed as falling into the interval. Similarly, an interval's real upper limit is the largest value that would be classed as being in the interval. For example, had we recorded reaction times to the nearest thousandth of a second, rather than to the nearest hun-

Histogram
Graph in which rectangles are used to represent frequencies of observations within each interval.

**Real lower limit
Real upper limit**
The points halfway between the top of one interval and the bottom of the next.

Table 3.3   Grouped Frequency Distribution

Interval	Mid-point	Fre-quency	Cumulative Frequency	Interval	Mid-point	Fre-quency	Cumulative Frequency
35–39	37	6	6	85–89	87	4	290
40–44	42	20	26	90–94	92	4	294
45–49	47	35	61	95–99	97	3	297
50–54	52	41	102	100–104	102	2	299
55–59	57	47	149	105–109	107	0	299
60–64	62	54	203	110–114	112	0	299
65–69	67	39	242	115–119	117	0	299
70–74	72	22	264	120–124	122	0	299
75–79	77	13	277	125–129	127	1	300
80–84	82	9	286				

dredth, the interval 35–39 would include all values between 34.5 and 39.5, because values falling between those points would be rounded up or down into that interval. (People often become terribly worried about what we would do if a person had a score of exactly 39.50000000 and therefore sat right on the breakpoint between two intervals. Don't worry about it. First, it is unlikely to happen. Second, you can always flip a coin. Third, there are many more important things to worry about. This is one of those nonissues that make people think the study of statistics is confusing, boring, or both.)

Midpoints
Center of interval—average of upper and lower limits.

The **midpoints** listed in Table 3.3 are the averages of the upper and lower limits and are presented for convenience. When we plot the data, we often plot the points as if they all fell at the midpoints of their respective intervals.

Table 3.3 also lists the frequencies with which scores fell in each interval. For example, there were six reaction times between 35/100 and 39/100 of a second. The distribution in Table 3.3 is shown as a histogram in Figure 3.2.

People often ask about the optimal number of intervals to use when grouping data. Although there is no right answer to this question, somewhere around 10 intervals is usually reasonable.[1] In this example I used 19 intervals because the numbers naturally broke that way, and because I had a lot of observations. In general and when practical it is best to use natural breaks in the number system (e.g., 0–9, 10–19, . . . or 100–119, 120–139) rather than to break up the range into exactly 10 arbitrarily defined intervals. However, if another kind of limit makes the data more interpretable, then use those limits. Remember

---

[1] One interesting scheme for choosing an optimal number of intervals is to set it equal to the integer closest to $\sqrt{N}$, where N is the number of observations. Applying that suggestion here would leave us with $\sqrt{300} = 17.32 = 17$ intervals, which is close to the 19 that I actually used.

Figure 3.2

Grouped Distribution of Reaction Times

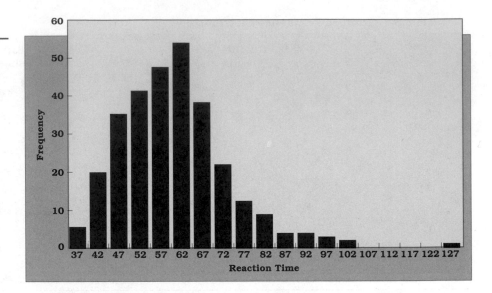

that you are trying to make the data meaningful—don't try to follow a rigid set of rules made up by someone who has never seen your problem.

Notice in Figure 3.2 that the reaction time data are generally centered on 50–70 hundredths of a second, that the distribution rises and falls fairly regularly, and that the distribution trails off to the right. We would expect such times to trail off to the right (referred to as being positively skewed) because there is some limit on how *quickly* the subject can respond, but really no limit on how *slowly* he can respond. Notice also the extreme value of 125 hundredths. This value is called an **outlier** because it is widely separated from the rest of the data. Outliers frequently represent errors in recording data, but in this particular case it was just a trial in which the subject couldn't make up his mind which button to push.

Outlier
An extreme point that stands out from the rest of the distribution.

3.3 Stem-and-Leaf Displays

Stem-and-leaf display
Graphical display presenting original data arranged into a histogram.

Exploratory data analysis (EDA)
A set of techniques developed by Tukey for presenting data in visually meaningful ways.

Although histograms and frequency distributions are commonly used methods of presenting data, each has its drawbacks. Because histograms portray grouped data, they lose the actual numerical values of the individual scores in each interval. Frequency distributions, on the other hand, retain the value of the individual observations, but they can be difficult to use when they do not summarize the data sufficiently. An alternative approach that avoids both of these criticisms is the **stem-and-leaf display**.

John Tukey (1977), as part of his general approach to data analysis, known as **exploratory data analysis (EDA),** developed a variety of methods for displaying data in visually meaningful ways. One of the simplest of these methods is a stem-and-leaf display. I can't start with the reaction time data here,

Figure 3.3

Stem-and-Leaf Display of Electronic Game Data

Raw Data	Stem	Leaf
.	0	00000000000233566678
.	1	2223555579
.	2	33577
40 41 41 42 43	3	22278999
43 44 46 46 46	4	01123346667899
47 48 49 49	5	24557899
52 54 55 55 57	6	37
58 59 59	7	1556689
63 67	8	34779
71 75 75 76 76	9	466
78 78	10	23677
.	11	3479
.	12	2557899
.	13	89

Leading digits (most significant digits)
Left-most digits of a number.

Stem
Vertical axis of display containing the leading digits.

Trailing digits (less significant digits)
Digits immediately to right of leading digits.

Leaves
Horizontal axis of display containing the trailing digits.

because that would require a slightly more sophisticated display because of the large number of observations. Instead, I'll use a hypothetical set of data in which we record the amount of time (in minutes per week) that each of 100 students spends playing electronic games. Some of the raw data are given in Figure 3.3. On the left side of the figure is a portion of the data (data from students who spend between 40 and 80 minutes per week playing games) and on the right is the complete stem-and-leaf display that results.

From the raw data in Figure 3.3, you can see that there are several scores in the 40s, another bunch in the 50s, two in the 60s, and some in the 70s. We refer to the tens' digits—here 4, 5, 6, and 7—as the **leading digits** (sometimes called the **most significant digits**) for these scores. These leading digits form the **stem**, or vertical axis, of our display. Within the set of 14 scores that were in the 40s, you can see that there was one 40, two 41s, one 42, two 43s, one 44, no 45s, three 46s, one 47, one 48, and two 49s. The units' digits 0, 1, 2, 3, and so on, are called the **trailing** (or **less significant**) **digits**. They form the **leaves**—the horizontal elements—of our display.[2]

On the right side of Figure 3.3 you can see that next to the stem entry of 4 you have a 0, two 1s, a 2, two 3s, a 4, three 6s, a 7, an 8, and two 9s. These leaf values correspond to the units' digits in the raw data. Similarly, note how the

---

[2]It is not always true that the tens' digits form the stem and the units' digits the leaves. For example, if the data ranged from 100 to 1000, the hundreds' digits would form the stem, the tens' digits the leaves, and we would ignore the units' digits.

Figure 3.4

Stem-and-Leaf Display for Reaction Time Data

Raw Data	Stem	Leaf
36 37 38 38 39 39 39 40	3s	67
40 40 40 41 41 41 42 42	3.	88999
42 43 43 43 43 43 44 44	4*	0000111
44 44 44 45 45 45 45 45	4t	22233333
45 46 46 46 46 46 46 46	4f	44444555555
46 46 46 46 47 47 47 47	4s	6666666666677777777777
47 47 47 47 47 48 48 48	4.	888899999
48 49 49 49 49 49 50 50	5*	00000111111111111
50 50 50 51 51 51 51 51	5t	222222222233333333
51 51 51 51 51 51 51 52	5f	4444445555555
52 52 52 52 52 52 52 52	5s	66666666667777777
52 53 53 53 53 53 53 53	5.	8888888888899999999999
53 54 54 54 54 54 54 55	6*	00000000000011111111111
55 55 55 55 55 55	6t	22222222222222233333333333
. . .	6f	444444455555555
	6s	66666666677777777777777
	6.	889999999
	7*	01111
	7t	22222222333
	7f	44444455
	7s	666677
	7.	88899
	8*	00011
	8t	2333
	8f	5
	8s	67
	8.	8
	9*	0
	9t	
	9f	4455
	9s	
	9.	8
	High	104; 104; 125

leaves opposite the stem value of 5 correspond to the units' digits of all responses in the 50s. From the stem-and-leaf display you could completely regenerate the raw data that went into that display. For example, you can tell that 11 students spent zero minutes playing electronic games, one student spent two minutes, two students spent three minutes, and so on. Moreover, the shape of the display looks just like a sideways histogram, giving you all of the benefits of that method of graphing data as well.

One apparent drawback of this simple stem-and-leaf display is that for some data sets it will lead to a grouping that is too coarse for our purposes. In fact, that is why I needed to use hypothetical data for this introductory example. When I tried to use the reaction time data, I found that the stem for 50 (i.e., 5) had 88 leaves opposite it, which was a little silly. Not to worry; Tukey was there before us and figured out a clever way around this problem.

If the problem is that we are trying to lump together everything between 50 and 59, perhaps what we should be doing is breaking that interval into smaller intervals. We *could* try using the intervals 50–54, 55–59, and so on. But then we couldn't just use 5 as the stem, because it would not distinguish between the two intervals. Tukey suggested using "5*" to represent 50–54, and "5." to represent 55–59. But that won't solve our problem, because the categories still are too coarse. So Tukey suggested an alternative scheme where "5*" represents 50–51, "5t" represents 52–53, "5f" represents 54–55, "5s" represents 56–57, and "5." represents 58–59. (Can you guess why he used those particular letters? Hint: "Two" and "three" both start with "t.") If we apply this scheme to the data on reaction times, we obtain the results shown in Figure 3.4. In that figure I have presented only some of the raw data for purposes of illustration, but the complete stem-and-leaf display is there, allowing you to reproduce the original data set. (In deciding on the number of stems to use, the problem is similar to selecting the number of categories in a histogram. Again, you want to do something that makes sense and that conveys information in a meaningful way. The one restriction is that the stems should be the same width. You would not let one stem be 50–54, and another 60–69.)

Notice that in Figure 3.4 I did not list the extreme values as I did the others. I used the word *high* in place of the stem and then inserted the actual values. I did this to highlight the presence of extreme values, as well as to conserve space.

Stem-and-leaf displays can be particularly useful for comparing two different distributions. Such a comparison is accomplished by plotting the two distributions on opposite sides of the stem. Figure 3.5 shows the actual distribution of numerical grades of males and females in a course on experimental methods that included a substantial statistics component. These are actual data. Notice the use of stems such as 6* (for 60–64), and 6. (for 65–69). In addition, notice the code at the bottom of the table that indicates how entries translate to raw scores. This particular code says that |4*| 1 represents 41, not 4.1 or 410. Finally, notice that the figure nicely illustrates the difference in performance between the male students and the female students.

Figure 3.5

Grades (in Percent) for an Actual Course in Experimental Methods, Plotted Separately by Gender

Male	Stem	Female
	3*	
6	3.	
	4*	1
	4.	
	5*	
	5.	
2	6*	03
	6.	568
32200	7*	0144
88888766666655	7.	555556666788899
4432221000	8*	00000111112222334444
7666666555	8.	55666666666667788888899
422	9*	000000000133
	9.	56

Code |4*| 1 = 41

3.4 Alternative Methods of Plotting Data

The previous sections dealt with only a few ways of plotting data. There is an almost unlimited number of other ways that data can be presented, some of which are quite ingenious and informative. A few examples are shown in Figures 3.6, 3.7, and 3.8. These examples were chosen because they illustrate how displays can be used to reveal interesting features of data.

Two comments are in order about how we plot data. First, the point of representing data graphically is to communicate to an audience. If there is a better way to communicate, then use it. Rules of graphical presentation are intended as guides to clearer presentation, not as prescriptive rules that may never be broken. This point was made earlier in the discussion about the number of intervals that should be used for a histogram, but it goes beyond histograms. So the first "rule" is this: *If it aids understanding, do it; if it doesn't, don't.*

The second rule is to keep things simple. Generally, the worst graphics are those that include irrelevant features that only add to the confusion. Tufte (1983) calls such material "chart junk," and you should avoid it. Perhaps the worst sin, in the opinion of many, is plotting something in three dimensions that could be better plotted in two. There are legitimate reasons for three-dimensional plots (the next example is one), but three dimensions are more likely to confuse the issue than to clarify it. Unfortunately, most graphics packages written for corporate users (often called "presentation graphics") encour-

Figure 3.6

**Major Causes of
Death in Vermont,
1900 and 1981**

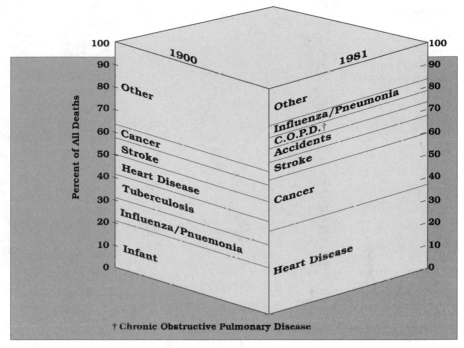

† Chronic Obstructive Pulmonary Disease

From *1981 Annual Report of Vital Statistics in Vermont*, Vermont Department of Health, 1982.

age the addition of unnecessary dimensions. Graphics should look utilitarian and, if possible, neat and orderly; they should rarely look "pretty."

Figure 3.6 is a comparison of the causes of death of Vermont residents in 1900 and 1981. Notice that the various causes have been ordered from bottom to top in terms of decreasing order of magnitude. From this figure it is immediately apparent that, whereas almost one-third of the deaths in 1900 were attributable to a high rate of infant mortality and to tuberculosis, neither of those sources contributed noticeably to death rates in 1981. On the other hand, cancer and heart disease, which together accounted for 60% of all deaths in 1981, played a much reduced role in 1900, accounting for less than 15% of all deaths.

Figure 3.7 is the distribution, by age and gender, of the populations of Mexico, Spain, the United States, and Sweden. This figure clearly portrays differences between countries in terms of their age distributions. (Compare Mexico and Sweden, for example.) By having males and females plotted back to back, we can also see the effects of gender differences in life expectancy. The older age groups in three countries contain more females than males. In Mexico it appears that men begin to outnumber women in their early twenties. This type of distribution was common in the past when many women died in childbirth, and we might start looking there for an explanation.

Figure 3.8 is included primarily as an example of how data are sometimes presented in an accurate but misleading manner. In an attempt to illustrate in a limited space the fact that consumers in one state pay less than consumers

Figure 3.7

Population, by Sex and Age, for Selected Countries: 1970

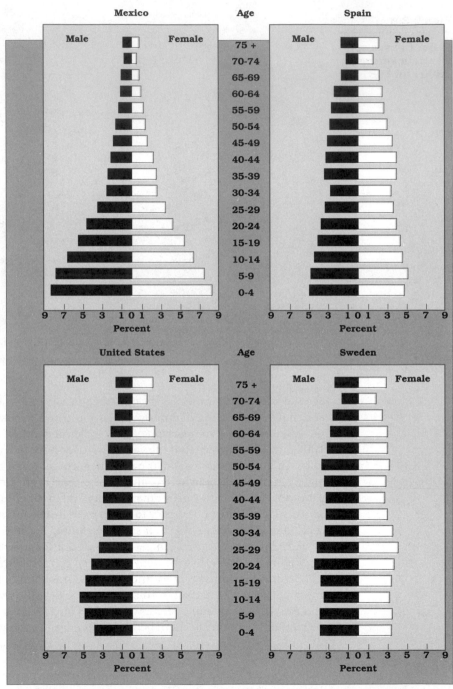

From *Social Indicators: 1976*. U.S. Department of Commerce. U.S. Government Printing Office, 1977.

Figure 3.8

**Average Monthly
Electric Bills in
New England**

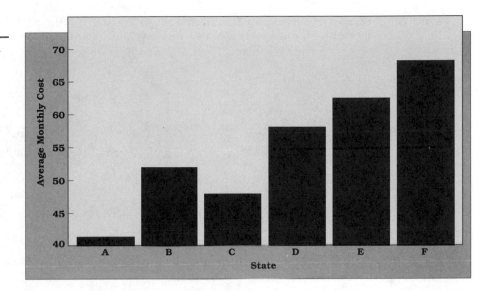

Figure 3.8

**Average Monthly
Electric Bills in
New England**

in other states for the same amount of electricity (750 kilowatt hours), a local utility company (which prefers to remain nameless) published a graph similar to the one shown in Figure 3.8. Although the *data* would be accurately portrayed in such a figure, the *relationships* among those data would not. For example, because the values on the ordinate start at $40, it appears that customers in State C pay about seven times as much (their bar is about seven times as tall) as do customers in State A. In fact, the charges were actually $41.02 and $47.11, with State C customers paying 15%, not 700%, more. When you are presenting data in a graph such as this, it is important to start the ordinate at zero or, if that is not practical, at least far enough from the smallest value to avoid giving an inaccurate visual message. More examples of distorted representation of data can be found in the excellent and entertaining paper by Wainer (1984).

3.5 Describing Distributions

The distributions of scores illustrated in Figures 3.1 and 3.2 were more or less regularly shaped distributions, rising to a maximum and then dropping away smoothly. Not all distributions are like that, however (see the stem-and-leaf display in Figure 3.3), and it is important to understand the terms used to describe different distributions. Consider the two distributions shown in Figure 3.9(a) and (b). These plots are of data that were computer generated to come from populations with specific shapes. These plots, and the other four in Figure 3.9, are based on samples of 1000 observations, and the slight irregularities are just random variability. Both of the distributions in Figure 3.9(a) and (b) are called **symmetric** because they have the same shape on both sides of the center. The distribution shown in Figure 3.9(a) came from what we will later refer to as a normal distribution. The distribution in Figure 3.9(b) is referred to

Symmetric
Having the same
shape on both sides
of the center.

Figure 3.9   Shapes of Frequency Distributions: (a) Normal, (b) Bimodal, (c) Negatively Skewed, (d) Positively Skewed, (e) Platykurtic, and (f) Leptokurtic

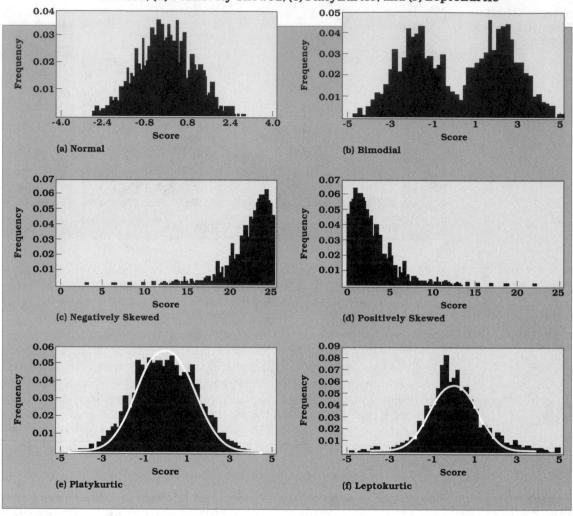

(a) Normal

(b) Bimodial

(c) Negatively Skewed

(d) Positively Skewed

(e) Platykurtic

(f) Leptokurtic

Bimodal
A distribution having two distinct peaks.

Unimodal
A distribution having one distinct peak.

Modality
The term referring to the number of major peaks in a distribution.

as **bimodal,** because it has two peaks. The term *bimodal* is used to refer to any distribution that has two predominant peaks, whether or not those peaks are of exactly the same height. If a distribution has only one major peak, it is called **unimodal**. The term used to refer to the number of major peaks in a distribution is **modality**.

Next consider Figure 3.9(c) and (d). These two distributions obviously are not symmetric. The distribution in Figure 3.9(c) has a tail going out to the left, whereas that in Figure 3.9(d) has a tail going out to the right. We say that the former is **negatively skewed** and the latter **positively skewed**. (Hint: To help you remember which is which, notice that negatively skewed distributions point to the negative, or small, numbers, and that positively skewed distributions point to the positive end of the scale.) There are statistical measures of

Figure 3.10

Frequency Distribution of Bradley's Reaction Time Data

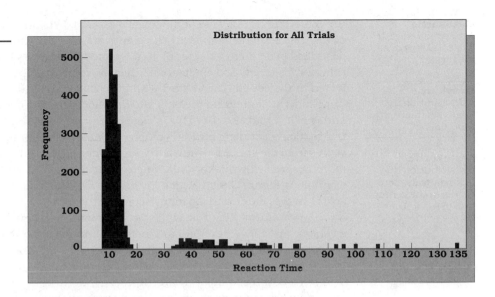

Negatively skewed
A distribution that trails off to the left.

Negatively skewed
A distribution that trails off to the left.

Positively skewed
A distribution that trails off to the right.

Skewness
A measure of the degree to which a distribution is asymmetrical.

the degree of asymmetry, or **skewness,** but they are not commonly used in the social sciences.

An interesting real-life example of a positively skewed bimodal distribution is shown in Figure 3.10. These data were generated by Bradley (1963), who instructed subjects to press a button as quickly as possible whenever a small light came on. Most of the data points are smoothly distributed between roughly 7 and 17 hundredths of a second, but a small but noticeable cluster of points lies between 30 and 70 hundredths, trailing off to the right. This second cluster of points was obtained primarily from trials on which the subject missed the button on the first try. Their inclusion in the data significantly affects the distribution's shape. An experimenter who had such a collection of data might seriously consider treating times greater than some maximum separately, on the grounds that those times were more a reflection of the *accuracy* of a psychomotor response than a measure of the *speed* of that response.

It is important to consider the difference between Bradley's data, shown in Figure 3.10, and the data that I generated, shown in Figures 3.1 and 3.2. Both distributions are positively skewed, but my data generally show longer reaction times without the second cluster of points. One difference was that I was making a decision on *which* button to press, whereas Bradley's subjects only had to press a single button whenever the light came on. In addition, the program I was using to present stimuli and record responses recorded data only from *correct* responses, not from errors. There was no chance to correct and hence nothing equivalent to missing the button on the first try and having to press it again. I point out these differences to illustrate that differences in the way in which data are collected can have noticeable effects on the kinds of data we see.

The last characteristic of a distribution that we will examine is kurtosis. **Kurtosis** has a specific mathematical definition, but basically it refers to the relative concentration of scores in the center, the upper and lower ends (tails), and the shoulders (between the center and the tails) of a distribution. In Fig-

Kurtosis
A measure of the peakedness of a distribution.

Mesokurtic
A distribution with a neutral degree of kurtosis.

Platykurtic
A distribution that is relatively thick in the "shoulders."

Leptokurtic
A distribution that has relatively more scores in the center and in the tails.

ure 3.9(e) and (f) I have superimposed a normal distribution on top of the plot of the data to make comparisons clear. A normal distribution (which will be described in detail in Chapter 6) is called **mesokurtic**. Its tails are neither too thin nor too thick, and there are neither too many nor too few scores concentrated in the center. If you start with a normal distribution and move scores from both the center and the tails into the shoulders, the curve becomes flatter and is called **platykurtic**. This is clearly seen in Figure 3.9(e), where the central portion of the distribution is much too flat. If, on the other hand, you moved scores from the shoulders into both the center and the tails, the curve becomes more peaked with thicker tails. Such a curve is called **leptokurtic,** and an example is Figure 3.9(f). Notice in this distribution that there are too many scores in the center *and* too many scores in the tails.[3]

Skewness and kurtosis, while not commonly used measures in the social sciences, are convenient verbal labels used to describe distributions. As an educated person, you should know what a positively skewed distribution is, even though it is unlikely that you will ever want to compute a numerical index of skewness. You should be aware, however, that these measures are important to statisticians, who might rightly be annoyed by the cavalier way I seem to be dismissing them. I downplay these measures because they are less useful to a user of statistics than to the professional.

It is important to recognize that relatively large samples of data are needed before we can have a good idea about the shape of a distribution, especially its kurtosis. With sample sizes of around 30, the best we can reasonably expect to see is whether the data tend to pile up in the tails of the distribution or are markedly skewed in one direction or another.

3.6   Using Computer Programs to Display Data

Almost all statistics texts assume that simple data analyses will be carried out by hand with the help of a standard calculator. This is probably the best approach to teaching, but today more and more analyses are carried out by computer programs. Thus it is important for you to be familiar with reading and interpreting the results of computer printouts. For that reason, most chapters in this book will include samples of computer solutions for examples previously analyzed by hand. These solutions will be obtained by using a variety of programs, to allow you to see different approaches. In the early chapters we will focus on a commonly available program called Minitab, since it is one of the easiest general-purpose programs to use and many students have access

---

[3] I would like to thank Karl Wuensch of East Carolina University for his helpful suggestions on understanding skewness and kurtosis. His ideas are reflected here, although I'm not sure that he would be satisfied by my statements on kurtosis. Karl has spent a lot of time thinking about kurtosis and made a good point recently when he stated in an electronic mail discussion, "I don't think my students really suffer much from not understanding kurtosis well, so I don't make a big deal out of it." You should have a general sense of what kurtosis is, but you should focus your attention on other, more important issues.

Figure 3.11

**Analysis of
Electronic Game
Data by Minitab**

```
MTB  > SET the following data in column C1
DATA > 15 23 7 0 8 43 . . .
DATA > 138 139
DATA > END
MTB  > HISTOGRAM on the data in column C1

Histogram of C1 N = 100

Midpoint    Count
     0       14      **************
    10       10      **********
    20        8      ********
    30        6      ******
    40       12      ************
    50        9      *********
    60        7      *******
    70        2      **
    80        8      ********
    90        4      ****
   100        4      ****
   110        5      *****
   120        3      ***
   130        6      ******
   140        2      **

MTB > STEM AND LEAF on the data in column C1

Stem-and-leaf of C1      N = 100
Leaf Unit = 1.0

    20       0    00000000000233566678  ←——— Modal interval
    30       1    2223555579
    35       2    33577
    43       3    22278999
   (14)      4    01123346667899  ‹———————— Interval containing median
    43       5    24557899
    35       6    37
    33       7    1556689
    26       8    34779
    21       9    466
    18      10    23677
    13      11    3479
     9      12    2557899
     2      13    89

MTB > STOP
```

to it. Along with the printout you will find the instructions required to produce the output.

Figure 3.11 shows a histogram and a stem-and-leaf display produced by Minitab for the electronic games data shown in Figure 3.3. Note that the raw data are entered first, in any order, using the SET command. (MTB> and DATA> are prompts supplied by Minitab that request input of either a command or data. The words in all capital letters are required; those with lower-case letters are optional.) Only the first few scores are shown to illustrate the use of the SET command, but the full set of observations could be reconstructed from Figure 3.3. Minitab chooses its own intervals for the histogram (in this case -5 to $+4.99$, 5 to 14.99, . . . , 135 to 144.99, which are not exactly the same intervals we chose in Figure 3.3) and lists each interval's midpoint. Since Minitab has chosen intervals that are different from ours, it produces a different (though still correct) histogram from the one we obtained.

The stem-and-leaf display generated by Minitab is equivalent to ours, although an additional column on the left contains cumulative frequencies (often referred to as **depth**) running inward from each end. For example, 20 people had scores less than or equal to 8, the largest entry for the first stem. In addition, 10 people had scores between 12 and 19, meaning a total of 30 people had scores less than or equal to 19. Similarly, we find that 43 people had scores less than or equal to 39. You should be able to find each of these values in the table. The number in parentheses is the frequency (noncumulative) for the interval that contains the middle value. In this case, 14 people fell in the interval containing the middle value. You can see that the distribution is positively skewed because the cumulative frequencies pile up much more quickly when we go from low scores toward the center than when we go from high scores toward the center. This is even more apparent in the stem-and-leaf display itself.

So far in our discussion almost no mention has been made of the numbers themselves. We have seen how data can be organized and presented in the form of distributions, and we have discussed a number of ways in which distributions can be characterized: symmetry or its lack (skewness), kurtosis, and modality. As useful as this information might be in certain situations, it is inadequate in others. We still do not know the average speed of a simple decision reaction time nor how alike or dissimilar are the reaction times for individual trials. To obtain this knowledge, we must reduce the data to a set of measures that carry the information we need. The questions to be asked refer to the location, or central tendency, and to the dispersion, or variability, of the distributions along the underlying scale. Measures of these characteristics will be considered in the next two chapters.

Depth
Cumulative frequency counting in from the nearer end.

3.7 Summary

In this chapter we discussed ways of describing distributions. All the techniques discussed here are intended primarily to organize and reduce the information contained in large sets of data to manageable proportions and to readily communicate some of that information to others. In examining these techniques we also looked briefly at stem-and-leaf displays (one small part of Tukey's exploratory data analysis) and examined a number of terms that are useful in characterizing the shapes of distributions.

Some important terms in this chapter are:

- Frequency distribution
- Histogram
- Real lower limit
- Real upper limit
- Midpoints
- Outlier
- Stem-and-leaf display
- Exploratory data analysis (EDA)
- Leading digits (most significant digits)
- Stem
- Trailing digits (less significant digits)

- Leaves
- Symmetric
- Modality
- Bimodal
- Unimodal
- Negatively skewed
- Positively skewed
- Skewness
- Kurtosis
- Mesokurtic
- Platykurtic
- Leptokurtic
- Depth

3.8 Exercises

3.1 Children differ from adults in that they tend to recall stories in terms of a sequence of actions rather than in terms of an overall plot. This means that their descriptions of a movie are filled with the phrase "and then. . . ." An experimenter with supreme patience asked 50 children to tell her about a given movie. Among other variables, she counted the number of "and then . . ." statements. The data follow.

```
18  15  22  19  18  17  18  20  17
12  16  16  17  21  23  18  20  21
20  20  15  18  17  19  20  23  22
10  17  19  19  21  20  18  18  24
11  19  31  16  17  15  19  20  18
18  40  18  19  16
```

(a) Plot an ungrouped frequency distribution for these data.

(b) What is the general shape of the distribution?

3.2 Make a histogram for the data in Exercise 3.1 using a reasonable number of intervals.

3.3 What is the difficulty with making a stem-and-leaf display of the data in Exercise 3.1?

3.4 As part of the study described in Exercise 3.1, the experimenter obtained the same kind of data for adults. Their data follow.

10	12	5	8	13	10	12	8	7
11	11	10	9	9	11	15	12	17
14	10	9	8	15	16	10	14	7
16	9	1	4	11	12	7	9	10
3	11	14	8	12	5	10	9	7
11	14	10	15	9				

(a) What can you tell just by looking at these numbers? Do children and adults seem to recall stories in the same way?

(b) Plot an ungrouped frequency distribution for these data using the same scale on the axes as you used for the children's data.

(c) Overlay this frequency distribution on the one from Exercise 3.1.

3.5 Use a back-to-back histogram (see Figure 3.7) to compare the data from Exercises 3.1 and 3.4.

3.6 Create a positively skewed set of data and plot it.

3.7 Create a bimodal set of data that represents some actual phenomenon and plot it. Why did you expect the data to be bimodal?

3.8 What would you predict to be the shape (e.g., skewness and modality) of the distribution of the number of cigarettes smoked per day for the next 200 people you meet?

The next two exercises refer to a large data set in Appendix C. These data come from a research study by Howell and Huessy, 1985, which is described at the beginning of the appendix.

3.9 Draw a histogram for the data for GPA in Appendix C, using reasonable intervals.

3.10 Create a stem-and-leaf display for the ADDSC score in Appendix C.

3.11 What three interesting facts about the populations of Mexico and Spain can be seen in Figure 3.7?

3.12 In some stem-and-leaf displays with one or two high values, the last stem is often written as HI and the complete values follow in the leaf section. Why might we do this?

3.13 How would you describe the skewness of the grades of males or females in Figure 3.5? Why would you have expected this kind of skewness even before you saw the data?

3.14 In Table 3.1 the reaction time data are broken down separately by the number of digits in the comparison stimulus. Create three side-by-side stem-and-leaf displays, one for each set of data. (Ignore the distinction between positive and negative instances.) What kinds of differences do you see between the reaction times under the three conditions?

3.15 Sternberg ran his original study (the one that is replicated in Table 3.1) to investigate whether people process information simultaneously or sequentially. He reasoned that if they process information simultaneously, they would compare the test stimulus against all digits in the comparison stimulus at the same time, and the time to decide whether a digit was part of the comparison set would not depend on how many digits were in the comparison. If people process information sequentially, the time to come to a decision would increase with the number of digits in the comparison. Which hypothesis do you think the figures you drew in Exercise 3.14 support?

3.16 In addition to comparing the three distributions of reaction times, as in Exercise 3.15, how else could you use the data from Table 3.1 to investigate how people process information?

3.17 One frequent assumption in statistical analyses is that observations are inde-

Figure 3.12

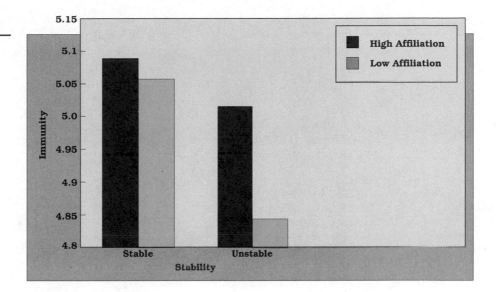

pendent of one another. (Knowing one re sponse tells you nothing about the magnitude of another response.) How would you characterize the reaction time data in Table 3.1, just based on what you know about how it was collected? (A lack of independence would not invalidate anything we have done with these data in this chapter.)

3.18 Figure 3.12 is adapted from a paper by Cohen, Kaplan, Cunnick, Manuck, and Rabin (1992), which examined the immune response of nonhuman primates raised in stable and unstable social groups. In each group animals were classed as high or low in affiliation, measured in terms of the amount of time they spent in close physical proximity to other animals. Higher scores on the immunity measure represent greater immunity to disease. How would you interpret these results?

3.19 Rogers and Prentice-Dunn (1981) had subjects deliver shock to their fellow subjects as part of a biofeedback study. They recorded the amount of shock that the subjects delivered to white participants and

black participants when the subjects had and had not been insulted by the experimenter. Their results are shown in Figure 3.13. Interpret these results.

3.20 The following data represent U.S. college enrollments by census categories as measured in 1982 and 1991. Plot the data in a form that represents the changing ethnic distribution of college students in the United States. (The data entries are in 1000s.)

Ethnic Group	1982	1991
White	9,997	10,990
Black	1,101	1,335
Native American	88	114
Hispanic	519	867
Asian	351	637
Foreign	331	416

3.21 The following data represent the number of AIDS cases in the United States among people aged 13–29. Plot these data to show the trend over time. (The data are in 1000s of cases.)

Figure 3.13

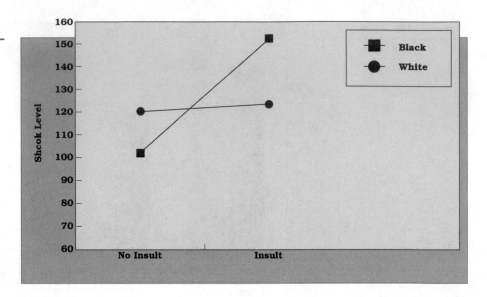

Year	Cases
1981–1982	196
1983	457
1984	960
1985	1685
1986	2815
1987	4385
1988	6383
1989	6780
1990	5483

3.22 The following data represent the total number of households, the number of households headed by women, and family size from 1960 to 1990. Present these data in such a way to reveal any changes in U.S. demographics. What do the data sug-gest about how a social scientist might look at the problems facing the United States? (Households are given in 1000s.)

Year	Total House-holds	House-holds Headed by Females	Family Size
1960	52,799	4,507	3.33
1970	63,401	5,591	3.14
1975	71,120	7,242	2.94
1980	80,776	8,705	2.76
1985	86,789	10,129	2.69
1987	89,479	10,445	2.66
1988	91,066	10,608	2.64
1989	92,830	10,890	2.62
1990	92,347	10,890	2.63

4

MEASURES OF CENTRAL TENDENCY

In Chapter 3 you saw how to display data in ways that allow us to begin to draw some conclusions about what the data have to say. Plotting data shows the general shape of the distribution and gives a visual sense of the general magnitude of the numbers involved.

In this chapter you will see several statistics that can be used to represent the "center" of the distribution. These statistics are called **measures of central tendency**. In the next chapter we will go a step further and look at measures that deal with how the observations are scattered around that central tendency, but first we must address identifying the center of the distribution.

The three common measures of central ten-

Measures of central tendency
Numerical values referring to the center of the distribution.

dency are the mode, the median, and the mean, and they will be discussed in turn. We will begin with what is probably the least used (and least useful) measure, the mode.

4.1 The Mode

Mode (Mo)
The most commonly occurring score.

The **mode** (Mo) can be defined simply as the most common score, that is, the score obtained from the largest number of subjects. Thus the mode is that value of X that corresponds to the highest point on the distribution. In the example in Chapter 3 that dealt with reaction times in a simple short-term memory task (see Table 3.2), this value is 67, because more trials (fourteen) had a reaction time of 67 hundredths of a second than had any other time. (The next most frequent reaction time, 62, occurred 13 times.)

If two *adjacent* times occur with equal (and greatest) frequency, a common convention is to take an average of the two values and call that the mode. If, on the other hand, two *nonadjacent* reaction times occur with equal (or nearly equal) frequency, we say that the distribution is bimodal and would most likely report both modes. For example, the distribution of time spent playing electronic games is roughly bimodal (see Figure 3.3), with peaks at the intervals of 0–9 minutes and 40–49 minutes. (You might argue that it is trimodal, with another peak at 120+ minutes, but that is a catchall interval for "all other values," so it does not make much sense to think of it as a modal value.)

One problem with the mode is illustrated in the reaction time data. For the same set of data the mode will change depending on how we plot the data. If you look at Table 3.3 or Figure 3.2, where we have grouped the data, you can see that the modal interval is the interval 60–64, with 54 reaction times falling in that interval. When many data points are examined in an ungrouped fashion, there is probably so much unimportant variability from one value to another that it doesn't make much sense to worry about the mode or to be very concerned with bimodality. When the data have been grouped into a reasonably stable looking plot, as in Figure 3.2, the mode is considerably more meaningful.

4.2 The Median

Median (Med)
The score corresponding to the point having 50% of the observations below it when observations are arranged in numerical order.

The **median (Med)** is the score that corresponds to the point at or below which 50% of the scores fall when the data are arranged in numerical order. By this definition, the median is also called the 50th percentile.[1] For example, consider the numbers (5 8 3 7 15). If the numbers are arranged in numerical order (3 5 7 8 15), half of the scores fall below 7, and it would be called the median. Suppose, however, that there were an even number of scores, for example,

---

[1] The specific percentile is defined as the point on a scale at or below which a specified percentage of the scores fall.

(5 11 3 7 15 14). Rearranging, we get (3 5 7 11 14 15), and no score has 50% of the values below it. That point actually falls between the 7 and the 11. In such a case the average (9) of the two middle scores (7 and 11) is commonly taken as the median.[2]

Median location
The location of the median in an ordered series.

A term that we will need shortly is the **median location**. The median location of N numbers is defined as follows:

$$\text{Median location} = \frac{N + 1}{2}$$

Thus, for five numbers the median location = $(5 + 1)/2 = 3$, which simply means that the median is the third number in an ordered series. For 12 numbers the median location = $(12 + 1)/2 = 6.5$; the median falls between, and is the average of, the sixth and seventh numbers.

For the data on reaction times in Table 3.2, the median location = $(300 + 1)/2 = 150.5$. When the data are arranged in order, both the 150th and 151st times are 60 hundredths of a second, which is the median. You can calculate this for yourself from Table 3.2. For the electronic games data there are 100 scores, and the median location is 50.5. We can tell from the stem-and-leaf display in Figure 3.3 that the fiftieth score is 44 and the fifty-first score is 46. The median would be 45, which is the average of these two values.

4.3 The Mean

The most common measure of central tendency, and one that really needs little explanation, is the mean, or what people generally have in mind when they use the word *average*. The **mean ($\overline{X}$)** is the sum of the scores divided by the number of scores and is usually designated $\overline{X}$ (read "X bar"). It is defined (using the summation notation given in Chapter 2) as follows:

Mean ($\overline{X}$)
The sum of the scores divided by the number of scores.

$$\overline{X} = \frac{\Sigma X}{N}$$

where ΣX is the sum of all values of X, and N is the number of X values. As an illustration, the mean of the numbers 3, 5, 12, and 5 is

$$\frac{3 + 5 + 12 + 5}{4} = \frac{25}{4} = 6.25$$

---

[2]The definition of the median is another one of those things over which statisticians love to argue. The definition given here, in which the median is defined as a *point* on a distribution of numbers, is the one most critics prefer. It is also in line with the statement that the median is the 50th percentile. On the other hand, there are many who are perfectly happy to say that the median is either the middle *number* in an ordered series (if N is odd) or the average of the two middle *numbers* (if N is even). Reading these arguments is a bit like going to a faculty meeting when there is nothing terribly important on the agenda. The less important the issue, the more there is to say about it.

For the reaction time data in Table 3.2, the sum of the observations is 18,078. When we divide that number by $N = 300$, we get $18{,}078/300 = 60.26$. Notice that this answer agrees well with the median, which we found to be 60. The mean and the median will be close whenever the distribution is nearly symmetric (as defined in Chapter 3). It also agrees reasonably well with the modal interval (60–64).

We could calculate the mean for the electronics game data by obtaining the raw data vales from the stem-and-leaf display, summing those values, and dividing by 100. For that example, the mean would be $5204/100 = 52.04$. Later in this chapter you will see how to use Minitab to save yourself considerable work in calculating the mean for large data sets.

4.4 Relative Advantages and Disadvantages of the Mode, the Median, and the Mean

Only when the distribution is symmetric will the mean and the median be equal, and only when the distribution is symmetric and unimodal will all three measures be the same. In all other cases—including almost all situations with which we will deal—some measure of central tendency must be chosen. A set of rules governing when to use a particular measure of central tendency would be convenient. However, there are no such rules. To make intelligent choices among the three measures, you must have some idea of the strengths and weaknesses of each.

The Mode

The mode is the most commonly occurring score. By definition, then, it is a score that actually occurred, whereas the mean and sometimes the median may be values that never appear in the data. The mode also has the obvious advantage of representing the largest number of people. Someone who is running a small store would do well to concentrate on the mode. If 80% of your customers want the giant economy family size and 20% want the teeny-weeny, single-person size, it wouldn't seem particularly wise to aim for the mean and stock only the regular size.

Related to these two advantages is the fact that, by definition, the probability that an observation drawn at random (X_i) will be equal to the mode is greater than the probability that it will be equal to any other specific score. Expressing this algebraically, we can say

$$p(X_i = \text{mode}) > p(X_i = \text{any other score})$$

Finally, the mode has the advantage of being applicable to nominal data, which, if you think about it, is obviously not true of the median or the mean.

The mode has its disadvantages, however. We have already seen that the mode depends on how we group our data. Another disadvantage is that it may not be particularly representative of the entire collection of numbers. This disadvantage is illustrated in the electronics game data (see Figure 3.11), in which the modal interval equals 0–9, which probably reflects the fact that a number of people do not play video games (difficult as that may be to believe). Using that interval as the mode would be to ignore all of those people who do play.

The Median

The major advantage of the median, which it shares with the mode, is the fact that it is unaffected by extreme scores. Thus the medians of both (5 8 9 15 16) and (0 8 9 15 206) are 9. Many experimenters find this characteristic to be useful in studies in which extreme scores occasionally occur but have no particular significance. For example, the average trained rat can run down a short runway in approximately 1 to 2 seconds. Every once in a while this same rat will inexplicably stop halfway down, scratch himself, poke his nose at the photocells, and lie down to sleep. In that instance it is of no practical significance whether he takes 30 seconds or 10 minutes to get to the other end of the runway. It may even depend on when the experimenter gives up and pokes him with a pencil—a common practice when stamping your feet, blowing on the rat, and tapping on the runway all fail. If we ran a rat through three trials on a given day and his times were (1.2, 1.3, and 20 seconds), that would have the same meaning to us—in terms of what it tells us about the rat's knowledge of the task—as if his times were (1.2, 1.3, and 136.4 seconds). In both cases the median would be 1.3. Obviously, however, his daily *mean* would be quite different in the two cases (7.5 versus 46.3 seconds). It is this problem that frequently induces experimenters to work with the median rather than the mean time per day.

The median has another point in its favor, when contrasted with the mean, which those writers who get excited over scales of measurement like to point out. The calculation of the median does not require any assumptions about the interval properties of the scale. With the numbers (5, 8, and 11), the object represented by the number 8 is in the middle, no matter how close or distant it is from objects represented by 5 and 11. When we say that the *mean* is 8, however, we may be making the implicit assumption that the underlying distance between objects 5 and 8 is the same as the underlying distance between objects 8 and 11. Whether or not this assumption is reasonable is up to the experimenter to determine. I prefer to work on the principle that if it is an absurdly unreasonable assumption, the experimenter will realize that and take appropriate steps. If it is not absurdly unreasonable, then its practical effect on the results most likely will be negligible. (This problem of scales of measurement was discussed in more detail in Chapter 2.)

A major disadvantage of the median is that it does not enter readily into equations and is thus more difficult to work with than the mean. It is also not as stable from sample to sample, as we will see in the next chapter.

The Mean

Of the three principal measures of central tendency, the mean is by far the most common. It would not be too much of an exaggeration to say that for many people statistics is (unfortunately) nearly synonymous with the study of the mean.

As we have already seen, certain disadvantages are associated with the mean. It is influenced by extreme scores, its value may not actually exist in the data, and its interpretation in terms of the underlying variable being measured requires at least some faith in the interval properties of the data. You might be inclined to politely suggest that if the mean has all the disadvantages I have just ascribed to it, then maybe it should be quietly forgotten and allowed to slip into oblivion along with statistics like the "critical ratio," a statistical concept that hasn't been heard of for years. The mean, however, is made of sterner stuff.

The mean has several important advantages that far outweigh its disadvantages. Probably the most important of these from a historical point of view (though not necessarily from your point of view) is that the mean can be manipulated algebraically. In other words, we can use the mean in an equation and manipulate it through the normal rules of algebra, specifically because we can write an equation that defines the mean. Since you cannot write a standard equation for the mode or the median, you have no real way of manipulating those statistics using standard algebra. Whatever the mean's faults, this accounts in large part for its widespread application. The second important advantage of the mean is that it has several desirable properties with respect to its use as an estimate of the population mean. In particular, if we drew many samples from some population, the sample means that resulted would be more stable (less variable) estimates of the central tendency of that population than would the sample medians or modes. The fact that the sample mean is in general a better estimate of the population mean than is the mode or the median is a major reason that it is so widely used.

4.5 Obtaining Measures of Central Tendency Using Minitab

For small sets of data it is perfectly reasonable to compute measures of central tendency by hand. With larger sample sizes or data sets with many variables, however, it is much simpler to let a computer program do the work. (It is also more fun.) Minitab is ideally suited to this purpose since it is easy to use, versatile, and widely available.

Suppose that as part of a large study on teaching effectiveness we asked each of 15 students in class to record the number of different annoying mannerisms exhibited by their instructor (e.g., dropping chalk, losing chalk, arranging and rearranging lecture notes, pacing, alternately standing and sitting, and all those other activities the counting of which makes the lecture pass more quickly). These data are illustrated in Figure 4.1, along with the com-

Figure 4.1

Minitab Program to Calculate Measures of Central Tendency on the Number of Annoying Mannerisms

```
MTB > Set the following data in Column C1
DATA> 12 18 19 15 18 14 17 20 18 15 17 11 23 19 10
DATA> end

MTB > name c1 'manner'

MTB > Mean of 'manner'  ←————— Mean
    MEAN  =    16.400

MTB > Median of 'manner'
    MEDIAN =    17.000   ←————— Median
MTB > Histogram of 'manner'

Histogram of manner N = 15


Midpoint  Count
      10     1 *
      11     1 *
      12     1 *
      13     0
      14     1 *
      15     2 **
      16     0
      17     2 **
      18     3 ***  ←————— Mode
      19     2 **
      20     1 *
      21     0
      22     0
      23     1 *

MTB > Save 'Manner.min'

MTB > Stop
```

mands required to produce the three common measures of central tendency. We can obtain the mean and the median directly, but to get the mode we need to produce a histogram (or a stem-and-leaf display) and then look for the most frequently appearing interval.

From the figure you can see that the mean (16.4), the median (17), and the mode (18) are all about the same, and that the distribution is fairly smooth but slightly negatively skewed. We can also see from the histogram that there is considerable disagreement among students concerning the number of annoying mannerisms exhibited by the instructor. This dispersion on either side of the mean is discussed in the next chapter.

4.6 Summary

In this chapter we considered several measures used to describe the center of a distribution. Each measure has its own particular strengths and weaknesses. One of these, the mean, forms the basis for much of the material discussed in the remainder of this book.

Some important terms in this chapter are:

• **Measures of central tendency**	• **Median location**
• **Mode (Mo)**	• **Mean ($\overline{X}$)**
• **Median (Med)**	

4.7 Exercises

4.1 Calculate the mode, the median, and the mean for the data in Exercise 3.1.

4.2 Calculate the mode, the median, and the mean for the data in Exercise 3.4.

4.3 Compare the answers in Exercises 4.1 and 4.2. What do they tell you about story-telling behavior in adults and children?

4.4 Make up a set of data for which the mean is greater than the median.

4.5 Make up a positively skewed set of data. Does the mean fall above or below the median?

4.6 Can you make up a unimodal set of data where the mean and median are equal but different from the mode?

4.7 A group of 15 rats running a straight-alley maze required the following number of trials to perform to a predetermined criterion. The frequency distribution follows:

Trials to reach criterion						
18	19	20	21	22	23	24
Number of rats (frequency)						
1	0	4	3	3	3	1

Calculate the mean and median number of trials to criterion for this group.

4.8 Given the following set of data, demonstrate that subtracting a constant (e.g., 5) from every score reduces all measures of central tendency by that amount.

8   7   12   14   3   7

4.9 Given the following data, show that multiplying each score by a constant multiplies all measures of central tendency by that constant.

8   3   5   5   6   2

4.10 Create a sample of ten numbers that has a mean of 8.6. Notice carefully how you did this—it will help you later to understand the idea of degrees of freedom.

4.11 Calculate the measures of central tendency for the data on ADDSC and GPA in Appendix C.

4.12 Why would it not make any sense to calculate the mean for SEX or ENGL in Appendix C? If we did go ahead and compute the mean for SEX, what would the value of ($\overline{X} - 1$) really represent?

4.13 Why is the mode an acceptable measure for nominal data? Why are the mean and the median not acceptable measures for nominal data?

4.14 In Table 3.1 the reaction time data are broken down separately by the number of digits in the comparison stimulus. Calculate the three main measures of central tendency for each set of data, ignoring the distinction between positive and negative instances. How well do these measures agree within each data set?

4.15 With reference to Exercise 4.14, if people process information in short-term memory in parallel, the mean reaction time should not depend on the number of digits in the comparison stimulus, whereas if we process information sequentially, reaction times should increase with increasing size of the comparison stimulus. What do the answers to Exercise 4.14 suggest about how we process information?

5

MEASURES OF VARIABILITY

In Chapter 4 we considered several measures related to the center of a distribution. However, an average value for a distribution (whether it be the mode, the median, or the mean) fails to give the whole story. We need some additional measure (or measures) to indicate the degree to which individual observations are clustered about or, equivalently, deviate from that average value. The average may reflect the general location of most of the scores, or the scores may be distributed over a wide range of values, and the "average" may not be very representative of the full set of observations. Probably everyone has had experience with examinations on which all students received approximately the same grade and with examinations on which the scores ranged from excellent to dreadful. Measures that refer to the differences between these two types of situations are what we have in mind when we speak of **dispersion**, or variability, around the median, the mode, or any other point we wish. In general we will refer specifically to dispersion around the mean.

As an example of a situation in which we might expect differences in variability from one group to another, consider the case in which two sections of Computer Science I are given the same exam. One section is told that the exam will count for 20% of their final grade, and the other section is told that it will count for 90%. It is probably reasonable to expect that the two sections will have roughly the same mean. However, because "pressure" has a facilitative effect on the performance of some people and a disruptive effect on the performance of others, we might expect more variability in the section for whom the exam counts for 90% of their final grade. Do these hypotheses correspond with your experience? If not, what would you expect to happen? Does your expectation lead to differences in means, variances, both, or neither?

As a second example, consider the following four sets of data:

A	B	C	D
4	3	2	1
5	5	5	5
6	7	8	9

A little calculation will show you that all four sets have the same mean (5), but that there is greater variability around that mean as you move from set A toward set D. You can see this visually by plotting the values on the same graph (Figure 5.1).

For our final illustration we will take some interesting data collected by Langlois and Roggman (1990) on the perceived attractiveness of faces. Think for a moment about some of the faces you consider attractive. Do they tend to have unusual features (e.g., prominent noses or unusual eyebrows), or are the features rather ordinary? Langlois and Roggman were interested in investigating what makes faces attractive. Toward that end they presented students with computer-generated pictures of faces. Some of these pictures had been created by averaging together snapshots of four different people to create a composite. We will label these photographs Set 4. Other pictures (Set 32) were created by averaging across snapshots of 32 different people. As you might suspect, when you average across four people, there is still room for individuality in the composite. For example, some composites show thin faces, while others show round ones. However, averaging across 32 people usually gives results that are very "average." Noses are neither too long nor too short, ears don't stick out too far nor sit too close to the head, and so on. Students were asked to examine the resulting pictures and rate each one on a 5-point scale of attractiveness. The authors were primarily interested in determining whether the *mean* rating of

Dispersion
The degree to which individual data points are distributed around the mean.

Figure 5.1

Plot of Four Sets of Data with Different Degrees of Variability

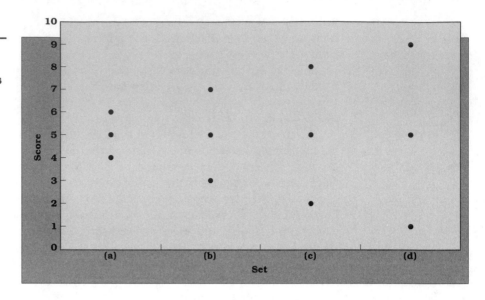

the faces in Set 4 was less than the mean rating of the faces in Set 32. It was, suggesting that faces with distinctive characteristics are judged as less attractive than more ordinary faces. In this chapter, however, we are interested in the degree of *similarity* in the ratings of faces. We suspect that composites of 32 faces would be more homogeneous, and thus would be rated more similarly, than composites of four faces.

The data are shown in Table 5.1.[1] From the table you can see that Langlois and Roggman were correct in predicting that Set 32 faces would be rated as more attractive than Set 4 faces. (The means were 3.26 and 2.64, respectively.) But notice also that the ratings for the composites of 32 faces are considerably more homogeneous than the ratings of the composites of four faces. We can plot these two sets of data as standard histograms, as in Figure 5.2.

While it is apparent from Figure 5.2 that there is greater variability in the rating of composites of four photographs than in the rating of composites of 32 photographs, some sort of measure is needed to reflect this difference in variability. A number of measures could be used, and they will be discussed in turn, starting with the simplest.

---

[1] These data are not the actual numbers that Langlois and Roggman collected, but they have been generated to have exactly the same mean and standard deviation as the original data. Langlois and Roggman used six composite photographs per set. I have used 20 photographs per set to make the data more applicable to my purposes in this chapter. The conclusions that you would draw from these data, however, are exactly the same as the conclusions you would draw from theirs.

Table 5.1

**Rated
Attractiveness of
Composite Faces**

	Set 4		Set 32	
Picture	Composite of 4 Faces	Picture	Composite of 32 Faces
1	1.20	21	3.13
2	1.82	22	3.17
3	1.93	23	3.19
4	2.04	24	3.19
5	2.30	25	3.20
6	2.33	26	3.20
7	2.34	27	3.22
8	2.47	28	3.23
9	2.51	29	3.25
10	2.55	30	3.26
11	2.64	31	3.27
12	2.76	32	3.29
13	2.77	33	3.29
14	2.90	34	3.30
15	2.91	35	3.31
16	3.20	36	3.31
17	3.22	37	3.34
18	3.39	38	3.34
19	3.59	39	3.36
20	4.02	40	3.38
Mean = 2.64		Mean = 3.26	

5.1 Range

Range
The distance from the lowest to the highest score.

Outliers
Unusually extreme observations.

The **range** is a measure of distance, namely the distance from the lowest to the highest score. For our data the range for Set 4 is $(4.02 - 1.20) = 2.82$ units; for Set 32 it is $(3.38 - 3.13) = 0.25$ units. The range is an exceedingly common measure and is illustrated in everyday life by such statements as, "The price of hamburger fluctuates over a 70¢ range from $1.29 to $1.99 per pound." The range suffers, however, from a total reliance on extreme values, or, if the values are *unusually* extreme, on what are called **outliers**. As a result, the range may give a distorted picture of the variability.

Figure 5.2

**Distribution
of Scores for
Attractiveness
of Composites**

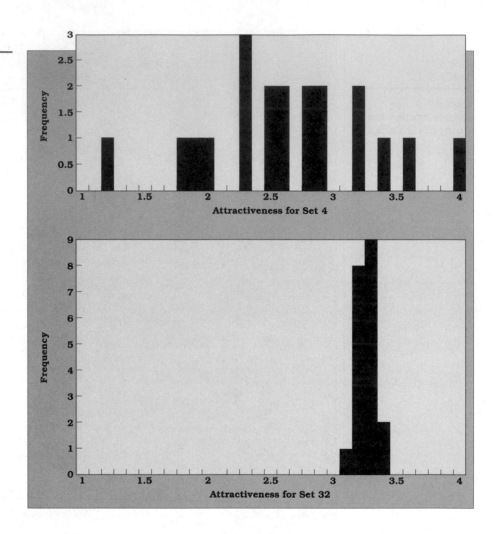

For examples of some of the difficulties with the range, consider the three sets of data shown in Table 5.2. The first two sets are exactly alike except for the last score, and they have nearly the same mean. However, the range for Group I is double that for Group II. The second and third groups have exactly the same mean and range, but almost all the scores for Group II are 9s and 11s, whereas the scores for Group III are fairly evenly spaced from 6 to 14.

5.2 Interquartile Range and Other Range Statistics

Interquartile range
The range of the
middle 50% of the
observations.

The **interquartile range** (which is closely related to something called the H-spread) represents an attempt to circumvent the problem of the range being heavily dependent on extreme scores. An interquartile range is obtained by discarding the upper and lower 25% of the distribution and taking the range of

Table 5.2

Sample Data Illustrating Problems with the Range

	Group I	Group II	Group III
	8	8	6
	9	9	6
	9	9	6
	9	9	9
	9	9	9
	9	9	9
	9	9	10
	9	9	10
	9	9	10
	9	9	10
	11	11	11
	11	11	11
	11	11	11
	11	11	14
	11	11	14
	24	16	14
Mean	10.5	10	10
Range	16	8	8

what remains. As such, it is the range of the middle 50% of the observations, or the difference between the 75th percentile and the 25th percentile. We can calculate the interquartile range for the data on attractiveness of faces by omitting the lowest five scores and the highest five scores and determining the range of the remainder. In this case the interquartile range for Set 4 would be 0.58 and the interquartile range for Set 32 would be only 0.11.

The interquartile range plays an important role in a useful graphical method known as a boxplot. This method will be discussed in Section 5.9.

In many ways the interquartile range suffers from problems that are just the opposite of those found with the range. Specifically, it discards too much of the data. If we want to know if one set of photographs is judged more variable than another, it does not make much sense to toss out those scores that are most extreme and thus vary the most from the mean.

There is nothing sacred about eliminating the upper and lower 25% of the distribution before calculating the range. In fact we could eliminate any percentage we wanted, as long as we could justify that number to ourselves and to others. What we really want to do is eliminate those scores that are likely to

Trimmed samples
Samples with a percentage of extreme scores removed.

be accidents without eliminating the variability that we seek to study. Samples that have had a certain percentage (e.g., 10%) of the values in each tail removed are called **trimmed samples**, and statistics calculated on such samples are called **trimmed statistics** (e.g., trimmed means or trimmed ranges).

Trimmed statistics
Statistics calculated on trimmed samples.

5.3 The Average Deviation

At first glance it would seem that if we want to measure how scores are dispersed around the mean (i.e., deviate from the mean) the most logical thing to do would be to obtain all the deviations (i.e., $X_i - \bar{X}$) and average them. The more widely the scores are dispersed, the greater the deviations and therefore the greater the average of the deviations—at least that is what you might think. However, common sense has led you astray here. If you calculate the deviations from the mean, some scores will be above the mean and have a positive deviation, while others will be below the mean and have negative deviations. In the end the positive and negative deviations will balance each other out and the sum of the deviations will be zero. This will not get us very far.

5.4 The Mean Absolute Deviation

If you think about the difficulty in trying to get something useful out of the average of the deviations, you might well be led to suggest that we could solve the whole problem by taking the absolute values of the deviations. (The absolute value of a number is the value of that number with any minus signs removed. The absolute value is indicated by vertical bars around the number, e.g., $|-3| = 3$.) The suggestion to use absolute values makes sense because we want to know *how much* scores deviate from the mean without regard to whether they are above or below it. The measure suggested here is a perfectly legitimate one and even has a name: the **mean absolute deviation (m.a.d.)**. The sum of the absolute deviations is divided by N (the number of scores) to yield an average (mean) deviation:

Mean absolute deviation (m.a.d.)
Mean of the absolute deviations about the mean.

$$\text{m.a.d.} = \frac{\Sigma|X - \bar{X}|}{N}$$

For the data on attractiveness of faces the mean absolute deviations are given in Table 5.3. For Set 4 the m.a.d. = 0.50, while for Set 32 it is only 0.06. This measure clearly reflects the fact that there is greater diversity in the judgments of pictures that contain less averaging, which is as we would expect.

For all its simplicity and intuitive appeal, the mean absolute deviation has not played an important role in statistical methods. Much more useful measures, the variance and the standard deviation, are normally used instead.

2.82

Table 5.3

Rated Attractiveness of Composite Faces

	Set 4			Set 32	
Picture	X	$|(X - \bar{X})|$	Picture	X	$|(X - \bar{X})|$
1	1.20	1.44	21	3.13	0.13
2	1.82	0.82	22	3.17	0.09
3	1.93	0.71	23	3.19	0.07
4	2.04	0.60	24	3.19	0.07
5	2.30	0.34	25	3.20	0.06
6	2.33	0.31	26	3.20	0.06
7	2.34	0.30	27	3.22	0.04
8	2.47	0.17	28	3.23	0.03
9	2.51	0.13	29	3.25	0.01
10	2.55	0.09	30	3.26	0.00
11	2.64	0.00	31	3.27	0.01
12	2.76	0.12	32	3.29	0.03
13	2.77	0.13	33	3.29	0.03
14	2.90	0.26	34	3.30	0.04
15	2.91	0.27	35	3.31	0.05
16	3.20	0.56	36	3.31	0.05
17	3.22	0.58	37	3.34	0.08
18	3.39	0.75	38	3.34	0.08
19	3.59	0.95	39	3.36	0.10
20	4.02	1.38	40	3.38	0.12

Mean = 2.64			Mean = 3.26		
Total absolute deviation = 9.91			Total absolute deviation = 1.15		
Mean absolute deviation = 0.50			Mean absolute deviation = 0.06		

5.5 The Variance

Sample variance (s^2)
Sum of the squared deviations about the mean divided by $N - 1$.

Population variance (σ^2)
Variance of the population—usually estimated, rarely computed.

The measure that we will consider in this section, the **sample variance (s^2)**, represents a different approach to the problem of the deviations themselves averaging to zero. (When we are referring to the **population variance**, we use σ^2 [lowercase sigma] as the symbol.) In the case of the variance we take advantage of the fact that the square of a negative number is positive. Thus we sum the *squared* deviations rather than the deviations themselves. Because we want an average, we next divide that sum by a function of N, the number of scores. Although you might reasonably expect that we would divide by N, we actually divide by ($N - 1$). We use ($N - 1$) as a divisor *for the sample variance only* because, as we will see shortly, it leaves us with a sample variance that is a better estimate of the corresponding population variance. (The population variance is calculated by dividing the sum of the squared deviations, for each value in the population, by N rather than $(N - 1)$. However, we only rarely calculate a population variance; we almost always estimate it from a sample variance.) If it is important to specify more precisely the variable to which s^2 refers, we can subscript it with a letter representing the variable. Thus, if we denote the data in Set 4 as X, the variance could be denoted as s_X^2. (You could refer to $s_{Set\ 4}^2$, but long subscripts are usually awkward. In general we label variables with simple letters like X and Y.)

For our example we can calculate the sample variances of Set 4 and Set 32 as follows:[2]

Set 4 (X)

$$s_X^2 = \frac{\Sigma(X - \bar{X})^2}{N - 1}$$

$$= \frac{(1.20 - 2.64)^2 + (1.82 - 2.64)^2 + \cdots + (4.02 - 2.64)^2}{20 - 1}$$

$$= \frac{8.1567}{19} = 0.4293$$

Set 32 (Y)

$$s_Y^2 = \frac{\Sigma(Y - \bar{Y})^2}{N - 1}$$

$$= \frac{(3.13 - 3.26)^2 + (3.17 - 3.26)^2 + \cdots + (3.38 - 3.26)^2}{20 - 1}$$

$$= \frac{0.0902}{19} = 0.0048$$

From these calculations we see that the difference in variances reflects the differences we see in the distributions.

Although the variance is an exceptionally important concept and one of the most commonly used statistics, it does not have the direct intuitive interpretation we would like. Because it is based on *squared* deviations, the result is in terms of squared units. Thus, Set 4 has a mean attractiveness rating of 2.64 and a variance of 0.4293 *squared* units. But squared units are awkward things

---

[2] In these calculations and others throughout the book, my answers may differ slightly from those that you obtain for the same data. If so, the difference is most likely due to rounding. If you repeat my calculations and arrive at a similar answer, that is sufficient.

to talk about and have little meaning with respect to the data. Fortunately the solution to this problem is simple: take the square root of the variance.

5.6 The Standard Deviation

**Standard deviation
(s or σ)**
Square root of the
variance.

The **standard deviation** (**s** or **σ**) is defined as the positive square root of the variance and, for a sample, is symbolized as *s* (with a subscript identifying the variable if necessary) or, occasionally, as S.D. (The notation *σ* is used in reference to a *population* standard deviation.) The following formula defines the standard deviation:

$$s_X = \sqrt{\frac{\Sigma (X - \bar{X})^2}{N - 1}}$$

For our example,

$$s_X = \sqrt{s_X^2} = \sqrt{0.4293} = 0.6552$$

$$s_Y = \sqrt{s_Y^2} = \sqrt{0.0048} = 0.0689$$

For convenience, I will round these answers to 0.66 and 0.07, respectively.

If you look at the formula for the standard deviation, you will see that the standard deviation, like the mean absolute deviation, is basically a measure of the average of the deviations of each score from the mean. Granted, these deviations have been squared, summed, and so on, but at heart they are still deviations. And even though we have divided by $(N - 1)$ instead of N, we still have obtained something very much like a mean or an "average" of these deviations. Thus we can say without too much distortion that attractiveness ratings for Set 4 deviated, on the average, 0.66 unit from the mean, whereas attractiveness ratings for Set 32 deviated, on the average, only 0.07 unit from the mean. This rather loose way of thinking about the standard deviation as a sort of average deviation goes a long way toward giving it meaning without doing serious injustice to the concept.

These results tell us two interesting things about attractiveness. If you were a subject in this experiment, the fact that computer averaging of many faces produces similar composites would be reflected in the fact that your ratings of Set 32 would not show much variability—all those images are judged to be pretty much alike. Second, the fact that those ratings have a higher mean than the ratings of faces in Set 4 reveals that averaging over many faces produces composites that seem more attractive. Does this conform to your everyday experience? I, for one, would have expected that faces judged attractive would be those with distinctive features, but I would have been wrong. Go back and think again about those faces you class as attractive. Are they really distinctive? If so, do you have an additional hypothesis to explain the findings?

We can also look at the standard deviation in terms of how many scores fall no more than a standard deviation above or below the mean. For a wide variety of reasonably symmetric and mound-shaped distributions, we can say that approximately two-thirds of the observations lie within one standard deviation of the mean (for a normal distribution, which will be discussed in Chapter 7, it is almost exactly two-thirds). Although there certainly are exceptions, especially for badly skewed distributions, this rule is still useful. If I told you that for traditional jobs the mean starting salary for college graduates this year is expected to be \$20,000 with a standard deviation of \$4000, you probably would not be far off to conclude that about two-thirds of graduates who take these jobs will earn between \$16,000 and \$24,000.

A third characteristic of the standard deviation is that it is usually about one-fifth or one-sixth of the range. While this is not a particularly useful way of interpreting the standard deviation, it is a handy way of checking your work. If a glance at the data shows that the range is about 20 units, and you have just calculated $s_X = 15$, I would strongly suggest that you check your work. You may be right, but probably are not. On the other hand, if you find that $s_X = 3.8$, you are justified in accepting that as at least a reasonable answer.

5.7 Computational Formulae for the Variance and the Standard Deviation

The previous expressions for the variance and the standard deviation, while perfectly correct, are incredibly unwieldy for any reasonable amount of data. They are also prone to rounding errors, since they usually involve squaring fractional deviations. They are excellent definitional formulae, but we will now consider a more practical set of calculational formulae. These formulae are algebraically equivalent to the ones we have seen, so they will give the same answers but with much less effort.

The definitional formula for the sample variance was given as

$$s_X^2 = \frac{\Sigma(X - \bar{X})^2}{N - 1}$$

A more practical computational formula is

$$s_X^2 = \frac{\Sigma X^2 - \dfrac{(\Sigma X)^2}{N}}{N - 1}$$

Similarly, for the sample standard deviation

$$s_X = \sqrt{\frac{\Sigma(X - \bar{X})^2}{N - 1}}$$

$$= \sqrt{\frac{\Sigma X^2 - (\Sigma X)^2/N}{N - 1}}$$

It would be an excellent idea for you to memorize these formulae, because these equations, or parts of them, will recur throughout this book and crop up in unexpected places. Applying the computational formula for the sample variance for Set 4, we obtain

$$s_X^2 = \frac{\Sigma X^2 - \dfrac{(\Sigma X)^2}{N}}{N - 1}$$

$$= \frac{1.20^2 + 1.82^2 + \cdots + 4.02^2 - \dfrac{52.89^2}{20}}{19}$$

$$\frac{148.0241 - \dfrac{52.89^2}{20}}{19} - 0.4293$$

Note that the answer we obtained here is exactly the same as the answer we obtained by the definitional formula. Note also, as pointed out in Chapter 2, that $\Sigma X^2 = 148.0241$ is quite different from $(\Sigma X)^2 = 52.89^2 = 2797.35$. I leave the calculation of the variance for Set 32 to you.

You might be somewhat reassured that the level of mathematics required for the previous calculations is about as much as you will need anywhere in this book. (I told you that you learned it all in high school.)

5.8 The Mean and the Variance as Estimators

Mention was made in Chapter 1 of the fact that we generally calculate measures such as the mean and the variance to use as *estimates* of the corresponding values in the populations. Characteristics of samples are called *statistics* and are designated by Roman letters (e.g., $\overline{X}$). Characteristics of populations, on the other hand, are called *parameters* and are designated by Greek letters. Thus the population mean is symbolized by μ (lowercase mu). In general, then, we use statistics as estimates of parameters.

If the purpose of obtaining a statistic is to use it as an estimator of a parameter, it should come as no surprise that our choice of a statistic (and even how we define it) is partly a function of how well that statistic functions as an estimator of the parameter in question. In fact, the mean is usually preferred over other measures of central tendency precisely because of its performance as an estimator of μ. The variance (s^2) is defined as it is specifically because of the advantages that accrue when s^2 is used to estimate the population variance, signified by σ^2.

Three properties of estimators are of particular interest to statisticians and heavily influence the choice of the statistics we compute. These properties are sufficiency, unbiasedness, and efficiency. They are discussed here simply to give you a feel for why some measures of central tendency and variability are seen as more important than others. It is *not* critical that you have a thorough understanding of estimation and related concepts, only that you have some general appreciation of the issues involved.

Sufficiency

Sufficient statistic
A statistic that uses all of the information in a sample.

A statistic is a **sufficient statistic** if it contains (makes use of) all the information in a sample. You might think this is pretty obvious, because it certainly seems reasonable to base your estimates on all the data. In fact, the mean does exactly that. The mode, however, uses only the most common observations, ignoring all others, while the median uses only the middle one, again ignoring the values of other observations. Similarly, the range, as a measure of dispersion, uses only the two most extreme (and thus most unrepresentative) scores. Here you see one of the reasons that we emphasize the mean as our measure of central tendency.

Unbiasedness

Suppose we have a population for which we somehow know the mean (μ), say, the heights of all basketball players in the NBA. If we were to draw one sample from that population and calculate the sample mean ($\overline{X}_1$), we would expect $\overline{X}_1$ to be reasonably close to μ, particularly if N is large, since it is an estimator of μ. So if the average height in this population is 7.0′ ($\mu = 7.0′$), we would expect a sample of, say, 10 players to have an average height of approximately 7.0′ as well, although it probably would not be exactly equal to 7.0′. (We can write $\overline{X}_1 \approx 7$, where the symbol $\approx$ means "approximately equal.") Now suppose we draw another sample and obtain its mean ($\overline{X}_2$). (The subscript here is used to differentiate the means of successive samples. Thus the mean of the 43d sample, if we drew that many, would be denoted by $\overline{X}_{43}$.) This mean would probably also be reasonably close to μ, but we would not expect it to be exactly equal to μ or to $\overline{X}_1$. If we were to keep up this procedure and draw sample means ad infinitum, we would find that *the average of the sample means would*

Expected value
The average value calculated for a statistic over an infinite number of samples.

be precisely equal to μ. Thus we say that the **expected value** (i.e., the long-range average of many, many samples) of the sample mean is equal to μ, the population mean that it is estimating. An estimator whose expected value equals the parameter to be estimated is called an **unbiased estimator** and that is a very important property for a statistic to possess. Both the sample mean and the sample variance are unbiased estimators of their corresponding parameters. (This is why we used ($N - 1$) as the denominator of the formula for the sample variance.) By and large, unbiased estimators are like unbiased people—they are nicer to work with than biased ones.

Unbiased estimator
A statistic whose expected value is equal to the parameter to be estimated.

Efficiency

Estimators are also characterized in terms of **efficiency**. Suppose that a population is symmetric: thus the values of the population mean and median are equal. Now suppose that we want to estimate the mean of this population (or,

Efficiency
The degree to which repeated values for a statistic cluster around the parameter.

equivalently, its median). If we drew many samples and calculated their means, we would find that the means ($\bar{X}$s) clustered relatively closely around μ. The medians of the same samples, however, would cluster more loosely around μ. This is so even though the median is also an unbiased estimator in this situation, because the expected value of the median in this case would also equal μ. The fact that the sample means cluster more closely around μ than do the sample medians indicates that the mean is more *efficient* as an estimator. (In fact, it is the most efficient estimator of μ.) Because the mean is more likely to be closer to μ (i.e., a more accurate estimate) than the median, it is a better statistic to use to estimate μ.

While it should be obvious that efficiency is a relative term (a statistic is more or less efficient than some other statistic), statements that such and such a statistic is "efficient" are common. Such usage of the term really means that the statistic is more efficient than all other statistics as an estimate of the parameter in question. Both the sample mean, as an estimate of μ, and the sample variance, as an estimate of σ^2, are efficient estimators in that sense. The fact that both the mean and the variance are unbiased and efficient is the major reason that they play such an important role in statistics. These two statistics will form the basis for most of the procedures discussed in the remainder of this book.

The Sample Variance as an Estimator of the Population Variance

The sample variance offers an excellent example of what was said in the discussion of unbiasedness. You may recall that I earlier sneaked in the divisor of $(N - 1)$ instead of N for the calculation of the variance and the standard deviation. Now is the time to explain why. Here, as was the case when I previously discussed the properties of estimators, I would like you just to have a general sense of the issues involved. Whenever you see a variance or a standard deviation, it will have been computed with $(N - 1)$ in the denominator. You can say "It's probably because of some obscure statistical argument," and skip this section, or you can read this section and see that $(N - 1)$ makes a good deal of sense.

There are a number of ways of explaining why sample variances require $(N - 1)$ as the denominator. Perhaps the simplest is in terms of what has been said already about the sample variance (s^2) as an unbiased estimate of the population variance (σ^2). Assume for the moment that we had an infinite number of samples (each containing N observations) from one population and that we knew the population variance. Suppose further that we were foolish enough to calculate sample variances as $\Sigma(X - \bar{X})^2/N$. (Note the denominator.) If we took the average of these samples' variances, we would find

$$\text{Average}\left(\frac{\Sigma(X - \bar{X})^2}{N}\right) = E\left(\frac{\Sigma(X - \bar{X})^2}{N}\right) = \frac{(N - 1)\sigma^2}{N}$$

where $E(\ )$ is read as "the expected value of" whatever is in parentheses.

This last point can be illustrated by a simple example. Suppose we had a population that consisted of only the numbers 1, 2, and 3. Because this is the entire population, we can calculate μ and σ^2 exactly: $\mu = 2$ and $\sigma^2 = 0.667$. (Remember that if, *and only if,* we have the entire population instead of a sample, $\sigma^2 = \Sigma(X - \mu)^2/N$.) Suppose further that we estimate the population variance on the basis of a sample of two observations. Only nine different samples of $N = 2$ could possibly be drawn from this population, and it is a simple matter in this case to list them and to compute the mean and the variance of each sample. For our example we will calculate s^2 using both N and $(N - 1)$ as the denominator. The data and the calculations are presented in Table 5.4.

Notice that, as predicted, the mean of the sample means is exactly equal to μ and the mean of the sample variances, using $(N - 1)$ as the denominator, is exactly equal to σ^2. Furthermore, the average of $\Sigma(X - \overline{X})^2/N$ (the biased statistic) is

$$E\left(\frac{\Sigma(X - \overline{X})^2}{N}\right) = \frac{(N - 1)\ \sigma^2}{N} = \frac{1}{2}\ \sigma^2 = \frac{1}{2}\ (0.667) = 0.333$$

Thus, the expected value of $\Sigma(X - \overline{X})^2/N$ is not σ^2, which is what we had hoped to estimate, but instead $\sigma^2(N - 1)/N$, as we saw a few paragraphs back. When we use N in the denominator, we are estimating the wrong thing and have a biased estimate of σ^2. This result does, however, provide us with a basis for estimating σ^2. If

$$E\left(\frac{\Sigma(X - \overline{X})^2}{N}\right) = \frac{(N - 1)\sigma^2}{N}$$

Table 5.4

The Results of Sampling from a Very Small Population

Sample		$\overline{X}$	s^2 Using $(N - 1)$	s^2 Using N
1	1	1.0	0.00	0.00
1	2	1.5	0.50	0.25
1	3	2.0	2.00	1.00
2	1	1.5	0.50	0.25
2	2	2.0	0.00	0.00
2	3	2.5	0.50	0.25
3	1	2.0	2.00	1.00
3	2	2.5	0.50	0.25
3	3	3.0	0.00	0.00
Average		2.0	0.667	0.333

then simple algebra will show that

$$E\left(\frac{\Sigma(X - \bar{X})^2}{N} \cdot \frac{N}{N-1}\right) = \sigma^2$$

and thus

$$E\left(\frac{\Sigma(X - \bar{X})^2}{N-1}\right) = \sigma^2$$

This last formula is our standard definitional formula for the variance. It shows us not only how to find the estimate of σ^2 but also that this estimate is unbiased.

5.9 Boxplots: Graphical Representations of Dispersions and Extreme Scores

Boxplot (box-and-whisker plot)
A graphical representation of the dispersion of a sample.

In Chapter 3 you saw how stem-and-leaf displays can represent data in several meaningful ways at the same time. Such displays combine data into something very much like a histogram, while retaining the individual values of the observations. In addition to the stem-and-leaf display, John Tukey has developed other ways of looking at data, one of which gives greater prominence to the dispersion of the data. This method is known as a **boxplot**, or, sometimes, **box-and-whisker plot**.

The data and the accompanying stem-and-leaf display in Table 5.5 were taken from normal- and low-birthweight infants participating in a study at the University of Vermont and represent preliminary data on the length of hospitalization of 38 normal-birthweight infants. Data on three infants are missing for this particular variable and are represented by an asterisk (*). (They are included to emphasize that we should not just ignore missing data.) Because the data vary from 1 to 10, with two exceptions, all the leaves are zero. The zeros really just fill in space to produce a histogram-like distribution. Examination of the data as plotted in the stem-and-leaf display reveals that the distribution is positively skewed with a median stay of three days. Near the bottom of the stem you will see the entry HI and the values 20 and 33. These are extreme values, or outliers, and are set off in this way to highlight their existence. Whether they are large enough to make us suspicious is one of the questions a boxplot is designed to address. The last line of the stem-and-leaf display indicates the number of missing observations.

To understand how a boxplot is constructed, we need to invoke a number of concepts we have already discussed and then add a few more. In Chapter 4 we defined the median location of a set of N scores as $(N + 1)/2$. When the median location is a whole number, as it will be when N is odd, then the median is simply the value that occupies that location in an ordered arrangement of

Table 5.5

Data and Stem-and-Leaf Display on Length of Hospitalization for Full-Term Newborn Infants (in Days)

Data			Stem-and-Leaf	
2	1	7	1	000
1	33	2	2	000000000
2	3	4	3	00000000000
3	*	4	4	0000000
3	3	10	5	00
9	2	5	6	0
4	3	3	7	0
20	6	2	8	
4	5	2	9	0
1	*	*	10	0
3	3	4	HI	20, 33
2	3	4		Missing = 3
3	2	3		
2	4			

data. When the median location is a decimal number (i.e., when *N* is even), the median is the average of the two values on either side of that location. For the data in Table 5.5 the median location is $(38 + 1)/2 = 19.5$, and the median is 3. To construct a boxplot we are also going to take what amounts to the medians of each half of the display and call those points the **hinges**. Hinges are closely related to the first and third **quartiles** (often designated Q_1 and Q_3), which are the values that cut off the lowest and highest 25% of the distributions. (The difference between the hinges and the quartiles is minor and tends to vanish with large sample sizes.) To calculate the hinges, we first need to obtain the **hinge location**, which is defined as

$$\text{Hinge location} = \frac{\text{Median location} + 1}{2}$$

Hinges (Quartiles)
Those points that cut off the bottom and top quarter of a distribution.

Hinge location
The location of the hinge in an ordered series.

If the median location is a fractional value, the fraction should be dropped from the numerator when you compute the hinge location. The hinge location is to the hinge what the median location is to the median. It tells us where, in an ordered series, the hinge values are to be found. For the data on hospital stay, the hinge location is $(19 + 1)/2 = 10$. Thus the hinges are going to be the tenth scores from the bottom and from the top. These values are 2 and 4, respectively. For data sets without tied scores, or for large samples, the hinges will bracket the middle 50% of the scores.

To complete the concepts required for understanding boxplots, we need to consider three more terms: H-spread, inner fences, and adjacent values. The

H-spread
The range between the two hinges.

Inner fences
Points that are 1.5 times the H-spread above and below the appropriate hinge.

Adjacent values
Actual data points that are no more extreme than the inner fences.

Whiskers
Lines drawn in a boxplot from hinges to adjacent values.

H-spread is simply the range between the two hinges and as such is basically just the interquartile range. For our data the H-spread is $4 - 2 = 2$. An **inner fence** is a point that falls 1.5 times the H-spread above or below the appropriate hinge. (If you can figure out why Tukey settled on the number 1.5, send me an electronic mail message at the Internet address given in the Preface. I have looked for that reason in vain.) Because the H-spread is 2 for our data, the inner fence is $2 \times 1.5 = 3$ points farther out than the hinges. Because our hinges are the values 2 and 4, the inner fences will be at $2 - 3 = -1$ and $4 + 3 = 7$. **Adjacent values** are those values in the data that are no more extreme (no farther from the median) than the inner fences. Because the smallest value we have is 1, that is the closest value to the lower inner fence and is the lower adjacent value. The higher inner fence is 7, and because we have a 7 in our data, that will be the higher adjacent value. The calculations for all the terms we have just defined are shown in Table 5.6.

Inner fences and adjacent values can cause some confusion. Think of a herd of cows scattered around a field. The fence around the field represents the inner fence of the boxplot. The cows closest to but still inside the fence are the adjacent values. Don't worry about the cows who have escaped outside the fence. They are not involved in the calculations at this point.

Now we are ready to draw the boxplot. First we draw and label a scale that covers the whole range of the obtained values. This has been done at the bottom of Table 5.6. We then draw a rectangular box from one hinge to the other, with a vertical line representing the location of the median. Next we draw lines (**whiskers**) from the hinges out to the adjacent values. Finally we plot the locations of all points that are more extreme than the adjacent values.

From Table 5.6 we can see several important things. First of all the central portion of the distribution is reasonably symmetric. This is indicated by the fact that the median lies in the center of the box and was apparent from the stem-and-leaf display. We can also see that the distribution is positively skewed,

Table 5.6

Calculation and Boxplots for Data from Table 5.5

Median location $= (N + 1)/2 = (38 + 1)/2 = 19.5$
Median $= 3$
Hinge location $=$ (median location† + 1)$/2 = (19 + 1)/2 = 10$
Lower hinge $= $ 10th lowest score $= 2$
Upper hinge $= $ 10th highest score $= 4$
H-spread $= $ upper hinge $- $ lower hinge $= 4 - 2 = 2$
H-spread $\times 1.5 = 2 \times 1.5 = 3$
Lower fence $= $ lower hinge $- 1.5$(H-spread)$ = 2 - 3 = -1$
Upper fence $= $ upper hinge $+ 1.5$(H-spread)$ = 4 + 3 = 7$
Lower adjacent value $= $ smallest value $\geq$ lower fence $= 1$
Upper adjacent value $= $ largest value $\leq$ upper fence $= 7$

0	5	10	15	20	25	30	35

$\dagger$ Drop any fractional values

because the whisker on the right is substantially longer than the one on the left. This also was apparent from the stem-and-leaf display, although not so clearly. Finally, we see that we have four outliers, where an outlier is defined here as any value more extreme than the whiskers (and therefore more extreme than the adjacent values). The stem-and-leaf display did not show the position of the outliers nearly so graphically as does the boxplot.

Outliers deserve special attention. An outlier could represent an error in measurement, in data recording, or in data entry, or it could represent a legitimate value that just happens to be extreme. For example, our data represent length of hospitalization, and a full-term infant might have been born with a physical defect that required extended hospitalization. Because these are actual data, it was possible to go back to hospital records and look more closely at the four extreme cases. On examination, it turned out that the two most extreme scores were attributable to errors in data entry and were readily correctable. The other two extreme scores were caused by physical problems of the infants. Here a decision was required by the project director as to whether the problems were sufficiently severe to cause the infants to be dropped from the study (both were retained as subjects). The two corrected values were 3 and 5 instead of 33 and 20, respectively, and a new boxplot on the corrected data is shown in Table 5.7. This boxplot is identical to the one shown in Table 5.6 except for the spacing and the two largest values. (You should verify for yourself that the corrected data set would indeed yield this boxplot.)

Table 5.7

Boxplot for Corrected Data from Table 5.6

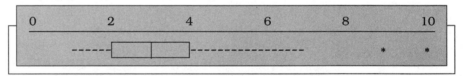

From what has been said, it should be evident that boxplots are extremely useful tools for examining data with respect to dispersion. I find them particularly useful for screening data for errors and for highlighting potential problems before subsequent analyses are carried out. Boxplots are presented often in the remainder of this book as visual guides to the data.

5.10 Obtaining Measures of Dispersion Using Execustat

We will use a program called Execustat to calculate measures of dispersion on the reaction time data discussed in Chapter 3 (see page 28). I have chosen Execustat because it not only gives measures of dispersion but also allows us to generate separate boxplots depending on the number of digits in the comparison set. In part (a) of Table 5.8 are the measures of central tendency and dispersion for the complete data set of 300 observations. The mode is not given here because there are so many different values of the reaction times that different ways of grouping the data would produce different values for the mode. (I would have called the mode 67 and been done with it.) Notice that

Table 5.8

Execustat Output for Measures of Central Tendency and Dispersion

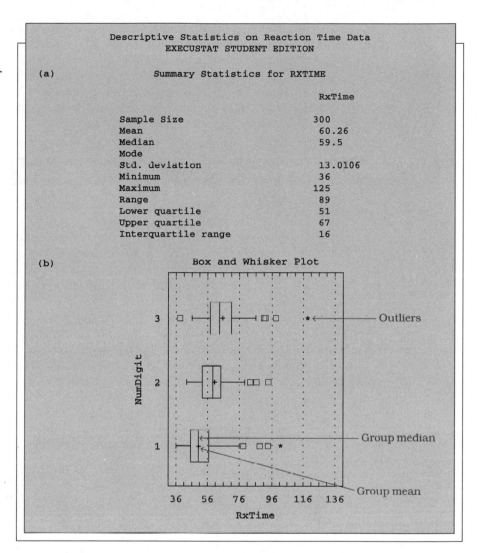

Descriptive Statistics on Reaction Time Data
EXECUSTAT STUDENT EDITION

(a)   Summary Statistics for RXTIME

                                                        RxTime

            Sample Size   300
            Mean   60.26
            Median   59.5
            Mode
            Std. deviation   13.0106
            Minimum   36
            Maximum   125
            Range   89
            Lower quartile   51
            Upper quartile   67
            Interquartile range   16

(b)   Box and Whisker Plot

the range is substantial (about 9/10 of a second), although this is reduced to 16/100 of a second when we ignore extreme scores by looking at the interquartile range. The standard deviation is 13.01/100 of a second, around a mean of 60.26/100.

In part (b) of Table 5.8 are the mean and the standard deviation for the different treatment conditions (the number of digits in the comparison set). Both the central tendency and the dispersion are seen clearly in the boxplots, where I have separated out each condition. The small squares are values beyond the inner fences, and the asterisk is a particularly extreme outlier. Notice how much different a picture you get of dispersion when you consider the range than when you consider other measures. In a different direction, notice the small "+" in each box. What would you guess they represent?

You should recall from Chapter 3 that if we process information sequentially, our reaction times would be expected to increase as the number of digits in the comparison set increases. On the other hand, if we engage in parallel processing, reaction times would not be expected to increase with a larger number of digits. What would you conclude from the output in Table 5.8? What, if anything, would you conclude from the fact that dispersion remained nearly constant as the number of digits increased?

5.11 A Final Worked Example

Why does the moon appear to be so much larger when it is near the horizon than when it is directly overhead? This simple question has produced a wide variety of theories from psychologists. One of the most complete series of studies was carried out by Kaufman and Rock (1962). They proposed that the moon illusion is caused by the greater apparent *distance* of the moon when it is at the horizon than when it is at its zenith. (Something along the idea that "if it is really that far away, it must be big.") When we discuss the *t* test in Chapters 12 through 14, we will examine Kaufman and Rock's data, but first we have to ask if the apparatus they used really produced a moon illusion in the first place. In Table 5.9 are measures of the moon illusion collected by Kaufman and Rock (1962). For these data a score of 1.73, for example, means that the moon appeared to the subject to be 1.73 times larger when on the horizon than when overhead. Ratios greater than 1.00 are what we would expect if the apparatus works correctly. And if the task given the subjects is a good one, we would hope that there would not be much variability in the scores.

For the data in Table 5.9 we can calculate the following statistics.

Table 5.9

Moon Illusion Data

Illusion (X)	X^2
1.73	2.9929
1.06	1.1236
2.03	4.1209
1.40	1.9600
0.95	0.9025
1.13	1.2769
1.41	1.9881
1.73	2.9929
1.63	2.6569
1.56	2.4336
$\Sigma X = 14.63$	$\Sigma X^2 = 22.4483$

Mean:

$$\bar{X} = \frac{\Sigma X}{N} = \frac{14.63}{10} = 1.463$$

Variance:

$$s^2 = \frac{\Sigma X^2 - \dfrac{(\Sigma X)^2}{N}}{N-1} = \frac{22.4483 - \dfrac{(14.63)^2}{10}}{9} = 0.1161$$

Standard deviation:

$$s = \sqrt{0.1161} = 0.3407$$

Boxplots:

First rearrange the observations in ascending order:

0.95   1.06   1.13   1.40   1.41   1.56   1.63   1.73   1.73   2.03

$$\text{Median location} = \frac{N+1}{2} = \frac{11}{2} = 5.5$$

$$\text{Median} = \frac{1.41 + 1.56}{2} = 1.485$$

$$\text{Hinge location} = \frac{\text{Median location} + 1}{2} = \frac{5+1}{2} = 3$$

(Drop fraction from median location if necessary.)

Hinges = the third observations from the top and the bottom of the ordered series = 1.13 and 1.73

H-spread = distance between upper and lower hinges = $1.73 - 1.13 = 0.60$

$1.5 \times$ H-spread = $1.5(0.60) = 0.90$

Inner fences = hinges $\pm$ 1.5(H-spread)

Upper inner fence = $1.73 + 0.90 = 2.63$

Lower inner fence = $1.13 - 0.90 = 0.23$

Adjacent values = values closest to *but not exceeding* inner fences

Lower adjacent value = 0.95

Upper adjacent value = 2.03

Resulting boxplot:

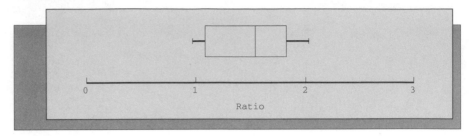

From these results we can see that the average moon illusion is well above 1.00; in fact only one measurement was less than 1. With a mean of 1.46, we can say that, on average, the horizon moon appears to be about half again as large (46%) as the zenith moon. More important for our puposes here, the variability of the illusion is reasonably small ($s = 0.34$), meaning that the measurements are in pretty good agreement with one another, and there are no outliers. It looks as if Kaufman and Rock's apparatus works well for their purpose.

5.12 Summary

In this chapter we considered a number of measures of the degree to which scores are distributed around the mean. Of these measures the standard deviation and the variance are the most important and will play a major role in the remainder of the text. We also examined how to use boxplots to highlight the shape of the distribution and to help in identifying outliers.

Some important terms in this chapter are:

- Dispersion
- Range
- Outliers
- Interquartile range
- Trimmed samples
- Trimmed statistics
- Mean absolute deviation (m.a.d.)
- Sample variance
- Population variance
- Standard deviation
- Sufficient statistic

- Expected value
- Unbiased estimator
- Efficiency
- Boxplot
- Hinges
- Hinge location
- H-spread
- Inner fence
- Adjacent values
- Whiskers

5.13 Exercises

5.1   Calculate the range, the variance, and the standard deviation for the data in Exercise 3.1.

5.2   Calculate the range, the variance, and the standard deviation for the data in Exercise 3.4.

5.3   Compare the answers to Exercises 5.1 and 5.2. Is the standard deviation for children substantially greater than the standard deviation for adults?

5.4   In Exercise 5.1 what percentage of the scores fall within two standard deviations from the mean?

5.5   In Exercise 5.2 what percentage of the scores fall within two standard deviations from the mean?

5.6   Given the following set of data, demonstrate that adding or subtracting a constant to each score does not change the standard deviation. What happens to the *mean* when a constant is added or subtracted?

   5   4   2   3   4   9   5

5.7   Given the data in Exercise 5.6, show that multiplying or dividing by a constant multiplies or divides the standard deviation by that constant. How does this relate to what happens to the *mean* under similar circumstances?

5.8   Using the results demonstrated in Exercises 5.6 and 5.7, transform the following set of data to a new set with a standard deviation of 1.00.

   5   8   3   8   6   9   9   7

5.9   Use the answers to Exercises 5.6 and 5.7 to modify the answer to Exercise 5.8 to have a mean of 0 and a standard deviation of 1.00. (*Note:* The solution to Exercises 5.8 and 5.9 will be important in Chapter 6.)

5.10   Create two sets of scores with equal ranges but different variances.

5.11   Create a boxplot for the data in Exercise 5.1.

5.12   Create a boxplot for the data in Exercise 5.2.

5.13   Create a boxplot for the variable ADDSC in Appendix C.

5.14 (a)   Calculate the variance and the standard deviation for ENGG in Appendix C.

(b)   These measures should be greater than the corresponding measures on GPA. Can you explain why this should be? (We will come back to this later in Chapter 12, but see if you can figure it out.)

5.15   The mean of the data used in Exercise 5.1 is 18.9. Suppose that we had an additional child who had a score of 18.9. Recalculate the variance for these data. (You can build on the intermediate steps used in Exercise 5.1.) What effect does this score have on the answers to Exercise 5.1?

5.16   Instead of adding a score equal to the mean (as in Exercise 5.15), add a score of 40 to the data used in Exercise 5.1. How does this score affect the answers to Exercise 5.1?

5.17   Repeat the computations used to generate Table 5.4, but this time let the population consist of the numbers 1, 2, 3, 4, and 5 and draw all possible samples of $N = 3$. (*Hint:* There are 125 possible samples, so this problem is best done by those who have access to a spreadsheet program like Lotus 1-2-3 or Excel.)

5.18 The discussion of an efficient statistic was phrased in terms of what would happen if we drew a very large number of samples. But we usually draw only one sample from any population. Why, then, do we care about the results from many samples?

5.19 Answer Exercise 5.18 with respect to unbiasedness rather than efficiency.

5.20 (a) Draw a boxplot for the following data:

$$1 \quad 3 \quad 3 \quad 5 \quad 8 \quad 8 \quad 9 \quad 12$$
$$13 \quad 16 \quad 17 \quad 17 \quad 18 \quad 20 \quad 21 \quad 30$$

(b) Calculate the standard deviation of these data and divide every score by the standard deviation.

(c) Draw a boxplot for the data in (b).

(d) Compare the two boxplots.

5.21 The following graph came from using a statistical package for the Macintosh called JMP with the data in Table 5.5. Notice the boxplot on the top of the figure. How does that boxplot compare with the ones we have been using? (*Hint:* The mean is 4.66.)

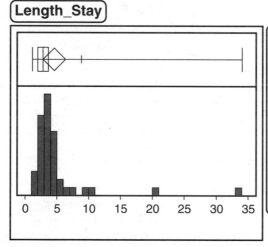

Quantiles		
maximum	100.0%	33.000
	99.5%	33.000
	97.5%	33.000
	90.0%	9.100
quartile	75.0%	4.000
median	50.0%	3.000
quartile	25.0%	2.000
	10.0%	1.900
	2.5%	1.000
	0.5%	1.000
minimum	0.0%	1.000

5.22 In Section 5.10 statistics were computed from the reaction time data in Chapter 3. What would you conclude from these data about how we process information in short-term memory?

6

THE NORMAL DISTRIBUTION

From what has been said in the preceding chapters, it is apparent that we are going to be very much concerned with distributions—distributions of data, hypothetical distributions of populations, and sampling distributions. Of all the possible forms that distributions can take, the class known as the **normal distribution** is by far the most important for our purposes.

Before elaborating on the normal distribution, however, it is worth a short digression to explain just why we are so interested in distributions in general. The critical factor is that there is an important link between distributions and probabilities. If we know something about the distribution of events (or of sample statistics), we know something about the probability that one of those events (or statistics) is likely to occur. To see the issue in

Figure 6.1

Pie Chart Showing Persons Under Correctional Supervision, by Type of Supervision, on December 31, 1982

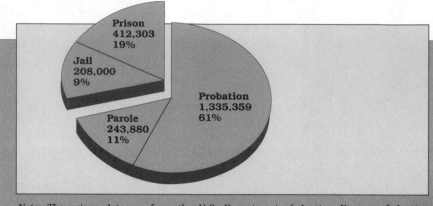

Note: The prison data are from the U.S. Department of Justice, Bureau of Justice Statistics, *Prisoners in 1982*, Bulletin NCJ-87933 (Washington, D.C.: U.S. Government Printing Office, 1983). The jail data are from the U.S. Department of Justice, Bureau of Justice Statistics, *Jail Inmates 1982*, Bulletin NCJ-87161 (Washington, D.C.: U.S. Department of Justice, February 1983). The parole data and the probation data are from the annual Uniform Parole Reports and National Probation Reports surveys.

Normal distribution
Specific distribution having a characteristic bell-shaped form.

its simplest form, take the lowly pie chart. (This is the only time you will see a pie chart in this book, because I find it very difficult to compare little slices of pie in different orientations to see which one is larger. There are much better ways to present data. However, the pie chart serves a useful purpose here.)

The pie chart shown in Figure 6.1 is taken from a U.S. Department of Justice report on probation and parole. It shows the status of all individuals convicted of a criminal offense. From this figure you can see that 9% were in jail, 19% were in prison, 61% were on probation, and the remaining 11% were on parole. You can also see that the percentages in each category are directly reflected in the percentage of the area of the pie that each wedge occupies. The area taken up by each segment is directly proportional to the percentage of individuals in that segment. Moreover, if we declare that the total area of the pie is 1.00 unit, the area of each segment is equal to the proportion of observations falling in that segment.

It is easy to go from speaking about areas to speaking about probabilities. The concept of probability will be elaborated in Chapter 7, but even without a precise definition of probability we can make an important point about areas of a pie chart. For now simply think of probability in its common everyday usage, referring to the likelihood that some event will occur. From this perspective it is logical to conclude that, because 19% of those convicted of a federal crime are currently in prison, if we were to randomly draw the name of one person from a list of convicted individuals, the probability is .19 that the individual would be in prison. To put this in slightly different terms, if 19% of the area of the pie is allocated to prison, then the probability that a person would fall in that segment is .19.

This pie chart also allows us to explore the addition of areas. It should be clear that if 19% are in prison and 9% are in jail, $19 + 9 = 28\%$ are incarcerated. In other words, we can find the percentage of individuals in one of several categories just by adding the percentages for each category. The same thing holds in terms of areas, in the sense that we can find the percentage of incarcerated individuals by adding the areas devoted to prison and to jail. And finally, if we can find percentages by adding areas, we can also find probabilities by adding areas. Thus the probability of being incarcerated is the probability of being in one of the two segments associated with incarceration, which we can get by summing the two areas (or their associated probabilities).

There are other ways to present data besides pie charts. Two of the simplest are a histogram (discussed in Chapter 3) and its closely related cousin, the bar chart. Figure 6.2 is a redrawing of Figure 6.1 in the form of a bar chart. Although this figure does not contain any new information, it has two advantages over the pie chart. First of all, it is easier to compare categories, because the only thing we need to look at is the height of the bar, rather than trying to compare the lengths of two different arcs in different orientations. The second advantage is that the bar chart is visually more like the common distributions we will deal with, in that the various levels or categories are spread out along the horizontal dimension, and the percentages in each category are shown along the vertical dimension. Here again you can see that the various areas of the distribution are related to probabilities. Further, you can see that we can meaningfully sum areas in exactly the same way that we did in the pie chart. When we move to more common distributions, particularly the normal distribution, the principles of areas, percentages, probabilities, and the addition of areas or probabilities carry over almost without change.

Figure 6.2

Bar Chart Showing Persons Under Correctional Supervision, by Type of Supervision

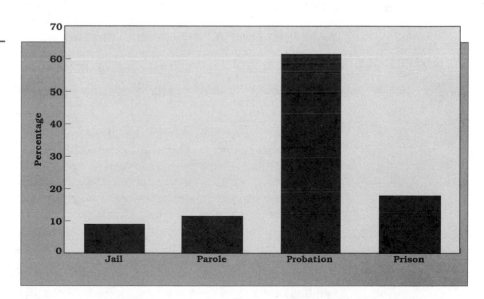

6.1 The Normal Distribution

Now let's move closer to the normal distribution. I stated earlier that the normal distribution is one of the most important distributions we will encounter. There are several reasons for this:

1. Many of the dependent variables with which we deal are commonly assumed to be normally distributed in the population. That is to say, we frequently assume that if we were to obtain the whole population of observations, the resulting distribution would closely resemble the normal distribution.

2. If we can assume that a variable is at least approximately normally distributed, then the techniques that are discussed in this chapter allow us to make a number of inferences (either exact or approximate) about values of that variable.

3. The theoretical distribution of the hypothetical set of sample means obtained by drawing an infinite number of samples from a specified population can be shown to be approximately normal under a wide variety of conditions. Such a distribution is called the sampling distribution of the mean and is discussed and used extensively throughout the remainder of this book.

4. Most of the statistical procedures we will employ have, somewhere in their derivation, an assumption that the population of observations is normally distributed.

To introduce the normal distribution, we will look at one additional data set that is approximately normal (and would be normal if we had more observations). The data we are going to look at were collected using the Achenbach Youth Self Report form (Achenbach, 1991). This is a frequently used measure of behavior problems that produces scores on a number of different dimensions. The one we are going to look at is the dimension of Total Behavior Problems, which represents the total number of behavior problems reported by the child (weighted by the severity of the problem). (Examples of Behavior Problem categories are "Argues," "Impulsive," "Shows off," and "Teases.") Figure 6.3 is a histogram of data from 289 junior high school students. A higher score represents more behavior problems. You can see that this distribution has a center very near 50 and is fairly symmetrically distributed on either side of that value, with the scores ranging between about 25 and 75. The standard deviation of this distribution is approximately 10. The distribution is not perfectly even—it has some bumps and valleys—but overall it is fairly smooth, rising in the center and falling off at the ends. (The actual mean and standard deviation for this particular sample are 50.98 and 10.42, respectively.)

One thing that you might note from this distribution is that if you add the frequencies of subjects falling in the intervals 52–53, 53–54, and 55–56, you will find that 64 students obtained scores between 52 and 56. Because there

Figure 6.3

Histogram Showing Distribution of Total Behavior Problem Scores

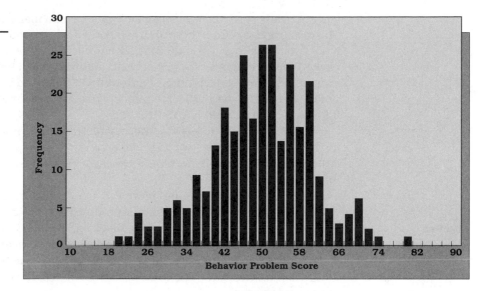

are 289 observations in this sample, $64/289 = 22\%$ of the observations fell in this interval. This illustrates the comments made earlier on the addition of areas.

If we take this same set of data and represent it by a frequency polygon rather than a histogram, we obtain Figure 6.4. There is absolutely no information in this figure that was not in Figure 6.3. I merely connected the tops of the bars in the histogram and then erased the bars themselves. Why, then, waste an artist's time by putting in a figure that has nothing new to offer? The reason is simply that I want to get people to see the transition from a histogram, which

Figure 6.4

Frequency Polygon Showing Distribution of Total Behavior Problem Scores

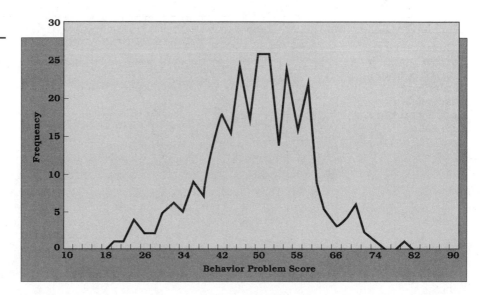

you see nearly every time you open a newspaper or a magazine, to a line graph. The next transition from there to the smoothed curves you will often see in the rest of the book (e.g., Figure 6.5) is straightforward. The major difference between the line graph (frequency polygon) and the smoothed curve is that the latter is a stylized version that leaves out the bumps and valleys. If you would prefer, you can always think of the smoothed curve as sitting on top of an invisible histogram (with very narrow bars).

Now we are ready to go to the normal distribution. First we will consider it in the abstract, and then we will take a concrete example making use of the Achenbach Youth Self Report Total Behavior Problem scores that we saw in Figures 6.3 and 6.4.

The distribution shown in Figure 6.5 is a characteristic normal distribution. It is a symmetric, unimodal distribution, frequently referred to as "bell shaped," and has limits of $\pm\infty$. The **abscissa**, or horizontal axis, represents different possible values of X, while the **ordinate**, or vertical axis, is referred to as the density and is related to (but not the same as) the frequency or probability of occurrence of X. The concept of density is discussed in further detail in the next chapter.

Abscissa
Horizontal axis.

Ordinate
Vertical axis.

The normal distribution has a long history. It was originally investigated by DeMoivre (1667–1754), who was interested in its use to describe the results of games of chance (gambling). The distribution was defined precisely by Pierre-Simon Laplace (1749–1827) and put in its more usual form by Carl Friedrich Gauss (1777–1855), both of whom were interested in the distribution of errors in astronomical observations. In fact, the normal distribution often is referred to as the Gaussian distribution and as the "normal law of error." Adolph Quetelet (1796–1874), a Belgian astronomer, was the first to apply the distribution

Figure 6.5

A Characteristic Normal Distribution with Values of X on the Abscissa and Density on the Ordinate

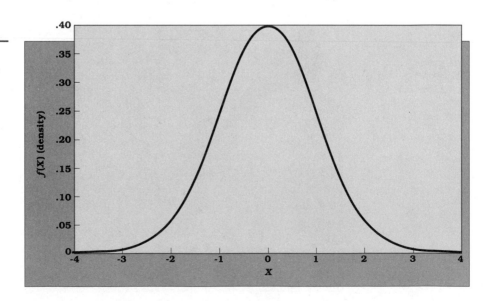

to social and biological data. He collected chest measurements of Scottish soldiers and heights of French soldiers. He found that both sets of measurements were approximately normally distributed. Quetelet interpreted the data to indicate that the mean of this distribution was the ideal at which nature was aiming, and observations to either side of the mean represented error (a deviation from nature's ideal). (For 5′8″ males like myself, it is somehow comforting to think of all those bigger guys as nature's mistakes.) Although we no longer think of the mean as nature's ideal, this is a useful way to conceptualize variability around the mean. In fact, we still use the word *error* to refer to deviations from the mean. Francis Galton (1822–1911) carried Quetelet's ideas further and gave the normal distribution a central role in psychological theory, especially the theory of mental abilities. Some would insist that Galton was *too* successful in this endeavor, and we tend to assume that measures are normally distributed even when they are not. I won't argue the issue here.

Mathematically the normal distribution is defined as

$$f(X) = \frac{1}{\sigma\sqrt{2\pi}}(e)^{-(X-\mu)^2/2\sigma^2}$$

where π and e are constants ($\pi = 3.1416$ and $e = 2.7183$), and μ and σ are the mean and the standard deviation, respectively, of the distribution. Given that μ and σ are known, the ordinate, $f(X)$, for any value of X is obtained simply by substituting the appropriate values for μ, σ, and X and solving the equation. This is not nearly as difficult as it looks, but in practice you are unlikely ever to have to make the calculations. The cumulative form of this distribution is tabled, and we can simply read the information we need from the table.

Those of you who have had a course in calculus may recognize that the area under the curve between any two values of X (say, X_1 and X_2), and thus the probability that a randomly drawn score will fall within that interval, could be found by integrating the function over the range from X_1 to X_2. Those of you who have not had such a course can take comfort from the fact that tables are readily available in which this work has already been done for us or by use of which we can easily do the work ourselves. Such a table appears in Appendix D (Table D.10).

You might be excused at this point for wondering why anyone would want to table such a distribution in the first place. Just because a distribution is common (or at least commonly assumed) doesn't automatically suggest a reason for having an appendix that tells all about it. The reason is quite simple. By using Table D.10, we can readily calculate the probability that a score drawn at random from the population will have a value lying between any two specified points (X_1 and X_2). Thus, by using statistical tables we can make probability statements in answer to a variety of questions. You will see examples of such questions in the rest of this chapter. They will also appear in many other chapters throughout the book.

6.2 The Standard Normal Distribution

A problem arises when we try to table the normal distribution, because the distribution depends on the values of the mean and the standard deviation (μ and σ) of the distribution. To do the job right, we would have to make up a different table for every possible combination of the values of μ and σ, which certainly is not practical. The solution to this problem is quite simple. What we actually have in the table is what is called the **standard normal distribution**, which has a mean of 0 and a standard deviation of 1. Such a distribution is often designated as $N(0, 1)$, where N refers to the fact that it is normal, 0 is the value of μ, and 1 is the value of σ^2. ($N(\mu, \sigma^2)$ is the more general expression.) Given the standard normal distribution in the appendix and a set of rules for transforming any normal distribution to standard form and vice versa, we can use Table D.10 to find the areas under any normal distribution.

Standard normal distribution
A normal distribution with a mean equal to 0 and variance equal to 1. Denoted $N(0,1)$.

Consider the distribution shown in Figure 6.6, with a mean of 50 and a standard deviation of 10 (variance of 100). It represents the distribution of *an entire population* of Total Behavior Problem scores from the Achenbach Youth Self Report form, of which the data in Figures 6.3 and 6.4 are a sample. If we knew something about the areas under the curve in Figure 6.6, we could say something about the probability of various values of Behavior Problem scores and could identify, for example, those scores that are so high that they are obtained by only 5% or 10% of the population.

The only tables of the normal distribution that are readily available are those of the *standard* normal distribution. Therefore, before we can answer questions about the probability that an individual will get a score above some particular value, we must first transform the distribution in Figure 6.6 (or at

Figure 6.6

A Normal Distribution with Various Transformations on the Abscissa

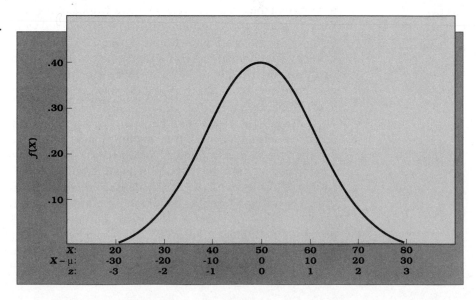

least specific points along it) to a standard normal distribution. That is, we want to be able to say that a score of X_i from a normal distribution with a mean of 50 and a variance of 100—often denoted $N(50,100)$—is comparable to a score of z_i from a distribution with a mean of 0 and a variance, and standard deviation, of 1—denoted $N(0,1)$. Then anything that is true of z_i is also true of X_i, and z and X are comparable variables.

From Exercise 5.6 we know that subtracting a constant from each score in a set of scores reduces the mean of the set by that constant. Thus, if we subtract 50 (the mean) from all the values for X, the new mean will be $50 - 50 = 0$. (More generally, the distribution of $(X - \mu)$ has a mean of 0.) The effect of this transformation is shown in the second set of values for the abscissa in Figure 6.6. We are halfway there, since we now have the mean down to 0, although the standard deviation (σ) is still 10. We also know from Exercise 5.7 that if we divide all values of a variable by a constant (e.g., 10), we divide the standard deviation by that constant. Thus, the standard deviation will now be $10/10 = 1$, which is just what we wanted. We will call this transformed distribution z and define it, on the basis of what we have done, as

$$z = \frac{X - \mu}{\sigma}$$

For our particular case, where $\mu = 50$ and $\sigma = 10$,

$$z = \frac{X - \mu}{\sigma} = \frac{X - 50}{10}$$

Linear transformation
A transformation involving addition, subtraction, multiplication, or division of or by a constant.

The third set of values (labeled z) for the abscissa in Figure 6.6 shows the effect of this transformation. Note that aside from a **linear transformation**[1] of the numerical values, the data have not been changed in any way. The distribution has the same shape and the observations continue to stand in the same relation to each other as they did before the transformation. It should not come as a great surprise that changing the unit of measurement does not change the shape of the distribution or the relative standing of observations. Whether we measure the quantity of alcohol that people consume per week in ounces or in milliliters really makes no difference in the relative standing of people. It just changes the numerical values on the abscissa. (The town drunk is still the town drunk, even if now his liquor is measured in milliliters.) It is important to realize exactly what converting X to z has accomplished. A score that used to be 60 is now 1. That is, a score that used to be one standard deviation (10 points) above the mean remains one standard deviation above the mean, but now is given a new value of 1. A score of 45, which was 0.5 standard devia-

---

[1]A linear transformation involves only multiplication (or division) of X by a constant and/or adding or subtracting a constant to or from X. Such a transformation leaves the relationship among the values unaffected. In other words, it does not distort values at one part of the scale more than values at another part. Changing units from inches to centimeters is a good example of a linear transformation.

Table 6.1   The Normal Distribution (Abbreviated Version of Table D.10)

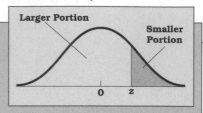

z	Mean to z	Larger Portion	Smaller Portion	z	Mean to z	Larger Portion	Smaller Portion
0.00	0.0000	0.5000	0.5000	0.45	0.1736	0.6736	0.3264
0.01	0.0040	0.5040	0.4960	0.46	0.1772	0.6772	0.3228
0.02	0.0080	0.5080	0.4920	0.47	0.1808	0.6808	0.3192
0.03	0.0120	0.5120	0.4880	0.48	0.1844	0.6844	0.3156
0.04	0.0160	0.5160	0.4840	0.49	0.1879	0.6879	0.3121
0.05	0.0199	0.5199	0.4801	0.50	0.1915	0.6915	0.3085
. . .	. . .	. . .	. . .	. . .	. . .	. . .	. . .
0.97	0.3340	0.8340	0.1660	1.42	0.4222	0.9222	0.0778
0.98	0.3365	0.8365	0.1635	1.43	0.4236	0.9236	0.0764
0.99	0.3389	0.8389	0.1611	1.44	0.4251	0.9251	0.0749
1.00	0.3413	0.8413	0.1587	1.45	0.4265	0.9265	0.0735
1.01	0.3438	0.8438	0.1562	1.46	0.4279	0.9279	0.0721
1.02	0.3461	0.8461	0.1539	1.47	0.4292	0.9292	0.0708
1.03	0.3485	0.8485	0.1515	1.48	0.4306	0.9306	0.0694
1.04	0.3508	0.8508	0.1492	1.49	0.4319	0.9319	0.0681
1.05	0.3531	0.8531	0.1469	1.50	0.4332	0.9332	0.0668
. . .	. . .	. . .	. . .	. . .	. . .	. . .	. . .
1.95	0.4744	0.9744	0.0256	2.40	0.4918	0.9918	0.0082
1.96	0.4750	0.9750	0.0250	2.41	0.4920	0.9920	0.0080
1.97	0.4756	0.9756	0.0244	2.42	0.4922	0.9922	0.0078
1.98	0.4761	0.9761	0.0239	2.43	0.4925	0.9925	0.0075
1.99	0.4767	0.9767	0.0233	2.44	0.4927	0.9927	0.0073
2.00	0.4772	0.9772	0.0228	2.45	0.4929	0.9929	0.0071
2.01	0.4778	0.9778	0.0222	2.46	0.4931	0.9931	0.0069
2.02	0.4783	0.9783	0.0217	2.47	0.4932	0.9932	0.0068
2.03	0.4788	0.9788	0.0212	2.48	0.4934	0.9934	0.0066
2.04	0.4793	0.9793	0.0207	2.49	0.4936	0.9936	0.0064
2.05	0.4798	0.9798	0.0202	2.50	0.4938	0.9938	0.0062

tion *below* the mean, now is given the value of −0.5, and so on. In other words, a z score represents the number of standard deviations that X_i is above or below the mean—a positive z score being above the mean and a negative z score being below the mean.

The equation for z is completely general. We can transform any distribution to a distribution of **z scores** simply by applying this equation. Keep in mind, however, the point that was just made. The *shape* of the distribution is unaffected by the transformation. That means that *if the distribution was not normal before it was transformed, it will not be normal afterward.* Some people believe that they can "normalize" (in the sense of producing a normal distribution) their data by transforming them to z. It just won't work.

z score
Number of standard deviations above or below the mean.

Using the Tables of the Standard Normal Distribution

As already mentioned, the standard normal distribution is extensively tabled. Such a table can be found in Table D.10, part of which is reproduced in Table 6.1. To see how we can make use of this table, consider the normal distribution represented in Figure 6.7. This might represent the standardized distribution of the Behavior Problem scores as seen in Figure 6.6. Suppose we want to know how much of the area under the curve is above one standard deviation from the mean, if the total area under the curve is taken to be 1.00. (We care about areas because they translate directly to probabilities.) We already have seen that z scores represent standard deviations from the mean, and thus we know that we want to find the area above $z = 1$.

Only the positive half of the normal distribution is tabled. Because the distribution is symmetric, any information given about a positive value of z applies equally to the corresponding negative value of z. From Table 6.1 (or Table D.10) we find the row corresponding to $z = 1.00$. Reading across that row, we can see that the area from the *mean to $z = 1$* is 0.3413, the area in the

Figure 6.7

Illustrative Areas Under the Normal Distribution

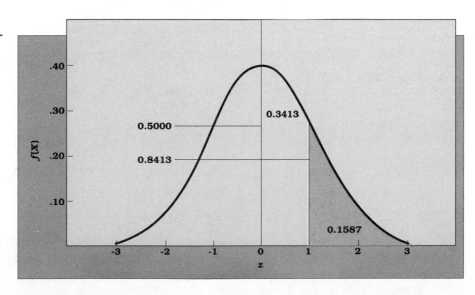

larger portion is 0.8413, and the area in the *smaller portion* is 0.1587. (If you visualize the distribution being divided into the segment below z = 1 [the unshaded part of Figure 6.7] and the segment above z = 1 [the shaded part], the meanings of the terms *larger portion* and *smaller portion* become obvious.) Thus, the answer to our original question is 0.1587. Because we already have equated the terms *area* and *probability* (see Chapter 3), we now can say that if we sample a child at random from the population of children, and if Behavior Problem scores are normally distributed, then the probability that the child will score more than one standard deviation above the mean of the population (i.e., above 60) is .1587. Because the distribution is symmetric, we also know that the probability that a child will score more than one standard deviation *below* the mean of the population is also .1587.

Now suppose that we want the probability that the child will be more than one standard deviation (10 points) from the mean *in either direction*. This is a simple matter of the summation of areas. Because we know that the normal distribution is symmetric, then the area below z = −1 will be the same as the area above z = +1. This is why the table does not contain negative values of z—they are not needed. We already know that the areas in which we are interested are each 0.1587. Then the total area outside z = ±1 must be 0.1587 + 0.1587 = 0.3174. The converse is also true. If the area outside z = ±1 is 0.3174, then the area between z = +1 and z = −1 is equal to 1 − 0.3174 = 0.6826. Thus, the probability that a child will score between 40 and 60 is .6826.

To extend this procedure, consider the situation in which we want to know the probability that a score will be between 30 and 40. A little arithmetic will show that this is simply the probability of falling between 1.0 standard deviation below the mean and 2.0 standard deviations below the mean. This situation is diagrammed in Figure 6.8. (*Hint:* It is always wise to draw simple dia-

Figure 6.8

Areas Between 1.0 and 2.0 Standard Deviations Below the Mean

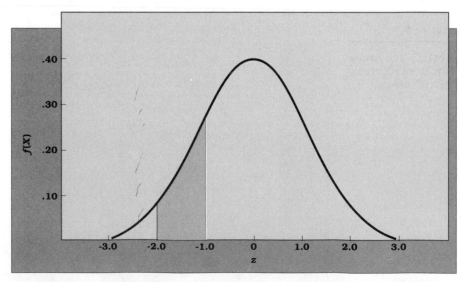

grams such as Figure 6.8. They eliminate many errors and make clear the area(s) for which you are looking.)

From Table D.10 we know that the area from the mean to $z = -2.0$ is 0.4772 and from the mean to $z = -1.0$ is 0.3413. The difference in these two areas must represent the area between $z = -2.0$ and $z = -1.0$. This area is $0.4772 - 0.3413 = 0.1359$. Thus, the probability that Behavior Problem scores drawn at random from a normally distributed population will be between 30 and 40 is .1359.

6.3 Setting Probable Limits on an Observation

For a final example, consider the situation in which we want to identify limits within which we have some specified degree of confidence that a child sampled at random will fall. In other words we want to make a statement of the form, "If I draw a child at random from this population, 95% of the time her score will lie between _____ and _____." From Figure 6.9 you can see the limits we want—the limits that include 95% of the scores in the population.

If we are looking for the limits within which 95% of the scores fall, we also are looking for the limits beyond which the remaining 5% of the scores fall. To rule out this remaining 5%, we want to find that value of z that cuts off 2.5% at each end, or "tail," of the distribution. (We do not need to use symmetric limits, but we typically do because they usually make the most sense and produce the shortest interval.) From Table D.10 we see that these values are $z \pm 1.96$. Thus, we can say that 95% of the time a child's score sampled at random will fall between 1.96 standard deviations above the mean and 1.96 standard deviations below the mean.

Figure 6.9

Values of z That Enclose 95% of the Behavior Problem Scores

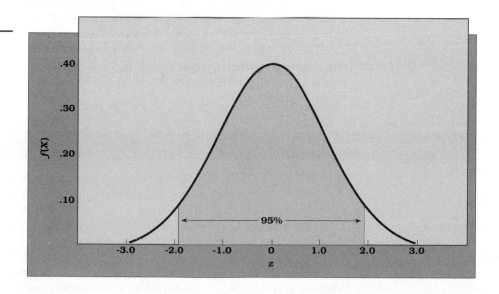

Because we generally want to express our answers in terms of raw Behavior Problem scores, rather than z scores, we must do a little more work. To obtain the raw score limits, we simply work the formula for z backward, solving for X instead of z. Thus, if we want to state the limits within which 95% of the population falls, we want to find those scores that are 1.96 standard deviations above or below the mean of the population. This can be written as

$$z = \frac{X - \mu}{\sigma}$$

$$\pm 1.96 = \frac{X - \mu}{\sigma}$$

$$X - \mu = +1.96\sigma$$

$$X = \mu \pm 1.96\sigma$$

where the values of X corresponding to $(\mu + 1.96\sigma)$ and $(\mu - 1.96\sigma)$ represent the limits we seek. For our example the limits will be

$$\text{Limits} = 50 \pm (1.96)(10) = 50 \pm 19.6 = 30.4 \text{ and } 69.6$$

So the probability is .95 that a child's score (X) chosen at random would be between 30.4 and 69.6. We may not be very interested in low scores, because they don't represent problems. But anyone with a score of 69.6 or higher is a problem to someone. Only 2.5% of children score that high.

What we have just discussed is closely related to, but not quite the same as, what we will later consider under the heading of confidence limits. The major difference is that here we knew the population mean and were trying to estimate where a single observation (X) would fall. When we discuss confidence limits, we will have a sample mean (or some other statistic) and will want to set limits that have a .95 probability of bracketing the population mean (or some other relevant parameter). You do not need to know anything at all about confidence limits at this point. I simply mention the issue to forestall any confusion in the future.

6.4 Measures Related to z

We already have seen that the z formula given earlier can be used to convert a distribution with any mean and variance to a distribution with a mean of 0 and a standard deviation (and variance) of 1. We frequently refer to such transformed scores as **standard scores**. There also are other transformational scoring systems with particular properties, some of which people use every day without realizing what they are.

Standard scores
Scores with a predetermined mean and standard deviation.

A good example of such a scoring system is the common IQ. The raw scores from an IQ test are routinely transformed to a distribution with a mean of 100 and a standard deviation of 15 (or 16 in the case of the Binet). Knowing this, you can readily convert an individual's IQ (e.g., 120) to his or her position in terms of standard deviations above or below the mean (i.e., you can calculate the z score). Because IQ scores are more or less normally distributed, you can then convert z into a percentage measure by use of Table D.10. (In this example, a score of 120 has approximately 91% of the scores below it. This is known as the 91st **percentile**.)

Percentile
The point below which a specified percentage of the observations fall.

Another common example is a nationally administered examination, such as the SAT. The raw scores are transformed by the producer of the test and reported as coming from a distribution with a mean of 500 and a standard deviation of 100 (at least when the tests were first developed). Such a scoring system is easy to devise. We start by converting raw scores to z scores (on the basis of the raw score mean and standard deviation). We then convert the z scores to the particular scoring system we have in mind. Thus

$$\text{New score} = \text{New S.D.}(z) + \text{New mean}$$

where z represents the z score corresponding to the individual's raw score. For the SAT

$$\text{New score} = 100(z) + 500$$

T scores
A set of scores with a mean of 50 and a standard deviation of 10.

Scoring systems such as the one used on Achenbach's Youth Self Report checklist, which have a mean set at 50 and a standard deviation set at 10, are called **T scores** (the T is always capitalized). These tests are useful in psychological measurement because they have a common frame of reference. For example, people become used to seeing a cutoff score of 63 as identifying the highest 10% of the subjects.

6.5 Summary

In this chapter we examined the normal distribution. I discussed how to use the tables of the standard normal distribution to obtain areas under any normal distribution and we saw that areas are directly related to probabilities. We also examined how to use the normal distribution to calculate percentages.

Some important terms in this chapter are:

• Normal distribution	• Linear transformation
• Abscissa	• z score
• Ordinate	• Standard scores
• Density	• Percentile
• Standard normal distribution	• T scores

6.6 Exercises

6.1 Assuming that the following data represent a population with $\mu = 4$ and $\sigma = 1.63$:

$X = 1\ \ 2\ \ 2\ \ 3\ \ 3\ \ 3\ \ 4\ \ 4\ \ 4\ \ 4\ \ 5$
$\ \ \ \ \ \ \ 5\ \ 5\ \ 6\ \ 6\ \ 7$

(a) Plot the distribution as given.

(b) Convert the distribution in Exercise 6.1(a) to a distribution of $X - \mu$.

(c) Go the next step and convert the distribution in Exercise 6.1(b) to a distribution of z.

6.2 Using the distribution in Exercise 6.1, calculate z scores for $X = 2.5$, 6.2, and 9. Interpret these results.

6.3 Suppose we want to study the errors found in the performance of a simple task. We ask a large number of judges to report the number of people seen entering a major department store in one morning. Some judges will miss some people, and some will count others twice, so we don't expect everyone to agree. Suppose we find that the mean number of shoppers reported is 975 with a standard deviation of 15. Assume that the distribution of counts is normal.

(a) What percentage of the counts will lie between 960 and 990?

(b) What percentage of the counts will lie below 975?

(c) What percentage of the counts will lie below 990?

6.4 Using the example from Exercise 6.3:

(a) What two values of X (the count) would encompass the middle 50% of the results?

(b) 75% of the counts would be less than _____.

(c) 95% of the counts would be between _____ and _____.

6.5 The person in charge of the project in Exercise 6.3 counted only 950 shoppers entering the store. Is this a reasonable answer if he was counting conscientiously? Why or why not?

6.6 A set of reading scores for fourth-grade children has a mean of 25 and a standard deviation of 5. A set of scores for ninth-grade children has a mean of 30 and a standard deviation of 10. Assume that the distributions are normal.

(a) Draw a rough sketch of these data, putting both groups in the same figure.

(b) What percentage of fourth graders score better than the average ninth grader?

(c) What percentage of the ninth graders score worse than the average fourth grader? (We will come back to the idea behind these calculations when we study power in Chapter 15.)

6.7 Under what conditions would the answers to (b) and (c) of Exercise 6.6 be equal?

6.8 A certain diagnostic test is indicative of problems only if a child scores in the lowest 10 percent of those taking the test (the 10th percentile). If the mean score is 150 with a standard deviation of 30, what would be the diagnostically meaningful cutoff?

6.9 A dean must distribute salary raises to her faculty for next year. She has decided that the mean raise is to be $2000, the standard deviation of raises is to be $400, and the distribution is to be normal.

(a) The most productive 10% of the faculty will have a raise equal to or greater than $____.

(b) The 5% of the faculty who have done nothing useful in years will receive no more than $____ each.

6.10 We have sent out everyone in a large introductory course to check whether people use seat belts. Each student has been told to look at 100 cars and count the number of people wearing seat belts. The number found by any given student is considered that student's score. The mean score for the class is 44, with a standard deviation of 7.

(a) Diagram this distribution, assuming that the counts are normally distributed.

(b) A student who has done very little work all year has reported finding 62 seat belt users out of 100. Do we have reason to suspect that the student just made up a number rather than actually counting?

6.11 Several years ago a friend of mine produced a diagnostic test of language problems. A score on her scale is obtained simply by counting the number of language constructions (e.g., plural, negative, passive) that the child produces correctly in response to specific prompts from the person administering the test. The test has a mean of 48 and a standard deviation of 7. Parents have trouble understanding the meaning of a score on this scale, and my friend wanted to convert the scores to a mean of 80 and a standard deviation of 10 (to make them more like the kinds of grades parents are used to). How could she have gone about her task?

6.12 Unfortunately the whole world is not built on the principle of a normal distribution. In the preceding example the real distribution is badly skewed because most children do not have language problems and therefore produce all constructions correctly.

(a) Diagram how this distribution might look.

(b) How would you go about finding the cutoff for the bottom 10% if the distribution is not normal?

6.13 In October of 1981 the mean and the standard deviation on the Graduate Record Exam (GRE) for all people taking the exam were 489 and 126, respectively. What percentage of students would you expect to have a score of 600 or less? (This is called the percentile rank of 600.)

6.14 In Exercise 6.13 what score would be equal to or greater than 75% of the scores on the exam? (This score is called the 75th percentile.)

6.15 For all seniors and nonenrolled college graduates taking the GRE in October 1981, the mean and the standard deviation were 507 and 118, respectively. How does this change the answers to Exercises 6.13 and 6.14?

6.16 What does the answer to Exercise 6.15 suggest about the importance of reference groups?

6.17 What is the 75th percentile for GPA in Appendix C? (This is the point below which 75% of the observations are expected to fall.)

6.18 Assuming that the Behavior Problem scores discussed in this chapter come from a population with a mean of 50 and a standard deviation of 10, what would be a diagnostically meaningful cutoff if you wanted to identify those children who score in the highest 2% of the population?

6.19 In Section 6.4 I said that T scores are designed to have a mean of 50 and a standard deviation of 10 and that the Achenbach Youth Self Report measure produces T scores. The data in Figure 6.3 do not have a mean and standard deviation of exactly 50 and 10. Why do you suppose that this is so?

7

BASIC CONCEPTS OF PROBABILITY

In Chapter 6 we began to make use of the concept of probability. For example, we saw that about 68% of children have Behavior Problem scores between 40 and 60 and thus concluded that if we chose a child at random, the probability that he or she would score between 40 and 60 is .68. When we begin concentrating on inferential statistics in Chapter 8, we will rely heavily on statements of probability. There we will be making statements of the form, "If this hypothesis were correct, the probability is only .015 that we would have obtained a result as extreme as the one we actually obtained." If we are to rely on statements of probability, it is important to understand what we mean by probability and to understand a few basic rules for computing and manipulating probabilities. That is the purpose of this chapter.

The material covered in this chapter has been selected for two reasons. First, it is directly applicable to an understanding of the material presented in the remainder of the book. Second, it is intended to allow you to make simple calculations of probabilities that are likely to be useful to you. Material that does not satisfy either of these qualifications has been deliberately omitted. For example, we will not consider such things as the probability of drawing the queen of hearts, given that 14 cards, including the four of hearts, have already been drawn. Nor will we consider the probability that your desk light will burn out in the next 25 hours of use, given that it has already lasted 250 hours. The student who is interested in those topics is encouraged to take a course in probability theory, in which such material can be covered in depth.

7.1 Probability

Analytic view
Definition of probability in terms of analysis of possible outcomes.

The concept of probability can be viewed in several different ways. There is not even general agreement as to what we mean by the word *probability*. The oldest and most common definition of a probability is what is called the **analytic view**. Let's take an example that I have used through five editions of two books. (It once was a true example, but regrettably I have improved my health habits over the years.) I have a bag of caramels hidden in the drawer of my desk (hidden because I have learned not to trust my colleagues). The bag contains 85 of the light caramels, which I like, and 15 of the dark ones, which I save for candy-grubbing colleagues. Being hungry, I reach into the bag and grab a caramel at random. What is the probability that I will pull out a light-colored caramel? Most of you could answer this without knowing anything more about probability. Because 85 of the 100 caramels are light, and because I am sampling at random, the probability (p) of drawing a light caramel is $85/100 = .85$. This example illustrates one definition of probability:

> If an event can occur in A ways and can fail to occur in B ways, and if all possible ways are equally likely (e.g., each caramel has an equal chance of being drawn), then the probability of its occurrence is $A/(A + B)$, and the probability of its failing to occur is $B/(B + A)$.

Relative frequency view
Definition of probability in terms of past performance.

Because there are 85 ways of drawing a light caramel (one for each of the 85 light caramels) and 15 ways of drawing a dark caramel, $A = 85$, $B = 15$, and $p(A) = 85/(85 + 15) = .85$.

Sample with replacement
Sampling in which the item drawn on trial N is replaced before the drawing on trial $N + 1$.

An alternative view of probability is the **relative frequency view**. Suppose that we keep drawing caramels from the bag, noting the color on each draw. In conducting this sampling study we **sample with replacement**, meaning that each caramel is replaced before the next one is drawn. If we made a very large number of draws, we would find that (approximately) 85% of the draws would result in a light caramel. Thus we might define probability as the limit[1] of the relative frequency of occurrence of the desired event that we approach as the number of draws increases.

Yet a third concept of probability is advocated by a number of theorists. That is the concept of **subjective probability**. By this definition probability represents an individual's subjective belief in the likelihood of the occurrence of an event. For example, the statement, "I think that tomorrow will be a good day," is a subjective statement of degree of belief, which probably has very little to do with the long-range relative frequency of the occurrence of good days, and in fact may have no mathematical basis whatsoever. This is not to say that such a view of probability has no legitimate claim for our attention. Subjective probabilities play an extremely important role in human decision making and govern all aspects of our behavior. Just think of the number of decisions you make based on subjective beliefs in the likelihood of certain outcomes. You order pasta for dinner because it is probably better than the mystery meat special; you plan to go skiing tomorrow because the weather forecaster says that there is an 80% chance of snow overnight; you bet your money on a horse because you think that the odds of its winning are better than the 6:1 odds the bookies are offering. Statistical decisions as we will make them here generally will be stated with more mathematical approaches, although even so the *interpretation* of those probabilities has a strong subjective component.

Although the particular definition that you or I prefer may be important to each of us, any of the definitions will lead to essentially the same result in terms of hypothesis testing, the discussion of which will begin in Chapter 8 and run through the rest of the book. (It should be said that those who favor subjective probabilities often disagree with the general hypothesis-testing orientation.) In actual fact most people use the different approaches interchangeably. When we say that the probability of losing at Russian roulette is 1/6, we are referring to the fact that one of the gun's six cylinders has a bullet in it. When we buy a particular car because *Consumer Reports* said it has a good repair record, we are responding to the fact that a high proportion of these cars have been relatively trouble-free. When we say that the probability of the Yankees winning the pennant is high, we are stating our subjective belief in the likelihood of that event. But when we reject some hypothesis because there is a very low probability that the actual data would have been obtained if the hypothesis had been true, it may not be important which view of probability we hold.

Subjective probability
Definition of probability in terms of personal subjective belief in the likelihood of an outcome.

---

[1]The word *limit* refers to the fact that as we sample more and more caramels, the proportion of light will get closer and closer to some value. After 100 draws, the proportion might be .83; after 1000 draws it might be .852; after 10,000 draws it might be .8496, and so on. Notice that the answer is coming closer and closer to $p = .8500000. \ldots$ The value that is being approached is called the limit.

7.2 Basic Terminology and Rules

Event
The outcome of a trial.

The basic bit of data for a probability theorist is called an **event**. The word *event* is a term that statisticians use to cover just about anything. An event can be the occurrence of a king when we deal from a deck of cards, a score of 36 on a scale of likability, a classification of "female" for the next person appointed to the Supreme Court, or the mean of a sample. Whenever you speak of the probability of something, the something is called an event. When we are dealing with a process as simple as flipping a coin, the event is the outcome of that flip— either heads or tails. When we draw caramels out of a bag, the possible events are light and dark. When we speak of a grade in a course, the possible events are the letters A, B, C, D, and F.

Independent events
Events are independent when the occurrence of one has no effect on the probability of the occurrence of the other.

Two events are said to be **independent events** when the occurrence or nonoccurrence of one has no effect on the occurrence or nonoccurrence of the other. The voting behaviors of two randomly chosen subjects normally would be assumed to be independent, especially with a secret ballot, because how one person votes could not be expected to influence how the other will vote. However, the voting behaviors of two members of the same family probably would not be independent events, because those people share many of the same beliefs and attitudes. This would be true even if those two people were careful not to let the other see their ballot.

Mutually exclusive
Two events are mutually exclusive when the occurrence of one precludes the occurrence of the other.

Two events are said to be **mutually exclusive** if the occurrence of one event precludes the occurrence of the other. For example, the standard college classes of First Year, Sophomore, Junior, and Senior are mutually exclusive because one person cannot be a member of more than one class. A set of events is said to be **exhaustive** if it includes all possible outcomes. Thus the four college classes in the previous example are exhaustive with respect to full-time undergraduates, who have to fall in one or another of those categories—if only to please the registrar's office. At the same time, they are not exhaustive with respect to total university enrollments, which include graduate students, medical students, nonmatriculated students, hangers-on, and so forth.

Exhaustive
A set of events that represents all possible outcomes.

As you already know—or could deduce from our definitions of probability—probabilities range between .00 and 1.00. If some event has a probability of 1.00, then it *must* occur. (Very few things have a probability of 1.00, including the probability that I will be able to keep typing until I reach the end of this paragraph.) If some event has a probability of .00, it is certain *not* to occur. The closer the probability comes to either extreme, the more likely or unlikely is the occurrence of the event.

Basic Laws of Probability

Two important theorems are central to any discussion of probability. (If my use of the word *theorems* makes you nervous, substitute the word *rules*.) They are often referred to as the additive and multiplicative rules.

The Additive Rule   To illustrate the additive rule, we will complicate the caramel example by eating many of the light candies and replacing them with wooden cubes. We now have 30 light caramels, 15 dark caramels, and 55 rather tasteless wooden cubes. Given these frequencies, we know from the analytic definition of probability that $p(\text{light}) = 30/100 = .30$, $p(\text{dark}) = 15/100 = .15$, and $p(\text{wooden}) = 55/100 = .55$. But what is the probability that I will draw a caramel, either light or dark, instead of a piece of wood? Here we need the **additive law of probability**.

Additive law of probability
The rule giving the probability of the occurrence of one or more mutually exclusive events.

> Given a set of mutually exclusive events, the probability of the occurrence of one event or another is equal to the sum of their separate probabilities.

Thus, $p(\text{light or dark}) = p(\text{light}) + p(\text{dark}) = .30 + .15 = .45$. Notice that we have imposed the restriction that the events must be mutually exclusive, meaning that the occurrence of one event precludes the occurrence of the other. If a caramel is light, it can't be dark. This requirement is important. About one-half of the population of this country are female, and about one-half of the population have traditionally feminine names. But the probability that a person chosen at random will be female *or* will have a feminine name is obviously not $.50 + .50 = 1.00$. Here the two events are *not* mutually exclusive. However, the probability that a girl born in Vermont in 1987 was named Ashley or Sarah, the two most common girls' names in that year, equals $p(\text{Ashley}) + p(\text{Sarah}) = .044 + .032 = .076$. Here the names are mutually exclusive because you can't have both Ashley *and* Sarah as your first name (unless your parents got carried away and combined the two with a hyphen).

The Multiplicative Rule   Let's continue with the bag of caramels in which $p(\text{light}) = .30$, $p(\text{dark}) = .15$, and $p(\text{wooden}) = .55$. Suppose I draw two caramels, replacing the first before drawing the second. What is the probability that I will draw a light caramel on the first trial *and* a light one on the second? Here we need to invoke the **multiplicative law of probability**.

Multiplicative law of probability
The rule giving the probability of the joint occurrence of independent events.

> The probability of the joint occurrence of two or more independent events is the product of their individual probabilities.

Thus $p(\text{light, light}) = p(\text{light}) \times p(\text{light}) = .30 \times .30 = .09$. Similarly, the probability of a light caramel followed by a dark one is $p(\text{light, dark}) = p(\text{light}) \times p(\text{dark}) = .30 \times .15 = .045$. Notice that we have restricted ourselves to independent events, meaning the occurrence of one event has no effect on the occurrence or nonoccurrence of the other. Because gender and name are not independent, it would be wrong to state that $p(\text{female with feminine name}) = .50 \times .50 = .25$. But it most likely would be correct to state that $p(\text{female, born in January}) = .50 \times .083 = .042$, because I know of no data to suggest that birth month is dependent on gender. (If month and gender were related, my calculation would be wrong.)

In Chapter 19 we will use the multiplicative law to answer questions about the independence of two variables. An example from that chapter will help illustrate a specific use of this law. In a study to be discussed there, Geller, Witmer, and Orebaugh (1976) wanted to test the hypothesis that what someone did with a supermarket flier depended on whether the flier contained a request not to litter. Geller et al. distributed fliers with and without this message and at the end of the day searched the store to find where the fliers had been left. Testing their hypothesis involves, in part, calculating the probability that a flier would contain a message about littering *and* would be found in a trash can. We need to calculate what this probability would be if the two events (contains message about littering and flier in trash) are independent. *If* we assume that these two events are independent, the multiplicative law tells us that p(message, trash) = p(message) $\times$ p(trash). In their study 49% of the fliers contained a message, so the probability that a flier chosen at random would contain the message is .49. Similarly, 6.8% of the fliers were later found in the trash, giving p(trash) = .068. Therefore, if the two events are independent, p(message, trash) = .49 $\times$ .068 = .033. (In fact, 4.5% of the fliers with messages were found in the trash, which is a bit higher than we would expect if the ultimate disposal of the flier was independent of the message. What does this suggest to you about the effectiveness of the message?)

Finally we can take a simple example that illustrates both the additive and the multiplicative laws. What is the probability that over two trials (sampling with replacement) I will draw one light caramel and one dark one, *ignoring the order in which they are drawn*? First we use the multiplicative rule to calculate

$$p(\text{light, dark}) = .30 \times .15 = .045$$

$$p(\text{dark, light}) = .15 \times .30 = .045$$

Because these two outcomes satisfy our requirement (and because they are the only ones that do), we now need to know the probability that one or the other of these outcomes will occur. Here we apply the additive rule:

$$p(\text{light, dark}) + p(\text{dark, light}) = .045 + .045 = .09$$

Thus the probability of obtaining one caramel of each color over two draws is .09—that is, it will occur a little less than one-tenth of the time.

Students sometimes get confused over the additive and multiplicative laws because they almost sound the same when you read them quickly. One useful idea is to realize the difference between the situations in which the rules apply. In those situations in which you use the additive rule, you know that you are going to have *one* outcome. A caramel that you draw may be dark or light, but there is only going to be one of them. In the multiplicative case, we are speaking about at least *two* outcomes (e.g., the probability that we will get one dark caramel *and* one light one). For single outcomes we add probabilities; for multiple outcomes we multiply them.

Joint and Conditional Probabilities

Two types of probabilities play an important role in discussions of probability: joint probabilities and conditional probabilities.

Joint probability
The probability of the co-occurrence of two or more events.

A **joint probability** is defined simply as the probability of the co-occurrence of two or more events. For example, in Geller's study of supermarket fliers, the probability that a flier would *both* contain a message about littering *and* be found in the trash is a joint probability, as is the probability that a flier would both contain a message about littering and be found stuffed down behind the Raisin Bran. Given two events, their joint probability is denoted as $p(A, B)$, just as we have used p(light, dark) or p(message, trash). If those two events are independent, then the probability of their joint occurrence can be found by using the multiplicative law, as we have just seen. If they are *not* independent, the probability of their joint occurrence is more complicated to compute and will differ from what it would be if the events were independent. We won't compute that probability here.

Conditional probability
The probability of one event *given* the occurrence of some other event.

A **conditional probability** is the probability that one event will occur *given* that some other event has occurred. The probability that a person will contract AIDS given that he or she is an intravenous drug user is a conditional probability. The probability that an advertising flier will be thrown in the trash given that it contains a message about littering is another example. A third example is a phrase that occurs repeatedly throughout this book: "If the null hypothesis is true, the probability of obtaining a result such as this is. . . ." Here I have substituted the word *if* for *given*, but the meaning is the same. (I'll define the phrase *null hypothesis* in Chapter 11.)

With two events, A and B, the conditional probability of A given B is denoted, by use of a vertical bar, as $p(A \mid B)$, for example, p(AIDS | Drug user) or p(trash | message).

We often assume, with some justification, that parenthood breeds responsibility. People who have spent years acting in careless and irrational ways somehow seem to turn into different people once they become parents, changing many of their old behavior patterns. (Just wait a few years.) Suppose that a radio station sampled 100 people, 20 of whom had children. They found that 30 of the people sampled used seatbelts, and that 15 of those people had children. The results are shown in Table 7.1.

The information in Table 7.1 allows us to calculate the simple, joint, and conditional probabilities. The simple probability that a person sampled at ran-

Table 7.1

The Relationship Between Parenthood and Seatbelt Use

Parenthood	Wear Seatbelt	Do Not Wear Seatbelt	Total
Children	15	5	20
No children	15	65	80
Total	30	70	100

dom will use a seatbelt is $30/100 = .30$. The joint probability that a person will have children *and* will wear a seatbelt is $15/100 = .15$. The conditional probability of a person using a seatbelt given that he or she has children is $15/20 = .75$. Do not confuse joint and conditional probabilities. As you can see, they are quite different. You might wonder why I didn't calculate the joint probability here by multiplying the appropriate simple probabilities. But the use of the multiplicative law requires that parenthood and seatbelt use be independent. In this example they are not, because the data show that whether people use seatbelts depends very much on whether or not they have children. (If I had assumed independence, I would have predicted the joint probability to be $.30 \times .20 = .06$, which is less than half the size of the actual obtained value.)

To take another example, the probability that you have been drinking alcoholic beverages and that you have an accident is a joint probability. This probability is not very high, because relatively few people are drinking at any one time and relatively few people have accidents. However, the probability that you have an accident given that you have been drinking, or, in reverse, the probability that you have been drinking given that you have an accident, are both much higher. At night the conditional probability of $p(\text{drinking} \mid \text{accident})$ approaches .50, since nearly half of all automobile accidents at night in the United States involve alcohol. I don't know the conditional probability of $p(\text{accident} \mid \text{drinking})$, but I do know that it is much higher than the **unconditional probability** of an accident, that is, $p(\text{accident})$.

Unconditional probability
The probability of one event *ignoring* the occurrence or nonoccurrence of some other event.

7.3 Discrete versus Continuous Variables

In Chapter 2 a distinction was made between discrete and continuous variables. As mathematicians view things, a discrete variable is one that can take on a countable number of different values, whereas a continuous variable is one that can take on an infinite number of different values. For example, the number of people attending a specific movie theater tonight is a discrete variable because we literally can count the number of people entering the theater, and there is no such thing as a fractional person. However, the distance between two people in a study of personal space is a continuous variable because the distance could be $2'$, or $2.8'$, or $2.8173754814'$. Although the distinction given here is technically correct, common usage is somewhat different.

In practice when we speak of a discrete variable, we *usually* mean a variable that takes on one of a relatively small number of possible values (e.g., a five-point scale of socioeconomic status). A variable that can take on one of many possible values is generally treated as a continuous variable if the values represent at least an ordinal scale. Thus we usually think of an IQ score as a continuous variable, even though we recognize that IQ scores come in whole units and we will not find someone with an IQ of 105.317.

The distinction between discrete and continuous variables is reintroduced here because the *distributions* of the two kinds of variables are treated somewhat differently in probability theory. With discrete variables we can speak of the probability of a specific outcome. With continuous variables, on the other hand, we need to speak of the probability of obtaining a value that falls within a specific *interval.*

7.4 Probability Distributions for Discrete Variables

An interesting example of a discrete probability distribution is seen in Figure 7.1. The data plotted in this figure come from a study by Campbell, Converse, and Rodgers (1976), in which they asked 2164 respondents to rate on a 1–5 scale the importance they attach to various aspects of their lives (1 = extremely important, 5 = not at all important). Figure 7.1 presents the distribution of responses for several of these aspects. The possible values of X (the rating) are presented on the abscissa, and the relative frequency (or probability) of people choosing that response is plotted on the ordinate. From the figure you can see that the distributions of responses to questions concerning health, friends, and savings are quite different. The probability that a person chosen at random will consider his or her health to be extremely important is .70, whereas the probability that the same person will consider a large bank account to be extremely important is only .16. (So much for the stereotypic American Dream.) Campbell et al. collected their data in the mid-1970s. Would you expect to find similar results today? How might they differ?

7.5 Probability Distributions for Continuous Variables

When we move from discrete to continuous probability distributions, things become more complicated. We dealt with a continuous distribution when we considered the normal distribution in Chapter 6. You may recall that in that

Figure 7.1

Distributions of Importance Ratings of Three Aspects of Life

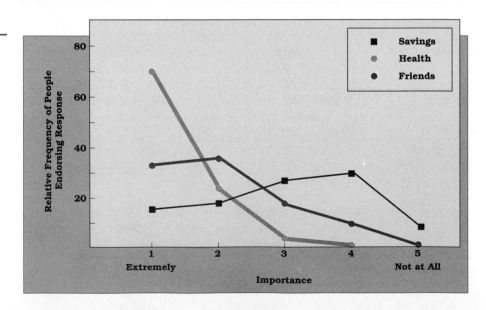

Figure 7.2

Age at Which a Child First Walks Unaided

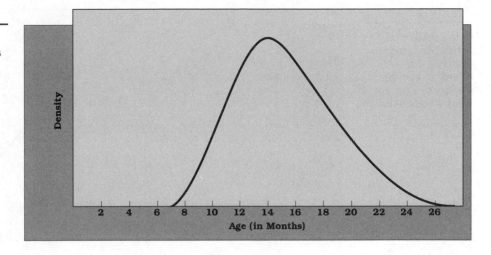

chapter we labeled the ordinate of the distribution "density." We also spoke in terms of intervals rather than in terms of specific outcomes. Now we need to elaborate somewhat on those points.

Figure 7.2 shows the approximate distribution of the age at which children first learn to walk (based on data from Hindley et al., 1966). The mean is approximately 14 months, the standard deviation is approximately three months, and the distribution is positively skewed. You will notice that in this figure the ordinate is labeled "density," whereas in Figure 7.1 it was labeled "relative frequency." **Density** is not synonymous with probability, and it is probably best thought of as merely the height of the curve at different values of X. At the same time, the fact that the curve is higher near 14 months than it is near 12 months tells us that children are more likely to walk at around 14 months than at about one year. The reason for changing the label on the ordinate is that we now are dealing with a continuous distribution rather than a discrete one. If you think about it for a moment, you will realize that although the highest point of the curve is at 14 months, the probability that a child picked at random will first walk at *exactly* 14 months (i.e., 14.00000000 months) is infinitely small—statisticians would argue that it is in fact 0. Similarly, the probability of first walking at 14.00000001 months also is infinitely small. This suggests that it does not make any sense to speak of the probability of any *specific* outcome. On the other hand we know that many children start walking at *approximately* 14 months, and it does make considerable sense to speak of the probability of obtaining a score that falls within some specified *interval*. For example, we might be interested in the probability that an infant will start walking at 14 months plus or minus one-half month. Such an interval is shown in Figure 7.3. If we arbitrarily define the total area under the curve to be 1.00, then the shaded area in Figure 7.3 between points a and b will be equal to the probability that an infant chosen at random will begin walking at this time. Those of you who have had calculus will probably recognize that if we knew the form of the equation that describes this distribution (i.e., if we knew the equation for the curve), we would simply need to integrate the function over the interval

Density
Height of the curve for a given value of X—closely related to the probability of an observation in an interval around X.

Figure 7.3

Probability of
First Walking
During One-
Week Intervals
Centered on 14
and 18 Months

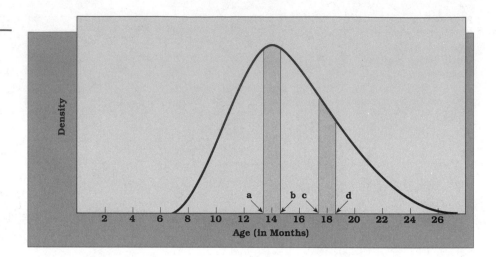

from a to b. Those of you who have not had calculus are not at any disadvantage, however, because the distributions with which we will work are adequately approximated by other distributions that have already been tabled. In this book we will never integrate functions, but we will often refer to tables of distributions. You have already had experience with this procedure with regard to the normal distribution in Chapter 6.

We have just considered the area of Figure 7.3 between a and b, which is centered on the mean. However, the same things could be said for any interval. In Figure 7.3 you can also see the area that corresponds to the period that is one-half month on either side of 18 months (denoted as the shaded area between c and d). Although there is not enough information in this example for us to calculate actual probabilities, it should be clear by inspection of Figure 7.3 that the one-month interval around 14 months has a higher probability (greater shaded area) than the one-month interval around 18 months.

A good way to get a feel for areas under a curve is to take a piece of transparent graph paper and lay it on top of the figure (or use a regular sheet of graph paper and hold the two up to a light). If you count the number of squares that fall within a specified interval and divide by the total number of squares under the whole curve, you will approximate the probability that a randomly drawn score will fall within that interval. It should be obvious that the smaller the size of the individual squares on the graph paper, the more accurate the approximation.

7.6 Summary

In this chapter we examined the various definitions of the term *probability* and a number of fundamental concepts and rules of probability theory. We also considered the differences between discrete and continuous variables and their distributions.

Some important terms in this chapter are:

- Analytic view
- Relative frequency view
- Sample with replacement
- Subjective probability
- Event
- Independent events
- Mutually exclusive

- Exhaustive
- Additive law of probability
- Multiplicative law of probability
- Joint probability
- Conditional probability
- Unconditional probability
- Density

7.7 Exercises

7.1 Give an example of an analytic, a relative frequency, and a subjective view of probability.

7.2 Say you bought a ticket for the local fire department lottery and your brother bought two tickets. You have just read that 1000 tickets were sold.

   (a) What is the probability that you will win?

   (b) What is the probability that your brother will win?

   (c) What is the probability that you *or* your brother will win?

7.3 Now suppose that in the previous question only 10 tickets were sold and that two prizes are to be awarded.

   (a) Given that you don't win first prize, what is the probability that you will win second prize? (The first-prize ticket is not put back into the hopper before the second-prize ticket is drawn.)

   (b) What is the probability that your brother will come in first and you will come in second?

   (c) What is the probability that you will

come in first and he will come in second?

   (d) What is the probability that the two of you will take first and second place?

7.4 Which parts of Exercise 7.3 dealt with joint probabilities?

7.5 Which parts of Exercise 7.3 dealt with conditional probabilities?

7.6 Make up a simple example of a situation in which you are interested in joint probabilities.

7.7 Make up a simple example of a situation in which you are interested in conditional probabilities.

7.8 In some homes a mother's behavior seems to be independent of her baby's and vice versa. If the mother looks at her child a total of 2 hours each day, and if the baby looks at the mother a total of 3 hours each day, and if they really do behave independently, what is the probability that they will look at each other at the same time?

7.9 In Exercise 7.8 assume that both mother and child sleep from 8:00 P.M. to 7:00 A.M. What would be the probability now?

7.10 In the example dealing with what happens to supermarket fliers, we found that the probability that a flier carrying a "do not litter" message would end up in the trash, *if what people do with fliers is independent of the message that is on them,* was .033. I also said that 4.5% of those messages actually ended up in the trash. What does this tell you about the effectiveness of messages?

7.11 Give an example of a common continuous distribution for which we have some real interest in the probability that an observation will fall within some specified interval.

7.12 Give an example of a continuous variable that we routinely treat as if it were discrete.

7.13 Give two examples of discrete variables.

7.14 A graduate admissions committee has finally come to realize that it cannot make valid distinctions among the top applicants. This year the committee rated all 1000 applicants and randomly chose 10 from those at or above the 80th percentile. (The 80th percentile is the point at or below which 80 percent of the scores fall.) What is the probability that any particular applicant will be admitted (assuming you have no knowledge of her rating)?

7.15 With respect to Exercise 7.14, determine the conditional probability that the person will be admitted given the following:

(a) that she has the highest rating

(b) that she has the lowest rating

7.16 In Appendix C, what is the probability that a person drawn at random will have an ADDSC score greater than 50?

7.17 In Appendix C, what is the probability that a male will have an ADDSC score greater than 50?

7.18 In Appendix C, what is the probability that a person will drop out of school given that he or she has an ADDSC score of at least 60?

7.19 How might you use conditional probabilities to determine if an ADDSC cutoff score in Appendix C of 66 is predictive of whether or not a person will drop out of school?

7.20 Compare the conditional probability from Exercise 7.19 with the unconditional probability of dropping out of school.

7.21 People who sell cars are often accused of treating male and female customers differently. Make up a series of statements to illustrate simple, joint, and conditional probabilities with respect to such behavior. How might we begin to determine if those accusations are true?

7.22 Assume you are a member of a local human rights organization. How might you use what you know about probability to examine discrimination in housing?

SAMPLING DISTRIBUTIONS AND HYPOTHESIS TESTING

In the last several chapters we examined a number of different statistics and how they might be used to describe a set of data or present the probability of the occurrence of some event. Although the description of data is important and fundamental to any analysis, it is not sufficient to answer many of the most interesting problems we encounter. In a typical experiment we might treat one group in a special way and then see if their scores differ from the scores of people in general. Descriptive statistics will not tell us, for example, whether the difference between a sample mean and a hypothesized population mean, or between two obtained sample means, is small enough to be explained on the basis of chance alone or represents a true difference that might be attributable to the effect of our experimental treatment(s). And as we will see in the next three chapters, descriptive statistics will not tell us if an apparent relationship between two or more variables is real or just a chance occurrence that would be difficult to reproduce on a second try.

Statisticians frequently use phrases such as "differ by chance" and "sampling error" and assume you know what they mean. Perhaps you do. But if you don't, you are headed for confusion in the remainder of this book unless we take a moment to clarify the meaning of these phrases. We will begin with a simple example. In Chapter 6 we considered the distribution of total Behavior Problem scores from Achenbach's Youth Self Report form. Total Behavior Problem scores are normally distributed in the population (i.e., the complete population of such scores is normally distributed) with a population mean (μ) of 50 and a population standard deviation (σ) of 10. We know that different children show different levels of problem behaviors and therefore have different scores. We also know that if we took a sample of children their sample mean would probably not equal exactly 50. One sample of children might have a mean of 49, while a second sample might have a mean of 52.3. The actual sample means would depend on the particular children who happened to be included in the sample. This expected variability that we see from sample to sample is what is meant when we speak of "variability due to chance." We are referring to the fact that statistics (in this case, means) obtained from samples naturally vary from one sample to another.

Sampling error
The variability of a statistic from sample to sample due to chance.

Along the same lines the term **sampling error** often is used in this context as a synonym for variability due to chance. It indicates that the value of a sample statistic probably will be in error (i.e., will deviate from the parameter it is estimating) as a result of the particular observations that happened to be included in the sample. In this context "error" does not imply carelessness or mistakes. In the case of behavior problems, one random sample might just happen to include an unusually obnoxious child, whereas another sample might happen to include an unusual number of relatively well-behaved children.

8.1 Two Simple Examples Involving Course Evaluations and Rude Motorists

One example that we will investigate near the end of the next chapter looks at the relationship between how students evaluate a course and the grade they expect to receive in that course. This is a topic that many faculty feel strongly about, because even the best instructors turn to the semiannual course evaluation forms with some trepidation—perhaps the same amount of trepidation with which many students open their grade report form. Some faculty think that a course is good or bad independently of how well a student feels he or she will do in terms of a grade. Others feel that a student who seldom came to class and who will do poorly as a result will also (unfairly?) rate the course as poor. Finally there are those who argue that students who do well and experience success take something away from the course other than just a grade and that those students will generally rate the course highly. But the relationship between course ratings and student performance is an empirical question and, as such, can be answered by looking at relevant data. Suppose that in a random sample of fifty courses we find a general trend for courses in which students expect to do well to rate the course highly and for courses in which students expect to do poorly to rate the overall quality of the course as low. How do we tell whether this trend in our small data set is representative of a trend among students in general or just a fluke that would disappear if we ran the study over? (For your own interest, make your prediction of what kind of results we will find. We will return to this issue in the next chapter.)

A second example comes from a study by Doob and Gross (1968), who investigated the influence of perceived social status. They found that if an old, beat-up (low-status) car failed to start when a traffic light turned green, 84% of the time the driver of the second car in line honked the horn. However, when the stopped car was an expensive, high-status car, only 50% of the time did the following driver honk. These results could be explained in one of two ways:

1. The difference between 84% in one sample and 50% in a second sample is attributable to sampling error (random variability among samples); therefore, we cannot conclude that perceived social status influences horn-honking behavior.

2. The difference between 84% and 50% is large. The difference is not attributable to sampling error; therefore, people are less likely to honk at drivers of high-status cars.

Although the statistical calculations required to answer this question are different from those used to answer the one about course evaluations (because the first deals with relationships and the second deals with proportions), the underlying logic is fundamentally the same.

Hypothesis testing
A process by which decisions are made concerning the values of parameters.

These examples of course evaluations and horn honking are two kinds of questions that fall under the heading of **hypothesis testing**. This chapter is intended to present the theory of hypothesis testing in as general a way as possible, without going into the specific techniques or properties of any particular test. I will focus largely on the situation involving differences instead of the situation involving relationships, but the logic is basically the same. You will see additional material on examining relationships in the next chapter.

The theory of hypothesis testing is so important in all that follows that a thorough understanding of it is essential. Many students who have had one or more courses in statistics and who know how to run a number of different statistical tests still do not have a basic knowledge of what it is they are doing. As a result they have difficulty interpreting statistical tables and must learn every new procedure in a step-by-step, rote fashion. This chapter is designed to avoid that difficulty by presenting the theory in its most general sense, without the use of any formulae. You can learn the formulae later, after you understand *why* you might want to use them. Professional statisticians might fuss over the looseness of the definitions, but any looseness will be set right in subsequent chapters. Others may object that we are considering hypothesis testing before we consider the statistical procedures that produce the test. That is precisely the intent. The material covered here cuts across all statistical tests and can be discussed independently of them. By separating the material in this way, you are free to concentrate on the underlying principles without worrying about the mechanics of calculation.

The important issue in hypothesis testing is to find some way of deciding whether we are looking at a small chance fluctuation between the horn-honking rates for low- and high-status cars or a difference that is sufficiently large for us to believe that people are much less likely to honk at those they consider higher in status.

8.2 Sampling Distributions

A third example is one that affects a large number of children in our society. Consider the situation in which we have five students from recently divorced households. These five children have a mean of 56 on the Achenbach Youth Self Report scale of Total Behavior Problems. This mean is over half a standard deviation above the mean (50) in the general population, and we want to know if this finding is sufficiently deviant for us to conclude that the stress associated with divorce tends to elicit behavior problems in children at higher than normal levels. Perhaps we just came up with a peculiar sample, and another sample of children from divorced households would show normal levels of behavior. Or perhaps divorce is a sufficiently stressful event in children's lives to produce serious behavior problems. To answer this kind of question, we have to use what are called **sampling distributions**, which tell us specifically what degree of sample-to-sample variability we can expect by chance as a function of sampling error.

Sampling distributions
The distribution of a statistic over repeated sampling from a specified population.

The most basic concept underlying all statistical tests is the sampling distribution of a statistic. It is fair to say that if we did not have sampling distributions, we would not have any statistical tests. Roughly speaking, sampling distributions tell us what values we might (or might not) expect to obtain for a particular statistic under a set of predefined conditions (e.g., what the obtained mean of five children might be *if* the true mean of the population from which those children come is 50). In addition, the standard deviation of that distribution (known as the "standard error" of the distribution) reflects the variability that we would expect to find in the values of that statistic over repeated trials. Sampling distributions provide the opportunity to evaluate the likelihood (given the value of a sample statistic) that such predefined conditions actually exist.

Basically, the sampling distribution of a statistic can be thought of as the distribution of values obtained for that statistic over repeated sampling (i.e., running the experiment, or drawing samples, an unlimited number of times). Although sampling distributions are almost always derived mathematically, it is easier to understand what they represent if we consider how they could, in theory, be derived empirically with a simple sampling experiment.

Sampling distribution of the mean
The distribution of sample means over repeated sampling from one population.

We will take as an illustration the **sampling distribution of the mean**, because it is the most easily understood and relates directly to the example of behavior problems. The sampling distribution of the mean is nothing more than the distribution of means of an infinite number of random samples drawn under certain specified conditions (e.g., under the condition that the true mean of our population is 50 and the standard deviation is 10). Suppose we have a population with a known mean ($\mu = 50$). Further suppose that we draw a very large number (theoretically an infinite number) of random samples from this population, each sample consisting of five scores. For each sample we will calculate its mean, and when we finish drawing all the samples, we will plot the distribution of these *means*. Such a distribution would be a sampling distribution of the mean and might look like the one presented in Figure 8.1. We can see from this figure that sample means between 48 and 52, for example, are quite likely to occur when we sample five children at random. We also can see that it is extremely unlikely that we would draw from this population a sample of five observations with a sample mean as high as 70, although there is some (quite small) probability of doing so. The fact that we know the kinds of values to expect for the mean of a sample drawn from this population is going to allow us to turn the question around and ask if an obtained sample mean can be taken as evidence in favor of the hypothesis that we actually are sampling from this population.

Figure 8.1

Distribution of Sample Means of Behavior Problems, Each Based on $n = 5$ Scores

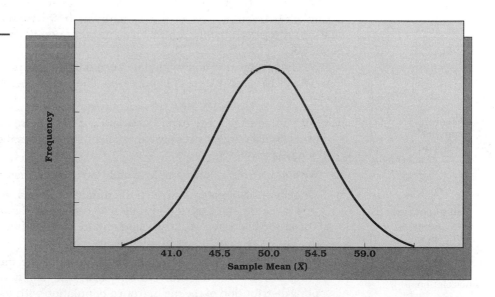

8.3 Hypothesis Testing

We do not go around obtaining sampling distributions, either mathematically or empirically, simply because they are interesting to look at. We have important reasons for doing so. The usual reason is that we want to test some hypothesis. Let's go back to the random sample of five highly stressed children with a mean behavior problem score of 56. We want to test the hypothesis that such a sample mean could reasonably have arisen had we drawn our sample from a population in which $\mu = 50$. This is another way of saying that we want to know whether the mean of stressed children is different from the mean of normal children. The only way we can test such a hypothesis is to have some idea of the probability of obtaining a sample mean as extreme as 56 *if* we actually sampled observations from a population in which $\mu = 50$. The answer to this question is precisely what a sampling distribution is designed to provide.

Suppose we obtained (constructed) the sampling distribution of the mean for samples of five children from a population whose mean (μ) is 50 (the distribution plotted in Figure 8.1). Suppose further we then determined from that distribution the probability of a sample mean as high as 56. For the sake of argument, suppose this probability is .15. Our reasoning could then go as follows: "If we did in fact sample from a population with $\mu = 50$, the probability of obtaining a sample mean as high as 56 is .15—a fairly likely event. Because a sample mean that high is often obtained from a population with a mean of 50, we have no reason to doubt that this sample came from such a population."

Alternatively, suppose we obtained a sample mean of 62 and calculated from the sampling distribution that the probability of a sample mean as high as 62 was only .004. Our argument could then go like this: "*If* we did sample from a population with $\mu = 50$, the probability of obtaining a sample mean as high as 62 is only .004—an unlikely event. Because a sample mean that high is unlikely to be obtained from such a population, we can reasonably conclude that this sample probably came from some other population (one whose mean is not 50)."

It is important to realize what has been done in this example, because the logic is typical of most tests of hypotheses. The actual test consisted of several stages:

Research hypothesis

The hypothesis that the experiment was designed to investigate.

1. We wanted to test the hypothesis, often called the **research hypothesis**, that children under stress are more likely than normal children to exhibit behavior problems.

2. We obtained a random sample of children under stress.

Null hypothesis (H_0)

The statistical hypothesis tested by the statistical procedure; usually a hypothesis of no difference or no relationship.

3. We set up the hypothesis (called the **null hypothesis**, H_0) that the sample was in fact drawn from a population whose mean, denoted μ_0, equals 50. This is the hypothesis that stressed children do not differ from normal children in terms of behavior problems.

4. We then obtained the sampling distribution of the mean under the assumption that H_0 (the null hypothesis) is true (i.e., we obtained the sampling distribution of the mean from a population with $\mu_0 = 50$).

5. Given the sampling distribution, we calculated the probability of a mean *at least as large* as our actual sample mean.

6. On the basis of that probability, we made a decision: to either reject or fail to reject H_0. Because H_0 states that $\mu = 50$, rejection of H_0 represents a belief that $\mu > 50$, although the actual value of μ remains unspecified.

The preceding discussion is oversimplified in the sense that we generally would prefer to test the research hypothesis that children under stress are *different from* (rather than just *higher than*) other children, but we will return to that point shortly. It is also oversimplified in the sense that in practice we also would need to take into account (either directly or by estimation) the value of σ^2, the population variance, and N, the sample size. But again, those are specifics we can deal with when the time comes. The logic of the approach is representative of the logic of most, if not all, statistical tests. In each case we begin with a research hypothesis, set up the null hypothesis, construct the sampling distribution of the particular statistic on the assumption that H_0 is true, collect some data, compare the sample statistic to that distribution, and reject or retain H_0, depending on the probability, under H_0, of a sample statistic as extreme as the one we have obtained.

8.4 The Null Hypothesis

As we have seen, the concept of the null hypothesis plays a crucial role in the testing of hypotheses. People frequently are puzzled by the fact that we set up a hypothesis that is directly counter to what we hope to show. For example, if we hope to demonstrate the research hypothesis that college students do not come from a population with a mean self-confidence score of 100, we immediately set up the null hypothesis that they do. Or if we hope to demonstrate the validity of a research hypothesis that the means (μ_1 and μ_2) of the population from which two samples are drawn are different, we state the null hypothesis that the population means are the same (or, equivalently, $\mu_1 - \mu_2 = 0$). (The term "null hypothesis" is most easily seen in this second example, in which it refers to the hypothesis that the difference between the two population means is zero, or *null*.) We use the null hypothesis for several reasons. The philosophical argument, put forth by Fisher when he first introduced the concept, is that we can never prove something to be true, but we can prove something to be false. Observing 3000 people with only one head does not prove the statement "Everyone has only one head." However, finding one person with two heads does disprove the original statement without any shadow of a doubt. While one might argue with Fisher's basic position—and many people have—the null hypothesis retains its dominant place in statistics.

A second and more practical reason for employing the null hypothesis is that it provides us with the starting point for any statistical test. Consider the case in which you want to show that the mean self-confidence score of college students is greater than 100. Suppose further that you were granted the privilege of proving the truth of some hypothesis. What hypothesis are you going to test? Should you test the hypothesis that $\mu = 101$, or maybe the hypothesis that $\mu = 112$, or how about $\mu = 113$? The point is that you do not have a *specific* alternative (research) hypothesis in mind, and without one you cannot construct the sampling distribution you need. However, if you start off by assuming $H_0:\mu = 100$, you can immediately set about obtaining the sampling distribution for $\mu = 100$ and then, with luck, reject that hypothesis and conclude that the mean score of college students is greater than 100, which is what you wanted to show in the first place.

8.5 Test Statistics and Their Sampling Distributions

Sample statistics
Statistics calculated from a sample and used primarily to describe the sample (e.g., $\overline{X}$).

Test statistics
The results of a statistical test (e.g., t).

We have been discussing the sampling distribution of the mean, but the discussion would have been essentially the same had we dealt instead with the median, the variance, the range, the correlation coefficient (as in our course evaluation example), proportions (as in our horn honking example), or any other statistic you care to consider. (Technically the shape of these distributions would be different, but I am deliberately ignoring such issues in this chapter.) The statistics just mentioned usually are referred to as **sample statistics** because they describe samples. There is a whole different class of statistics called **test statistics**, which are associated with specific statistical procedures and which have their own sampling distributions. Test statistics are statistics such as t, F, χ^2, which you may have run across in the past. If you are not familiar with them, don't worry—we will consider them separately in later chapters. This is not the place to go into a detailed explanation of any test statistics (I put this chapter where it is because I didn't want readers to think that they were supposed to worry about technical issues). This chapter is the place, however, to point out that the sampling distributions for test statistics are obtained and used in essentially the same way as the sampling distribution of the mean.

As an illustration, consider the sampling distribution of the statistic t, which will be discussed in Chapters 12 through 14. For those who have never heard of the t test, it is sufficient to say that the t test is often used, among other things, to determine whether two samples were drawn from populations with the same means. Let μ_1 and μ_2 represent the means of the populations from which the two samples were drawn. The null hypothesis is the hypothesis that the two population means are equal, in other words, $H_0:\mu_1 = \mu_2$ (or $\mu_1 - \mu_2 = 0$). If we were extremely patient, we could empirically obtain the sampling distribution of t when H_0 is true by drawing an infinite number of pairs of samples, all from one population, calculating t for each pair of samples (by methods to be discussed later), and plotting the resulting values of t. In that case H_0 must be true because the samples came from the same population. The resulting distribution is the sampling distribution of t when H_0 is true. If we had two samples that produced a particular value of t, we would test the null hypothesis by comparing our sample t to the sampling distribution of t. We would reject the null hypothesis if our obtained t did not look like the kinds of t values that the sampling distribution told us to expect when the null hypothesis is true.

I could rewrite the preceding paragraph substituting χ^2, or F, or any other test statistic in place of t, with only minor changes dealing with how the statistic is calculated. Thus, you can see that all sampling distributions can be obtained in basically the same way (calculate and plot an infinite number of statistics by sampling from a known population). Once you understand that fact, much of the remainder of the book is an elaboration of methods for calculating the desired statistic and a description of characteristics of the appropriate sampling distribution.

8.6 Using the Normal Distribution to Test Hypotheses

Much of the discussion so far has dealt with statistical procedures that you do not yet know how to use. I did this deliberately to emphasize the point that the logic and the calculations behind a test are two separate issues. However, we now can use what you already know about the normal distribution to test some simple hypotheses. In the process we can deal with several fundamental issues that are more easily seen by use of a concrete example.

An important use of the normal distribution is to test hypotheses, either about individual observations or about sample statistics such as the mean. In this chapter we will deal with individual observations, leaving the question of testing sample statistics until later chapters. Note, however, that in the general case we test hypotheses about sample statistics such as the mean rather than about individual observations. I am starting with an example of an individual observation because the explanation is somewhat clearer. Since we are dealing with only single observations, the sampling distribution invoked here will be the distribution of individual scores (rather than the distribution of means). The basic logic is the same, and we are using an example of individual scores only because it simplifies the explanation and is something with which you have had experience.

For a simple example assume we know that the mean rate of finger tapping of normal healthy adults is 100 taps in 20 seconds, with a standard deviation of 20, and that tapping speeds are normally distributed in the population. Assume further that we know that the tapping rate is slower among people with certain neurological problems. (In fact, tapping speeds really are an important diagnostic indicator of neurological damage, although the difference in rates between left and right hands is more important than the absolute rate of either hand.) Finally, suppose that an individual has just been sent to us who taps at a rate of 70 taps in 20 seconds. Is his score sufficiently below the mean for us to assume that he did not come from a population of neurologically healthy people? This situation is diagrammed in Figure 8.2, in which the arrow indicates the location of our piece of data (the person's score).

The logic of the solution to this problem is the same as the logic of hypothesis testing in general. We begin by assuming that the individual's score does

Figure 8.2

Location of a Person's Tapping Score on a Distribution of Scores of Neurologically Healthy People

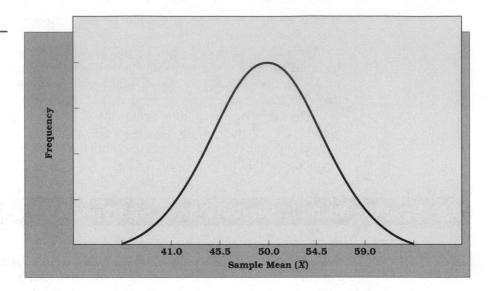

come from the population of healthy scores. This is the null hypothesis (H_0). If H_0 is true, we automatically know the mean and the standard deviation of the population from which he was supposedly drawn (100 and 20, respectively). With this information we are in a position to calculate the probability that a score *as low as* his would be obtained from this population. If the probability is very low, we can reject H_0 and conclude that he did not come from the healthy population. Conversely, if the probability is not particularly low, then the data represent a reasonable result under H_0, and we would have no reason to doubt its validity and thus no reason to doubt that the person is healthy. Keep in mind that we are not interested in the probability of a score *equal* to 70 (which, because the distribution is continuous, would be infinitely small) but rather in the probability that the score would be at least as low as (i.e., less than or equal to) 70.

The individual had a score of 70. We want to know the probability of obtaining a score *at least as low as* 70 if H_0 is true. We already know how to find this—it is the area below 70 in Figure 8.2. All we have to do is convert 70 to a z score and then refer to Appendix D, Table D.10.

$$z = \frac{X - \mu}{\sigma} = \frac{70 - 100}{20} = \frac{-30}{20} = -1.5$$

Decision making
A procedure for making logical decisions on the basis of sample data.

From Table D.10, we can see that the probability of a z score of -1.5 or below is .0668. (Locate $z = 1.50$ in the table and then read across to the column headed "Smaller Portion.")

At this point we have to become involved in the **decision-making** aspects of hypothesis testing. We must decide if an event with a probability of .0668 is sufficiently unlikely to cause us to reject H_0. Here we will fall back on arbitrary conventions that have been established over the years. The rationale for these conventions will become clearer as we go along, but for the time being keep in mind that they are merely conventions. One convention calls for rejecting H_0 if the probability under H_0 is less than or equal to .05 ($p \le .05$), while another convention—one that is more conservative with respect to the probability of rejecting H_0—calls for rejecting H_0 whenever the probability under H_0 is less than or equal to .01. These values of .05 and .01 are often referred to as the **rejection level**, or **significance level**, of the test. Whenever the probability obtained under H_0 is less than or equal to our predetermined significance level, we will reject H_0. Another way of stating this is to say that any outcome whose probability under H_0 is less than or equal to the significance level falls in the **rejection region**, since such an outcome leads us to reject H_0. For the purpose of setting a standard level of rejection for this book, we will use the .05 level of significance, keeping in mind that some people would consider this level to be too lenient.[1] For our particular example we have obtained a probability value of .0668, which obviously is greater than .05. Because we have specified that we will not reject H_0 unless the probability of the data under H_0 is less than .05, we must conclude that we have no reason to decide that the person did not come from a population of healthy people. More specifically, we conclude that a finger-tapping rate of 70 reasonably could have come from a population of scores with a mean equal to 100 and a standard deviation equal to 20. It is important to note that we have not shown that this person is healthy, but only that we have insufficient reason to believe that he is not. It may be that he is just acquiring the disease and therefore is not quite as different from normal as is usual for his condition. Or maybe he has the disease at an advanced stage but just happens to be an unusually fast tapper. This is an example of the fact that we can never say that we have proved the null hypothesis. We can conclude only that this person does not tap sufficiently slowly for an illness, if any, to be statistically detectable.

The theory of significance testing as just outlined was popularized by R. A. Fisher in the first third of the 20th century. The theory was expanded and cast in more of a decision framework by Jerzy Neyman and Egon Pearson between 1928 and 1938, often against the loud and abusive objections of Fisher. Current statistical practice more closely follows the Neyman-Pearson approach,

---

Rejection level (significance level)
The probability with which we are willing to reject H_0 when it is in fact correct.

Rejection region
The set of outcomes of an experiment that will lead to rejection of H_0.

---

[1]The particular view of hypothesis testing described here is the classical one that a null hypothesis is rejected if its probability is less than the predefined significance level, and not rejected if its probability is greater than the significance level. Currently a substantial body of opinion holds that such cut-and-dried rules are inappropriate and that more attention should be paid to the probability value itself. In other words, the classical approach (using a .05 rejection level) would declare $p = .051$ and $p = .150$ to be (equally) "nonsignificant" and $p = .048$ and $p = .0003$ to be (equally) "significant." The alternative view would think of $p = .051$ as "nearly significant" and $p = .0003$ as "very significant." While this view has much to recommend it, it will not be wholeheartedly adopted here. Most computer programs do print out exact probability levels, and those values, when interpreted judiciously, can be useful. The difficulty comes in defining what is meant by "interpreted judiciously."

Alternative hypothesis (H_1)
The hypothesis that is adopted when H_0 is rejected; usually the same as the research hypothesis.

which emphasizes more than did Fisher the fact that we also have an **alternative hypothesis (H_1)** that is contradictory to the null hypothesis (H_0). Thus if the null hypothesis is

$$H_0: \mu = 100$$

then the alternative hypothesis could be

$$H_1: \mu \neq 100$$

or

$$H_1: \mu < 100$$

or

$$H_1: \mu > 100$$

We will discuss alternative hypotheses in more detail shortly.

8.7 Type I and Type II Errors

Whenever we reach a decision with a statistical test, there is always a chance that our decision is the wrong one. While this is true of almost all decisions, statistical or otherwise, the statistician has one point in her favor that other decision makers normally lack. She not only makes a decision by some rational process but she can also specify the conditional probabilities of a decision's being in error. In everyday life we make decisions with only subjective feelings about what is probably the right choice. (I had one excellent student who went around with the feeling that whatever his choice, it was probably the wrong one.) The statistician, however, can state quite precisely the probability that she erroneously rejected H_0 in favor of the alternative (H_1). This ability to specify the probability of error follows directly from the logic of hypothesis testing.

Consider the finger-tapping example, this time ignoring the score of the individual sent to us. The situation is diagrammed in Figure 8.3, in which the distribution is the distribution of scores from healthy subjects, and the shaded portion represents the lowest 5% of the distribution. The actual score that cuts off the lowest 5% is called the **critical value.** Critical values are those values of X (the variable) that describe the boundary or boundaries of the rejection region(s). For this particular example the critical value is 67.

Critical value
The value of a test statistic at or beyond which we will reject H_0.

If we have a decision rule that says to reject H_0 whenever an outcome falls in the lowest 5% of the distribution, we will reject H_0 whenever an individual's score falls in the shaded area; that is, whenever a score as low as his has a probability of .05 or less of coming from the population of healthy scores. Yet

Figure 8.3

Lowest 5% Of Scores from Clinically Healthy People

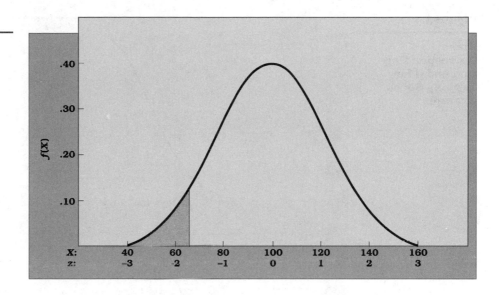

by the very nature of our procedure, 5% of the scores from perfectly healthy people will themselves fall in the shaded portion. Thus if we actually have sampled a person who is healthy, we stand a 5% chance of his score being in the shaded tail of the distribution, causing us erroneously to reject the null hypothesis. This kind of error (rejecting H_0 when in fact it is true) is called a **Type I error,** and its conditional probability (the probability of rejecting the null hypothesis given that it is true) is designated as α **(alpha)**, the size of the rejection region. In the future, whenever we represent a probability by α, we will be referring to the probability of a Type I error.

Keep in mind the "conditional" nature of the probability of a Type I error. I know that sounds like jargon, but what it means is that you should be sure you understand that when we speak of a Type I error we mean the probability of rejecting H_0 *given that it is true*. We are not saying that we will reject H_0 on 5% of the hypotheses we test. We would hope to run experiments on important and meaningful variables and, therefore, to often reject H_0. But when we speak of a Type I error we are speaking only about rejecting H_0 in those situations in which the null hypothesis happens to be true.

You might feel that a 5% chance of making an error is too great a risk to take and suggest that we make our criterion much more stringent, by rejecting, for example, only the lowest 1% of the distribution. This procedure is perfectly legitimate, but realize that the more stringent you make your criterion, the more likely you are to make another kind of error—failing to reject H_0 when it is in fact false and H_1 is true. This type of error is called a **Type II error**, and its probability is symbolized by β **(beta)**.

The major difficulty in terms of Type II errors stems from the fact that if H_0 is false, we almost never know what the true distribution (the distribution under H_1) would look like for the population from which our data came. We know only the distribution of scores under H_0. Put in the present context, we know

Type I error
The error of rejecting H_0 when it is true.

α (alpha)
The probability of a Type I error.

Type II error
The error of not rejecting H_0 when it is false.

β (beta)
The probability of a Type II error.

Figure 8.4

Areas Corresponding to α and β for Tapping Speed Example

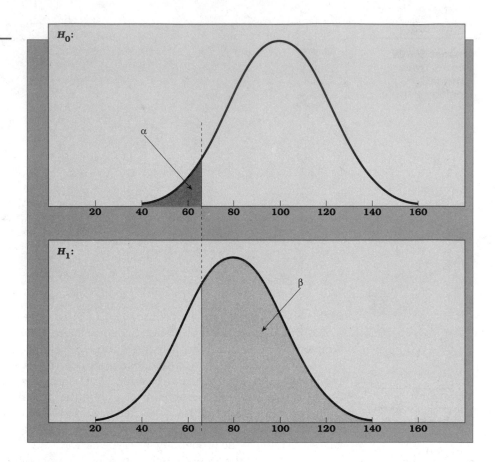

the distribution of scores from healthy people but not from nonhealthy people. It may be that people suffering from some neurological disease tap, on average, considerably more slowly than healthy people, or it may be that they tap, on average, only a little more slowly. This situation is illustrated in Figure 8.4, in which the distribution labeled H_0 represents the distribution of scores from healthy people (the set of observations expected under the null hypothesis), and the distribution labeled H_1 represents our hypothetical distribution of nonhealthy scores (the distribution under H_1). Remember that the curve H_1 is only hypothetical. We really do not know the location of the nonhealthy distribution, other than that it is lower (slower speeds) than the distribution of H_0. (I have arbitrarily drawn that distribution with a mean of 80 and a standard deviation of 20.)

The darkly shaded portion in the top half of Figure 8.4 represents the rejection region. Any observation falling in that area (i.e., to the left of about 67) would lead to rejection of the null hypothesis. If the null hypothesis is true, we know that our observation will fall in this area 5% of the time. Thus, we will make a Type I error 5% of the time.

The lightly shaded portion in the bottom half of Figure 8.4 represents the probability (β) of a Type II error. This is the situation of a person who was actually drawn from the nonhealthy population but whose score was not sufficiently low to cause us to reject H_0.

In the particular situation illustrated in Figure 8.4, we can in fact calculate β by using the normal distribution to calculate the probability of obtaining a score *greater than* 67 (the critical value) if $\mu = 80$ and $\sigma = 20$. The actual calculation is not important for your understanding of β; because this chapter was designed specifically to avoid calculation, I will simply state that this probability (i.e., the area labeled β) is .74. Thus for this example, 74% of the time when we have a person who is actually nonhealthy (i.e., H_1 is actually true), we will make a Type II error by failing to reject H_0 when it is false (as medical diagnosticians, we leave a lot to be desired).

From Figure 8.4 you can see that if we were to reduce the level of α (the probability of a Type I error) from .05 to .01 by moving the rejection region to the left, it would reduce the probability of Type I errors but would increase the probability of Type II errors. Setting α at .01 would mean that $\beta = .908$. Obviously there is room for debate over what level of significance to use. The decision rests primarily on your opinion concerning the relative importance of Type I and Type II errors for the kind of study you are conducting. If it is important to avoid Type I errors (such as telling someone that he has a disease when he does not), then you would set a stringent (i.e., small) level of α. If, on the other hand, you want to avoid Type II errors (telling someone to go home and take an aspirin when in fact he needs immediate treatment), you might set a fairly high level of α. (Setting $\alpha = .20$ in this example would reduce β to .44.) Unfortunately in practice most people choose an arbitrary level of α, such as .05 or .01, and simply ignore β. In many cases this may be all you can do. (In fact you will probably use the alpha level that your instructor recommends.) In other cases, however, there is much more you can do, as you will see in Chapter 15.

I should stress again that Figure 8.4 is purely hypothetical. I was able to draw the figure only because I arbitrarily decided that speeds of nonhealthy people were normally distributed with a mean of 80 and a standard deviation of 20. In most everyday situations we do not know the mean and the variance of that distribution and can make only educated guesses, thus providing only crude estimates of β. In practice we can select a value of μ under H_1 that represents the *minimum* difference we would like to be able to detect, since larger differences will have even smaller βs.

From this discussion of Type I and Type II errors we can summarize the decision-making process with a simple table. Table 8.1 presents the four pos-

Table 8.1

Possible Outcomes of the Decision-Making Process

	True State of the World	
Decision	H_0 **True**	H_0 **False**
Reject H_0	Type I error $p = \alpha$	Correct decision $p = 1 - \beta =$ Power
Fail to reject H_0	Correct decision $p = 1 - \alpha$	Type II error $p = \beta$

sible outcomes of an experiment. The items in this table should be self-explanatory, but there is one concept—power—that we have not yet discussed. The **power** of a test is the probability of rejecting H_0 when it is actually false. Because the probability of *failing* to reject a false H_0 is β, then power must equal $1 - \beta$. Those who want to know more about power and its calculation will find the material in Chapter 15 relevant.

Power
The probability of correctly rejecting a false H_0.

8.8 One- and Two-Tailed Tests

The preceding discussion brings us to a consideration of one- and two-tailed tests. In our tapping example we knew that nonhealthy subjects tapped more slowly than healthy subjects; therefore, we decided to reject H_0 only if a subject tapped too slowly. However, suppose our subject had tapped 180 times in 20 seconds. Although this is an exceedingly unlikely event to observe from a healthy subject, it did not fall in the rejection region, which consisted *solely* of low rates. As a result we find ourselves in the position of not rejecting H_0 in the face of a piece of data that is very unlikely, but not in the direction expected.

The question then arises as to how we can protect ourselves against this type of situation (if protection is thought necessary). The answer is to specify before we run the experiment that we are going to reject a given percentage (say 5%) of the *extreme* outcomes, both those that are extremely high and those that are extremely low. But if we reject the lowest 5% and the highest 5%, then we would in fact reject H_0 a total of 10% of the time when it is actually true, that is, $\alpha = .10$. We are rarely willing to work with α as high as .10 and prefer to see it set no higher than .05. The only way to accomplish this criterion is to reject the lowest 2.5% and the highest 2.5%, making a total of 5%.

One-tailed test (directional test)
A test that rejects extreme outcomes in only one specified tail of the distribution.

The situation in which we reject H_0 for only the lowest (or only the highest) tapping speeds is referred to as a **one-tailed**, or **directional**, **test**. We make a prediction of the direction in which the individual will differ from the mean and our rejection region is located in only one tail of the distribution. When we reject extremes in both tails, we have what is called a **two-tailed**, or **nondirectional**, **test**. It is important to keep in mind that while we gain something with a two-tailed test (the ability to reject the null hypothesis for extreme scores in either direction), we also lose something. A score that would fall in the 5% rejection region of a one-tailed test may not fall in the rejection region of the corresponding two-tailed test, because now we reject only 2.5% in each tail.

Two-tailed test (nondirectional test)
A test that rejects extreme outcomes in either tail of the distribution.

In the finger tapping example, the decision between a one- and a two-tailed test might seem reasonably clear-cut. We know that people with a given disease tap more slowly; therefore we care only about rejecting H_0 for low scores—high scores have no diagnostic importance. In other situations, however, we do not know which tail of the distribution is important (or both are), and we need to guard against extremes in either tail. The situation might arise when we are considering a campaign to persuade children to brush their teeth more often. We might find that the campaign leads to an increase in the desired behavior. Or, we might find that kids hate to be told to brush their teeth and therefore brush even less frequently just to spite us. In either case we would want to reject H_0.

In general, two-tailed tests are far more common than one-tailed tests for several reasons. First, the investigator may have no idea what the data will look like and therefore has to be prepared for any eventuality. Although this situation is rare, it does occur in some exploratory work.

Another common reason for preferring two-tailed tests is that the investigators are reasonably sure the data will come out one way but want to cover themselves in the event that they are wrong. This type of situation arises more often than you might think. (Carefully formed hypotheses have an annoying habit of being phrased in the wrong direction, for reasons that seem so obvious after the event.) A frequent question that arises when the data may come out the other way around is, "Why not plan to run a one-tailed test and then, if the data come out the other way, just change the test to a two-tailed test?" This kind of question comes from people who have no intention of being devious but who just do not understand the logic of hypothesis testing. If you start an experiment with the extreme 5% of the left-hand tail as your rejection region and then turn around and reject any outcome that happens to fall in the extreme 2.5% of the right-hand tail, you are working at the 7.5% level. In that situation you will reject 5% of the outcomes in one direction (assuming that the data fall in the desired tail), and you are willing also to reject 2.5% of the outcomes in the other direction (when the data are in the unexpected direction). There is no denying that 5% + 2.5% = 7.5%. To put it another way, would you be willing to flip a coin for an ice cream cone if I have choose "heads" but also reserve the right to switch to "tails" after I see how the coin lands? Or would you think it fair of me to shout, "Two out of three!" when the coin toss comes up in your favor? You would object to both of these strategies, and you should. For the same reason the choice between a one-tailed test and a two-tailed one is made *before* the data are collected. It is also one of the reasons that two-tailed tests are usually chosen.

Although the preceding discussion argues in favor of two-tailed tests, and although in this book we generally confine ourselves to such procedures, there are no hard and fast rules. The final decision depends on what you already know about the relative severity of different kinds of errors. It is important to keep in mind that with respect to a given tail of a distribution, the difference between a one-tailed test and a two-tailed test is that the latter just uses a different cutoff. A two-tailed test at $\alpha = .05$ is more liberal than a one-tailed test at $\alpha = .01$.[2]

---

[2] One of the reviewers of an earlier edition of this book made the case for two-tailed tests even more strongly: "It is my (minority) belief that what an investigator *expects to be true* has absolutely no bearing *whatsoever* on the issue of one- versus two-tailed tests. Nature couldn't care less what psychologists' theories predict, and will often show patterns/trends in the opposite direction. Since our goal is to know the truth (not to prove we are astute at predicting), our tests must always allow for testing *both* directions. I say *always* do two-tailed tests, and if you are worried about β, jack the sample size up a bit to offset the loss in power" (D. Bradley, personal communication, 1983). I am personally inclined toward this point of view. Nature is notoriously fickle, or else we are notoriously inept at prediction. On the other hand, a second

If you have a sound grasp of the logic of testing hypotheses by use of sampling distributions, the remainder of this course will be relatively simple. For any new statistic you encounter, you will need to ask only two basic questions.

1.   How and with which assumptions is the statistic calculated?

2.   What does the statistic's sampling distribution look like under H_0?

If you know the answers to these two questions, your test is accomplished by calculating the test statistic for the data at hand and comparing the statistic to the sampling distribution. Because the relevant sampling distributions are tabled in the appendices, all you really need to know is which test is appropriate for a particular situation and how to calculate its test statistic. (Keep in mind, however, there is a great deal more to understanding the field of statistics than how to calculate, and evaluate, a specific statistical test.)

8.9 A Final Worked Example

A number of years ago the mean on the verbal section of the Graduate Record Exam (GRE) was 489 with a standard deviation of 126. The statistics were based on all students taking the exam in that year, the vast majority of whom were native speakers of English. Suppose we have an application from an individual with a Chinese name who scored particularly low (e.g., 220). If this individual is a native speaker of English, that score would be sufficiently low for us to question his suitability for graduate school unless the rest of the documentation is considerably better. If, however, this student is not a native speaker of English, we would probably disregard the low score entirely, on the grounds that it is a poor reflection of his abilities.

We have two possible choices here, namely that the individual (1) is or (2) is not a native speaker of English. If he is a native speaker, we know the mean and the standard deviation of the population from which his score was sampled: 489 and 126, respectively. If he is not a native speaker, we have no idea what the mean and the standard deviation are for the population from which his score was sampled. To help us to draw a reasonable conclusion about this person's status, we will set up the null hypothesis that this individual is a native speaker, or, more precisely, $H_0{:}\mu = 489$. We will identify H_1 with the hypothesis that the individual is not a native speaker ($\mu \neq 489$).

---

reviewer (J. Rodgers, personal communication, 1986) takes exception to this position. While acknowledging that Bradley's point is well considered, Rodgers argues, "To generate a theory about how the world works that implies an expected direction of an effect, but then to hedge one's bet by putting some (up to 1/2) of the rejection region in the tail other than that predicted by the theory, strikes me as both scientifically dumb and slightly unethical. . . . Theory generation and theory testing are much closer to the proper goal of science than truth searching, and running one-tailed tests is quite consistent with those goals." Neither Bradley nor I would accept the judgment of being "scientifically dumb and slightly unethical," but I presented the two positions in juxtaposition because doing so gives you a flavor of the debate. Obviously there is room for disagreement on this issue.

We now need to choose between a one-tailed and a two-tailed test. In this particular case we will choose a one-tailed test on the grounds that the GRE is given in English, and it is difficult to imagine that a population of nonnative speakers would have a mean higher than the mean of native speakers of English on a test that is given in English. (Note: This does not mean that non-English speakers may not, singly or as a population, outscore English speakers on a fairly administered test. It just means that they are unlikely to do so, especially as a population, when both groups take the test in English.) Because we have chosen a one-tailed test, we have set up the alternative hypothesis as $H_1: \mu < 489$.

Before we can apply our statistical procedures to the data at hand, we must make one additional decision. We have to decide on a level of significance for our test. In this case I have chosen to run the test at the 5% level, because I am using $\alpha = .05$ as a standard for this book and also because I am more worried about a Type II error than I am about a Type I error. If I make a Type I error and erroneously conclude that the student is not a native speaker when in fact he is, it is very likely that the rest of his credentials will exclude him from further consideration anyway. If I make a Type II error and do not identify him as a nonnative speaker, I am doing him a real injustice.

Next we need to calculate the probability of a student receiving a score *at least as low as* 220 when $H_0: \mu = 489$ is true. We first calculate the z score corresponding to a raw score of 220:

$$z = \frac{(X - \mu)}{\sigma} = \frac{(220 - 489)}{126} = \frac{-269}{126} = -2.13$$

We then go to tables of z to calculate the probability that we would obtain a z value less than or equal to -2.13. From Table D.10 we find that this probability is .017. Because this probability is less than the 5% significance level we chose to work with, we will reject the null hypothesis on the grounds that it is too unlikely that we would obtain a score as low as 220 if we had sampled an observation from a population of native speakers of English who had taken the GRE. Instead we will conclude that we have an observation from an individual who is not a native speaker of English.

It is important to note that in rejecting the null hypothesis we could have made a Type I error. We know that if we do sample speakers of English, 1.7% of them will score this low. It is possible that our applicant was a native speaker who just did poorly. All we are saying is that such an event is sufficiently unlikely that we will place our bets with the alternative hypothesis.

8.10 Back to Course Evaluations and Rude Motorists

We started this chapter with a discussion of the relationship between how students evaluate a course and the grade they expect to receive in that course. Our second example looked at the probability of motorists honking their horns at low- and high-status cars that did not move when a traffic light changed to green. As you will see in the next chapter, the first example uses a correlation coefficient to represent the degree of relationship. The second example simply compares two proportions. Both examples can be dealt with using the techniques discussed in this chapter. In the first case, if there is no relationship between the two variables, we would expect that the true correlation in the population of students is 0.00. We simply set up the null hypothesis that the population correlation is 0.00 and then ask about the probability that a sample of 15 observations would produce a correlation as large as the one we obtained. In the second case, we set up the null hypothesis that there is no difference between the proportion of motorists *in the population* who honk at low- and high-status cars. Then we ask what is the probability of obtaining a difference in sample proportions as large as the one we obtained (in our case 0.34) if the null hypothesis is true. I do not expect you to be able to run these tests now, but you should have a general sense of the way we will set up the problem when we do learn to run them.

8.11 Summary

The purpose of this chapter has been to examine the general theory of hypothesis testing without becoming involved in the specific calculations required to actually carry out a test. We first considered the concept of the sampling distribution of a statistic, which is the distribution that the statistic in question would have if it were computed repeatedly from an infinite number of samples under certain specified conditions. The sampling distribution basically tells us what kinds of values are reasonable to expect for the statistic if the conditions under which the distribution was derived are met. We then examined the null hypothesis and the role it plays in hypothesis testing. We saw that we can test any null hypothesis by asking what the sampling distribution of the relevant statistic would look like if the null hypothesis were true and then comparing our particular statistic to the distribution. We next saw how a simple hypothesis actually could be tested using what we already know about the normal distribution. Finally we considered Type I and Type II errors and one- and two-tailed tests.

Some important terms in this chapter are:

- Sampling error

- Hypothesis testing

- Sampling distributions

- Sampling distribution of the mean

- Research hypothesis

- Null hypothesis (H_0)

- Sample statistics

- Test statistics

- Decision making

- Rejection level (significance level)

- Rejection region
- Alternative hypothesis (H_1)
- Critical value
- Type I error
- α (alpha)
- Type II error

- β (beta)
- Power
- One-tailed test (directional test)
- Two-tailed test (nondirectional test)

8.12 Exercises

8.1 Suppose I told you that last night's NHL hockey game resulted in a score of 26–13. You would probably decide that I had misread the paper and was discussing something other than a hockey score. In effect you have just tested and rejected a null hypothesis.

   (a) What was the null hypothesis?

   (b) Outline the hypothesis-testing procedure that you have just applied.

8.2 For the past year I have spent about $4.00 a day for lunch, give or take a quarter or so.

   (a) Draw a rough sketch of this distribution of daily expenditures.

   (b) If, without looking at the bill, I paid for my lunch with a $5 bill and received $.75 in change, should I worry that I was overcharged?

   (c) Explain the logic involved in your answer to Exercise 8.2(b).

8.3 What would be a Type I error in Exercise 8.2?

8.4 What would be a Type II error in Exercise 8.2?

8.5 Using the example in Exercise 8.2, describe what we mean by the rejection region and the critical value.

8.6 Why might I want to adopt a one-tailed test in Exercise 8.2, and which tail should I choose? What would happen if I chose the wrong tail?

8.7 A recently admitted class of graduate students at a large state university has a mean Graduate Record Exam verbal score of 650 with a standard deviation of 50. (The scores are reasonably normally distributed.) One student, whose mother just happens to be on the board of trustees, was admitted with a GRE score of 490. Should the local newspaper editor, who loves scandals, write a scathing editorial about favoritism?

8.8 Why is such a small standard deviation reasonable in Exercise 8.7?

8.9 Why might (or might not) the GRE scores be normally distributed for the restricted sample (admitted students) in Exercise 8.7?

8.10 Imagine that you have just invented a statistical test called the Mode Test to test whether the mode of a population is some value (e.g., 100). The statistic (M) is calculated as

$$M = \frac{\text{Sample mode}}{\text{Sample range}}$$

Describe how you could obtain the sampling distribution of M. (*Note:* This is a purely fictitious statistic as far as I am aware.)

8.11 In Exercise 8.10 what would we call M in the terminology of this chapter?

8.12 Describe a situation in daily life in which we routinely test hypotheses without realizing it.

8.13 In Exercise 8.7 what would be the alternative hypothesis (H_1)?

8.14 Define "sampling error."

8.15 What is the difference between a "distribution" and a "sampling distribution"?

8.16 How would decreasing α affect the probabilities given in Table 8.1?

8.17 Give two examples of research hypotheses and state the corresponding null hypotheses.

8.18 For the distribution in Figure 8.4 I said that the probability of a Type II error (β) is .74. Show how this probability was obtained.

8.19 Rerun the calculations in Exercise 8.18 for $\alpha = .01$.

8.20 In the example in Section 8.9 how would the test have differed if we had chosen to run a two-tailed test?

8.21 Describe the steps you would go through to flesh out the example given in this chapter about the course evaluations. In other words, how might you go about determining if there truly is a relationship between grades and course evaluations?

8.22 Describe the steps you would go through to test the hypothesis that motorists are ruder to fellow drivers who drive low-status cars than to those who drive high-status cars.

9

CORRELATION

The previous chapters have dealt in one way or another with describing data on a single variable. We have discussed the distribution of a variable and how to find its mean and standard deviation. However, some studies are designed to deal with not one dependent variable, but with two or more. In such cases we often are interested in knowing the *relationship* between two variables, rather than what each variable looks like on its own. To illustrate the kinds of studies that might involve two variables (denoted X and Y), consider the following research questions:

- Does driving ability (Y) depend on the amount of alcohol (X) consumed?
- Does admission to college (Y) relate to the number of extracurricular activities (X) a student engaged in while attending high school?
- Does an individual's rated "likability" (Y) have anything to do with physical attractiveness (X)?
- Does degree of hoarding behavior in hamsters (Y) vary as a function of level of deprivation (X) during development?
- Does the accuracy of performance (Y) decrease as speed of response (X) increases?
- Does the average life span (Y) in a given country increase as the country's per capita health expenditure (X) increases?

Correlation
The relationship between variables.

In each case we are asking if one variable (Y) is related to another variable (X). When we are dealing with the relationship between two variables, we are concerned with **correlation**, and our measure of the degree or strength of this relationship is represented by a **correlation coefficient**. There are a number of different correlation coefficients, depending primarily on the underlying nature of the measurements, but we will see later that in many cases the distinctions among these different coefficients are more apparent than real. For the present we will be concerned with the most common correlation coefficient—the **Pearson product–moment correlation coefficient (r)**.

Correlation coefficient
A measure of the relationship between variables.

Pearson product–moment correlation coefficient (r)
The most common correlation coefficient.

9.1 Scatter Diagrams

Scatter diagram (scatterplot, scattergram)
A figure in which the individual data points are plotted in two-dimensional space.

When we collect measures on two variables for the purpose of examining the relationship between those variables, one of the most useful techniques for gaining some insight into the relationship is the preparation of a **scatter diagram** (also called a **scatterplot** or **scattergram**). Examples of four such diagrams appear in Figure 9.1. In this figure every experimental subject or other unit of observation is represented by a point in two-dimensional space, the coordinates of this point (X_i and Y_i) being the individual's (or object's) scores on variables X and Y, respectively.

Predictor variable
The variable from which a prediction is made.

In preparing a scatter diagram, the **predictor variable** is traditionally represented on the abscissa, or X axis, and the **criterion variable** on the ordinate, or Y axis. If the eventual purpose of the study is the prediction of one variable from knowledge of the other, the distinction is obvious since the criterion variable is that variable to be predicted, while the predictor is that variable from which the prediction is made. If the problem is simply one of obtaining a correlation coefficient, the distinction may be obvious (incidence of cancer would depend on amount smoked rather than the reverse) or it may not (neither running speed nor number of correct choices—common dependent variables in an animal learning study—is obviously in a dependent position relative to the other). Where the distinction is not obvious, it is irrelevant which variable is

Criterion variable
The variable to be predicted.

Figure 9.1

**Scatter Diagrams
Illustrating
Various Degrees
of Relationship**

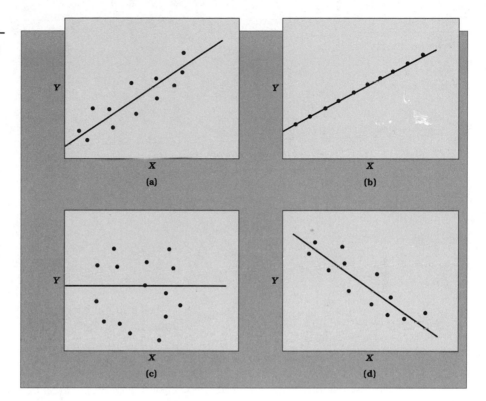

labeled X and which Y. By saying that we want to look at cancer as dependent on smoking, I do not mean to imply that a correlation coefficient will establish cause-and-effect relationships. It won't. I merely mean that we are much more likely to want to see if incidence of cancer varies with smoking (regardless of causation) than to see if smoking varies with incidence of cancer. Both of them may be "caused" by some third variable (e.g., lifestyle), though in this particular example there is convincing evidence in the literature for a causal link.

Consider the four hypothetical scatter diagrams in Figure 9.1. Figure 9.1(a) represents a case in which there is a relatively strong relationship between X and Y. Although the relationship is not perfect, it is generally true that as X increases Y also increases. Figure 9.1(b) illustrates the case of a perfect relationship. Every increase in X is accompanied by an exactly proportional increase in Y, with all the points falling on a straight line. You will probably never see two real variables exhibiting this kind of relationship except in the most trivial of circumstances—you would need to look at something as uninteresting as height in inches plotted against height in centimeters. This does, however, frame the upper limit of the kinds of relationships that we will be considering. In Figure 9.1(c) we have a situation in which there is no relationship between X and Y. There is no systematic tendency for Y to vary with X, and knowing the value of X tells us nothing about the corresponding value of Y.

A fascinating real-world example of the kind of relationship shown in Figure 9.1(c) is found in Figure 9.2. Here I have plotted data on the relationship

Figure 9.2

Life Expectancy as a Function of Health Care Expenditures

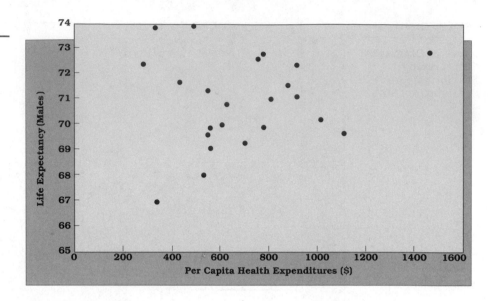

between life expectancy (for males) and per capita expenditure on health care for 23 developed (mostly European) countries. Each data point represents a different country. (The data are taken from a paper by St. Leger, Cochrane, and Moore, 1978. The data are about 15 years old, but more recent data show that the relationship has not changed.) At a time when there is considerable discussion nationally about the cost of health care, these data give us pause. If we measure the health of a nation by life expectancy (admittedly not the only and certainly not the best measure), it would appear that the total amount of money we spend on health care bears no relationship to the resultant quality of health (assuming that different countries apportion their expenditures in similar ways). (Several hundred thousand dollars spent on transplanting an organ from a baboon into a 57-year-old male may increase *his* life expectancy by a few years, but it is not going to make a dent in the *nation's* life expectancy. A similar amount of money spent on prevention efforts with young children, however, may eventually have a very substantial effect.) The two countries with the longest life expectancy (Iceland and Japan) spend nearly the same amount of money on health care as the country with the shortest life expectancy (Portugal). The United States has the second highest rate of expenditure but ranks 17th in life expectancy. Figure 9.2, then, represents a situation in which there is no apparent relationship between the two variables under consideration.

Finally, Figure 9.1(d) represents a relatively strong **negative relationship** between *X* and *Y*. In fact, the degree of relationship, though not its direction, is exactly the same as that shown in Figure 9.1(a) (the points have merely been rotated 90°). In this situation an increase in *X* corresponds to a general decrease in *Y*.

An interesting example of a relationship of about the same magnitude as those shown in Figures 9.1(a) and 9.1(d) can be seen in Figure 9.3. Here I have used the data gathered by St. Leger et al. and plotted infant mortality, adjusted

Negative relationship
A relationship in which increases in one variable are associated with decreases in the other.

Figure 9.3

Adjusted Infant Mortality as a Function of Number of Physicians

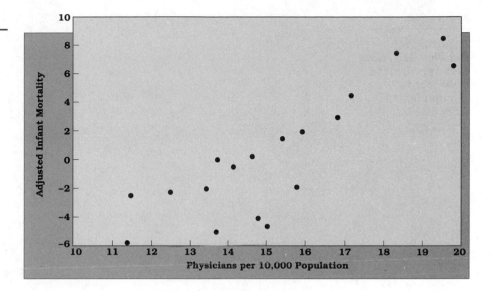

for gross national product (a measure of a country's wealth), as a function of the number of physicians per 10,000 population. Notice the fascinating result that infant mortality *increases* with the number of physicians. That is certainly an unexpected result, but it is almost certainly not due to chance. As you look at these data and read the chapter, you might think about possible explanations for this surprising result.

The lines superimposed on the scatter diagrams in Figure 9.1 represent those straight lines that "best fit the data" (how to determine the best fit will be discussed in the next chapter). These lines are often included in scatterplots because they help to clarify the relationship. The correlation coefficient itself is a measure of how well the line fits the data. Correlation coefficients range between +1.00 and −1.00. In Figure 9.1(a) the points cluster reasonably closely about the line, and the correlation is high ($r = .81$). In Figure 9.3, in which adjusted infant mortality has been plotted against the number of physicians per 10,000 population, the correlation is .86. In Figure 9.1(b) the points fall exactly on the line, and the correlation is perfect ($r = 1.00$). In Figure 9.1(c) the points do not cluster at all around the line and the correlation is 0. This is the same general level of correlation that we found in Figure 9.2, which plots life expectancy against health care expenditures. For those data the correlation is .14, which is not reliably different from zero. Using only those data and accepting life expectancy as our measure of health, we cannot say that a nation's life expectancy is in any way dependent on the amount that that country spends on health care. (A different criterion variable might reveal a different story.) Finally, in Figure 9.1(d) the degree of clustering is the same as in Figure 9.1(a), but the relationship is negative so the correlation is negative ($r = -.81$).

An alternative approach to interpreting scatter diagrams is shown in Figures 9.4 and 9.5. These figures are based on data from the Achenbach Teacher Report form (Achenbach, 1991), which is a rating form for behavior problems

Figure 9.4

Relationship Between Learning and Appropriate Behavior in Normal Boys, Ages 12–16

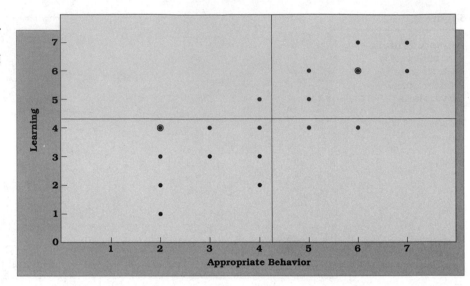

Figure 9.5

Relationship Between Happiness and Appropriate Behavior in Normal Boys, Ages 12–16

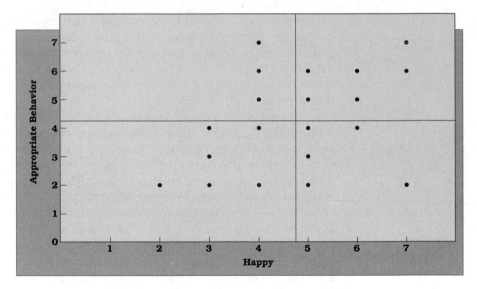

similar to the Achenbach Youth Self Report form. This form, however, is filled out by the teacher rather than the child. (The data have been modified somewhat for this example.) In Figure 9.4 I have plotted the relationship between the teacher's rating of the degree to which the child exhibits behavior appropriate to the situation and the teacher's rating of how much the child is learning. All ratings are on 7-point scales. The dots with circles around them represent children who happen to have the same scores, and are thus plotted on top of one another. In Figure 9.5 I have plotted the degree to which the teacher rates the child as happy and the degree to which that child shows appropriate behavior.

In Figures 9.4 and 9.5 I have drawn vertical and horizontal grid lines to divide both axes at their means. For example, the vertical line in Figure 9.4 divides those children who were below the mean on appropriate behavior from those who were above the mean on that variable. Similarly, the horizontal line separates those children who were below the mean on the learning variable from those who were above it. In both cases that variable we would most likely think of as the dependent variable is on the Y axis, and the other is on the X axis. Admittedly the choice is somewhat arbitrary, and again I do not mean to imply that one variable causes the other.

If there were a strong positive relationship between learning and appropriate behavior, for example, we would expect that most of the children who were high (above the mean) on one variable would be high on the other. Likewise, most of those who were below the mean on one variable should be below it on the other. Such an idea can be represented by a simple table in which we count the number of children who were above the mean on both variables, the number below the mean on both variables, and the number above the mean on one and below the mean on the other. Such a table is shown in Table 9.1 for the data in Figures 9.4 and 9.5.

With a strong positive relationship between the two variables, we would expect most of the data points in Table 9.1 to fall in the "Above–Above" and "Below–Below" cells, with only a smattering in the "Above–Below" and "Below–Above" cells. Conversely, if the two variables are not related to each other, we would expect to see approximately equal numbers of data points in the four cells of the table (or quadrants of the scatter diagram). From Table 9.1 we see that for the relationship between appropriate behavior and learning, 17 out of the 20 children fall in the cells associated with a positive relationship between the variables. In other words, if they are below the mean on one variable they

Table 9.1

Examining Scatter Diagrams by Division into Quadrants

		Appropriate Behavior versus Learning (Figure 9.4)	
		Appropriate Behavior	
		Below Mean	**Above Mean**
Learning	**Above Mean**	1	7
	Below Mean	10	2
		Happiness versus Appropriate Behavior (Figure 9.5)	
		Happy	
		Below Mean	**Above Mean**
Appropriate Behavior	**Above Mean**	3	6
	Below Mean	6	5

are most likely below the mean on the other and vice versa. Only 3 of the children break this pattern. However, for the data plotted in Figure 9.5, Table 9.1 shows that only 12 children are on the same side of the mean on both variables, while 5 children are below the mean on appropriate behavior but above it on happiness, and 3 children show the opposite pattern.

These two examples, then, illustrate in a simple way the interpretation of scatter diagrams and the relationship between variables. In the first case there is a strong positive relationship between the variables. In the second case the relationship, although positive, is considerably weaker. This result is reflected in the correlation between the variables. For Figure 9.4 the correlation is .78, whereas the correlation among the data points in Figure 9.5 is .38.[1] (Keep in mind that I have used small samples for ease of discussion, and these correlations might well be different if we had larger samples. This is especially true because I hunted around to find somewhat extreme examples and thus may have found unrepresentative ones. We will address the issue of the unreliability of sample results in later chapters.)

9.2 An Example: The Relationship Between Speed and Accuracy

Many cognitive psychologists doing research on problem solving have been concerned with the variable of impulsivity and have suggested that impulsive subjects use less effective problem-solving strategies than do nonimpulsive subjects. In a study on the relationship between impulsivity and problem-solving strategies, Knehr-McDonald (1984) assessed impulsivity by means of Jerome Kagan's Matching Familiar Figures Test (MFFT). In this task subjects are shown a simple line-drawn figure (the standard) and eight similar comparison figures. The task is to identify the comparison figure that exactly matches the standard. (Subjects continue answering until they are correct.) This task is repeated with 12 different sets of figures. Two of the dependent variables are the total time to the first response (summed over all 12 figures) and the total number of errors. By plotting these two variables against each other, it is possible to identify groups of subjects with different response styles. Knehr-McDonald's data on this task, very slightly modified for the sake of our example, are shown in Table 9.2 and plotted in Figure 9.6. In Table 9.2 you will also see the mean and the standard deviation of each variable, along with some intermediate calculations that will prove useful.

Figure 9.6, which was produced by a software package called JMP for the Macintosh, contains the correlation between time and errors and a scatterplot of the relationship. Because of the way JMP presents results, we see both the

---

[1] It is of interest to note that in the days before computers and electronic calculators, many textbooks showed how to estimate the correlation coefficient by breaking the scatterplot into squares and counting the number of observations in each square. The breakdown was finer than the four quadrants that we used, but the idea was the same.

Table 9.2

Data on Total Errors and Total Response Time (in Seconds) for the Matching Familiar Figures Test

Subject #	Time (X)	Errors (Y)	Subject #	Time (X)	Errors (Y)
1	285	11	30	973	0
2	599	9	31	571	8
3	1001	5	32	832	6
4	324	15	33	1352	1
5	595	5	34	813	2
6	363	9	35	603	5
7	361	4	36	866	4
8	870	4	37	1357	2
9	531	2	38	1220	1
10	526	6	39	635	7
11	749	3	40	1105	5
12	852	5	41	242	15
13	514	7	42	371	8
14	856	1	43	951	1
15	467	6	44	1183	1
16	449	12	45	1184	7
17	949	2	46	977	1
18	929	1	47	411	12
19	776	1	48	989	2
20	348	10	49	930	1
21	507	13	50	519	5
22	640	5	51	485	9
23	474	4	52	434	7
24	497	11	53	710	3
25	953	1	54	708	2
26	575	7	55	941	5
27	1253	2	56	170	10
28	762	8	57	889	1
29	827	5			

$\Sigma X = 41,253$　　　$\Sigma Y = 305$　　　$\Sigma XY = 174,474$
$\Sigma X^2 = 34,673,815$　　$\Sigma Y^2 = 2,483$　　$N = 57$
$\bar{X} = 723.74$　　　$\bar{Y} = 5.351$
$s_X = 293.20$　　　$s_Y = 3.90$

Curvilinear relationship
A situation that is best represented by something other than a straight line.

Linear relationship
A situation in which the best-fitting regression line is a straight line.

correlation of time with errors and the correlation of errors with time. The same holds true for the scatterplot. This produces duplicate information because the two correlations must be the same. Note that the upper right scatterplot shows time on the Y axis and errors on the X axis. In the lower left, we have errors on the X axis and time on the Y axis.

From an inspection of Figure 9.6 you can see a strong negative relationship between time and errors—as time increases, errors decrease, and vice versa. The relationship is slightly **curvilinear** (i.e., the best-fitting "line" might in fact be curved), but there is a sufficient enough **linear relationship** between the two variables that a straight line fits the data quite well as a first approximation. (We say that a relationship is linear if the criterion variable increases in a straight-line fashion with increases in the predictor variable.) I have drawn in this line to make the relationship clearer. Look at the lower left scatterplot in

Figure 9.6

**Correlation and
Scatter Diagram
of Time (X) and
Errors (Y)**

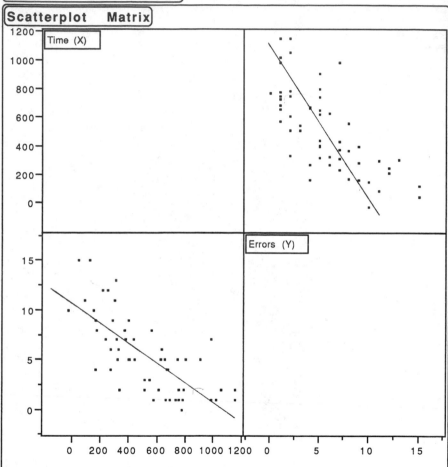

Figure 9.6. Those people whose data points fall in the upper left of the scatter diagram are what Kagan called "impulsives"—they act impulsively, with short response times and many errors. (Impulsives are always sure that "This time I'm right," but it never seems to work out that way. I should know—I'm a prime example, hence the occasional dumb error in past editions of the text, but *this* time. . . .) In the lower right are data points from the "reflectives." These people take a lot of time to think things out, but when they finally do come to a decision, it is usually correct. Away from the line toward the upper right are data points of two or three people who take a long time to think things out and then blow it anyway. Finally, in the lower left are a few of those fast and accurate people who make the rest of us look bad.

9.3 The Covariance

Covariance
A statistic representing the degree to which two variables vary together.

The correlation coefficient that we want to compute on these data is itself based on a statistic called the **covariance**. The covariance is basically a number that reflects the degree to which two variables vary together. If, for example, high scores on one variable tend to be paired with high scores on the other, the covariance will be large and positive. If, as happens in our example, high scores on one variable are paired with low scores on the other, the covariance will be large but negative. Finally, when high scores on one variable are paired about equally often with both high and low scores on the other, the covariance will be near zero.

To define the covariance mathematically we can write

$$\text{cov}_{XY} = \frac{\Sigma(X - \bar{X})(Y - \bar{Y})}{N - 1}$$

From this equation it is apparent that the covariance is similar in form to the variance. If we changed both of the Ys in the equation to Xs, we would have $s_x{}^2$. It is also apparent that the covariance is based on how an observation deviates from the mean on each variable, which is the point that was illustrated in Figures 9.4 and 9.5 and Table 9.1. (An expression of the form $(X - \bar{X})$ is called a deviation score because it measures the degree to which X deviates from the mean, $\bar{X}$. You can see here that the numerator for the covariance is the product of two deviation scores.) You can gain some insight into the meaning of the covariance by considering what we would expect to find in the case of a high negative correlation, such as the data in Table 9.2. In that situation high times will be paired with low errors. Thus for a slow, accurate subject $(X - \bar{X})$ will be positive, $(Y - \bar{Y})$ will be negative, and their product will be negative. For a fast, inaccurate subject $(X - \bar{X})$ will be negative, $(Y - \bar{Y})$ will be positive, and the product will again be negative. Thus we will find that the sum of $(X - \bar{X})$ $(Y - \bar{Y})$ will be large and negative, giving a large negative covariance. (To help you see this, take a few of the data points from Figure 9.4 or Table 9.2 and work out their contribution to the covariance.)

Next consider the case of a strong positive relationship. Here large positive values of $(X - \bar{X})$ will be paired with large positive values of $(Y - \bar{Y})$ and vice versa. The sum of products of the deviations will be large and positive, indicating a high positive relationship. Such a situation was illustrated in Figure 9.3, where we saw the relationships between infant mortality and the number of physicians.

Finally, consider a situation in which there is no relationship between X and Y. In that case a positive value of $(X - \bar{X})$ will sometimes be paired with a positive value of $(Y - \bar{Y})$ and sometimes with a negative value. The result is that the products of the deviations will be positive about half the time and negative about half the time, producing a near-zero sum and indicating no relationship between the variables. A slightly less extreme instance of this case was illustrated in Figure 9.5.

It is possible to show that the covariance will be at its positive maximum whenever X and Y are perfectly positively correlated ($r = +1.00$) and at its negative maximum whenever they are perfectly negatively correlated ($r = -1.00$). When the two variables are perfectly uncorrelated ($r = 0$), the covariance will be zero.

For computational purposes a simple expression for the covariance is given by

$$\text{cov}_{XY} = \frac{\Sigma(X - \bar{X})(Y - \bar{Y})}{N - 1} = \frac{\Sigma XY - \dfrac{(\Sigma X)(\Sigma Y)}{N}}{N - 1}$$

As you should remember from Chapter 2, ΣXY is calculated by multiplying each subject's X score by his or her Y score and then summing the results across subjects. For the data in Table 9.2, $\Sigma XY = 285 \cdot 11 + 599 \cdot 9 + 1001 \cdot 5 + \ldots + 889 \cdot 1 = 174{,}474$. Using the results for the data in Table 9.2, the covariance is

$$\text{cov}_{XY} = \frac{\Sigma XY - \dfrac{(\Sigma X)(\Sigma Y)}{N}}{N - 1}$$

$$= \frac{174{,}474 - \dfrac{(41{,}253)(305)}{57}}{56} = -826.17$$

9.4 The Pearson Product–Moment Correlation Coefficient (r)

What I have just said about the covariance might suggest that we could use the covariance as a measure of the degree of relationship between two variables. An immediate difficulty arises, however, in that the absolute value of cov_{XY} is also a function of the standard deviations of X and Y. For example, $\text{cov}_{XY} = 20$ might reflect a high degree of correlation when the standard deviations are small, but a low degree of correlation when the standard deviations are large. To resolve this difficulty, we will divide the covariance by the standard deviations and make the result our estimate of correlation. (Technically, this is known as *scaling* the covariance by the standard deviations, because we basically are changing the scale on which it is measured.) Thus we will define what is known as the Pearson product–moment correlation coefficient (r)[2] as

$$r = \frac{\text{cov}_{XY}}{s_X s_Y}$$

The maximum value of cov_{XY} turns out to be $\pm s_X s_Y$. (This can be shown mathematically, but for now just trust me.) Because the maximum of cov_{XY} is $\pm s_X s_Y$,

---

[2]This coefficient is named after its creator (Karl Pearson). Deviations of the form $(X - \bar{X})$ and $(Y - \bar{Y})$ are called "moments," hence the phrase "product–moment."

it follows that the limits on r are ± 1.00. One interpretation of r, then, is that it is a measure of the degree to which the covariance approaches its maximum.

An equivalent way of writing the preceding equation would be to replace the variances and covariances by their computational formulae and then simplify by cancellation. If we do this, we will arrive at

$$r = \frac{N\Sigma XY - \Sigma X \Sigma Y}{\sqrt{[N\Sigma X^2 - (\Sigma X)^2][N\Sigma Y^2 - (\Sigma Y)^2]}}$$

While this formula is useful if you are calculating correlations by hand, it is becoming uncommon to do hand calculation, at least without an electronic calculator. And since most calculators produce the means and standard deviations automatically, it is usually much simpler to use the first formula in this section. That one at least has the advantage of making it clear what is happening. Both equations for r will produce exactly the same answers; the choice is up to you. I prefer the expression in terms of the covariance and the standard deviations.

Applying the first equation to the data in Table 9.2, we have

$$r = \frac{\text{cov}_{XY}}{s_X s_Y} = \frac{-826.17}{(293.303)(3.898)} = -.722$$

I leave the calculations using the second formula to you. You will find that it will give exactly the same result.

The correlation coefficient must be interpreted cautiously so as not to attribute to it meaning that it does not possess. Specifically, $r = .72$ should *not* be interpreted to mean that there is 72% of a relationship (whatever that might mean) between time and errors. The correlation coefficient is simply a point on the scale between -1.00 and $+1.00$, and the closer it is to either of those limits, the stronger is the relationship between the two variables. For a more specific interpretation we will prefer to speak in terms of r^2, which is discussed in the next chapter.

9.5 Correlations with Ranked Data

In the previous example the data for each subject were recorded in everyday units such as time and number of errors. Sometimes, however, we ask judges to rank items on two dimensions; we then want to correlate the two sets of ranks. For example, we might ask one judge to rank the quality of the "Statement of Purpose" found in 10 applications to graduate school in terms of clarity, specificity, and apparent sincerity. The weakest would be assigned a rank of 1, the next weakest a rank of 2, and so on. Another judge might rank the overall acceptability of these same 10 applicants based on all available information, and we might be interested in the degree to which well-written statements of purpose are associated with highly admissible applicants. When we

Ranked data
Data for which the observations have been replaced by their numerical ranks from lowest to highest.

Spearman's correlation coefficient for ranked data (r_S)
A correlation coefficient on ranked data.

have such **ranked data**, we frequently use what is known as **Spearman's correlation coefficient for ranked data**, denoted r_S. (This is not the only coefficient that can be calculated from ranked data, nor even the best, but it is one of the simplest.)

In the past when people obtained correlations by hand, we had a special formula for calculating r_S, because when you know that the data are ranks, you know that they are the first N integers. We have formulae that tell us the sum of the first N (e.g., 10) integers and the sum of squares of the first N integers, so we could substitute those in place of ΣX and ΣX^2 in our regular formula for r. This simplified the calculations somewhat when people were solving problems with pencil and paper, but we rarely do such calculations by hand anymore; if we do, we can still use the regular formula for r. When people use a special formula, they tend to think that they are doing something different and treat r_S as if it is something special. In fact, no matter how you calculate it, r_S is still a plain old Pearson product–moment correlation coefficient, only this time it is calculated on ranks rather than on measured variables.

The Interpretation of r_S

Spearman's r_S and other coefficients calculated on ranked data are slightly more difficult to interpret than Pearson's r, partly because of the nature of the data. In the example that I have described, the data occurred naturally in the form of ranks because that is the task that we set our judges. In this situation r_S is a measure of the *linear* (straight line) relationship between one set of *ranks* and another set of *ranks*.

In other cases the data may not naturally occur in ranks; instead, we might convert raw data to ranks. (We might do this because we are unhappy with the peculiar distribution of one or the other of our variables.) For example, we might measure a person's "sociability" by the number of friends he claims to have and measure his physical attractiveness by asking an independent judge to assign a rating on a 10-point scale. Having very little faith in the underlying properties of either scale, we might then simply convert the raw data on each variable to ranks (e.g., the person reporting the fewest friends is assigned a rank of 1, and so on) and carry out our correlations with those ranks. In that case the value of r_S is a measure of the *linearity* of the relationship between the *ranks*, but it is only a measure of the **monotonic relationship** between the original variables. (A monotonic relationship is one that is continuously rising or continuously falling—the line does not need to be straight; it can go up for a while, level off, and then rise again. It just can't reverse direction and start falling.) This relationship should not surprise you. A correlation coefficient tells us directly only about the variables on which it is computed. It cannot be expected to give very precise information about variables on which it was not computed. As discussed in Chapter 2, it is essential to keep in mind the similar distinction between the variables that you have actually measured (e.g., number of friends) and the underlying property that you want to examine (e.g., sociability).

Monotonic relationship
A relationship represented by a regression line that is continually increasing (or decreasing), but perhaps not in a straight line.

9.6 Factors That Affect the Correlation

The correlation coefficient can be importantly affected by characteristics of the sample. Three of these characteristics are the restriction of the range (or variance) of X and/or Y, nonlinearity of relationship, and the use of heterogeneous subsamples.

The Effect of Range Restrictions and Nonlinearity

Range restrictions
Artificial limitations on the range over which X or Y varies.

A common problem that arises in many instances concerns restrictions on the range over which X and Y vary. The effect of such **range restrictions** is to alter the correlation between X and Y from what it would have been if the range had not been so restricted. Depending on the nature of the data, the correlation may either rise or fall as a result of such restrictions, although most commonly r is reduced.

With the exception of very unusual circumstances, restricting the range of X will increase r only when the restriction results in eliminating some *curvilinear* relationship. For example, if we correlated height with age, where age ran from 0 to 70, the data would be decidedly curvilinear (rising to about 17 years of age and then leveling off or even declining), and the correlation, which measures *linear* relationships, would be quite low. If, however, we restricted the range of ages to 4 to 17, the correlation would be quite high, because we have eliminated those values of Y that were not varying linearly with X.

The more usual effect of restricting the range of X or Y is to reduce the correlation. This problem is especially important in the area of test construction, because in that area the criterion measure (Y) may be available for only the higher values of X. Consider the hypothetical data in Figure 9.7. This figure represents the relationship between college grade point averages and scores on a standard achievement test (such as the SAT) for a sample of students. In the ideal world of the test constructor, all people who took the exam would then be sent to college and receive a grade point average, and the correlation between test scores and grade point averages would be computed. As can be seen from Figure 9.7, this correlation would be reasonably high ($\pm = .65$).

In the real world, however, not everyone is admitted to college. Colleges take only the more able students, whether this ability is measured by achievement test scores, high school performance, or whatever. That means college grade point averages are available mainly for students having relatively high scores on the standardized test. This has the effect of allowing us to evaluate the relationship between X and Y for only those values of, say, $X > 400$. From Figure 9.7 you can see that in this case the correlation is relatively low, not because the test is worthless, but because the range has been restricted. In other words, when we use the entire sample of points in Figure 9.7, the correlation is .65; when we restrict the sample to those students having SAT scores of at least 400, the correlation drops to only .43. (This is easier to see if you cover up all data points for $X < 400$.)

Figure 9.7

Hypothetical Data Illustrating the Effect of Restricted Range

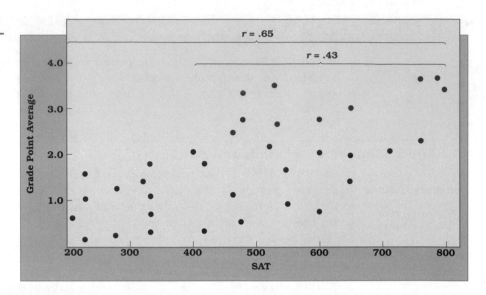

The effect of range restrictions must be taken into account whenever we see a coefficient based on a restricted sample. The coefficient might be quite inappropriate for the question at hand. Essentially what we have done is to ask how well a standardized test predicts a person's suitability for college, but we have answered that question by reference only to those people who are actually admitted to college. At the same time, it is sometimes useful to deliberately restrict the range of one of the variables. For example, if we wanted to know the way in which reading ability increases linearly with age, we probably would restrict the age range by using only subjects who are at least 5 years old and less than 20 years old (or some other reasonable limits). We presumably would never expect reading ability to continue to rise indefinitely.

The Effect of Heterogeneous Subsamples

Heterogeneous subsamples
Data in which the sample of observations could be subdivided into two distinct sets on the basis of some other variable.

Another important consideration in evaluating the results of correlational analyses deals with **heterogeneous subsamples.** This point can be illustrated with a simple example involving the relationship between height and weight in male and female subjects. These variables may appear to have little to do with psychology, but considering the important role both variables play in the development of people's images of themselves, the example is not as far afield as you might expect. The data plotted in Figure 9.8, using Minitab, come from sample data from the Minitab manual (Ryan et al., 1985). These are actual data from 92 college students who were asked to report height, weight, gender, and several other variables. (Keep in mind that these are self-report data, and there may be systematic reporting biases.)

When we combine the data from both males and females, the relationship is strikingly good, with a correlation of .78. When you look at the data from the two genders separately, however, the correlations fall to .60 for males and .49

Figure 9.8

Relationship Between Height and Weight for Males and Females Combined

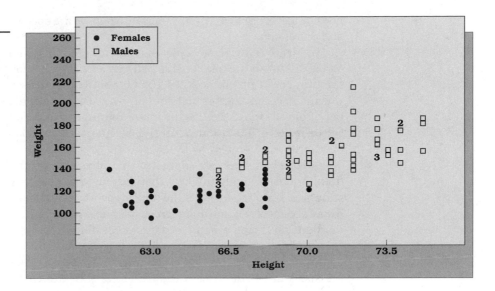

for females. (Males and females have been plotted using different symbols, with data from females primarily in the lower left.) The important point is that the high correlation we found when we combined genders is not due purely to the relation between height and weight. It is also due largely to the fact that men are, on average, taller and heavier than women. In fact, a little doodling on a sheet of paper will show that you could create artificial, and improbable, data where within each gender weight is negatively related to height, while the relationship is positive when you collapse across gender. (There is an example of this kind of relationship in the exercises at the end of the chapter.) The point I am making here is that experimenters must be careful when they combine data from several sources. The relationship between two variables may be obscured or enhanced by the presence of a third variable. Such a finding is important in its own right.

A second example of heterogeneous subsamples that makes a similar point is the relationship between cholesterol consumption and cardiovascular disease in men and women. If you collapse across both genders, the relationship is not impressive. But when you separate the data by male and female, there is a distinct trend for cardiovascular disease to increase with increased consumption of cholesterol. This relationship is obscured in the combined data because men, regardless of cholesterol level, have an elevated level of cardiovascular disease compared to women.

9.7 If Something Looks Too Good to Be True, Perhaps It Is

Not all statistical results mean what they seem to mean; in fact, not all results are meaningful. This is a point that will be made repeatedly throughout this book, and it is particularly appropriate when we are speaking about correlation and regression.

In Figure 9.3 we saw a plot of data collected by Cochrane, St. Leger, and Moore (1978) on the relationship between a country's infant mortality rate and the number of physicians per 10,000 population. This correlation ($r = .88$) was not only remarkably high, but positive. The data indicate that as the number of physicians increases the infant mortality rate also increases. What are we to make of such data? Are physicians really responsible for deaths of children?

No one has seriously suggested that physicians actually do harm to children, and it is highly unlikely that there is a causal link between these two variables. For our purposes the data are worth study more for what they have to say about correlation and regression than what they have to say about infant mortality, and it is worth considering possible explanations. In doing so, we have to keep several facts in mind. First, these data are all from developed countries, primarily but not exclusively in Western Europe. In other words we are speaking of countries with high levels of health care. Although undoubtedly there are substantial differences in infant mortality (and the number of physicians) among these countries, these differences are nowhere near as large as we would expect if we took a random sample of all countries. This suggests that at least some of the variability in infant mortality that we are trying to explain is probably more meaningless random fluctuation in the system than meaningful variability. The second thing to keep in mind is that these data are selective. Cochrane et al. did not simply take a random sample of developed countries—they chose carefully what data to include. We might, and indeed would, obtain somewhat less dramatic relationships if we looked at a more inclusive group of developed countries. A third consideration is that Cochrane et al. selected this particular relationship from among many that they looked at because it was a surprising finding. If you look hard enough, you are likely to find something interesting in any set of data, even when there is nothing really important going on.

In terms of explanations for the finding shown in Figure 9.3, let's consider a few possible—though not terribly good—ones. In the first place it might be argued that we have a reporting problem. With more physicians we stand a better chance of having infant deaths reported, causing the number of *reported* deaths to increase with increases in physicians. This would be a reasonable explanation if we were speaking of underdeveloped countries, but we are not. It is probably unlikely that many deaths would go unreported in Western Europe or North America even if there weren't so many physicians. Another possibility is that physicians go where the health problems are. This argument implies a cause-and-effect relationship, but in the opposite direction—high infant mortality causes a high number of physicians. A third possibility is that high population densities tend to lead to high infant mortality and also tend to attract physicians. In the United States both urban poverty and physicians tend to congregate in urban centers. (How would you go about testing such a hypothesis?)

9.8 Testing the Significance of a Correlation Coefficient

The fact that a sample correlation coefficient is not exactly zero does not necessarily mean that those variables are truly correlated *in the population*. For example, I just wrote a simple program that drew 25 numbers from a random number generator and arbitrarily named that variable "income." I then drew another 25 random numbers and named that variable "musicality." When I paired the first number of each set with the first number of the other set, the second with the second, and so on, and calculated the correlation between the two variables, I obtained a correlation of .278. That seems pretty good. It looks as if I've shown that the more musical a person is the greater his or her income (and vice versa). But we know these data are just random numbers, and there really isn't any true correlation between two sets of random numbers. I just happened to get a reasonably large value of *r* by chance.

The point of this example is to illustrate that correlation coefficients, like all other statistics, suffer from sampling error. They deviate from the true correlations in the population (in this case zero) by some amount. Sometimes they are too high, sometimes too low, and sometimes, but rarely, right on. If I drew a new set of data in the previous example, I might get $r = -.15$, or maybe $r = .03$, or maybe $r = -.20$. But I probably would *not* get $r = .95$ or $r = -.87$. Small deviations from the true value of zero are to be expected; large deviations are not.

But how large is large? When do we decide that our correlation coefficient is far enough from zero that we can no longer believe it likely that the true correlation in the population is zero? This is where we come to the issue of hypothesis testing developed in Chapter 8.

You may recall that I began Chapter 8 with an example about course evaluations and students' anticipated grades. For each of 50 courses I know the mean overall course evaluation rating and the mean anticipated grade—in both cases averaging across all students in the course. (These are actual data.) I also know that for this sample the correlation between evaluations and anticipated grades is .30. But I want to know whether those variables are truly correlated in the whole population of courses, and I will set up my null hypothesis that the population correlation coefficient (denoted ρ) is 0 (i.e., $H_0:\rho = 0$). If I am able to reject H_0, I will be able to conclude that how a course is evaluated is related to how well the students expect to do in terms of grades. If I cannot reject H_0, I will have to conclude that I have insufficient evidence to show that these variables are related, and I will treat them as linearly independent.

I prefer to use two-tailed tests, so I will choose to reject H_0 if the obtained correlation is too large in either a positive or a negative direction. In other words I am testing

$$H_0:\rho = 0$$

against

$$H_0:\rho \neq 0$$

But we are still left with the question, "How big is too big?" There are at least three ways to answer, and I have chosen to discuss the two simplest ways. I'll start with the use of tables.

Table D.2 in the Appendices shows how large a sample correlation coefficient must be before we declare the null hypothesis to be rejected. To use this table, we have to know the degrees of freedom, which are directly linked to the sample size. When we are predicting one variable from one other variable, as we are in this chapter, the degrees of freedom $= N - 2$, where N is the size of our sample. We are using an example where $N = 50$, so we would look up the critical value for 48 df, which we find to be approximately .279. (I say "approximately" because the table lists 40 and 50 df but not 48, so I need to interpolate. Since 48 is eight-tenths of the way between 40 and 50, I'll take as my critical value the value that is eight-tenths of the way between .304 and .273, which is .279.) Thus a sample correlation greater than or equal to .279 is significant at the 5% level of significance, meaning we can reject H_0 at $\alpha = .05$. Our sample correlation was .30, which is more extreme than .279, so we will reject H_0. To say this a little differently, if we take a situation in which we know the null hypothesis ($H_0{:}\rho = 0$) to be true (as, for example, the random number example that started this section), and if we have 50 cases with scores on the two variables, only 5% of the time will we obtain a sample correlation greater than or equal to .279. Thus a correlation of $r = .30$ or more would occur less than 5% of the time if H_0 were true, so we can reject H_0.

I can state all this in terms of a rule. First, calculate the sample correlation and compute $df = N - 2$, where N is the number of *pairs* of observations. Next look in Table D.2 and find the critical value of r. We then reject $H_0{:}\rho = 0$ whenever the absolute value of r (i.e., ignore its sign) is greater than or equal to the tabled critical value.

The alternative approach to hypothesis testing is even simpler when you use almost any computer program. Most programs will print out the probability (either one-tailed or two-tailed) associated with the computed value of r. This is the probability of obtaining that value of r or a more extreme one when H_0 is true. In our case a program would give a two-tailed probability of .0338. This means that if H_0 is true, the probability that we would obtain a sample correlation at least as large (positive or negative) as the one obtained is .0338. We reject H_0 whenever this value is less than .05. As an example, look ahead to Figure 9.11, where you will see that SPSS gives the correlation between life expectancy and expenditures as .138. Below this correlation is the entry of .265, which is the *one-tailed* probability of the obtained correlation if H_0 is true. We would double this value to get the two-tailed probability of .53. A correlation coefficient of .138 with 23 cases is quite common when H_0 is true, so we have no reason to reject H_0. (Most programs would print the two-tailed probability, but SPSS chose to go with one-tailed probabilities. You have to be careful and make sure you know what you are seeing. Notice that you are told this in the line above the correlations.)

9.9 Intercorrelation Matrices

So far we have largely been speaking about the relationship between two variables. Often, however, we have a whole set of variables and want to know how they relate to each other in a pairwise fashion. In Figure 9.9 I have used JMP to plot, in one table, the correlations among several variables concerned with course evaluation. Above the plots is a matrix of correlations among a set of

Figure 9.9

Matrix of Intercorrelations Among Course Evaluation Variables

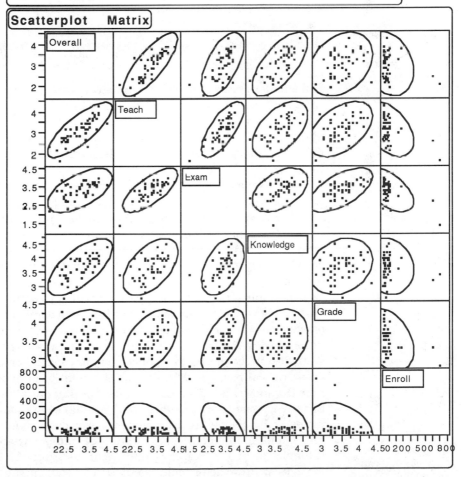

Correlations

Variable	Overall	Teach	Exam	Knowledge	Grade	Enroll
Overall	1.0000	0.8039	0.5956	0.6818	0.3008	-0.2396
Teach	0.8039	1.0000	0.7197	0.5263	0.4691	-0.4511
Exam	0.5956	0.7197	1.0000	0.4515	0.6100	-0.5581
Knowledge	0.6818	0.5263	0.4515	1.0000	0.2242	-0.1279
Grade	0.3008	0.4691	0.6100	0.2242	1.0000	-0.3371
Enroll	-0.2396	-0.4511	-0.5581	-0.1279	-0.3371	1.0000

Intercorrelation matrix
A matrix (table) that shows the pairwise correlations between all variables.

variables. This is known as an **intercorrelation matrix**. These data are a sample of 50 courses from a complete set of course evaluations performed on several hundred classes in a major state university. They relate to the overall quality of the course (Overall), the rating of the skills of the teacher (Teach), the fairness of the exams (Exam), the instructor's apparent knowledge of the material (Knowledge), the student's expected grade (Grade), and class size (Enroll). The curved lines in each little box are portions of ellipses that include 95% of the data points. (The ellipses are cut off at the borders of the boxes, which is what makes them look so odd.) In these plots you can see how each variable is related to each of the other variables. (Notice that the correlation between the overall rating and the anticipated grade is given as .3008, the value we used earlier.) You can see that class size and students' expected grades in the course seem less related to the overall rating of the course than do characteristics of the instructor. Notice also that students' ratings of the fairness of exams is closely related to the grades that they anticipate receiving. For our data set pay particular attention to the two apparent outliers in the Enroll variable, which are clearly visible in the scatterplots.

9.10 Other Correlation Coefficients

The standard correlation coefficient is Pearson's r, which applies primarily to variables distributed more or less along interval or ratio scales of measurement. We also have seen that the same formula will produce a statistic called Spearman's r_s when the variables are in the form of ranks. You should be familiar with two other correlation coefficients, although here again there is little that is new.

When we have one variable measured on a continuous scale and one variable measured as a dichotomy (i.e., that variable has only two levels), then the correlation coefficient that we produce is called the **point biserial correlation** (r_{pb}). For example, we might perform an analysis of test items by correlating the total score on the test (X) with "right/wrong" on a particular item (Y). In this case X values might run from roughly 60 to 100, but Y values would be either 0 (wrong) or 1 (right). Although special formulae exist for calculating r_{pb}, you can accomplish the same thing just as easily by computing r. The only difference is that we call the answer r_{pb} instead of r to point out the nature of the data on which it was computed. Don't let the point about the calculation of r_{pb} pass by too quickly. I belong to several electronic mail discussion groups dealing with statistics and computing, and once every few weeks someone asks if a particular statistical package will calculate the point biserial correlation. And every time the answer is, "Yes it will, just use the standard Pearson r procedure." In fact, this is such a frequently asked question ("FAQ," for those who like to be insiders) that people are beginning to be less patient with their answers.

Point biserial correlation (r_{pb})
The correlation coefficient when one of the variables is measured as a dichotomy.

Dichotomous variables
Variables that can take on only two different values.

A point is in order here about **dichotomous variables**. In the preceding example I scored "*wrong*" as 0 and "*right*" as 1 to make the arithmetic simple for those who are doing hand calculations. I could just as easily score them as 1 and 2 or even as 87 and 213—just as long as all the "*right*" scores receive the

Table 9.3

Various Correlation Coefficients

		Variable X	
Variable Y		Continuous	Dichotomous	Ranked
Continuous	Pearson	Point biserial	
Dichotomous	Point biserial	Phi	
Ranked			Spearman

same number and all the "*wrong*" scores receive the same (but different) number. The correlation coefficient itself will be exactly the same no matter what pair of numbers we use.

A slightly different correlation coefficient, ϕ (**phi**), arises when *both* variables are measured as dichotomies. For example, in studying the relationship between gender and religiosity we might correlate gender (coded Male = 1, Female = 2) with regular church attendance (No = 0, Yes = 1). Again it makes no difference what two values we use to code the dichotomous variables. Although phi has a special formula, it is just as easy and correct to use Pearson's formula but label the answer phi.

ϕ (phi)
The correlation coefficient when both variables are measured as dichotomies.

There are a number of other correlation coefficients, but the ones given here are the most common. All those in this text are special cases of Pearson's *r*, and all can be obtained by using the formulae discussed in this chapter. These coefficients are the ones that are usually generated when a large set of data is entered into a computer data file and a correlation or regression program is run. Table 9.3 shows a diagram that illustrates the relationships among these coefficients. The empty spaces of the table reflect the fact that we do not have a good correlation coefficient to use when we have one ranked variable and one continuous or dichotomous variable. In each case you could use the standard Pearson correlation coefficient, but remember the kinds of variables you have when it comes to interpreting the result. Keep in mind that all the correlations shown in this table can be obtained by using the standard Pearson formula.

9.11 Using Minitab and SPSS to Obtain Correlation Coefficients

Figures 9.6 and 9.9 showed the computer printouts of a statistical package called JMP. Figures 9.10 and 9.11 show correlational analyses produced by Minitab and SPSS, respectively. The data are the data on life expectancy and expenditures on health care that we saw earlier. In the SPSS printout (Figure 9.11) the scatterplot looks a bit different from what you would expect. This is caused by the fact that SPSS expresses scores in terms of the number of standard deviation units they are from the mean (i.e., in standardized form) rather than in raw scores. This has the effect of making distances on the two axes comparable. Notice also that SPSS has a legend on the right side of the

Figure 9.10

Minitab Analysis of the Relationship Between Life Expectancy and Health Expenditures

Descriptive statistics →

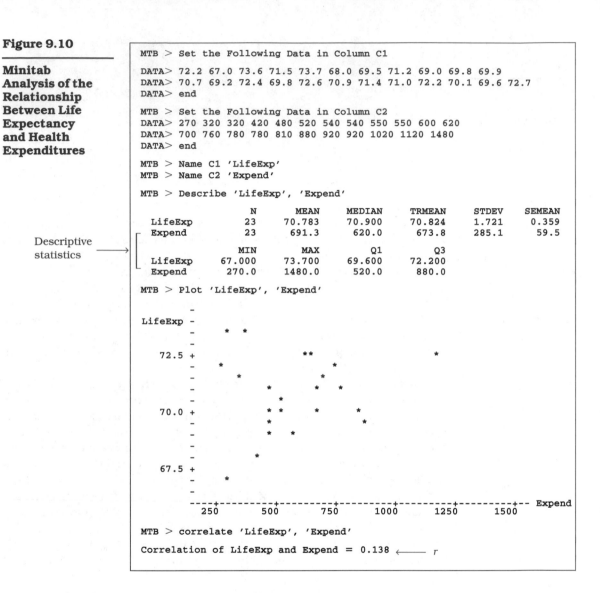

```
MTB > Set the Following Data in Column C1
DATA> 72.2 67.0 73.6 71.5 73.7 68.0 69.5 71.2 69.0 69.8 69.9
DATA> 70.7 69.2 72.4 69.8 72.6 70.9 71.4 71.0 72.2 70.1 69.6 72.7
DATA> end
MTB > Set the Following Data in Column C2
DATA> 270 320 320 420 480 520 540 540 550 550 600 620
DATA> 700 760 780 780 810 880 920 920 1020 1120 1480
DATA> end
MTB > Name C1 'LifeExp'
MTB > Name C2 'Expend'
MTB > Describe 'LifeExp', 'Expend'

                N       MEAN     MEDIAN     TRMEAN     STDEV    SEMEAN
LifeExp        23     70.783     70.900     70.824     1.721     0.359
Expend         23      691.3      620.0      673.8     285.1      59.5

              MIN        MAX         Q1         Q3
LifeExp    67.000     73.700     69.600     72.200
Expend      270.0     1480.0      520.0      880.0

MTB > Plot 'LifeExp', 'Expend'
```

```
          -
LifeExp   -
          -        *   *
          -
   72.5   +                        **
          -      *                      *
          -          *              *
          -            *         *    *
          -             *
   70.0   +           *  *      *         *
          -           *
          -           *    *
          -
          -        *
   67.5   +
          -      *
          ----+---------+---------+---------+---------+---------+-- Expend
            250       500       750      1000      1250      1500
```

```
MTB > correlate 'LifeExp', 'Expend'
Correlation of LifeExp and Expend = 0.138 ←—— r
```

scatterplot showing that two overlapping points are represented by a colon (:) instead of an asterisk (*). Notice that the output from the two procedures is quite similar and that the numerical answers agree (as they should).

9.12 A Final Worked Example

We have used an example in this chapter of the relationship between course evaluations and students' anticipated grades, but we never actually saw data or the calculation of the correlation. The following set of observations are actual data on 50 courses taken from a large data set on the evaluation of several hun-

Figure 9.11

**SPSS Analysis of
the Relationship
Between Life
Expectancy
and Health
Expenditures**

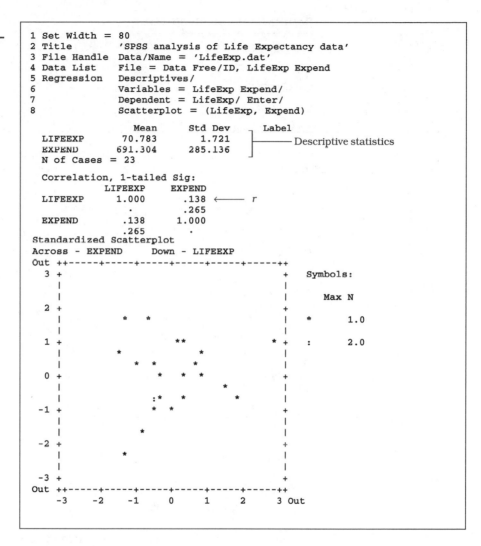

dred courses. (I have shown only the first 15 cases to save space, but have given
the calculated values for all 50 cases.) The complete data set is available on disk.

Expected Grade (X)	Overall Quality (Y)	Expected Grade (X)	Overall Quality (Y)
3.5	3.4	3.0	3.8
3.2	2.9	3.1	3.4
2.8	2.6	3.0	2.8
3.3	3.8	3.3	2.9
3.2	3.0	3.2	4.1
3.2	2.5	3.4	2.7
3.6	3.9	3.7	3.9
4.0	4.3		

Results Based on All 50 Cases

$\Sigma X = 174.3$

$\Sigma X^2 = 613.65$

$\Sigma Y = 177.5$

$\Sigma Y^2 = 648.57$

$\Sigma XY = 621.94$

Our first step is to calculate the mean and the standard deviation of each variable, as follows:

$$\bar{Y} = 177.5/50 = 3.550$$

$$s_Y = \sqrt{\frac{648.57 - 177.5^2/50}{49}} = 0.6135$$

$$\bar{X} = 174.3/50 = 3.486$$

$$s_X = \sqrt{\frac{613.65 - 174.3^2/50}{49}} = 0.3511$$

The covariance is given as

$$\text{cov}_{XY} = \frac{621.94 - (174.3)(177.5)/50}{49} = 0.0648$$

Finally, the correlation is given by

$$r = \frac{\text{cov}_{XY}}{s_X s_Y} = \frac{0.0648}{(0.3511)(0.6135)} = .3008$$

This is a moderate correlation, one that would lend support to the proposition that courses that have higher mean grades also have higher mean ratings. As we saw in Section 9.8, this correlation is significant. You should realize that this correlation does not mean higher grades cause higher ratings. It is just as plausible that more advanced courses are rated more highly, and it is often in these courses that students do their best work.

Summary and Conclusions of Course Evaluation Study

If you were asked to write up the study on course evaluations concisely but accurately, how would you do it? Presumably you would want to say something about the research hypothesis that you were testing, the way you collected your data, the statistical results that followed, and the conclusions you would draw. The two paragraphs that follow are an abbreviated form of such a report. A regular report would include a review of the background literature and considerably more information on data collection. It might also speculate on future research.

It is often thought by course instructors that the way in which students evaluate a course will be related, in part, to the grades that are given in that course. In an attempt to test this hypothesis we collected data on 50 courses in a major state university located in the Northeast, asking students to rate the overall quality of the course (on a five-point scale) and their anticipated grade (A = 4, B = 1, etc.) in that course. For each of the 50 courses we calculated the overall mean rating and the mean anticipated grade. Those means were the observations used in the analysis.

A Pearson correlation between mean rating and mean anticipated grade produced a correlation of $r = .30$, and this correlation was significant at $\alpha = .05$ ($r(48) = .30$, $p < .05$). From this result we can conclude that course ratings do vary with anticipated grades, with courses giving higher grades having higher overall ratings. The interpretation of this effect is unclear. It may be that students who expect to receive good grades have a tendency to "reward" their instructors with higher grades. But it is equally likely that students learn more in better courses and rate those courses accordingly.

9.13 Summary

In this chapter we dealt with the correlation coefficient as a measure of the relationship between two variables. You saw how to draw a scatterplot of the variables and how to compute the correlation coefficient. We followed this up with a discussion of how to test for the significance of a correlation coefficient. We also considered the correlation of ranked data and saw that Pearson's original formula is appropriate for this purpose. Finally, we considered factors that affect the magnitude of the correlation, some cautions concerning interpretation, and the treatment of dichotomous variables.

Some important terms in this chapter are:

- Correlation

- Correlation coefficient

- Scatter diagram

- Predictor variable

- Criterion variable

- Negative relationship

- Curvilinear relationship

- Linear relationship

- Covariance

- Pearson product–moment correlation coefficient (r)

- Ranked data

- Spearman's correlation coefficient for ranked data (r_s)

- Monotonic relationship

- Range restrictions

- Heterogeneous subsamples

- Intercorrelation matrix

- Point biserial correlation (r_{pb})

- Dichotomous variables

- Phi (ϕ)

9.14 Exercises

9.1 The state of Vermont is divided into ten Health Planning Districts, corresponding roughly to counties. The following data for 1980 represent the percentage of births under 2500 grams (Y), the fertility rate for females ≤ 17 or ≥ 35 years of age (X_1), and the percentage of births to unmarried mothers (X_2) for each district.

District	Y	X_1	X_2
1	6.1	43.0	9.2
2	7.1	55.3	12.0
3	7.4	48.5	10.4
4	6.3	38.8	9.8
5	6.5	46.2	9.8
6	5.7	39.9	7.7
7	6.6	43.1	10.9
8	8.1	48.5	9.5
9	6.3	40.0	11.6
10	6.9	56.7	11.6

(a) Make a scatter diagram of Y and X_1.
(b) Draw (by eye) the line that appears to best fit the data.

9.2 Calculate the correlation between Y and X_1 in Exercise 9.1.

9.3 Calculate the correlation between Y and X_2 in Exercise 9.1.

9.4 Divide the scatter diagram for Y and X_1 from Exercise 9.1 into quadrants, as in Figure 9.4, and count the observations in each quadrant. What do these results suggest?

9.5 Divide the scatter diagram for Y and X_2 from Exercise 9.1 into quadrants, as in Figure 9.4, and count the observations in each quadrant. What do these results suggest?

9.6 Compare the answers to Exercises 9.4 and 9.5. Do they reflect the differences between the answers to Exercises 9.2 and 9.3?

9.7 Draw scatter diagrams for the following sets of data:

1		2		3	
X	Y	X	Y	X	Y
2	2	2	4	2	8
3	4	3	2	3	6
5	6	5	8	5	4
6	8	6	6	6	2

(a) Calculate the covariance for each set of data using the definitional formula.
(b) Calculate the covariance for each set of data using one of the computational formulae.

9.8 Calculate the correlation for each data set in Exercise 9.7. How can the values of Y in Exercise 9.7 be rearranged to produce the smallest possible positive correlation?

9.9 The following data represent the percentage of voluntary homework problems completed by each of 20 students and their final grade at the end of the course (converted to a 100-point scale).

Problems completed	50	60	80	70	90
Final grade	75	75	90	80	85

Problems completed	40	100	85	90	80
Final grade	60	98	95	95	80

Problems completed	50	95	40	80	85
Final grade	75	90	60	50	70

Problems completed	95	70	40	80	30
Final grade	85	75	60	80	55

(a) Plot the data points.
(b) Compute the correlation between the amount of homework completed and the final grade.
(c) Is the obtained correlation significantly different from zero?
(d) Interpret the correlation.

Exercises 9.10 through 9.15 involve an unusual amount of work. However, the data are real and the answers are important.[3] Once the data have been entered into a computer file, the rest is not at all difficult. These data are available on a diskette, which your instructor may have. I would not suggest working these problems unless you have access to computer software and to the data in a usable form. The questions are instructive, but it is too much work to do by hand.

Sternglass and Bell (1983) published a controversial paper arguing that "the principal new factor in the sharp decline [of SAT scores] during the 1970s was the fallout from the massive nuclear bomb tests in the 1950s and early 1960s." As support for this hypothesis they reported a correlation of .55 between the iodine-131 levels (by state) in 1962 (when nuclear testing was briefly resumed in Nevada) and the decline from 1978 to 1979 in verbal SAT scores. Their argument was that exposure early in life led to poor performance later in life. The correlations for declines in 1978 and 1979 were reported as .2956 and .3300, respectively. The raw data for math and verbal SAT scores for the school years 1972–1973 to 1978–1979 for those states from which SAT data were reported are shown in Table 9.4, along with the iodine-131 levels. (In these data each row represents a state. Also, because most students take the SAT exams in the fall, only the first year of the pair is listed, e.g., the 1972–1973 year is listed as 72.)

9.10 Calculate the *decline* for both math and verbal scores from 1978 to 1979, and correlate the decline with I-131 levels. Does this answer agree with the reported results?

9.11 Make a stem-and-leaf display for the variable I-131 and for the change in math scores from 1977 to 1979.

9.12 Draw a scatter diagram of the relation between the 1977–1978 to 1978–1979 decline in math SAT and the I-131 level. What does this diagram suggest?

9.13 The data for the most extreme data point in the scatter diagram in Exercise 9.12 was based on 4% of the high school seniors in that state. What problems does this present? (The other extreme point was based on 31% of that state's high school seniors.)

9.14 Omit the two extreme data points identified in Exercise 9.12 and rerun the correlations.

9.15 Use any statistical package to correlate the 1962 I-131 levels and changes in math and verbal SAT scores from year to year during the 1970s. What, if anything, does this tell you?

9.16 In 1957 there was also a substantial increase in nuclear testing in Nevada compared to the previous year. If we assume that the distribution of I-131 across states would have been similar to the distribution in 1962 (and that may not be a fair assumption), what would you expect to see in the data? Use the answers to Exercise 9.15 to evaluate this expectation.

9.17 Plot and calculate the correlation for the relationship between ADDSC and GPA for the data in Appendix C. Is this relationship significant?

---

[3]I do not happen to agree with the conclusions of the authors who reported these data, but I do think that it is important for you to see the kinds of data on which questions of some national importance are argued. The conclusions we draw are in some ways secondary to the process by which we draw those conclusions.

Table 9.4   Data on SAT Scores and Radioactive Fallout

V72	V73	V74	V75	V76	V77	V78	M72	M73	M74	M75	M76	M77	M78	I-131
464	474	461	454	459	458	452	486	495	481	485	487	485	478	104
502	501	496	491	492	492	485	534	534	525	532	531	529	524	12
478	484	482	485	480	483	478	511	512	510	518	519	514	513	37
452	450	435	430	427	427	428	485	484	473	470	470	466	473	13
485	484	479	476	469	473	469	521	522	515	521	518	516	513	15
451	452	442	439	437	438	435	482	480	471	473	468	469	465	21
447	449	439	437	438	436	433	482	479	476	476	477	477	468	32
417	420	414	409	401	398	396	481	481	478	479	473	468	467	12
484	492	493	483	489	488	480	520	518	524	519	530	521	518	25
472	471	460	464	459	463	462	509	513	510	509	507	511	511	38
429	423	418	415	412	413	412	470	469	463	460	458	457	455	33
525	526	523	523	513	516	518	565	570	568	572	563	569	567	59
441	441	437	437	431	429	430	481	477	471	476	471	467	468	22
454	452	436	432	431	431	426	488	485	471	470	469	466	464	24
444	445	434	432	429	430	428	481	477	469	469	465	465	463	22
450	458	451	453	454	459	456	491	502	498	506	508	511	508	30
506	512	506	504	500	497	497	552	556	552	557	556	550	549	43
475	475	465	464	464	465	461	509	510	500	505	506	506	504	58
505	512	500	490	493	493	487	553	558	547	545	550	549	541	40
475	476	465	456	457	457	449	501	502	497	497	498	494	486	*
459	461	449	446	443	446	444	497	496	485	488	484	486	483	20
438	436	424	422	422	419	419	469	464	454	456	455	451	452	22
482	492	486	481	481	485	486	522	525	516	522	521	524	521	21
452	452	441	437	434	431	426	495	495	484	484	479	471	469	28
458	459	456	457	459	459	457	496	500	499	504	506	504	502	35
491	492	480	482	483	483	486	528	527	514	515	525	527	522	48
445	446	440	432	432	437	434	482	475	468	469	468	469	466	27
443	442	430	431	429	427	426	479	477	470	470	468	467	464	36
442	439	432	429	424	425	424	477	471	469	469	461	463	459	23
438	439	431	427	424	425	418	474	475	467	466	464	460	456	38
528	532	516	506	515	516	507	561	560	553	545	550	564	538	87
448	445	439	435	435	434	434	483	478	476	474	475	473	472	23
484	496	489	479	480	484	481	523	528	522	522	525	525	525	43
496	502	492	483	479	479	476	548	552	544	546	545	540	535	39
516	500	506	486	501	498	488	559	547	548	545	555	542	532	55
448	454	459	466	476	484	487	498	506	507	518	533	538	538	53
401	401	386	387	376	*	381	422	418	403	403	377	*	401	23
504	510	503	496	503	*	498	545	546	540	543	550	*	541	59
477	484	470	476	480	*	*	511	517	507	517	520	*	*	29
456	455	456	464	466	*	460	491	488	491	501	505	*	495	23
426	466	477	470	466	*	468	460	493	503	499	501	*	497	23
522	519	510	504	501	*	525	568	558	554	548	561	*	570	41
398	386	367	363	354	*	*	437	430	428	417	420	*	*	14
515	528	523	515	534	*	531	552	573	561	586	586	*	570	39
473	479	462	466	459	*	461	505	514	502	510	499	*	494	19

9.18 Rank the data in Exercise 9.1 and compute Spearman's r_S for Y and X_1.

9.19 Rank the data in Exercise 9.1 and compute Spearman's r_S for Y and X_2.

9.20 Assume that a set of data contains a slightly curvilinear relationship between X and Y (the best-fitting line is slightly curved). Would it ever be appropriate to calculate r on these data?

9.21 Several times in this chapter I referred to the fact that a correlation based on a small sample might not be reliable.

    (a) What does "reliable" mean in this context?

    (b) Why do you think that a correlation based on a small sample might not be reliable?

9.22 What reasons might there be for the finding that the amount of money that a country spends on health care is not correlated with life expectancy?

9.23 What would you expect the relationship to be between a state's welfare budget (per capita) and its mortality rate? What, if anything, does this say about efforts at prevention?

9.24 Considering the data relating height to weight, what effect would systematic reporting biases from males and females have on our conclusions?

9.25 Draw a figure using a small number of data points to illustrate the argument that you could have a negative relationship between weight and height within each gender and yet still have a positive relationship overall.

9.26 Sketch a rough diagram to illustrate the point made in the section on heterogeneous subsamples about the relationship between cholesterol consumption and cardiovascular disease for males and females.

9.27 Give an example of a situation in which you would expect a high correlation between two variables, where it is clear that neither variable is *caused* by the other.

10

REGRESSION

If you think of all the people you know, you are aware that there are individual differences in people's mental health. Some are cheerful and outgoing, some are depressed and withdrawn, some are aggressive and even unpleasant, some have trouble sleeping and spend their nights worrying about things over which they have no control. How do we predict what any specific individual will be like?

This question is really too big and too general, so let's narrow it down. Suppose we take a standard checklist and ask a large number of students to indicate whether they have experienced a variety of psychological symptoms in the past month. Each person's score will be a weighted sum of reported symptoms. The higher the score, the more problems he or she has; conversely, the lower the score, the better that person's state of mental health. But again, how do we predict a person's score?

If all that we have is a set of symptom scores, the best prediction we can make for any one individual is the group's mean. Since I have never met you and don't know anything about you, I will be less in error, *on average,* if I predict the mean than if I predict any other value. Obviously I won't always be right, but it's the best I can do.

But let's be a little more specific and assume that I know whether you are male or female. Here I have another variable I can use in making my prediction. In other words I can use one variable to help me predict another. In this case what prediction do you think I should make? If you say that I should use the mean of males to make a prediction about males and the mean of females to make a prediction about females, you are right. On the average I will do better than if I just use the overall mean. Notice that my prediction is conditional on gender. My prediction would be of the form, "Given that you are female, I would predict. . . ." How does this statement relate to how we defined conditional probabilities?

Now let's go one more step and instead of using a dichotomous variable like gender, we will use a continuous variable like stress. We know that psychological health varies with stress, in that people who experience a great deal of stress tend to have more symptoms than those who do not. Therefore, we can use people's stress levels to refine our prediction of symptoms. The process is more complicated and sophisticated than using a dichotomous variable such as gender, but the underlying idea is similar. We want to write an equation that explains how differences in one variable relate to differences in another and that allows us to predict a person's score on one variable from knowledge of that person's score on another variable. When we are interested in deriving an equation for predicting one variable from another, we are dealing with **regression**, the topic of this chapter.

Just as we did in our discussion of correlation, we will restrict our coverage of regression to those cases in which the best-fitting line through the scatter diagram is a straight line. This means that we will deal only with **linear regression**. This restriction is not as serious as you might expect because a surprisingly high percentage of sets of data turn out to be basically linear. Even in those cases in which the relationship is *curvilinear* (i.e., where the best-fitting line is a curve), a straight line often will provide a very good approximation, especially if we eliminate the extremes of the distribution of one or both of the variables.

Regression
The prediction of one variable from knowledge of one or more other variables.

Linear regression
Regression in which the relationship is linear.

10.1 The Relationship Between Stress and Health

Wagner, Compas, and Howell (1988) investigated the relationship between stress and mental health in first-year college students. Using a scale developed to measure the frequency, perceived importance, and desirability of recent life events, they created a measure of negative life events weighted by the reported frequency of each event and the respondent's subjective estimate of its impact. In other words, more weight was given to those events that occurred frequently and/or that the student felt had an important impact. This served as their measure of the subject's perceived social and environmental stress. The researchers also asked students to complete the Hopkins Symptom Checklist, assessing the presence or absence of 57 psychological symptoms. The stem-and-leaf displays and boxplots for the measures of stress and symptoms are shown in Table 10.1.

Table 10.1   Description of Data on the Relationship Between Stress and Mental Health

Stem-and-Leaf for Stress		Stem-and-Leaf for Symptoms	
0*	01222234	5.	8
0.	556677888899	6*	112234
1*	0111222222333444444	6.	55668
1.	5556666777888999	7*	00012334444
2*	0001111223333334	7.	57788899
2.	556778999	8*	00011122233344
3*	012233444	8.	5666677888899
3.	56677778	9*	0111223344
4*	23444	9.	556679999
4.	55	10*	0001112224
		10.	567799
HI	57, 74	11*	112
		11.	78
Code:	2.|5 = 25	12*	11
		12.	57
		13*	1
		HI	135, 135, 147, 186
		Code:	5.|8 = 58

Boxplot for Stress

```
         0    10    20    30    40    50    60    70
         |---------|---------|---------|---------|---------|---------|---------|----
       -----------|   |----|--------------|                *           *
```

Boxplot for Symptoms

```
    50    60    70    80    90   100   110   120   130   140   150      180
    |---------|---------|---------|---------|---------|---------|---------|---------|---------|-----/   /--|-----
             ------------------|     |----|-------------------------------2       *               *
```

Before we consider the relationship between these variables, we need to examine the variables individually. The stem-and-leaf displays for both variables show that the distributions are unimodal but slightly positively skewed. Except for a few extreme values, there is nothing about either variable that should disturb us, such as extreme skewness or bimodality. Note that there is a fair amount of variability in each variable. This variability is important, because if we want to show that different stress scores are associated with differences in symptoms, we need to have differences to explain in the first place.

The boxplot in Table 10.1 reveals the presence of outliers on both variables. (The "2" indicates the presence of two overlapping data points.) The existence of outliers should alert us to *potential* problems that these scores may cause. The first thing we could do is to check the data to see whether these few subjects were responding in unreasonable ways; for example, do they report the occurrence of all sorts of unlikely events or symptoms, making us question the legitimacy of their responses? (Difficult as it may be to believe, some subjects have been known to treat psychological experiments with something less than the respect and reverence that psychologists think that they deserve.) The second thing to check is whether the same subject produced outlying data points on both variables. That would suggest that the subject's data, although legitimate, might have a disproportionate influence on the resulting correlations. (To put this in everyday terms, think about how you form stereotypes. The person who is really "nerdy" and who does brilliantly in class has a disproportionate role in establishing in our minds the association between nerdiness and intelligence. We forget about all those people who are brilliant but not nerdy or nerdy but not intellectually outstanding.) The third thing to do is to make a scatterplot of the data, again looking for the undue influence of particular extreme data points. (Such a scatterplot will appear later in Figure 10.1.) Finally, we can run our analyses including and excluding extreme points to see what differences appear in the results. If you carry out each of these four steps on the data, you will find nothing to suggest that the outliers we have identified influenced the resulting correlation or regression equation in any important way. These steps are important precursors to any good analysis, if only because they give us greater faith in our final results.

10.2 The Basic Data

A portion of the data on stress and symptoms appears in Table 10.2. The full data set is available on disk. Since the complete data for 107 subjects would take too much space, I have given an abbreviated data set in the table. Here you see how the data would be set up in a data file, along with the means, the standard deviations, and the covariance.

From these data you can calculate the correlation (covered in Chapter 9):

$$r = \frac{\text{cov}_{XY}}{s_X s_Y}$$

Table 10.2

First 10 Cases from Data of Wagner et al. (1988)

Subject	Stress (X)	Symptoms (Y)
1	30	99
2	27	94
3	9	80
4	20	70
5	3	100
6	15	109
7	5	62
8	10	81
9	24	74
10	34	121

Descriptive Statistics for Full Data Set

Mean	21.467	90.701
Standard deviation	13.096	20.266
Covariance	134.301	

For our data the result would be

$$r = \frac{134.301}{(13.096)(20.266)} = .506$$

This correlation is fairly substantial for real data on psychological variables such as these. Using Table D.2 in the Appendices with $N = 107$ ($df = 105$) and $\alpha = .05$, two-tailed, we see that any correlation greater than about .195 would be significant. We can therefore reject $H_0 : \rho = 0$ and conclude that there is a significant relationship between stress and symptoms. As we saw in the last chapter, it does not tell us that stress *causes* symptoms, although that is a possibility.

10.3 The Regression Line

We have just seen that there is a significant degree of relationship between stress and psychological symptoms. We can obtain a better idea of what this relationship is like by looking at a scatterplot of the two variables and the regression line for predicting Symptoms (Y) on the basis of Stress (X). The scatterplot is shown in Figure 10.1, where the best-fitting line for predicting Y on the basis of X has been superimposed. You will see shortly where this line came from, but notice first the way in which the Symptom scores increase linearly with increases in Stress scores. Our correlation coefficient told us that such a

Figure 10.1

**Scatterplot of
Symptoms as
a Function
of Stress**

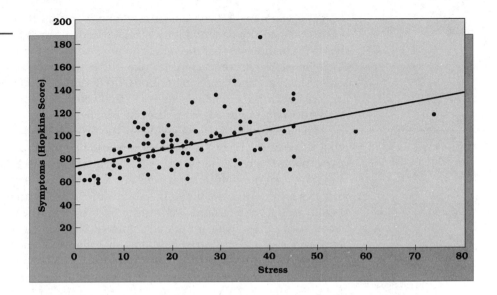

relationship existed, but it is easier to appreciate just what it means when you see it presented graphically. Notice also that the degree of scatter of points about the regression line remains about the same as you move from low values of stress to high values, although with a correlation of approximately .50 the scatter is fairly wide. We will discuss scatter again in more detail when we consider the assumptions on which our procedures are based.

As you may remember from high school, the equation for a straight line is of the form $Y = bX + a$. (You may have used other letters in place of a and b, but most statisticians use a and b.) For our purposes we will write the equation as

$$\hat{Y} = bX + a$$

where

$\hat{Y}$ = the *predicted* value of Y

Slope
The amount of change
in Y for a one-unit
change in X.

b = the **slope** of the regression line (the amount of difference in $\hat{Y}$ associated with a one-unit difference in X)

a = the **intercept** (the value of $\hat{Y}$ when $X = 0$)

Intercept
The value of Y when
X is 0.

X is simply the value of the predictor variable, in this case, stress. Our task will be to solve for those values of a and b that will produce the best-fitting linear function. In other words, we want to use our existing data to solve for the values of a and b such that the line (the values of $\hat{Y}$ for different values of X) will come as close as possible to the actual obtained values of Y.

Why, you may ask, did I use the symbol $\hat{Y}$, rather than Y, in my equation when I defined the equation for a straight line in terms of Y? The reason for using $\hat{Y}$ is to indicate that the values we are searching for are *predicted* values. The symbol Y represents, in this case, the actual *obtained* values for Symptoms. These are the values that our 107 different subjects reported. What we are looking for are predicted values ($\hat{Y}$) that come as close as possible to the Y values actually obtained, hence the different symbol.

Having said that we are looking for the best-fitting line, we have to define what we mean by "best." A logical way would be in terms of **errors of prediction**, that is, in terms of the $(Y - \hat{Y})$ deviations. Since $\hat{Y}$ is the value of the symptom variable that our equation would predict for a given level of stress, and Y is a value that we actually obtained, $(Y - \hat{Y})$ is an error of prediction, usually called the **residual**. We want to find the line (the set of $\hat{Y}$s) that minimizes such errors. We cannot just minimize the *sum* of the errors, however, because for an infinite variety of lines—any line that goes through the point $(\overline{X}, \overline{Y})$—that sum will be zero. Instead, we will look for the line that minimizes the sum of the squared errors, that is, that minimizes $\Sigma(Y - \hat{Y})^2$. (I said much the same thing in Chapter 6 when I discussed the variance. There I was discussing deviations from the mean, and here I am discussing deviations from the regression line—sort of a floating or changing mean. These two concepts— errors of prediction and variance—have much in common.)

It is not difficult to derive the equations for the optimal values for a and b, but I will not do so here. As long as you keep in mind that they are derived in such a way as to minimize squared errors in predicting Y, it is sufficient to state simply

$$b = \frac{\mathrm{cov}_{XY}}{s_X^2}$$

and

$$a = \overline{Y} - b\overline{X} = \frac{\Sigma Y - b\Sigma X}{N}$$

You should note that the equation for a includes the value of b, so you need to solve for b first. Also note that the equation for b resembles the equation for r, except that the denominator is s_X^2 instead of $s_X s_Y$. Another way of writing an equation for b is to write

$$b = r\frac{s_Y}{s_X}$$

(What does that tell you about the relationship between r and b when $s_X = s_Y$?)

If we apply these equations (using the covariance and the variance) to the data, we obtain

$$b = \frac{\mathrm{cov}_{XY}}{s_X^2} = \frac{134.301}{13.096^2} = 0.7831$$

Errors of prediction
The difference between Y and $\hat{Y}$.

Residual
The difference between the obtained value and the predicted value of Y, i.e., $Y - \hat{Y}$.

and

$$a = \bar{Y} - b\bar{X} = 90.701 - (0.7831)(21.467) = 73.891$$

We can now write

$$\hat{Y} = 0.7831X + 73.891$$

Regression equation
The equation that predicts Y from X.

Regression coefficients
The general name given to the slope and the intercept; most often refers just to the slope.

This equation is our **regression equation**, and the values of a and b are called the **regression coefficients**. The interpretation of this equation is straightforward. Consider the intercept (a) first. If $X = 0$ (i.e., if the subject reports no stressful events in the past month), the predicted value of $\hat{Y}$ (Symptoms) is 73.891, quite a low score on the Hopkins Symptom Checklist. In other words the intercept is the predicted level of symptoms when the predictor (Stress) is 0.0. Next consider the slope (b). You may know that a slope is often referred to as the *rate of change*. In this example $b = 0.7831$. This means that for every 1-point difference in Stress, we predict a 0.7831-point difference in Symptoms. This is the rate at which symptom scores change with changes in stress scores. Most people think of the slope as just a numerical constant in a mathematical equation, but it really makes more sense to think of it as how much different you expect Y to be for a one-unit difference in X.

Although we rarely work with standardized data (data that have been transformed so as to have a mean of 0 and a standard deviation of 1 on each variable), it is worth considering what b would represent if the data for each variable were standardized separately. In that case, a difference of one unit in X or Y would represent a difference of one standard deviation. Thus, if the slope were 0.75 for standardized data, we would be able to say that a one standard deviation increase in X will be reflected in three-quarters of a standard deviation increase in $\hat{Y}$. When speaking of the slope coefficient for standardized data,

Standardized regression coefficient, or β (beta)
The regression coefficient that results from data that have been standardized.

we often refer to the **standardized regression coefficient** as β **(beta)** to differentiate it from the coefficient for nonstandardized data (b). We will return to the idea of standardized variables when we discuss multiple regression. (What would the intercept be if the data were standardized?)

The interesting thing about β is that *when we have one predictor variable* it is equivalent to r, the correlation coefficient. Therefore, we can say that if $r = .506$, a one standard deviation difference between two students in terms of their Stress scores would be associated with a predicted difference of about one-half a standard deviation unit in terms of Symptoms. That gives us some idea of what kind of a relationship we are speaking about. When we come to multiple regression in the next chapter, we will find other uses of β.

A word is in order here about actually plotting the regression line. To plot the line, you can simply take any two values of X (preferably at opposite ends of the scale), calculate $\hat{Y}$ for each, mark the coordinates on the figure, and connect them with a straight line. I generally use three points, just as a check for accuracy. For the data on stress and symptoms, we have

$$\hat{Y} = 0.7831X + 73.891$$

When $X = 0$,

$$\hat{Y} = 0.7831 \cdot 0 + 73.891 = 73.891$$

When $X = 50$,

$$\hat{Y} = 0.7831 \cdot 50 + 73.891 = 113.046$$

The line then passes through the points ($X = 0$, $Y = 73.891$) and ($X = 50$, $Y = 113.046$), as shown in Figure 10.1. An even easier way is to pass the line through the intercept and the point ($\overline{X}$, $\overline{Y}$), provided that these points are far enough apart to lead to a sufficient degree of accuracy in drawing the line.

It is important to point out that we have constructed a line to predict symptoms from stress, not the other way around. Our line minimizes the sum of the squared deviations of predicted symptoms from actual symptoms. If we wanted to turn things around and predict stress ratings from symptoms, we could not use this line—it wasn't derived for that purpose. Instead we would have to find the line that minimizes the squared deviations of predicted stress from actual stress. The simplest way to do this is just to go back to the equations for a and b, reverse which variable is labeled X and which is labeled Y, and solve for the new values of a and b. You then can use the same formulae that we have already used.

10.4 The Accuracy of Prediction

The fact that we can fit a regression line to a set of data does not mean that our problems are solved. On the contrary, they have just begun. The important point is not whether a straight line can be drawn through the data (you can always do that), but whether that line represents a reasonable fit to the data—in other words, whether our effort was worthwhile.

Before we discuss errors of prediction, however, it is instructive to go back to the situation in which we want to predict Y without *any* knowledge of the value of X, which we considered at the very beginning of this chapter.

The Standard Deviation as a Measure of Error

Assume that you were given the complete data set illustrated in Table 10.1 and asked to predict a particular individual's level of symptoms (Y) without being told what he or she reported in terms of stress for the past month. Your best prediction in that case would be the mean symptom score ($\overline{Y}$). You predict the mean because it is closer, on average, to all the other scores than any other prediction would be. Think how badly you would generally do if your prediction were the smallest score or the largest one. Once in a while you would be exactly right, but most of the time you would be absurdly off. With the mean you will probably be exactly right more often (because more people actually fall in the center of the distribution), and when you are wrong you likely won't be off by as much as if you had made an extreme prediction. The error associated with your prediction will be the standard deviation of Y (s_Y). This is true because your prediction is the mean, and s_Y deals with deviations around the mean. Examining s_Y, we know that it is defined as

$$s_Y = \sqrt{\frac{\Sigma(Y - \overline{Y})^2}{N - 1}}$$

and that the variance is defined as

$$s_Y^2 = \frac{\Sigma(Y - \overline{Y})^2}{N - 1}$$

The numerator is the sum of squared deviations from $\overline{Y}$ (the point you would have predicted in this particular example), which we refer to as the sum of squares of Y (SS_Y).

The Standard Error of Estimate

Now suppose we want to make a prediction about the level of psychological distress (as measured by symptoms) that a person is likely to experience given that we know his or her reported level of stress. Suppose that the person's X value (Stress) is 15. In this situation we know the relevant value of X and the regression equation, and our best prediction would be $\hat{Y}$. In this case $X = 15$, and $\hat{Y} = 0.7831 \cdot 15 + 73.891 = 85.64$. In line with our previous measure of error (the standard deviation), the error associated with this prediction will again be a function of the deviations of Y about the predicted point; however, in this case the predicted point is $\hat{Y}$ rather than $\overline{Y}$. Specifically, a measure of error can now be defined as

$$s_{Y-\hat{Y}} = \sqrt{\frac{\Sigma(Y - \hat{Y})^2}{N - 2}}$$

Standard error of estimate
The average of the squared deviations about the regression line.

and again the sum is of squared deviations about the prediction ($\hat{Y}$). The statistic $s_{Y-\hat{Y}}$ is called the **standard error of estimate** and is sometimes written $s_{Y \cdot X}$ to indicate that it is the standard deviation of Y *predicted from* X. It is the most common (though not always the best) measure of the error of prediction. Its square, $s^2_{Y-\hat{Y}}$, is called the **residual variance**, or **error variance**.

Residual variance (error variance)
The square of the standard error of estimate.

Table 10.3 shows how to calculate directly the standard error of estimate. The raw data for the first 10 cases are given in columns 2 and 3, and the predicted values of $\hat{Y}$ (obtained from $\hat{Y} = 0.7831X + 73.891$) are given in column 4. Column 5 contains the values of $Y - \hat{Y}$ for each observation. Note that the sum

Table 10.3

First 10 Cases from Data of Wagner et al. (1988), Including $\hat{Y}$ and Residuals

Sub-ject	Stress (X)	Symptoms (Y)	$\hat{Y}$	$(Y - \hat{Y})$
1	30	99	97.383	1.617
2	27	94	95.034	−1.034
3	9	80	80.938	−0.938
4	20	70	89.552	−19.552
5	3	100	76.239	23.761
6	15	109	85.636	23.364
7	5	62	77.806	−15.806
8	10	81	81.721	−0.721
9	24	74	92.684	−18.684
10	34	121	100.515	20.485

Descriptive Statistics for the Full Data Set

Mean	21.467	90.701	$\Sigma(Y - \hat{Y}) = 0.000$
Standard deviation	13.096	20.266	$\Sigma(Y - \hat{Y})^2 = 32388.049$
Covariance		134.301	

of that column ($\Sigma(Y - \hat{Y})$) is 0, as stated previously. If we square and sum the deviations we obtain $\Sigma(Y - \hat{Y})^2 = 32388.049$. From this sum we can calculate

$$s_{Y-\hat{Y}} = \sqrt{\frac{\Sigma(Y - \hat{Y})^2}{N - 2}} = \sqrt{\frac{32388.049}{105}} = \sqrt{308.458} = 17.563$$

Finding the standard error this way is hardly the most enjoyable way to spend a winter evening, and I don't recommend that you do so. I present it because it makes clear what the term represents. Fortunately a much simpler calculational procedure exists that not only represents a way of obtaining the standard error of estimate, but also leads directly to even more important matters.

r^2 and the Standard Error of Estimate

We have defined the residual, or error, variance as

$$s^2_{Y-\hat{Y}} = \frac{\Sigma(Y - \hat{Y})^2}{N - 2}$$

From here a small amount of algebraic substitution and manipulation, which I am omitting, will bring us to

$$s_{Y-\hat{Y}} = s_Y\sqrt{(1 - r^2)\left(\frac{N - 1}{N - 2}\right)}$$

or, as most texts present it (although not quite accurately),

$$s_{Y-\hat{Y}} = s_Y\sqrt{(1 - r^2)}$$

This last equation is arrived at by treating the term $(N - 1)/(N - 2)$ as 1.0, which it is for all practical purposes when N is large.

From our data we now can calculate $s_{Y-\hat{Y}}$ three different ways:

1.
$$s_{Y-\hat{Y}} = \sqrt{\frac{\Sigma(Y - \hat{Y})^2}{N - 2}}$$

$$= \sqrt{\frac{32388.049}{105}} = 17.563$$

2.
$$s_{Y-\hat{Y}} = s_Y\sqrt{(1 - r^2)\left(\frac{N - 1}{N - 2}\right)}$$

$$= 20.266\sqrt{(1 - .506^2)\left(\frac{106}{105}\right)} = 17.563$$

3. $$s_{Y-\hat{Y}} \cong s_Y\sqrt{(1 - r^2)}$$

$$\cong 20.266\sqrt{1 - .506^2} \cong 17.480$$

The third solution differs from the other two because it is based on a formula that ignores the constant $\sqrt{(N - 1)/(N - 2)}$. That is why the "approximately equals" sign ($\cong$) was used. For large sample sizes the difference will be minor, but not for small sample sizes.

Now that we have computed the standard error of estimate, we can interpret it as a form of standard deviation. Thus it is reasonable to say that the standard deviation of points about the regression line is 17.563. Another way of saying this is to say that $s_{Y-\hat{Y}}$ is the standard deviation of the errors that we make when using our regression equation. If all our predictions were perfect, all the errors would be zero, as would $s_{Y-\hat{Y}}$. Because the regression line represents our set of predictions, a standard deviation of approximately 18 points should make us a bit uncomfortable. Being off by 18 units, on average, is not a particularly happy state of affairs, especially given the fact that even without knowing the stress level we would have a level of inaccuracy that is only slightly greater (i.e., the standard deviation, which is 20.266).

I have a specific reason for pointing out the substantial amount of error that is left in our predictions even after taking X (Stress) into account. Most people think that if we have a regression equation, we can make a prediction and that's that. Although it is true that a regression equation yields better predictions than predictions made without one, a substantial amount of error remains in the system (and in this case the correlation between the two variables was a respectable .506). However, there are many things that could lead college students to show moderate levels of depression, anxiety, and other psychological symptoms, and we can hardly expect stress to explain it all.

r^2 as a Measure of Predictable Variability

Sum of squares
The sum of the squared deviations around some point (usually $\overline{Y}$ or $\hat{Y}$).

SS$_{error}$
The sum of the squared residuals, i.e., $\Sigma(Y - \hat{Y})^2$.

SS$_Y$
The sum of the squared deviations, i.e., $\Sigma(Y - \overline{Y})^2$.

From the preceding equation that expresses residual error in terms of r^2, it is possible to derive an extremely important interpretation of the correlation coefficient. To avoid having to write several convoluted sentences that you would hate, I am forced to introduce a new term: **sum of squares**, which is the sum of squared deviations. (You will see a similar term when we come to the analysis of variance.) Let the notation **SS$_{error}$** stand for $\Sigma(Y - \hat{Y})^2$ and **SS$_Y$** stand for $\Sigma(Y - \overline{Y})^2$. SS_{error} represents deviations between actual values of Y and our predictions ($\hat{Y}$). SS_Y represents deviations between observed values of Y and the mean ($\overline{Y}$) that would have been our prediction if we had not taken stress into account. SS_Y is also called SS_{total} in some contexts because it stands for the total variability in Y. It is possible to show, although I will not do so here, that

$$SS_{error} = SS_Y(1 - r^2)$$

Expanding and rearranging, we have

$$SS_{error} = SS_Y(1 - r^2)$$

$$r^2 = \frac{SS_Y - SS_{error}}{SS_Y}$$

In this equation SS_Y (the sum of squares of Y) represents the total of both of the following:

1.   the part of the variability in Y that is related to X
2.   the part of the variability in Y that is independent of X, which is SS_{error}

Those parts of SS_Y are probably not immediately obvious. In the context of our example, we are talking about the level of symptoms related to an individual's daily stress and the level of symptoms attributable (or at least related) to other things. These concepts can be made clearer with a second example.

Suppose we are interested in studying the relationship between cigarette smoking (X) and age at death (Y). As we watch people die off over time, we notice several things. First we see that not all die at precisely the same age—there is variability in age at death regardless of smoking behavior. This variability is measured by $SS_Y = \Sigma(Y - \bar{Y})^2$. We also notice the obvious fact that some people smoke more than others. This is variability in smoking behavior regardless of age at death and is measured by $SS_X = \Sigma(X - \bar{X})^2$. We further find that cigarette smokers die earlier than nonsmokers, and heavy smokers earlier than light smokers. Thus we write a regression equation to predict Y from X. Because people differ in their smoking behavior, they will also differ in their *predicted* life expectancy ($\hat{Y}$), and we label this variability $s_{\hat{Y}}^2 = \Sigma(\hat{Y} - \bar{\hat{Y}})^2 = \Sigma(\hat{Y} - \bar{Y})^2$. This last measure is variability in Y that is directly attributable to variability in X, since different values of $\hat{Y}$ arise from different values of X, and the same values of $\hat{Y}$ arise from the same value of X—that is, $\hat{Y}$ does not vary unless X varies. (To see this more clearly, make predictions for two people who have stress scores of 50 and one person who has a stress score of 100. How and when do these predictions differ?)

We have one last source of variability, the variability in the life expectancy of those people who smoke exactly the same amount. It is measured by SS_{error} and is variability in Y that cannot be explained by variability in X, because these people did not differ in the amount they smoked. These several sources of variability (i.e., sums of squares) are summarized in Table 10.4.

If we consider the absurd extreme in which all nonsmokers die at exactly age 72 and all smokers smoke precisely the same amount and die at exactly age 68, then all the variability in life expectancy is directly predictable from variability in smoking behavior. If you smoke you will die at 68, and if you don't smoke you will die at 72. Here $SS_{\hat{Y}} = SS_Y$, and $SS_{error} = 0$.

In a more realistic example smokers might tend to die earlier than nonsmokers, but within each group there would be a certain amount of variability in life expectancy. In this situation, some of SS_Y is attributable to smoking ($SS_{\hat{Y}}$) and some is not (SS_{error}). We want to be able to specify the percentage of the overall variability in life expectancy attributable to variability in smoking behavior. In other words we want a measure that represents

$$\frac{SS_{\hat{Y}}}{SS_Y} = \frac{SS_Y - SS_{error}}{SS_Y}$$

Table 10.4

Sources of Variance in Regression

SS_X = variability in amount smoked = $\Sigma(X - \bar{X})^2$

SS_Y = variability in life expectancy = $\Sigma(Y - \bar{Y})^2$

$SS_{\hat{Y}}$ = variability in life expectancy directly attributable to variability in smoking behavior = $\Sigma(\hat{Y} - \bar{Y})^2$

SS_{error} = variability in life expectancy that cannot be attributable to variability in smoking behavior = $\Sigma(Y - \hat{Y})^2 = SS_Y - SS_{\hat{Y}}$

As we have seen, that measure is r^2. In other words

$$r^2 = \frac{SS_{\hat{Y}}}{SS_Y}$$

This interpretation of r^2 is extremely useful. If, for example, the correlation between amount smoked and life expectancy were an unrealistically high .80, we could say that $.80^2 = 64\%$ of the variability in life expectancy is directly predictable from the variability in smoking behavior. Obviously, this is a substantial exaggeration of the real world. If the correlation were a more likely $r = .20$, we could say that $.20^2 = 4\%$ of the variability in life expectancy is related to smoking behavior, whereas the other 96% is related to other factors. While 4% may seem to you to be an awfully small amount, when we are talking about how long people will live, it is far from trivial, especially to those people.

One problem associated with focusing on the squared correlation coefficient is maintaining an appropriate sense of perspective. If it were true that smoking accounted for 4% of the variability in life expectancy, it might be tempting to dismiss smoking as a minor contributor to life expectancy. You have to keep in mind, however, that an enormous number of variables contribute to life expectancy, including such things as automobile accidents, homicide, cancer, heart disease, and stroke. Some of those are related to smoking and some are not, and one that accounts for 4% or even 1% of the variability is a fairly powerful predictor. In fact, it has been suggested that 30% of the cancers in the United States are caused by smoking. A variable that accounts for 4% of something like your grade in a course is probably minor. But something that accounts for 4% of the variability in life expectancy is not to be dismissed so easily.

It is important to note that phrases such as "accountable for," "attributable to," "predictable from," and "associated with" are not to be interpreted as statements of cause and effect. You could say that pains in your shoulder account for 10% of the variability in the weather without meaning to imply that sore shoulders cause rain, or even that rain itself causes sore shoulders. For example, your shoulder might hurt when it rains because carrying an umbrella aggravates your bursitis.

10.5 Hypothesis Testing in Regression

In the last chapter we saw how to test a correlation coefficient for significance. We tested $H_0: \rho = 0$, because if $\rho = 0$ the variables are linearly independent, and if $\rho \neq 0$ the variables are related. When we come to regression problems, we have both a correlation coefficient and a slope, and it makes sense to ask if either is different from zero.[1] You know how to deal with ρ, but what about b?

---

[1] You could also test the intercept, but such a test is usually uninteresting.

The simplest approach to testing the slope is just to say that when you have only one predictor you don't need a separate test on *b*. If the *correlation* between Stress and Symptoms, for example, is significant, it means that Symptoms are related to Stress. If the *slope* is significant it means that the predicted number of symptoms increases (or decreases) with the amount of stress. But that's saying the same thing! As you will see in a moment, the test for the slope is numerically equal to the test for the correlation coefficient. The easy answer, then, is to test the correlation. If that test is significant, then both the correlation in the population and the slope in the population are nonzero. But keep in mind that this is true only when we have one predictor.

An alternative approach is to use a test statistic we have not yet covered. I suggest that you just skim these two paragraphs and come back to them after you have read about *t* tests in Chapter 12. What we are going to do is calculate a statistic called *t* (using the slope, *b*) and look up *t* in a table. If the *t* we calculated is larger than the tabled *t*, we will reject H_0. Notice that this is the same kind of procedure we went through when we tested *r*. Our formula for *t* is:

$$t = \frac{b}{\frac{s_{Y-\hat{Y}}}{s_X\sqrt{N-1}}} = \frac{b(s_X)\sqrt{N-1}}{s_Y\sqrt{(1-r^2)\dfrac{N-1}{N-2}}}$$

I mention the *t* test here, without elaborating on it, because you are about to see that same *t* appear in the computer printout in the next section. To jump ahead, if you look at Figure 10.2, the last few lines show the values for the slope (labeled "Stress") and the intercept (labeled "Constant"). To the right is a column labeled "T" and another labeled "Sig T." The entries under "T" are the *t* tests just referred to. (The test on the intercept is somewhat different, but it is still a *t* test.) The entries under "Sig. T" are the probabilities associated with those *t*s under H_0. If the probability is less than .05, we can reject H_0. Here we will reject H_0 and conclude that the slope relating symptoms to stress is not zero. People with higher stress scores are predicted to have more symptoms.

10.6 Computer Solution Using SPSS

Figure 10.2 contains the printout from an SPSS analysis of the Symptoms and Stress data. The top part of the table contains the program and the bottom contains the printout. The output starts by presenting the mean, the standard deviation, and the sample size of all cases, followed by the correlation coefficient matrix. Here you can see that the correlation of .506 agrees with our own calculation. The next section presents the correlation coefficient again. (Here it is labeled "Multiple R." Ignore the word "Multiple"; that would be applicable only if we had more than one predictor.) This section also gives you the squared correlation (.25608), the adjusted *r* squared, which we will skip, and the standard error of estimate ($S_{Y-\hat{Y}}$). These values agree with those that we have cal-

Figure 10.2

**Regression
Analysis of
Relationship
Between
Symptoms
and Stress**

```
Set Width = 80
Title          'SPSS analysis of Wagner, Compas, & Howell Stress Data'
File Handle    Data/Name = '[d_howell.book]Stresswag.dat'
Data List      File = Data Free/
               Stress Symptoms
Regression     Descriptives = defaults sig/
               Variables = Stress Symptoms/
               Dependent = Symptoms/ Enter/
               Scatterplot = (Symptoms, Stress)

          * * * *  M U L T I P L E   R E G R E S S I O N  * * * *

Listwise Deletion of Missing Data

                   Mean       Std Dev      Label      Correlation,
                                                      1-tailed Sig:

STRESS          21.467       13.096          ⌉
SYMPTOMS        90.701       20.266          ├── Descriptive statistics
N of Cases = 107                             ⌋

Correlation, 1-tailed Sig:

                STRESS      SYMPTOMS

STRESS          1.000         .506    ←──── r
                  .            .000

SYMPTOMS         .506        1.000
                 .000          .

Variable(s) Entered on Step Number
1..      STRESS

Multiple R               .50605   ←──── r
R Square                 .25608
Adjusted R Square        .24900
Standard Error         17.56242

Analysis of Variance
                   DF      Sum of Squares      Mean Square
Regression          1        11148.38159      11148.38159
Residual          105        32386.04831        308.43856

F = 36.14458           Signif F = .0000   ←──── Test on H₀:ρ = 0

-------------------- Variables in the Equation --------------------
         Slope
Variable             B          SE B         Beta          T       Sig T
STRESS          .783115       .130258       .506045      6.012     .0000
(Constant)    73.889588      3.271360                   22.587     .0000
```
       Intercept

culated. The section headed "Analysis of Variance" is simply a test on the significance of the correlation coefficient. The entry "Signif F" is the probability,
under H_0, of a correlation as large as .506. Since the probability is less than
.05, we will reject H_0 and conclude that there is a significant relationship between Symptoms and Stress. Finally, in the section headed "Variables in the
Equation" we see the slope (in column B, next to the word STRESS) and the
intercept right below the slope. Skipping the next two columns we come to the
t tests on these coefficients and the probability of those ts. I have already dis-

cussed the t on the slope. This is the same value you would have calculated using the formula given in Section 10.5. The t test on the intercept is simply a test that the true intercept is zero. We rarely would expect it to be, so this test is not particularly useful for most purposes.

We might write up these results this way:

> In a study examining the relationship between stress and mental health in college students, we asked students to complete a checklist assessing the number and severity of negative life events that they had recently experienced. We also asked that they complete a checklist of psychological symptoms. The relationship between these two variables addresses the issue of stress and mental health. The analyses produced a correlation of .506 between the two variables ($r^2 = .256$), which is significant ($F(1105) = 36.14$, $p = .0000$). The regression equation has a slope $= 0.78$ ($t(105) = 6.012$, $p = .0000$). Higher levels of stress are associated with higher levels of psychological symptoms.

10.7 A Final Worked Example

In Chapter 9 we obtained the correlation coefficient for the relationship between the rated quality of a course and the difficulty of that course (as reflected in the average expected grade for students taking the course). The data are repeated in Table 10.5, which shows only the first 15 cases to conserve space, but the calculations are based on all 50 cases in my sample. Here we will solve for the regression equation for predicting rated Overall Quality (Y) from Ex-

Table 10.5

A Worked Example of Predicting Course Quality from Grades

Expected Grade (X)	Overall Quality (Y)	Expected Grade (X)	Overall Quality (Y)
3.5	3.4	3.0	3.8
3.2	2.9	3.1	3.4
2.8	2.6	3.0	2.8
3.3	3.8	3.3	2.9
3.2	3.0	3.2	4.1
3.2	2.5	3.4	2.7
3.6	3.9	3.7	3.9
4.0	4.3		

Results Based on All 50 Cases

$$\Sigma X = 174.3$$
$$\Sigma X^2 = 613.65$$
$$\Sigma Y = 177.5$$
$$\Sigma Y^2 = 648.57$$
$$\Sigma XY = 621.94$$
$$N = 50$$

pected Grade (X). We will then consider the interpretation of the coefficients in that equation.

Our first step is to calculate the mean and the standard deviation of each variable, as follows:

$$\overline{Y} = 177.7/50 = 3.550$$

$$s_Y = \sqrt{\frac{648.57 - 177.5^2/50}{49}} = 0.6135$$

$$\overline{X} = 174.3/50 = 3.486$$

$$s_X = \sqrt{\frac{613.65 - 174.3^2/50}{49}} = 0.3511$$

The covariance is given as

$$\text{cov}_{XY} = \frac{621.94 - (174.3)(177.5)/50}{49} = .0648$$

To calculate the slope, we have

$$b = \frac{\text{cov}_{XY}}{s_X^2} = \frac{0.0648}{0.3511^2} = 0.5257$$

We calculate the intercept as

$$a = \overline{Y} - b(\overline{X}) = 3.55 - 0.5257(3.486) = 1.7174$$

Our equation is then

$$\hat{Y} = 0.5257(X) + 1.7174$$

We can interpret the result as follows. If we had a course in which students expected a grade of 0, our best guess is that the expected course rating would be 1.7174. That is not a particularly meaningful statistic as far as interpretation is concerned because it is difficult to imagine a course in which everyone would expect to fail. In this case the intercept merely serves to anchor the regression equation.

A slope of 0.5257 can be interpreted to mean that if two courses differ by one point in expected grades, their overall ratings would be expected to differ by a little over one-half a point. Such a difference, then, would be expected between a course in which students anticipate a grade of C (2.0) and a course in which students anticipate a grade of B (3.0). Keep in mind, however, the remarks in Chapter 9 about the fact that we are not making a causal statement here. We have no particular reason to conclude that lower expected grades *cause* lower ratings, although they are *associated* with lower ratings. Poor teaching could easily lead to both.

10.8 Summary

In this chapter we expanded on the relationship between two variables to cover the situation in which we want to predict one variable from our knowledge of the other variable. We examined how to calculate the equation for a regression line and looked at the standard error of estimate ($s_{Y-\hat{Y}}$) as a measure of the accuracy of the prediction. You saw that r^2 is an important index of the percentage of variability in one variable that can be accounted for by variability in the other. The use of r^2 instead of r adds considerable meaning to the correlation coefficient, although it must be interpreted with caution. Finally, we discussed the role and procedures of hypothesis testing in regression.

Some important terms in this chapter are:

- Regression
- Linear regression
- Slope
- Intercept
- Errors of prediction
- Residual
- Regression equation
- Regression coefficients

- Standardized regression coefficient, or β (beta)
- Standard error of estimate
- Residual variance (error variance)
- Sum of squares
- SS_{error}
- SS_Y

10.9 Exercises

10.1 From the data in Exercise 9.1 compute the regression equation for predicting the percentage of births of infants weighing under 2500 grams (Y) on the basis of fertility rate for females whose ages are ≤ 17 or ≥ 35 (X_1). (X_1 is known as the "high-risk fertility rate.")

10.2 Calculate the standard error of estimate for the regression equation in Exercise 10.1.

10.3 If, as a result of ongoing changes in the role of women in society, we saw a change in the age of childbearing such that the high-risk fertility rate jumped to 70 in Exercise 9.1, what would we predict for the incidence of birthweight <2500 grams?

10.4 Why should you feel uncomfortable making a prediction in Exercise 10.3 for a rate of 70?

10.5 Compute a regression equation for predicting the final grade for the data in Exercise 9.9. Is the slope significantly different from zero?

10.6 Compute a regression equation for predicting the number of problems completed from the final grade for the data in Exercise 9.9. Is the slope significantly different from zero?

10.7 Using the data in Table 10.2 predict the Symptom score for a stress level of 45.

10.8 The mean Stress score in Table 10.2 was 21.467. What would your prediction be for a Stress score of 21.467? How does this compare to the mean Symptom score?

10.9 Use the data in Exercise 9.10 to fit a regression equation for predicting the decline in SAT math scores from 1978 to 1979 on the basis of I-131 levels.

10.10 With regard to the previous exercise, ignore I-131 and write an equation to predict a state's mean 1978 SAT math score from the corresponding SAT verbal score.

10.11 Interpret the results of the answer in Exercise 10.10.

10.12 Subtract 100 points from each 1978 verbal score in Exercise 10.10. Then run the correlation between M78 and both the old and the new V78.

10.13 Generate $\hat{Y}$ and $Y - \hat{Y}$ for the first five cases of the data in Table 10.2.

10.14 Using the data in Appendix C, compute the regression equation for predicting GPA from ADDSC.

10.15 Show that the two equations for b (i.e., $b = \text{cov}_{XY}/s_X^2$ and $b = r\,s_Y/s_X$) are equivalent. (I couldn't resist bringing in a small amount of algebra.)

10.16 Within a group of 200 faculty members who have been at a well-known univer-

sity for less than 15 years (i.e., before the salary curve starts leveling off), the equation relating salary (Y) (in thousands of dollars) to years of service (X) is $\hat{Y} = 0.9X + 28$. For administrative staff at the same university the equation is $\hat{Y} = 1.5X + 18$. Assuming that all differences are significant (the slope and intercept are significantly different from zero), interpret the meaning of these two equations. How many years must pass for an administrator and a faculty member to earn roughly the same salary?

10.17 In Exercise 10.16 there is a reference to whether the slope is significantly different from zero. State in your own terms what it means if the slope is or is not different from zero.

10.18 The following data represent the actual heights and weights referred to in Chapter 9, for male college students.

Height	Weight	Height	Weight
70	150	73	170
67	140	74	180
72	180	66	135
75	190	71	170
68	145	70	157
69	150	70	130
71.5	164	75	185
71	140	74	190
72	142	71	155
69	136	69	170
67	123	70	155
68	155	72	215
66	140	67	150
72	145	69	145
73.5	160	73	155
73	190	73	155
69	155	71	150
73	165	68	155
72	150	69.5	150
74	190	73	180
72	195	75	160
71	138	66	135

74	160	69	160
72	155	66	130
70	153	73	155
67	145	68	150
71	170	74	148
72	175	73.5	155
69	175		

(a) Make a scatterplot of the data.

(b) Calculate the regression equation of weight predicted from height for these data. Interpret the slope and the intercept.

(c) What is the correlation coefficient for these data?

(d) Are the correlation coefficient and the slope significantly different from zero?

10.19 The following data are the actual heights and weights, referred to in Chapter 9, of female college students:

Height	Weight	Height	Weight
61	140	65	135
66	120	66	125
68	130	65	118
68	138	65	122
63	121	65	115
70	125	64	102
68	116	67	115
69	145	69	150
69	150	68	110
67	150	63	116
68	125	62	108
66	130	63	95
65.5	120	64	125
66	130	68	133
62	131	62	110
62	120	61.75	108
63	118	62.75	112
67	125		

(a) Make a scatterplot of the data.

(b) Calculate the regression coefficients for these data. Interpret the slope and the intercept.

(c) What is the correlation coefficient for these data? Is the slope significantly different from zero?

10.20 Using your own height and the appropriate regression equation from Exercise 10.18 or 10.19, predict your own weight. (If you are uncomfortable reporting your own weight, predict mine—I am 5′8″ and weigh 146 pounds.)

(a) How much is your actual weight greater than or less than your predicted weight? (You have just calculated a residual.)

(b) What effect will biased reporting on the part of the students who produced the data play in your prediction of your own weight?

10.21 Use your scatterplot of the data for students of your own gender and observe the size of the residuals. (*Hint:* You can see the residuals in the vertical distance of points from the line.) What is the largest residual for your scatterplot?

10.22 Given a male and a female student who are both 5′6″, how much would they be expected to differ in weight? (*Hint:* Calculate a predicted weight for each of them using the regression equation specific to gender.)

10.23 The slope (*b*) used to predict the weights of males from their heights is greater than the slope for females. What does this tell us about male weights relative to female weights?

10.24 Back in Chapter 3 I presented data on the speed of deciding whether a briefly presented letter was part of a comparison set and gave data from trials on which the comparison set had contained one, three, or five letters. Eventually, I would like to compare the three conditions (using only the data from trials on which the stimulus letter had in fact been a part of that set), but I worry that the trials are not independent. If the subject (myself) was improving as the task went along, he would do better on later trials, and how he did would in some way be related to the number of the trial. If so, we would not be able to say that the responses were independent. Using only the data from the trials labeled Y in the condition in which there were five letters in the comparison set, obtain the regression of response on trial number. Was performance improving significantly over trials? Can we assume that there is no systematic linear trend over time?

10.25 Write a paragraph summarizing the results in Table 10.5 that is comparable to the paragraph in Chapter 9, Section 9.12, describing the results of the correlational analysis.

11

MULTIPLE REGRESSION*

$\mathbf{I}$n Chapters 9 and 10 we dealt with the case in which we were looking at the relationship between one variable and another. We wanted either to determine the degree to which the two variables were correlated or to predict one criterion (dependent) variable from one predictor (independent) variable. In this situation we have a correlation coefficient (r) and regression equation of the form $\hat{Y} = bX + a$. But there is no good reason why we must limit ourselves to having only one predictor. It is perfectly appropriate to ask how well some linear combination of two, three, four, or more predictors will predict the criterion. To take a greatly oversimplified example, we could

*Optional. This chapter may be omitted by an instructor with no loss of continuity.

ask how well I could do if I just added together the number of stressful events you report experiencing over the last month, the number of close friends you have, and your score on a measure assessing how much control you feel you have over events in your life and then used that composite score to predict your level of psychological symptoms. There is no reason why I should have to give equal weight to each of those predictor variables. It might make much more sense to pay more attention to some variables than to others. Perhaps your sense of personal control over events is twice as important in predicting psychological distress as is the number of stress events, and perhaps both of those are more important than the number of your friends.

If we let the letters *S, F,* and *C* represent "stress," "friends," and "control," we could have a regression equation of the form

$$\hat{Y} = b_1 S + b_2 F + b_3 C + a$$

Regression coefficients
The slopes and the intercept in a regression equation.

where b_1, b_2, and b_3 are the weights for predictors *S, F,* and *C*. In other words, they are slopes, or **regression coefficients**. The coefficient *a* is simply the intercept, with the same meaning that it has had throughout our discussion of regression (although in multiple regression it is usually denoted b_0 instead of *a*).

Multiple regression solutions are usually quite cumbersome to compute by hand, especially with more than two predictors, but they can be readily computed with any of the widely available statistical programs. In this chapter we will focus exclusively on solutions generated by computer software.

How do people decide who will be offered admission to graduate school? Several years ago I collected data on admission to one graduate program. All faculty in that department rated several hundred graduate applications on a scale from 1 to 7, where 1 represented "reject immediately," and 7 represented "accept immediately." For a random sample of 100 applications I attempted to predict the mean rating (Rating) for each application (averaged over judgments based on all available information) on the basis of Graduate Record Exam Verbal score (GREV), a numerical rating of the combined letters of recommendation (Letters), and a numerical rating of the statements of purpose (Purpose). The obtained regression equation was

$$\hat{Y} = 0.009 \cdot \text{GREV} + 0.51 \cdot \text{Letters} + 0.43 \cdot \text{Purpose} - 1.87$$

Multiple correlation coefficient (R)
The correlation between one variable (*Y*) and a set of predictors.

In addition, the correlation between Rating and the three predictors considered simultaneously (the **multiple correlation coefficient**, **R**) was .775.

We can square the correlation coefficient, just as we do in the one-predictor case, with a similar interpretation. The squared correlation coefficient (R^2) is .60. The interpretation of R^2 is the same as for the case of r^2 with one predictor. In other words, 60% of the variability in ratings can be accounted for by variability in the three predictors considered together. Put slightly differently, using GREV, Letters, and Purpose *simultaneously* as predictors, we can account for 60% of the variability in ratings of admissability.

The regression equation in multiple regression is interpreted in much the same way it was interpreted in simple regression, where we had only one predictor. To make a prediction, we multiply the student's GREV score by 0.009. We also multiply the rating of that student's letters of recommendation by 0.51 and the rating of the statement of purpose by 0.43. We then sum those results and subtract 1.87 (the intercept). For every one-unit change in GREV the predicted rating will increase by 0.009 unit, *assuming that Letters and Purpose remain unchanged.* Similarly, for every one-unit change in the rating of the letters of recommendation there will be a 0.51-unit change in the ratings, again assuming that the other two predictors are held constant.

In Chapter 10 I mentioned the standardized regression coefficient (β) and said that it represents the regression coefficient we would obtain if we standardized the variables, that is, converted the variables (separately) to z scores. Here is a good place to say something meaningful about β. In the equation given for predicting ratings from GREV, Letters, and Purpose, you might at first be inclined to suggest that GREV must not be very important as a predictor because it has such a small (unstandardized) regression coefficient (0.009). On the other hand the regression coefficient for Letters is 0.51, which is over 50 times greater. As we just saw, this regression equation tells us that a one-point difference in GREV would make (only) a 0.009 difference in our prediction, whereas a one-point difference in the rating of Letters would make a difference of about half a point in our prediction. But keep in mind that the variability of GREV is considerably greater than the variability of ratings of Letters. It is trivial to do one point better or worse on GREV (does anyone really care if you got a 552 instead of a 553 Verbal score—even ignoring the fact that the way the test is scored, values are rounded to the nearest 10's digit)? But Letters were rated on a seven-point scale, where a one-point difference is a big deal. This difference between the variances of our two measures is one major reason why we can't meaningfully compare regular regression coefficients.

If I now told you that the *standardized* regression coefficient (β) for GREV was 0.72, while the β for Letters was 0.61, you would see that, *after we take the difference in the standard deviations of the variables into account,* the weights for these variables are approximately equal. In this sense the two variables contribute about evenly to the prediction. But be careful of overinterpreting what I have said. Using standardized weights (β) does make it easier to keep the contributions of the variables in perspective. But this scheme is not foolproof. For reasons that I will gloss over by mumbling something about the intercorrelations of the predictor variables, β weights are not perfectly related to the contribution that each variable makes to the prediction. They are a good rough guide, but don't conclude that just because the value of 0.72 is greater than 0.61, GREV is more important than Letters. In the first place it is not clear just what "more important than" means here. Moreover, some other measure of the contribution of each variable might favor Letters over GREV. The task of deciding on the relative importance of predictors is a difficult one (for predictors that are themselves highly correlated, maybe even a meaningless one). A much more extensive discussion of this problem is found in Howell (1992).

An important consideration in a multiple regression problem is the degree of correlation among the predictors. When the predictors are highly correlated with each other (a condition known as **multicollinearity**), the regression equation is very unstable from one sample of data to another. In other words, two random samples from the same population might produce regression equations that appear to be totally different from one another. I would strongly advise you to avoid using highly correlated predictors and even to avoid moderate intercorrelations when possible.

Multicollinearity
A condition in which a set of predictor variables are highly correlated among themselves.

11.1 Course Evaluations Again

In the previous chapter we looked at the prediction of course evaluations as a function of a student's anticipated grade in the course. Here we will extend that example to take into account information we have on other variables related to the nature of the course. The data in Table 11.1 are real and represent the mean rating of each of 50 courses on six different variables. These variables were (1) overall quality of lectures (Overall), (2) teaching skills of the instructor (Teach), (3) quality of the tests and exams (Exam), (4) instructor's perceived knowledge of the subject matter (Knowledge), (5) the student's expected grade in the course on a scale of 1–5, with F = 1 and A = 5 (Grade), and (6) the enrollment of the course (Enroll). On the assumption that the best available rating of the course is the overall rating of the lectures (Overall), we will use that as the dependent variable (Y) and derive a regression equation predicting Y on the basis of other predictors. In this example I will use just three predictors, Teach, Knowledge, and Grade, but I have presented all the data so you can try other predictors.

Before we consider the regression solution itself, we need to look at the distribution of each variable. These are shown as stem-and-leaf displays in Table 11.2. (Notice that the display for Enroll contains a discontinuity because the few very large enrollments require the scale to move from increments of ten to increments of 100.) From these displays it is apparent that the criterion variable and four of the predictors are fairly well distributed. They are all more or less symmetric with a reasonable amount of variability. Notice that the center of each distribution is noticeably above 3.0, which was labeled on the scale as "average." Thus, there is some positive response bias in the data. This result is interesting, but it should have no important effect on the multiple regression solution; it will merely change the intercept from what it would be if each variable had a mean of 3.0. It is encouraging to notice that the distribution for scores on the instructors' knowledge of their subject matter is particularly biased upward. It is nice to see that students think their instructors know the material, even when they think the instructor is not very good at teaching it. The Teach and Exam variables each have one score that is unusually low relative to the others, but these are not so low as to bring their accuracy into question. The Enroll variable is unusually distributed; 46 of the 50 courses have

Table 11.1   Course Evaluation Data

Overall	Teach	Exam	Knowl-edge	Grade	Enroll	Overall	Teach	Exam	Knowl-edge	Grade	Enroll
3.4	3.8	3.8	4.5	3.5	21	4.4	4.4	4.3	4.4	2.9	25
2.9	2.8	3.2	3.8	3.2	50	3.1	3.4	3.6	3.3	3.2	55
2.6	2.2	1.9	3.9	2.8	800	3.6	3.8	4.1	3.8	3.5	28
3.8	3.5	3.5	4.1	3.3	221	3.9	3.7	4.2	4.2	3.3	28
3.0	3.2	2.8	3.5	3.2	7	2.9	3.1	3.6	3.8	3.2	27
2.5	2.7	3.8	4.2	3.2	108	3.7	3.8	4.4	4.0	4.1	25
3.9	4.1	3.8	4.5	3.6	54	2.8	3.2	3.4	3.1	3.5	50
4.3	4.2	4.1	4.7	4.0	99	3.3	3.5	3.2	4.4	3.6	76
3.8	3.7	3.6	4.1	3.0	51	3.7	3.8	3.7	4.3	3.7	28
3.4	3.7	3.6	4.1	3.1	47	4.2	4.4	4.3	5.0	3.3	85
2.8	3.3	3.5	3.9	3.0	73	2.9	3.7	4.1	4.2	3.6	75
2.9	3.3	3.3	3.9	3.3	25	3.9	4.0	3.7	4.5	3.5	90
4.1	4.1	3.6	4.0	3.2	37	3.5	3.4	4.0	4.5	3.4	94
2.7	3.1	3.8	4.1	3.4	83	3.8	3.2	3.6	4.7	3.0	65
3.9	2.9	3.8	4.5	3.7	70	4.0	3.8	4.0	4.3	3.4	100
4.1	4.5	4.2	4.5	3.8	16	3.1	3.7	3.7	4.0	3.7	105
4.2	4.3	4.1	4.5	3.8	14	4.2	4.3	4.2	4.2	3.8	70
3.1	3.7	4.0	4.5	3.7	12	3.0	3.4	4.2	3.8	3.7	49
4.1	4.2	4.3	4.7	4.2	20	4.8	4.0	4.1	4.9	3.7	64
3.6	4.0	4.2	4.0	3.8	18	3.0	3.1	3.2	3.7	3.3	700
4.3	3.7	4.0	4.5	3.3	260	4.4	4.5	4.5	4.6	4.0	27
4.0	4.0	4.1	4.6	3.2	100	4.4	4.8	4.3	4.3	3.6	15
2.1	2.9	2.7	3.7	3.1	118	3.4	3.4	3.6	3.5	3.3	40
3.8	4.0	4.4	4.1	3.9	35	4.0	4.2	4.0	4.4	4.1	18
2.7	3.3	4.4	3.6	4.3	32	3.5	3.4	3.9	4.4	3.3	90

enrollments below about 100, whereas the other 4 have enrollments ranging from 220 to 800. We will consider these extreme values later.

Although each of these variables taken alone (with the possible exception of Enroll) is reasonably behaved, what is particularly noteworthy is the behavior of the third course listed in Table 11.1. This course accounts for the two extreme scores on the variables Teach and Exam, and also has the most extreme score on Enroll. It is important to keep this course in mind, since it may well contribute more than its share of influence to the final results.

Table 11.2   Stem-and-Leaf Displays for All Variables for the Data in Table 11.1

	Overall (Y)		Teach (X₁)		Exam (X₂)
1.		1.		1.	9
2*	1	2*		2*	
2t		2t	2	2t	
2f	5	2f		2f	
2s	677	2s	7	2s	7
2.	889999	2.	899	2.	8
3*	000111	3*	111	3*	
3t	3	3t	222333	3t	2223
3f	44455	3f	4444455	3f	455
3s	6677	3s	7777777	3s	6666666777
3.	88889999	3.	88888	3.	888889
4*	000111	4*	0000011	4*	00000111111
4t	22233	4t	22233	4t	222223333
4f	444	4f	4455	4f	4445
4s		4s		4s	
4.	8	4.	8	4.	
5*		5*		5*	

	Knowledge (X₃)		Grade (X₄)		Enroll (X₅)
2*		2*		0	7
2t		2t		1	245688
2f		2f		2	0155577888
2s		2s		3	257
2.		2.	89	4	079
3*	1	3*	00011	5	00145
3t	3	3t	222222233333333	6	45
3f	55	3f	4445555	7	00356
3s	677	3s	6666777777	8	35
3.	8888999	3.	88889	9	0049
4*	000011111	4*	0011	1	00001
4t	2222333	4t	23	2	26
4f	4444555555555	4f		3	
4s	66777	4s		4	
4.	9	4.		5	
5*	0	5*		6	
				7	0
				8	0

Code: (Y to X₄) $3*|1 = 3.1$ Code: X_5 9|0 = 90

1 |0 = 100

(Underlined values would be shown as outliers in a boxplot.) Notice that the stems have been divided into five intervals per decade. The * stands for 0 and 1, t for 2 and 3, f for 4 and 5, s for 6 and 7, and . for 8 and 9.

Figure 11.1   Printout from Systat Analysis of Data from Table 11.1

```
PEARSON CORRELATION MATRIX

               OVERALL    TEACH   KNOWLEDG    GRADE

  OVERALL      1.000
    TEACH      0.804     1.000                            ──── Correlations
 KNOWLEDG      0.682     0.526     1.000
    GRADE      0.301     0.469     0.224     1.000

MATRIX OF PROBABILITIES

               OVERALL    TEACH   KNOWLEDG    GRADE

  OVERALL      0.000
    TEACH      0.000     0.000                            ──── Significance tests
 KNOWLEDG      0.000     0.000     0.000
    GRADE      0.034     0.001     0.118     0.000

NUMBER OF OBSERVATIONS:    50                   ⟋ Multiple correlation

DEP VAR: OVERALL   N:   .50   MULTIPLE R: 0.863   SQUARED MULTIPLE R: 0.745
ADJUSTED SQUARED MULTIPLE R: 0.728     STANDARD ERROR OF ESTIMATE   0.320
```

VARIABLE	COEFFICIENT	STD ERROR	STD COEF	TOLERANCE	T	P(2 TAIL)
Intercept						
CONSTANT	-0.927	0.596	0.000	.	-1.556	0.127
TEACH	0.759	0.112	0.658	0.593	6.804	0.000
KNOWLEDG	0.534	0.132	0.355	0.722	4.052	0.000
GRADE	-0.153	0.147	0.088	0.779	-1.037	0.305

Regression
coefficients (slopes)

ANALYSIS OF VARIANCE

Test on
$H_0 : \rho = 0$

SOURCE	SUM-OF-SQUARES	DF	MEAN-SQUARE	F-RATIO	P
REGRESSION	13.737	3	4.579	44.741	0.000
RESIDUAL	4.708	46	0.102		

The printout of the multiple regression analysis using Systat is presented in Figure 11.1. This printout closely resembles the printout you would get using any similar package. The first part of the printout gives the correlations among the variables involved. The section headed "Matrix of Probabilities" tells the probability of obtaining a correlation as large as each of those we obtained when H_0 is true. Notice in particular that the correlation and the probability given for the correlation between Overall and Grade ($r = .301$, $p = .034$) agree with the values we found in Chapter 9. Since most of these probabilities are less than $\alpha = .05$, we can conclude that most of the correlations are significant. The one exception is the correlation between Knowledge and Grade ($r = .224$, $p = .118$).

We can see that all three predictors are individually correlated with Overall, but what happens when we use all of them at the same time to predict Overall? Will our prediction, as reflected in the *multiple* correlation coefficient, improve? Will all three predictors still play a significant role in that prediction? To answer these questions, we need to look at the rest of Figure 11.1.

Notice that in the center of Figure 11.1 the multiple correlation is given as .863, which squared is .745. This is the correlation between the best linear combination of the predictors and the criterion. For example, I previously showed you a regression equation for predicting rating for admission to graduate school on the basis of three pieces of information (GREV, Letters, and Purpose). If we made a prediction for every applicant and correlated the predicted rating with the actual rating, that correlation would be the multiple correlation coefficient. Similarly in this case, if we used our regression equation to predict overall ratings, the correlation between the predicted rating and the overall rating would be .863. (When we speak of multiple correlation, we signify the correlation coefficient with R instead of r, but the meaning is the same.)

We can treat the squared multiple correlation the same way we treated the squared simple (one-predictor) correlation in Chapter 9. With $R^2 = .745$ we can say that 74.5% of the variability in Overall ratings can be accounted for by variability in Teach ratings, the perceived Knowledge of the instructor, and the expected Grade. This is a substantial amount of expected variability.

In the next line of the table is the adjusted squared multiple correlation coefficient. We will not make use of that statistic in this book, but it includes an adjustment for chance. If you have many predictors relative to the number of subjects, there is a reasonable likelihood that you will have a high correlation just by chance. (Try correlating any two variables with data on only two subjects.) The adjusted R^2 is an attempt to adjust for that effect.

The next section of the table gives the regression coefficients and related statistics. The coefficients are given in the second column, with their labels in the first column. The word "constant" can be read as "intercept," so the intercept for the regression equation is -0.927. The next three entries are the slopes for Teach, Knowledge, and Grade, giving us the following regression equation:

$$\hat{Y} = 0.759 \cdot \text{Teach} + 0.534 \cdot \text{Knowledge} - 0.153 \cdot \text{Grade} - 0.927$$

We can make a prediction for any course simply by plugging in that course's ratings for Teach, Knowledge, and Grade. For example, the first course in Table 11.1 had a mean Teach score of 3.8, a mean Knowledge rating of 4.5, and a mean anticipated Grade of 3.5. Therefore, we would predict that this course would have an Overall rating of

$$\hat{Y} = 0.759 \cdot 3.8 + 0.534 \cdot 4.5 - 0.153 \cdot 3.5 - 0.927 = 3.82$$

In fact that course had an overall rating of 3.4, so our prediction was in error by

$$Y - \hat{Y} = 3.4 - 3.82 = -0.42$$

which means that our prediction overshot the actual rating by 0.42 point. We could make a similar prediction for every course in Table 11.1, or we could use what we have learned here to make predictions about future courses. We would expect our accuracy to be somewhat less on predictions for the future, because the regression equation that we derived maximized the fit to the existing data, and therefore it should fit those data better than it would fit data for which it was not optimized.

11.2 Residuals

When we make a prediction from a set of data, we don't expect to be right all the time. Sometimes our prediction will be a bit high, sometimes a bit low. And sometimes the actual data point will be far away from what we have predicted. It is worth looking briefly at these predictions and the errors of prediction (called **residuals**) because they tell us something about multiple regression.

Residuals
The set of deviations between the obtained value and the predicted value of Y.

In Table 11.3 I used the regression equation found in Figure 11.1 to predict Overall on the basis of Teach, Knowledge, and Grade:

$$\text{Predicted Overall} = 0.759 \cdot \text{Teach} + 0.534 \cdot \text{Knowledge} - 0.153 \cdot \text{Grade} - 0.927$$

and substituted the Teach, Knowledge, and Grade scores for each course. (You could do the same for a course you are currently taking, although it probably wouldn't be politic to use your Statistics course. First assign a rating from 1 to 5 for the overall quality of the course and then for the teaching skills of the instructor, your estimate of the instructor's knowledge of the material, and the grade you expect to receive. Then use the above equation to make your prediction and compare the prediction with your actual rating.) Table 11.3 shows the results for selected cases for the data in my sample.

Notice in Table 11.3 that some of the predictions were quite accurate (e.g., the rating for Course 34 was only .013 unit higher than the predicted rating), while others were not very good. For example, Course 15 was more than three quarters of a point higher than we predicted, and Course 44 was almost two-thirds of a point higher than predicted. On the other hand, Course 36 was two-thirds of a point lower than predicted. These may be just random deviations, or these courses may have something about them that we are not taking into account.[1] Here is a case where you might want to go back to the courses themselves and try to identify what is going on. Perhaps these "errors" are the most useful part of the study, in that they may offer insights into features of a course or an instructor that make them more effective than we would expect.

Notice also that the particularly large courses (enrollment >100) were predicted about as well as other courses. Thus we have no particular reason to think that large-enrollment courses follow a different regression model than other courses. (If we omitted the four largest courses and reran the analysis, there would be no major difference in the results.)

---

[1] See Howell (1992) for a discussion of how to evaluate the magnitude of the deviation from prediction.

Table 11.3   Predicted Values and Residuals for Selected Courses

Course	Overall	Teach	Knowledge	Grade	Enroll	Predicted	Residual
1	3.4	3.8	4.5	3.5	21	3.825	−0.425
2	2.9	2.8	3.8	3.2	50	2.738	0.162
3	2.6	2.2	3.9	2.8	800	2.397	0.208
4	3.8	3.5	4.1	3.3	221	3.414	0.386
5	3.0	3.2	3.5	3.2	7	2.881	0.119
6	2.5	2.7	4.2	3.2	108	2.876	−0.376
7	3.9	4.1	4.5	3.6	54	4.037	−0.137
8	4.3	4.2	4.7	4.0	99	4.159	0.141
9	3.8	3.7	4.1	3.0	51	3.612	0.188
10	3.4	3.7	4.1	3.1	47	3.596	−0.196
11	2.8	3.3	3.9	3.0	73	3.201	−0.401
12	2.9	3.3	3.9	3.3	25	3.155	−0.255
13	4.1	4.1	4.0	3.2	37	3.831	0.269
14	2.7	3.1	4.1	3.4	83	3.095	−0.395
15	3.9	2.9	4.5	3.7	70	3.111	0.789
⋮	⋮	⋮	⋮	⋮	⋮	⋮	⋮
34	3.7	3.8	4.3	3.7	28	3.687	0.013
35	4.2	4.4	5.0	3.3	85	4.578	−0.378
36	2.9	3.7	4.2	3.6	75	3.573	−0.673
37	3.9	4.0	4.5	3.5	90	3.977	−0.077
⋮	⋮	⋮	⋮	⋮	⋮	⋮	⋮
44	4.8	4.0	4.9	3.7	64	4.160	0.640
45	3.0	3.1	3.7	3.3	700	2.847	0.103
46	4.4	4.5	4.6	4.0	27	4.333	0.067
47	4.4	4.8	4.3	3.6	15	4.462	−0.062
48	3.4	3.4	3.5	3.3	40	3.018	0.382
49	4.0	4.2	4.4	4.1	18	3.983	0.017
50	3.5	3.4	4.4	3.3	90	3.498	0.200

11.3 The Visual Representation of Multiple Regression

Another way to think about multiple regression, which will help us think about residuals, is to plot the data. When we had only two variables, plotting was relatively easy. We could plot Y on the vertical axis and X on the horizontal axis

Figure 11.2

Three-Dimensional Plot of Teaching Evaluation Data

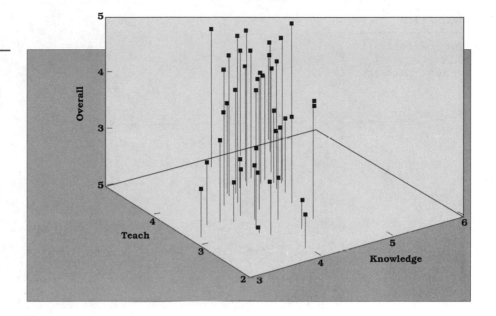

and make a scatter plot of the points in two dimensions. With three variables (one criterion and two predictors) we can plot in three dimensions. This is harder on paper than it is with a three-dimensional model, but it can be done. Such a plot is seen in Figure 11.2, where I have plotted Overall on the vertical axis and Teach and Knowledge on the other two axes. (I have ignored Grade because I can plot only three variables, and Grade does not make a major contribution anyway.) Each point can be thought of as a ball on the top of a flagpole, with the height of the flagpole corresponding to the course's Overall evaluation, and the base of the flagpole positioned in two-dimensional space corresponding to the evaluations of Teach and Knowledge.

Now imagine that you had a rigid sheet of paper that you could position so that it would go through most of the points. This sheet would form a plane, which is called the **regression surface**. It is analogous to the regression line that we had with one predictor. This plane would slope up from front to back, and this slope would be the slope for Teach in an equation using only these two predictors. (You will see such an equation in Table 11.4.) The plane would also slope up from left to right, and this slope would correspond to the one in our equation for Knowledge. The fact that some of the points would be above this sheet of paper and some below is a statement about the residuals. In other words, the residuals are the deviations of the points from the regression surface.

Another way to look at residuals is to make a simple two-dimensional plot with the predicted values on the horizontal axis and the obtained values on the vertical axis. Such a plot is shown in Figure 11.3. The advantage of this plot is that you can easily see the large residuals just by looking at the vertical deviation of each point from the regression line. You can also see that there is substantial spread among the points. I mention the spread among the points

Regression surface
The equivalent of the regression line in multidimensional space.

Figure 11.3

Plot of Actual Ratings Against Predicted Ratings

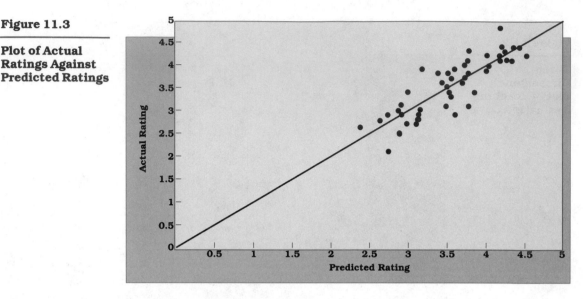

to make it clear that simply because we have a regression equation and even a substantial R^2 does not mean that all our predictions will be close to the mark. I have already pointed to some relatively large residuals, and I now have shown them graphically in two different ways. Two courses with the same values on all the predictors, and hence the same prediction, may still differ substantially in their actual Overall evaluation.

11.4 Hypothesis Testing

You saw in Chapter 10 that we can ask if the regression coefficient is significantly different from zero. In other words, we can ask if differences in one variable are related to differences in another. If the slope is not significantly different from zero, we have no reason to believe that the criterion is related to the predictor. That works very cleanly when we have only one predictor variable; in fact, I told you that a test on the correlation coefficient and a test on the regression coefficient are equivalent in the one-predictor case. But the situation is distinctly different when we have more than one predictor.

To address the problem of the significance of individual predictors, we have to stop and look a little more closely at the meaning of the regression coefficients. When we say that the regression coefficient for Teach in Figure 11.1 is 0.759, we are saying that there will be a 0.759-unit change in $\hat{Y}$ for every one-unit change in Teach *if we hold Knowledge and Grade constant.* The italicized portion of the preceding sentence is very important. It says that if we have two classes that have exactly the same rated Knowledge and anticipated Grade, then a one-unit difference in Teach is associated with a 0.759-unit difference in Overall. Similarly, if we have two classes with the same ratings for Teach and Grade, then a course that is one unit higher in Knowledge will have a predicted Overall rating that is .534 unit higher.

Now we can ask if each of those three slopes is significant. For classes that are equal on Knowledge and Grade, does a difference in Teach lead to significant differences on Overall? And are classes that are equivalent on Teach and Knowledge but different on Grade predicted to be significantly different on Overall? Put more directly, we want to test the hypotheses

$$H_0 : b_1 = 0 \qquad H_0 : b_2 = 0 \qquad H_0 : b_3 = 0$$

against the alternative hypotheses

$$H_1 : b_1 \neq 0 \qquad H_1 : b_2 \neq 0 \qquad H_1 : b_3 \neq 0$$

Tests on these hypotheses were given in the column labeled T (for t test) in Figure 11.1, along with the associated two-tailed probabilities in the next column. These tests are the same kinds we saw in the last chapter, except that we are testing three slopes instead of one. Here you can see that the test for the slope for Teach is significantly different from zero because the probability value ($p = .000$) is less than .05. (The probability is not exactly 0, but it rounds to 0 for three decimal places.) Similarly the slope of Knowledge is also significant. The slope for Grade, however, is not significantly different from zero ($p = .305$).

You might be puzzled that in the last chapter we saw that there was a significant relationship between Overall and Grade, but here I have just said that it is not significant. The difference is that in this chapter we are including Teach and Knowledge as additional predictors. While Grade may be significantly related to Overall when taken on its own, it loses that significance when we take Teach and Knowledge into account. Once we have controlled for these two variables, Grade no longer has a significant role to play. Another way of saying this is that Grade does not explain variability in the Overall rating *above and beyond* what can be explained by Teach and Knowledge.

You might find it easier to understand the nonsignificance of Grade in this case when you realize that Teach and Grade are correlated ($r = .469$), as are Knowledge and Grade ($r = .224$). In general instructors who are perceived as better teachers are also perceived as giving higher grades (and vice versa). Therefore, in using Teach to predict Overall, we are already taking into account some of the variability related to Grade. To put this in more everyday terms, both your mother and your father *each* know something about you—you might be surprised how much—and they share much of that knowledge in common. If I ask your father alone, he can probably tell me a great deal. But if I ask your father after taking into account what your mother knows, he may have very little to add. It's not that dads don't know much; it's that moms know most of what dads do and then some.

One more major piece of information is given in Figure 11.1 in the section "Analysis of Variance." This section is a test on the null hypothesis that there is no correlation between the set of predictors (Teach, Knowledge, and Grade) taken together and the criterion. A significant effect here would mean that we reject that null hypothesis. In the table we see $F = 44.741$ with an associated probability of .000. Since this probability is less than $\alpha = .05$, we will reject H_0

and conclude that Overall is predicted at better than chance levels by these three predictors taken together. In other words, we will conclude that the true correlation in the population is not zero.

These two kinds of significance tests (tests on slopes and tests on the multiple correlation) are presented in virtually all regression analyses. I have covered them in the order they were presented in the printout, but in general if the Analysis of Variance test on the relationship is not significant, it usually doesn't make much sense even to worry about the significance of individual predictors. Fortunately, for most of the regression problems we see, the overall relationship is significant and the real issue is the role of individual predictors.

11.5 Refining the Regression Equation

In Figure 11.1, we saw that Teach and Knowledge were significant predictors of Overall, but that Grade had little additional information to offer (the probability value for the slope relating Grade to Overall was .305). Since Grade does not add significant new information over and above Teach and Knowledge, there really is no particular reason to leave it in the equation. We might be better off to drop that predictor and simply use Teach and Knowledge as the only predictors.

The results of dropping Grade from the regression equation are shown in Figure 11.4. Here you can see that both Teach and Knowledge continue to be significant predictors (the *t* tests on both slopes are significant at $\alpha = .05$). You can also see that there is very little change in the multiple correlation. We do almost as well with the two predictors as we did with the three. (*R* has dropped from .863 to .860, which is certainly a minor change.) In fact when we look at the adjusted R^2, we see that it has remained exactly the same. Moreover, the

Figure 11.4   Regression Analysis Using Teach and Knowledge to Predict Overall

```
                                        Multiple correlation              Tests on
                                                                          slopes
DEP VAR: OVERALL   N:   50   MULTIPLE R: 0.860   SQUARED MULTIPLE R: 0.739
ADJUSTED SQUARED MULTIPLE R: 0.728    STANDARD ERROR OF ESTIMATE    0.320

VARIABLE   COEFFICIENT   STD ERROR   STD COEFF   TOLERANCE          T    P(2 TAIL)
            Intercept
CONSTANT      -1.298       0.477       0.000         .          -2.720     0.009
TEACH          0.710       0.101       0.616       0.723         7.021     0.000
KNOWLEDG       0.538       0.132       0.358       0.723         4.082     0.000
          Regression
          coefficients                                                 Test on
          (slopes)            ANALYSIS OF VARIANCE                     multiple
                                                                       correlation
SOURCE     SUM-OF-SQUARES         DF      MEAN-SQUARE      F-RATIO     P

REGRESSION      13.627            2         6.814          66.467      0.000
RESIDUAL         4.818           47         0.103
```

analysis of variance test on the significance of the relationship has an even larger *F*, suggesting that doing this well with two predictors is even more impressive than predicting slightly better with three predictors.

What we have just done in this example is to search for a regression equation (a model of the data) that best predicts the criterion variable. We did this by starting with three variables, seeing that one variable was not making a significant contribution, dropping that variable, and settling on an equation where the two remaining predictors play a significant role. There is a substantial literature on the topic of choosing an optimum regression equation. Many of the techniques are known as **stepwise procedures**. An introduction to this literature and additional references can be found in Howell (1992). The only point to be made here is that automatic computational procedures for identifying regression models can be seductive. They often produce a nice-looking model, but they also capitalize on chance differences in the data. This produces a model that fits the current data well but that might not fit a new set of data nearly as well. In trying to construct an optimal model, it is important to realize that what you know about the variables and the theoretical constructs in the field is far more important than the statistical vagaries of a set of data. You should treat stepwise regression with considerable caution.

Stepwise procedures
A set of rules for deriving a regression equation by adding or subtracting one variable at a time from the regression equation.

11.6 A Second Example: Height and Weight

In Section 9.6 we briefly considered a dataset on the height and weight of college students. Height and weight are variables that often are used as the classic example of correlation and regression, and we usually don't take such data seriously. These data, however, actually can teach us a good deal about concepts in regression; when we add gender as a variable, it makes an even better example. The data we are using were taken from data supplied with the Minitab program in a file named "Pulse." As I said in Chapter 9, these data were generated by students as a classroom exercise. Given people's attitudes toward weight in particular, you should treat the data with caution. If you weigh more than people in their sample, perhaps they "rounded" up or down in reporting their data. I have extracted the variables Height, Weight, and Gender from the dataset and presented them in Table 11.4. Here males are coded 1 and females are coded 2. (These data can also be found in Exercises 10.8 and 10.9.)

The results of the prediction of Weight on the basis of Height and Gender are given in Figure 11.5. You can see that all three variables are highly intercorrelated and that these correlations are all significant. From the analysis of variance portion of the table you can see that there is a significant relationship between Weight and the two predictors ($F = 86.678$, $p = .000$). The multiple correlation is .813, which is a substantial correlation, accounting for 66% of the variability in weight. Finally, we can see that our regression equation is

$$\text{Predicted Weight} = 3.691 \cdot \text{Height} - 14.700 \cdot \text{Gender} - 88.199$$

Table 11.4   Data on Gender, Height, and Weight for College Students

Gender	Height	Weight	Gender	Height	Weight	Gender	Height	Weight
1	70	150	1	66	135	2	70	125
1	67	140	1	71	170	2	68	116
1	72	180	1	70	157	2	69	145
1	75	190	1	70	130	2	69	150
1	68	145	1	75	185	2	67	150
1	69	150	1	74	190	2	68	125
1	71.5	164	1	71	155	2	66	130
1	71	140	1	69	170	2	65.5	120
1	72	142	1	70	155	2	66	130
1	69	136	1	72	215	2	62	121
1	67	123	1	67	150	2	62	130
1	68	155	1	69	145	2	63	118
1	66	140	1	73	155	2	67	125
1	72	145	1	73	155	2	65	135
1	73.5	160	1	71	150	2	66	125
1	73	190	1	68	155	2	65	118
1	69	155	1	69.5	150	2	65	122
1	73	165	1	73	180	2	65	115
1	72	150	1	75	160	2	64	102
1	74	190	1	66	135	2	67	115
1	72	195	1	69	160	2	69	150
1	71	138	1	66	130	2	68	110
1	74	160	1	73	155	2	63	116
1	72	155	1	68	150	2	62	108
1	70	153	1	74	148	2	63	95
1	67	145	1	73.5	155	2	64	125
1	71	170	2	61	140	2	68	133
1	72	175	2	66	120	2	62	110
1	69	175	2	68	130	2	61.75	108
1	73	170	2	68	138	2	62.75	112
1	74	180	2	63	121			

Figure 11.5   Prediction of Weight on the Basis of Height and Gender

```
PEARSON CORRELATION MATRIX

              WEIGHT       HEIGHT      GENDER

WEIGHT       1.000
HEIGHT       0.785        1.000                    ⌐ Intercorrelations
GENDER      -0.709       -0.714       1.000        ⌐

MATRIX OF PROBABILITIES

              WEIGHT       HEIGHT      GENDER

WEIGHT       0.000
HEIGHT       0.000        0.000
GENDER       0.000        0.000        0.000

NUMBER OF OBSERVATIONS:     92


DEP VAR: WEIGHT  N:   92  MULTIPLE R: 0.813  SQUARED MULTIPLE R: 0.661       Tests on
ADJUSTED SQUARED MULTIPLE R: 0.653    STANDARD ERROR OF ESTIMATE  13.981     predictors

VARIABLE     COEFFICIENT      STD ERROR     STD COEF    TOLERANCE       T    P(2 TAIL)
             ⌐ Intercept
CONSTANT        -88.199        43.777        0.000         .         -2.015    0.047
GENDER ⌐        -14.700         4.290       -0.302       0.490       -3.426    0.001
HEIGHT ⌐          3.691         0.572        0.569       0.490        6.450    0.000

        Regression
        coefficients                                                    Test on
        (slopes)              ANALYSIS OF VARIANCE                      multiple
                                                                       correlation
SOURCE         SUM-OF-SQUARES        DF        MEAN-SQUARE      F-RATIO      P

REGRESSION        33886.657          2          16943.328       86.670    0.000
RESIDUAL          17397.213         89            195.474
```

The intercept in our regression equation is meaningless, regardless of the fact that it is significant. Since we can not imagine an individual who is zero inches tall and neither male nor female (i.e., coded 0 for Gender), it is not useful to ask what his or her predicted weight would be. On the other hand, the intercept is a necessary part of the regression equation, so we don't completely ignore it.

The regression coefficients for Height and Gender are given in the table and are readily interpretable and informative. For people who are all the same gender (e.g., for all females), a difference of 1 inch in height is associated with a 3.691 difference in weight. Put slightly differently, if we had a large number of women for whom we knew their heights, our best guess is that the regression line relating weight to height would have a slope of 3.691. Similarly, if we had a large number of men, we would also expect that the line relating their weight to their heights would also have a slope of 3.691. This is what we mean by "holding gender constant." (Another phrase used in this context is "controlling for gender.")

The coefficient for Gender is -14.700. This means that if we hold height constant (i.e., select a large number of subjects who are all the same height), a difference of 1 unit in gender is associated with a difference of 14.7 pounds. But since males are coded 1 and females 2, this really means that if we go from males to females (with height held constant) our predicted weights will differ by 14.7 pounds. And to say it in yet a simpler way, *when we control for height,* women are 14.7 pounds lighter than men.

Let's explore this last idea just a bit further. Simple descriptive statistics will show us that the mean weight for males in our sample is 158.26 pounds, while the mean weight for females is 123.80 pounds. Thus women are, on average, 34.46 pounds lighter than men. But of course men are, on average, taller than women by about 5 inches, and some of the difference in weight is due to that height difference. Perhaps all of it? No! We have just seen that when we control for height there is a difference of 14.7 pounds. That is a difference in weight between men and women that cannot be explained on the basis of differences in height.

In the exercises in Chapter 10 I asked you to use a regression equation to estimate your own weight using the appropriate regression equation (the one derived from subjects of your own sex). In those cases we were artificially holding gender constant by deriving separate regression equations for males and females. But now we can accomplish the same thing by using one equation, but one that includes gender as a predictor. I'll hold off asking you to do this for your own height and weight until we get to the exercises, but let's take an example of a male who happens to be 68 inches tall. We can make a prediction by inserting the appropriate values for Gender (1) and Height (68) into the equation derived above:

$$\text{Predicted weight} = 3.691 \cdot \text{Height} - 14.7 \cdot \text{Gender} - 88.199$$
$$= 3.691 \cdot 68 - 14.7 \cdot 1 - 88.199$$
$$= 148.089$$

For this person we would expect a weight of about 148.1 pounds. Suppose this person stepped on the scales today and weighed 145.5. Then our residual would be

$$\text{Residual} = \text{Actual weight} - \text{Predicted weight}$$
$$= 145.5 - 148.1 = -2.6$$

Our prediction was too high by about 2.5 pounds, which is a pretty good prediction.

11.7 A Third Example: Psychological Symptoms in Cancer Patients

There can be no doubt that a diagnosis of cancer is a disturbing event, and many, though not all, cancer patients show elevated levels of psychological symptoms. If we could understand the variables associated with psychological distress, perhaps we could implement intervention programs to prevent that distress. That is the subject of this example.

Malcarne, Compas, Epping, and Howell (in press) examined 126 cancer patients soon after they were diagnosed with cancer and at a four-month follow-up. At the initial interviews (Time 1) they collected data on the patients' current levels of distress (Distress1), the degree to which they attributed the blame for the cancer to the type of person they are (BlamPer), and the degree to which they attributed the cancer to the kind of behaviors in which they had engaged (e.g., smoking) (BlamBeh). At the four-month follow-up (Time 2) they again collected data on the levels of psychological distress that the patients reported. (They also collected data on a number of other variables, which do not concern us here.)

A major purpose of this study was to test the hypothesis that psychological distress at follow-up (Distress2) was related to the degree to which the subjects blamed cancer on the type of person they are. It was hypothesized that those who blame themselves (rather than their actions) will show greater distress, in part because we do not easily change the kind of person we are, and therefore we have little control over the course, or the recurrence, of the disease.

If we want to predict distress at follow-up, one of the most important predictors is likely to be the level of distress at the initial interview. It makes sense to include this Time 1 distress measure (Distress1) in the prediction along with the initial level of personal blame (BlamPer). The dependent variable is distress at follow-up (Distress2). Because only 80 subjects completed measures at follow-up, the resulting analysis is based on a sample size of 80. (You might ask yourself what might be wrong with drawing conclusions on only the 80 subjects, out of an initial 126, who participated after four months of treatment.) The results of this analysis are shown in Figure 11.6. The analysis was carried out using Minitab.

The first line in Figure 11.6 tells Minitab to regress (predict) Distress2 on two variables, Distress1 and BlamPer. Below this you can see the regression equation, with the intercept and the two slope coefficients. Immediately below that are the coefficients written out in a different form. Here the word "Constant" is used in place of the word "Intercept," and the two slopes are identified by means of the variable names to which they apply. Notice that we have a t test on all three coefficients and that the three t values are all significantly different from 0.00. This tells us that higher distress at Time 2 is associated with higher distress at Time 1 and with a greater tendency for patients to blame the type of person they are for the cancer. The intercept is also significantly different from 0.00, but this is not of interest. As always the intercept represents the predicted value of the dependent variable (Distress2) when each of the others is equal to 0. Because it is difficult to imagine a person with absolutely no distress and no personal blame at Time 1, we really don't care about the value of the intercept.

In the next portion of the table we see that the squared multiple correlation is .434 (accounting for 43.4% of the variation in Distress2) and that R^2 adjusted for the number of subjects and the number of variables is .418.

Figure 11.6   Distress at Follow-up as a Function of Distress and Self-Blame at Diagnosis

```
     MTB > Regress 'Distress2' 2 'Distress1' 'BlamPer'.

     The regression equation is
     Distress2 = 14.2 + 0.642 Distress1 + 2.60 BlamPer
```
Intercept
```
     Predictor        Coef       Stdev    t-ratio          p
     Constant        14.209      5.716       2.49      0.015
     Distress1       0.6424      0.1024      6.27      0.000
     BlamPer         2.5980      0.8959      2.90      0.005
```
Regression coefficients (slope)
```
     s = 7.610     R-sq = 43.4%     R-sq(adj) = 41.8%
```
                                         Squared multiple correlation
```
     Analysis of Variance

     SOURCE          DF          SS           MS          F           p

     Regression       2        3157.0       1578.5      27.25      0.000
     Error           71        4112.0         57.9
     Total           73        7269.0
```
                                                    Test on
```
     SOURCE          DF       SEQ SS                 multiple correlation
     Distress1        1       2669.9
     BlamPer          1        487.1


     Unusual Observations
     Obs.    Distress1   Distress2        Fit     Stdev.Fit      Residual     St.Resid
      31        54.0      33.000       51.496       1.032       -18.496       -2.45R
      51        57.0      64.000       63.816       3.158         0.184        0.03 X
      52        57.0      71.000       53.424       1.055        17.576        2.33R
      59        63.0      39.000       57.278       1.333       -18.278       -2.44R
      73        80.0      69.000       68.199       2.784         0.801        0.11 X
      74        80.0      80.000       73.395       2.775         6.605        0.93 X

     R denotes an obs. with a large st. resid.
     X denotes an obs. whose X value gives it large influence.

     MTB >
```

The Analysis of Variance table represents a test on the null hypothesis that the true multiple correlation coefficient in the population is 0. Because we have a large value of F and a very small value of p, we can reject that hypothesis in favor of the hypothesis that there is a true correlation between Distress2 and the combination of Distress1 and BlamPer.

In the section titled "Unusual Observations" are six cases that Minitab has singled out as worthy of note. These are cases either where the regression equation does a particularly bad job of predicting Distress2 or cases that deviate sufficiently from the rest of the subjects for us to worry that they could have an undue influence on the outcome of the regression. We might want to inspect these cases closely to see if there is anything unusual about them that can, perhaps, be attributed to some other variable or to erroneous data points.

You might be tempted to ask if perhaps additional predictors might improve our regression solution. For example, we also have data on the degree to which patients blame their cancer on their own behaviors (BlamBeh), and we might want to add that predictor to the ones we have already used. Although I strongly caution against throwing in additional variables just because you have them—your set of predictors should make some sort of logical sense on *a priori* grounds—I have added BlamBeh to the regression to illustrate what happens. Those results are presented in Figure 11.7.

I will not discuss this figure in detail because it is essentially the same as the previous figure. I will point out the magnitude of R^2 and the probability value associated with the test on BlamPer. Notice that R^2 is virtually unchanged by the addition of BlamBeh, going from .434 to .435. This is our first indication that BlamBeh is not contributing noticeably to the prediction of Distress2 *over and above the predictors that were already in the equation.* This does not mean that BlamBeh is not related to Distress2, but only that it has nothing to add beyond what we can tell from the other two predictors.

Notice also that the probability value associated with the BlamPer predictor (and the associated regression coefficient) has changed somewhat. This says nothing more than that the contribution of BlamPer is somewhat, though not much, reduced when a similar variable (BlamBeh) is added to the model.

Figure 11.7   Prediction of Distress2 as a Function of Distress1, BlamBeh, and BlamPer

```
MTB > Regress 'Distress2' 3 'Distress1' 'BlamBeh' 'BlamPer'.

The regression equation is
Distress2 = 14.1 + 0.640 Distress1 + 0.272 BlamBeh + 2.45 BlamPer

Predictor          Coef        Stdev     t-ratio          p
Constant         14.052        5.782        2.43      0.018
Distress1        0.6399       0.1035        6.18      0.000
BlamBeh          0.2720       0.9900        0.27      0.784  ←——— Test on BlamBeh
BlamPer           2.451        1.048        2.34      0.022

s = 7.660    R-sq = 43.5%    R-sq(adj) = 41.1%

Analysis of Variance

SOURCE           DF          SS           MS          F          p

Regression        3       3161.4       1053.8      17.96      0.000
Error            70       4107.6         58.7
Total            73       7269.0

SOURCE           DF       SEQ SS
Distress1         1       2669.9
BlamBeh           1        170.7
BlamPer           1        320.8

Unusual Observations
Obs.    Distress1   Distress2        Fit    Stdev.Fit    Residual     St.Resid
 31        54.0      33.000       51.599       1.104     -18.599      -2.45R
 51        57.0      64.000       63.051       4.226       0.946       0.15 X
 52        57.0      71.000       53.518       1.117      17.482       2.31R
 59        63.0      39.000       57.357       1.372     -18.357      -2.44R

R denotes an obs. with a large st. resid.
X denotes an obs. whose X value gives it large influence.

MTB >
```

This is quite common and reflects the fact that BlamPer and BlamBeh are correlated ($r = .521$) and, to some extent, account for overlapping portions of the variability in Distress2. To put this in terms of an everyday example, consider how much you can tell me that I don't already know about an English class you are taking. But if I first ask your roommate about that class, even if she is not taking it, the amount you can tell me *that was not covered by what she said* is reduced. That is what is happening here, though in a small way.

11.8 Summary

In this chapter we examined the prediction of one criterion variable on the basis of two or more predictor variables. We considered the interpretation of the regression equation and saw that the multiple correlation coefficient is interpreted in the same way we interpreted the simple correlation coefficient in Chapter 9. We looked at how we might plot such data and how the residuals can be interpreted with respect to such plots and investigated two forms of hypothesis testing. The important thing about almost everything in this chapter is that it is just a logical extension of the material in the preceding two chapters.

Some important terms in this chapter are:

- Regression coefficients

- Multiple correlation coefficient (R)

- Multicollinearity

- Residuals

- Regression surface

- Stepwise procedures

11.9 Exercises

11.1 A psychologist studying perceived "quality of life" in a large number of cities ($N = 150$) came up with the following equation using mean temperature (Temp), median income in $1000 (Income), per capita expenditure on social services (SocSer), and population density (Popul) as predictors.

$$\hat{Y} = 5.37 - 0.01\text{Temp} + 0.05\text{Income} + 0.003\text{SocSer} - 0.01\text{Popul}$$

(a) Interpret the regression equation in terms of the coefficients.

(b) Assume a city has a mean temperature of 55 degrees, a median income of $12,000, spends $500 per capita on social services, and has a population density of 200 people per block. What is its predicted quality of life score?

(c) What would we predict in a different city that is identical in every way except that it spends $100 per capita on social services?

11.2 A large corporation is interested in predicting a measure of job satisfaction among its employees. Data have been collected on 75 employees who each supplied information on job satisfaction, level of responsibility, number of people supervised, rating of working environment, and years of service. The following is an abbreviated printout from BMDP1R, one of the BMDP statistical programs. (You will not understand parts of the printout, but that will be true of other printouts you will see, so I left them in for realism.)

```
DEPENDENT VARIABLE  .........  1 SATISF
TOLERANCE  ...................  0.0100
ALL DATA CONSIDERED AS A SINGLE GROUP
MULTIPLE R                     0.6974
MULTIPLE R-SQUARE              0.4864

ANALYSIS OF VARIANCE
                   SUM OF SQUARES    DF  MEAN SQUARE   F RATIO    P(TAIL)
     REGRESSION           40.078      4       10.020    16.57      .000
     RESIDUAL             42.322     70        0.605

                                       STD. REG
   VARIABLE      COEFFICIENT STD. ERROR   COEFF      T     P(2 TAIL)  TOLERANCE
INTERCEPT          1.66926
RESPON             0.60516     0.428     0.624    1.414    0.188     0.263940
NUMSUP            -0.33399     0.537    -0.311   -0.622    0.548     0.205947
ENVIR              0.48552     0.160     0.514    3.034    0.109     0.600084
YRS                0.07023     0.013     0.263    5.402    0.000     0.919492
```

(a) Is there reason to believe that we are predicting at better than chance levels?

(b) Write out the regression equation for the values given in this table.

(c) What is the multiple correlation coefficient?

11.3 In Exercise 11.2 which variables make a significant contribution to the prediction of job satisfaction as judged by the test on their slopes?

11.4 In Exercise 11.2 the column headed "Tolerance" gives you 1 minus the squared multiple correlation of that predictor with all other predictors. What can you now say about the relationships among the set of predictors?

11.5 On the basis of your answer to Exercise 11.4 can you speculate on one of the reasons why Years of Service might be an important predictor of Satisfaction, while Responsibility is not?

11.6 Substitute your own height and gender in the regression equation we computed in Section 11.6 and predict your weight. (Feel free to lie if using your actual data makes you feel uncomfortable.) How do your actual and predicted weights compare?

11.7 Your predictions of your weight using the multiple regression equation that involves both gender and height is different from the prediction you made in Chapter 10, when you used an equation built solely on people of your own sex. Can you speculate why there was a difference and under what very limited set of conditions the two predictions would be equal? (*Hint:* Compare the slopes for height in the two cases.)

11.8 The state of Vermont is divided into 10 Health Planning Districts, which correspond roughly to counties. The following data represent the percentage of live births of babies weighing under 2500 grams (Y), the fertility rate for females 17 years of age or younger (X_1), total high-risk fertility rate for females younger than 17 or older than 35 years of age (X_2), percentage of mothers with fewer than 12 years of education (X_3), percentage of births to unmarried mothers (X_4), and percentage of mothers not seeking medical care until the third trimester (X_5). (There are too few observations for a meaningful analysis, so do not put faith in the results.) The data follow.

Y	X_1	X_2	X_3	X_4	X_5
6.1	22.8	43.0	23.8	9.2	6
7.1	28.7	55.3	24.8	12.0	10
7.4	29.7	48.5	23.9	10.4	5
6.3	18.3	38.8	16.6	9.8	4
6.5	21.1	46.2	19.6	9.8	5
5.7	21.2	39.9	21.4	7.7	6
6.6	22.2	43.1	20.7	10.9	7
8.1	22.3	48.5	21.8	9.5	5
6.3	21.8	40.0	20.6	11.6	7
6.9	31.2	56.7	25.2	11.6	9

Use any regression program to compute the multiple regression predicting the percentage of births under 2500 grams.

11.9 Using the output from Exercise 11.8, interpret the results as if they were significant.

11.10 Mireault (1990) studied students who had lost a parent to death during their childhood, students who came from divorced families, and students who came from intact families. Among other things she collected data on their current perceived sense of vulnerability to future loss (PVLoss), their level of social support (SuppTotl), and the age at which they lost a parent during childhood (AgeAtLos). The accompanying data disk contains these data. Use the Mireault.dat dataset and any available regression program to evaluate a model that says that depression (DepressT) is a function of these three variables. (Since only subjects in Group 1 lost a parent, you will need to restrict your analysis to those cases.)

11.11 Interpret the results of the analysis in Exercise 11.10.

12

HYPOTHESIS TESTS APPLIED TO MEANS: ONE SAMPLE

In Chapter 8 we considered the general logic of hypothesis testing and ignored the specific calculations involved. In Chapters 9, 10, and 11 we looked at measures that indicate the relationship between variables and considered hypothesis testing as a way of asking whether there is a reliable nonzero correlation between variables in the population (not just in our sample) and whether the regression coefficients (slopes and intercepts) are reliably different from zero. In this chapter we will begin concentrating on hypothesis tests about means. In particular we will focus on testing a null hypothesis about the value of a population mean.

We will start with an example referred to in Chapter 8. There we considered the case in which we know that Total Behavior Problem scores on the Youth Self Report form are nearly normally distributed with a mean of 50 and a standard deviation of 10. In Chapter 8 we dealt with that example in a general way. Here we will start over and deal with it more precisely.

Because there is evidence in the psychological literature that stress in a child's life may lead to subsequent behavior problems, it might be expected that a sample of children who have been subjected to an unusual amount of stress would show an unusually high level of behavior problems. On the other hand, such children could feel that they have enough going on in their lives without complicating matters further, in which case they might show an unusually low number of behavior problems. That latter possibility does not seem terribly likely, but it is worth guarding against. This means we are interested **Experimental** in examining a two-tailed **experimental hypothesis** that the number of behavior problems among stressed children is different from the number of behavior problems among children in general. We can't test the experimental hypothesis directly, however. Instead we will test the null hypothesis (H_0) that the scores of stressed children came from a population of scores with the *same* mean as the population of scores of normal children. More specifically, we want to decide between

Experimental hypothesis
Another name for the research hypothesis.

$$H_0 : \mu = 50$$

and

$$H_1 : \mu \neq 50$$

I have chosen the two-tailed alternative form of H_1 because I want to reject H_0 if $\mu < 50$ *or* if $\mu > 50$.

To investigate this problem I drew a sample of five children, each of whom is under a high level of stress of one kind or another. I asked the children to complete the Youth Self Report form and obtained the following scores:

48   62   53   66   51

This sample of five observations has a mean of 56.0 and a standard deviation of 7.65. Thus the five children have an average score six points above the mean of the population of normal children. But because this result is based on a sample of only five children, it is quite conceivable that the deviation from 50 could be due to chance (or, phrased differently, due to sampling error). Even if $H_0 : \mu = 50$ is true, we certainly would not expect our sample mean to be exactly 50.000. We probably wouldn't be particularly surprised to find a mean of 49 or 51. But what about 56? Is that surprisingly large? If so, perhaps we should not be willing to continue to entertain the idea that $\mu = 50.0$. Before we can draw any conclusions, however, we will have to know what values we reasonably could expect sample means to have if we really sampled from a population of normal children.

12.1 Sampling Distribution of the Mean

As you should recall from Chapter 8, the sampling distribution of a statistic is the distribution of values we would expect to obtain for that statistic if we drew an infinite number of samples from the population in question and calculated the statistic on each sample. Because we are concerned here with sample *means*, we need to know something about the **sampling distribution of the mean**. Fortunately all the important information about the sampling distribution of the mean can be summed up in one very important theorem: the **Central Limit Theorem**. The Central Limit Theorem is a factual statement about the distribution of means. It states:

Sampling distribution of the mean
The distribution of sample means over repeated sampling from one population.

> Given a population with mean μ and variance σ^2, the sampling distribution of the mean (the distribution of sample means) will have a mean equal to μ (i.e., $\mu_{\bar{x}} = \mu$) and a variance ($\sigma^2_{\bar{x}}$) equal to σ^2/N (and standard deviation, $\sigma_{\bar{x}}$, equal to $\sigma/\sqrt{N}$). The distribution will approach the normal distribution as N, the *sample size*, increases.

Central Limit Theorem
The theorem that specifies the nature of the sampling distribution of the mean.

The Central Limit Theorem is one of the most important theorems in statistics, because it not only tells us what the mean and the variance of the sampling distribution of the sample mean must be for any given sample size but also states that as N increases, the shape of this sampling distribution approaches normal, *whatever* the shape of the parent population. The importance of these facts will become clear shortly.

The rate at which the sampling distribution of the mean approaches normal is a function of the shape of the parent population. If the population itself is normal, the sampling distribution of the mean will be exactly normal regardless of N. If the population is symmetric but nonnormal, the sampling distribution of the mean will be nearly normal even for quite small sample sizes, especially if the population is unimodal. If the population is markedly skewed, we may require sample sizes of 30 or more before the means closely approximate a normal distribution.

To illustrate the Central Limit Theorem we will leave the behavior problem example temporarily and consider a more general example. Suppose we take an infinitely large population of random numbers evenly distributed between 0 and 100. This population will have what is called a **rectangular distribution**—every value between 0 and 100 being equally likely. The distribution of this population is shown in Figure 12.1, where it is evident why we call this distribution "rectangular." In this population the mean (μ) is 50, the standard deviation (σ) is 28.87, and the variance (σ^2) is 833.33.

Rectangular distribution
A distribution in which all outcomes are equally likely.

Now suppose we draw with replacement 5000 samples of size 5 (i.e., $N = 5$) from this population and plot the resulting sample means. Such sampling can be easily accomplished with the aid of a computer—the results of just such a procedure are presented in Figure 12.2(a). From Figure 12.2(a) it is apparent that the distribution of means, although not exactly normally distributed, at least peaks in the center and trails off toward the extremes. If you were to go to the effort of calculating the mean and the variance of this distribution, you

Figure 12.1

**Rectangular
Distribution with
$\mu = 50$ and $\sigma =$
28.87**

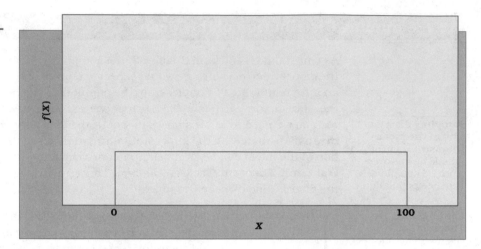

Figure 12.2

**Computer-
Generated
Sampling
Distribution
of the Mean**

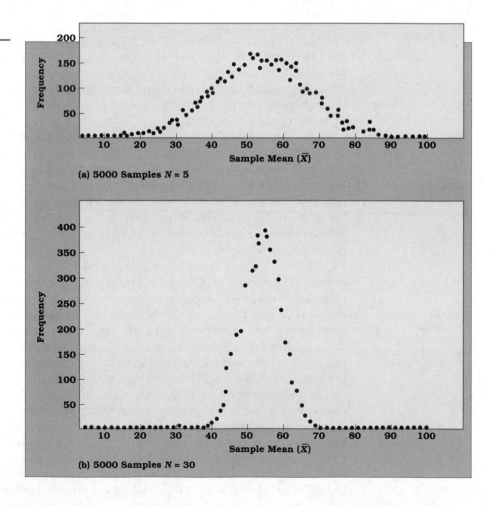

(a) 5000 Samples $N = 5$

(b) 5000 Samples $N = 30$

would find that they are extremely close to $\mu = 50$ and $\sigma^2_{\bar{X}} = \sigma^2/N = 833.33/5 = 166.67$. (Remember that μ and $\sigma^2_{\bar{X}}$ refer to the mean and the variance of the distribution of means.)

Now suppose we repeat the entire procedure, only this time we draw 5000 samples, each with 30 observations. Again, I have actually done this; the results are plotted in Figure 12.2(b). There you can see that, just as the Central Limit Theorem predicted, the distribution is approximately normal, the mean (μ) is again 50, and the variance has been reduced to $833.33/30 = 27.78$.

12.2 Testing Hypotheses About Means When σ Is Known

From the Central Limit Theorem we know all the important characteristics of the sampling distribution of the mean (its shape, its mean, and its standard deviation). On the basis of this information we are in a position to begin testing hypotheses about means. For the sake of continuity it might be well to go back to something we discussed with respect to the normal distribution. In Chapter 8 we saw that we could test a hypothesis about the population from which a single score (in that case a finger-tapping score) was drawn by calculating

$$z = \frac{X - \mu}{\sigma}$$

and then obtaining the probability of a value of z as low as or lower than the one obtained by using of the tables of the standard normal distribution. Thus we ran a one-tailed test on the hypothesis that the tapping rate (70) of a single individual was drawn at random from a normally distributed population of healthy tapping rates with a mean of 100 and a standard deviation of 20. We did this by calculating

$$z = \frac{X - \mu}{\sigma} = \frac{70 - 100}{20} = \frac{-30}{20} = -1.5$$

and then using Table D.10 in the Appendices to find the area below $z = -1.5$. This value is .0668. Thus approximately 7% of the time we would expect a score this low or lower if we were sampling from a healthy population. Because this probability was greater than our selected significance level of $\alpha = .05$, we would not reject the null hypothesis. Instead we would conclude that we have insufficient evidence to diagnose the person's response rate as abnormal. The tapping rate for the person we examined was not an unusual rate for healthy subjects. (But what would we have concluded had the probability been calculated as .004?) Although in this example we were testing a hypothesis about a single observation, exactly the same logic applies to testing hypotheses about sample means.

In most situations in which we test a hypothesis about a population mean we don't have any knowledge about the variance of that population. (This is the primary reason that we have t tests, which are the main focus of this chapter.) In a limited number of situations, however, we do know σ for some reason, and a discussion of testing a hypothesis when σ is known provides a good transition from what we already know about the normal distribution to what we want to know about t tests. The example of behavior problems is useful for this purpose because we know both the mean and the standard deviation for the population of Total Behavior Problem scores ($\mu = 50$ and $\sigma = 10$). We also know that our random sample of children who were under stress had a mean score of 56.0, and we want to test the null hypothesis that these five children are a random sample from a population of normal children (i.e., normal with respect to their general level of behavior problems). In other words, we want to test H_0: $\mu = 50$ against the alternative $H_1: \mu \neq 50$.

Because we know the mean and standard deviation of the population of general behavior problem scores, we can use the Central Limit Theorem to obtain the sampling distribution of the mean when the null hypothesis is true. The Central Limit Theorem states that if we obtain the sampling distribution of the mean from this population, it will have a mean of 50, a variance of $\sigma^2/N = 10^2/5 = 100/5 = 20$, and a standard deviation (usually referred to as the **standard error**) of $\sigma/\sqrt{N} = 4.47$. This distribution is diagrammed in Figure 12.3. The arrow in the figure points to the location of the sample mean.

A short digression is in order here about the standard error, because this is a concept that runs throughout statistics. The standard deviation of any sampling distribution is normally referred to as the standard error of that distribution. Thus the standard deviation of means is called the standard error of the mean (symbolized by $\sigma_{\bar{x}}$), whereas the standard deviation of differences between means, which will be discussed in Chapter 14, is called the standard error of differences between means and is symbolized $\sigma_{\bar{x}_1 - \bar{x}_2}$. Standard errors are critically important because they tell us how variable statistics such as the

Standard error
The standard deviation of a sampling distribution.

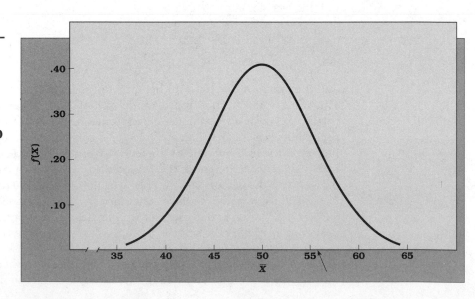

Figure 12.3

Sampling Distribution of the Mean for Samples of $N = 5$ Drawn from a Population with $\mu = 50$ and $\sigma = 10$

mean are from one sample to another. If the standard error is large, that means that whatever sample mean you happened to find, someone else doing the same study may find quite a different one. On the other hand, if the standard error is small, another person is likely to find a value fairly similar to yours. Minor changes in terminology such as calling a standard deviation a standard error really are not designed to confuse students. They just have that effect.

Because we know that the sampling distribution is normally distributed with a mean of 50 and a standard error of 4.47, we can find areas under the distribution by referring to tables of the standard normal distribution. For example, because two standard errors is 2(4.47) = 8.94, the area to the right of $\overline{X} = 58.94$ is simply the area under the normal distribution greater than two standard deviations above the mean.

For our particular situation we first need to know the probability of a sample mean greater than or equal to 56; thus we need to find the area above $\overline{X} = 56$. We can calculate this the same way we did with individual observations, with only a minor change in the formula for z.

$$z = \frac{X - \mu}{\sigma_X}$$

becomes

$$z = \frac{\overline{X} - \mu}{\sigma_{\overline{X}}}$$

which can also be written as

$$z = \frac{\overline{X} - \mu}{\dfrac{\sigma}{\sqrt{N}}}$$

For our data this becomes

$$z = \frac{56 - 50}{4.47} = \frac{6}{4.47} = 1.34$$

You will note that the equation for z used here has the same form as our earlier formula for z. The only differences are that X has been replaced by $\overline{X}$ and σ has been replaced by $\sigma_{\overline{X}}$. These differences occur because we now are dealing with a distribution of means; thus the data points are now means, and the standard deviation in question is now the standard error of the mean (the standard deviation of means). The formula for z continues to represent (1) a point on a distribution, minus (2) the mean of that distribution, all divided by (3) the standard deviation of the distribution. Now rather than being concerned specifically with the distribution of $\overline{X}$, we have reexpressed the sample mean in terms of z scores and can now answer the question with regard to the standard normal distribution.

From Table D.10 in the Appendices we find that the probability of a z as large as 1.34 is .0901. Because we want a two-tailed test of H_0 we need to double the probability to obtain the probability of a deviation as large as 1.34 standard errors in *either direction* from the mean. This is $2(.0901) = .1802$. Thus with a two-tailed test (that stressed children have a mean behavior problem score that is different *in either direction* from that of normal children) at the .05 level of significance we would not reject H_0 because the obtained probability is greater than .05. We would conclude that we have insufficient evidence in our small sample of five children to conclude that stressed children show more or fewer behavior problems than other children.

The test of one sample mean against a known population mean, which we have just performed, is based on the assumption that the sample means are normally distributed, or at least that the distribution is sufficiently normal that we will be only negligibly in error when we refer to the tables of the standard normal distribution. Many textbooks state that we assume we are sampling from a normal population (i.e., behavior problem scores themselves are normally distributed), but this is not strictly necessary in practical terms. All that is necessary to assume is that the sampling distribution of the mean (Figure 12.3) is normal. This assumption can be satisfied in two ways: if either (1) the population from which we sample is normal or (2) the sample size is sufficiently large to produce at least approximate normality by way of the Central Limit Theorem. This is one of the great benefits of the Central Limit Theorem: it allows us to test hypotheses even if the parent population is not normal, provided only that N is sufficiently large.

12.3 Testing a Sample Mean When σ Is Unknown (The One-Sample Test)

The previous example was chosen deliberately from among a fairly limited number of situations in which the population standard deviation (σ) is known. In the general case, we rarely know the value of σ and usually will have to estimate it by way of the *sample* standard deviation (s). When we replace σ with s in the formula, however, the nature of the test changes. We can no longer declare the answer to be a z score and evaluate it with reference to tables of z. Instead we denote the answer as t and evaluate it with respect to tables of t, which are somewhat different. The reasoning behind the switch from z to t is really rather simple, although most introductory texts tend to ignore it. The basic problem that requires this change to t is related to the sampling distribution of the sample variance.

The Sampling Distribution of s^2

Because the t test uses s^2 as an estimate of σ^2, it is important that we first look at the sampling distribution of s^2. This sampling distribution gives us some insight into the problems we are going to encounter. You saw in Chapter 6 that s^2 is an *unbiased* estimate of σ^2, meaning that with repeated sampling the av-

Figure 12.4

Sampling Distribution of s^2 from a Normally Distributed Population with $\mu = 50$, $\sigma^2 = 138.89$, and $N = 5$

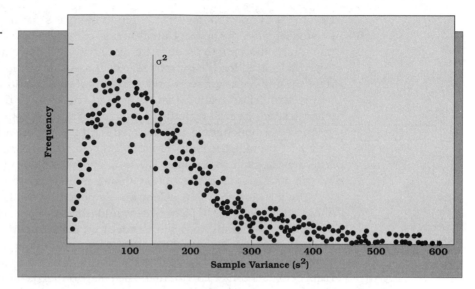

erage value of s^2 will equal σ^2. Although an unbiased estimator is nice, it is not everything. The problem is that the shape of the sampling distribution of s^2 is quite positively skewed, especially for small sample sizes. An example of a computer-generated sampling distribution of s^2 (where $\sigma^2 = 138.89$) is shown in Figure 12.4. Because of the skewness of this distribution, an individual value of s^2 is more likely to underestimate σ^2 than to overestimate it, especially for small samples. (s^2 remains unbiased because when it overestimates σ^2 it does so to such an extent as to balance off the more numerous but less drastic underestimates.) Can you see what the problem is going to be if we just take our sample estimate (s^2) and substitute it for the unknown σ^2 and pretend that nothing has changed? As a result of the skewness of the sampling distribution of the variance, the resulting value of t is likely to be larger than the value of z we would have obtained had σ been known, because any one sample variance (s^2) has a better than 50:50 chance of underestimating the population variance (σ^2).

The t Statistic

We will take the formula that we just developed for z,

$$z = \frac{\overline{X} - \mu}{\sigma_{\overline{X}}} = \frac{\overline{X} - \mu}{\dfrac{\sigma}{\sqrt{N}}} = \frac{\overline{X} - \mu}{\sqrt{\dfrac{\sigma^2}{N}}}$$

and substitute s^2 to give

$$t = \frac{\overline{X} - \mu}{s_{\overline{X}}} = \frac{\overline{X} - \mu}{\dfrac{s}{\sqrt{N}}} = \frac{\overline{X} - \mu}{\sqrt{\dfrac{s^2}{N}}}$$

Because we know that for any particular sample s^2 is more likely than not to be smaller than the appropriate value of σ^2, we can see that the t formula is more likely than not to produce a larger answer than we would have obtained if we had solved for t using σ^2 itself. As a result it would not really be fair to treat the answer as a z score and use the table of z. To do so would give us too many "significant" results, that is, we would make more than 5% Type I errors when testing the null hypothesis at significance level $\alpha = .05$. (For example, when we were calculating z, we rejected H_0 at the .05 level of significance whenever z fell outside the limits of ± 1.96. If we create a situation in which H_0 is true, repeatedly draw samples of $N = 5$, use s^2 in place of σ^2, and calculate t, we will obtain a value of ± 1.96 or greater more than about 10% of the time.)

The solution to this problem was supplied by William Gossett. Gossett showed that using s^2 in place of σ^2 would lead to a particular sampling distribution, now generally known as **Student's t distribution**.[1] As a result of Gossett's work, all we have to do is stick in our s^2, denote the answer as t, and evaluate t with respect to its own distribution, much as we evaluated z with respect to the normal distribution. The t distribution is tabled in Table D.6, and examples of the actual distribution of t for various sample sizes are shown graphically in Figure 12.5.

As you can see from Figure 12.5, the distribution of t varies as a function of the **degrees of freedom (df)**, which for the moment we will define as one less than the number of observations in the sample. Because the skewness of the sampling distribution of s^2 disappears as the number of degrees of freedom increases, the tendency for s to underestimate σ will also disappear. Thus for

Student's t distribution
The sampling distribution of the t statistic.

Degrees of freedom (df)
The number of independent pieces of information remaining after estimation of one or more parameters.

---

[1] It is called "Student's t" because Gossett worked for the Guinness Brewing Company, which would not let him publish his results under his own name. He published under the pseudonym of "Student," hence our present-day reference to Student's t.   •

Figure 12.5

t Distribution for 1, 30, and ∞ Degrees of Freedom

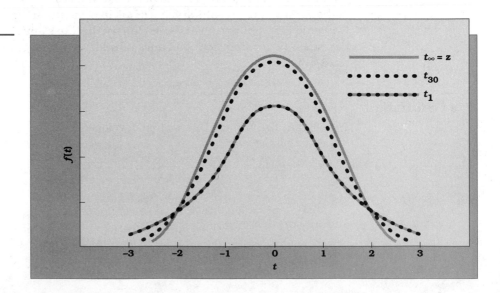

an infinitely large number of degrees of freedom t will become normally distributed and equivalent to z.

Degrees of Freedom

I have mentioned that the t distribution is a function of its degrees of freedom. For the one-sample case, $df = N - 1$; the one degree of freedom is lost because we use the sample mean in calculating s^2. To be more precise, we obtain the variance (s^2) by calculating the deviations of the observations from their own mean $(X - \bar{X})$, rather than from the population mean $(X - \mu)$. Because the sum of the deviations about the mean, $\Sigma(X - \bar{X})$, always equals 0, only $N - 1$ of the deviations are free to vary (the Nth is determined if the sum of the deviations is to be zero). For an illustration of this point consider the case of five scores whose mean is 10. Four of these scores can be anything you want (e.g., 18, 18, 16, 2), but the fifth score cannot be chosen freely. Here it must be -4 if the mean is going to be 10. In other words, there are only four free numbers in that set of five scores once the mean has been determined; therefore, we have four degrees of freedom. This is the reason the formula for s^2 (defined in Chapter 5) used $N - 1$ in the denominator. Because s^2 is based on $N - 1$ df, we have $N - 1$ degrees of freedom for t.

Example of the Use of t : Do Children Always Say What They Feel?

On several occasions throughout this book I have referred to studies of children and adults under stressful situations. Often we find that stress produces negative reactions in the form of depression, anxiety, behavior problems, and so on. But in an ongoing study of the families of cancer patients, Compas and others have observed that young children do not report an unusual number of symptoms of depression or anxiety. If fact they even look slightly better than average. Is it really true that young children somehow escape the negative consequences of this kind of family stressor? Can you think of an alternative hypothesis that might explain these results?

One of the commonly used measures of anxiety in children is called the Children's Manifest Anxiety Scale (CMAS) (Reynolds and Richmond, 1978). Nine items on this scale form what is often called the "Lie Scale." These items are intended to identify children who seem to be giving socially desirable responses rather than answering honestly. (Calling it a "lie" scale is not really being fair to the children; they are just trying to tell you what they think you want to hear.) Could it be that young children under stress have low anxiety scores not because they have very little anxiety, but because the anxiety is masked by an attempt to give socially appropriate answers? One way of addressing this question is to ask if these children have unusually high scores on the Lie Scale. If so, it would be easier to defend the argument that children are just not telling us about their anxiety, not that they don't have any.

Compas et al. (unpublished) collected data on 36 children from families in which one parent had recently been diagnosed with cancer. Each child completed the CMAS, and their Lie Scale scores, among others, were computed. For this group of children the mean Lie Scale score was 4.39, with a standard deviation of 2.61. Reynolds and Richmond report a population mean for elementary school children of 3.87, but from their data it is not possible to determine the population variance for only this age range of children. Therefore, we are required to estimate the variance from the sample variance and use the t test.

We want to test the null hypothesis that the Lie Scale scores are a random sample from a population with a mean (μ) of 3.87. Therefore,

$$H_0: \mu = 3.87$$

$$H_1: \mu \neq 3.87$$

We will use a two-tailed test and work at the 5% level of significance.

From the previous discussion we have

$$t = \frac{\bar{X} - \mu}{s_{\bar{X}}} = \frac{\bar{X} - \mu}{\dfrac{s}{\sqrt{N}}}$$

Notice that the numerator of the formula for t represents the distance between the sample mean and the population mean given by H_0 and the denominator represents an estimate of the standard deviation of the distribution of sample means. This is the same thing that we had with z, except that the sample variance (or standard deviation) has been substituted for the population variance (or standard deviation). For our data we have

$$t = \frac{\bar{X} - \mu}{\dfrac{s}{\sqrt{N}}} = \frac{4.39 - 3.87}{\dfrac{2.61}{\sqrt{36}}} = \frac{0.52}{0.435} = 1.20$$

A t value of 1.20 in and of itself is not particularly meaningful unless we can evaluate it against the sampling distribution of t. For this purpose the critical values of t are presented in Table D.6, a portion of which is shown in Table 12.1. This table differs in form from the table of the normal distribution (z) because, instead of giving the area above and below each specific value of t, which would require too much space, the table gives those values of t that cut off particular critical areas, for example, the .05 and .01 levels of significance. Also, in contrast to z, a different t distribution is defined for each possible number of degrees of freedom. We want to work at the two-tailed .05 level. The critical value generally is denoted t_α or, in this case, $t_{.05}$.

To use the t tables we must enter the table with the appropriate degrees of freedom. We have 36 observations in our data, so we have $N - 1 = 36 - 1 =$

Table 12.1   Abbreviated Version of Table D.6, Percentage Points of the t Distribution

	\.25	\.20	\.15	\.10	\.05	\.025	\.01	\.005	\.0005
df	\.50	\.40	\.30	\.20	\.10	\.05	\.02	\.01	\.001
1	1.000	1.376	1.963	3.078	6.314	12.706	31.821	63.657	63.662
2	0.816	1.061	1.386	1.886	2.920	4.303	6.965	9.925	31.599
3	0.765	0.978	1.250	1.638	2.353	3.182	4.541	5.841	12.924
4	0.741	0.941	1.190	1.533	2.132	2.776	3.747	4.604	8.610
5	0.727	0.920	1.156	1.476	2.015	2.571	3.365	4.032	6.869
6	0.718	0.906	1.134	1.440	1.943	2.447	3.143	3.707	5.959
⋮	⋮	⋮	⋮	⋮	⋮	⋮	⋮	⋮	⋮
23	0.685	0.858	1.060	1.319	1.714	2.069	2.500	2.807	3.768
24	0.685	0.857	1.059	1.318	1.711	2.064	2.492	2.797	3.745
25	0.684	0.856	1.058	1.316	1.708	2.060	2.485	2.787	3.725
26	0.684	0.856	1.058	1.315	1.706	2.056	2.479	2.779	3.707
27	0.684	0.855	1.057	1.314	1.703	2.052	2.473	2.771	3.690
28	0.683	0.855	1.056	1.313	1.701	2.048	2.467	2.763	3.674
29	0.683	0.854	1.055	1.311	1.699	2.045	2.462	2.756	3.659
30	0.683	0.854	1.055	1.310	1.697	2.042	2.457	2.750	3.646
40	0.681	0.851	1.050	1.303	1.684	2.021	2.423	2.704	3.551
50	0.679	0.849	1.047	1.299	1.676	2.009	2.403	2.678	3.496
100	0.677	0.845	1.042	1.290	1.660	1.984	2.364	2.626	3.390
∞	0.674	0.842	1.036	1.282	1.645	1.960	2.326	2.576	3.291

Header spanning note: **Level of Significance for One-Tailed Test** (over first set .25–.0005) and **Level of Significance for Two-Tailed Test** (over second set .50–.001).

35 df for this example. Because we want $t_{.05}$, Table D.6 (or Table 12.1) tells us that the critical value for $t_{.05}(35)$ is ±2.03. (I obtained that value by taking the average of the critical values for 30 and 40 df, because the table does not contain an entry for exactly 35 df.)

The number in parentheses after $t_{.05}$ is the degrees of freedom. Our result tells us that if H_0 is true only 5% of the time would a t computed on a sample of 36 cases lie outside ±2.03. Because the value we computed (1.20) was less than 2.03, we will not reject H_0. We do not have sufficient evidence to conclude that young children under stress perform any differently from a random sample of normal children. We will have to look elsewhere for an explanation of the low anxiety scores of these children. (To see if these children's anxiety scores really are below the population average, see Exercise 12.22.)

12.4 Factors That Affect the Magnitude of t and the Decision About H_0

Several factors affect the magnitude of the t statistic and/or the likelihood of rejecting H_0:

1.   the actual obtained difference $(\overline{X} - \mu)$
2.   the magnitude of the sample variance (s^2)
3.   the sample size (N)
4.   the significance level (α)
5.   whether the test is a one- or a two-tailed test

It should be obvious that the obtained difference between $\overline{X}$ and the mean (μ) given by H_0 is important. This follows directly from the fact that the larger the numerator, the larger the t value. But it is also important to keep in mind that the value of $\overline{X}$ is in large part a function of the mean of the population from which the sample was drawn. If this mean is denoted μ_1 and the mean given by the null hypothesis is denoted μ_0, then the likelihood of obtaining a significant result will increase as $\mu_1 - \mu_0$ increases.

When you look at the formula for t, it should be apparent that as s^2 decreases or N increases, the denominator $(\sigma/\sqrt{N})$ itself will decrease and the resulting value of t will increase. Because variability introduced by the experimental setting itself (caused by ambiguous instructions, poorly recorded data, distracting testing conditions, and so on) is superimposed on whatever variability there is among subjects, we try to reduce s by controlling as many sources of variability as possible. By obtaining as many subjects as possible, we also make use of the fact that increasing N decreases $s_{\overline{X}}$.

Finally, it should be evident that the likelihood of rejecting H_0 will depend on the size of the rejection region, which in turn depends on α and the location of that region (whether a one-tailed or two-tailed test is used).

12.5 A Second Example: The Moon Illusion

It may be useful to consider a second example, this one taken from a classic paper by Kaufman and Rock (1962) on the moon illusion. The moon illusion is the commonly observed fact that the moon near the horizon appears larger than the moon at its zenith. (We examined this study in Chapter 5, p. 78.) Kaufman and Rock concluded that the moon illusion could be explained on the basis of the greater *apparent* distance of the moon when it is at the horizon. As part of a very complete series of experiments the authors initially sought to estimate the moon illusion by asking subjects to adjust a variable "moon" appearing to be on the horizon to match the size of a standard "moon" appearing at its zenith, or vice versa. (In these measurements they did not use the actual moon, but an artificial one created with a special apparatus.) One of the first questions we might ask is whether there really is a moon illusion, that is, whether a larger setting is required to match a horizon moon than to match a zenith moon. The following data for ten subjects are taken from Kaufman and Rock's paper and represent the ratio of the diameter of the variable moon and the standard moon. A ratio of 1.00 would indicate no illusion; a ratio other than 1.00 would represent an illusion. For example, a ratio of 1.5 would mean that the horizon moon appeared to have a diameter 1.5 times the diameter of the zenith moon. Evidence in support of an illusion would require that we reject $H_0 : \mu = 1.00$ in favor of $H_1 : \mu \neq 1.00$.

Obtained Ratio: 1.73 1.06 2.03 1.40 0.95 1.13 1.41 1.73 1.63 1.56

For these data $N = 10$, $\overline{X} = 1.463$, and $s = 0.341$. A t test on $H_0 : \mu = 1.00$ is given by

$$t = \frac{\overline{X} - \mu}{s_{\overline{X}}} = \frac{\overline{X} - \mu}{\dfrac{s}{\sqrt{N}}} = \frac{1.463 - 1.000}{\dfrac{0.341}{\sqrt{10}}} = \frac{0.463}{0.108} = 4.29$$

From Table D.6 in the Appendices, we see that with $10 - 1 = 9$ df for a two-tailed test at $\alpha = .05$ the critical value of $t_{.05}(9) = \pm 2.262$. The obtained value of t (often denoted t_{obt}) is 4.29. Because $4.29 > 2.262$, we can reject H_0 at $\alpha = .05$ and conclude that the true mean ratio under these conditions is not equal to 1.00. In fact it is greater than 1.00, which is what we would expect on the basis of our experience. (It is always comforting to see science confirm what we have all known since childhood, but the results also mean that Kaufman and Rock's experimental apparatus performs as it should.) What would we have concluded if t had been equal to -4.29?

12.6 Confidence Limits on the Mean

Point estimate

The specific value taken as the estimate of a parameter.

Interval estimate

A range of values estimated to include the parameter.

Confidence limits and confidence interval

An interval, with limits at either end, with a specified probability of including the parameter being estimated.

The moon illusion is an excellent example of a case in which we are particularly interested in estimating the true value of μ, in this case the true ratio of the perceived size of the horizon moon to the perceived size of the zenith moon. The sample mean $(\overline{X})$, as you already know, is an unbiased estimate of μ. When we have one specific estimate of a parameter, we call it a **point estimate**. There are also **interval estimates**, which set limits by a procedure that has a high probability of including the true (population) value of the mean (the mean, μ, of a whole population of observations). What we want, then, are **confidence limits** on μ. These limits enclose what is called a **confidence interval**. In Chapter 7 we saw how to set what were called "probable limits" on an observation. A similar line of reasoning will apply here.

If we want to set limits on μ, given the data at hand, what we really want to do is to ask how large or small μ could be without causing us to reject H_0 if we ran a t test on the obtained sample mean. In other words if μ is actually quite small, we would have been unlikely to obtain the sample data. The same would be true if μ is quite large. But there is a whole range of values for μ for which data such as those we obtained would not be particularly unusual. We want to calculate those values of μ.

An easy way to see what we are doing is to start with the formula for t.

$$t = \frac{\bar{X} - \mu}{s_{\bar{X}}} = \frac{\bar{X} - \mu}{\dfrac{s}{\sqrt{N}}}$$

Because we have collected the data, we already know $\bar{X}$, s, and $\sqrt{N}$. We also know that the critical two-tailed value for t at $\alpha = .05$ is $t_{.05}(9) = \pm 2.262$. We will substitute these values in the formula for t and solve for μ.

$$t = \frac{\bar{X} - \mu}{\dfrac{s}{\sqrt{N}}}$$

$$\pm 2.262 = \frac{1.463 - \mu}{\dfrac{0.341}{\sqrt{10}}} = \frac{1.463 - \mu}{0.108}$$

Rearranging to solve for μ, we have

$$\mu = \pm 2.262(0.108) + 1.463 = \pm 0.244 + 1.463$$

Using the $+0.244$ and -0.244 separately to obtain the upper and lower limits for μ, we have

$$\mu_{upper} = +0.244 + 1.463 = 1.707$$

$$\mu_{lower} = -0.244 + 1.463 = 1.219$$

Thus we can write the 95% confidence limits as 1.219 and 1.707 and the confidence interval as

$$CI_{.95} = 1.219 \le \mu \le 1.707$$

or, to write a general expression,

$$CI_{.95} = \bar{X} \pm t_{.05}s_{\bar{X}} = \bar{X} \pm t_{.05}\frac{s}{\sqrt{N}}$$

We have a 95% confidence interval because we used the two-tailed critical value of t at $\alpha = .05$. For the 99% limits we would take $t_{.01} = \pm 3.250$. Then the 99% confidence interval is

$$CI_{.99} = \bar{X} \pm t_{.01}s_{\bar{X}} = 1.463 \pm 3.250(0.108) = 1.112 \le \mu \le 1.814$$

We now can say that the probability is .95 that an interval such as 1.219–1.707 includes the true mean ratio for the moon illusion, while the probability

Figure 12.6

Confidence Limits Computed on 25 Samples from a Population with $\mu = 5.00$

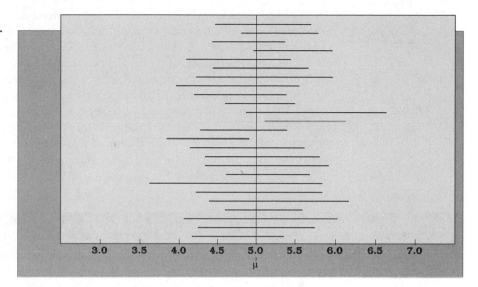

is .99 that an interval such as 1.112–1.814 includes μ. Note that neither interval includes the value 1.00, which represents no illusion. We already knew this for the 95% confidence interval because we had rejected that null hypothesis when we ran the t test.

A graphic demonstration of confidence limits is shown in Figure 12.6. To generate this figure I drew 25 samples of $N = 4$ from a population with a mean (μ) of 5. For every sample a 95% confidence interval on μ was calculated and plotted. For example, the limits produced from the first sample were approximately 4.46 and 5.72, whereas for the second sample the limits were 4.83 and 5.80. Because in this case we know that the value of μ equals 5, I have drawn a vertical line at that point. Notice that the limits for samples 12 and 14 do not include $\mu = 5$. We would expect that the confidence limits would encompass μ 95 times out of 100. Therefore, two misses out of 25 seems reasonable. Notice also that the confidence intervals vary in width. This variability can be explained by the fact that the width of an interval is a function of the standard deviation of the sample, and some samples have larger standard deviations than others.[2]

---

[2] Many statisticians would correctly object to my statement of the meaning of confidence limits as I have written it. They would argue that *before* the experiment is run and the calculations are made, an interval of the form

$$\bar{X} \pm t_{.05}s_{\bar{x}}$$

has a probability of .95 of encompassing μ. However, once the data are in, an interval such as 1.219–1.707 either includes the value of μ (probability = 1.00) or it doesn't (probability = 0.00). Put slightly differently

$$\bar{X} \pm t_{.05}s_{\bar{x}}$$

is a *random variable*, but the specific interval 1.219–1.707 is not a random variable and therefore does not have a probability associated with it. However, as mentioned in Chapter 7, there

A comment is in order here about the interpretation of confidence limits. Statements of the form $p(1.219 < \mu < 1.707) = .95$ are not to be interpreted in the usual way. The parameter μ is not a variable. It does not jump around from experiment to experiment. Rather μ is a constant, and the *interval* is what varies from experiment to experiment. Think of the parameter as a stake and the experimenter, in computing confidence limits, as tossing rings at that stake (parameter). Ninety-five percent of the time a ring of specified width will encircle the stake, and 5% of the time it will miss. A confidence statement is a statement of the probability that the ring has landed on the stake (i.e., the interval includes the parameter) and *not* a statement of the probability that the stake (parameter) landed inside the ring (interval).

12.7 Using Minitab to Run One-Sample *t* Tests

When you have large amounts of data, it is often much more convenient to use a program such as Minitab to compute *t* values. Figure 12.7 is an illustration of the use of Minitab to obtain a one-sample *t* test and confidence limits for the moon illusion data. Notice that Minitab's results agree, within rounding error, with those we obtained by hand. Notice also that Minitab computes the exact probability of a Type I error (the ***p* value**) rather than comparing *t* to a tabled value. Although we concluded that the probability of a Type I error was less than .05, Minitab reveals that the actual probability is .0020.[3] Most computer programs operate in this way.

From the output in Figure 12.7 we could conclude that the mean ratio settings for the moon illusion, based on 10 subjects, was significantly greater than 1.00, which would be the expected setting if there were in fact no moon illusion. This could be written as $t(9) = 4.30$, $p = .002$, where the value in parentheses (9) is the degrees of freedom for *t*.

p **value**
The probability that a particular result would occur by chance if H_0 is true; the exact probability of a Type I error.

12.8 A Final Worked Example

We now will return to the *t* test on means and work through an example of a *t* test on a null hypothesis about a single population mean (μ). Consider the following example.

A psychologist hypothesizes that with changes in diet and patterns of exercise and other differences between life in the 1980s and life in the 1950s, women should be healthier and even taller. He knows that in the 1950 the mean height of American women was 64 inches, but the tables don't give the

---

are different ways of defining what we mean by a probability. In *subjective* probability terms it is perfectly reasonable to say that my subjective probability is .95 that if you were to tell me the true value of μ it would be found to lie between 1.219 and 1.707.

[3]We could have approximated this probability roughly by use of Table D.6 in the Appendices. For 9 *df* a *t* of 3.250 would have had a *two-tailed* probability of .01, and a value of $t = 4.781$ would have had a two-tailed probability of .001. Because the obtained *t* falls between these two values, its probability is somewhere between .01 and .001.

Figure 12.7   Minitab Analysis for One-Sample t Tests and Confidence Limits

```
MTB > Set the following data in Column C1
DATA> 1.73 1.06 2.03 1.40 0.95 1.13 1.41 1.73 1.63 1.56
DATA> end
MTB > Name c1 'Illusion'

MTB > ttest against mu = 1.00 for 'Illusion' data
                                              t statistic
TEST OF MU = 1.000 VS MU N.E. 1.000

              N      MEAN    STDEV   SE MEAN      T    P VALUE
Illusion     10     1.463    0.341    0.108     4.30    0.0020 ←── Probability of t ≥ 4.30 if H₀: true

MTB > tinterval for 95 percent confidence interval on 'Illusion'

              N      MEAN    STDEV   SE MEAN     95.0 PERCENT C.I.
Illusion     10     1.463    0.341    0.108    (  1.219,   1.707)

MTB > tinterval for 99 percent confidence interval on 'Illusion'  95% confidence limits

              N      MEAN    STDEV   SE MEAN     99.0 PERCENT C.I.
Illusion     10     1.463    0.341    0.108    (  1.113,   1.813)
```

standard deviation. To test his hypothesis he sampled 16 women from local medical records and recorded their heights. Would these data lead our experimenter to reject the null hypothesis that women, on average, are the same height that they were 40 years ago?

First we need to set up the null hypothesis. The psychologist wants to test the hypothesis that women's average height is different from what it was in 1950, so he will set up the null hypothesis that it is the same, with the hope of being able to reject it. Thus we have $H_0: \mu = 64$. Next we need to decide on a one-tailed or two-tailed test and a significance level. For reasons that were given earlier, we will use a two-tailed test and set $\alpha = .05$.

From the data we will first calculate the mean and the standard deviation, and then we will calculate t.

Data: 63   65   64   66   67   61   60   66   63   65   68   67   68   63   62   66

$$\overline{X} = \frac{\Sigma X}{N} = \frac{1034}{16} = 64.625$$

$$s^2 = \frac{\Sigma X^2 - \dfrac{(\Sigma X)^2}{N}}{N - 1} = \frac{66912 - \dfrac{1034^2}{16}}{15} = 5.9833$$

$$s = \sqrt{s^2} = \sqrt{5.9833} = 2.446$$

We are now in a position to solve for t:

$$t = \frac{\overline{X} - \mu}{s/\sqrt{N}} = \frac{64.625 - 64}{2.446/\sqrt{16}} = \frac{0.625}{0.612} = 1.02$$

From Table D.6 in the Appendices we find that for $N - 1 = 16 - 1 = 15$ df at $\alpha = .05$, the two-tailed critical value of t is 2.131. Thus we would reject H_0 if our value of t had exceeded ± 2.131. Because t_{obt} was less than the critical value we cannot reject the null hypothesis. We have insufficient reason to conclude that women are, on average, taller than they were 40 years ago. One way to write this up would be to say that we examined the heights of 16 women in 1990. Their mean height was 64.625 inches with a standard deviation of 2.446 inches. When this sample mean was compared to the mean height, taken from insurance tables, of women in 1950, there was a difference of 0.625 inch. A t test comparing heights in 1990 and 1950 produced $t(15) = 1.02$, $p > .05$. We conclude that the difference between the heights in those two years is not a reliable difference, and we have no reason to believe that changes in diet and other aspects of daily life have led women to be taller.

12.9 Summary

We began this chapter by considering the sampling distribution of the mean and how the information it gives is useful in testing hypotheses. We then discussed how we could combine what we know about z and what we know about the sampling distribution of the mean to produce a test of a null hypothesis concerning μ. Next we examined how we could go beyond z to make use of a t test when the population standard deviation is not known and must be estimated by the sample standard deviation. We considered the factors that influence the magnitude of t in a particular experiment. Next we considered the construction of confidence limits on the value of a population mean.

Some important terms in this chapter are:

* **Experimental hypothesis**

* **Sampling distribution of the mean**

* **Central Limit Theorem**

* **Rectangular distribution**

* **Standard error**

* **Student's t distribution**

* **Degrees of freedom (df)**

* **Point estimate**

* **Interval estimate**

* **Confidence limits and confidence interval**

* **p value**

12.10 Exercises

12.1 Using Table D.9 in the Appendices (or any other source of more or less random numbers), plot the distribution of the first 100 least significant (rightmost) digits.

12.2 Repeat Exercise 12.1, except calculate

and plot the means for 25 samples of five least significant digits. (Group the means into appropriate intervals.)

12.3 Compare the means and the standard deviations for the distribution of digits in Exercise 12.1 and the sampling distribution of the mean in Exercise 12.2. Do these answers agree with what the Central Limit Theorem would lead you to expect?

12.4 In what way would the result in Exercise 12.2 differ if you had drawn more samples of size 5?

12.5 In what way would the result in Exercise 12.2 differ if you had drawn 25 samples of size 15?

12.6 In 1979 the 238 students from North Dakota who took the verbal portion of the SAT exam had a mean of 525. The standard deviation was not reported.

(a) Is this result consistent with the idea that North Dakota's students are a random sample from a population of students having a mean of 500 and a standard deviation of 100?

(b) Would you have rejected H_0 had you been looking for evidence that SAT scores in general have been declining over the years from a mean of 500?

(c) If you rejected H_0 in part (a) you might draw some conclusions about North Dakota's students or our assumption about the general population of students. What are those possible conclusions?

12.7 Why do the data in Exercise 12.6 not really speak to the issue of whether American education in general is in a terrible state?

12.8 In 1979 the 2345 students from Arizona who took the math portion of the SAT had a mean of 524. Is this consistent with the notion of a population mean of 500 if we assume that $\sigma = 100$?

12.9 Why does the answer to Exercise 12.8 differ substantially from the answer to Exercise 12.6 even though the means are virtually the same?

12.10 It is commonly assumed that Graduate Record Exams produce scores with a mean of 500. In October 1981 the mean verbal score of 5701 college seniors and nonenrolled college graduates in the biological sciences was 503 with a standard deviation of 104. Is our common belief about the mean of the GRE justified, at least for the biological sciences? How does this question relate to Exercise 12.6(c)?

12.11 What are the null hypothesis (H_0) and the alternative hypothesis (H_1) in Exercise 12.10?

12.12 Would it have made sense to run a one-tailed test for Exercise 12.10?

12.13 If you had rejected the null hypothesis in Exercise 12.10, would that be an important finding? Why or why not?

12.14 In a large corporation the mean salary for all males with 3 to 5 years of experience is $27,000. Salaries (expressed in thousands) for a random sample of 10 women also having 3 to 5 years of experience were

23 26 30 20 18 25 29 21 14 35

Is there evidence of different salary practices for males and females?

12.15 Although most of the salaries in Exercise 12.14 were less than $27,000, you could not reject H_0. Why might that be?

12.16 Compute 95% confidence limits on μ for the data in Exercise 12.6.

12.17 Compute 95% confidence limits on μ for the data in Exercise 12.10.

12.18 How did your approaches to Exercise 12.16 and 12.17 differ?

12.19 For the IQ data on females in Appendix C, test the null hypothesis that $\mu_{female} = 100$.

12.20 In Exercise 12.19 you probably solved for t instead of z. Why was that necessary?

12.21 Describe the procedures that you would go through to reproduce the results in Figure 12.4.

12.22 In Section 12.3 we ran a t test to test the hypothesis that young children under stress give more socially desirable answers on an anxiety measure than normal children. We never really tested the hypothesis that they report lower levels of anxiety. For the data on these children the mean anxiety score was 11.00, with a standard deviation of 6.085. The population mean anxiety score for elementary school–aged children on this measure is reported as 14.55. Do our children show significantly lower levels of anxiety than children in the general population?

13

HYPOTHESIS TESTS APPLIED TO MEANS: TWO RELATED SAMPLES

In Chapter 12 we considered the situation in which we had one sample mean ($\overline{X}$). We wanted to test to see if it was reasonable to believe that such a sample mean would have occurred if we had been sampling from a population with some specified mean (often denoted μ_0). Another way of phrasing this is to say that we were testing to determine if the mean of the population from which we sampled (call it μ_1) was equal to some particular value given by the null hypothesis (μ_0).

In this chapter we will move away from the case in which we perform a test on the mean of one sample of data. Instead we will consider the case

Related samples (repeated measures, matched samples) An experimental design in which the same subject is observed under more than one treatment.

in which we have two **related samples** and we wish to perform a test on the difference between their two means. (The same analyses apply to what are variously called **repeated measures**, **matched samples**, correlated samples, paired samples, dependent samples, randomized blocks, or split plots, depending in part on the speaker's background.) As you will see, this test is similar to the test discussed in the previous chapter.

13.1 Related Samples

In many (but certainly not all) situations in which we will use the form of the *t* test discussed in this chapter we will have two sets of data from the same subjects. For example, we might ask 20 people to rate their level of anxiety before and after donating blood. Or we might record ratings of level of disability made using two different ratings systems for each of 20 handicapped individuals in an attempt to see whether one rating system leads to generally lower assessments than the other. In both examples we would have 20 sets of numbers, two numbers for each person, and we would expect these two sets of numbers (variables) to be correlated. We need to take this correlation into account in planning our *t* test. In the example of anxiety about donating blood, people differ widely in level of anxiety. Some seem to be anxious all the time no matter what happens, and others just take things as they come and don't worry about anything. Thus, there should be a relationship between an individual's anxiety level before donating blood and the anxiety level after donating blood. In other words if we know what a person's anxiety score was before donation, we can make a reasonable guess what it was after donation. Similarly, some people are severely handicapped, whereas others are only mildly so. If we know that a particular person received a high assessment using one system, it is likely that person also received a relatively high assessment using another system. The relationship between data sets doesn't have to be perfect—in fact it probably never will be. The fact that we can make better-than-chance predictions is sufficient to classify two sets of data as related or matched. (To put this another way, we have related or matched samples whenever the two variables, such as the two sets of anxiety scores, are significantly correlated.)

In the two preceding examples I have chosen situations in which each person in the study contributed two scores. Although this is the most common way of obtaining related samples, it is not the only way. For example, a study of marital relationships might involve asking husbands and wives to rate their satisfaction with their marriage, with the goal of testing to see whether wives are, on average, more or less satisfied than husbands. Here each individual would contribute only one score, but the couple as a unit would contribute a pair of scores. It is very probable that if the wife is very dissatisfied with the marriage, her husband isn't likely to be too happy either, and vice versa.

There are many examples of experimental designs involving related samples. They all have one thing in common, and that is the fact that knowing one member of a pair of scores tells you something—maybe not much, but something—about the other member. Whenever this is the case, we say that the samples are related. This chapter deals with *t* tests on the difference between the means of two related samples.

13.2 Student's *t* Applied to Difference Scores

As an example of the analysis of related samples we will consider an intervention study designed to promote certain social skills among high school freshmen (a group that gives us ample room for improvement). Before we begin the program, we take the group of 15 subjects to a shopping mall, to dinner at the local branch of Hamburger Heaven, and to a movie. We also take a set of judges who count the number of socially inappropriate behaviors exhibited by each subject (running five abreast through the mall, yelling at passing cars, smearing catsup on the salt shaker, putting out cigarettes in coffee cups, making comments behind necking couples in the movie, and all those other unlovable behaviors that each of us engaged in when we were that age). After a two-week intervention program, during which we try to instill in our subjects a whole array of adult social behaviors that we think they should adopt (and omitting all the adult social behaviors that we don't wish to nurture), we take the same subjects shopping, eating, and movie-watching again and let the same judges again count socially inappropriate behaviors.

The data from this hypothetical study are presented in Table 13.1, in

Table 13.1

Data and Difference Scores on Number of Socially Inappropriate Behaviors

	Before (X_1)	After (X_2)	Difference (*D*)
	18	12	6
	5	4	1
	19	17	2
	13	11	2
	12	8	4
	17	12	5
	26	27	−1
	3	3	0
	1	3	−2
	20	14	6
	15	12	3
	18	14	4
	10	11	−1
	8	10	−2
	15	9	6
Mean	13.333	11.133	2.200
s	6.914	5.998	2.933

which the first set of scores is designated X_1 and the second set is designated X_2. The null hypothesis that we want to test is the hypothesis that the mean (μ_1) of the population of scores from which the first set of data was drawn is equal to the mean (μ_2) of the population from which the second set of data was drawn. In other words we want to test $H_0: \mu_1 = \mu_2$ (or, equivalently, $H_0: \mu_1 - \mu_2 = 0$). Note that we have no interest in the values of μ_1 and μ_2, only in whether they are equal. Note also that we will be testing this null hypothesis using data from related samples, because the same subjects were tested on two separate occasions.

Difference Scores

Difference scores
The set of scores that represents the difference between the subjects' performance on two occasions.

Although it would seem obvious to view the data as representing two samples of scores, one set obtained before the training program and one after, it is also possible, and very profitable, to transform the data into one set of scores—the set of differences between X_1 and X_2 for each subject. These differences are called **difference scores** and are shown in the third column of Table 13.1. Think of them as the degree of improvement between one measurement session and the next—presumably as a result of our intervention. If in fact the intervention program had *no* effect (i.e., if H_0 is true), the average score would not change from session to session. By chance some subjects would happen to have a higher score on X_2 than on X_1, and some would have a lower score, but *on the average* there would be no difference.

If we now think of our data as being the column of difference scores, the null hypothesis becomes the hypothesis that the mean of a population of difference scores (denoted μ_D) equals 0. Because it can be shown that $\mu_D = \mu_1 - \mu_2$, we can write $H_0: \mu_D = \mu_1 - \mu_2 = 0$. But now we can see that we are testing a hypothesis using *one* sample of data (the sample of difference scores), and we already know how to do that from Chapter 12.

The t Statistic

We are now at precisely the same place we were in the last chapter when we had a sample of data and a null hypothesis ($\mu = 0$). The only difference is that in this case the data are difference scores, and the mean and the standard deviation are based on the differences. Recall that t was defined as the difference between a sample mean and a population mean, divided by the standard error of the mean. Then we have

$$t = \frac{\bar{D} - 0}{s_{\bar{D}}} = \frac{\bar{D} - 0}{\frac{s_D}{\sqrt{N}}}$$

Where $\bar{D}$ and $s_{\bar{D}}$ are the mean and the standard deviation of the difference scores and N is the number of difference scores (i.e., the number of *pairs*, not the number of raw scores). For our data

$$t = \frac{\overline{D} - 0}{\frac{s_D}{\sqrt{N}}} = \frac{2.20 - 0}{\frac{2.933}{\sqrt{15}}} = 2.91$$

Degrees of Freedom

The degrees of freedom for the matched-sample case are exactly the same as they were for the one-sample case. Because we are working with the difference scores, N will be equal to the number of differences (or the number of *pairs* of observations, or the number of *independent* observations—all of which amount to the same thing.). Because the variance of these difference scores (s^2_D) is used as an estimate of the variance of a population of difference scores (σ^2_D) and because this sample variance is obtained using the sample mean ($\overline{D}$), we will lose one *df* to the mean and have $N - 1$ *df.* In other words $df =$ number of *pairs* minus 1.

We have 15 difference scores in this example, so we will have 14 degrees of freedom. From Table D.6 in the Appendices, we find that for a two-tailed test at the .05 level of significance, $t_{.05}(14) = \pm 2.145$. Our obtained value of t (2.91) exceeds 2.145, so we will reject H_0 and conclude that the difference scores were not sampled from a population of difference scores where $\mu_D = 0$. In practical terms this means that the subjects showed fewer socially undesirable behaviors after the intervention program than before it. Although we would like to think that this means that the program was successful, it may just mean that the students finally noticed that someone was recording their behavior, that we happened to make our second observation on a day when everyone was too tired to do much of anything, or something else we have not even considered. The fact remains, however, that for whatever reason, the scores were sufficiently lower on the second occasion to allow us to reject $H_0: \mu_D = \mu_1 - \mu_2 = 0$.

13.3 A Second Example: The Moon Illusion Again

For a second example we will return to the work by Kaufman and Rock (1962) on the moon illusion. An important earlier hypothesis about the source of the moon illusion had been put forth by Holway and Boring (1940), who suggested that the illusion was due to the fact that when the moon was on the horizon, the observer looked straight at it with eyes level, whereas when it was at its zenith, the observer had to elevate his eyes as well as his head to see it. Holway and Boring proposed that this difference in the elevation of the eyes was the cause of the illusion. To test this hypothesis, Kaufman and Rock (1962) devised an apparatus that allowed them to present two artificial moons (one at the horizon and one at the zenith) and to control whether or not the subjects elevated their eyes to see the zenith moon. In one case the subject was able to see the zenith moon with eyes level. In the other case the subject was forced to see the zenith moon with eyes raised. (The horizon moon was always viewed with eyes level.) In both cases the dependent variable was the ratio of the perceived size of the horizon moon to the perceived size of the zenith moon (a ratio of 1.00 would represent no illusion). If Holway and Boring were correct, there should be a greater illusion (larger ratio) in the eyes-elevated condition than in the eyes-level condition, although the "moon" was always perceived to be in the same place, the zenith. If Kaufman and Rock (with their "apparent distance" hypothesis) were correct, there should be no differences between the "eyes-level" and "eyes-elevated" conditions. The actual data for this experiment are given in Table 13.2.

In this example we want to test the *null* hypothesis that the means are equal under the two viewing conditions. Because we are dealing with related observations (each subject served under both conditions), we will work with the difference scores and test $H_0 : \mu_D = 0$. Using a two-tailed test at $\alpha = .05$, the alternative hypothesis is $H_1 : \mu_D \neq 0$.

From the formula for a t test on related samples we have

$$t = \frac{\bar{D} - 0}{\dfrac{s_D}{\sqrt{N}}} = \frac{0.019 - 0}{\dfrac{0.137}{\sqrt{10}}} = \frac{0.019}{0.043} = 0.44$$

From Table D.6 we find that $t_{.05}(9) = \pm 2.262$. Because our obtained t (t_{obt}) =

Table 13.2	Subject	Eyes Elevated	Eyes Level	Difference (D)
Magnitude of the Moon Illusion When Zenith Moon Is Viewed with Eyes Level and with Eyes Elevated	1	1.65	1.73	−0.08
	2	1.00	1.06	−0.06
	3	2.03	2.03	0.00
	4	1.25	1.40	−0.15
	5	1.05	0.95	0.10
	6	1.02	1.13	−0.11
	7	1.67	1.41	0.26
	8	1.86	1.73	0.13
	9	1.56	1.63	−0.07
	10	1.73	1.56	0.17

$$\bar{D} = 0.019$$
$$s_D = 0.137$$
$$s_{\bar{D}} = 0.043$$

0.44 is less than 2.262, we will fail to reject H_0 and decide that we have no evidence to suggest that the illusion is affected by the elevation of the eyes.[1] (These data, moreover, included a second test of Holway and Boring's hypothesis, since Holway and Boring would have predicted that there would not be an illusion if subjects viewed the zenith moon with eyes level. In fact the data reveal a considerable illusion under this condition. Would this illusion be significant by the t test discussed in the preceding chapter? A test of the significance of the illusion level can be obtained by the methods in Chapter 12, and the illusion is in fact significant.)

13.4 Advantages and Disadvantages of Using Related Samples

In the next chapter we will consider experimental designs in which we use two independent groups of subjects rather than testing the same subjects twice (or some other method of having related samples of data). In many cases independent samples are useful, but before considering that topic, it is important that you understand the strengths and weaknesses of related samples.

Probably the most important advantage of designing an experiment around related samples is that such a procedure allows us to avoid problems associated with variability from subject to subject. Return for a moment to the data on social behaviors in adolescents in Table 13.1. Notice that some subjects (e.g., the eighth and ninth subjects) engage in almost no undesirable behaviors. On the other hand, the seventh and tenth subjects are candidates for some unpleasant action on the part of people around them. The advantage of related-samples designs is that these differences between subjects do not enter into the data we analyze—the difference scores. A change from 26 to 24 is treated exactly the same as a change from 6 to 4. In not allowing variability from subject to subject in overall level of obnoxious behavior to influence the data by producing a large sample variance, related-samples designs have a considerable advantage over independent samples in terms of the ability to reject a false null hypothesis (power).

A second advantage of related samples over two independent samples is the fact that related samples allow us to control for extraneous variables. Had we measured one group of subjects before they received our intervention and a different group after, there may have been any number of differences between the groups that had nothing to do with our intervention but that would influence the results. That was not a problem in our study because we used the same subjects for both measurement sessions.

---

[1] Note: A glance at Table D.6 in the Appendices will reveal that any t less than 1.96 (the critical value for z) will never be significant at $\alpha = .05$, regardless of the number of degrees of freedom. Moreover, unless you have at least 50 degrees of freedom, t values less than 2.00 will not be significant, thus often making it unnecessary for you to even bother looking at the table of t.

A third advantage of related-measures designs is that they require fewer subjects than do independent-sample designs for the same degree of power. This is a substantial advantage, as anyone who has ever tried to recruit subjects can attest. It is usually a much easier task to get 20 people to do something twice than to get 40 people to do it once.

Order effect
The effect on performance attributable to the order in which treatments were administered.

Carry-over effect
The effect of previous trials (conditions) on a subject's performance in subsequent trials.

The primary disadvantage of related-measures designs is that there may be either an **order effect** or a **carry-over effect** from one session to the next, or the first measurement may influence the treatment itself though processes such as sensitization. For example, if we plan to give a test of knowledge of current events, followed by a crash course in current events, and then follow that with a retest using the same test, it is reasonable to conclude that subjects will be more familiar with the items the second time around and may even have looked up answers during the interval between the two administrations. Similarly in drug studies the effects of the first drug may not have worn off by the next test session. A common problem with related-measures designs arises when a pretest "tips off" subjects as to the purpose of the intervention. For example, a pretest on attitudes toward breastfeeding might make you a wee bit suspicious when a stranger sits down beside you the next day and just happens to launch into a speech on the virtues of breastfeeding. Whenever you have concerns that your study could be contaminated by carry-over effects or that treatment effects might be influenced by pretreatment measures, a related-measures design is not recommended. There are techniques for controlling, though not eliminating, order and carry-over effects, but we will not discuss them here. Would you anticipate that either of these effects might influence the data on the moon illusion? If so, how might we control for such effects?

13.5 Using SPSS for *t* Tests on Related Samples

Figure 13.1 is the printout of an SPSS computation of a *t* test on two related samples. The data in this example are those we have already seen on the moon illusion. The data collected in the eyes-level and eyes-elevated conditions are entered as two separate variables, and the important command is the one that says

    "T-Test   Pairs = Elev Level"

This command simply tells SPSS to run a related-samples *t* test comparing the two variables, Elev and Level. The Options command simply controls how the output is positioned on the page. Notice that the result ($t = 0.44$) agrees with the result in Section 13.3.

Figure 13.1 SPSS Analysis of *t* Tests on Related Samples

```
Data File Moon.Dat

1.65 1.73
1.00 1.06
2.03 2.03
1.25 1.40
1.05 0.95
1.02 1.13
1.67 1.41
1.86 1.73
1.56 1.63
1.73 1.56


SPSS Program

Title           "Related sample t test on moon illusion data"
File Handle     MoonData/Name = 'Moon.dat'
Data List       File = MoonData List/Elev Level
Var Labels      Elev, Estimate with eyes elevated/
                Level, Estimate with eyes level/
T-Test          Pairs = Elev Level
Option          4

SPSS Output

        ---t-tests for paired samples---
```

Variable	Number of Cases	Mean	Standard Deviation	Standard Error	
ELEV	Estimate with eyes elevated				
	10	1.4820	.374	.118	Descriptive statistics
LEVEL	Estimate with eyes level				
	10	1.4630	.341	.108	

(Difference) Mean	Standard Deviation	Standard Error	2-tail Corr. Prob.	t Value	Degrees of Freedom	2-tail Prob.
.0190	.137	.043	.931 .000	.44	9	.672

Correlation between Elev and Level   t statistic

13.6 Summary

In this chapter we considered the analysis of data involving two related samples. You saw that the data easily can be reduced to one set of difference scores and that the standard one-sample *t* test can be applied to those difference scores to test the null hypothesis that the mean of the differences does not deviate from 0 more than would be predicted by chance. We then examined the strengths and weaknesses of experimental designs using related-measures designs. Finally, you saw how to use SPSS to perform *t* tests for related samples.

Some important terms in this chapter are:

- Related samples
- Repeated measures
- Matched samples
- Difference scores
- Order effect
- Carry-over effect

13.7 Exercises

13.1 For six months we worked with a group of 15 severely retarded individuals in an attempt to train them in self-care skills through imitation. For a second six-month period we used physically guided practice with the same individuals. For each six-month session we have ratings on the level of required assistance (high scores = bad) for each person. The data for each individual follow:

Subject	Imitation	Physical Guidance
1	14	10
2	11	13
3	19	15
4	8	5
5	4	3
6	9	6
7	12	7
8	5	9
9	14	16
10	17	10
11	18	13
12	0	1
13	2	2
14	8	3
15	6	6

Have we found that the level of assistance the subjects require has been reduced in the second six-month period?

13.2 Does the study described in Exercise 13.1 give us a clear answer concerning the relative quality of the two approaches? If not, why not?

13.3 How could we improve the study described in Exercise 13.1?

13.4 Use techniques developed in Chapter 12 to construct 95% confidence limits on the true mean difference between the treatments described in Exercise 13.1.

13.5 As part of a study to reduce smoking, a national organization ran an advertising campaign to convince people to quit smoking. To evaluate the effectiveness of their campaign, they had 15 subjects record the average number of cigarettes smoked per day in the week before and the week after exposure to the ad. The data follow:

Subject	Before	After
1	45	43
2	16	20
3	20	17
4	33	30
5	30	25
6	19	19
7	33	34
8	25	28
9	26	23
10	40	41
11	28	26
12	36	40
13	15	16
14	26	23
15	32	34

Run the appropriate t test.

13.6 Assume the data in Exercise 13.5 had come out differently. The new data follow:

Subject	Before	After
1	45	59
2	16	35
3	20	30
4	33	40
5	30	20
6	19	10
7	33	20
8	25	20
9	26	36
10	40	46
11	28	10
12	36	25
13	15	8
14	26	35
15	32	46

Run the appropriate t test.

13.7 Compare the conclusions a careful experimenter would draw from Exercises 13.5 and 13.6.

13.8 Give an example of an experiment in which using related samples would be ill advised because of carry-over effects.

13.9 Using the data for the first 20 subjects in Appendix C, test the hypothesis that English grades are generally higher than the overall GPA.

13.10 Assume that the mean and the standard deviation of the difference scores in Exercise 13.5 would remain the same if we added more subjects. How many subjects would we need to obtain a significant t? (We will return to this general problem in Chapter 15.)

13.11 Modify the data in Exercise 13.5 by shifting around the entries in the "Before" row so that occasionally high "Before" scores are paired with low "After" scores. Run a t test on the modified data and notice the effect on t.

13.12 Putting together the answer to Exercise 13.11 and what you know about correlation, how would you expect the degree of correlation between two variables (sets of data) to affect the magnitude of the t test between them?

13.13 In Section 13.4 I explained that by removing subject-to-subject variability from the data, related-samples designs prevent this variability from influencing the data on which the t test is run. This increases our ability to reject a false null hypothesis. Explain in your own words why this is so.

13.14 In Section 13.3 I discussed a second test of the Holway and Boring (1940) experiment using a one-sample t test on the "eyes-level" condition. Run this t test and draw the appropriate conclusions.

13.15 If there were reason to believe that carry-over effects could influence the data on the moon illusion referred to in Section 13.3, how might we control such effects?

14

HYPOTHESIS TESTS APPLIED TO MEANS: TWO INDEPENDENT SAMPLES

In Chapter 13 we considered a study in which we obtained a set of measures of socially undesirable behavior before and after an intervention program. In that example the *same* subjects were observed both before and after the intervention. While that may have been the best way to evaluate the effects of the intervention program, in a great many experiments it is either impossible or undesirable to obtain data using repeated measurements of the same subjects. For example, if we want to determine if males are more socially inept than females, it clearly would be impossible to test the same people as males and then as females. Instead we would need a sample of males and a second, *independent* sample of females.

One of the most common uses of the t test involves testing the difference between the means of two independent groups. We might want to compare the mean number of trials needed to reach criterion in a simple visual discrimination task for two groups of rats—one raised under normal conditions and one raised under conditions of sensory deprivation. Or in a memory study we might want to compare levels of retention for a group of college students asked to recall active declarative sentences and a group asked to recall passive negative sentences. As a final example, we might place subjects in a situation in which another person needed help. We could compare the latency of helping behavior when subjects were tested alone and when they were tested in groups.

In conducting any experiment with two independent groups, we would most likely find that the two sample means differed by some amount. The important question, however, is whether that difference is sufficiently large to justify the conclusion that the two samples were drawn from different populations—for example, using the case of helping behavior, is the mean of the population of latencies from singly-tested subjects different from the mean of the population of latencies from group-tested subjects? Before we consider a specific example, we will need to examine the sampling distribution of differences between means and the t test that results from that sampling distribution.

14.1 Distribution of Differences Between Means

Sampling distribution of differences between means
The distribution of the differences between means over repeated sampling from the same population(s).

When we are interested in testing for a difference between the mean of one population (μ_1) and the mean of a second population (μ_2), we will be testing a null hypothesis of the form $H_0: \mu_1 - \mu_2 = 0$ or, equivalently, $\mu_1 = \mu_2$. Because the test of this null hypothesis involves the difference between independent sample means, it is important that we digress for a moment and examine the **sampling distribution of differences between means**. Suppose we have two populations labeled X_1 and X_2 with means μ_1 and μ_2 and variances σ_1^2 and σ_2^2. We now draw pairs of samples of size N_1 from population X_1 and of size N_2 from population X_2 and record the means and the differences between the means for each pair of samples. Because we are sampling independently from each population, the sample means will be independent. (Means are paired only in the trivial and presumably irrelevant sense of being drawn at the same time.) Because we are only supposing, we might as well go all the way and suppose that we repeated this procedure an infinite number of times. The results are presented schematically in Figure 14.1. In the lower portion of this figure the first two columns represent the sampling distributions of $\overline{X}_1$ and $\overline{X}_2$, and the third column represents the sampling distribution of differences in means ($\overline{X}_1 - \overline{X}_2$). It is this third column in which we are most interested, because we are concerned with testing differences between means. The mean of this distribution

Figure 14.1

Hypothetical Set of Means and Differences Between Means When Sampling from Two Populations

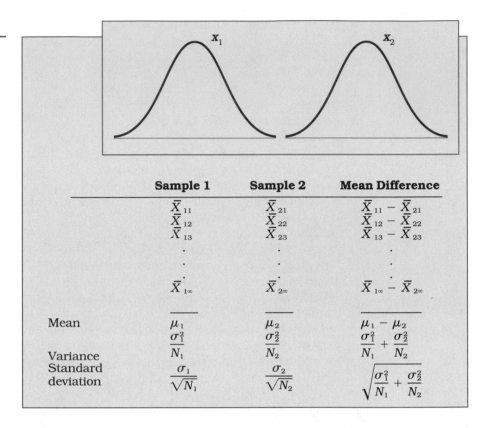

	Sample 1	Sample 2	Mean Difference
	$\bar{X}_{11}$	$\bar{X}_{21}$	$\bar{X}_{11} - \bar{X}_{21}$
	$\bar{X}_{12}$	$\bar{X}_{22}$	$\bar{X}_{12} - \bar{X}_{22}$
	$\bar{X}_{13}$	$\bar{X}_{23}$	$\bar{X}_{13} - \bar{X}_{23}$
	.	.	.
	.	.	.
	.	.	.
	$\bar{X}_{1\infty}$	$\bar{X}_{2\infty}$	$\bar{X}_{1\infty} - \bar{X}_{2\infty}$
Mean	μ_1	μ_2	$\mu_1 - \mu_2$
Variance	$\dfrac{\sigma_1^2}{N_1}$	$\dfrac{\sigma_2^2}{N_2}$	$\dfrac{\sigma_1^2}{N_1} + \dfrac{\sigma_2^2}{N_2}$
Standard deviation	$\dfrac{\sigma_1}{\sqrt{N_1}}$	$\dfrac{\sigma_2}{\sqrt{N_2}}$	$\sqrt{\dfrac{\sigma_1^2}{N_1} + \dfrac{\sigma_2^2}{N_2}}$

Variance Sum Law
The rule giving the variance of the sum of (or difference between) two or more variables.

can be shown to equal $\mu_1 - \mu_2$. The variance of this distribution is given by what is commonly called the **Variance Sum Law**, a limited form of which states:

> The variance of the sum or difference of two *independent* variables is equal to the sum of their variances.[1]

We know from the Central Limit Theorem that the variance of the distribution of $\bar{X}_1$ is σ_1^2/N_1 and the variance of the distribution of $\bar{X}_2$ is σ_2^2/N_2. Because the variables (sample means) are independent, the variance of the difference of these two variables is the sum of their variances. Thus

$$\sigma^2_{\bar{X}_1 \pm \bar{X}_2} = \sigma^2_{\bar{X}_1} + \sigma^2_{\bar{X}_2} = \frac{\sigma_1^2}{N_1} + \frac{\sigma_2^2}{N_2}$$

---

[1]The complete form of the law omits the restriction that the variables must be independent and states that the variance of their sum or difference is

$$\sigma^2_{\bar{X}_1 \pm \bar{X}_2} = \sigma^2_{\bar{X}_1} + \sigma^2_{\bar{X}_2} \pm 2\rho\sigma_{\bar{X}_1}\sigma_{\bar{X}_2}$$

where ρ is the correlation coefficient in the population between $\bar{X}_1$ and $\bar{X}_2$. The minus signs apply when considering differences.

Figure 14.2

Sampling Distribution of Differences Between Means

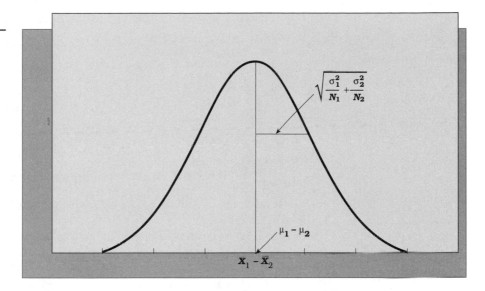

$$\sqrt{\frac{\sigma_1^2}{N_1} + \frac{\sigma_2^2}{N_2}}$$

$\mu_1 - \mu_2$

$\overline{X}_1 - \overline{X}_2$

Having found the mean and the variance of a set of differences between means, we know most of what we need to know to test a hypothesis about differences between means. The general form of the sampling distribution of mean differences is presented in Figure 14.2.

The final point to be made about this distribution concerns its shape. An important theorem in statistics states that the sum or difference of two independent normally distributed variables is itself normally distributed. Because Figure 14.2 represents the difference between two sampling distributions of means, and because we know the sampling distribution of means is at least approximately normal for reasonable sample sizes, then the distribution in Figure 14.2 must itself be at least approximately normal.

The t Statistic

Given the information we now have about the sampling distribution of differences between means, we can proceed to develop the appropriate test procedure. Assume *for the moment* that knowledge of the population variances (σ_1^2 and σ_2^2) is not a problem. We have earlier defined z as a statistic (a point on the distribution) minus the mean of the distribution, divided by the standard error of the distribution. Our statistic in the present case is ($\overline{X}_1 - \overline{X}_2$), the observed difference between the sample means. The mean of the sampling distribution is ($\mu_1 - \mu_2$), and, as we saw, the **standard error of differences between means** is

Standard error of differences between means

The standard deviation of the sampling distribution of the differences between means.

$$\sigma_{\overline{x}_1 - \overline{x}_2} = \sqrt{\frac{\sigma_1^2}{N_1} + \frac{\sigma_2^2}{N_2}}$$

Remember, the standard error of any statistic (in this case the difference between two sample means) is the standard deviation of the sampling distribution of that statistic. As such it is a measure of how stable we expect that statistic to be.

Given what we know, we can write

$$z = \frac{(\bar{X}_1 - \bar{X}_2) - (\mu_1 - \mu_2)}{\sigma_{\bar{X}_1 - \bar{X}_2}}$$

$$= \frac{(\bar{X}_1 - \bar{X}_2) - (\mu_1 - \mu_2)}{\sqrt{\dfrac{\sigma_1^2}{N_1} + \dfrac{\sigma_2^2}{N_2}}}$$

The critical value for $\alpha = .05$ is $z = \pm 1.96$, as it was for the one-sample tests discussed in Chapter 12.

The preceding formula is not particularly useful, except for the purpose of showing the origin of the appropriate t test, because we rarely know the necessary population variances. (Such knowledge is so rare that it isn't even worth imagining cases in which we would have it, although a few do exist.) However, just as we did in the one-sample case, we can circumvent this problem by using the sample variances as estimates of the population variances. For the same reasons discussed earlier for the one-sample t, this means that the result will be distributed as t rather than z.

$$t = \frac{(\bar{X}_1 - \bar{X}_2) - (\mu_1 - \mu_2)}{s_{\bar{X}_1 - \bar{X}_2}}$$

$$= \frac{(\bar{X}_1 - \bar{X}_2) - (\mu_1 - \mu_2)}{\sqrt{\dfrac{s_1^2}{N_1} + \dfrac{s_2^2}{N_2}}}$$

Because the null hypothesis is generally the hypothesis that $\mu_1 - \mu_2 = 0$, we usually drop that term from the equation and write

$$t = \frac{(\bar{X}_1 - \bar{X}_2)}{s_{\bar{X}_1 - \bar{X}_2}}$$

$$= \frac{(\bar{X}_1 - \bar{X}_2)}{\sqrt{\dfrac{s_1^2}{N_1} + \dfrac{s_2^2}{N_2}}}$$

Pooling Variances

Although the equation for t that we just developed is quite appropriate when the sample sizes are equal, it requires some modification for unequal sample sizes. This modification is designed to provide a better estimate of the population variance. One of the assumptions required for the use of t for two indepen-

Homogeneity of variance
The situation in which two or more populations have equal variances.

dent samples is that $\sigma_1^2 = \sigma_2^2$ (i.e., the samples come from populations with equal variances), regardless of the truth or falsity of H_0. Such an assumption is often a reasonable one and is called the assumption of **homogeneity of variance**. We often begin an experiment with two groups of subjects who are equivalent and then do something to one (or both) group(s) that will raise or lower the subjects' scores. In such a case it often makes sense to assume that the variances will remain unaffected. (You should recall that adding or subtracting a constant to a set of scores has no effect on its variance.) Because the population variances are assumed to be equal, this common variance can be represented by the symbol σ^2, without a subscript.

In our data we have two estimates of σ^2, namely s_1^2 and s_2^2. It seems appropriate to obtain some sort of an average of s_1^2 and s_2^2 on the grounds that this average should be a better estimate of σ^2 than either of the two separate estimates. We do not want to take the simple arithmetic mean, however, because doing so would give equal weight to the two estimates, even if one were based on considerably more observations. What we want is a **weighted average**, in which the sample variances are weighted by their degrees of freedom ($N_i - 1$). If we call this new estimate s_p^2, then

Weighted average
The mean of the form $(a_1X_1 + a_2X_2)/(a_1 + a_2)$, where a_1 and a_2 are weighting factors and X_1 and X_2 are the values to be averaged.

$$s_p^2 = \frac{(N_1 - 1)s_1^2 + (N_2 - 1)s_2^2}{N_1 + N_2 - 2}$$

The numerator represents the sum of the variances, each weighted by its degrees of freedom, and the denominator represents the sum of the weights or, equivalently, the degrees of freedom for s_p^2.

The weighted average of the two sample variances is usually referred to as a **pooled variance** estimate (a rather inelegant name, but reasonably descriptive). Having defined our pooled estimate (s_p^2), we can now replace s_i^2 with

Pooled variance
A weighted average of the separate sample variances.

$$t = \frac{(\overline{X}_1 - \overline{X}_2)}{s_{\overline{X}_1 - \overline{X}_2}} = \frac{(\overline{X}_1 - \overline{X}_2)}{\sqrt{\dfrac{s_p^2}{N_1} + \dfrac{s_p^2}{N_2}}} = \frac{(\overline{X}_1 - \overline{X}_2)}{\sqrt{s_p^2\left(\dfrac{1}{N_1} + \dfrac{1}{N_2}\right)}}$$

Notice that both this formula for t and the one we used in the previous section involve dividing the difference between the sample means by an estimate of the standard error of the difference between means. The only difference concerns the way in which this standard error is estimated. When sample sizes are equal, it makes absolutely no difference whether you pool variances; the resulting t will be the same. When the sample sizes are unequal, however, pooling can make quite a difference.

Degrees of Freedom for t

You will note that two sample variances (s_1^2 and s_2^2) have gone into calculating t. Each of these variances is based on squared deviations about their corresponding sample means; therefore, each sample variance has $N_i - 1$ df. Across the two samples, therefore, we will have $(N_1 - 1) + (N_2 - 1) = N_1 + N_2 - 2 \; df$. Thus the t for two independent samples will be based on $N_1 + N_2 - 2$ degrees of freedom.

Let's Stop to Review

We have just covered unusually more formulae, with somewhat more emphasis on derivation, than you have seen previously in this book. It might be smart to stop and say something about what all of that is for. It isn't as messy and cumbersome as it looks.

I started out by saying that if I want to know whether the means of two independent samples are significantly different, I need to know something about what differences between two means look like. In other words, I need to know the sampling distribution of differences between means. Such a distribution would have a mean equal to the difference between the population means and a standard error equal to the square root of the sum of the population variances each divided by the corresponding sample size. Such a distribution would be at least approximately normal.

At this point I know the mean, the standard error, and the shape of the sampling distribution of differences between means. I can now compute a z score as the difference in sample means, minus the difference in population means, divided by the standard error. This is the same kind of z score we have been seeing all along.

This formula is not adequate by itself, because it assumes we know the population variances, which we don't. So we do the same thing we did for earlier t tests—we substitute the sample variances for the population variances and call the result t.

Finally, when you have two sample variances, you usually want to average them to get a better estimate of the population variance. We call this averaging "pooling." We use the pooled version whenever the sample variances are in general agreement with one another, especially when sample sizes are about equal.

You should stop at this point and go back through the last few pages to see how the review I just gave you fits with the formulae we've covered so far in this chapter.

Example: Recall of Active and Passive Sentences

To illustrate the use of t as a test of the difference between two independent means, let's consider a hypothetical example from the field of verbal learning. Suppose an investigator has a fight with a journal editor who insists on using the passive voice in the third person ("It was found that . . .") rather than the active voice in the first person ("I found that . . ."). (Journal editors can be as stuffy as other people and, as bureaucrats learned long ago, elaborate sentence structures make even meaningless prose look more impressive.) You may have had the opposite experience with an instructor in English 101 who objected to any use of the passive. Our investigator wants to show that people recall active

Table 14.1

Recall of Active Declarative and Passive Negative Sentences

	Group AD		Group PN	
	17	18	13	13
	17	20	18	15
	21	21	17	14
	18	16	13	16
	22	15	14	15
	18	16	13	15
	16	20	18	13
	15		19	17
			16	17
			14	15
Mean	18.00		15.25	
Variance	5.286		3.671	

declarative sentences ("Joe rang the bell") better than passive negative sentences ("The bell was not rung by Amy"). The experimenter obtained 35 subjects and assigned them at random to two groups. By chance the first group (Group AD) had 15 subjects and the second (Group PN) had 20. Group AD was read 25 active declarative sentences and was given a recall test after each sentence. Group PN heard and recalled passive negative forms of the sentences used for Group AD. The dependent variable was the number of sentences correctly recalled by each subject. The data are presented in Table 14.1.

Before we consider any statistical test—and ideally even before the data are collected—we must specify several features of the test. First we must specify the null and alternative hypotheses:

$$H_0 : \mu_{AD} = \mu_{PN}$$

$$H_1 : \mu_{AD} \neq \mu_{PN}$$

The alternative hypothesis is bidirectional (we will reject H_0 if $\mu_{AD} < \mu_{PN}$ or if $\mu_{AD} > \mu_{PN}$); thus we are using a two-tailed test. For the sake of consistency with other examples in this book, we will let $\alpha = .05$. (It is important to keep in mind that there is nothing particularly sacred about these two decisions.[2]) Given the null hypothesis as stated, we can now calculate t:

---

[2] If we had a good reason for testing the hypothesis that μ_{AD} was five points higher than μ_{PN}, for example, we could set $H_0 : \mu_{AD} - \mu_{PN} = 5$, although this type of situation is extremely rare. Similarly, we could set α at .01, .001, or even .10, although this last value is higher than most people would accept.

$$t = \frac{\overline{X}_1 - \overline{X}_2}{s_{\overline{X}_1 - \overline{X}_2}}$$

$$= \frac{\overline{X}_1 - \overline{X}_2}{\sqrt{\dfrac{s_1^2}{N_1} + \dfrac{s_2^2}{N_2}}}$$

Because we are testing $H_0: \mu_{AD} - \mu_{PN} = 0$, the $\mu_{AD} - \mu_{PN}$ term has been dropped from the equation. When we pool the variances, we obtain

$$s_p^2 = \frac{(N_1 - 1)s_1^2 + (N_2 - 1)s_2^2}{N_1 + N_2 - 2}$$

$$= \frac{14(5.286) + 19(3.671)}{15 + 20 - 2} = \frac{74.004 + 69.749}{33} = 4.356$$

Note that the pooled variance is somewhat closer in value to s_2^2 than s_1^2 because of the greater weight given s_2^2 in the formula. Then

$$t = \frac{\overline{X}_1 - \overline{X}_2}{\sqrt{\dfrac{s_p^2}{N_1} + \dfrac{s_p^2}{N_2}}}$$

$$= \frac{18.00 - 15.25}{\sqrt{\dfrac{4.356}{15} + \dfrac{4.356}{20}}}$$

$$= \frac{2.75}{\sqrt{0.5082}} = \frac{2.75}{0.713} = 3.86$$

For this example we have $N_1 - 1 = 14$ df for Group AD and $N_2 - 1 = 19$ df for Group PN, making a total of $N_1 - 1 + N_2 - 1 = 33$ df. From the sampling distribution of t in Table D.6 in the Appendices, $t_{.05}(33) = \pm 2.04$ (with linear interpolation). Because the value of t_{obt} far exceeds t_α, we will reject H_0 (at $\alpha = .05$, two-tailed) and conclude that there is a difference between the means of the populations from which our observations were drawn. In other words, we will conclude (statistically) that $\mu_{AD} \neq \mu_{PN}$ and (practically) that $\mu_{AD} > \mu_{PN}$. In terms of the experimental variables, active declarative sentences are recalled better than passive negative sentences.[3]

Confounded
Term used to describe two variables when they are varied simultaneously and their effects cannot be separated.

---

[3]Because active declarative sentences are generally shorter than passive negative sentences, our interpretation of the results could be open to question. Unless our sentences were equated for length, we have no defense against the argument that we have shown merely that shorter sentences are remembered better than longer ones. We have **confounded** the variables of syntax and sentence length.

14.2 Heterogeneity of Variance

Heterogeneity of variance
A situation in which samples are drawn from populations having different variances.

As we have seen, one of the assumptions behind the t test for two independent samples is the assumption of homogeneity of variance ($\sigma_1^2 = \sigma_2^2$). When this assumption does not hold (i.e., when $\sigma_1^2 \neq \sigma_2^2$), we have what is called **heterogeneity of variance**. Considerable work has been done examining the practical effect of heterogeneity of variance on the t test. As a result of this work we can come to some general conclusions about the analysis of data that is appropriate with heterogeneous variances.

The first point to keep in mind is that our homogeneity assumption refers to population variances and not to sample variances—we would expect the sample variances to be equal only rarely even if the population variances were. On the basis of sampling studies that have been conducted, the general rule of thumb is that if one sample variance is no more than four[4] times the other *and* if the sample sizes are equal or approximately equal, you may go ahead and compute t as you would normally. Heterogeneity of variance is not likely to have a serious effect on your results under these conditions. On the other hand, if one sample variance is more than four times the other, or if the variances are quite unequal and the sample sizes are also quite unequal, then an alternative procedure may be necessary. This procedure is easy to apply, however. Simply compute t using the *separate* variance estimates (i.e., do not pool). Then go to the t tables using the *smaller* of $N_1 - 1$ and $N_2 - 1$ as the degrees of freedom (rather than $N_1 + N_2 - 2$). This is a conservative test, meaning that if H_0 is true you are less likely to commit a Type I error than the nominal value of α would suggest. As an example of this procedure, suppose we have the following data:

$$\bar{X} = 111.53 \quad \bar{X} = 108.38$$
$$s_1^2 = 19.65 \quad s_2^2 = 3.06$$
$$N_1 = 10 \quad N_2 = 18$$

$$t = \frac{\bar{X}_1 - \bar{X}_2}{\sqrt{\dfrac{s_1^2}{N_1} + \dfrac{s_2^2}{N_2}}}$$

$$= \frac{111.53 - 108.38}{\sqrt{\dfrac{19.65}{10} + \dfrac{3.06}{18}}}$$

$$= \frac{3.15}{1.461} = 2.16$$

---

[4]The use of the number four here is probably conservative. Some people would argue for using the standard approach when variances are considerably more different than this.

Because the variances were very unequal (one was more than six times the other), we did not pool them. The values of $N_1 - 1$ and $N_2 - 1$ are 9 and 17, respectively, and we will evaluate t by going to Table D.6 with 9 df (the smaller of 9 and 17). Here we find that $t_{.05}(9) = \pm 2.262$, which is larger than the obtained value. Thus we will not reject H_0.[5]

There are more accurate (less conservative) solutions to the problem of heterogeneity of variance, which rely on calculating an adjusted degrees of freedom lying between the smaller of $N_1 - 1$ and $N_2 - 1$, on the one hand, and $N_1 + N_2 - 2$ on the other. Many computer programs, including SAS, SPSS, Minitab, and the BMDP series, supply such an adjustment. For most purposes the conservative approach suggested here is sufficient. (A more complete discussion of the problem of heterogeneity of variance can be found in Howell, 1992.)

14.3 Nonnormality of Distributions

We saw earlier that another assumption required for the correct use of the t test is the assumption that the population(s) from which the data are sampled is (are) normally distributed—or at least that the sampling distribution of differences between means is normal. In general, as long as the distributions of sample data are roughly mound-shaped (high in the center and tapering off on either side), the test is likely to be valid. This is especially true for large samples (N_1 and N_2 greater than 30), because then the Central Limit Theorem almost guarantees near normality of the sampling distribution of differences between means.

14.4 A Second Example with Two Independent Samples

Earlier we briefly considered a study by Doob and Gross (1968) that investigated the effects of status on horn-honking behavior. In the study the driver of either a low- or a high-status car remained stopped when a traffic light turned green, and the experimenter observed the behavior of the driver of the following car. One of the measures was the number of seconds that elapsed between the time the light turned green and the time the driver of the following car honked the horn. The data shown in Table 14.2 have been created to have essentially the same means and standard deviations as those reported by Doob and Gross, although their study involved larger sample sizes. (The conclusions that follow are the same as theirs.)

Doob and Gross were interested in testing the null hypothesis that the mean latency (in the population) to respond to a stopped high-status car was equal to the mean latency to respond to a low-status car (i.e., $H_0: \mu_1 = \mu_2$). They chose a two-tailed alternative hypothesis ($H_0: \mu_1 \neq \mu_2$) and set $\alpha = .05$. Visual

---

[5]Note that if we had not had a problem with heterogeneity of variance, we would have used $N_1 + N_2 - 2 = 26$ df, and the difference would have been significant.

Table 14.2

Latency (in Seconds) of Horn Honking as a Function of Status

Low-Status Group ($N = 15$)				High-Status Group ($N = 20$)			
1.68	6.42	8.58	6.85	9.10	7.83	11.22	5.29
10.59	3.26	9.44	4.84	13.20	11.79	3.87	7.41
4.98	12.31	9.01	6.13	8.40	14.05	4.44	8.11
7.86	6.71	8.14		9.81	11.79	6.84	12.64
				8.68	10.66	9.95	9.53

$$\overline{X}_1 = 7.12 \qquad s_1 = 2.77 \qquad \overline{X}_2 = 9.23 \qquad s_2 = 2.82$$
$$s_1^2 = 7.69 \qquad\qquad\qquad s_2^2 = 7.95$$

inspection of the data suggests that the sample variances are nearly equal ($s_1^2 = 7.69$, $s_2^2 = 7.95$) and that the data are at least unimodal and symmetric, so a t test seems appropriate. Because we have unequal sample sizes, we will pool the sample variances. The pooled variance is given by

$$s_p^2 = \frac{(N_1 - 1)s_1^2 + (N_2 - 1)s_2^2}{N_1 + N_2 - 2}$$

$$= \frac{14(7.69) + 19(7.95)}{15 + 20 - 2} = \frac{107.66 + 151.05}{33} = \frac{258.71}{33}$$

$$= 7.84$$

Then t, using the pooled variances, is

$$t = \frac{\overline{X}_1 - \overline{X}_2}{\sqrt{\dfrac{s_p^2}{N_1} + \dfrac{s_p^2}{N_2}}}$$

$$= \frac{7.12 - 9.23}{\sqrt{\dfrac{7.84}{15} + \dfrac{7.84}{20}}}$$

$$= \frac{-2.11}{\sqrt{0.9147}} = \frac{-2.11}{0.9564}$$

$$= -2.21$$

From Table D.6, with $\alpha = .05$ and $df = 33$, we have $t_{.05}(33) = \pm 2.04$. Because $t_{obt} = -2.21$ lies in the rejection region, we will reject H_0 and conclude that $\mu_1 \neq \mu_2$. In practical terms this means that we will conclude that a driver is quicker to blow his or her horn when a low-status car is blocking the intersection than when the car is of high status. (It is interesting to note that this experiment suggests unobtrusive ways in which we could examine discriminatory behavior. This approach could be applied in a variety of situations—do drivers honk more readily at women or members of minority groups? Do male drivers honk more readily than female drivers?)

14.5 Confidence Limits on $\mu_1 - \mu_2$

In addition to testing a null hypothesis about population means (i.e., testing $H_0: \mu_1 - \mu_2 = 0$), it is sometimes useful to set confidence limits on the difference between μ_1 and μ_2. The logic for setting these confidence limits is exactly the same as it was for the one-sample case in Chapter 12. The calculations are also exactly the same except that we use the *difference* between the means and the standard error of *differences* between means in place of the mean and the standard error of the mean. Thus, for the 95% confidence limits on $\mu_1 - \mu_2$ we have

$$CI_{.95} = (\bar{X}_1 - \bar{X}_2) \pm t_{.05}s_{\bar{x}_1 - \bar{x}_2}$$

For the horn-honking example we have

$$CI_{.95} = (7.12 - 9.23) \pm 2.04 \sqrt{\frac{7.84}{15} + \frac{7.84}{20}}$$

$$= -2.11 \pm 2.04 \,(0.9564) = -2.11 \pm 1.96$$

$$-4.05 \le (\mu_1 - \mu_2) \le -0.17$$

The probability is .95 that an interval such as the interval -4.05 to -0.17 encloses the difference in latency between honking at low- and at high-status cars.

14.6 Use of Computer Programs for Analysis of Two Independent Sample Means

To illustrate how different computer programs analyze the same data set, I have chosen two programs that approach t tests on two independent groups differently. The differences in their output, and even in their answers, are of interest.

Figure 14.3 illustrates the use of Minitab to analyze the results of the horn-honking experiment. In the upper portion of the table you will see the stem-and-leaf and boxplot displays for the data for each group separately. From these displays we can see that the data are symmetrically distributed with no outliers. The pooled t test is shown in the lower portion of the table along with

Figure 14.3   Minitab Analysis of Horn-Honking Data

```
MTB > Stem-and-Leaf 'Delay' ;
SUBC> By 'Group'.

Stem-and-leaf of Delay    Group = 1    N = 15
Leaf Unit = 0.10

    1      1 6
    1      2
    2      3 2
    4      4 89
    4      5
   (4)     6 1478
    7      7 8
    6      8 15
    4      9 04
    2     10 5
    1     11
    1     12 3

Stem-and-leaf of Delay    Group = 2    N = 20
Leaf Unit = 0.10

    1      3 8
    2      4 4
    3      5 2
    4      6 8
    6      7 48
    9      8 146
   (4)     9 1589
    7     10 6
    6     11 277
    3     12 6
    2     13 2
    1     14 0
```

```
Group
1    Low     -----------------[    +    ]-----------------

2    High        --------------[    +    ]----------

        ---------------|---------------|---------------|---------------|---------------|-------------- Delay
                     3.5            7.0           10.5           14.0
```

```
MTB > TwoSample 95.0 'Delay' 'Group'
SUBC>    Alternative 0;
SUBC>    Pooled.

TWOSAMPLE T FOR Delay
Group    N       MEAN      STDEV     SE MEAN
1        15      7.12      2.77      0.72
2        20      9.23      2.82      0.63
```

95 PCT CI FOR MU 1 — MU 2: (−4.06, −0.16) $\leftarrow$ *t* when variances are pooled

TTEST MU 1 = MU 2 (VS NE): T= −2.21 P=0.034 DF= 33 $\leftarrow$
                                                  df when variances are pooled

```
POOLED STDEV = 2.80

MTB > TwoSample 95.0 'Delay' 'Group';
SUBC>    Alternative 0.

TWOSAMPLE T FOR Delay
Group    N       MEAN      STDEV     SE MEAN
1        15      7.12      2.77      0.72
2        20      9.23      2.82      0.63
```

95 PCT CI FOR MU 1 — MU 2: (−4.06, −0.16) $\leftarrow$ *t* when variances not pooled

TTEST MU 1 = MU 2 (VS NE): T= −2.21 P=0.035 DF= 30 $\leftarrow$
                                                  df when variances not pooled

```
MTB >
```

the 95% confidence limits on $\mu_1 - \mu_2$. You can see that these results agree with the ones we obtained earlier. Also included in Figure 14.3 for illustrative purposes is a t test using the separate variance estimates (rather than pooling). This procedure leads to essentially the same results, although you can see that, as suggested earlier, the degrees of freedom have been adjusted slightly due to the small differences in the sample variances.[6]

Figure 14.4 contains output from the student version of a program named Stata. Both Stata and Minitab are highly sophisticated programs that can do

---

[6] If you were to run this analysis using a different statistical package, the adjusted df most likely would not be a whole integer. Minitab calculates the adjusted df and then rounds down to the nearest whole integer. (It really makes no difference except to the purists among us.)

Figure 14.4   Stata Analysis of Horn-Honking Data

```
. use doob.dta
(Data from Study on Horn-Honking)

. stem delay if status == 1          . stem delay if status == 2

Stem and leaf plot for delay in      Stem and leaf plot for delay in
units of 0.1                         units of 0.1

1 | 6
2 |
3 | 2                                3 | 8
4 | 89                               4 | 4
5 |                                  5 | 2
6 | 1478                             6 | 8
7 | 8                                7 | 48
8 | 15                               8 | 146
9 | 04                               9 | 1589
1 | | 05,23                          1 | | 06,12,17,17,26,32,40

. ttest delay, by(status)
```

Variable	Obs	Mean	Std. Dev.
1	15	7.12	2.772742
2	20	9.2305	2.820255
combined	35	8.326	2.955231

H_0: mean(x) = mean(y) (assuming equal variances)
          t = −2.21 with 33 d.f.
       Pr > |t| = 0.0344 ← t with pooled variances

```
. ttest delay, by(status) unequal
```

Variable	Obs	Mean	Std. Dev.
1	15	7.12	2.772742
2	20	9.2305	2.820255
combined	35	8.326	

H_0: mean(x) = mean(y) (assuming unequal variances)
          t = −2.21 with 33 d.f. ← df with separate variances (erroneous)
       Pr > |t| = 0.0340 ← t with separate (unpooled) variances

```
. exit, clear
```

very complex analyses. They do differ from one another superficially in their output. (I have not tried to match each step in the analyses, partly because Stata's boxplots are high-quality graphics that cannot be saved or printed from the student version that I have.)

There is an important difference between the way you would think of the data if you were calculating t by hand and the way we usually calculate it using computer software. By hand, we usually think of two columns of data and run a t test between the means of the two columns. The standard way to run analyses via software is to have one column of data that represents the dependent variable (Delay) and another column that represents group membership (usually coded 1 and 2). You then ask the program to look at the data in the dependent variable, broken down by group. In Figure 14.3 each stem-and-leaf display represents a different group. There is a similar pattern for the boxplots and for the t tests. That is the normal way of doing things.

Notice the difference in how the two programs print their stem-and-leaf displays. Minitab uses more categories and adds a column to the left, which we labeled *depth* in Chapter 3. When Stata comes to what would otherwise be two-digit stems, it doubles the vertical line and uses two-digit leaves instead. This is not a critical difference, but it is an example of what you often find when you compare different software. (I placed Stata's stem-and-leaf displays side by side to conserve space and adjusted the second one vertically to make comparisons of the distributions easier.)

Notice that both programs produce the same t values when they use either pooled or separate variance estimates. In both cases I first solved using the pooled variance approach and then using the separate (nonpooled) variance approach. Notice that when separate variance estimates were used the two sets of results differ on the degrees of freedom for those ts and on the resulting probabilities. (These are the adjusted degrees of freedom referred to on p. 256.) The differences may be small, but the fact that they are different at all is important. *They should not differ*, and in this case Minitab is correct. This is a small lesson in the fallibility of computer programs. Put not your faith in software—at least not uncritical faith.

14.7 A Final Worked Example

The following data are based on a study by Eysenck (1974) that among other things, compared the levels of recall of older and younger subjects. (We will have more to say about this study in Chapters 16 and 17.) Eysenck wanted to test the hypothesis that when subjects were required to process verbal information (lists of words), older subjects did less processing and therefore recalled fewer words. (In this study he also showed that there were no differences in recall between the two age groups when in-depth processing was *not* required.) The data in Table 14.3 have been constructed to have the same means and standard deviations as two of the conditions in Eysenck's study and refer to groups who were told to memorize the words so that they could be recalled later. The dependent variable is the number of items correctly recalled.

Table 14.3

Data from Eysenck (1974)

Younger Subjects				Older Subjects			
21	19	17	15	10	19	14	5
22	16	22	22	10	11	14	15
18	21			11	11		
	ΣX_1	193			ΣX_2	120	
	ΣX_1^2	3789			ΣX_2^2	1566	
	N_1	10			N_2	10	

First we need to specify the null hypothesis, the significance level, and whether we will use a one- or a two-tailed test. We want to test the null hypothesis that the two age groups recall the same amount of information, so we have $H_0: \mu_1 = \mu_2$. We will set alpha at $\alpha = .05$, in line with what we have been using. Finally, we will choose to use a two-tailed test because it is reasonably possible for either group to show superior recall.

Next we need to calculate the means and the variances.

$$\bar{X}_1 = \frac{193}{10} = 19.3 \qquad \bar{X}_2 = \frac{120}{10} = 12.0$$

$$s_1^2 = \frac{3789 - \frac{193^2}{10}}{9} \qquad s_2^2 = \frac{1566 - \frac{120^2}{10}}{9}$$

$$= 7.122 \qquad\qquad = 14.00$$

With equal sample sizes we do not need to bother pooling the variances, because the resulting t would be the same in either event. However, for the sake of an example I will do so here:

$$s_p^2 = \frac{(N_1 - 1)(s_1^2) + (N_2 - 1)(s_2^2)}{N_1 + N_2 - 2} = \frac{9(7.122) + 9(14.000)}{18} = 10.561$$

Finally, we can calculate t using the pooled variance estimate:

$$t = \frac{(\bar{X}_1 - \bar{X}_2)}{\sqrt{\frac{s_p^2}{N_1} + \frac{s_p^2}{N_2}}} = \frac{19.3 - 12.0}{\sqrt{\frac{10.561}{10} + \frac{10.561}{10}}} = \frac{7.300}{\sqrt{2.112}} = 5.02$$

For this example we have $N_1 + N_2 - 2 = 18$ degrees of freedom. From Table D.6 in the Appendices we find $t_{.05} = 2.101$. Because $5.02 > 2.101$, we will reject H_0 and conclude that the two population means are not equal.

If you were writing up the results of this experiment, you might write something like the following:

In an attempt to test the hypothesis that older subjects process and store information less completely than younger subjects, we asked two groups of 10 subjects each (differing only in age) to study and then recall a list of words that required a moderate level of verbal processing. The results showed that younger subjects recalled a mean of 19.3 words, while older subjects recalled a mean of 12.0 words. (The two standard deviations were 2.67 and 3.74, respectively.) A t test comparing the two groups was significant ($t(18) = 5.02$, $p < .05$). The results demonstrated that younger subjects recalled significantly more words than did older subjects. This is not to say that older subjects are not as smart as younger ones, but only that for some reason they did not perform as well on this task. Because other data revealed no differences on tasks that did not require in-depth processing, it would appear that processing of information is a relevant variable. It may well be that older subjects are not willing to process information to the same extent that younger subjects are, possibly because they are not really interested in the experiment.

14.8 Summary

In this chapter we considered the use of the t test for testing the null hypothesis that two population means are equal. This test is based on sample means from two independent samples and is probably the most common form of the t test. We also considered the assumptions underlying the use of t, procedures to be applied when the assumption of homogeneity of variance is not met, and confidence limits for mean differences.

Some important terms in this chapter are:

- Sampling distribution of differences between means

- Variance Sum Law

- Standard error of differences between means

- Homogeneity of variance

- Weighted average

- Pooled variance

- Confounded

- Heterogeneity of variance

14.9 Exercises

14.1 Suppose we redesigned the study described in Exercise 13.1 to have different subjects serve under the Imitation and Physical Guidance conditions. We obtained the following data:

Imitation		Physical Guidance	
14	14	10	0
11	17	14	1
19	18	5	4
8	0	8	2
4	2	1	3
9	8	10	4
12	6	13	14
5		14	

What would you conclude?

14.2 What is the most obvious problem with the data in Exercise 14.1 in terms of finding a significant difference?

14.3 Why was the experimental design used in Exercise 13.1 able to produce a statistically significant difference when there wasn't one for Exercise 14.1?

14.4 We randomly assigned nine children to two groups and asked each child to feed his or her pet every day for one week. The children in one group were praised each time their pets were fed; those in the other group were praised only at the end of the week. The following data represent the number of times each child forgot to do his or her task.

Daily Reward	Weekly Reward
3	1
3	3
2	2
2	1
3	0
4	3
3	1
1	0
0	2

Run the appropriate t test.

14.5 What is the role of random assignment in Exercise 14.4?

14.6 In a comparison of different programs advocated by two organizations concerned with weight loss, 20 subjects were enrolled in Program A and 20 in Program B. The amount of weight lost in the next six months is shown for those subjects who completed the program.

Program A	Program B	
25	15	14
21	17	18
18	9	16
20	12	10
22	11	5
30	19	13

Run the appropriate t test after considering the group variances.

14.7 The following data represent alternative data that might have been obtained in the study described in Exercise 14.6.

Program A	Program B	
25	15	14
21	17	18
8	9	16
20	12	10
12	11	15
30	19	13

Calculate and evaluate t after considering the two sample variances.

14.8 In Exercise 14.7 the means are not the only important statistics. What might be considered more important?

14.9 Much has been made of the concept of *experimenter bias*, which refers to the fact that for even the most conscientious experimenters there seems to be a tendency for the data to come out in the desired direction. Suppose we use students as experimenters. All the experimenters are told that subjects will be given caffeine before the experiment, but half the experimenters are told that we expect caffeine to lead to good performance, and half are told that we expect it to lead to poor performance. The dependent variable is the number of simple arithmetic problems the subject can solve in 2 minutes. The obtained data are as follows:

Expect Good Performance		Expect Poor Performance	
19	15	14	21
15	20	18	24
22	25	17	14
13	22	12	
18		21	

What would you conclude?

14.10 Calculate the 95% confidence limits on $\mu_1 - \mu_2$ for the data in Exercise 14.9.

14.11 Calculate the 95% confidence limits on $\mu_1 - \mu_2$ for the data in Exercise 14.7.

14.12 Using the data in Appendix C, use a t test to compare ADDSC scores of males and females.

14.13 Using the data in Appendix C, compare grade point averages for those having ADDSC scores of 65 or less with those having ADDSC scores of 66 or more.

14.14 What does the answer to Exercise 14.13 tell you about the predictive utility of the ADDSC score?

14.15 An experimenter working in the area of decision making asked ten children to solve as many problems as they could in ten minutes. Half of the children were told this was a test of their innate problem-solving ability, and the other half were told this was just a time-filling task. Compute and interpret the appropriate t test. The dependent variable is the number of problems solved. The data are as follows:

Innate Ability	Time Filling
4	11
5	6
8	9
3	7
7	9

14.16 A second experimenter repeated the experiment described in Exercise 14.15 and obtained exactly the same results. However, she felt that it would be more appropriate to record the data in terms of minutes per problem. (For example, four problems in ten minutes = 10/4 = 2.50 minutes per problem.) Her data are as follows:

Innate Ability	Time Filling
2.50	0.91
2.00	1.67
1.25	1.11
3.33	1.43
1.43	1.11

Analyze and interpret these data with the appropriate t test.

14.17 Given the definition of a weighted average (see page 251) show what the pooled variance estimate (s_p^2) would be if the two sample sizes were equal. (*Hint:* Replace N_1 and N_2 with N.)

14.18 With respect to the previous exercise, what would happen if $s_1^2 = s_2^2$, regardless of N_i?

14.19 What does a comparison of Exercises 14.15 and 14.16 show?

14.20 Demonstrate that, *because we have equal sample sizes*, I would have arrived at the same answer in Section 14.7 if I had not pooled the variances, although the degrees of freedom would probably differ.

15

Power

$\mathbf{M}$ost applied statistical work as it is actually carried out in analyzing experimental results is concerned primarily with minimizing (or at least controlling) the probability of a Type I error (α). When it comes to designing experiments, people generally tend to ignore that there is a probability (β) of another kind of error, a Type II error. Whereas Type I errors deal with the problem of *finding* a difference that is *not* there, Type II errors concern the equally serious problem of *not finding* a difference that *is* there. When we consider the substantial cost in time and money that goes into a typical experiment, it is remarkably shortsighted of experimenters not to recognize that they may, from the start, have a very small chance of finding the effect for which they are looking, even if such an effect actually exists in the population and even if it is a nontrivial effect worth finding.

Investigators historically have tended to avoid concerning themselves with Type II errors. Until recently many textbooks ignored the problem altogether. Those books that did discuss the material discussed it in ways not easily understood by the book's intended audience. In the past 20 years, however, Jacob Cohen, a psychologist, has discussed the problem clearly and lucidly in several publications. Cohen (1988) presents a thorough and rigorous treatment of the material. In Welkowitz, Ewen, and Cohen (1991) the material is treated in a slightly simpler way, through the use of an approximation technique, which is the approach adopted in this chapter. This approximation is based on the use of the normal distribution, and differences between the level of power computed with this method and with the more exact approach are generally negligible. Most recently, Cohen (1992) has written an excellent five-page paper that is quite accessible, and I hand it out to anyone who asks me about statistical power. If you become interested in this topic or need to consider power in greater depth than we do in this chapter, you should have no difficulty with the sources just mentioned or with any of the many excellent papers Cohen has published on a wide variety of topics.

Speaking in terms of Type II errors is a negative way of approaching the problem, since it focuses on our mistakes. The more positive approach is to speak in terms of **power**, which is defined as the probability of *correctly* rejecting a *false H_0*. Put another way, power equals $1 - \beta$. When we say that the power of a particular experimental design is .65, we mean that if the null hypothesis is false to the degree we expect, the probability is .65 that the results of the experiment will lead us to reject H_0. A more powerful experiment is one that has a greater probability of rejecting a false H_0 than does a less powerful experiment.

Power
The probability of correctly rejecting a false H_0.

This chapter will take the approach of Welkowitz, Ewen, and Cohen (1991) and work with an approximation to the true power of a test. This approximation is an excellent one, especially because we do not really care whether power equals .85 or .83, but rather if it is in the .80s or in the .30s. For purposes of exploring the basic material, let's assume for the moment that we are interested in using a t test for testing one sample mean against a specified population mean, although the approach immediately generalizes to the testing of other hypotheses.

15.1 The Basic Concept

To review briefly what we have already covered in Chapter 11, consider the two distributions in Figure 15.1. The distribution to the left (labeled H_0) represents the sampling distribution of the mean when the null hypothesis is true and

Figure 15.1

Sampling Distributions of $\bar{X}$ Under H_0 and H_1

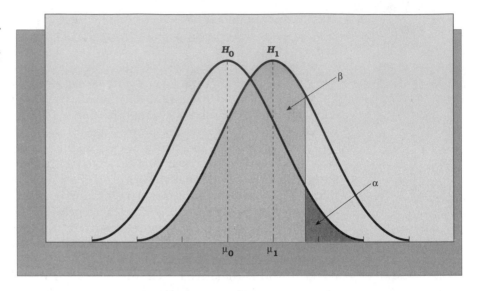

the population mean equals μ_0.[1] The right-hand tail of this distribution (the darker-shaded area) represents α, the probability of a Type I error, assuming that we are using a one-tailed test (otherwise it represents $\alpha/2$). This area contains the values of a sample mean that would result in significant values of t.

The second distribution (H_1) represents the sampling distribution of the mean when H_0 is false and when the true mean is μ_1. It is readily apparent that even when H_0 is false, many of the sample means (and therefore the corresponding values of t) will nonetheless fall to the left of the critical value, causing us to fail to reject a false H_0, thereby committing a Type II error. The probability of this error is indicated by the lighter-shaded area in Figure 15.1 and is labeled β.

Finally, when H_0 is false and the test statistic falls to the right of the critical value, we will correctly reject a false H_0. The probability of doing this is what we mean by power and is shown in the unshaded area of the H_1 distribution.

15.2 Factors That Affect the Power of a Test

As you might expect, power is a function of several variables:

1. the probability of a Type I error (α), the *a priori* level of significance and the criterion for rejecting H_0

2. the true difference between the null hypothesis and an alternative hypothesis ($\mu_0 - \mu_1$)

---

[1] If you are not sure that you remember what a sampling distribution is, look back at Chapter 11. Briefly, a sampling distribution is the distribution that a statistic (such as the mean) will have over repeated sampling.

3. the sample size (N) and σ^2

4. the particular test to be employed and whether we are using a one- or a two-tailed test

We will discuss the fourth relationship only with respect to the relative power of independent versus related (matched) samples. In general, when the assumptions behind a particular test are met, the procedures presented in this book (with the possible exception of those discussed in Chapter 20) can be shown to have more power to answer the question at hand than other available tests.

Power as a Function of α

With the aid of Figure 15.1 it is easy to see why we say that power is a function of α. If we are willing to increase α, the cutoff point moves to the left, simultaneously decreasing β and increasing power. Unfortunately this is accompanied by a corresponding rise in the probability of a Type I error.

Power as a Function of $\mu_0 - \mu_1$

The fact that power is a function of the nature of the true alternative hypothesis—more precisely, ($\mu_0 - \mu_1$)—is illustrated by a comparison of Figures 15.1 and 15.2. In Figure 15.2 the distance between μ_0 and μ_1 has been increased, resulting in a substantial increase in power. This is not particularly surprising, since all we are saying is that the chances of finding a difference depend on how large the difference is. (It is easier to distinguish between oranges and apples than between oranges and tangerines.)

Figure 15.2

Effect on Power of Increasing Distance Between μ_0 and μ_1

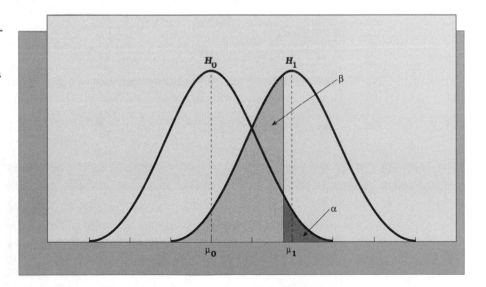

Figure 15.3

Effect on Power of a Decrease in the Standard Error of the Mean

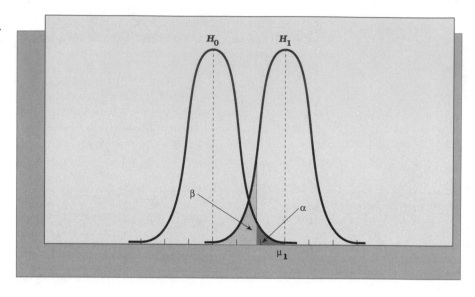

Power as a Function of the Sample Size (N) and σ^2

The relationship between power and sample size (and between power and σ^2) is only a little subtler. Because we are interested in means or differences between means, we are interested, directly or indirectly, in the sampling distribution of the mean. We know that $\sigma_{\bar{X}}^2 = \sigma^2/N$. From this equation we can see that the variance of the sampling distribution of the mean decreases either as N increases or as σ^2 decreases. Figure 15.3, in comparison with Figure 15.2, illustrates what happens to the two sampling distributions (H_0 and H_1) as we increase N or decrease σ^2. In Figure 15.3 we see that as $\sigma_{\bar{X}}^2$ decreases, the overlap between the two distributions is reduced, with a resulting increase in power.

An experimenter concerned with the power of a test most likely will be interested in those variables governing power that she can manipulate easily. Because N is more easily manipulated than either σ^2 or ($\mu_0 - \mu_1$), and because tampering with α produces undesirable side effects (increasing the probability of a Type I error), discussions of power are generally concerned with the effects of varying sample size.

15.3 Effect Size

As we have seen in Figures 15.1 through 15.3, power depends on the degree of overlap between the sampling distributions under H_0 and H_1. Furthermore, this overlap is a function of *both* the distance between μ_0 and μ_1 (the population mean if H_0 is true and the population mean if H_1 is true) and the standard error of the mean (the standard deviation of either of these sampling distributions). One measure, then, of the degree to which H_0 is false would be the difference in population means under H_0 and H_1, which is ($\mu_0 - \mu_1$), expressed in terms of the number of standard errors (i.e., ($\mu_0 - \mu_1$)/$\sigma_{\bar{x}}$). The problem with this measure is that the denominator ($\sigma_{\bar{x}} = \sigma/\sqrt{N}$) includes the sample size. In practice we usually will want to keep N separate from ($\mu_0 - \mu_1$) and σ so we can solve for the power associated with a given value of N or else for that value of N required for a given level of power. For that reason we will take as our distance measure, or **effect size**,

Effect size
The difference between two population means divided by the standard deviation of either population.

$$\gamma = \frac{\mu_1 - \mu_0}{\sigma}$$

Gamma (γ)
The symbol for the effect size.

We will ignore the sign of γ (**gamma**), attending only to its absolute value. Gamma is a measure of the degree to which μ_1 and μ_0 differ in terms of the standard deviation of the parent population. For example, if we expect a group of children who have suffered from malnutrition to have a mean IQ 8 points below normal (where $\sigma = 16$), we are talking about an effect size of one-half a standard deviation (i.e., the malnourished group will be below average by $8/16 = 1/2$ a standard deviation). Then $\gamma = 1/2 = 0.5$. From our equation we see that γ is estimated independently of N, simply by estimating μ_1 and σ. We will incorporate N at a later date.

Estimating the Effect Size

The first task becomes that of estimating γ, because it will form the basis for future calculations. We can do this in one of three ways.

1. *Prior research.* We often can obtain at least a rough approximation of γ by looking at past data. Thus we could look at sample means and variances from other studies and make an informed guess at the values we might expect for $\mu_1 - \mu_0$ and for σ. In practice this task is not as difficult as it might seem, especially when you realize that even a rough approximation is far better than no approximation at all.

2. *Personal assessment of what difference is important.* In many cases an investigator is able to say, "I am interested in detecting a difference of at least ten points between μ_1 and μ_0." The investigator is saying essentially that smaller differences have no important or useful meaning, whereas differences greater than ten points do. Here we are given the value of $\mu_1 - \mu_0$ directly, without any necessary knowledge of the particular values of μ_1 and μ_0. All that remains is to estimate σ from other data. For example, an investigator might say that he is interested in finding a study guide that will raise scores on the College Board Examination (SAT) by 40 points above average. We already know that the standard deviation for this test is approximately 100. Thus $\gamma = 40/100 = 0.40$. If, instead of saying that he wanted to raise scores by 40 points, the experimenter said he wanted to raise them by $4/10$ of a standard deviation, he would have been giving us γ directly.

3.   *The use of special conventions.* When we encounter a situation in which there is no way that we can estimate the required parameters, we can fall back on a set of conventions given by Cohen (1988). Cohen has defined three values of γ for use when testing means. For a justification of these levels the reader is referred to Cohen's work. Cohen's rule of thumb is

Effect Size	γ
Small	.20
Medium	.50
Large	.80

Thus when all else fails, experimenters simply can decide whether they are after a small, medium, or large effect and set γ accordingly. Although it is common to see reference to these estimates, it must be emphasized that this solution should be chosen only when the other alternatives are not feasible.

You might think it is peculiar to be asked to define the difference you are looking for before the experiment is conducted. Many people would respond by claiming that if they knew how the experiment would come out, they wouldn't have needed to run it in the first place. Although many experimenters behave as if this were true, if you consider the excuse carefully you should start to question its validity. Do we really not know, at least vaguely, what will happen in our experiments, and if not, why are we running them? And even if we have no idea what to expect, we should at least consider the minimum effect we would be interested in detecting. While there is an occasional legitimate "I wonder what would happen if" experiment, "I don't know" usually translates to "I haven't thought that far ahead." Remember that most experiments are run to demonstrate to the rest of the world that a particular theory is correct, and that theory often tells us what kind of results to expect.

Combining the Effect Size and N

Delta (δ)
A value used in calculating power that combines gamma and the sample size.

In our discussion of the effect size (γ), we split off the sample size from the effect size to make it easier to deal with N separately. The final thing we will need is a method for combining the effect size with the sample size to determine the power of an experiment for a given N and effect size. For this we will use the symbol δ (**delta**):

$$\delta = \gamma[f(N)]$$

where the particular function of N, $f(N)$, will be defined differently for each individual test.[2] In this equation the notation $f(N)$—read "f of N"—is used as a

---

[2] I'm sure a lot of students out there just groaned that they had finished with their math requirement and thought they were safely away from things like $f(N)$—or else they skipped math entirely because they didn't want to worry about such stuff. Just think of $f(N)$ as a shorthand way of writing, "some value based on N that I don't want to specify more precisely here."

general way of stating that δ depends not only on γ but also in some unspecified way on N. For example, you will see that in the one-sample t test we will compute δ by replacing $f(N)$ with $\sqrt{N}$, whereas in the two-sample t test we will replace $f(N)$ with $\sqrt{(N/2)}$. The nice thing about this system is that it allows us to use the same table of δ for power calculations for all the statistical procedures to be considered. How we will actually use δ is illustrated in the next section.

It is probably worth restating why we have gone to all this work to define γ without regard to N and have then put N back in when it comes to defining δ. When you are planning an experiment, $(\mu_1 - \mu_0)$ and σ, and therefore γ, are more or less fixed. But the choice of N is up to you. We want to be able to compute power, by way of δ, for a given γ when N is 20, for example, and then when N is 50. We don't want to have to repeat a set of calculations every time we change N. By defining γ independently of N and then having a simple formula to put the two together, we save ourselves a lot of work.

15.4 Power Calculations for the One-Sample *t* Test

For our first example we will examine the calculation of power for the one-sample t test. In the previous section you saw that δ is based on γ and some function of N. For the one-sample t test, that function will be $\sqrt{N}$, and δ will then be defined as

$$\delta = \gamma\sqrt{N}$$

A small amount of algebra will show that δ is now the difference between μ_1 and μ_0 divided by the standard error of the mean (recall that $\gamma = \mu_1 - \mu_0$ divided by the standard deviation).

$$\delta = \gamma\sqrt{N} = \frac{\mu_1 - \mu_0}{\sigma}\sqrt{N} = \frac{\mu_1 - \mu_0}{\left(\dfrac{\sigma}{\sqrt{N}}\right)} = \frac{\mu_1 - \mu_0}{\sigma_{\bar{x}}}$$

Now, assume a clinical psychologist wants to test the hypothesis that individuals who seek treatment for psychological problems have a higher IQ than normal. Using the IQs of 25 randomly selected clients drawn from a wide variety of clinical settings, she is interested in finding the power of detecting a difference of 5 points between the mean of the general population and the mean of the population from which her sample of clients is drawn. The parameters are $\mu_1 = 105$, $\mu_0 = 100$, and $\sigma = 15$, the last two being the mean and the standard deviation of most IQ tests when administered to the general population. Thus,

$$\gamma = \frac{105 - 100}{15} = 0.33$$

Then

$$\delta = \gamma\sqrt{N}$$
$$= 0.33\sqrt{25} = 0.33(5) = 1.65$$

Although the experimenter expects the sample mean to be above the mean of the general population, she plans to use a two-tailed test at $\alpha = .05$ to protect against unexpected events. Given δ, we immediately can determine the power of the test from Table D.5 in the Appendices. A portion of this table is reproduced in Table 15.1. To use either table, simply go down the left-hand margin until you come to the value of $\delta = 1.65$ and then read across to the column headed .05; that entry will be the power of the test. Neither table has an entry for $\delta = 1.65$, but they do have entries for $\delta = 1.60$ and $\delta = 1.70$. For $\alpha = .05$ this means that power is between 0.36 and 0.40. By linear interpolation we will say that for $\delta = 1.65$, power is equal to 0.38. This means that if H_0 is really false and $\mu_1 = 105$, only 38% of the time will the clinician obtain data that will produce a significant value of t when testing the difference between her *sample* mean and that specified by H_0. This is a rather discouraging result, because it means that if the true mean is really 105, 100% − 38% = 62% of the time the study as designed will *not* obtain a significant result.

Because the experimenter was intelligent enough to examine the question of power before she began her experiment, she still has the chance to make changes that will lead to an increase in power. She could, for example, set α at .10, thus increasing power to approximately 0.50, but this is probably unsatisfactory. (Journal editors, for example, generally hate to see α set at any value greater than .05.) Alternatively the experimenter could make use of the fact that power increases as N increases.

Table 15.1

Abbreviated Version of Table D.5, Power as a Function of δ and Significance Level (α)

	Alpha for Two-Tailed Test			
δ	.10	.05	.02	.01
1.00	0.26	0.17	0.09	0.06
1.10	0.29	0.20	0.11	0.07
1.20	0.33	0.22	0.13	0.08
1.30	0.37	0.26	0.15	0.10
1.40	0.40	0.29	0.18	0.12
1.50	0.44	0.32	0.20	0.14
1.60	0.48	**0.36**	0.23	0.17
1.70	0.52	**0.40**	0.27	0.19
1.80	0.56	0.44	0.30	0.22
1.90	0.60	0.48	0.34	0.25
⋮	⋮	⋮	⋮	⋮

Estimating Required Sample Sizes

It is fine to say that a thoughtful experimenter can increase power by increasing N, but how large an N is needed? The answer to that question depends simply on the level of power that is acceptable. Suppose you wanted to modify the previous example to have power equal to 0.80. The first thing you need to do is read Table D.5 backward to find what value for δ is associated with the specified degree of power. From the table we see that for power equal to 0.80, δ must equal 2.80. Thus we have δ and can simply solve for N by a minor algebraic manipulation:

$$\delta = \gamma\sqrt{N}$$

$$N = \left(\frac{\delta}{\gamma}\right)^2$$

$$= \left(\frac{2.80}{0.33}\right)^2 = 8.40^2 = 70.56$$

Because clients generally come in whole units, we will round off to 71. Thus if the experimenter wants to have an 80% chance of rejecting H_0 when $\gamma = 0.33$ (i.e., when $\mu_1 = 105$ or 95), she will have to obtain the IQs of 71 randomly selected clients. Although she may feel that this is a large number of clients, there is no alternative other than to settle for a lower level of power and increase the chance of not finding anything.

You might wonder why we selected power equal to 0.80 in the previous example. Remember that with this degree of power we still run a 20% chance of making a Type II error. The answer lies in the question of practicality. Suppose, for example, that our experimenter had wanted power to equal 0.95. A few simple calculations will show that this would require a sample of $N = 119$; for power equal to 0.99 she would need approximately 167 subjects. These may well be unreasonable sample sizes for a particular experimental situation or for the resources of the experimenter. While increases in power are generally bought by increases in N, at very high levels of power the cost can be very high. In addition, it is a case of diminishing returns because δ increases as a function of the square root of N. If you are taking data from tapes supplied by the U.S. Census Bureau, that is one thing. It is quite a different matter when you are studying identical twins reared apart.

15.5 Power Calculations for Differences Between Two Independent Means

The treatment of power in a situation in which we want to test the difference between two independent means is similar to our treatment of the case in which we had only one mean. In the previous section we obtained γ by taking the difference between μ under H_1 (i.e., μ_1) and μ under H_0 (i.e., μ_0) and dividing by σ. In this section we will do something similar, although this time we are going to be working with differences between means. In this case we want the difference between the two population means $(\mu_1 - \mu_2)$ under H_1 minus the difference $(\mu_1 - \mu_2)$ under H_0, again divided by σ. (You should recall that we assume $\sigma_1^2 = \sigma_2^2 = \sigma^2$.) But $(\mu_1 - \mu_2)$ under H_0 is zero in all usual applications, so we can drop that term from the formula. Thus

$$\gamma = \frac{(\mu_1 - \mu_2) - 0}{\sigma} = \frac{\mu_1 - \mu_2}{\sigma}$$

The numerator is the expected difference between population means under H_1, and the denominator is the common standard deviation of both populations.

Equal Sample Sizes

For the sake of an example, assume that we want to test the difference in amount of hoarding behavior between normal rats and rats who were deprived during infancy. A somewhat similar experiment conducted by Hunt (1941) would suggest that the mean number of food pellets hoarded by the deprived group would be approximately 35 and for the nondeprived group approximately 15. In addition, Hunt's data would suggest a value of 17 for σ. Thus, at least as a rough approximation, we expect $\mu_1 = 35$, $\mu_2 = 15$, and $\sigma = 17$. Then

$$\gamma = \frac{(\mu_1 - \mu_2)}{\sigma} = \frac{20}{17} = 1.18$$

We are saying that we expect a difference of 1.18 standard deviations between the two means. (That is a fairly substantial difference, as you can see by comparing this value to Cohen's rule of thumb for effect sizes.)

First we will investigate the power of an experiment with 10 observations in each of two groups. We will define δ in the two-sample case as

$$\sigma = \sqrt{\frac{N}{2}}$$

where N equals the number of cases *in any one sample* (there are $2N$ cases in all). Thus

$$\delta = \gamma\sqrt{\frac{N}{2}} = 1.18\sqrt{\frac{10}{2}}$$

$$= 1.18\sqrt{5} = 1.18(2.236) = 2.64$$

From Table D.5 in the Appendices we see by interpolation that for $\delta = 2.64$ with a two-tailed test at $\alpha = .05$, power equals 0.75. Thus if we actually run this experiment with 10 subjects in each group and if the estimate of δ is correct, then we have a 75% chance of actually rejecting H_0. This is a high degree of power for so few subjects, but we are dealing with a fairly large effect.

We next want to turn the question around and ask how many subjects would be needed for power equal to 0.90. (It is reasonable here to try to boost power to 0.90 [reduce β to 0.10] because we already know that as few as 10 subjects per group would give us power equal to 0.75 with the effect size that we have.) From Table D.5 we see that this would require δ equal to 3.25.

$$\delta = \gamma \sqrt{\frac{N}{2}}$$

Squaring for easier rearrangements of terms, we have

$$\delta^2 = \frac{\gamma^2\, N}{2}$$

Then

$$N = \frac{2\delta^2}{\gamma^2} = \frac{2(3.25^2)}{1.18^2} = \frac{2(10.5625)}{1.3924} - 15.17$$

Because N refers to the number of subjects per sample, we would need 15 subjects per group, for a total of 30 subjects, if power is to be 0.90. That is slightly on the large side for a typical study using laboratory rats, which must be bought, housed, and fed at considerable expense. Whether it is worth the expense depends on the importance of the research.

Unequal Sample Sizes

In the previous section we dealt with the case in which the two samples are of equal size. We also run experiments, however, in which the two sample sizes are unequal because of the nature of the experiment and/or events beyond our control. Unequal size samples obviously present difficulties when we try to solve for δ, because we need one value for N to insert into the formula. What value can we use?

The simplest solution is to let N be the **harmonic mean** of the two sample sizes. In general the harmonic mean of k numbers $(X_1, X_2, \ldots X_k)$ is defined as

Harmonic mean
The number of elements to be averaged divided by the sum of the reciprocals of the elements.

$$\overline{X}_h = \frac{k}{\sum \dfrac{1}{X_i}}$$

For example, for the numbers 8, 12, and 13 the harmonic mean is

$$\overline{X}_h = \frac{3}{\dfrac{1}{8} + \dfrac{1}{12} + \dfrac{1}{13}} = 10.52$$

For the case of two sample sizes (N_1 and N_2) the formula reduces to

$$\bar{N}_h = \frac{2}{\dfrac{1}{N_1} + \dfrac{1}{N_2}}$$

Multiplying the numerator and the denominator by $N_1 N_2$ yields a simpler formula:

$$\bar{N}_h = \frac{2N_1 N_2}{N_1 + N_2}$$

We then can use the harmonic mean of N in place of N itself in calculating δ. Notice that the harmonic mean deals with terms of the form $1/N$. Because the standard error of the mean also varies as a function of $1/N$, we use the harmonic mean rather than the usual arithmetic mean in calculating δ.

An interesting finding arises from playing with different values of N in the preceding formula. For a fixed total number of subjects, we will have the greatest degree of power when the subjects are divided equally between the two groups. When you have unequal sample sizes and can add more subjects to the study, you will maximize your power by adding them in such a way as to balance the groups.

15.6 Power Calculations for the *t* Test for Related Samples

When we move to the situation in which we want to test the difference between two matched samples, the problem becomes somewhat more difficult, and an additional parameter must be considered. For that reason the analysis of power for this case is frequently impractical. However, the general solution to the problem illustrates an important principle of experimental design and thus justifies close examination of the related-sample case. (This section was not written with the expectation that everyone will run out and compute power calculations for a related-sample experiment—most experimenters don't do that either. The important thing is *not* the arithmetic but the conclusions that follow.)

We are going to define γ as

$$\gamma = \frac{\mu_1 - \mu_2}{\sigma_D}$$

where $\mu_1 - \mu_2$ represents the expected mean difference (the expected mean of the difference scores). A problem arises from the fact that σ_D is not the standard deviation of the populations of X_1 and X_2 but rather the standard deviation of difference scores drawn from these populations. Although we might be able to make an intelligent guess at σ_1 or σ_2, we probably have no idea about σ_D.

If we are willing to make the assumption that the two sets of scores have the same population standard deviations ($\sigma_1 = \sigma_2 = \sigma$), it is easy to show that

$$\sigma_D = \sigma\sqrt{2(1 - \rho)}$$

where ρ (rho) is the correlation in the population between X_1 and X_2 and can take on values between $+1$ and -1, being positive for almost all situations in which we would likely want a related-sample *t*. In this formula σ is the standard deviation of the population of scores for X_1 or X_2 (because $\sigma_1 = \sigma_2 = \sigma$).

Assuming for the moment that we can estimate ρ, from here on the procedure is the same as for the case of the one-sample *t* test. We define

$$\gamma = \frac{\mu_1 - \mu_2}{\sigma_D} = \frac{\mu_1 - \mu_2}{\sigma\sqrt{2(1 - \rho)}}$$

and

$$\delta = \gamma\sqrt{N}$$

We then can refer to Table D.5 for the value of δ.

For an example, assume that we want to see if cognitive performance of young children is better in the morning than at night. Consequently we want to administer a commonly used standardized achievement test to a sample of 20 children just before their bedtime and then readminister the test a week later early in the morning. (To control for practice effects, half the children will be tested in the reverse order.) Suppose we want to evaluate the power for finding a difference between means as great as three points—more than a three point difference seems unlikely. Information on most standardized tests is available in many textbooks. From such a source we might find that the standard deviation of test scores is 10. The correlation between scores on two administrations of the test is nothing but the short-term reliability of the test, and a reasonable value for the reliability is 0.92. Thus

$$\sigma_D = \sigma\sqrt{2(1 - \rho)}$$
$$= 10\sqrt{2(1 - 0.92)} = 10\sqrt{2(0.08)} = 4.0$$

$$\gamma = \frac{\mu_1 - \mu_2}{\sigma_D}$$

$$= \frac{3}{4.0} = 0.75$$

$$\delta = \gamma\sqrt{N}$$
$$= 0.75\sqrt{20} = 3.35$$

From Table D.5 in the Appendices we find that power = 0.92 for $\alpha = .05$.

Suppose on the other hand that we had used a less reliable test for which $\rho = 0.50$. We will assume that σ remains unchanged. Then

$$\sigma_D = \sigma\sqrt{2(1 - \rho)}$$
$$= 10\sqrt{2(1 - 0.50)} = 10\sqrt{2(0.50)} = 10.0$$

$$\gamma = \frac{\mu_1 - \mu_2}{\sigma_D}$$

$$= \frac{3}{10.0} = 0.30$$

$$\delta = \gamma\sqrt{N}$$

$$= 0.30\sqrt{20} = 1.34$$

Here power $= 0.27$ for $\alpha = .05$.

You can see that as the correlation between the two variables (in this case the reliability of the test) drops, so does power. When $\rho = 0$, the two samples are (linearly) independent, and thus the related-sample case has been reduced to the independent-sample case except for the difference in the degrees of freedom, which would be obscured anyway by the approximation used to generate Table D.5. The important point to be made here (and the reason behind all these calculations) is that for all practical purposes the minimum power for the related-sample case occurs when ρ is 0 and we have independent samples. Thus for all situations in which we are even remotely likely to use related samples (i.e., when we expect a positive correlation between X_1 and X_2), the related-sample design is more powerful than the corresponding independent-groups design. This illustrates one of the main advantages of designs that use related samples.

15.7 Power Considerations in Terms of Sample Size

Our discussion of power here illustrates that reasonably large sample sizes are almost a necessity if you are to run experiments that have a good chance of rejecting H_0 when it is in fact false, especially if the effect is small. A few minutes with a calculator will show you that if we want to have power equal to 0.80 and if we accept Cohen's definitions for small, medium, and large effects, our samples must be quite large. Table 15.2 presents the total Ns required (at power $= .80$, $\alpha = .05$) for small, medium, and large effects for the tests we have been discussing. These figures indicate that power (at least a substantial amount of it) is a very expensive commodity, especially for small effects. While it could be argued that this is actually a good thing, since otherwise the literature would contain many more trivial results than it already does, that will come as little comfort to most experimenters. The general rule is to look for big effects, to use large samples, or to employ sensitive experimental designs such

Effect Size	γ	One-Sample t	Two-Sample t
Small	0.20	196	784
Medium	0.50	32	126
Large	0.80	13	49

Table 15.2

Total Sample Sizes Required for Power = .80, α = .05, Two-Tailed

as those that involve the use of repeated measurements on the same subjects, reducing experimental error and thus making small differences translate into large effect sizes.

15.8 Summary

In this chapter we considered those factors that contribute to the power of a test. You saw that the most easily manipulated factor is the sample size, and we considered ways of calculating the power for a given sample size and, conversely, the sample size need for a specified level of power. Finally, we considered the unwelcome conclusion that high levels of power often may require more subjects than we can reasonably expect.

Some important terms in this chapter are:

- Power
- Effect size
- Gamma (γ)

- Delta (δ)
- Harmonic mean

15.9 Exercises

15.1 Over the past 10 years a small New England college has been able to hold its mean SAT score (and, by inference, the mean of the population from which it draws its applicants) at 520 with a standard deviation of 80. A major competitor would like to demonstrate that the school's standards have slipped and that it is now really drawing from a population of applicants with a mean of 500. They plan to run a t test on the mean SAT of next fall's entering class.

(a) What is the effect size in question?

(b) What is the value of δ if the size of next fall's class is 100?

(c) What is the power of the test?

15.2 Diagram the situation described in Exercise 15.1 along the lines of Figure 15.1.

15.3 In Exercise 15.1 what sample sizes would be needed to raise power to 0.70, 0.80, and 0.90?

15.4 Unbeknownst to the competition, the first college referred to in Exercise 15.1 has started a major campaign to increase the quality of its new students. The college is hoping to show a 30-point gain in the mean SAT score for next year. If 100 students enroll next fall, what is the power of a t test used to test the significance of any increase?

15.5 Diagram the situation described in Exercise 15.4 along the lines of Figure 15.1.

15.6 A neuroscience laboratory has been studying avoidance behavior in rabbits for several years and has published numerous papers on the topic. It is clear from this research that the mean response latency for a particular task is 5.8 seconds with a standard deviation of 2 seconds (based on a large number of rabbits). Now the investigators want to create lesions in certain areas of the amygdala and demonstrate poorer avoidance conditioning in those animals. They expect latencies to decrease by about 1 second (i.e., rabbits will repeat the punished response sooner), and they plan to run a one-sample t test (with $H_0 : \mu_0 = 5.8$).

(a) How many subjects do they need to have at least a 50:50 chance of success?

(b) How many subjects do they need to have at least an 80:20 chance of success?

15.7 Suppose the laboratory referred to in Exercise 15.6 decided that instead of running one group and comparing it against $\mu_0 = 5.8$ they would run two groups (one with and one without lesions). They still expect the same degree of difference, however.

(a) How many subjects do they now need (overall) if they are to have power equal 0.60?

(b) How many subjects do they now need (overall) if they are to have power equal 0.90?

15.8 As it turns out, a research assistant has just finished running the experiment described in Exercise 15.7 without having carried out any power calculations. He tried to run 20 subjects in each group, but he accidentally tipped over a rack of cages and had to void 5 subjects in the experimental group. What is the power of this experiment?

15.9 I have just conducted a study comparing cognitive development of low-birthweight (premature) and normal-birthweight babies at one year of age. Using a score of my own devising, I found the sample means of the two groups to be 25 and 30, respectively, with a pooled standard deviation of 8. There were 20 subjects in each group. If we assume that the true means and standard deviations have been estimated exactly, what was the *a priori* probability (the probability before the experiment was conducted) that this study would find a significant difference?

15.10 Let's modify Exercise 15.9 to have sample means of 25 and 28, with a pooled standard deviation of 8 and sample sizes of 20 and 20.

(a) What is the *a priori* power of this experiment?

(b) Run the t test on the data.

(c) What, if anything, does the answer to (a) have to say about the answer to (b)?

15.11 Two graduate students have recently completed their dissertations. Each used a t test for two independent groups. One found a barely significant t using 10 subjects per group. The other found a barely significant t using 45 subjects per group. Which result impresses you more?

15.12 Draw a diagram (analogous to Figure

15.1) to defend your answer to Exercise 15.11.

15.13 Make up a simple two-group example to demonstrate that for a total of 30 subjects power increases as the sample sizes become more nearly equal.

15.14 A beleaguered Ph.D. candidate has the impression that he must find significant results if he wants to defend his dissertation successfully. He wants to show a difference in social awareness, as measured by his own scale, between a normal group of students and a group of ex-delinquents. He has a problem, however. He has data to suggest that the normal group has a true mean equal to 38, and he has 50 of those subjects. For the other group he has access either to 100 college students who have been classed as delinquent in the past or to 25 high school dropouts with a history of delinquency. He suspects that the scores of the college group come from a population with a mean of approximately 35, whereas the scores of the dropout group come from a population with a mean of approximately 30. He can use only one of these groups—which should it be?

15.15 Generate a table analogous to Table 15.2 for power equal to 0.80, with $\alpha = .01$, two-tailed.

15.16 Generate a table analogous to Table 15.2 for power equal to 0.60, with $\alpha = .05$, two-tailed.

15.17 Assume we want to test a null hypothesis about a single mean at $\alpha = .05$, one-tailed. Further assume that all necessary assumptions are met. Is there ever a case in which we are more likely to reject a true H_0 than we are to reject H_0 if it is false? (In other words, can power ever be less than α?)

15.18 If $\sigma = 15$, $N = 25$, and we are testing $H_0: \mu = 100$ versus $H_1: \mu > 100$, what value of the mean under H_1 would result in power being equal to the probability of a Type II error? (*Hint:* This is most easily solved by sketching the two distributions. Which areas are you trying to equate?)

16

ONE-WAY ANALYSIS OF VARIANCE

The **analysis of variance (ANOVA)** currently enjoys the status of being probably the most used (some would say abused) statistical technique in psychological research. The popularity and usefulness of this technique can be attributed to two facts. First of all the analysis of variance, like t, deals with differences between sample means, but unlike t, it has no restriction on the number of means. Instead of asking merely whether two means differ, we can ask whether two, three, four, five, or k means differ. Second, the analysis of variance allows us to deal with two or more independent variables simulta-

Analysis of variance (ANOVA)
A statistical technique for testing for differences in the means of several groups.

One-way ANOVA
An analysis of variance where the groups are defined on only one independent variable.

fects of each variable separately but also about the interacting effects of two or more variables.

This chapter will be concerned with the underlying logic of the analysis of variance (which is really quite simple) and the analysis of the results of experiments that employ only one independent variable. In addition we will deal with a few related topics that are most easily understood in the context of a one-variable analysis (**one-way ANOVA**). Subsequent chapters will deal with the analysis of experiments that involve two or more variables and with designs in which repeated measurements are made on each subject.

16.1 The General Approach

Many features of the analysis of variance can be best illustrated by a simple example, so we will begin with a study by M. W. Eysenck (1974) on recall of verbal material as a function of the level of processing. The data we will use have the same group means and standard deviations as those reported by Eysenck, but the individual observations are fictional.

Craik and Lockhart (1972) proposed as a model of memory that the degree to which verbal material is remembered by the subject is a function of the degree to which it was processed when it was initially presented. You have probably noticed that I frequently insert questions to you in the text, asking about alternative interpretations of the data, about what it would mean if the test statistic came out differently, and so on. The main purpose of these questions is to encourage you to "process" the information you have just read rather than to just let it flow past. I'm talking here about the same thing that Craik and Lockhart were. But to put the example in their terms, imagine that you are asked to memorize a list of words. Repeating a word to yourself (a low level of processing) would not be expected to lead to as good recall as thinking about each word and trying to form associations between that word and some other word. Eysenck (1974) was interested in testing this model and, more important, in looking to see whether it could help to explain reported differences between young and old subjects in their ability to recall verbal material. An examination of Eysenck's data on age differences will be postponed until Chapter 17; we will concentrate here on differences due to the level of processing.

Eysenck randomly assigned 50 subjects between the ages of 55 and 65 years to one of five groups: four incidental-learning groups and one intentional-learning group. (Incidental learning is learning in the absence of the expectation that the material will need to be recalled later.) The Counting group was asked to read through a list of words and simply count the number of letters in each word. This involved the lowest level of processing, since subjects did not need to deal with each word as anything more than a collection of letters. The Rhyming group was asked to read each word and to think of a word that rhymed with it. This task involved considering the sound of each word but not its meaning. The Adjective group had to process the words to the extent of giving an adjective that could reasonably be used to modify each word on the list.

Table 16.1   Number of Words Recalled as a Function of the Level of Processing

	Counting	Rhyming	Adjective	Imagery	Intentional	Total
	9	7	11	12	10	
	8	9	13	11	19	
	6	6	8	16	14	
	8	6	6	11	5	
	10	6	14	9	10	
	4	11	11	23	11	
	6	6	13	12	14	
	5	3	13	10	15	
	7	8	10	19	11	
	7	7	11	11	11	
Total	70	69	110	134	120	503
Mean	7.00	6.90	11.00	13.40	12.00	10.06
Standard deviation	1.83	2.13	2.49	4.50	3.74	4.01
Variance	3.33	4.54	6.22	20.27	14.00	16.06

The Imagery group was instructed to try to form vivid images of each word, and this condition was assumed to require the deepest level of processing. None of these four groups was told that they would later be asked to recall the items. Finally, the Intentional group was told to read through the list and to memorize the words for later recall. After the subjects had gone through the list of 27 items three times, they were given a sheet of paper and asked to write down all the words they could remember. If learning involves nothing more than being exposed to the material (the way most of us read a newspaper or, heaven forbid, a class assignment), then the five groups should have shown equal recall—after all, they all saw all the words. If the level of processing of the material is important, then there should have been noticeable differences among the group means. The data are presented in Table 16.1.

The Null Hypothesis

Eysenck was interested in testing the null hypothesis that the level of recall was equal under the five conditions. In other words, if μ_1 represents the population mean for all subjects who could potentially be testing under the Counting conditions, μ_2 represents the population mean corresponding to the Rhyming condition, and so on, up to μ_5 (for the Intentional condition), then the null hypothesis is

$$H_0: \mu_1 = \mu_2 = \mu_3 = \mu_4 = \mu_5$$

Figure 16.1 Graphical Representation of Populations of Recall Scores

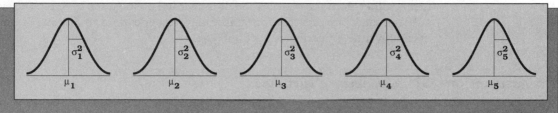

The alternative hypothesis will be the hypothesis that *at least* one mean is different from the others. The five hypothetical populations of recall scores are illustrated in Figure 16.1. The placement of these populations from left to right is not intended to suggest that one population mean is necessarily larger than the population mean to its left. At this point I am saying nothing about the relative magnitude of the population means.

The analysis of variance is a technique for using differences between sample means to draw inferences about the presence or absence of differences between population means. The null hypothesis could be false in a number of ways (e.g., all means could be different from each other, or the first two could be equal to each other but different from the last three), but for now we are going to be concerned only with the problem of whether the null hypothesis is completely true or false. Later in this chapter we will deal with the problem of whether only some of the means are equal.

The Population

One of the difficulties people frequently encounter in the study of statistics concerns the meaning of the word *population.* As mentioned in Chapter 1, a population is a collection of *numbers,* not a collection of rats or people or anything else. Strictly speaking, we are not trying to say that a population of people who learned a list under one condition is the same population as the population of people who learned under a different condition—obviously they are not. Rather we want to be able to say that a population of *scores* obtained under one condition has a mean greater than or less than the mean of a population of scores obtained under another condition. This may appear to be a rather trivial point, but it isn't. If you were to compare people of different ages, for example, as we will in the next chapter, the populations of people certainly would differ in a variety of ways. However, it is not obvious that the recall scores will be different between the populations.

The Assumption of Normality

For reasons dealing with our final test of significance, we will make the assumption that recall scores in each population are normally distributed around the population mean (μ_j). This is no more than the assumption that the observations in Figures 16.1 are normally distributed. As with t, the assumption of normality deals primarily with the normality of the sampling distribution of the mean rather than the distribution of individual observations. Moreover, even substantial departures from normality may, under certain conditions, have remarkably little influence on the final result.

The Assumption of Homogeneity of Variance

A second major assumption that we will make is that each population of scores has the same variance, specifically

$$\sigma_1^2 = \sigma_2^2 = \sigma_3^2 = \sigma_4^2 = \sigma_5^2 = \sigma_e^2$$

Here the notation σ_e^2 indicates the common value held by the five variances. The subscript e is an abbreviation for *error*, since this variance is error variance, that is, variance unrelated to any group differences.[1] Homogeneity of variance would be expected to occur if the effect of a treatment is to add a constant to everyone's score—if, for example, everyone who thought of adjectives in Eysenck's study recalled five more words than they otherwise would have recalled. As you will see later, under certain conditions this assumption also can be relaxed without doing too much damage to the final result. In other words the analysis of variance is robust with respect to violations of the normality and homogeneity of variance assumptions.

The Assumption of Independence of Observations

Our third important assumption is that the observations are all independent of one another. For any two observations in an experimental treatment, we assume that knowing how one observation stands relative to the treatment (or population) mean tells us nothing about the other observation. (This assumption would be violated if, for example, subjects cheated and copied off their neighbors or overheard each other's answers.) This assumption is one of the important reasons why subjects are usually randomly assigned to groups. Violation of the independence assumption can have serious consequences for an analysis.

16.2 The Logic of the Analysis of Variance

The logic underlying the analysis of variance is really very simple—once you understand it, the rest of the discussion will make considerably more sense. In this section I will simplify the presentation slightly by assuming that all groups have the same number of observations, though that is not a requirement of the

---

[1] In terms of the discussion in Chapter 10, this is error variance in the sense that it is variability that cannot be predicted from group membership, since people in the same group (population) obviously don't differ on the grouping variable.

analysis of variance. Consider for a moment the effect of our three major assumptions: normality, homogeneity of variance, and the independence of observations. By making the first two of these assumptions, we have said that the five populations represented in Figure 16.1 have the same shape and the same dispersion. As a result, the only way left for them to differ is in terms of their means.

We will begin by making no assumption about H_0—it may be true or false. For any one treatment, the variance of the 10 scores in that group would be an estimate of the variance of the population from which the scores were drawn. Because we have assumed that all populations have the same variance, it is also one estimate of the common population variance σ_e^2. If you prefer, you can think of

$$\sigma_1^2 \doteq s_1^2 \qquad \sigma_2^2 \doteq s_2^2 \ \cdots \ \sigma_5^2 \doteq s_5^2$$

where $\doteq$ is read "is estimated by." Because of our homogeneity assumption, all of these are estimates of σ_e^2. For the sake of increased reliability, we can pool the five estimates by taking their mean, if $n_1 = n_2 = \ldots = n_5 = n$, and thus

$$\sigma_e^2 \doteq \overline{s}_j^2 = \frac{s_1^2 + s_2^2 + s_3^2 + s_4^2 + s_5^2}{5}$$

This is our best estimate of σ_e^2. Pooling of variances is exactly equivalent to what we did when we pooled variances in the t test (although here we have more than two variances). This average value of the five sample variances (s_j^2) is one estimate of the population variance (σ_e^2) and is what we will later refer to as **MS**$_{within}$ or **MS**$_{error}$ (read "mean square within" or "mean square error"). It is important to note that this estimate does *not* depend on the truth or falsity of H_0, because s_j^2 is calculated on each sample separately. For the data from Eysenck's study, our pooled estimate of σ_e^2 will be

$$\overline{s}_j^2 = (3.33 + 4.54 + 6.22 + 20.27 + 14.00)/5 = 9.67$$

Now let us assume that H_0 *is true.* If that is the case, then the five samples of 10 cases can be thought of as five independent samples from the same population, and we have another estimate of σ_e^2. We can examine the variance of means. Remember from earlier discussions that means are not as variable as observations. (Why should this be?) In fact, the Central Limit Theorem states that the variance of *means* drawn from the same population equals the variance of the population divided by the sample size. If H_0 is true, the sample means have been drawn from the same population (or identical populations, which amounts to the same thing), and therefore

$$s_{\overline{X}}^2 \doteq \frac{\sigma_e^2}{n}$$

MS$_{within}$ (**MS**$_{error}$)
Variability among subjects in the same treatment group.

Figure 16.2

Illustration of the Meaning of MS_{error} and MS_{group} When Sample Sizes Are Equal

$$
\begin{aligned}
&s_1^2 \leftarrow \text{Sample 1} \rightarrow \bar{X}_1 \\
&s_2^2 \leftarrow \text{Sample 2} \rightarrow \bar{X}_2 \\
&s_3^2 \leftarrow \text{Sample 3} \rightarrow \bar{X}_3 \quad\Bigg\} \quad \text{Variance of } \bar{X}_i = s_{\bar{X}}^2 \\
&s_4^2 \leftarrow \text{Sample 4} \rightarrow \bar{X}_4 \\
&s_5^2 \leftarrow \text{Sample 5} \rightarrow \bar{X}_5
\end{aligned}
$$

$$\text{Average } s_j^2 = MS_{error} \qquad n(s_{\bar{X}}^2) = MS_{group}$$

where n is the size of each sample. Here all samples will have the same size. We can reverse the usual order of things and, instead of estimating the variance of means from the variance of the population, we can estimate the variance of the population(s) from the variance of the sample means ($s_{\bar{X}}^2$). If we simply clear fractions in the previous formula we have

$$\sigma_e^2 \doteq ns_{\bar{X}}^2$$

$MS_{between\,groups}$ (MS_{group})
Variability among group means.

This term is commonly known as $MS_{between\,groups}$ or more simply MS_{group}.

These few steps can be illustrated easily, as has been done for five equal-sized groups in Figure 16.2. This figure emphasizes that the average of the sample variances is MS_{error} and the variance of the sample means *multiplied by the sample size* is MS_{group}.

We now have two estimates of the population variance (σ_e^2). One of these estimates, MS_{error}, is independent of the truth or falsity of H_0. It is *always* an estimate of the population variance. The other, MS_{group}, is an estimate of σ_e^2 *only as long as* H_0 *is true* (only as long as the conditions assumed by the Central Limit Theorem are met, namely that the samples are drawn from one population). Otherwise, MS_{group} would estimate the variability of group means in addition to σ_e^2. If the two estimates (MS_{error} and MS_{group}) are roughly in agreement, we will have support for the truth of H_0; and if they disagree substantially, we will have support for the falsity of H_0. I can illustrate the logic just described by way of two very simple examples that have been deliberately constructed to represent more or less ideal results under the conditions H_0 true and H_0 false. Never in practice will data be as neat and tidy as in these examples.

Example: The Case of a True H_0

Assume that we have an experiment involving three groups. As we saw earlier, when H_0 is true, $\mu_1 = \mu_2 = \mu_3$, and any samples drawn from these three populations can be thought of as coming from just one population. In the first example three samples of $n = 9$ have been chosen to resemble data that might be drawn from the same normally distributed population with a mean of 5 and a variance of 10. For example, these data might represent the number of information-seeking comments uttered by nine subjects in each of three groups prior to the onset of a socialization-training experiment. Because the

Table 16.2

Representative Data for the Case in Which H_0: True

Group 1	Group 2	Group 3
3	1	5
6	4	2
9	7	8
6	4	8
3	1	2
12	10	8
6	4	5
3	1	2
9	7	8

$\overline{X}_j =$ 6.3333 | 4.3333 | 5.3333
$s_j^2 =$ 10.000 | 10.0000 | 7.750

Grand Mean $(GM) = 5.3333$

$$s_{\overline{X}}^2 = \frac{\Sigma(\overline{X}_j - GM)^2}{k - 1} = 1.000$$

$$\overline{s}_j^2 = \frac{10.00 + 10.00 + 7.75}{3} = 9.250$$

$$MS_{error} = \overline{s}_j^2 = 9.25$$

$$MS_{group} = ns_{\overline{X}}^2 = 9(1) = 9$$

experiment has not yet begun, we hope not to find group differences. The data are presented in Table 16.2 for the $k = 3$ groups. From this table we can see that the average variance in each group is 9.250, a respectable estimate of $\sigma_e^2 = 10$. The variance of the group means is 1.000, and because we know H_0 to be true,

$$s_{\overline{X}}^2 \doteq \frac{\sigma_e^2}{n}$$

$$\sigma_e^2 \doteq ns_{\overline{X}}^2 = 9(1) = 9$$

This is our value for MS_{group}. This value is also reasonably in agreement with σ_e^2 and with our other estimate based on the variability within treatments. Because these two estimates agree, we would conclude that we have no reason to doubt the truth of H_0. Put another way, the three sample means do not vary more than we would expect if H_0 were true.

Table 16.3

Representative Data for the Case in Which H_0: False

Group 1	Group 2	Group 3
5	0	5
8	3	2
11	6	8
8	3	8
5	0	2
14	9	8
8	3	5
5	0	2
11	6	8
$\overline{X}_J =$ 8.3333	3.3333	5.3333
$s_j^2 =$ 10.000	10.0000	7.750

Grand Mean $(GM) = 5.6667$

$$s_{\overline{X}}^2 = \frac{\Sigma(\overline{X}_J - GM)^2}{k - 1} = 6.333$$

$$\overline{s}_j^2 = \frac{10.00 + 10.00 + 7.75}{3} = 9.250$$

$$MS_{error} = \overline{s}_j^2 = 9.25$$

$$MS_{group} = ns_{\overline{X}}^2 = 9(6.333) = 57$$

Example: The Case of a False H_0

Next consider an example in which I know H_0 to be false because I made it false. The data in Table 16.3 have been obtained by adding or subtracting constants to or from the data in Table 16.2. These data might represent the number of information-seeking comments uttered by people in three different groups at the *end* of our socialization-training sessions. We now have data that might have been produced by sampling from three normally distributed populations, all with variance equal to 10. However, Group 1 scores might have come from a population with $\mu = 8$, whereas scores for Groups 2 and 3 might have come from a population, or populations, with $\mu = 4$. This represents a substantial departure from H_0, which stated that all population means were equal to each other.

From Table 16.3 you will note that the variance within each treatment remains unchanged, since adding or subtracting a constant has no effect on the variance within groups. This illustrates the earlier statement that the variance within groups (MS_{error}) is independent of the truth or falsity of the null hypothesis. The variance among the groups, however, has increased substantially, reflecting the differences among the population means. In this case the estimate of σ_e^2 based on sample means is $ns_{\bar{X}}^2 = 9(6.333) = 57$, a value that is way out of line with the estimate of 9.25 given by the variance within groups (MS_{error}). The most logical conclusion would be that $ns_{\bar{X}}^2$ is not merely estimating population variance (σ_e^2), but is estimating σ_e^2 *plus* the variance of the population means themselves. In other words, the scores differ not only because of random error but also because we have been successful in teaching some of our subjects to ask information-seeking questions. We know this to be the case because the data have been deliberately manufactured for that purpose.

Summary of the Logic of the Analysis of Variance

From the preceding discussion we can state the logic of the analysis of variance concisely. To test H_0 we calculate two estimates of the population variance; one (MS_{error}) is independent of the truth or falsity of H_0, while the other (MS_{group}) is dependent on H_0. If the two are in approximate agreement, we have no reason to reject H_0. The means differ only to the extent that the sample distribution of the mean leads us to expect when H_0 is true. If MS_{group} is much larger than MS_{error}, we conclude that underlying differences in treatment means must have contributed to the second estimate, inflating it and causing it to differ from the first. We therefore reject H_0. This illustrates how an analysis of *variance* allows us to draw inferences about *means*.

16.3 Calculations for the Analysis of Variance

The calculations for the analysis of variance are quite simple and straightforward. The formulae appear to be different from the kinds of formulae you saw for t tests, but this difference is really a function of the fact that here we are going to emphasize the use of totals and sums of squares instead of means and variances.

Sums of Squares

In the analysis of variance most of our computations deal with sums of squares, which, in this context, are merely the sum of squared deviations about the mean $\Sigma(X - \bar{X})^2$ or some multiple of that. The advantage of sums of squares and the reason that we begin by calculating them is that they can be added and subtracted, whereas mean squares usually cannot. In Chapter 5 you saw that we can write $\Sigma(X - \bar{X})^2 = \Sigma X^2 - (\Sigma X)^2/N$ and use that formula for computational purposes. We will do exactly the same thing here except that to avoid a proliferation of summation signs we will replace ΣX with **G** (for **Grand total**) and have $\Sigma X^2 - G^2/N$ instead. We will calculate all sums of squares using either this formula or a variation of it.

G (Grand total)
The sum of all the observations.

Totals

Although we have been speaking of group *means,* we actually will carry out our calculations in terms of group *totals.* This distinction is one of convenience rather than substance, since totals are linearly related to means. If two groups of the same size have different totals, they obviously have different means.

The Calculations

At this point we will return to the example from Eysenck on recall of verbal material. The data have been reproduced in Table 16.4 with the resulting computations, which we will discuss in detail.

In section (a) of Table 16.4 you can see the observations, the individual group totals (T_j), and the grand total ($G = \Sigma X$). The use of the notation T_j to represent the total of the jth group will be followed throughout our discussion of the analysis of variance. In analyses in which there is more than one independent variable (factor), T_j can be extended to $T_{row\ i}$ and $T_{column\ j}$ without confusion and without any loss of clarity.

The means and the variances are exactly those found by Eysenck, but since the data points are fictitious, there is little to be gained by examining the distribution of observations within individual groups—the data were actually drawn from normally distributed populations and then rounded to whole numbers. With real data it is important to examine these distributions first to make sure they are not seriously skewed, bimodal, or, even more important, skewed in different directions. Even for this example, it is useful to examine the individual group variances as a check on the assumption of homogeneity of variance. Although the variances are not as similar as we might like (the variance for Imagery is noticeably larger than the others), they do not appear to be so drastically different as to cause concern. As you will see later, the analysis of variance is robust against violations of assumptions, especially when we have the same number of observations in each group.

SS_{total}
The sum of squares of all the scores, regardless of group membership.

SS_{total}   The **SS_{total}** (read "total sum of squares") represents the sum of squares of all the observations, regardless of which treatment produced them. It is the sum of all the squared observations, minus the grand total squared divided by N:

$$SS_{total} = \Sigma X^2 - \frac{G^2}{N}$$

SS_{group}
The sum of squares of group totals divided by the number of scores per group minus G^2/N.

SS_{group}   The **SS_{group}** term is a measure of differences due to groups (in effect, differences between group means) and is directly related to the variability of the group totals. To calculate SS_{group}, we simply square and then sum the group totals, divide by the number of observations on which each total is based (in this case n) and subtract G^2/N. (In the analysis of variance we use lowercase n

Table 16.4 Calculations of Analysis of Variance for Data in Table 16.1

(a) Data

	Counting	Rhyming	Adjective	Imagery	Intentional	Total	
	9	7	11	12	10		
	8	9	13	11	19		
	6	6	8	16	14		
	8	6	6	11	5		
	10	6	14	9	10		
	4	11	11	23	11		
	6	6	13	12	14		
	5	3	13	10	15		
	7	8	10	19	11		
	7	7	11	11	11		
Total (T_j)	70	69	110	134	120	503	$= \Sigma X = G$
Mean	7.00	6.90	11.00	13.40	12.00	10.06	
Standard deviation	1.83	2.13	2.49	4.50	3.74	4.01	
Variance	3.33	4.54	6.22	20.27	14.00	16.058	

(b) Calculations

$$SS_{total} = \Sigma X^2 - \frac{(G)^2}{N} = (9^2 + 8^2 + \cdots + 11^2) - \frac{503^2}{50}$$

$$= 5847 - 5060.18 = 786.82$$

$$SS_{group} = \frac{\Sigma T_j^2}{n} - \frac{(G)^2}{N} = \frac{(70^2 + 69^2 + 110^2 + 134^2 + 120^2)}{10} - \frac{503^2}{50}$$

$$= 5411.7 - 5060.18 = 351.52$$

$$SS_{error} = SS_{total} - SS_{group} = 786.82 - 351.52 = 435.30$$

(c) Summary Table

Source	df	SS	MS	F
Group	4	351.52	87.88	9.08
Error	45	435.30	9.67	
Total	49	786.82		

to stand for the number of observations in a group and uppercase N to stand for the total number of observations.) To gain a better appreciation of exactly what SS_{group} represents, the formula for it could be written somewhat differently (where k represents the number of groups):

$$SS_{group} = \frac{\Sigma T_j^2}{n} - \frac{G^2}{N}$$

$$= \frac{\Sigma T_j^2}{n} - \frac{(\Sigma T_j)^2}{nk} = \frac{\Sigma T_j^2 - \dfrac{(\Sigma T_j)^2}{k}}{n} = \frac{\Sigma(T_j - \overline{T})^2}{n}$$

From this equation we can see that SS_{group} represents the sum of squared deviations of the treatment totals about the mean of the totals (T bar), divided by n. The n in this case is exactly the same divisor that we discussed in connection with the Central Limit Theorem (Chapter 12, p. 215). (It appears in the denominator rather than in the numerator simply because we are working with totals rather than means.) Its purpose is eventually to produce an estimate of σ_e^2. In all the sums of squares discussed in the analysis of variance, the same general principle applies.

General Rule for the Calculation of Any Sums of Squares In conjunction with this discussion of SS_{group} it is now possible to lay down a general rule for the calculation of any sum of squares (SS) other than those we will calculate by subtraction:

> For any SS except SS_{error}, square the relevant totals, divide by the number of observations on which each total is based, sum the results, and subtract G^2/N.

This rule will allow you to calculate the SS for any example in this book, no matter how complex the experimental design. In the one-way analysis of variance the "relevant totals" just referred to are the totals for the various groups. When we come to the two-way analysis of variance in the next chapter, we will just generalize this rule to allow for different dimensions along which groups are formed. (The rule also applies to the calculation of SS_{total}, but there the relevant totals become the individual observations, and the divisor is therefore 1, which is usually not shown.) The only exceptions will be sums of squares obtained by subtraction, and we will consider those as we go along.

SS_{error}
The sum of the sums of squares within each group.

SS_{error} In practice **SS_{error}** is usually obtained by subtraction. Because it can be shown easily that

$$SS_{total} = SS_{group} + SS_{error}$$

then it must also be true that

$$SS_{error} = SS_{total} - SS_{group}$$

This is the procedure presented in Table 16.4. An alternative method of calculation is also available. As you will recall from earlier discussions, we seek a term that is not influenced by differences among treatments and therefore a term that represents the variability within each of the three treatments separately. To that end we could calculate a sum of squares within Treatment 1 (SS_{error_1}) and a similar term for the SS within each of the other treatments.

$$SS_{within\ Counting} = 9^2 + 8^2 + \cdots + 7^2 - \frac{70^2}{10} = 520 - 490 \qquad = 30.00$$

$$SS_{within\ Rhyming} = 7^2 + 9^2 + \cdots + 7^2 - \frac{69^2}{10} = 517 - 476.1 \qquad = 40.90$$

$$SS_{within\ Adjective} = 11^2 + 13^2 + \cdots + 11^2 - \frac{110^2}{10} = 1266 - 1210 \quad = 56.00$$

$$SS_{within\ Imagery} = 12^3 + 11^2 + \cdots + 11^2 - \frac{134^2}{10} = 1978 - 1795.6 = 182.40$$

$$SS_{within\ Intentional} = 10^2 + 19^2 + \cdots + 11^2 - \frac{120^2}{10} = 1566 - 1440 \quad = 126.00$$

$$\overline{}$$

$$SS_{error} = \qquad\qquad\qquad\qquad\qquad\qquad\qquad 435.30$$

The sum of these individual terms is 435.30, which agrees exactly with the answer we obtained in Table 16.4. This simply goes to show that SS_{error} is a measure of the variability within each group.

The Summary Table

Part (c) of Table 16.4 is the summary table for the analysis of variance. It is called a summary table for the rather obvious reason that it summarizes a series of calculations, making it possible to tell at a glance what the data have to offer.

Sources of Variation The first column of the summary table contains the sources of variation—I use the word "variation" as being synonymous with the phrase "sum of squares." As you can see from the table, there are three sources of variation: the total variation, the variation due to groups (variation between group means), and the variation due to error (variation within groups). These sources reflect the fact that we have partitioned the total sum of squares into two portions, one portion representing variability between the several groups and the other representing variability within the individual groups.

Degrees of Freedom The degrees of freedom column shows the allocation of the degrees of freedom between the two sources of variation. The calculation of df is probably the easiest part of our task. The total degrees of freedom (**df_{total}**) are always $N - 1$, where N is the total number of observations. The degrees of freedom between groups (**df_{group}**) always equal $k - 1$, where k is the number of groups. The degrees of freedom for error (**df_{error}**) are most easily thought of as what is left over, although they can be calculated more directly as the sum of the degrees of freedom within each treatment. In our example $df_{total} = 50 - 1 = 49$. Of these 49 df, 4 are associated with differences among the five groups and the remaining 45 are associated with variability within groups.

For those students who are interested in understanding why the degrees of freedom are assigned as they are, a short explanation is in order. SS_{total} is the sum of N-squared deviations around one point—the grand mean. The fact that we have taken deviations around this one (estimated) point has cost us 1 df, leaving $N - 1$ df. SS_{group} is the sum of deviations of the k group means around one point (again the grand mean), and again we have lost 1 df in estimating this point, leaving us with $k - 1$ df. SS_{error} represents k sets of n deviations about one point (the group mean), losing us 1 df for each group and leaving $k(n - 1) = N - k$ df. To repeat this in a slightly different form, the total variability is based on N scores and therefore has $N - 1$ df. The variability of treatment means is based on k scores (means or totals) and therefore has $k - 1$ df. The variability within any one treatment is based on n scores and thus has $n - 1$ df, but because we sum k of these within-treatment terms, we will have k times $n - 1 = k(n - 1)$ df.

Sums of Squares There is little to be said about the column labeled SS. It simply contains the sums of squares obtained in part (b) of the table.

Mean Squares The column of mean squares contains the two estimates of σ_e^2. These values are obtained by dividing the sums of squares by their corresponding df. Thus $351.52/4 = 87.88$ and $435.30/45 = 9.67$. We typically do not calculate a MS_{total}, because we have no use for it. It would represent the variance of all N observations.

While it is true that mean squares are variances, it is important to keep in mind what these terms are variances of. Thus MS_{error} is the (average) variance of the observations within each treatment. However, MS_{group} is not the variance of group means or totals but rather the variance of those means (or totals) corrected by n to produce an estimate of the population variance (σ_e^2); in other words it is an estimate of σ_e^2 based on the variance of group means.

The F Statistic The last column, headed F, is the most important one in terms of testing the null hypothesis. **F** is obtained by dividing MS_{group} by MS_{error}. As noted earlier, MS_{error} is an estimate of the population variance (σ_e^2). MS_{group} is also an estimate of population variance (σ_e^2) *if* H_0 is true, but not if H_0 is false. If H_0 is true, then both MS_{error} and MS_{group} are estimating the same thing,

df_{total}
Degrees of freedom associated with
$SS_{total} = N - 1$.

df_{group}
Degrees of freedom associated with
$SS_{group} = k - 1$.

df_{error}
Degrees of freedom associated with
$SS_{error} = k(n - 1)$.

$N - k$

F statistic
The ratio of MS_{group} over MS_{error}.

and as such they should be approximately equal. If that is the case, the ratio of one to the other will be approximately 1, give or take a fair amount for sampling error. All we have to do is compute the ratio and determine whether it is close enough to 1 to indicate support for the null hypothesis.

When we spoke about a t test, it was pretty clear what a one-tailed test meant. It meant that we would reject H_0 if the difference between the means was in the predicted direction. It also meant that we would reject H_0 if the value of t was of the correct sign, in both cases assuming that the difference (or t) was large enough. When we have multiple groups, however, the use of the label "one-tailed" is less clear. In one sense we are running a one-tailed test because we will reject H_0 only if the computed value of F is significantly *greater* than 1.0. On the other hand we could obtain a large value of F for a variety of reasons. In the analysis of variance we reject H_0 when the means are sufficiently far apart, without regard to which one(s) is (are) larger than others. Thus we have a one-tailed test of a nondirectional H_0.

The question remains as to how much larger than 1.0 our value of F needs to be before we decide that there are differences among the population means and thus reject H_0.[2] The answer to this lies in the fact that if H_0 is true, the ratio

$$F = \frac{MS_{group}}{MS_{error}}$$

is distributed as the F distribution tabled in Table D.3 in the Appendices. It will have df_{group} and df_{error} degrees of freedom. A portion of Table D.3 is reproduced as Table 16.5. Because the shape of the F distribution, and thus areas under it, depend on the degrees of freedom for the two mean squares, this table looks somewhat different from other tables you have seen. In this case we select the column that corresponds to the degrees of freedom for the mean square in the numerator of F (i.e., $k - 1$) and the row that corresponds to the degrees of freedom for the mean square in the denominator (i.e., $k(n - 1)$). The intersection of the row and the column gives us the critical value of F at the level of α shown at the top of the table.

To use Table D.3 (and Table 16.5), we first have to select the particular table corresponding to our level of α (in Table D.3 $\alpha = .05$, and in Table D.4 $\alpha = .01$). Then, because we have 4 df for the numerator (MS_{group}) and 45 df for the denominator (MS_{error}), we move down the fourth column to the row labeled 45. But there is no row that corresponds to exactly 45 df, so we will average the entries for the rows corresponding to 40 df and 50 df. The intersections of those rows and column 4 contain the entries 2.61 and 2.56, the average of which rounds to 2.58. This is the critical value of F. We would expect to exceed an F of 2.58 only 5% of the time if H_0 were true. Because our obtained $F = 9.08$ exceeds $F_{.05} = 2.58$, we will reject H_0 and conclude that the groups

---

[2] If H_0 is true, the expected value of F is not exactly 1.00, but it is so close that it doesn't make any difference to the point being made here. Also, there is usually no meaning to be assigned to an F very much less than 1.0, though we might be puzzled if our group means were much *closer* to each other than we would expect.

Table 16.5   Abbreviated Version of Table D.3, Critical Values of the F Distribution Where $\alpha = .05$

					Degrees of Freedom for Numerator						
	1	**2**	**3**	**4**	**5**	**6**	**7**	**8**	**9**	**10**	**15**
1	161.4	199.5	215.8	224.8	230.0	233.8	236.5	238.6	240.1	242.1	$\cdots$
2	18.51	19.00	19.16	19.25	19.30	19.33	19.35	19.37	19.38	19.40	$\cdots$
3	10.13	9.55	9.28	9.12	9.01	8.94	8.89	8.85	8.81	8.79	$\cdots$
4	7.71	6.94	6.59	6.39	6.26	6.16	6.09	6.04	6.00	5.96	$\cdots$
5	6.61	5.79	5.41	5.19	5.05	4.95	4.88	4.82	4.77	4.74	$\cdots$
6	5.99	5.14	4.76	4.53	4.39	4.28	4.21	4.15	4.10	4.06	$\cdots$
7	5.59	4.74	4.35	4.12	3.97	3.87	3.79	3.73	3.68	3.64	$\cdots$
8	5.32	4.46	4.07	3.84	3.69	3.58	3.50	3.44	3.39	3.35	$\cdots$
9	5.12	4.26	3.86	3.63	3.48	3.37	3.29	3.23	3.18	3.14	$\cdots$
10	4.96	4.10	3.71	3.48	3.33	3.22	3.14	3.07	3.02	2.98	$\cdots$
11	4.84	3.98	3.59	3.36	3.20	3.09	3.01	2.95	2.90	2.85	$\cdots$
12	4.75	3.89	3.49	3.26	3.11	3.00	2.91	2.85	2.80	2.75	$\cdots$
13	4.67	3.81	3.41	3.18	3.03	2.92	2.83	2.77	2.71	2.67	$\cdots$
14	4.60	3.74	3.34	3.11	2.96	2.85	2.76	2.70	2.65	2.60	$\cdots$
15	4.54	3.68	3.29	3.06	2.90	2.79	2.71	2.64	2.59	2.54	$\cdots$
16	4.49	3.63	3.24	3.01	2.85	2.74	2.66	2.59	2.54	2.49	$\cdots$
17	4.45	3.59	3.20	2.96	2.81	2.70	2.61	2.55	2.49	2.45	$\cdots$
18	4.41	3.55	3.16	2.93	2.77	2.66	2.58	2.51	2.46	2.41	$\cdots$
19	4.38	3.52	3.13	2.90	2.74	2.63	2.54	2.48	2.42	2.38	$\cdots$
20	4.35	3.49	3.10	2.87	2.71	2.60	2.51	2.45	2.39	2.35	$\cdots$
22	4.30	3.44	3.05	2.82	2.66	2.55	2.46	2.40	2.34	2.30	$\cdots$
24	4.26	3.40	3.01	2.78	2.62	2.51	2.42	2.36	2.30	2.25	$\cdots$
26	4.23	3.37	2.98	2.74	2.59	2.47	2.39	2.32	2.27	2.22	$\cdots$
28	4.20	3.34	2.95	2.71	2.56	2.45	2.36	2.29	2.24	2.19	$\cdots$
30	4.17	3.32	2.92	2.69	2.53	2.42	2.33	2.27	2.21	2.16	$\cdots$
40	4.08	3.23	2.84	**2.61**	2.45	2.34	2.25	2.18	2.12	2.08	$\cdots$
50	4.03	3.18	2.79	**2.56**	2.40	2.29	2.20	2.13	2.07	2.03	$\cdots$
60	4.00	3.15	2.76	2.53	2.37	2.25	2.17	2.10	2.04	1.99	$\cdots$
120	3.92	3.07	2.68	2.45	2.29	2.18	2.09	2.02	1.96	1.91	$\cdots$
200	3.89	3.04	2.65	2.42	2.26	2.14	2.06	1.98	1.93	1.88	$\cdots$
500	3.86	3.01	2.62	2.39	2.23	2.12	2.03	1.96	1.90	1.85	$\cdots$
1000	3.85	3.01	2.61	2.38	2.22	2.11	2.02	1.95	1.89	1.84	$\cdots$

Degrees of Freedom for Denominator

were sampled from populations with different means. Had we chosen to work at $\alpha = .01$, Table D.4 in the Appendices shows that $F_{.01}(4,45) = 3.78$, and we would still reject H_0. (Notice the format for reporting the significance level and the degrees of freedom for F in the preceding sentence. That is the standard way of writing them.)

Conclusions

On the basis of a significant value of F, we have rejected the null hypothesis that the treatment means in the population are equal. Strictly speaking, this conclusion indicates that at least one of the population means is different from at least one other mean, but we don't know exactly which means are different from which other means. We will pursue this question shortly with a different example. For the moment I'm going to take some liberties and speak about group differences as if I had already shown that they are significantly different.

It is evident from an examination of the data in Table 16.4 that increased processing of the material is associated with increased levels of recall. For example, a strategy that involves associating images with items to be recalled leads to nearly twice as good recall as does merely counting the letters in the items. Results such as these give us important hints about how to go about learning any material and point out the poor recall to be expected from passive studying. Good recall, whether it be of lists of words or complex statistical concepts, requires active and "deep" processing of the material, which in turn is facilitated by noting associations between to-be-learned material and other material that you already know. You have probably noticed that sitting in class and dutifully recording everything that the instructor says doesn't usually lead to the grades that you think such effort deserves. Now you know a bit about why. (You'll do much better if you tell yourself silly little stories about the material. Writing down that the Congress of Vienna ended in 1815 probably will not help you much at exam time. Imagining your instructor dressed up in a 1800s wig with knee-high stockings, looking 15 years old, just might.)

If you were writing up the results of this study, you might say something like the following:

> In an attempt to investigate the role of the processing of verbal material on recall, five groups of subjects were asked to study lists of words. The instructions to the subjects differed in the amount of processing of the material that they were to do. The dependent variable was the level of recall, and an analysis of variance was run to compare group means. The results showed a significant difference in the means of the groups—$F(4,45) = 9.08$, $p < .05$—with groups instructed to do higher levels of processing showing better recall.

16.4 Unequal Sample Sizes

Most experiments are designed originally with the idea of having the same number of observations in each treatment. Frequently, however, things do not work out that way. Subjects in an experiment are often remarkably unreliable, and many fail to arrive for testing or are eliminated for failure to follow instructions. There is even a report in the literature in which an experimental animal was eliminated from the study for repeatedly biting the experimenter (Sgro and Weinstock, 1963). Moreover, in studies conducted on intact groups, such as school classes, groups are nearly always unequal in size for reasons that, again, have nothing to do with the experiment.

If the sample sizes are not equal, the analysis discussed earlier is not appropriate without modification. For the case of one independent variable, however, this modification is relatively minor.

For the case of equal sample sizes we defined

$$SS_{group} = \frac{\Sigma T_j^2}{n} - \frac{G^2}{N}$$

where n is the number of observations in each group. We were able to divide each of the T_j^2 (and therefore ΣT_j^2) by n because n was common to all treatments. If the sample sizes differ, however, and we define n_j as the number of subjects in the jth treatment ($\Sigma n_j = N$), we can rewrite the equation as

$$SS_{group} = \Sigma \left(\frac{T_j^2}{n_j} \right) - \frac{G^2}{N}$$

which, when all n_j are equal, reduces to the original form. All we are doing here is dividing each squared total by its own sample size as we go along.

An Additional Example: Adaptation to Maternal Roles

An additional example of a one-way analysis of variance will illustrate the treatment of unequal sample sizes. In a study of the development of low-birthweight (LBW) infants (Nurcombe, Howell, Rauh, Teti, Ruoff, and Brennan, 1984), three groups of newborn infants differed in terms of birthweight and whether their mothers had participated in a training program about the special needs of low-birthweight infants. The mothers were then interviewed when the infants were 6 months old. There were three groups in the experiment—an LBW Experimental group, an LBW Control group, and a Full-Term Control group. The two control groups received no special training, and so serve as reference points against which to compare the performance of the trained (experimental) group. The LBW Experimental group was part of the intervention program, and we hoped to show that those mothers would adapt to their new role as well as mothers of full-term infants. On the other hand, we expected that mothers of low-birthweight infants who did not receive the intervention program would have some trouble adapting. (Being a parent of a low-birthweight baby is not an easy task, especially for the first few months. For rather dramatic results from tracking these children for nine years, see Achenbach, Howell, Aoki, and Rauh, 1993.)

The actual data from this study are presented in part (a) of Table 16.6. Part (b) of the table shows the calculations for the analysis of variance, and

Table 16.6 Adaptation to Maternal Role in Three Groups of Mothers (Low Scores Are Associated with Better Adaptation)

(a) Data

Group 1 LBW Experimental			Group 2 LBW Control			Group 3 Full-Term			
24	10	16	21	17	13	12	12	12	
13	11	15	19	18	25	25	17	20	
29	13	12	10	18	16	14	18	14	
12	19	16	24	13	18	16	18	14	
14	11	12	17	21	11	13	18	12	
11	11	12	25	27	16	10	15	20	
12	27	22	16	29	11	13	13	12	
13	13	16	26	14	21	11	15	17	
13	13	17	19	17	13	20	13	15	
13	14					23	13	11	
						16	10	13	
						20	12	11	
						11			

$\Sigma X = 434$		495		549		$G = 1478$	
$n_j = 29$		27		37		$N = 93$	
$\overline{X} = 14.97$		18.33		14.84			

(b) Calculations

$$SS_{total} = \Sigma X^2 - \frac{(G)^2}{N}$$

$$= 24^2 + 10^2 + \cdots + 11^2 + 11^2) - \frac{1478^2}{93}$$

$$= 25,562 - 23,489.075$$

$$- 2072.925$$

$$SS_{group} = \Sigma \frac{T_j^2}{n_j} - \frac{G^2}{N}$$

$$= \frac{434^2}{29} + \frac{495^2}{27} + \frac{549^2}{37} - \frac{1478^2}{93}$$

$$= 23,716.007 - 23,489.075$$

$$= 226.932$$

$$SS_{error} = SS_{total} - SS_{group}$$

$$= 2072.925 - 226.932$$

$$= 1845.993$$

continued

Table 16.6   Continued

(c) Summary Table

Source	df	SS	MS	F
Group	2	226.932	113.466	5.53
Error	90	1845.993	20.511	
Total	92	2072.925		

part (c) contains the summary table. Notice that the calculations are carried out just as they would be for the case of equal sample sizes except that for SS_{group} each value of T_j^2 is divided by the corresponding sample size as we progress.

From the summary table we can see that the obtained F value is 5.53 and that it is based on 2 and 90 degrees of freedom. From Table D.3 in the Appendices we get through interpolation $F_{.05}(2,90) = 3.11$. (Here 90 degrees of freedom is halfway between 60 and 120 df, so we take as our critical value the value halfway between 3.15 and 3.07, which is 3.11.) Because $5.53 > 3.11$, we will reject H_0 and conclude that not all the scores were drawn from populations with equal means. In fact it looks as if the first and third groups are about equal, whereas the second (the LBW Control group) has a higher mean (poorer adaptation). However, the F tells us only that we can reject $H_0 : \mu_1 = \mu_2 = \mu_3$. It does *not* tell us which groups are different from which other groups. To draw those kinds of conclusions, we will need to use special techniques known as multiple comparison procedures.

16.5 Multiple Comparison Procedures

Multiple comparison techniques
Techniques for making comparisons between two or more group means subsequent to an analysis of variance.

When we run an analysis of variance and obtain a significant F value, we have shown simply that the overall null hypothesis is false. We do not know which of a number of possible alternative hypotheses (e.g., $H_1 : \mu_1 \neq \mu_2 \neq \mu_3 \neq \mu_4 \neq \mu_5$; $H_2 : \mu_1 \neq \mu_2 = \mu_3 = \mu_4 = \mu_5$) is true. **Multiple comparison techniques** allow us to investigate hypotheses that involve means of individual groups or sets of groups. For example, we might be interested in whether Group 1 is different from Group 2 or whether the combination of Groups 1 and 2 is different from Group 3.

One of the major problems with making comparisons among groups is that unrestricted use of these comparisons can lead to an excessively high probability of a Type I error. For example, if we have 10 groups where the complete null hypothesis is true ($H_0 : \mu_1 = \mu_2 = \mu_3 = \ldots = \mu_{10}$), t tests between all pairs of means will lead to making *at least* one Type I error 57.8% of the time. In other words the experimenter who thinks she is working at the $\alpha = .05$ level of significance is actually working at $\alpha = .578$. Figure 16.3 shows how the proba-

Figure 16.3

Probability of a Type I Error as a Function of the Number of Pairwise Comparisons Where $\alpha = .05$ for Any One Comparison

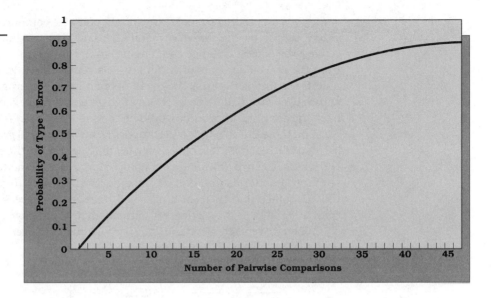

bility of making at least one Type I error increases as we increase the number of *independent* t tests we make between pairs of means. While it is nice to find significant differences, it is not nice to find ones that are not really there. Psychologists have enough trouble explaining all the real differences that we find without having to worry about spurious differences as well. We need to find some way to make the comparisons we need but keep the probability of incorrect rejections of H_0 under control.

In an attempt to control the likelihood of Type I errors, statisticians have developed a large number of procedures for comparing individual means. (For a discussion of many of these techniques see Howell, 1992.) Fortunately two relatively simple techniques provide reasonable control of the probability of Type I errors and are applicable to most multiple comparison problems you are likely to encounter. The first procedure is often referred to as the **protected t** or Fisher's **least significant difference (LSD) test**. (If your instructor looks a little pale at the suggestion to use Fisher's least significant difference test, just wait a bit and I'll defend that suggestion. It is not as outrageous as people may think.) Fisher's procedure is one of the most liberal multiple comparison tests we have. Following the discussion of that test I will go to the other extreme and present Scheffé's test, one of our most conservative. Finally, I will discuss the Bonferroni procedure, which is particularly useful when you use any standard statistical computer package to solve your problem. We will look at Fisher's LSD test first.

The procedures for using a protected t, or LSD test, are really very simple. *The first requirement for a protected t is that the F for the overall analysis of variance must be significant.* If the F was not significant, no comparisons between pairs of means are allowed. You simply declare that there are no group differences and stop right there. On the other hand, if the overall F is signifi-

Protected t (least significant difference test)
A technique in which we run t tests between pairs of means only if the analysis of variance was significant.

cant, you can proceed to make any (or all) pairwise comparisons between individual means by the use of a modified t test. The modification is simply to replace the pooled variance estimate (s_p^2) in the standard t formula with MS_{error} from the overall analysis of variance. This replacement is a perfectly reasonable thing to do. Because MS_{error} is defined as the average of the variances within each group, if there were only two groups in the experiment, the MS_{error} from the analysis of variance would be the same as the s_p^2 from the two-sample t test on those group means. In comparing among several groups we use MS_{error} instead of s_p^2 because it is based on variability within *all* the groups rather than within just the two groups we are comparing at the moment. As such it is presumably a better estimate of σ_e^2. Along with the use of this error term comes the advantage that the resulting t will have df_{error} degrees of freedom rather than just the $n_1 + n_2 - 2$ degrees of freedom it would have had otherwise.

When we replace s_p^2 with MS_{error}, the formula for t becomes

$$t = \frac{\overline{X}_i - \overline{X}_j}{\sqrt{\dfrac{MS_{error}}{n_i} + \dfrac{MS_{error}}{n_j}}} = \frac{\overline{X}_i - \overline{X}_j}{\sqrt{MS_{error}\left(\dfrac{1}{n_i} + \dfrac{1}{n_j}\right)}}$$

To illustrate the use of the protected t, let's take the data on maternal adaptation from the previous example. In that case we did find a significant overall F, which will allow us to look further in our analysis. Given the nature of that study, we would be interested in asking two questions:

1. Are there differences between mothers in the LBW Control group and mothers in the Full-Term group?

2. Are there differences between the mean of mothers in the LBW Control group and the mean of mothers in the Experimental group?

The first question asks whether mothers of low-birthweight infants have more difficulty adapting than do mothers of full-term infants. The second question asks whether the intervention program makes a difference in adaptation for mothers of low-birthweight infants. Note that it makes little sense to compare the LBW Experimental group with the Full-Term group because if we did find a difference we could not tell whether it was due to intervention effects or to birthweight effects. In this comparison intervention and birthweight are *confounded.*

The results on maternal adaptation are presented in Table 16.7, in which the obtained values of t are -2.77 and 3.04 for the two comparisons. We will use a two-tailed test at $\alpha = .05$, and we have 90 degrees of freedom for our error term. From Table D.3 we find that $t_{.05}(90) = \pm 1.99$ by interpolation. Thus for both comparisons we can reject the null hypothesis, because both values of the obtained t (t_{obt}) are more extreme (further from 0) than ± 1.99. We will therefore conclude that there is a difference in adaptation between mothers of low-birthweight babies and those of full-term infants, with the full-term mothers showing better adaptation. We will also conclude that the intervention program is effective for mothers of low-birthweight infants.

Table 16.7   Fisher's Least Significant Difference Test Applied to Low-Birthweight and Full-Term Groups

	Group 1 LBW Experimental	Group 2 LBW Control	Group 3 Full-Term
$\bar{X}_j =$	14.97	18.33	14.84
$n_j =$	29	27	37
$MS_{error} =$	20.511		
$df_{error} =$	90		

(a) μ_1 versus μ_2

$$t = \frac{\bar{X}_1 - \bar{X}_2}{\sqrt{MS_{error}\left(\dfrac{1}{n_1} + \dfrac{1}{n_2}\right)}}$$

$$= \frac{14.97 - 18.33}{\sqrt{20.511\left(\dfrac{1}{29} + \dfrac{1}{27}\right)}}$$

$$= \frac{3.36}{\sqrt{1.467}} = \frac{-3.36}{1.21} = -2.77$$

(b) μ_2 versus μ_3

$$t = \frac{\bar{X}_2 - \bar{X}_3}{\sqrt{MS_{error}\left(\dfrac{1}{n_2} + \dfrac{1}{n_3}\right)}}$$

$$= \frac{18.33 - 14.84}{\sqrt{20.511\left(\dfrac{1}{27} + \dfrac{1}{37}\right)}}$$

$$= \frac{3.49}{\sqrt{1.314}} = \frac{3.49}{1.15} = 3.04$$

You might ask why we call this particular multiple comparison procedure a "protected t." Or you may have heard somewhere that it is a bad idea to run all sorts of t tests between pairs of means, and it often is. This is a good place to address both these concerns at the same time.

One of the primary considerations in running a set of multiple comparisons is to hold down the probability of making *at least* one Type I error. In other words if we ran an analysis of variance and then three comparisons, we would want to ensure that the probability is high that we have not made a Type I error *anywhere*, either in the original F or in any of the three comparisons. The probability of making such an error is called the **familywise error rate**, because it deals with the probability that the *family* of comparisons contains *at*

Familywise error rate
The probability that a family of comparisons contains at least one Type I error.

least one Type I error. For familywise error rates making ten Type I errors is no worse than making one. (Or perhaps I should phrase that in reverse—making one Type I error is as bad as making ten.) If we just ran t tests between all pairs of means, the familywise error rate would become unacceptably high, especially if there were lots of means to compare. We need to impose some conditions to prevent that from happening, which is what a protected t test does by the simple expedient of requiring that no tests may be run unless the overall F from the analysis of variance is significant. To see why this simple step works, consider the following examples.

Suppose we have only two means and *the null hypothesis is true.* The probability of making a Type I error would be the probability that the original F was significant by chance, which is .05. If that F was significant, we have already made our Type I error, and even if we went on and ran a t test, we couldn't make the situation worse. If the F was not significant, we cannot run the protected t and so do not increase the error rate.[3] Thus with two means the familywise error rate is .05.

Now suppose we have three means. First assume that the complete null hypothesis is true—that is, suppose that $\mu_1 = \mu_2 = \mu_3$. First we run the overall F. The probability of finding a significant difference (which would be a Type I error because H_0 is true) is .05, and that represents our first Type I error out of the "at least one" that the familywise error rate protects against. If the F is not significant, we stop right there and have no further chances of making a Type I error. In other words when the complete null hypothesis is true, the probability of making *at least one* Type I error is limited by our rule to .05, which is what we want. Next suppose that the complete null hypothesis is false and that one mean is different from the other two (e.g., $\mu_1 = \mu_2 \neq \mu_3$). Then, because the complete null hypothesis is not true, it is impossible to make a Type I error with our overall F test. If we have a significant F, which we would hope to be the case, we can go on and test, for example, each pair of means—Group 1 versus Group 2, Group 1 versus Group 3, and Group 2 versus Group 3. But there is only one of those tests for which the null hypothesis is true, and therefore there is only one chance of making a Type I error. Here again the probability of at least one Type I error is only .05. Finally, suppose that all means are different from each other. Here we have no possibility of making a Type I error, because there is no true null hypothesis to erroneously declare false. From examination of these possibilities we can conclude that with three means the familywise error rate is also at most .05.

So we have seen that with two or three groups, Fisher's LSD test guarantees that the probability of making at least one Type I error will not exceed .05. But suppose we had four groups. In that case it is possible that there is more than one true null hypothesis. For example, Groups 1 and 2 could be equal and Groups 3 and 4 could be equal. If $\mu_1 = \mu_2$ and $\mu_3 = \mu_4$, you have two

---

[3]With only two means the t and the analysis of variance are equivalent tests, but that is not important here. The point is that if there is a Type I error on the F, we already have at least one error, and if F is not significant we cannot test further.

chances of making a Type I error, and the true familywise error rate is nearly .10. But I would submit that this is not an outrageous error rate given four means, and I would not cringe at using such a test, although it is not my favorite. Now if you want to talk about ten means, that's a different story, and anyone who would use Fisher's test with ten groups is asking for trouble. This is the complaint that is often raised against Fisher, but it's not really fair. If you look through the psychological literature (and I suspect it's true for all the behavioral sciences), you'll have a hard time finding experiments with even four groups. Ten-group experiments are almost unheard of, so why reject a test on the grounds that it doesn't work well with ten groups? Simply demanding a significant overall F before running multiple comparisons (which is where the protection comes from) is surprisingly effective in controlling familywise error rates when we have only a few groups. That is the reason I have stressed the protected t in this chapter. It does a good job of controlling the familywise error rate if you have a relatively small number of groups while at the same time being a test that you can easily apply and that has a reasonable degree of power.

The Scheffé Test

Scheffé test
A relatively conservative multiple comparison procedure.

Not everyone likes the protected t test, and people have requested that I include a conservative procedure for those who would prefer more stringent control over familywise error rates. I have chosen to include the **Scheffé test** because it is easy to use and popular with people who prefer stringent control. The presentation here is slightly different from that of other books, but it is algebraically equivalent to more traditional presentations, and it builds nicely on what you have already learned about computing the protected t.

First of all, with the Scheffé test we drop the requirement that the overall F from the analysis of variance be significant. We can run multiple comparisons with the Scheffé test regardless of whether or not the overall F is significant.

Next, you run any and all comparisons you want among pairs of means exactly as you did with the protected t. In other words you apply exactly the same formula. The only difference is that when you calculate your t, you square it and treat it as a legitimate value of F. (When we compare two groups, t^2 and F will be identical.)

Finally, you compare that F to the critical values of F in Table D.3 in the Appendices. But here is where the difference comes in. In the ordinary course of events it would not make any difference if you compared your t to $t_{.05}$ on $k(n - 1)$ degrees of freedom or compared your F to $F_{.05}$ on 1 and $k(n - 1)$ degrees of freedom. The result would be the same. But we are *not* going to compare our F to the critical value of $F_{.05}$ on 1 and $k(n - 1)$ df. Instead we are going to compare our F to $(k - 1)$ *times* the $F_{.05}$ on $(k - 1)$ and $k(n - 1)$ df. (Notice that I have used the df from the analysis of variance, as well as multiplying the critical value by $k - 1$.) In other words we are doing everything we did with the protected t (except no longer requiring the overall F to be significant), but now we are changing the critical value to make the test more conservative. For the comparison of the two LBW groups, $t = -2.77$, and thus $F = (-2.77)^2 = 7.67$. The $F_{.05}$ for 2 and 90 $df = 3.11$ (by interpolation), and two times that F is 6.22. Since $7.67 > 6.22$, we can reject H_0. Our t for LBW Experimental versus Full-Term would be evaluated against the same standard and is also significant.

A second worked example using the Scheffé test appears near the end of this chapter. An important point to keep in mind is that in holding down the familywise error rate, Scheffé has also made his test much more conservative. By that I mean he has made it harder to reject a true null hypothesis by making it harder to reject *any* null hypothesis—even a false one.

The Bonferroni Test

Bonferroni test
A multiple comparison procedure in which the familywise error rate (α) is divided by the number of comparisons.

The **Bonferroni test** is a nice compromise between the Fisher and Scheffé tests. As in the others, you calculate a standard t test between those pairs of means in which you are interested. But in this case you must either (1) compare every mean with every other mean or, better, (2) decide *before you collect the data* what groups you will compare. There is a good reason for this restriction, but elaborating that reason often seems to derail the discussion and lose the forest for the trees, so we will skip it. In this case you reject H_0 only if the difference is significant at α/c, where c is the number of comparisons you are running. For example, if we made the two tests shown in Table 16.7, we would reject H_0 only if that test were significant at the $.05/2 = .025$ level. If we wanted to make all three comparisons (1 versus 2, 1 versus 3, and 2 versus 3)—and I have suggested that this probably does not make much sense—we would calculate three t's and reject each if they were significant at the $.05/3 = .01667$ level.

You may have noticed a major difficulty here. Your tables don't give you the critical value of t at $\alpha = .01667$ or at most of the other levels of α you might need. Such tables do exist and can be found in many statistics texts (e.g., see Howell, 1992). Alternatively almost every computer program that calculates a t prints out not only the value of t but its probability (significance level) as well. Simply compare that probability value to α/c; if your obtained probability is less than α/c, reject H_0. I have calculated the probabilities for the two ts that we find in Table 16.7. For $t = -2.77$, the two-tailed probability under H_0 is .0068; for $t = 3.04$ the corresponding probability is .0031. Since both of these are less than $\alpha/2 = .05/2 = .025$, we can reject H_0 just as we did with Fisher's test.

16.6 Violations of Assumptions

As we have seen, the analysis of variance is based on the assumptions of normality and homogeneity of variance. In practice, however, the analysis of variance is a robust statistical procedure, and the assumptions can frequently be violated with relatively minor effects.

In general, if the populations can be assumed to be either symmetric or at least similar in shape (e.g., all negatively skewed) and if the largest variance is no more than four or five times the smallest, the analysis of variance is most likely to be valid. (Some argue that it would be valid for even greater differences between the variances.) It is important to note, however, that serious heterogeneity of variance and unequal sample sizes do not mix. If you have reason to anticipate noticeably unequal variances, make every effort to keep your sample sizes as equal as possible. This is particularly true when you plan to run a series of multiple comparisons.

For those situations in which the assumptions underlying the analysis of variance are seriously violated, there are alternative procedures for handling the analysis. Some of these procedures involve transforming the data (e.g., converting X to $\log(X)$) and then performing standard statistical tests on the transformed data. Other procedures involve using quite different tests, which are discussed in Chapter 20. (Also see the discussion of the Behrens-Fisher problem in Howell, 1992.)

16.7 Magnitude of Effect

Simply because we obtain a significant difference among our treatment means does not mean that the differences are large or important. There are many real differences that are trivial. No statistic can tell us whether a difference, no matter how large, is of any practical importance to the rest of the world. However, there are procedures that give us some help in this direction.

Magnitude of effect
A measure of the degree to which variability among observations can be attributed to treatments.

η^2 (eta squared)
A measure of the magnitude of effect.

One of the simplest measures of the **magnitude of effect** is η^2 (**eta squared**). While η^2 is a biased measure (in the sense that it tends to overestimate the value we would obtain if we were able to measure whole populations of scores), its calculation is so simple and it is so useful as a first approximation that it is worth discussing. In any analysis of variance, SS_{total} tells us how much overall variability there is in the data. Some of that variability is due to the fact that different groups of subjects are treated differently and therefore have different scores, and some of it is due just to random error—differences among people who are treated alike. The differences of importance are the differences among scores that can be attributed to our treatment, or group, effects, and they are measured by SS_{group}. If we form the ratio

$$\eta^2 = \frac{SS_{group}}{SS_{total}}$$

we can say what percentage of the variability among observations can be attributed to group effects.[4] For our maternal adaptation data

$$\eta^2 = \frac{SS_{group}}{SS_{total}} = \frac{226.932}{2072.925} = .11$$

---

[4] If you had *two* groups and created a variable (X) by entering 1 for all subjects in Group 1 and 2 for all subjects in Group 2, and if you let Y be the dependent variable (e.g., maternal adaptation), then the squared correlation (r^2) between X and Y would be equivalent to η^2. This relationship does not work in the same way for more than two groups.

Thus we can conclude that 11% of the variability in adaptation scores can be attributed to group membership. Although that might appear at first to be a small percentage, if you stop and think about the high level of variability among mothers you have known, explaining even 11% of it is a noteworthy accomplishment.

Although η^2 is a quick and easy measure to calculate, one you can estimate in your head when reading research reports, it is a biased statistic. It will tend to overestimate the true value in the population. A much less biased estimate is afforded by another statistic, ω^2 (**omega squared**). For the analysis of variance discussed in this chapter we can define

ω^2 (omega squared)
A less biased measure of the magnitude of effect.

$$\omega^2 = \frac{SS_{group} - (k - 1)MS_{error}}{SS_{total} + MS_{error}}$$

where k stands for the number of groups. For our example

$$\omega^2 = \frac{SS_{group} - (k - 1)MS_{error}}{SS_{total} + MS_{error}} = \frac{226.932 - (3 - 1)(20.511)}{2072.925 + 20.511} = 0.089$$

This value is somewhat lower than the value we obtained for η^2. However, it still suggests that we are accounting for approximately 9% of the variability.

16.8 The Use of BMDP for a One-way Analysis of Variance

An illustration of how BMDP computer software can be used to run a one-way analysis of variance is presented in Figure 16.4 for the maternal adaptation data. The output includes the mean and the standard deviation of each group, followed by the analysis of variance summary table. This figure agrees with the analysis in Table 16.6 but with two important differences. Notice that the first line of the summary table refers to an effect called MEAN. This is a test of the null hypothesis that the grand mean across all scores is 0.00. In our case we would not seriously entertain such a hypothesis because we expect the mean to be well above 0. The test on it is presented nonetheless. You can generally ignore the test on the grand mean. The other thing worth noting is that the program prints out the probability value associated with an F of 5.53. When we ran the analysis by hand and referred to Table D.3, we simply declared the difference to be significant with a probability less than .05. In other words we said that the probability of differences among means at least as great as we found is something less than .05. From this printout we have a more specific answer. Here we learn that the probability of difference among means at least as great as we found is exactly .0054. Since this is less than .05, we can reject H_0.

Figure 16.4   BMDP Analysis of Maternal Adaptation Data

```
BMDP2V - ANALYSIS OF VARIANCE AND COVARIANCE WITH REPEATED MEASURES.

PROGRAM INSTRUCTIONS

    /Problem    Title is 'BMDP2V Analysis of Maternal Adaptation Data.'.
    /Input      Variables are 2.
                Format is free.
                Cases are 93.
                File is 'Maternal.dat'.
    /Variable   Names are Group, Adapt.
    /Design     Dependent is Adapt.
                Grouping is Group.
    /End

DESCRIPTIVE STATISTICS OF DATA
----------- ---------- -- ----


CELL MEANS             FOR 1-ST DEPENDENT VARIABLE
-------------------
    Group =    *1            *2            *3            MARGINAL

    Adapt     14.96552      18.33333      14.83784     15.89247
    COUNT         29            27            37            93

STANDARD DEVIATIONS FOR 1-ST DEPENDENT VARIABLE
---------------- ---
    Group =    *1            *2            *3

    Adapt      4.84387       5.16646       3.70820

ANALYSIS OF VARIANCE FOR THE 1-ST DEPENDENT VARIABLE
--------------------

THE TRIALS ARE REPRESENTED BY THE VARIABLES:
Adapt
```

Test on $H_0 \, \mu = 0$

SOURCE	SUM OF SQUARES	D.F.	MEAN SQUARE	F	TAIL PROB.
MEAN	23513.09467	1	23513.09467	1146.36	0.0000
Group	226.93219	2	113.46609	5.53	0.0054
1 ERROR	1845.99254	90	20.51103		

} — P values

MS_{error}

Test on Group differences

16.9 A Final Worked Example

The following example illustrates a one-way analysis of variance with unequal sample sizes. It also illustrates the use of the Scheffé test.

What does marijuana do, and how does it do it? Aside from its better known effects, marijuana increases or in some cases decreases locomotor (walking around) behavior. The nucleus accumbens is a forebrain structure that has been shown to be involved in locomotor activity in rats. (It is also thought to control feelings of pleasure.) Administration of low doses of tetra-hydrocannabinol (THC, the major active ingredient in marijuana) is known to

Table 16.8   Data from the Study by Conti and Musty (1984)

	Placebo	0.1 μg	0.5 μg	1 μg	2 μg	
	30	60	71	33	36	
	27	42	50	78	27	
	52	48	38	71	60	
	38	52	59	58	51	
	20	28	65	35	29	
	26	93	58	35	34	
	8	32	74	46	24	
	41	46	67	32	17	
	49	63	61		50	
	49	44			53	
Total	340	508	543	388	381	2160 = G
Mean	34.00	50.80	60.33	48.50	38.10	45.96
n	10	10	9	8	10	47

increase locomotor activity, whereas high doses are known to lead to a decrease in activity. In an attempt to examine whether THC is acting within the nucleus accumbens to produce its effects on activity, Conti and Musty (1984) bilaterally injected either a placebo or 0.1, 0.5, 1, or 2 micrograms (μg) of THC directly into the nucleus accumbens of rats. The investigators recorded the change in the activity level of the animals after injection. It was expected that activity would increase more with smaller injections than with larger ones. The data in Table 16.8 represent the amount of change (decrease) in each animal.[5]

First we will set up the null hypothesis, which states that all these samples were drawn from populations with the same mean. In other words $H_0 : \mu_1 = \mu_2 = \mu_3 = \mu_4 = \mu_5$. For consistency we will test this null hypothesis with a significance level of $\alpha = .05$.

Next we will run the overall analysis of variance, starting with the calculation of the sums of squares:

$$SS_{total} = \Sigma X^2 - \frac{G^2}{N} = (30^2 + 27^2 + \cdots + 53^2) - \frac{2160^2}{47}$$

$$= 113,556 - 99,268.085 = 14,287.91$$

---

[5]Although THC is expected to *increase* activity, the dependent variable is measured as a *decrease* in overall activity because the animals were becoming acclimated to a new situation and were thus exploring less. Thus rather than an increase in activity, we actually are looking for less of a decrease. It's confusing!

$$SS_{groups} = \sum\left(\frac{T_j^2}{n_j}\right) - \frac{G^2}{N} = \left(\frac{340^2}{10} + \frac{508^2}{10} + \frac{543^2}{9} + \frac{388^2}{8} + \frac{381^2}{10}\right) - \frac{2160^2}{47}$$

$$= 103,461.50 - 99,268.085 = 4193.41$$

$$SS_{error} = SS_{total} - SS_{groups} = 14,287.91 - 4193.41 = 10,094.50$$

We can now put these terms in a summary table.

Source	df	SS	MS	F
Groups	4	4,193.41	1048.35	4.36
Error	42	10,094.50	240.35	
Total	46	14,287.91		

Finally, we compare $F = 4.36$ to the critical value from Table D.3 in the Appendices. We have 4 df for Groups and 42 df for Error. The critical value from Table D.3 is 2.61, if we round off to 40 degrees of freedom for the denominator. Because our obtained value exceeds 2.61, we will reject the null hypothesis and conclude that there are differences in activity levels among the five drug groups, presumably reflecting differences due to the dosage of THC administered.

The experimental hypothesis had predicted that the low-dose groups would show greater increases (or smaller decreases) in activity than the high-dose groups. Therefore, we might want to compare the 0.5-μg group with the 2-μg group. It would also be interesting to compare the 2-μg group with the placebo group to see if those groups were different. We will make both these comparisons using the Scheffé test. As discussed in the text, we will perform this test by first running t tests between the groups, just as we did with the protected t.

Comparison of Groups 3 and 5 (0.5 μg versus 2 μg):

$$t = \frac{\overline{X}_3 - \overline{X}_5}{\sqrt{MS_{error}\left(\frac{1}{n_3} + \frac{1}{n_5}\right)}}$$

$$= \frac{60.33 - 38.10}{\sqrt{240.35\left(\frac{1}{9} + \frac{1}{10}\right)}}$$

$$= \frac{22.23}{\sqrt{240.35(0.2111)}} = \frac{22.23}{\sqrt{50.74}} = \frac{22.23}{7.12} = 3.12$$

$$F = t^2 = 3.12^2 = 9.73$$

Comparison of Groups 1 and 5 (placebo versus 2 μg):

$$t = \frac{\overline{X}_1 - \overline{X}_5}{\sqrt{MS_{error}\left(\dfrac{1}{n_1} + \dfrac{1}{n_5}\right)}}$$

$$= \frac{34.00 - 38.10}{\sqrt{240.35\left(\dfrac{1}{10} + \dfrac{1}{10}\right)}}$$

$$= \frac{-4.10}{\sqrt{240.35(0.20)}} = \frac{-4.10}{\sqrt{48.07}} = \frac{-4.10}{6.93} = -0.59$$

$$F = t^2 = (-0.59)^2 = 0.35$$

Notice that for both tests I have squared the resulting values of t to obtain an F. These two values of F can be compared to Table D.3. To do this we first need the critical value of F on 4 and 42 degrees of freedom. This value (if we round the denominator degrees of freedom to 40) is 2.61. We next multiply this critical value of F by $k - 1 = 4$ to obtain 10.44. Any value of F that exceeds this value will be declared significant. Because our two values of F are 9.73 and 0.35, we will not reject the null hypothesis in either case.

You might wonder why we did not reject the null hypothesis for either of these comparisons, although we would have rejected it for the comparison of Groups 3 and 5 had we been using a protected t. The major reason is that the Scheffé test is a more conservative test. In the first place it does a better job than the protected t of keeping the familywise error rate in this case below $\alpha = .05$. But beyond that it is still a very conservative test, which is why I prefer the protected t when we have only a few groups. I would rather let the familywise error rate creep up too much than find myself with such a conservative test that I have difficulty finding *any* differences to be significant. However, many people would disagree with me, and they are the people for whom I presented this test in the first place. My own preference is to choose the Bonferroni test over either of the other two tests, but you need either special tables or the actual probability of t under H_0, and you should plan your tests in advance.

16.10 Summary

The analysis of variance is one of our most powerful statistical tools. In this chapter we began by examining the logic behind the analysis and then turned to the calculations. After considering the calculations for the case of equal sample sizes, we took up the problem of unequal sample sizes and saw that for the one-way analysis of variance we need to make only minor changes in the formulae. We then considered the problem of isolating group differences by means of multiple comparison procedures. After discussing the effects of violating the assumptions behind the test, we considered the problem of estimating the magnitude of experimental effects.

Some important terms in the chapter are:

- Analysis of variance (ANOVA)
- One-way ANOVA
- MS_{within} (MS_{error})
- $MS_{between\ groups}$ (MS_{groups})
- G (Grand total)
- SS_{total}
- SS_{group}
- SS_{error}
- df_{total}
- df_{group}
- df_{error}

- F statistic
- Multiple comparison techniques
- Protected t (least significant difference test)
- Familywise error rate
- Scheffé test
- Bonferroni test
- Magnitude of effect
- η^2 (eta squared)
- ω^2 (omega squared)

16.11 Exercises

16.1 To investigate maternal behavior of laboratory rats, we separated the rat pup from the mother and recorded the time (in seconds) required for the mother to retrieve the pup. We ran the study with 5-, 20-, and 35-day-old pups because we were interested in whether retrieval time varies with the age of the pup. The data are given below, with six pups per group. (The data are artificial, but they were created to ease computation and to demonstrate a point with respect to unequal sample sizes in a later exercise.)

5 Days Old	20 Days Old	35 Days Old
15	30	40
10	15	35
25	20	50
15	25	43
20	23	45
18	20	40

Run a one-way analysis of variance with $\alpha = .05$.

16.2 Use a protected t with the data in Exercise 16.1 to evaluate the difference between 5- and 20-day-old pups and the difference between 20- and 35-day-old pups.

16.3 Assume that you have just collected data to answer the question of whether the person paying a restaurant bill (Host) orders a less expensive meal than his or her partner (Guest). To avoid confusing the issue, you chose to look at only same-sex pairs and to record the price of the meal for only one person in each pair. Subjects are assigned to groups on the basis of whether or not the subject eventually picked up the tab. The dependent variable is the cost of the entrée.

Host	Guest
9.50	10.75
8.75	9.50
10.25	8.50
9.00	10.50
9.25	12.25

(a) Run the analysis of variance on the two groups.

(b) Run a two-sample t test on the same data, square the t, and compare the results. (*Note:* This relationship between t and F holds only when we have two groups.)

(c) Why was it necessary to ensure that you had data on only one member of each pair? (Answer with respect to what you know about t.)

16.4 It might be predicted that consumer buying behavior would vary with the location of a product in the store, even if the product in question has a high degree of brand loyalty. We therefore look at the purchases of well-known and unknown brands of candy bars when they are in their usual place next to the check-out counter and when they are in an awkward location behind a counter. The dependent variable is the number of candy bars of each brand sold per day. (For the time being we will ignore that this design might be analyzed by techniques to be discussed in Chapter 17.)

Known Brand/ Usual Location	Known Brand/ Awkward Location	Unknown Brand/ Usual Location	Unknown Brand/ Awkward Location
15	24	10	15
23	14	5	13
18	15	8	10
16	19	12	17
25	30	13	18
29	26	6	11
17	18	10	15

(a) Run a one-way analysis of variance.

(b) Now run a one-way analysis of variance on Groups 1 and 3 combined versus Groups 2 and 4 combined. What question does this test ask?

16.5 Refer to Exercise 16.1. Assume that for reasons beyond our control the data for the last pup in the 5-day-old group could not be used, nor could the data for the last two pups in the 35-day-old group. Rerun the analysis of variance using the remaining data.

16.6 Refer to Exercise 16.3. Suppose we collected two additional data points for the host group. The data now look like the following:

Host	Guest
9.50	10.75
8.75	9.50
10.25	8.50
9.00	10.50
9.25	12.25
11.75	
9.00	

(a) Rerun the analysis of variance.

(b) Run an independent t without pooling the variance.

(c) Run an independent t after pooling the variance.

(d) Which of these values of t corresponds (after squaring) to the F in part (a)?

16.7 Calculate η^2 and ω^2 for the data in Exercise 16.3.

16.8 Some words in a prose passage are particularly important for the meaning of the passage, whereas other words are of no real importance. It is hypothesized that good readers read primarily the important words and that if those words are capitalized and the other words are not the passage can be read more rapidly. We define three groups that read the same passage. For Group 1 no words are capitalized. For Group 2 a random selection of words are capitalized. For Group 3 the important words are capitalized. The dependent variable is the time to read the passage (in seconds).

	n	Mean	Standard Deviation
Group 1	10	30.2	6.21
Group 2	10	38.3	7.55
Group 3	10	25.6	5.75

(a) Run the analysis and draw whatever conclusions seem warranted.

(b) Point out at least one major failing in the design of this experiment as it relates to the hypothesis that good readers look for important words.

(c) What does rejection of H_0 mean in this case?

16.9 What would we conclude if we had the same means and standard deviations as in Exercise 16.8 but n equaled 5 instead of 10?

16.10 Use protected t tests for the data in Exercise 16.8 to clarify the meaning of the significant F.

16.11 The data in Exercise 16.9 also produced a significant F. Do you have more or less faith in the effect? Why?

16.12 Using the data in Appendix C, compare the grades in English (ENGG) for the three different levels of English (ENGL).

16.13 Why should you feel a bit uncomfortable about the answer to Exercise 16.12?

16.14 For the data in Appendix C, form three groups. Group 1 has ADDSC scores of 40 or below, Group 2 has ADDSC scores between 41 and 59, and Group 3 has ADDSC scores of 60 or above. Run an analysis of variance on the GPA scores for these three groups.

16.15 Compute η^2 and ω^2 from the results in Exercise 16.14.

16.16 Darley and Latané (1968) recorded the speed with which subjects summoned help for a person in trouble. Subjects thought that they were alone with the person (Group 1, $n = 13$), that one other person was there (Group 2, $n = 26$), or that four other people were there (Group 3, $n = 13$). The dependent variable was speed ($1/\text{time} \times 100$). The mean speed scores for the three groups were 0.87, 0.72, and 0.51, respectively. The MS_{error} was 0.053. Reconstruct the analysis of variance. (*Hint:* Compute group totals first.) What would you conclude?

16.17 Using the data in Exercise 16.1, calculate SS_{error} directly rather than by subtraction and show that this is the same answer you found in that exercise.

16.18 Use the Scheffé test for the data in Exercise 16.1 and compare your answer to the answer in Exercise 16.2.

16.19 Use the Scheffé test for the data in Exercise 16.8. What would you conclude? How does this compare to the answer for Exercise 16.10?

16.20 Would you find significant differences for the two comparisons we made for the data in Table 16.8 if you used the Bonferroni test? (*Hint:* In this particular case you will not need special tables because the t tables you have will suffice.)

16.21 What effect does smoking have on performance? Spilich, June, and Renner (1992) asked nonsmokers (NS), smokers who had delayed smoking for three hours (DS), and smokers who were actively smoking (AS) to perform a pattern recognition task in which they had to locate a target on a screen. The dependent variable was latency (in seconds). The data are presented below. Plot the resulting means and run the analysis of variance. On the basis of these data is there support for the hypothesis that smoking has an effect on performance?

Active Smokers	Delayed Smokers	Nonsmokers
9	12	8
8	7	8
12	14	9
10	4	1
7	8	9
10	11	7
9	16	16
11	17	19
8	5	1
10	6	1
8	9	22
10	6	12
8	6	18
11	7	8
10	16	10

16.22 In the study referred to in Exercise 16.21, Spilich et al. (1992) also investigated performance on a cognitive task that required the subject to read a passage and then to recall it later. This task has much greater information processing demands than the pattern recognition task. The independent variable was the three smoking groups referred in Exercise 16.21. The dependent variable was the number of propositions recalled from the passage. The data follow.

Active Smokers	Delayed Smokers	Nonsmokers
27	48	34
34	29	65
19	34	55
20	6	33
56	18	42
35	63	54
23	9	21
37	54	44
4	28	61
30	71	38
4	60	75
42	54	61
34	51	51

19	25	32
49	49	47

Run the analysis of variance on these data and draw the appropriate conclusions.

16.23 Use the Fisher LSD test to compare smokers with nonsmokers and to compare the two groups of smokers on the data in Exercise 16.22. What do these data suggest about the advisability of smoking while you are studying for an exam and the advisability of smoking just before you take an exam?

16.24 Spilich et al. (1992) ran a third experiment in which the three groups of smokers participated in a driving simulation video game. The AS group smoked immediately before the game but not during it. The data follow, where the dependent variable is an adjusted score related to the number of collisions. Run the analysis of variance and draw the appropriate conclusions.

Active Smokers	Delayed Smokers	Nonsmokers
15	7	3
2	0	2
2	6	0
14	0	0
5	12	6
0	17	2
16	1	0
14	11	6
9	4	4
17	4	1
15	3	0
9	5	0
3	16	6
15	5	2
13	11	3

16.25 The three experiments by Spilich et al. (1992) on the effects of smoking on performance find conflicting results. Can you suggest why the results are different?

17

FACTORIAL ANALYSIS OF VARIANCE

In Chapter 16 we dealt with a one-way analysis of variance, which is an experimental design having only one independent variable. In this chapter we will extend the analysis of variance to cover experimental designs involving two or more independent variables. For purposes of simplicity we will consider only experiments involving two independent variables, although the extension to more complex designs is quite simple (see Howell, 1992).

Why do older people often seem not to remember things as well as younger people? Do they not pay attention? Do they just not process the material as thoroughly? Do they know less? Or do they really do just as well, but are we more likely to notice when they forget than when younger people do? In Chapter 16 we considered a study by Eysenck (1974) in which he asked subjects to recall lists of words to which they had been exposed under one of several different conditions. In that example we were interested in determining whether recall was related to the level at which material was processed initially. Eysenck's study was actually more complex. He was interested in whether level-of-processing notions could explain differences in recall between older and younger subjects. If older subjects do not process information as deeply, they might be expected to recall fewer items than would younger subjects, especially in conditions that entail greater processing. This study now has two independent variables (Age and recall Condition), which we will refer to as **factors**. The experiment is an instance of what is called a **two-way factorial design**.

To expand this experiment even further, we could classify subjects additionally as male and female. We then would have what is called a *three-way factorial design*, with Age, Condition, and Gender as factors.

Factors
Another word for independent variables in the analysis of variance.

Two-way factorial design
An experimental design involving two independent variables in which every level of one variable is paired with every level of the other variable.

17.1 Factorial Designs

Factorial design
An experimental design in which every level of each variable is paired with every level of each other variable.

An experimental design in which every level of every factor is paired with every level of every other factor is called a **factorial design**. In other words a factorial design is one in which we include all *combinations* of the levels of the independent variables. Table 17.1 illustrates the two-way design of Eysenck's study. In the factorial designs discussed in this chapter, we will consider only the case in which different subjects serve under each of the treatment combinations. For instance, in our example one group of younger subjects will serve in the Counting condition, a different group of younger subjects in the Rhyming condition, and so on. Since we have 10 combinations of our two factors (5 recall Conditions × 2 Ages), we will have 10 different groups of subjects. When a research plan calls for the *same* subject to be included under more than one treatment combination, we speak of repeated-measures designs. Repeated-measures designs will be discussed in Chapter 18.

Factorial designs have several important advantages over one-way designs. First, they allow greater generalizability of the results. Consider Eysenck's study for a moment. If we were to run a one-way analysis using the five Conditions with only older subjects, as in Chapter 16, our results would apply only to older subjects. When we use a factorial design with both older and younger

Table 17.1

Diagrammatic Representation of Eysenck's Two-way Factorial Study

	Counting	Rhyming	Adjective	Imagery	Intentional
Younger					
Older					

subjects, we are able to determine whether differences between Conditions apply to younger subjects as well as older ones. We are also able to determine whether age differences in recall apply to all tasks, or whether younger (or older) subjects excel on only certain kinds of tasks. Thus factorial designs allow for a much broader interpretation of the results and at the same time give us the ability to say something meaningful about the results for each of the independent variables.

Interaction
A situation in a factorial design in which the effects of one independent variable depend upon the level of another independent variable.

The second important feature of factorial designs is that they allow us to look at the **interaction** of variables. We can ask whether the effect of Condition is independent of Age or whether there is some interaction between Condition and Age. For example, we would have an interaction if younger subjects showed much greater (or smaller) differences across the five recall Conditions than did older subjects. For example, the younger subjects might have had much better recall scores with high levels of processing than with low levels, while the older subjects did about the same under all levels of the Condition factor. Interaction effects are often among the most interesting results we obtain.

A third advantage of a factorial design is its economy. Since we are going to average the effects of one variable across the levels of the other variable, a two-variable factorial will require fewer subjects than would two one-ways for the same degree of power. Essentially, we are getting something for nothing. Suppose we had no reason to expect an interaction of Age and Condition. Then, with ten older subjects and ten younger subjects in each Condition, we would have 20 scores for each of the five conditions. If we instead ran a one-way with younger subjects and then another one-way with older subjects, we would need twice as many subjects overall for each of our experiments to have 20 subjects per condition, and we would have two experiments.

As mentioned earlier, factorial designs are labeled by the number of factors involved. A factorial design with two independent variables, or factors, is called a two-way factorial, and one with three factors is called a three-way factorial. An alternative method of labeling designs is in terms of the number of levels of each factor. Eysenck's study had two levels of Age and five levels of Condition.

2 × 5 factorial
A factorial design with one variable having two levels and the other having five levels.

As such, it is a **2 × 5 factorial**. A study with three factors, two of them having three levels and one having four levels, would be called a 3 × 3 × 4 factorial. The use of such terms as "two-way" and "2 × 5" are common ways of designating designs, and both will be used throughout this book.

In much of what follows, we will concern ourselves primarily with the two-way analysis. Higher-order analyses follow almost automatically once you understand the two-way, and many of the related problems we will discuss are most simply explained in terms of two factors.

Notation

In this chapter I will keep the notation as simple as possible to avoid unnecessary confusion. Names of factors generally are designated by the first letter (capitalized) of the factor name, and the individual levels of each factor are indicated by that capital letter with the appropriate subscript (e.g., for Condition,

Table 17.2   Factorial Design of Eysenck's Study

Age	Conditions					Totals
	Counting	**Rhyming**	**Adjective**	**Imagery**	**Intentional**	
Younger	T_{11}	T_{12}	T_{13}	T_{14}	T_{15}	T_{A1}
Older	T_{21}	T_{22}	T_{23}	T_{24}	T_{25}	T_{A2}
Totals	T_{C1}	T_{C2}	T_{C3}	T_{C4}	T_{C5}	$G = \Sigma X$

Cell
The combination of a particular row and column: the set of observations obtained under identical treatment conditions.

Counting would be designated as C_1, Rhyming as C_2, and Intentional as C_5). The number of levels of the factor will be denoted by a lowercase letter corresponding to that factor. Thus Condition (C) has $c = 5$ levels, whereas Age (A) has $a = 2$ levels. Any specific combination of one level of one factor and one level of another factor (e.g., Older subjects in the Rhyming condition) is called a **cell**, and the number of observations per cell will be denoted by n. The total number of observations is N, and in our example, $N = acn = 2 \times 5 \times 10 = 100$ because there are $a \times c = 10$ cells, each with 10 subjects. Table 17.2 shows the factorial design of Eysenck's study.

The subscripts i and j are used as general (nonspecific) notations for the level of rows and columns. Thus, cell$_{ij}$ is the cell in the ith row and the jth column. For example, cell$_{22}$ in Table 17.2 would be the Older subjects (row 2) in the Rhyming Condition (column 2). The totals for the individual levels of Age will be denoted as T_{Ai}, and the totals for the individual levels of Condition will be denoted as T_{Cj}. The subscripts A and C refer to the variable names, and T stands for "total." Cell totals are denoted as T_{ij}, and the grand total (the total of all N scores) is shown as either G or ΣX. Needless subscripts serve only as a source of confusion, and wherever possible I will leave them out.

The notation described here will be used throughout our discussion of the analysis of variance, and it is important that you thoroughly understand it before proceeding. The advantage of this system is that it easily generalizes to other examples. For example, if we had a Drug $\times$ Gender factorial, it should be clear that T_{D1} and T_{G2} refer to the totals of the first level of the Drug variable and the second level of the Gender variable, respectively.

17.2 The Extension of the Eysenck Study

As we have been discussing, Eysenck actually conducted a study varying Age as well as recall Condition. The study included 50 subjects 18–30 years of age and 50 subjects 55–65 years of age. The data in Table 17.3 have been created to have the same means and standard deviations as those reported by Eysenck. The table contains all the calculations for the standard analysis of variance, and we will discuss each of those in turn. Before we begin the analysis, it is important to note that the data themselves are approximately normally distributed with acceptably homogeneous variances. The boxplots are not given in the table because the individual data points are artificial; for real data it would be well worth your effort to compute them. You can tell from the cell and marginal totals that recall appears to increase with greater processing, and younger subjects seem to recall more items than do older subjects. Notice also

Table 17.3   Data and Calculations for Example from Eysenck (1974)

(a) Data

Age	Counting	Rhyming	Adjective	Imagery	Intentional	T_{A_i}
			Recall Conditions			
Older	9	7	11	12	10	
	8	9	13	11	19	
	6	6	8	16	14	
	8	6	6	11	5	
	10	6	14	9	10	
	4	11	11	23	11	
	6	6	13	12	14	
	5	3	13	10	15	
	7	8	10	19	11	
	7	7	11	11	11	
	70	69	110	134	120	503
Younger	8	10	14	20	21	
	6	7	11	16	19	
	4	8	18	16	17	
	6	10	14	15	15	
	7	4	13	18	22	
	6	7	22	16	16	
	5	10	17	20	22	
	7	6	16	22	22	
	9	7	12	14	18	
	7	7	11	19	21	
	65	76	148	176	193	658
T_{c_j}	135	145	258	310	313	$1161 = \Sigma X$

(Continued)

Table 17.3   (Continued)

(b) Calculations

$$\Sigma X^2 = 16{,}147 \qquad (\Sigma X)^2/N = 1161^2/100 = 13{,}479.21$$

$$SS_{total} = \Sigma X^2 - (\Sigma X)^2/N = 16{,}147 - 13{,}479.21 = 2667.79$$

$$SS_A = \frac{\Sigma T_A^2}{nc} - \frac{(\Sigma X)^2}{N} = \frac{503^2 + 658^2}{50} - \frac{1161^2}{100}$$

$$= 13{,}719.46 - 13{,}479.21 = 240.25$$

$$SS_C = \frac{\Sigma T_C^2}{na} - \frac{(\Sigma X)^2}{N} = \frac{135^2 + 145^2 + 258^2 + 310^2 + 313^2}{20} - \frac{1161^2}{100}$$

$$= 14{,}994.15 - 13{,}479.21 = 1514.94$$

$$SS_{cells} = \frac{\Sigma T_{ij}^2}{n} - \frac{(\Sigma X)^2}{N} = \frac{70^2 + 69^2 + \cdots + 176^2 + 193^2}{10} - \frac{1161^2}{100}$$

$$= 15{,}424.70 - 13{,}479.21 = 1945.49$$

$$SS_{AC} = SS_{cells} - SS_A - SS_C$$

$$= 1945.49 - 240.25 - 1514.94 = 190.30$$

$$SS_{error} = SS_{total} - SS_{cells} = 2667.79 - 1945.49 = 722.30$$

(c) Summary Table

Source	df	SS	MS	F
A (Age)	1	240.25	240.250	29.94*
C (Condition)	4	1514.94	378.735	47.19*
AC	4	190.30	47.575	5.93*
Error	90	722.30	8.026	
Total	99	2667.79		

*$p < .05$

---

that the difference between younger and older subjects seems to depend on the task, with greater differences for those tasks that involve deeper processing. We will consider these results further after we consider the analysis itself.

It will avoid confusion later if I take the time here to define two important terms. As I have said, we have two factors in this experiment—Age and Condition. If we look at the differences between older and younger subjects, *ignoring the particular conditions,* we are dealing with what is called the **main effect** of Age. Similarly if we look at differences among the five Conditions, ignoring the Age of the subjects, we are dealing with the main effect of Conditions.

An alternative method of looking at the data would be to compare the

Main effect
The effect of one independent variable averaged across the levels of the other independent variable(s).

means of the five conditions for only the older subjects. (This is what we did in Chapter 16.) Or we might compare older and younger subjects for only the data from the Counting task, for example, or we might compare older and younger subjects on the Intentional task. In these three examples we are looking at the effect of one factor for the data at only *one* level of the other factor. When we do this, we are dealing with a **simple effect**—the effect of one factor at one level of the other factor. A main effect, on the other hand, is that of a factor *ignoring* the other factor. If we say that tasks that involve more processing lead to better recall, we are speaking of a main effect. If we conclude that for younger subjects tasks that involve more processing lead to better recall, we are speaking about a simple effect. We will have more to say about simple effects and their calculations shortly. For now it is important only that you understand the terminology.

Simple effect
The effect of one independent variable at one level of another independent variable.

Calculations

The calculations for the sums of squares appear in part (b) of Table 17.3. Many of these calculations should be familiar, since they resemble the procedures used with a one-way design. For example, SS_{total} is computed the same way it was in Chapter 16, which is the same way it is always computed. We sum all the squared observations and subtract $(\Sigma X)^2/N$, the correction factor.

The sum of squares for the Age factor (SS_A) is nothing but the SS_{group} that we would obtain if this were a one-way analysis of variance without the Condition factor. In other words we simply sum the squared Age totals, divide by the number of observations on which each Age total is based (= nc), and subtract the correction factor. The same thing can be said for SS_C, except that there we ignore the presence of the Age variable.

You will notice that ΣT_A^2 is divided by nc and ΣT_C^2 is divided by na, where A and C represent Age and Condition, respectively. If you try to remember these denominators as formulae, you will be wasting your time. The denominators represent the number of scores per total and nothing more. They are exactly analogous to the denominator (n) we used in the one-way when we wanted to turn a variance of totals into an estimate of σ_e^2. The only difference is that in a one-way, n represented the number of observations per treatment, and here it represents the number of observations per cell—since c cells are involved with each Age level, there must be nc observations for each Age total (T_{Ai}).

After more than 20 years of teaching this material, I have concluded that confusion about denominators in the analysis of variance is innate. In fact, such confusion probably is a result of people learning to memorize formulae in high school math class. *Whenever you square any total in the analysis of variance, divide that square by the number of observations on which the total was based.* Above all, never try to memorize formulae for denominators. They exist only so that textbook writers have a way of writing equations precisely.

Having obtained SS_{total}, SS_A, and SS_C, we come to an unfamiliar term, **SS_{cells}**. SS_{cells} represents the variability of the individual cell totals and is in fact only a dummy term; it will not appear in the summary table. It is calcu-

SS_{cells}
The sum of squares assessing differences among cell totals.

lated just like any other sum of squares. We take the *cell totals*, square and sum them, divide by the number of observations per total, and subtract the correction factor. Although it might not be readily apparent why we want this term, its usefulness will become clear when we calculate a sum of squares for the interaction of Age and Condition. (It may be easier to understand the calculation of SS_{cells} if you think of it as what you would have if you viewed this as a study with 10 "groups" and calculated SS_{group}.)

SS_{cells} is a measure of how much the cell totals (and thus the cell means) differ. Two cell totals may differ for any of three reasons, other than sampling error: (1) they come from different levels of A; (2) they come from different levels of C; (3) there is an interaction between A and C. We already have a measure of how much the cells differ, since we know SS_{cells}. SS_A tells us how much of this difference can be attributed to difference in Age, and SS_C tells us how much can be attributed to differences in Condition. Whatever cannot be attributed to Age or Condition must be attributable to the interaction between Age and Condition (SS_{AC}). Thus, SS_{cells} is partitioned into its three constituent parts—SS_A, SS_C, and SS_{AC}. To obtain SS_{AC}, we simply subtract SS_A and SS_C from SS_{cells}. Whatever is left over is SS_{AC}. In our example

$$SS_{AC} = SS_{cells} - SS_A - SS_C$$
$$= 1945.49 - 240.25 - 1514.94 = 190.30$$

All we have left to calculate is the sum of squares due to error. Just as in the one-way analysis, we will obtain this by subtraction. The total variation is represented by SS_{total}. Of this total we know how much can be attributed to A, C, and AC. What is left over represents unaccountable variation or error. Thus

$$SS_{error} = SS_{total} - (SS_A + SS_C + SS_{AC})$$

However, since $SS_A + SS_C + SS_{AC} = SS_{cells}$, it is simpler to write

$$SS_{error} = SS_{total} - SS_{cells}$$

This equation provides us with our sum of squares for error, and we now have all the necessary sums of squares for our analysis.

Part (c) of Table 17.3 is the summary table for the analysis of variance. The source column and the sum of squares column are fairly obvious from what has already been said. The degrees of freedom column should also be familiar from what you know about the one-way. The total degrees of freedom (df_{total}) are always equal to $N - 1$. The degrees of freedom for Age and Condition are the number of levels of the variable minus 1. Thus, $df_A = a - 1 = 1$ and $df_C = c - 1 = 4$. The number of degrees of freedom for any interaction is simply the product of the degrees of freedom for the components of that interaction. Thus, $df_{AC} = df_A \times df_C = (a - 1)(c - 1) = 1 \times 4 = 4$. Finally, the degrees of freedom for error can be obtained by subtraction. Thus $df_{error} = df_{total} - df_A - df_C - df_{AC}$. Alternatively because MS_{error} is the average of the AC cell variances, and because each cell variance has $n - 1$ df, MS_{error} has $ac(a - 1)$ degrees of freedom. These rules for degrees of freedom apply to any factorial analysis of variance, no matter how complex.

Just as with the one-way analysis of variance, the mean squares are obtained by dividing the sums of squares by the corresponding degrees of freedom. This is the same procedure we will use in any analysis.

Finally, to calculate F, we divide each MS by MS_{error}. Thus, for Age, $F_A = MS_A/MS_{error}$; for Condition, $F_C = MS_C/MS_{error}$; and for AC, $F_{AC} = MS_{AC}/MS_{error}$. Each F is based on the number of degrees of freedom for the term in question and the df_{error}. Thus the F for Age is on 1 and 90 df, and the F for Condition and the F for the Age $\times$ Condition interaction are based on 4 and 90 df. From Table D.3 in the Appendices, we find that the critical values of F are $F_{.05}(1,90) = 3.96$ (by interpolation) and $F_{.05}(4,90) = 2.49$ (again by interpolation).

Interpretation

From part (c) of Table 17.3, the summary table, you can see that there were significant effects for Age, Condition, and their interaction. In conjunction with the cell totals, it is clear that younger subjects recall more items overall than do older subjects. It is also clear that those tasks that involve greater depth of processing lead to better recall overall than do tasks that involve less processing, which is in line with the differences we found in Chapter 16. The significant interaction tells us that the effect of one variable depends on the level of the other variable. For example, differences between older and younger subjects on the easier tasks such as counting and rhyming are less than the age-related differences on those tasks that involve greater depths of processing, such as imagery and intentional. Another view is that differences among the five conditions are less extreme for the older subjects than they are for the younger ones.

The results support Eysenck's hypothesis that older subjects do not perform as well as younger subjects on tasks that involve a greater depth of processing of information but do perform about equally with younger subjects when the tasks do not involve much processing. These results do not mean that older subjects are not *capable* of processing information as deeply. Older subjects simply may not make the effort that younger subjects do. Whatever the reason, they do not perform as well on those tasks.

You could write up the results of this study as follows:

> In an attempt to investigate the reported differences between older and younger people in the ability to recall verbal material, we asked five groups of older subjects and five groups of younger subjects to study and recall textual material under a variety of conditions. The conditions varied in terms of the degree to which the instructions called for the material to be processed mentally. There were ten subjects in each Age $\times$ Condition combination. The results showed significant differences due to Age ($F(1,90) = 29.94$, $p < .05$) and due to Conditions ($F(4,90) = 47.19$, $p < .05$). These differences reveal better overall recall for younger subjects and better re-

call of tasks that require greater processing. There was also a significant Age × Condition interaction ($F(4,90) = 5.93$, $p < .05$) reflecting the fact that differences between the two age groups generally were greater for those conditions in which greater mental processing of the material was required.

17.3 Interactions

A major benefit of factorial designs is that they allow us to examine the interaction of variables. Indeed in many cases the interaction term may be of greater interest than are the main effects (the effects of factors taken individually). Consider, for example, the study by Eysenck. The means are plotted in Figure 17.1 for each age group separately. Here you can see clearly what I referred to in the interpretation of the results when I said that the differences due to Conditions were greater for younger subjects than for older ones. The fact that the two lines are not parallel is what we mean when we speak of an interaction. If Condition differences were the same for the two Age groups, the lines would be parallel—whatever differences between Conditions existed for younger subjects would be equally present for older subjects. This would be true regardless of whether younger subjects were generally superior to older subjects or whether the two groups were comparable. Raising or lowering the entire line for younger subjects would change the main effect of Age, but it would have no effect on the interaction.

It may make the situation clearer if you consider several plots of cell means that represent the presence or absence of an interaction. In Figure 17.2 the first three plots represent the case in which there is no interaction. In all three cases the lines are parallel, even when they are not straight. Another way of

Figure 17.1

Cell Means for Data in Table 17.3

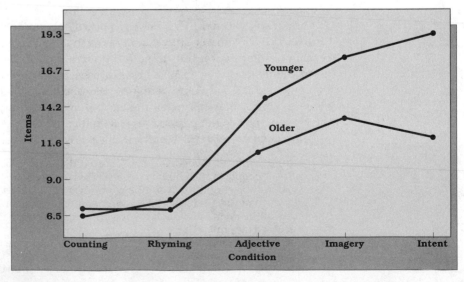

Figure 17.2

**Illustration
of Possible
Noninteractions
and Interactions**

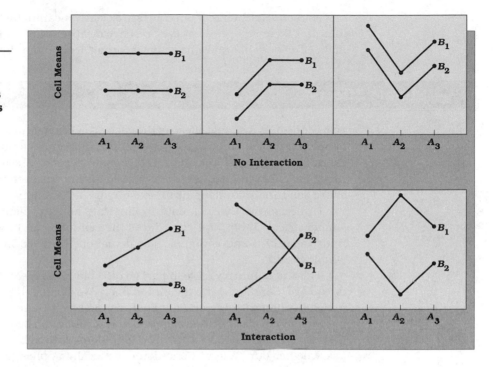

looking at this is to say that the difference between B_1 and B_2 (the effect of factor B) at A_1 is the same as it is at A_2 and at A_3. In the second set of three plots the lines clearly are not parallel. In the first plot one line is flat and the other rises. In the second plot the lines actually cross. In the third plot the lines do not cross, but they move in opposite directions. In every case the effect of B is *not* the same at the different levels of A. Whenever the lines are (significantly) nonparallel, we say that we have an interaction.

Many people will argue that if you find a significant interaction the main effects should be ignored. It is not reasonable, however, to automatically exclude interpretation of main effects in the presence of *any* significant interaction. In the Eysenck study we had a significant interaction, but for both younger and older subjects the tasks that involved greater processing led to greater recall. The fact that this effect was more pronounced in the younger group does not negate the fact that it was also clearly present in the older subjects. Here it is perfectly legitimate to speak about the main effect of Condition, even in the presence of an interaction. Had the younger group shown better recall with more demanding tasks while the older group showed poorer recall, it might not actually be of interest whether the main effect of Condition was significant or not, and we would instead concentrate on discussing the simple effects of differences among Conditions for the younger and older subjects separately. (Interactions in which group differences reverse their sign at some level of the other variable—that is, when the lines cross—are sometimes referred to as **"disordinal" interactions**.) In general the interpretation depends

**Disordinal
interaction**
An interaction in
which group differ-
ences reverse their
sign at some level of
the other variable.

on common sense. If the main effects are clearly meaningful, it makes sense to interpret them regardless of the presence or absence of an interaction. If the main effect does not really have any meaning, it should be ignored.

17.4 Simple Effects

I earlier defined a simple effect as the effect of one factor (independent variable) at one level of the other factor, for example, differences among Conditions for the younger subjects. The analysis of simple effects can be an important technique for analyzing data that contain significant interactions. In a very real sense such analysis allows us to "tease apart" interactions.

I will use the Eysenck data to illustrate how to calculate and interpret simple effects. Table 17.4 reproduces the cell totals and the summary table from Table 17.3 and contains the calculations involved in obtaining all the simple effects.

The first summary table in part (c) of Table 17.4 reveals significant effects due to Age, Condition, and their interaction. We discussed these results earlier in conjunction with the original analysis. As I said there, the presence of an interaction means that there are different Condition effects for the two Ages and different Age effects for the five Conditions. It thus becomes important to ask whether our general Condition effect really applies for older as well as younger subjects and whether there really are Age differences under all Conditions. The analysis of these simple effects is found in part (b) of Table 17.4 and in the second summary in part (c). I have shown all possible simple effects for the sake of completeness. In practice you should examine only those effects in which you are interested.

Calculation

In part (b) of Table 17.4 you can see that $SS_{C\,at\,Old}$ is calculated in the same way as any sum of squares. We simply calculate SS_C using only the data for the older subjects. If we consider only those data, the five Condition totals are 70, 69, 110, 134, and 120. Thus, the sum of squares will be

$$SS_{C\ at\ Old} = \frac{(\Sigma T^2_{C\ at\ Old})}{n} - \frac{(\Sigma T_{Old})^2}{cn}$$

$$= \frac{70^2 + 69^2 + 110^2 + 134^2 + 120^2}{10} - \frac{503^2}{(5)(10)} = 351.52$$

The other simple effects are calculated in the same way, by ignoring all data in which you are not interested at the moment. Notice that the sum of squares for the simple effect of Condition for older subjects (351.52) is the same value as that we obtained in Chapter 16 when we ran a one-way analysis of variance on only the data from older subjects.

Table 17.4   Calculation of Simple Effects for Data from Table 17.3

(a) Cell Totals (n = 10)

	Counting	Rhyming	Adjective	Imagery	Intentional	Totals
Older	70	69	110	134	120	503
Younger	65	76	148	176	193	658
Totals	135	145	258	310	313	1161

(b) Calculations

Conditions at Each Age

$$SS_{C \ at \ Old} = \frac{70^2 + 69^2 + \cdots + 120^2}{10} - \frac{503^2}{50}$$

$$= 5411.70 - 5060.18 = 351.52$$

$$SS_{C \ at \ Young} = \frac{65^2 + 76^2 + \cdots + 193^2}{10} - \frac{658^2}{50}$$

$$= 10{,}013.00 - 8659.28 = 1353.72$$

Age at Each Condition

$$SS_{A \ at \ Counting} = \frac{70^2 + 65^2}{10} - \frac{135^2}{20}$$

$$= 912.50 - 911.25 = 1.25$$

$$SS_{A \ at \ Rhyming} = \frac{69^2 + 76^2}{10} - \frac{145^2}{20}$$

$$= 1053.70 - 1051.25 = 2.45$$

$$SS_{A \ at \ Adjective} = \frac{110^2 + 148^2}{10} - \frac{258^2}{20}$$

$$= 3400.40 - 3328.20 = 72.2$$

$$SS_{A \ at \ Imagery} = \frac{134^2 + 176^2}{10} - \frac{310^2}{20}$$

$$= 4893.20 - 4805.00 = 88.20$$

$$SS_{A \ at \ Intentional} = \frac{120^2 + 193^2}{10} - \frac{313^2}{20}$$

$$= 5164.90 - 4898.45 = 266.45$$

(Continued)

Table 17.4 (Continued)

(c) Summary Tables

Overall Analysis

Source	df	SS	MS	F
A (Age)	1	240.25	240.250	29.94*
C (Condition)	4	1514.94	378.735	47.19*
AC	4	190.30	47.575	5.93*
Error	90	722.30	8.026	
Total	99	2667.79		

*$p < .05$

Simple Effects

Source	df	SS	MS	F
Conditions				
C at Old	4	351.52	87.88	10.95*
C at Young	4	1353.72	338.43	42.15*
Age				
A at Counting	1	1.25	1.25	<1
A at Rhyming	1	2.45	2.45	<1
A at Adjective	1	72.20	72.20	9.00*
A at Imagery	1	88.20	88.20	10.99*
A at Intentional	1	266.45	266.45	33.20*
Error	90	722.30	8.03	

*$p < .05$

The degrees of freedom for the numerator of simple effects are calculated in the same way as for the corresponding main effects. This makes sense because the number of means we are comparing remains the same. Whether we use all the subjects or only part of them, we still are comparing five conditions and have $5 - 1 = 4$ *df* for Conditions.

To test the simple effects we use the error term from the overall analysis of variance (MS_{error}). This produces the *F*s shown in Table 17.4. Note that the denominator had 90 *df* because we used MS_{error} from the overall analysis.

Interpretation

From the column labeled F in the simple effects summary table in Table 17.4, it is evident that differences due to Conditions occur for both ages, although the sum of squares for the older subjects is only about one-quarter of what it is for the younger ones. With regard to the Age effects, however, no differences occur on the lower-level tasks of counting and rhyming, but differences do occur on the higher-level tasks. In other words differences between age groups show up only for those tasks involving higher levels of processing. This result is basically what Eysenck set out to demonstrate.

17.5 Unequal Sample Sizes

When we were dealing with a one-way analysis of variance, unequal sample sizes did not present a serious problem—we simply adjusted our formula accordingly. That is definitely *not* the case with factorial designs. Whenever we have a factorial design with unequal cell sizes, the calculations become considerably more difficult, and the interpretation can be very unclear. The best solution is not to have unequal ns in the first place. Unfortunately the world is not always cooperative, and unequal ns are often the result. An extensive discussion of this problem is contained in Howell (1992).[1]

17.6 Magnitude of Effect

The methods for estimating the magnitude of effect for variables in a factorial design are simple extensions of the methods used with a one-way design. The most easily computed measure is again η^2 (eta squared) although it is still a biased estimate of the value that we would get if we obtained observations on whole populations. For each effect (main effects and interactions) in the factorial design we compute η^2 by dividing the sum of squares for that effect by SS_{total}. For our example

$$\eta_A^2 = \frac{SS_A}{SS_{total}} = \frac{240.25}{2667.79} = 0.09$$

$$\eta_C^2 = \frac{SS_C}{SS_{total}} = \frac{1514.94}{2667.79} = 0.57$$

$$\eta_{AC}^2 = \frac{SS_{AC}}{SS_{total}} = \frac{190.30}{2667.79} = 0.07$$

---

[1] If you use computer programs to handle data with unequal ns—and you probably will—I recommend the BMDP series. If you use the SPSS package, be sure to request /Method = unique for the ANOVA program. (The default option tests silly null hypotheses.) For SAS request Type III sums of squares.

Thus within this experiment differences due to Age account for 9% of the variability, differences due to Condition account for 57% of the variability, and differences due to the Age $\times$ Condition interaction account for 7% of the variability. The remaining 27% of the variability in this experiment is assigned to error variance.

As with the one-way analysis, η^2 is handy for making rough estimates of the contribution of variables. But a considerably less biased estimate is given by ω^2 (omega squared). The calculations, though somewhat more cumbersome, are straightforward.

$$\omega_A^2 = \frac{SS_A - (a - 1)MS_{error}}{SS_{total} + MS_{error}} = \frac{240.25 - (1)8.026}{2667.79 + 8.026} = 0.087$$

$$\omega_C^2 = \frac{SS_C - (c - 1)MS_{error}}{SS_{total} + MS_{error}} = \frac{1514.94 - (4)8.026}{2667.79 + 8.026} = 0.554$$

$$\omega_{AC}^2 = \frac{SS_{AC} - (a - 1)(c - 1)MS_{error}}{SS_{total} + MS_{error}} = \frac{190.30 - (4)8.026}{2667.79 + 8.026} = 0.059$$

Notice that these values are slightly smaller than the values for η^2, although their interpretation is basically the same.

17.7 A Second Example: Maternal Adaptation Revisited

In Chapter 16 we considered an example of actual data on maternal adaptation for mothers of LBW (low-birthweight) infants from Experimental and Control groups and Full-Term infants (Nurcombe *et al.*, 1984). We saw there that mothers in the Experimental (Intervention) and Full-Term treatment groups adapted better than those in the LBW Control group. A more complete analysis of those data might involve breaking down the treatment groups by Maternal Education (High School or Less versus More than High School). The authors of the study thought that the mothers with less education might benefit more from the Experimental program than would more highly educated mothers. If this were true, the LBW Control versus LBW Experimental differences would be larger for the Low Education group than for the High Education group, giving us a significant interaction. The data and calculations for this analysis are presented in Table 17.5. These data are a subset of the real data, from which only the first eight observations in each cell have been selected. (The results agree with the results of the full data set.) You will note that there are both a Group effect and an Education effect (as indicated by the asterisks (*) following the F values), but that there is no interaction. (When F is less than 1, we normally report "$F < 1$" rather than give the actual value.) The lack of an interaction means that group differences do not depend on Education level, which runs counter to our experimental hypothesis. We would conclude from this analysis that both the amount of Education and the presence or absence of the inter-

Table 17.5   Data on Maternal Adaptation as a Function of Group and Education

(a) Data

	Group 1 LBW Experimental	Group 2 LBW Control	Group 3 Full-term	Education Totals
High School Education or Less	14	25	18	
	20	19	14	
	22	21	18	
	13	20	20	
	13	20	12	
	18	14	14	
	13	25	17	
	14	18	17	
	127	162	130	419
More Than High School Education	11	18	16	
	11	16	20	
	16	13	12	
	12	21	14	
	12	17	18	
	13	10	20	
	17	16	12	
	13	21	13	
	105	132	125	362
Group Totals	232	294	255	781 = G

(b) Calculations

$$SS_{total} = \Sigma X^2 - \frac{G^2}{N}$$

$$= 14^2 + \cdots + 13^2 - \frac{781^2}{48}$$

$$= 13,363 - 12,707.52 = 655.48$$

$$SS_{cells} = \frac{\Sigma T_{ij}^2}{n} - \frac{G^2}{N}$$

$$= \frac{127^2 + \cdots + 125^2}{8} - \frac{781^2}{48}$$

$$= 12,918.375 - 12,707.52 = 210.86$$

(Continued)

Table 17.5   **(Continued)**

$$SS_{error} = SS_{total} - SS_{cells}$$

$$= 655.48 - 210.86 = 444.62$$

$$SS_{educ} = \frac{\Sigma T_E^2}{ng} - \frac{G^2}{N}$$

$$= \frac{419^2 + 362^2}{(8)(3)} - \frac{781^2}{48}$$

$$= 12,775.21 - 12,707.52 = 67.69$$

$$SS_{group} = \frac{\Sigma T_G^2}{ne} - \frac{G^2}{N} = \frac{232^2 + 294^2 + 255^2}{(8)(2)} - \frac{781^2}{48} = 122.79$$

$$SS_{EG} = SS_{cells} - SS_{educ} - SS_{group} = 210.86 - 67.69 - 122.79 = 20.38$$

(c) Summary Table

Source	df	SS	MS	F
Education	1	67.69	67.69	6.39*
Group	2	122.79	61.40	5.80*
E × G	2	20.38	10.19	< 1
Error	42	444.62	10.59	
Total	47	655.48		

*$p < .05$

vention program had an effect on maternal adaptation. However, differences in adaptation observed among the groups did not depend on the level of education of the mother.

17.8 Using SPSS for Factorial Analysis of Variance

The printout from an SPSS analysis of the data in the previous example is shown in Figure 17.3. A sample of the raw data are shown at the top of the table. The first column of the data file indicates whether the subject had a high school education or less (1) or more than a high school education (2). The second column indicates whether the subject was in the LBW-Experimental (1), the LBW-Control (2), or the Full-Term group (3). The third column contains the

Figure 17.3   SPSS Analysis of Maternal Adaptation Data

```
Raw Data:

1 1 14
1 1 20
. . .
2 3 13

Printout:

6-Jun-93 SPSS RELEASE 4.1 FOR VAX/VMS          Page 1

   1 0 Title        'SPSS Analysis of Low BirthWeight Data'
   2 0 File Handle  Data / Name = '[D_Howell.book]LBW.dat'
   3 0 Data List    File = Data/
   4 0              Educ 1 Treat 3 Adapt 5-6
   5 0 Value Labels Educ (1) 'HS or Less' (2) '> HS'/
   6 0              Treat (1) 'LBW Exper' (2) 'LBW Control' (3) 'Full-Term'
   7 0 Anova        Adapt by Educ (1,2) Treat (1,5)
   8 0              /Method = unique ──── Specifies most common
                                         method for analysis
```

**** ANALYSIS OF VARIANCE ****

ADAPT
by EDUC
  TREAT

SS for combined main effects

Source of Variation		Sum of Squares	DF	Mean Square	F	Sig of F
Main Effects B/W		190.479	3	63.493	5.998	.002
EDUC	$SS_{educ} \rightarrow$	67.687	1	67.687	6.394	.015
TREAT	$SS_{treat} \rightarrow$	122.792	2	61.396	5.800	.006
2-Way Interactions		20.375	2	10.188	.962	.390
EDUC TREAT	$SS_{interaction} \rightarrow$	20.375	2	10.188	.962	.390
Explained		210.854	5	42.171	3.984	.005
Residual w/in		444.625	42	10.586 $\leftarrow MS_{error}$		
						p values
Total		655.479	47	13.946		

```
48 cases were processed.
0 cases (.0 pct) were missing.
```

dependent variable. The program itself tells where the data file can be found, where the individual variables are located within that file, labels for the various values of the independent variable, and instructions for running the analysis. Notice that I have included "/Method = unique" in my program. This option is not required in this case because I have equal sample sizes. It will do no harm, however, and routinely including it ensures that I will use it in the unequal sample size case, where it is required to produce a meaningful analysis.

The summary table is somewhat different from the ones you are used to seeing. SPSS first tells you how much of the variability can be attributed to the two main effects. For the equal sample size case this value is simply the sum of the sums of squares for the main effects. Then, after reporting the two main effects, SPSS reports the total variability that can be accounted for by all the interactions. Since in a two-way design there is only one interaction, this row is the same as the single interaction that follows. Notice that, within rounding, the answers on this printout agree completely with the answers in Table 17.4.

17.9 Summary

In this chapter we extended the discussion of the analysis of variance to include designs involving two independent variables. In the factorial analysis we assumed that there are still different subjects in the different cells. We considered some of the advantages of factorial designs, especially that they allow us to look at the interaction effects of two variables. We also considered briefly the topic of simple effects (the effect of one variable at *one* level of the the other variable), the problems posed by unequal sample sizes, and procedures for estimating the magnitude of experimental effects.

Some important terms in this chapter are:

- Factors
- Two-way factorial design
- Factorial design
- Interaction
- 2×5 factorial

- Cell
- Main effect
- Simple effect
- SS_{cells}
- Disordinal interactions

17.10 Exercises

17.1 In a more complete study of restaurant behavior than we had in Chapter 16 (Exercise 16.3) we observe restaurant patrons who sit as same-sex couples. We record the price of the entreé ordered by one person in each pair and categorize subjects on the basis of the subject's gender and whether or not the subject pays the bill. The data follow:

Host		Guest	
Male	**Female**	**Male**	**Female**
8.00	8.25	9.75	8.75
7.00	8.75	10.25	9.00
8.25	9.75	9.50	9.25
9.00	8.00	9.00	8.50
8.25	9.25	10.50	8.75

Run a two-way analysis of variance on these data.

17.2 In a study of mother-infant interaction, mothers are rated by trained observers on the quality of their interactions with their infants. Mothers were classified on the basis of whether this was their first child (primiparous versus multiparous) and whether the infant was low-birth-weight (LBW) or full-term (FT). The data represent a score on a 12-point scale, on which a higher score represents better mother-infant interaction.

Primiparous		Multiparous	
LBW	**FT**	**LBW**	**FT**
6	8	7	9
5	7	8	8
5	7	8	9
4	6	9	9
9	7	8	3
6	2	2	10
2	5	1	9
6	8	9	8
5	7	9	7
5	7	8	10

Run and interpret the appropriate analysis of variance.

17.3 Referring to Exercise 17.2, it seems obvious that the sample sizes do not reflect the relative frequency of these characteristics in the population. Would you expect the mean for all these primiparous mothers to be a good estimate of the population of primiparous mothers? Why or why not?

17.4 Use simple effect procedures to compare low-birthweight and normal-birthweight conditions for multiparous mothers.

17.5 In a study of memory processes, animals were tested on a one-trial avoidance learning task. The animals were presented with a fear-producing stimulus on the *learning* trial as soon as they stepped across a line in the test chamber. The dependent variable was the time it took them to step across the line on the subsequent (*test*) trial. Three groups of animals differed in terms of the area in which electrodes were implanted in their cortex (Neutral Site, Area A, Area B). Each group was further divided and given electrical stimulation either 50, 100, or 150 msec after crossing the line and being presented with the fear-inducing stimulus. If the brain area that was stimulated is involved in memory, stimulation would be expected to interfere with memory consolidation and retard learning of the avoidance response, and the animal should not show any hesitancy in recrossing the line. The data on latency to recross the line are as follows:

			Stimulation Area					
Neutral Site			**Area A**			**Area B**		
50	**100**	**150**	**50**	**100**	**150**	**50**	**100**	**150**
25	30	28	11	31	23	23	18	28
30	25	31	18	20	28	30	24	21
28	27	26	26	22	35	18	9	30
40	35	20	15	23	27	28	16	30
20	23	35	14	19	21	23	13	23

Run the analysis of variance.

17.6 Plot the cell means in Exercise 17.5.

17.7 For Exercise 17.5 use the protected t test to compare the Neutral Site to each of the other sites, ignoring Delay of Stimulation. (*Hint:* Follow the procedures outlined in Chapter 16, but be sure you take n_i as the number of scores on which X_i is based.)

17.8 Use the Scheffé test in place of the protected t in Exercise 17.7.

17.9 For Exercise 17.5, use simple effects to examine the effect of Delay of Stimulation in Area A.

17.10 If you go back to Exercise 16.4 in Chapter 16, you will see that it really forms a 2×2 factorial. Run the factorial analysis and interpret the results.

17.11 In Exercise 16.4, you ran a test between Groups 1 and 3 combined versus Groups 2 and 4 combined. How does that test compare to testing the main effect of Location in Exercise 17.10? Is there any difference?

17.12 Calculate η^2 and ω^2 for the Maternal Adaptation data in Section 17.7.

17.13 Make up a set of data for a 2×2 design that has two main effects but no interaction.

17.14 Make up a set of data for a 2×2 design that has no main effects but does have an interaction.

17.15 Describe a reasonable experiment in which the primary interest would be in the interaction effect.

17.16 Calculate η^2 and ω^2 for the data in Exercise 17.1.

17.17 Calculate η^2 and ω^2 for the data in Exercise 17.2.

17.18 In Exercises 16.21–16.24 we examined data from three different experiments on smoking and performance. Combine those data into a two-way analysis of variance, with Smoking Group as one variable and Task as the second.

(a) Why do we not have any interest in the main effect of Task?

(b) Run the analysis of variance and interpret the other two effects.

(c) Plot the means for these data.

17.19 Calculate η^2 and ω^2 for the data in Exercise 17.18.

17.20 By comparing the formulae for η^2 and ω^2, tell when these two different statistics would be in close agreement and when they would disagree noticeably.

17.21 In the Eysenck (1974) study analyzed in Section 17.1, the real test of Eysenck's hypothesis about changes with age is found in the interaction. Why?

18

REPEATED-MEASURES ANALYSIS OF VARIANCE

In the previous two chapters we have been concerned with experimental designs in which there are different subjects in each group or cell. These designs are called **between-subjects designs** because they involve comparisons between different groups of subjects. However, many experimental designs involve having the same subject serve under more than one treatment condition. For example, we might take a baseline measurement of some behavior (i.e., a measurement before any treatment program begins), take another measurement at the end of a treatment program, and yet a third measurement at the end of a six-month follow-up

Between-subjects designs
Designs in which different subjects serve under the different treatment levels.

Repeated-measures designs
An experimental design in which each subject receives all levels of at least one independent variable.

period. Designs such as this one, in which subjects are measured repeatedly, are called **repeated-measures designs** and are the subject of this chapter. You may recognize that what I have just described as a repeated-measures analysis of variance is very much like what I earlier called a *t* test for related samples, although we are not restricted to only two measurements. In fact this is just the general case of that test. In the same vein everything I said about the *t* test for related samples applies here. In other words if two or more samples are related in any way—not just multiple measures on the same subjects—then this design applies. By far the most common use of this design is in cases in which the same set of subjects are measured repeatedly on the same dependent variable, and that is the model followed in this chapter.

There are a wide variety of repeated-measures designs, depending on whether each subject serves under all levels of all variables or whether some variables involve different groups of subjects while others involve the same subjects. In this chapter we will be concerned only with the simplest case, in which there is one independent variable and each subject serves under all levels of that variable. For analysis of more complex designs you can refer to Howell (1992) or Winer (1971).

18.1 An Example: The Treatment of Migraine Headaches

Migraine headaches are a problem for many people, and one way of treating them involves relaxation therapy. But does relaxation therapy actually work? And if it does, how can we tell? A study of the effectiveness of relaxation techniques by Blanchard, Theobald, Williamson, Silver, and Brown (1978) addressed this problem, and I have modified the design of their experiment to illustrate the use and analysis of a repeated-measures design. The data described here have been generated to be in agreement with those found by Blanchard *et al.*, although they are not the actual data. (Their study was actually more complex than the one examined here.)

The example I use involves nine migraine sufferers who were asked to record the frequency and duration of their migraine headaches. After four weeks of baseline recording, during which no training was given, each subject had a six-week period of relaxation training. (Each experimental subject participated in the program at a different time, so things such as changes in climate and holidays (e.g., Christmas and Hanukkah) should not *systematically* influence the data. For our example we will analyze the data for the last two weeks of baseline and the last three weeks of training. The dependent variable is the duration (hours/week) of headaches in each of those five weeks. The data and the calculations are shown in Table 18.1.

Look first at part (a) in Table 18.1. You will notice that there is a great deal of variability in the data, but much of that variability comes from the fact that some people have more and/or longer-duration headaches than others, which really has very little to do with the intervention program. The fact that you have more headaches in *general* than I do does not speak at all to the issue of

Table 18.1   Analysis of Data on Migraine Headaches

(a) *Data*

| Subject | Baseline | | Training | | | Subject Totals |
	Week 1	Week 2	Week 3	Week 4	Week 5	
1	21	22	8	6	6	63
2	20	19	10	4	9	62
3	7	5	5	4	5	26
4	25	30	13	12	4	84
5	30	33	10	8	6	87
6	19	27	8	7	4	65
7	26	16	5	2	5	54
8	13	4	8	1	5	31
9	26	24	14	8	17	89
Week Totals	187	180	81	52	61	561 = G
Week Means	20.78	20.00	9.00	5.78	6.78	12.47

(b) *Calculations*

$$SS_{total} = \Sigma X^2 - \frac{G^2}{N}$$

$$= 21^2 + 20^2 + \cdots + 5^2 + 17^2 - \frac{561^2}{45}$$

$$= 10{,}483 - 6993.8 = 3489.2$$

$$SS_{subjects} = \frac{\Sigma T_S^2}{w} - \frac{G^2}{N}$$

$$= \frac{63^2 + \cdots + 89^2}{5} - \frac{561^2}{45}$$

$$= 7827.4 - 6993.8 = 833.6$$

$$SS_{weeks} = \frac{\Sigma T_W^2}{n} - \frac{G^2}{N}$$

$$= \frac{187^2 + \cdots + 61^2}{9} - \frac{561^2}{45}$$

$$= 8928.3 - 6993.8 = 1934.5$$

$$SS_{error} = SS_{total} - SS_{subjects} - SS_{weeks}$$

$$= 3489.2 - 833.6 - 1934.5 = 721.1$$

(Continued)

Table 18.1   (Continued)

(c) Summary Table

Source	df	SS	MS	F
Subjects	8	833.6		
Weeks	4	1934.5	483.625	21.46*
Error (S×W)	32	721.1	22.534	
Total	44	3489.2		

*$p < .05$

whether relaxation therapy is effective in reducing headaches from the baseline phase to the training phase. These are just individual differences in headache severity. What we are able to do with a repeated-measures design that we were not able to do with between-subjects designs is to remove this variability in people's general level of migraine headaches from SS_{total}. This has the effect of removing subject differences from the error term and producing a smaller MS_{error} than we would have otherwise. We do this by calculating a term called $SS_{subjects}$, which measures differences among people in terms of their reported headache durations. The $SS_{subjects}$ term is then subtracted from SS_{total}, along with SS_{weeks}, when we calculate SS_{error}. (In the previous design, in which every score represented a different subject, if we had calculated $SS_{subjects}$ it would have been the same thing as SS_{total}.)

From Table 18.1 you can see that SS_{total} is calculated in the usual manner. Similarly $SS_{subjects}$ and SS_{weeks} are calculated just as main effects always are (square the relevant totals, sum, divide by the number of observations per total, and subtract G^2/N). Finally the error term is obtained by subtracting $SS_{subjects}$ and SS_{weeks} from SS_{total}.

The summary table, part (c) of Table 18.1, shows that I have computed an F for Weeks but not for Subjects. The reason is that MS_{error} is not an appropriate denominator for an F on subjects. Therefore we cannot test the Subjects variable. This is not a great loss, however, because we rarely are concerned with determining whether subjects are different from one another. We computed $SS_{subjects}$ only to allow us to compute an appropriate error term to test Weeks.

The F value for Weeks is 21.46, based on 4 and 32 degrees of freedom. The critical value of F on 4 and 32 df is $F_{.05}(4,32) = 2.68$. We can therefore reject $H_0: \mu_1 = \mu_2 = \ldots = \mu_5$ and conclude that the relaxation program led to a reduction in the duration per week of headaches reported by subjects. Examination of the means in Table 18.1 reveals that during the last three weeks of training the amount of time per week involving migraine headaches was about one-third what it was during baseline.

You may have noticed that no Subjects × Weeks interaction is shown in the summary table. With only one score per cell, the interaction term *is* the error term; in fact some people prefer to use S × W instead of Error. No matter whether you think of it as Error or as the S × W interaction, this term is still the appropriate denominator for the F on Weeks.

18.2 Multiple Comparisons

If we wanted to carry the analysis further and make comparisons among means, we could use the protected t procedure discussed in Chapter 16. The MS_{error} in this analysis would be the appropriate term to use in the protected t. For our data the results are clear-cut, and there is little or nothing to be gained by making multiple comparisons. It is useful, however, to demonstrate the procedure, because it allows us to check on one of our methodological assumptions and also to see how to test means of combined groups.

The first comparison we might want to make is between the two means for the Baseline period. We want to be sure that there was no improvement even before treatment began simply as a result of being in an experimental situation. Because the overall F was significant, we can use the protected t to make this comparison. For t we have

$$t = \frac{\overline{X}_i - \overline{X}_j}{\sqrt{MS_{error}\left(\frac{1}{n_i} + \frac{1}{n_j}\right)}} = \frac{\overline{X}_1 - \overline{X}_2}{\sqrt{MS_{error}\left(\frac{1}{n_1} + \frac{1}{n_2}\right)}}$$

$$= \frac{20.78 - 20.00}{\sqrt{22.53\left(\frac{1}{9} + \frac{1}{9}\right)}} = \frac{0.78}{\sqrt{5.01}} = \frac{0.78}{2.24} = 0.35$$

This t has df_{error} degrees of freedom because MS_{error} was used in place of the pooled variance. A t of 0.35 clearly is not significant at $\alpha = .05$. Thus we have no reason to suspect an improvement before the introduction of treatment. Note that we were able to run the protected t test *as if* the means were from two independent samples because the error term has been adjusted accordingly.

The most obvious comparison, given the nature of the experiment, is between the Baseline trials and the Training trials. First we will manually compute the means of those blocks of trials. The 18 Baseline observations have a mean of 20.39, and the 27 Training trials have a mean of 7.19. Thus

$$t = \frac{\overline{X}_i - \overline{X}_j}{\sqrt{MS_{error}\left(\frac{1}{n_i} + \frac{1}{n_j}\right)}}$$

$$= \frac{20.39 - 7.19}{\sqrt{22.53\left(\frac{1}{18} + \frac{1}{27}\right)}} = \frac{13.20}{\sqrt{2.086}} = \frac{13.20}{1.44} = 9.17$$

Again this t has 32 degrees of freedom because it uses MS_{error}. This t is definitely significant at $\alpha = .05$, indicating a difference in the mean duration of headaches between the Baseline and the Training phases of the study. Notice how easy it was to create and test a pair of means from five different levels of the treatment variable.

You might wonder how we can apply what *appears* to be a standard independent-groups t test when we know that the data are not independent. You will recall that in Chapter 13 we handled dependent observations by forming differences and then taking the standard deviation of the differences. In footnote 1 in Chapter 14 (p. 248) I pointed out that this had been necessary because we could not easily calculate the variances of differences (of *dependent* samples) directly from variables X_1 and X_2 unless we knew the correlations between X_1 and X_2. However, for a repeated-measures analysis of variance, MS_{error} is in fact an estimate of the standard error of the differences, even though we don't use difference scores to calculate it. You can easily demonstrate this to yourself by running a repeated-measures analysis of variance and a t test for two related samples on the same set of data (e.g., use Baseline data from this experiment) and noting the similarities among the terms you calculate. (With one df in the numerator, $F = t^2$.)

18.3 Assumptions Involved in Repeated-Measures Designs

Repeated-measures designs involve the same assumptions of normality and homogeneity of variance required for any analysis of variance. In addition they also require (for most practical purposes) the assumption that the correlations among pairs of levels of the repeated variable are constant. In the case of our example this would mean that we assume that (in the population) the correlation between Week 1 and Week 2 is the same as the correlation between Weeks 2 and 3, and so on. For example, if the correlation between Duration at Week 1 and Duration at Week 2 is 0.50, then the correlation between Duration for any other pairs of Weeks should also be about 0.50. This is a rather stringent assumption and one that probably is violated at least as often as it is met. The test is not seriously affected unless this assumption is seriously violated. If it is seriously violated, there are two things you can do to ease the situation. The first thing you can do is to limit the levels of the independent variable to those that have a chance of meeting the assumption. For example, if you are running a learning study in which *everyone* starts out knowing nothing and ends up knowing everything, the correlation between early and late trials will be near zero, whereas the correlations between pairs of intermediate trials probably will be high. In that case, do not include the earliest and latest trials in your analysis. (They wouldn't tell you much anyway.)

The second thing you can do is to use a conservative procedure proposed by Greenhouse and Geisser (1959). For our example we had $(w - 1)$ and $(w - 1) \times (n - 1)$ df for our F. Greenhouse and Geisser showed that if you took the same F but evaluated it on 1 and $(n - 1)$ df, you would have a conservative test no matter how serious the violation. For our example this would mean evaluating our obtained F against $F(1,8) = 5.32$. We would still reject our null hypothesis even using this more conservative test. Greenhouse and Geisser (and later Huynh and Feldt, [1976]) also derived less conservative corrections to the degrees of freedom. We will see a reference to this shortly. For a further discussion of these corrections, see Howell (1992).

18.4 Advantages and Disadvantages of Repeated-Measures Designs

The major advantage of repeated-measures designs has already been discussed. Where there are large individual differences among subjects, these differences lead to large variability in the data. When subjects are measured only once, we cannot separate subject differences from random error, and everything goes into the error term. When we measure subjects repeatedly, however, we can assess subject differences and separate them from error. This produces a more powerful experimental design and thus makes it easier to reject H_0.

The disadvantages of repeated-measures designs are similar to the disadvantages we discussed with respect to related-sample t tests (which are just special cases of repeated-measures designs). When subjects are used repeatedly, there is always the risk of carry-over effects from one trial to the next. For example, the drug you administer on Trial 1 may not have worn off by Trial 2. Similarly a subject may learn something in early trials that will help her in later trials. In some situations this problem can be reduced by **counter-balancing** the order in which treatments are administered. Thus half the subjects might have Treatment A followed by Treatment B, and the other half might receive Treatment B followed by Treatment A. This counter-balancing will not make carry-over effects disappear, but it may make them affect both treatments equally. Although there are disadvantages associated with repeated-measures designs, in most situations the advantages outweigh the disadvantages, and such designs are popular and extremely useful in experimental work.

Counter-balancing
An arrangement of treatment conditions designed to balance out practice effects.

18.5 Using BMDP to Analyze Data in a Repeated-Measures Design

One of my favorite statistical packages for analyzing repeated-measures designs is the BMDP package. This is one of the original large statistical packages and is extremely powerful. One of its best features is that the printout looks more or less like what you expect it to (with some packages you have to hunt through the printout for the various pieces you require). That doesn't mean that BMDP gives you exactly what you saw in Table 18.1. There are a number of differences, and these differences are instructive.

The output from a BMDP analysis on the data of Table 18.1 is shown in Figure 18.1, along with the data file and the program that generated the analysis. Notice that I have entered all five scores for each subject on the same line and that I began the line with a subject ID number. Notice also that the data

Figure 18.1   BMDP Analysis of Migraine Data

```
DATA:

1 21 22  8  6  6
2 20 19 10  4  9
3  7  5  5  4  5
4 25 30 13 12  4
5 30 33 10  8  6
6 19 27  8  7  4
7 26 16  5  2  5
8 13  4  8  1  5
9 26 24 14  8 17

PROGRAM INSTRUCTIONS


/Program    Title is 'Analysis of Migraine Headache Study'.
/Input      Variables are 6.
            Format is '(F1.0, 5F4.0)'
            Cases are 9.
            File is 'Headache.dat'.
/Variable   Names are SubjID, Wk1, Wk2, Wk3, Wk4, Wk5.
/Design     Dependent are Wk1, Wk2, Wk3, Wk4, Wk5.
            Levels are 5.
            Name is Weeks.
/End


A N A L Y S I S   O F   V A R I A N C E FOR THE 1-ST DEPENDENT VARIABLE


THE TRIALS ARE REPRESENTED BY THE VARIABLES:
Wk1      Wk2      Wk3      Wk4      Wk5
```

F for test on $H_0: \mu = 0$

SOURCE	SUM OF SQUARES	D.F.	MEAN SQUARE	F	TAIL PROB.	GREENHOUSE GEISSER PROB.	HUYNH FELDT PROB.
MEAN	6993.80000	1	6993.80000	67.12	0.0000		
1 ERROR	833.60000	8	104.20000				
Weeks	1934.53333	4	483.63333	21.46	0.0000	0.0001	0.0000
2 ERROR	721.06667	32	22.53333				

SS_{weeks} MS_{weeks} F for test on Weeks   Adjusted p values

```
ERROR                EPSILON FACTORS FOR DEGREES OF FREEDOM ADJUSTMENT
TERM                 GREENHOUSE-GEISSER              HUYNH-FELDT
 2                        0.4218                        0.5222
```

p value for F

are aligned vertically so you can read a week's worth of data down a column. The program itself is largely self-explanatory. There is a title for clarity on the printout, and the program is told that there are six variables to be read. The Format statement tells how those variables are to be read, the Cases statement tells how many cases to read, and the File statement gives the name of the file that contains the data. The names of the variables are given by the Variable statement. The Design paragraph tells the program which variables to use for the analysis, how many there are, and what to call the variable in the analysis of variance summary table.

One odd thing you will see in the summary table is the effect labeled "Mean" and an error term that goes with it. We saw a similar test in Figure 16.4, although that was not a repeated-measures analysis. This is really just a test on the null hypothesis that the mean headache score is 0.00; with an F of 67.12 there is not much doubt about its significance. This is not usually a null hypothesis that we care about, because most of the time our grand mean is well above zero. When the test is not of interest, you can just ignore it. Next you will note the sum of squares for Weeks. This value agrees with the result in Table 18.1, again with a significant F. Notice that next to each F is a column headed Tail Prob. This is the probability of obtaining an F as large as the one we obtained if the null hypothesis were true, and it saves us going to the F tables to test for significance. If this value is less than 0.05 we can reject H_0. In fact the probability here is so small that it is reported as 0.0000. (The probability is not exactly zero, but the first nonzero value would not show up until at least the fifth decimal place.)

Next to the Tail Prob. column are two other columns with probability values. One lists the Greenhouse-Geisser probability, and the other the Huynh-Feldt probability. A few paragraphs back I said that we assumed the correlations among the five trials were all about equal. If that assumption is not met, at least approximately, the computed F is not strictly accurate and its probability is not the actual probability value we seek. Both Greenhouse and Geisser and Huynh and Feldt have proposed corrections that can be applied to evaluate the F properly. The probabilities that you see here are the probabilities obtained with the two different corrections. Note that regardless of which correction we make, we would still reject H_0 with a very low p value. (The correction factors computed by these two approaches are given at the bottom of the table.)

18.6 A Final Worked Example

As a final example I will adapt an example from Chapter 16 to illustrate the differences and similarities between the repeated-measures design and the more traditional between-subjects design. In Chapter 16 we used the data from Eysenck (1974) on recall as a function of depth of processing and examined the effect of recall Condition on older subjects. In Table 18.2 I use the same set of numbers for the sake of continuity. However, I have rearranged the data points to look like what we would expect if the data came from 10 subjects who served under each of the five recall conditions, rather than from 50 subjects who each served under only one condition.[1] I have merely shifted scores up and down in a column so that an individual who was one of the poor scorers under one condition is also a poor scorer under the other conditions, and similarly for the subjects showing good recall. The numbers in each group are still the same. (If you moved these new data back into Chapter 16, you would obtain exactly the same results that we found there.) The data follow, with an additional column on the right for the subject totals.

---

[1] We would never cavalierly rearrange real data like this. I did it here only to show the differences and similarities between the two experimental situations.

Table 18.2   Repeated-Measures Analysis Applied to Eysenck Example

Subject	Count	Rhyming	Adjective	Imagery	Intent	Total
1	4	3	6	9	5	27
2	5	6	8	12	10	41
3	6	6	10	11	15	48
4	6	8	11	11	11	47
5	7	6	14	11	11	49
6	7	7	11	10	11	46
7	8	7	13	19	14	61
8	8	6	13	16	14	57
9	9	9	13	12	10	53
10	10	11	11	23	19	74
Totals	70	69	110	134	120	503

First we will calculate the SS_{total}:

$$SS_{total} = \Sigma X^2 - \frac{G^2}{N} = 4^2 + 5^2 + \cdots + 19^2 - \frac{503^2}{50}$$

$$= 5847 - 5060.18 = 786.82$$

We now have two main effects to calculate, one based on the Condition totals and one based on the Subject totals:

$$SS_{Conditions} = \frac{\Sigma T_C^2}{n} - \frac{G^2}{N} = \frac{70^2 + 69^2 + \cdots + 120^2}{10} - \frac{503^2}{50}$$

$$= 5411.70 - 5060.18 = 351.52$$

$$SS_{Subjects} = \frac{\Sigma T_S^2}{c} - \frac{G^2}{N} = \frac{27^2 + 41^2 + \cdots + 74^2}{5} - \frac{503^2}{50}$$

$$= 5339 - 5060.18 = 278.82$$

The error term can now be obtained by subtraction:

$$SS_{error} = SS_{total} - SS_{Conditions} - SS_{Subjects}$$

$$= 786.82 - 351.52 - 278.82 = 156.48$$

This error term is also equivalent to the Conditions × Subjects interaction, as described in the text.

We now set up the summary table:

Source	df	SS	MS	F
Subjects	9	278.82	——	——
Conditions	4	351.52	87.88	20.22
Error	36	156.48	4.35	
Total	49	786.82		

To test the F for the Conditions effect, we go to the F table with 4 and 36 degrees of freedom. From Table D.3 in the Appendices, we find through interpolation that the critical value of F is 2.65. Because $20.22 > 2.65$, we will reject the null hypothesis and conclude that recall of verbal material varies with the conditions under which that material is learned.

If you go back to Chapter 16, Section 16.3, you will see that when I analyzed the same basic data set as a between-subjects design I obtained an F of 9.08 instead of 20.22. The difference is that in this analysis I have treated the data as if they were repeated measures and thus subtracted out differences due to subjects from the error term. Notice two things. In the earlier analysis the $SS_{Conditions}$ was 351.52, which is exactly what it is here. SS_{error} in the earlier analysis was 435.30. If you were to subtract from that the $SS_{Subjects}$ (278.82) that we have here, you would get 156.48, which is the present SS_{error}. So you can see that we literally have subtracted out the sum of squares due to individual differences from our error term to make a more powerful test.

It is important to keep in mind that I have moved the data around slightly to produce subjects who were consistently poor or consistently good. But this is nothing more than you would expect to find if you used the same subjects under all conditions. From a comparison of the F here and the one in Chapter 16, you can see that you generally increase the power of an experiment and therefore the probability of finding a significant difference by using a repeated-measures design, if it is practical and appropriate.

18.7   Summary

In this chapter you saw how to handle data in which individual subjects served under all levels of one or more independent variables. We examined a simple case of a repeated-measures design and saw that such designs remove differences among subjects from the error term. By eliminating individual differences from MS_{error}, repeated-measures designs generally are more powerful than comparable between-subjects designs.

Some important terms in this chapter are:

- **Between-subjects designs**
- **Repeated-measures designs**
- **Counter-balancing**

18.8 Exercises

18.1 It is at least part of the folklore that repeated experience with the Graduate Record Examination (GRE) leads to better scores, even without any intervening study. We obtained eight subjects and gave them the GRE Verbal exam every Saturday morning for three weeks. The data are given in the following table:

	Sessions		
Subject	1	2	3
1	550	570	580
2	440	440	470
3	610	630	610
4	650	670	670
5	400	460	450
6	700	680	710
7	490	510	510
8	580	550	590

Run the appropriate analysis of variance. What, if anything, would you conclude about practice effects on the GRE?

18.2 Use the data from Exercise 18.1 to answer (a) and (b).

(a) Delete the data for the third session and run a (related-samples) t test between sessions 1 and 2.

(b) Now run a repeated-measures analysis of variance on those same two columns and compare this F with the square of the preceding t.

18.3 In an attempt to demonstrate the practical uses of basic learning principles, a psychologist with an interest in behavior modification has collected data on a study designed to teach self-care skills to severely disabled children. He collected data during a baseline phase, at the end of a training phase, and at a follow-up session six months after training ended. The children were scored (blind) by a rater who rated them on a 10-point scale of self-sufficiency. The data are given below. Run and interpret the appropriate analysis.

Baseline	Training	Follow-up
8	9	7
5	7	5
3	2	3
5	7	2
2	9	5
6	7	9
5	8	6
6	5	7
4	7	3
4	9	5

18.4 Use the protected t tests with the data in Exercise 18.3 to help you interpret the results. (*Hint:* As I pointed out, you can calculate the t test as if these were independent samples because MS_{error} has been adjusted accordingly by removing subject differences.)

18.5 Give an example of a situation in which you might profitably use a repeated-measures analysis of variance.

18.6 Using the data on the data disk available to your instructor, analyze the data from variables V72 to V78. Run a repeated-measures analysis of variance to test the experimental hypothesis that SAT verbal scores changed across time. See the discussion preceding Exercise 9.10 for a description of these variables. (*Note:* In this case repeated measurements are made on States rather than on Subjects.)

18.7 What null hypothesis did you test in Exercise 18.6?

18.8 In Exercise 18.6 why did we treat Years as a repeated measure rather than as a between-subjects measure?

18.9 Use protected *t* tests with the data in Table 18.1 to compare performance at the following points:

(a) the beginning and end of Baseline

(b) the beginning and end of Training (*Hint:* See the hint in Exercise 18.4.)

18.10 Run the repeated-measures analysis of variance and the *t* test for two related samples on the two Baseline weeks in Table 18.1. Note the similarities.

18.11 Shift the data around (within columns) for Exercise 18.3 in such a way as to maximize the correlations between trials. Then rerun the analysis and note the changes in *F*.

18.12 Run both a repeated-measures analysis of variance and a *t* test for two related measures on the Baseline data from Table 18.1. Show that for these analyses $F = t^2$.

Chi-Square

In Saint-Exupery's *The Little Prince* the narrator, remarking that he believes the prince came from an asteroid known as B-612, explains his attention to such a trivial detail as the precise number of the asteroid with the following comment:

> Grown-ups love figures. When you tell them you have made a new friend, they never ask you any questions about essential matters. They never say to you, "What does his voice sound like? What games does he love best? Does he collect butterflies?" Instead they demand: "How old is he? How many brothers has he? How much does he weigh? How much does his father make?" Only from these figures do they think they have learned anything about him.[1]

In some ways the first chapters of this book have concentrated on dealing with the kinds of numbers Saint-Exupery's grown-ups like so much. This chapter will be devoted to the analysis of largely nonnumerical data.

In Chapter 1 I drew a distinction between measurement data (sometimes called quantitative data) and categorical data (sometimes called frequency data). When we deal with measurement data, each observation represents a score along some continuum, and the most common statistics are the mean and the standard deviation. When we deal with categorical data, on the other hand, the data consist of the frequencies of observations that fall into each of two or more categories ("Does your friend have a gravelly voice or a high-pitched voice?" or "Is he a collector of butterflies, coins, or baseball cards?").

As an example, we could ask 100 subjects to classify a vaguely worded newspaper editorial as to whether it favored or opposed unrestricted dissemination of birth control information (no neutral or undecided response is allowed). The results might look as follows:

Editorial View Seen As		
In Favor of	Opposed	Total
58	42	100

Here the data are the numbers of observations that fall into each of the two categories. Given such data, we might be interested in asking whether significantly more people view the editorial as in favor of the issue than view it as opposed or whether the editorial is really neutral and the frequencies just represent a chance deviation from a 50:50 split. (Recall that subjects were forced to choose between "*in favor of*" and "*opposed*.")

A differently designed study might collect the same data on the newspaper editorial but try to relate those data to the individual's own views on the topic. Thus we might also classify respondents with respect to their own views about the dissemination of birth control information. This study might arrive at the following data:

Respondent	Editorial View Seen As		
	In Favor of	Opposed	Total
In Favor of	46	24	70
Opposed	12	18	30
Total	58	42	100

Here we see that people's judgments of the editorial depend on their own point of view, with the majority (46/70) of those in favor of the unrestricted dissemination of birth control information viewing the editorial as being on their side and those opposed generally seeing the editorial as siding with them (18/30).

---

[1] Antoine de Saint-Exupery, *The Little Prince*, trans. Katherine Woods (New York: Harcourt Brace Jovanovich, Inc., 1943), pp. 15–16.

In other words, respondents' personal opinions and their judgments about the editorial are not independent of one another.

Although these two examples appear somewhat different in terms of the way the data are arranged and in terms of the experimental questions being asked, the same statistical technique—the **chi-square test**—is applicable to both. However, because the research questions we are asking and the way that we apply the test are different in the two situations, we will deal with them separately.

Chi-square test
A statistical test often used for analyzing categorical data.

19.1 One Classification Variable: The Chi-Square Goodness-of-Fit Test

The following example is based on one of the most famous experiments in animal learning, conducted by Tolman, Ritchie, and Kalish (1946). At the time of the original study Tolman was engaged in a theoretical debate with Clark Hull and the latter's students on whether a rat in a maze learns a discrete set of motor responses (Hull) or forms some sort of cognitive map of the maze and responds on the basis of that map (Tolman). At issue was the fundamental question of whether animals learn by stimulus-response conceptions or whether there is room for a cognitive interpretation of animal behavior. (To put this in less academic language, "Do animals think?") The statistical test in question is called a **goodness-of-fit test** because it asks whether there is a "good fit" between the data (observed frequencies) and the theory (expected frequencies).

Goodness-of-fit test
A test for comparing observed frequencies with theoretically predicted frequencies.

In a simple and ingenious experiment, Tolman and his colleagues first taught a rat to run down a starting alley of a maze into a large circular area. From the circular area another alley exited straight across from the entrance but then turned and ended up in a goal box, which was actually to the right of the circular area. After the rats had learned the task ("go to the circular area and exit straight across"), Tolman changed the task by making the original exit alley a dead end and by adding several new alleys, one of which pointed in the direction of the original goal box. Thus, the rat had several choices, one of which included the original alley and one of which included a new alley that pointed directly toward the goal. The maze is shown in Figure 19.1, with the original exit alley drawn with solid lines and the new alleys drawn with dotted lines. If Hull was correct, the rat would learn a stimulus-response sequence during the first part of the experiment and would therefore continue to make the same set of responses, thus entering the now dead-end alley. If Tolman was right and the rat learned a cognitive map of the situation, then the rat would enter the alley on the *right* because it knew that the food was "over there to the right." Since Tolman was the one who published the study, you can probably guess how it came out—the rats chose the alley on the right. But we still need some way of testing whether the preference for the alley on the right was due to chance (the rats entered the alleys at random) or whether the data support a general preference for the right alley. Do the data represent a "good fit" to the model?

Figure 19.1

Schematic View of Tolman's Maze

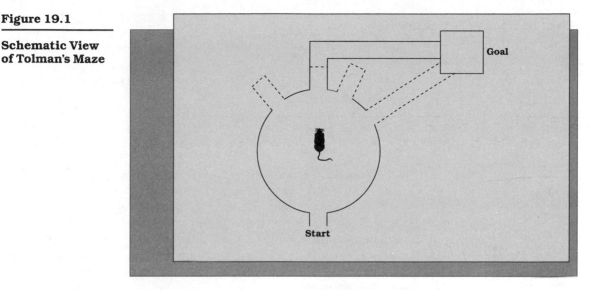

For the sake of this example I have modified the study slightly to include only two alleys in the second part of the experiment (Tolman *et al.* used 18). Let A represent the original exit and B the alley on the right. The choices for the 32 rats in the study are as follows (these are not Tolman's original data, which showed an even more dramatic difference):

	Alley Chosen		
	A	**B**	**Total**
Observed	9	23	32
Expected	16	16	32

The first line of this table shows the number of rats observed entering each alley in the second part of the experiment. This row sums to 32 because there were 32 rats in the experiment. We will take as our null hypothesis (H_0) for this test the hypothesis that the rats showed no preference for either of the two alleys. (Hull predicted that the rats would favor Alley A, whereas Tolman predicted that they would favor Alley B. We are testing the null hypothesis that they do not favor either alley.) In other words H_0 states that there is no difference between p (the probability of choosing Alley A) and q (the probability of choosing Alley B) and therefore that $p = q = .50$. In terms of **expected frequencies** this means that under H_0 we would expect half of the 32 rats to choose Alley A and half to choose Alley B. These expected frequencies are shown in the second row of the table. Since Tolman *et al.* used 32 *different* rats, the observations should be independent; there is no reason to expect that one rat's behavior would influence another rat's behavior. (If the study used eight rats four times each, we would have strong reservations about the independence of the observation.)

Expected frequencies
The expected value for the number of observations in a cell if H_0 is true.

The Chi-Square (χ^2) Statistic

We will approach this problem by use of the chi-square (χ^2) statistic, which is defined as

$$\chi^2 = \Sigma \frac{(O - E)^2}{E}$$

where

O = the observed frequency in each category
E = the expected frequency in each category

and the summation is taken over all categories.

Examination of this equation will make it clear why it is applicable to the question we want to ask. Notice that in the numerator we are directly measuring how far the observed frequencies deviate from the expected frequencies. The greater the deviations, the larger the value of χ^2. The denominator plays a useful role in terms of keeping the deviations in perspective. If we had expected 5 observations in a given category and obtained 15, that 10-point difference is substantial. On the other hand, if we had expected 500 and obtained 510, that 10-point difference would be brushed aside as inconsequential. When we divide by E, we are weighting the size of the squared deviations from the expected frequency by the size of the expected frequency.

From our formula for the chi-square test, we can calculate

$$\chi^2 = \Sigma \frac{(O - E)^2}{E}$$

$$= \frac{(9 - 16)}{16} + \frac{(23 - 16)^2}{16}$$

$$= 6.125$$

The Chi-Square Distribution

To test the null hypothesis that the probabilities of choosing the two alleys are equal, we need to evaluate the obtained χ^2 against the sampling distribution of chi-square in Table D.1 in the Appendices. A portion of that table is presented in Table 19.1. The chi-square distribution, like other distributions we have seen, depends on the degrees of freedom. For the goodness-of-fit test the degrees of freedom are defined as $k - 1$, where k is the number of categories (in our example, 2). Examples of the chi-square distribution for four different degrees of freedom are shown in Figure 19.2, along with the critical values and shaded rejection regions for $\alpha = .05$. You can see that the critical value for a specified level of α (e.g., $\alpha = .05$) will be larger for larger degrees of freedom. For our example we have $k - 1 = 2 - 1 = 1$ df. From Table D.1 (or Table 19.1) you

Table 19.1   Abbreviated Version of Table D.1, Upper Percentage Points of the χ^2 Distribution

df	.995	.990	.975	.950	.900	.750	.500	.250	.100	.050	.025	.010	.005
1	0.00	0.00	0.00	0.00	0.02	0.10	0.45	1.32	2.71	**3.84**	5.02	6.63	7.88
2	0.01	0.02	0.05	0.10	0.21	0.58	1.39	2.77	4.61	5.99	7.38	9.21	10.60
3	0.07	0.11	0.22	0.35	0.58	1.21	2.37	4.11	6.25	7.82	9.35	11.35	12.84
4	0.21	0.30	0.48	0.71	1.06	1.92	3.36	5.39	7.78	9.49	11.14	13.28	14.86
5	0.41	0.55	0.83	1.15	1.61	2.67	4.35	6.63	9.24	11.07	12.83	15.09	16.75
6	0.68	0.87	1.24	1.64	2.20	3.45	5.35	7.84	10.64	12.59	14.45	16.81	18.55
7	0.99	1.24	1.69	2.17	2.83	4.25	6.35	9.04	12.02	14.07	16.01	18.48	20.28
8	1.34	1.65	2.18	2.73	3.49	5.07	7.34	10.22	13.36	15.51	17.54	20.09	21.96
9	1.73	2.09	2.70	3.33	4.17	5.90	8.34	11.39	14.68	16.92	19.02	21.66	23.59

Figure 19.2

Chi-Square Distribution for $df = 1, 2, 4$, and 8 with Critical Values for $\alpha = .05$

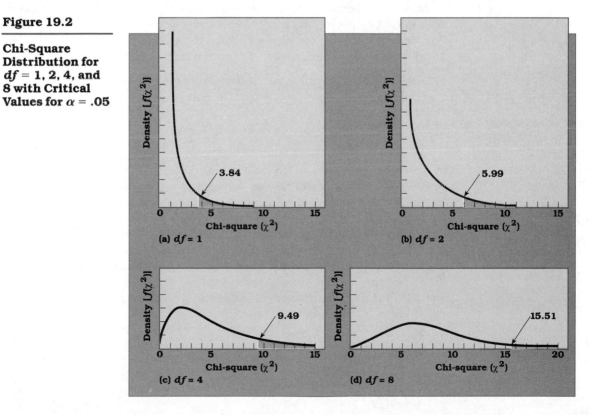

(a) $df = 1$

(b) $df = 2$

(c) $df = 4$

(d) $df = 8$

will see that, at $\alpha = .05$, $\alpha_{.05}(1) = 3.84$. Thus when H_0 is true, only 5% of the time would we obtain a value of $\chi^2 \geq 3.84$. Because our obtained value is 6.125, we will reject H_0 and conclude that the two alleys are not equally likely to be chosen. Tolman's rats chose Alley B at greater than chance levels. (I should note that here, as in the analysis of variance, we are using a one-tailed test of a nondirectional null hypothesis. By that I mean that we reject only for large values of χ^2, not for small ones. In that sense the test is one-tailed. However, we will obtain large values of χ^2, in the two-category case, regardless of which category has the larger obtained frequency. In that sense the test is two-tailed. With multiple categories there are a wide variety of patterns of differences that would lead to rejection, and the test could be thought of as multi-tailed or nondirectional.)

Extension to the Multicategory Case

Multicategory case
A situation in which data can be sorted into more than two categories.

In the example of place learning in rats we had a situation in which the data fell into one of two categories. We can easily extend this example to the **multi-category case**, in which data can be classified into three or more categories, the number being signified by k.

As an example, we can expand the place-learning problem to allow for multiple alleys running off the circular area. (Remember, Tolman used 18.) We will let Alley A be the one that was originally correct and now has a dead end. Alley D will be the one on the right, which rats would be expected to choose if they were trying to go to the place where the goal box previously had been. Alleys B and C are located midway between the other two. The data follow:

	Alley Chosen				
	A	**B**	**C**	**D**	**Total**
Observed	4	5	8	15	32
Expected	8	8	8	8	32

You can see that approximately half the rats chose the alley that Tolman would have predicted they would choose, whereas only four animals chose Alley A, the one that Hull's "response-learning" hypothesis would have predicted.

As in the first example, we have 32 animals. But this time we have four alleys. If the rats were responding at random—that is, if our null hypothesis were true—we would expect one-quarter of them to choose each alley. This leads to the expected frequency of eight for each alley. Our calculations for the chi-square test are the same as those followed in the earlier example, except that this time we will sum over four categories instead of two.

$$\chi^2 = \Sigma \frac{(O - E)^2}{E}$$

$$= \frac{(4 - 8)^2}{8} + \frac{(5 - 8)^2}{8} + \frac{(8 - 8)^2}{8} + \frac{(15 - 8)^2}{8}$$

$$= 9.25$$

From Table D.1, we see that for $k - 1 = 3$ df, $\chi^2_{.05} = 7.82$. Our value of 9.25 is greater than 7.82, so once again we will reject H_0. Again we have shown that our rats are not choosing at random. They are choosing the alley that leads in the correct direction at greater than chance levels, supporting Tolman's cognitive learning theory over Hull's response-learning model.

The thoughtful reader might ask why we analyzed the data this way rather than lumping Alleys A, B, and C together into one category labeled "wrong alley." There is no particularly convincing statistical answer to this question other than to say that it depends on what you know about the behavior of your animals and what you expect the data to look like. In our example the fact that about as many rats chose one of the three wrong alleys as chose the right one does not seem as relevant as the fact that about three times as many rats chose Alley D as chose any of the other alleys. (If you were to collapse back to "right" and "wrong," the *expected* frequency for "wrong" would be 24, because there are three wrong alleys, each with an expectancy of 8.)

19.2 Two Classification Variables: Contingency Table Analysis

Contingency table
A two-dimensional table in which each observation is classified on the basis of two variables simultaneously.

In the two previous examples we considered the case in which data are categorized along only one dimension (classification variable). Often, however, data are categorized with respect to two (or more) variables, and we are interested in asking whether those variables are independent of one another. To put this in the reverse, we often are interested in asking whether the distribution of one variable is *contingent* on a second variable. In this situation we will construct a **contingency table** showing the distribution of one variable at each level of the other. We saw one example of this kind of question when we wondered if the choices people made about the orientation of a newspaper editorial on birth control information depended on (was contingent on) the individual's own personal beliefs. Another example is offered by a study by Pugh (1983) on the "blaming the victim" phenomenon in prosecutions for rape.

Pugh conducted a thorough and complex study examining how juries come to decisions in rape cases. She examined a number of variables, but we will collapse two of them and simply look at her data in terms of (1) whether the defendant was found guilty, and (2) whether the defense alleged that the victim was somehow partially at fault for the rape. Pugh's actual data follow in the form of a contingency table.

Fault	Verdict		Total
	Guilty	**Not Guilty**	**Total**
Low	153 (127.559)	24 (49.441)	177
High	105 (130.441)	76 (50.559)	181
Total	258	100	358

This table shows some evidence that jurors assign guilt partly on the basis of the perceived faults of the victim. Notice that when the victim was seen as low in fault, approximately 86% (153/177) of the time the defendant is found guilty. On the other hand, when the victim is seen as high in fault, the defendant is found guilty only 58% (105/181) of the time.

Expected Frequencies for Contingency Tables

Marginal totals
Totals for the levels of one variable summed across the levels of the other variable.

For a contingency table the expected frequency for a given cell is obtained by multiplying together the totals for the row and column in which the cell is located and dividing by the total sample size (N). (These totals are known as **marginal totals**, because they sit at the margins of the table.) If E_{ij} is the expected frequency for the cell in row i and column j, R_i and C_j are the corresponding row and column totals, and N is the total number of observations, we have the following formula[2]:

$$E_{ij} = \frac{R_i C_j}{N}$$

For our example

$$E_{11} = \frac{177 \times 258}{358} = 127.559$$

$$E_{12} = \frac{177 \times 100}{358} = 49.441$$

$$E_{21} = \frac{181 \times 258}{358} = 130.441$$

$$E_{22} = \frac{181 \times 100}{358} = 50.559$$

Calculation of Chi-Square

Now that we have the observed and expected frequencies in each cell, the calculation of χ^2 is straightforward. We simply use the same formula that we have been using all along, although we sum our calculations over all cells in the table.

$$\chi^2 = \Sigma \frac{(O - E)^2}{E}$$

$$= \frac{(153 - 127.559)^2}{127.559} + \frac{(24 - 49.441)^2}{49.441} + \frac{(105 - 130.441)^2}{130.441} + \frac{(76 - 50.559)^2}{50.559}$$

$$= 35.93$$

[2]This formula for the expected values is derived directly from the formula for the probability of the joint occurrence of two *independent* events given in Chapter 7 on probability. For this reason the expected values that result are those that would be expected if H_0 were true and the variables were independent. A large discrepancy in the fit between expected and observed would reflect a large departure from independence, which is what we want to test.

Degrees of Freedom

Before we can compare our value of χ^2 to the value in Table D.1, we must know the degrees of freedom. For the analysis of contingency tables, the degrees of freedom are given by

$$df = (R - 1)(C - 1)$$

where

R = the number of rows in the table

and

C = the number of columns in the table

For our example we have $R = 2$ and $C = 2$; therefore, we have $(2 - 1)(2 - 1) = 1$ df. It may seem strange to have only 1 df when we have four cells, but you can see that once you know the row and column totals, you need to know only one cell frequency to be able to determine the rest.

Evaluation of χ^2

With 1 df the critical value of χ^2, as found in Table D.1, is 3.84. Because our value of 35.93 exceeds the critical value, we will reject the null hypothesis that the variables are independent of each other. In this case we will conclude that whether a defendant is found guilty depends in part on whether the victim is portrayed as being at fault for the rape. How do these results fit with how you think you would judge the case?

19.3 The Special Case of 2 × 2 Tables

In this book I have deliberately avoided discussing formulae that apply to special cases when a general formula will accomplish the same thing. I did this in part to relieve you of the need to memorize additional formulae, and in part because many analyses are obtained using computer software, and the actual formula is not particularly important. In the case of a 2 × 2 table, however, there is a formula that allows you to skip the calculation of expected frequencies and in fact allows you to determine χ^2 on a calculator without ever writing down intermediate results.

Let's imagine a 2 × 2 table with the cells and marginal totals labeled as follows:

A	B	$A + B$
C	D	$C + D$
$A + C$	$B + D$	N

Then

$$\chi^2 = \frac{N(AD - BC)^2}{(A + B)(C + D)(A + C)(B + D)}$$

Using the "blaming the victim" example,

Fault	Verdict		Total
	Guilty	**Not Guilty**	**Total**
Low	153	24	177
High	105	76	181
Total	258	100	358

$$\chi^2 = \frac{N(AD - BC)^2}{(A + B)(C + D)(A + C)(B + D)}$$

$$= \frac{358[(153 \times 76) - (24 \times 105)]^2}{177 \times 181 \times 258 \times 100}$$

$$= 35.93$$

This is exactly the same value of χ^2 that we obtained in the previous calculations.

People often have trouble with this formula because they forget which letter refers to which cell of the table. So do I. But notice what you are doing. You are multiplying cells that are diagonal to each other and then subtracting one product from the other. (It doesn't even matter which you subtract from which, because you are going to square the result anyway.) Next you multiply the squared answer by N and then divide by all the row and column totals. If you really become confused and divide when you should have multiplied or vice versa, you generally will obtain such an outlandish answer that you will know something is wrong.

Correction for Continuity

Some books advocate that for 2×2 tables you apply what is called a correction for continuity (also known as Yates's Correction), which simply amounts to reducing the numerator by one-half unit before squaring. This correction used to be quite common, but it has lost favor as we have learned more about the analysis of contingency tables. As Camilli and Hopkins (1978) pointed out, such a correction makes sense only if we have what are called "fixed marginal totals." Put differently, we would use the correction only if we found ourselves in a situation where we knew exactly what the row and column totals would be *before* we ran the experiment. Because such situations are rare, I am not going to cover the correction in more detail. For more extensive coverage see Howell (1992), who generally doesn't recommend it either.

19.4 Chi-Square for Larger Contingency Tables

The previous example involved two variables (Fault and Verdict), each of which had two levels. This particular design is referred to as a 2×2 contingency analysis and is a special case of more general $R \times C$ designs (where R and C represent the number of rows and columns). For an example of the analysis of a larger contingency table we can analyze data collected by Darley and Latané (1968) on bystander intervention. Why is it that bystanders who witness attacks and other negative events seem reluctant to intervene even in life-threatening situations? Are there any variables that can be shown to play a role in governing such bystander behavior?

Darley and Latané asked subjects to participate in a discussion carried on over an intercom system (supposedly to preserve confidentiality). One group of subjects was led to believe that they were speaking with only the discussion leader (later termed the victim); a second group of subjects thought one other person was involved in the discussion; and a third group thought that four other people were involved. In fact the subject was alone in all cases. Partway through the discussion the victim on the other end of the line pretended to have a seizure and began asking for help. He even stated that he was afraid that he might die without help. One of the dependent variables was the number of subjects in each group who tried to obtain help for the victim. The results are hardly encouraging for those of us who like to believe in the kindness of our fellow creatures. For the group of subjects each of whom thought he or she was alone with the victim, 85% tried to obtain help (the other 15% apparently decided to let nature take its course). For those subjects who thought one other person was listening, the response rate dropped to 62%. Worst of all when the subjects thought there were four other listeners, the response rate was a meager 31%. Although it is conceivable that these differences were due to chance, that doesn't seem likely. We can use chi-square to test the null hypothesis that helping behavior is independent of the number of bystanders. The data are presented in Table 19.2. The expected frequencies were obtained the same way they were obtained in the 2×2 case. In other words the expected frequency in the upper left cell is $(13 \times 31)/52 = 7.75$.

$$\chi^2 = \Sigma \frac{(O - E)^2}{E}$$

$$= \frac{(11 - 7.75)^2}{7.75} + \frac{(2 - 5.25)^2}{5.25} + \frac{(16 - 15.50)^2}{15.50}$$

$$+ \frac{(10 - 10.50)^2}{10.50} + \frac{(4 - 7.75)^2}{7.75} + \frac{(9 - 5.25)^2}{5.25}$$

$$= 1.36 + 2.01 + 0.02 + 0.02 + 1.81 + 2.68$$

$$= 7.90$$

Table 19.2

Observed and Expected Frequencies for Helping Behavior as a Function of the Number of Bystanders

	Observed Sought Assistance		Expected Sought Assistance		
Number of Bystanders	Yes	No	Yes	No	Total
0	11	2	7.75	5.25	13
1	16	10	15.50	10.50	26
4	4	9	7.75	5.25	13
Total	31	21	31	21	52

In this example we have $(3 - 1)(2 - 1) = 2$ df, and the critical value of χ^2 is 5.99. Because the obtained value of χ^2 (7.90) is greater than the critical value, we will reject H_0. If you expect something unpleasant to happen to you, be sure there are not too many people around—one person is about right.

19.5 The Problem of Small Expected Frequencies

Chi-square is an important and valid test for examining either goodness of fit or the independence of variables (contingency tables). However, the test is not as good as we would like when the *expected* frequencies are too small. The chi-square test is based in part on the assumption that if an experiment were repeated an infinite number of times with the same number of subjects, the obtained frequencies in any given cell would be normally distributed around the expected frequency. But if the expected frequency is small (e.g., 1.0), there is no way that the observed frequencies *could* be normally distributed around it. In cases in which the expected frequencies are too small, chi-square may not be a valid statistical test. The problem, however, is how we define "too small." There are almost as many definitions as there are statistics textbooks, and the issue still is being debated in the statistical journals. Here I take the admittedly conservative position that for small contingency tables (nine or fewer cells) all expected frequencies should be at least 5. For larger tables this restriction can be relaxed somewhat. There are people who argue that the test is conservative and produces few Type I errors, even with much smaller expected frequencies, but even they are forced to admit that when the total sample size is very small—as is frequently the case when the expected frequencies are small—the test has remarkably little power to detect false null hypotheses. (See Camilli and Hopkins, 1978, for a more complete discussion of this issue.)

19.6 The Use of Chi-Square as a Test on Proportions

The chi-square test can be used as a test on proportions or differences between two independent proportions. This is the same test we have been using all along. We simply change the way we conceive of our proportions (i.e., we change proportions to frequencies). Two simple examples make the point easily.

The first example involves a single proportion. A developer wants to build a large office building on what is now a city park. The building will bring in a large number of jobs, but it will also ruin the park, and there is considerable difference of opinion about the project. The developer has hired a well-respected polling agency, which has interviewed a random sample of 40 residents of the area. They found that 60% of those polled favored the project, while 40% of those polled opposed it. Is the developer safe in claiming that the majority opinion in the area is on her side, or could these results have occurred by chance if the residents were evenly divided? We will use chi-square to test the null hypothesis that the population is evenly split, that is, that the true value of P (the proportion in the population in favor of the project) is 0.50.

Because 40 people were polled and the proportion in favor was 60%, then $40 \times .60 = 24$ people were in favor and 16 were opposed. If H_0 were true, we would have an expected frequency of 20 for each alternative. Thus

	In Favor of	Opposed	Total
Obtained	24	16	40
Expected	20	20	40

Now we can compute

$$\chi^2 = \Sigma \frac{(O - E)^2}{E} = \frac{(24 - 20)^2}{20} + \frac{(16 - 20)^2}{20} = 1.60$$

We have 1 df in this case, and from the tables of χ^2 we find that at $\alpha = .05$ the critical value of $\chi^2 = 3.84$. Thus we cannot reject $H_0 : P = .50$. The developer does not have reliable evidence that more than half the population favors the project.

The second example involves testing the difference between two independent proportions and is based on a study of helping behavior by Latané and Dabbs (1975). In that study experimenters were instructed to walk into elevators and, just after the elevator started, drop a handful of pencils or coins on the floor. The dependent variable was whether bystanders helped pick up the pencils; one of the independent variables was the gender of the bystanders. The study was conducted in three cities (Columbus, Seattle, and Atlanta), but we will concentrate on the data from Columbus, where gender differences were least. We will also ignore any effect of the gender of the experimenter. Basically Latané and Dabbs found that 23% of the female bystanders and 28% of the male bystanders helped pick up the dropped items. (It is interesting that about three-quarters of the bystanders just stood there staring at the ceiling as if nothing had happened.) The question of interest is whether the difference between 23% and 28% is statistically significant. To answer this question, we must know the total sample sizes. In this case there were 1303 female bystanders and 1320 males. (Notice the large sample sizes that are easily obtained in this type of experiment.) Because we know the sample sizes, we can convert the proportions to frequencies easily.

	Sex of Bystander	
	Female	Male
Help	23%	28%
No help	77%	72%
Number	1303	1320

	Sex of Bystander		
	Female	Male	Total
Help	300	370	670
No help	1003	950	1953
Number	1303	1320	2623

The entry of 300 in the upper left corner of the table was obtained by taking 23% of 1303. The other entries were obtained in a similar way.

Because this is a 2×2 table, we can simplify the calculations by using the formula

$$\chi^2 = \frac{N(AD - BC)^2}{(A + B)(C + D)(A + C)(B + D)}$$

$$= \frac{2623[(300)(950) - (370)(1003)]^2}{(670)(1953)(1303)(1320)}$$

$$= \frac{2623(-86,110)^2}{(670)(1953)(1303)(1320)} = 8.64$$

Because the critical value on 1 df at $\alpha = .05$ is 3.84, I will reject H_0 and conclude that the proportions are significantly different. We can conclude that under the conditions of this study males are more willing to help than females.

A word of warning when using proportions. You will have noticed that we converted proportions to frequencies and then ran the chi-square test on the frequencies. This is the *only* right way to do that. I sometimes see people form a contingency table with the proportions themselves as cell entries and then go ahead and compute χ^2 as if nothing were wrong. But something *is* very wrong. They will not have a legitimate value of χ^2, and their test will be incorrect. Proportions, even if you throw away the decimal point and pretend that they are whole numbers, are not legitimate data for a chi-square test. You must use frequencies.

19.7 Nonindependent Observations

Aside from questions about small expected frequencies, the chi-square test also is based on the assumption that observations are independent of one another. In practical terms what this means is that subjects must contribute one, *and only one*, observation to the data. If in their bystander study Darley and

Latané had decided to use each subject two or three times to save the effort of recruiting more subjects, a chi-square analysis of the data would not have been appropriate. Fortunately they knew better, but this problem has a habit of sneaking into analyses carried out by even experienced investigators. The simplest rule is that N (the total of the row or column totals) must be equal to the number of *subjects* (not observations) in the experiment. If it is too large, you are probably using more than one observation from each subject. If it is too small, you have omitted some data (such as counting only how many subjects sought help for the victim and forgetting about counting those who did not seek help).

19.8 Minitab Analysis of Contingency Tables

Minitab does not have a procedure for running goodness-of-fit tests, but it does have two procedures for analyzing contingency tables, depending upon how the data are presented. The procedure most likely to be useful to you is shown in Figure 19.3 and is self-explanatory. The data analyzed there are the

Figure 19.3   Minitab Analysis of Bystander Data

```
MTB > Read the Data into Columns c1 and c2
DATA> 11 2
DATA> 16 10
DATA> 4 9
DATA> End
  3 ROWS READ

MTB > Name c1 'Yes'
MTB > Name c2 'No'

MTB > ChiSquare 'Yes' 'No'.

Expected counts are printed below observed counts

              Yes        No      Total
     1         11         2        13
              7.75      5.25

     2         16        10        26
             15.50     10.50

     3          4         9        13
              7.75      5.25

   Total       31        21        52
```

ChiSq = 1.363 + 2.012 +
    0.016 + 0.024 +
    1.815 + 2.679 = 7.908 ←———— χ^2
df = 2 ←———— degrees of freedom

```
MTB > PDF 7.908;
SUBC> Chisquare 2.
  7.9080 0.0096
MTB >
```
←———— p level

data from the first bystander study (see Table 19.2). The commands and the response

```
MTB > PDF 7.908;
SUBC> Chisquare 2.
 7.9080 0.0096
```

calculate the probability of a value of χ^2 of 7.908 on 2 df. This probability is .0096, which, because it is less than .05, will lead to rejection of H_0.

19.9 A Final Worked Example

We will take as our final example a study by Geller, Witmer, and Orebaugh (1976). These authors were studying littering behavior and were interested in, among other things, whether a message about not littering would be effective if placed on the handbills often given out in supermarkets advertising the daily specials. (This experiment was used in Chapter 7 to illustrate probability concepts.) To oversimplify a more complex study, two of Geller's conditions involved passing out handbills in a supermarket. Under one condition (Control) the handbills contained only a listing of the daily specials. In the other condition (Message), the handbills also included the notation, "Please don't litter. Please dispose of this properly." At the end of the day Geller and his students searched the store for handbills. They recorded the number found in trashcans; the number left in shopping carts, on the floor, and in various other places where they didn't belong (denoted Litter); and the number that could not be found and were apparently removed from the premises. The data obtained under the two conditions are shown in Table 19.3 and are taken from a larger table reported by Geller et al. Would you expect that such a notice on a handbill would have much effect on what *you* did with that handbill when you were finished with it?

We can analyze this contingency table appropriately by using the chi-square test because we have 1772 independent observations falling into six

Table 19.3   Data from Study by Geller, Witmer, and Orebaugh (1976)

	Trashcan	Litter	Removed	Total
Control	41 (61.66)*	385 (343.98)	477 (497.36)	903
Message	80 (59.34)	290 (331.02)	499 (478.64)	869
Total	121	675	976	1772

*Numbers in parentheses are expected frequencies.

mutually exclusive cells. We will test the null hypothesis that the location of the fliers at the end of the day is independent of the instructions on the flier, and we will set $\alpha = .05$.

We calculate the expected frequencies by the same procedure we have used before. Namely for a contingency table the expected frequencies are given $E = RT \times CT/GT$, where RT, CT, and GT stand for row, column, and grand totals, respectively. Therefore, if H_0 were true, the expected number of fliers from the Control group (the fliers without the message) found in the trashcan, would be $E_{11} = (903)(121)/1772 = 61.66$. Similarly, the number of people who received the antilittering message and removed their fliers would be expected to be $E_{23} = (869)(976)/1772 = 478.64$.

The calculation of χ^2 is based on the same formula we have been using all along:

$$\chi^2 = \Sigma \frac{(O - E)^2}{E} = \frac{(41 - 61.66)^2}{61.66} + \frac{(385 - 343.98)^2}{343.98} + \cdots + \frac{(499 - 478.64)^2}{478.64}$$

$$= 25.79$$

There are 2 df for this analysis because $(R - 1)(C - 1) = (2 - 1)(3 - 1) = 2$. The critical value of $\chi^2 = 5.99$, so we are led to reject H_0 and to conclude that the location in which handbills were left depended on the instructions given. In other words Instruction and Location are not independent. From the data it is evident that when subjects were asked not to litter a higher percentage of handbills were thrown into the trashcan or taken out of the store, and fewer were left lying in the shopping carts or on the floors and shelves.

If you were writing up these results, you would probably want to say something like the following:

> In an attempt to investigate whether people respond to antilittering messages on handbills, 1772 shoppers at a local supermarket were given handbills advertising daily specials. Approximately half of these fliers contained a message asking people not to litter and to dispose of the handbill in an appropriate place, while the other half did not contain such a message. At the end of the day a count was made of the number of messages found in the trash, the number that were found as litter, and the number that were removed from the store. These were classified by the presence or absence of the message on the flier, and a chi-square test was applied to the results. For these data $\chi^2(2) = 25.79$, $p < .05$. Examination of the results indicated that a smaller percentage of the handbills containing the antilittering message were found as litter, and a higher percentage were placed in the trash or removed from the store.

19.10 Summary

This chapter discussed the use of the chi-square test for the analysis of frequency data. We first considered the test for goodness of fit for the situation in which there is only one variable of classification. We then dealt with the use of chi-square for testing the independence of two variables, which is the way the test is most commonly used. Finally we considered the problem of small expected frequencies and the need for the independence of observations.

Some important terms in this chapter are:

- Chi-square test
- Goodness-of-fit test
- Expected frequencies
- Multicategory case
- Contingency table
- Marginal totals

19.11 Exercises

19.1 The chair of a psychology department suspects that some of his faculty are more popular than others. There are three sections of Introductory Psychology (taught at 10:00 AM, 11:00 AM, and noon) by Professors Anderson, Klansky, and Kamm. The number of students who enroll for each section are given below:

Professor Anderson	Professor Klansky	Professor Kamm
25	32	10

Run the appropriate chi-square test and interpret the results.

19.2 From the point of view of designing a valid experiment there is an important difference between Exercise 19.1 and a similar example used in this chapter. The data in Exercise 19.1 will not really answer the question that the chair wants answered. What is the problem and how could the experiment be improved?

19.3 I have a theory that if you ask subjects to sort one-sentence characteristics of people (e.g., "I eat too fast") into five piles ranging from *not at all like me* to *very much like me,* the percentage of items placed in each pile will be approximately 10%, 20%, 40%, 20%, and 10% for the

five piles. I have one of my children sort 50 statements and obtain the following data:

$$8 \quad 10 \quad 20 \quad 8 \quad 4$$

Do these data support my hypothesis?

19.4 To what population does the answer to Exercise 19.3 generalize?

19.5 In an old study by Clark and Clark (1939) black children were shown black dolls and white dolls and were asked to select one to play with. Out of 252 children, 169 chose the white doll and 83 chose the black doll. What can we conclude about the behavior of these children?

19.6 Following up the study referred to in Exercise 19.5, Hraba and Grant (1970) repeated the Clark and Clark study. The studies were not exactly equivalent, but they were close enough and the results are interesting. They found that out of 89 black children, 28 chose the white doll and 61 chose the black doll. Run the appropriate chi-square test on their data and interpret the results.

19.7 Combine the data from Exercises 19.5 and 19.6 into a two-way contingency table and run the appropriate test. How does the question that the two-way classification addresses differ from the questions addressed by Exercises 19.5 and 19.6?

19.8 Community mental health centers see a variety of problems, but some centers seem to see more of one kind of problem than others. Out of the last 100 clients seen by each of three centers, a count has been made of those classed as having Social Adjustment Problems, Problems with Living, and Other Problems. The data follow:

Mental Health Center

	A	B	C	Total
Social adjustment	50	40	40	130
Problems with living	26	34	20	80
Other problems	24	26	40	90
Total	100	100	100	300

(a) What null hypothesis would the chi-square test on this table actually test?

(b) Run the appropriate analysis.

(c) Interpret the results.

19.9 Use the data in Exercise 19.8 to demonstrate how chi-square varies as a function of sample size.

(a) Cut each cell entry in half and recompute chi-square.

(b) What does this have to say about the role of the sample size in hypothesis testing?

19.10 Howell and Huessy (1985) used a rating scale to classify children as to whether or not they showed Attention Deficit Disorder (ADD)–like behavior in the second grade. They then classified these same children again in the fourth and fifth grades. At the end of the ninth grade they examined school records and noted which children were enrolled in remedial English. In the following data all children who were ever classified as ADD have been combined into one group (labeled ADD):

Classifi-cation	Remedial English	Nonre-medial English	Total
Normal	22	187	209
ADD	19	74	93
Total	41	261	302

Does ADD classification in elementary school predict enrollment in remedial and nonremedial English in high school?

19.11 In Exercise 19.10 children were classified as those who never showed ADD-like behavior and those who showed ADD behavior at least once in the second, fourth, or fifth grade. If we do not collapse across categories, we obtain the following data:

Exhibition of ADD-Like Behavior

	Remedial English	Nonremedial English
Never	22	187
Grade 2	2	17
Grade 4	1	11
Grades 2 & 4	3	16
Grade 5	2	9
Grades 2 & 5	4	7
Grades 4 & 5	3	8
Grades 2, 4, & 5	4	6

(a) Run the chi-square test.

(b) What would you conclude, ignoring the small expected frequencies?

(c) How comfortable do you feel with these small expected frequencies? How might you handle the problem?

19.12 It would be possible to calculate a one-way chi-square test on the data in row 1 of Exercise 19.11. What hypothesis would you be testing if you did that? How would that hypothesis differ from the one you tested in Exercise 19.11?

19.13 In a study of eating disorders in female adolescents, Gross (1985) asked each of her subjects whether they would prefer to gain weight, lose weight, or maintain their current weight. (*Note:* Only 12% of the girls in Gross's sample were actually more than 15% above what normative tables say they should weigh, a common cutoff for a label of "overweight.") When she broke down the data for girls by race (African-American versus white), she obtained the following results. (Other races have been omitted because of small sample sizes.)

	Reducers	Maintainers	Gainers	Total
White	352	152	31	535
African-American	47	28	24	99
Total	399	180	55	634

(a) What conclusions can you draw from these data?

(b) Ignoring race, what conclusions can you draw about adolescent girls' attitudes toward their own weight?

19.14 Stress has long been known to influence physical health. Visintainer, Volpicelli, and Seligman (1982) investigated the hypothesis that rats given 60 trials of inescapable shock would be less likely to later reject an implanted tumor than would rats who had received 60 trials of escapable shock or 60 no-shock trials. They obtained the following data:

	Inescapable Shock	Escapable Shock	No Shock	Total
Reject	8	19	18	45
No Reject	22	11	15	48
Total	30	30	33	93

What would you conclude from these data?

19.15 Suppose that in the study by Latané and Dabbs (1975), referred to in Section 19.6, only 100 males and 100 females were involved. Compute χ^2.

19.16 What does the answer to Exercise 19.15 say about the effects of sample size on the power of an experiment?

19.17 In a recent survey of 150 students in a large lecture course, 45% thought the course needed major improvement, and 55% thought it was just fine. Is this difference significant?

19.18 In what way does the answer to Exercise 19.17 miss the point?

19.19 Dabbs and Morris (1990) examined archival data from military records to study the relationship between high testosterone levels and antisocial behavior in males. Out of the 4016 men in the normal testosterone group, 10.0% had a record of adult delinquency. Out of the 446 men in the high testosterone group, 22.6% had a record of adult delinquency.

(a) Create a contingency table of *frequencies* classifying men by high and normal testosterone levels and by delinquency and nondelinquency.

(b) Compute χ^2 for this table.

(c) Draw the appropriate conclusions.

19.20 In the study described in Exercise 19.19, 11.5% of the normal testosterone group and 17.9% of the high testosterone group had a history of childhood delinquency.

(a) Is there a significant relationship between these two variables?

(b) Interpret this relationship.

(c) How does this result expand on what we already know from Exercise 19.19?

19.21 Let's see how students and faculty compare on a basic statistical question. Zuckerman, Hodgins, Zuckerman, and Rosenthal (1993) surveyed 550 people and asked a number of questions on statistical issues. In one question a reviewer warned a researcher that she had a high probability of a Type I error because she had a small sample size. The researcher disagreed. Subjects were asked, "Was the researcher correct?" The proportions of respondents, partitioned among students, assistant professors, associate professors, and full professors, who sided with the researcher and the total number of respondents in each category were as follows:

	Students	Assistant Professors	Associate Professors	Full Professors
Proportion	.59	.34	.43	.51
Sample size	17	175	134	182

(*Note:* These data mean that 59% of the 17 students who responded sided with the researcher. When you calculate the actual *obtained* frequencies, round to the nearest whole person.)

(a) Who do you think was correct?

(b) What do these data tell you about differences among groups of respondents? (*Note:* The *researcher* was correct. Our tests are specifically designed to hold the probability of a Type I error at α, regardless of the sample size.)

19.22 The Zuckerman et al. paper referred to in the previous question hypothesized that faculty were less accurate than students because they have a tendency to give negative responses to such questions. ("There must be a trick.") How would you test such a hypothesis?

20

NONPARAMETRIC AND DISTRIBUTION-FREE STATISTICAL TESTS

Most of the statistical procedures we have discussed in the preceding chapters have involved the estimation of one or more parameters of the distribution of scores in the population(s) from which the data were sampled and assumptions concerning the shape of that distribution. For example, the *t* test makes use of the sample variance (s^2) as an estimate of the population variance (σ^2) and also requires the assumption that the population from which we sampled is normal (or at least that the sampling distribution of the mean is normal). Tests, such as the *t* test, that involve either assumptions about specific parameters or their distribution are referred to as **parametric tests**.

One class of tests, however, relies less on pa-

Parametric tests
Statistical tests that involve assumptions about or estimation of population parameters.

Nonparametric tests (distribution-free tests)
Statistical tests that do not rely on parameter estimation or precise distributional assumptions.

rameter estimation and/or distribution assumptions. Such tests usually are referred to as **nonparametric tests** or **distribution-free tests**. By and large if a test is nonparametric, it is also distribution-free; in fact it is the distribution-free nature of the test that is most valuable to us. Although the two names often are used interchangeably, these tests will be referred to here as distribution-free tests.

The argument over the value of distribution-free tests has gone on for many years, and it certainly cannot be resolved in this chapter. Many experimenters feel that, for the vast majority of cases, parametric tests are sufficiently robust to make distribution-free tests unnecessary. Others, however, believe just as strongly in the unsuitability of parametric tests and the overwhelming superiority of the distribution-free approach. (Bradley, 1968, is a forceful and articulate spokesman for the latter group.) Regardless of the position you take on this issue, it is important that you are familiar with the most common distribution-free procedures and their underlying rationale. These tests are too prevalent in the experimental literature simply to be ignored.

The major advantage generally attributed to distribution-free tests is also the most obvious—they do not rely on any seriously restrictive assumptions concerning the shape of the sampled population(s). This is not to say that distribution-free tests do not make *any* distribution assumptions, only that the assumptions they do require are far more general than those required for the parametric tests. The exact null hypothesis being tested may depend, for example, on whether two populations are symmetric or have a similar shape. None of these tests, however, makes an *a priori* assumption about the specific shape of the distribution; that is, the validity of the test is not affected by whether the distribution of the variable in the population is normal. A parametric test, on the other hand, usually includes some type of normality assumption; if that assumption is false, the conclusions drawn from the test may be inaccurate. Another characteristic of distribution-free tests that often acts as an advantage is that many of them, especially the ones discussed in this chapter, are more sensitive to medians than to means. Thus if the nature of your data is such that you are interested primarily in medians, the tests presented here may be particularly useful to you.

Those who favor using parametric tests in every case do not deny that the distribution-free tests are more liberal in the assumptions they require. They do argue, however, that the assumptions normally cited as being required of parametric tests are overly restrictive in practice and that the parametric tests are remarkably unaffected by violations of distribution assumptions.

The major disadvantage generally attributed to distribution-free tests is their lower power relative to the corresponding parametric test. In general, when the assumptions of the parametric test are met, the distribution-free test requires more observations than the comparable parametric test for the same level of power. Thus for a given set of data the parametric test is more likely to lead to rejection of a false null hypothesis than is the corresponding distribution-free test. Moreover, even when the distribution assumptions are violated to a moderate degree, the parametric tests are thought to maintain their advantage.

It often is claimed that the distribution-free procedures are particularly useful because of the simplicity of their calculations. However, for an experimenter who has just invested six months collecting data, a difference of five minutes in computation time hardly justifies the use of a less desirable test.

There is one other advantage of distribution-free tests. Because many of them rank the raw scores and operate on those ranks, they offer a test of differences in central tendency that are not affected by one or a few very extreme scores (outliers). An extreme score in a set of data actually can make the parametric test *less* powerful, because it inflates the variance and hence the error term, as well as biasing the mean by shifting it toward the outlier (the latter may increase or decrease the difference between means).

In this chapter we will be concerned with four of the most important distribution-free methods. The first two are analogues of the t test, one for independent samples and one for matched samples. The next two tests are distribution-free analogues of the analysis of variance, the first for k independent groups and the second for k repeated measures. All these tests are members of a class known as **rank-randomization tests** because they deal with ranked data and take as the distribution of their test statistic, when the null hypothesis is true, the theoretical distribution of randomly distributed ranks. Because these tests convert raw data to ranks, the shape of the underlying distribution of scores in the population becomes less important. Thus both the sets

Rank-randomization tests
A class of nonparametric tests based on the theoretical distribution of randomly assigned ranks.

11   14   15   16   17   22
(data that might have come from a normal distribution)

and

11   12   13   30   31   32
(data that might have come from a bimodal distribution)

reduce to the ranks

1   2   3   4   5   6

20.1 The Mann-Whitney Test

Mann-Whitney test
A nonparametric test for comparing the central tendency of two independent samples.

One of the most common and best-known distribution-free tests is the **Mann-Whitney test** for two independent samples. This test often is thought of as the distribution-free analogue of the t test for two independent samples, although it tests a slightly different, and broader, null hypothesis. Its null hypothesis is the hypothesis that the two samples were drawn at random from identical populations (not just populations with the same mean), but it is especially sensitive to population differences in central tendency. Thus rejection of H_0 generally is interpreted to mean that the two distributions had different central tendencies, but it is possible that rejection actually resulted from some other difference between the populations. Notice that when we gain one thing (freedom from assumptions), we pay for it with something else (loss of specificity).

The Mann-Whitney test is a variation on a test originally devised by Wilcoxon called the Rank-Sum test. Because Wilcoxon also devised another test, to be discussed in the next section, we will refer to this variation as the Mann-Whitney test to avoid confusion. Although the test as devised by Mann and Whitney used a slightly different test statistic, the statistic used in this chapter (the sum of the ranks of the scores in one of the groups) is often advocated because it is much easier to calculate. Either test statistic would lead to exactly the same conclusions when applied to the same set of data.

The logical basis of the Mann-Whitney test is particularly easy to understand. Assume that we have two independent treatment groups, with n_1 observations in Group 1 and n_2 observations in Group 2. Further assume that the null hypothesis is false to a substantial degree and that the population from which Group 1 scores have been sampled contains values generally lower than the population from which Group 2 scores were drawn. If we were to rank all $n_1 + n_2 = N$ scores from lowest to highest without regard to group membership, we would expect that the lower ranks generally would fall to Group 1 scores and the higher ranks to Group 2 scores. Going one step further, if we were to sum the ranks assigned to each group, the sum of the ranks in Group 1 would be expected to be appreciably smaller than the sum of the ranks in Group 2.

Now consider the case in which the null hypothesis is true and the scores for the two groups were sampled from identical populations. In this situation if we were to rank all N scores without regard to group membership, we would expect some low ranks and some high ranks in each group, and the sum of the ranks assigned to Group 1 would be roughly equal to the sum of the ranks assigned to Group 2. These situations are illustrated in Table 20.1.

Mann and Whitney (and Wilcoxon) based their tests on the logic just described, using the sum of the ranks in one of the groups as the test statistic. If that sum is too small relative to the other sum, we will reject the null hypothe-

Table 20.1   Illustration of Typical Results to Be Expected Under H_0 False and H_0 True

					H_0 **False**							
			Group 1						**Group 2**			
Raw data	10	12	17	13	19	20	30	26	25	33	18	27
Ranks (R_i)	1	2	4	3	6	7	11	9	8	12	5	10
ΣR_i				23						55		
					H_0 **True**							
			Group 1						**Group 2**			
Raw data	22	28	32	19	24	33	18	25	29	20	23	34
Ranks (R_i)	4	8	10	2	6	11	1	7	9	3	5	12
ΣR_i				41						37		

sis. More specifically, we will take as our test statistic the sum of the ranks assigned to the *smaller* group, or if $n_1 = n_2$ the *smaller* of the two sums. Given this value, we can use tables of the Mann-Whitney statistic (W_S) to test the null hypothesis.

To take a specific example, consider the following hypothetical data on the number of recent stressful life events reported by a group of cardiac patients in a local hospital and a control group of orthopedic patients in the same hospital. It is well known that stressful life events (marriage, new job, death of a spouse, etc.) are associated with illness, and it is reasonable to expect that many cardiac patients would have experienced more recent stressful events than orthopedic patients (who just happened to break an ankle while tearing down a building or a collarbone while skiing). It would appear from the data that this expectation is borne out. Because we have some reason to suspect that life stress scores probably are not symmetrically distributed in the population (especially for cardiac patients if our research hypothesis is true), we will choose to use a distribution-free test. In this case we will use the Mann-Whitney test because we have two independent groups.

	Cardiac Patients						**Orthopedic Patients**				
Raw data	32	8	7	29	5	0	1	2	2	3	6
Ranks	11	9	8	10	6	1	2	3.5	3.5	5	7

To apply the Mann-Whitney test we first rank all 11 scores from lowest to highest, assigning tied ranks to tied scores (see the discussion on ranking in Chapter 9). The orthopedic group is the smaller of the two, and if those patients generally have had fewer recent stressful life events, then the sum of the ranks assigned to that group would be relatively low. Letting W_S stand for the sum of the ranks in the smaller group (the orthopedic group), we find

$$W_S = 2 + 3.5 + 3.5 + 5 + 7 = 21$$

We can evaluate the obtained value of W_S by using Table D.8 in the Appendices, which gives the *smallest* value of W_S we would expect to obtain by chance if the null hypothesis were true. From Table D.8 we find that for $n_1 = 5$ subjects in the smaller group and $n_2 = 6$ subjects in the larger group (n_1 is *always* used to represent the number of subjects in the smaller group) the entry for $\alpha = .025$ (one-tailed) is 18. This means that for a difference between groups to be significant at the one-tailed .025 level (or the two-tailed .05 level), W_S must be less than or equal to 18. Because we found W_S to be 21, we cannot reject H_0. (By way of comparison, if we ran a t test on these data, ignoring that one sample variance is almost 50 times the other and that the data suggest that our prediction of the shape of the distribution of cardiac scores may be correct, t would be 1.52 on 9 df, a nonsignificant result.)

As an aside, I should point out that we just rejected H_0 because our value of W_S was *smaller* than the tabled value. Until now you have been rejecting H_0 when the obtained test statistic was *larger* than the corresponding tabled value. When we work with nonparametric tests the tables have been set up to lead to rejection for small obtained values. If I were redesigning statistical procedures, I would set the tables up differently, but nobody asked me. Just get used to the fact that parametric tables are set up such that you reject H_0 for *large* obtained values, and nonparametric tables are set up so that you reject for *small* values. That's just the way it is.

The entries in Table D.8 are for a one-tailed test and will lead to rejection of the null hypothesis only if the sum of the ranks for the smaller group is sufficiently *small*. It is possible, however, that the larger ranks could be congregated in the smaller group, in which case if H_0 is false, the sum of the ranks would be larger than chance expectation rather than smaller. One rather awkward way around this problem would be to rank the data all over again, this time from high to low. If we did that, the smaller ranks would appear in the smaller group, and we could proceed as before. We do not have to go through the process of reranking data, however. We can accomplish the same thing by making use of the symmetric properties of the distribution of the rank sum by calculating a statistic called W_S'. W_S' is the sum of the ranks for the smaller group that we would have found if we had reversed our ranking and ranked from highest to lowest:

$$W_S' = 2\overline{W} - W_S$$

where $2\overline{W} = n_1(n_1 + n_2 + 1)$ and is tabled in Table D.8. We then can evaluate W_S against the tabled value and have a one-tailed test on the *upper* tail of the distribution. For a two-tailed test of H_0 (which is what we normally want) we calculate W_S and W_S', enter the table with whichever is smaller, and double the listed value of α.

For an illustration of W_S and W_S', consider the following two sets of data:

	Set 1								
	Group 1				**Group 2**				
X	2	15	16	19	18	23	25	37	82
Ranks	1	2	3	5	4	6	7	8	9

$W_S = 11$ $W_S' = 29$

	Set 2								
	Group 1				**Group 2**				
X	60	40	24	21	23	18	15	14	4
Ranks	9	8	7	5	6	4	3	2	1

$W_S = 29$ $W_S' = 11$

Notice that the two data sets exhibit the same degree of *extremeness*, in the sense that for the first set four of the five lowest ranks are in Group 1, and in the second set four of the five highest ranks are in Group 1. Moreover, W_S for

Set 1 is equal to W'_s for Set 2 and vice versa. Thus if we establish the rule that we will calculate both W_s and W'_s for the *smaller* group and refer the *smaller* of W_s and W'_s to the tables, we will come to the same conclusion with respect to the two data sets.

The Normal Approximation

Table D.8 in the Appendices is suitable for all cases in which n_1 and n_2 are less than or equal to 25. For larger values of n_1 and/or n_2 we can make use of the fact that the distribution of W_s approaches a normal distribution as sample sizes increase. This distribution has

$$\text{Mean} = \frac{n_1(n_1 + n_2 + 1)}{2}$$

and

$$\text{Standard error} = \sqrt{\frac{n_1 n_2(n_1 + n_2 + 1)}{12}}$$

Because the distribution is normal and we know its mean and its standard deviation (the standard error), we can calculate z:

$$z = \frac{\text{Statistic} - \text{Mean}}{\text{Standard deviation}}$$

$$= \frac{W_s - \dfrac{n_1(n_1 + n_2 + 1)}{2}}{\sqrt{\dfrac{n_1 n_2(n_1 + n_2 + 1)}{12}}}$$

and obtain from the tables of the normal distribution an approximation of the true probability of a value of W_s at least as low as the one obtained.

To illustrate the computations for the case in which the larger ranks fall in the smaller group and to illustrate the use of the normal approximation (although we don't really need to use an approximation for such small sample sizes), consider the data in Table 20.2. These data are hypothetical (but probably reasonable) data on the birthweights (in grams) of children born to mothers who did not seek prenatal care until the third trimester and of children born to mothers who received prenatal care starting in the first trimester.

For the data in Table 20.2 the sum of the ranks in the smaller group equals 100. From Table D.8 we find $2W = 152$; thus $W'_s = 2\overline{W} - W_s = 52$. Because 52 is smaller than 100, we go to Table D.8 with $W_s = 52$, $n_1 = 8$, and $n_2 = 10$. (Remember, n_1 is defined as the smaller sample size.) Because we want a two-tailed test, we will double the tabled value of α. The critical value of W_s (or W'_s)

Table 20.2

Hypothetical Data on Birthweight of Infants Born to Mothers with Different Levels of Prenatal Care

	Beginning of Care		
Third Trimester		**First Trimester**	
Birthweight	**Rank**	**Birthweight**	**Rank**
1680	2	2940	10
3830	17	3380	16
3110	14	4900	18
2760	5	2810	9
1700	3	2800	8
2790	7	3210	15
3050	12	3080	13
2660	4	2950	11
1400	1		
2775	6		

$$W_S = \Sigma(\text{ranks in Group 2}) = 100$$

$$W_S' = 2\overline{W} - W_S = 152 - 100 = 52$$

$$z = \frac{W_S - \dfrac{n_1(n_1 + n_2 + 1)}{2}}{\sqrt{\dfrac{n_1 n_2(n_1 + n_2 + 1)}{12}}}$$

$$= \frac{100 - \dfrac{8(8 + 10 + 1)}{2}}{\sqrt{\dfrac{8(10)(8 + 10 + 1)}{12}}}$$

$$= \frac{100 - 76}{\sqrt{126.6667}} = 2.13$$

for a two-tailed test at $\alpha = .05$ is 53, meaning that only 5% of the time would we expect a value of W_S or W_S' less than or equal to 53 when H_0 is true. Our obtained value of W_S is 52, which falls in the rejection region, so we will reject H_0. We will conclude that mothers who do not receive prenatal care until the third trimester tend to give birth to smaller babies. This probably does not mean that not having care until the third trimester causes smaller babies, but only that variables associated with delayed care (e.g., young mothers, poor nutrition, and poverty) also are associated with lower birthweight.

The use of the normal approximation for evaluating W_S is illustrated in the lower section of Table 20.2. Here we find that $z = 2.13$. From Table D.10, we find that the probability of W_S or W_S' at least as small as 52 (a z at least as extreme as ± 2.13) is $2(0.0166) = 0.033$. Because this value is smaller than our traditional cutoff of $\alpha = .05$, we will reject H_0 and again conclude that there is sufficient evidence to say that failing to seek early prenatal care is related to lower birthweight. Note that both the exact solution and the normal approximation lead to the same conclusion with respect to H_0. (With the normal approximation it is not necessary to calculate and use W_S' because use of W_S will lead to the same value of z except for the reversal of its sign. It would be instructive for you to calculate t for the same set of data.)

The Treatment of Ties

When the data contain tied scores, any test that relies on ranks is likely to be somewhat distorted. There are several different ways of dealing with ties. You can assign tied ranks to tied scores (as we have been doing), you can flip a coin and assign consecutive ranks to tied scores, or you can assign untied ranks in whatever way will make it hardest to reject H_0. In actual practice most people simply assign tied ranks. Although that may not be the statistically best way to proceed, it is the most common and the method we will use here.

The Null Hypothesis

The Mann-Whitney test evaluates the null hypothesis that the two sets of scores were sampled from identical populations. This is broader than the null hypothesis tested by the corresponding t test, which dealt specifically with means (primarily as a result of the underlying assumptions that ruled out other sources of difference). If the two populations are assumed to have the same shape and dispersion, then the null hypothesis tested by the Mann-Whitney test would actually deal with the central tendency (in this case the medians) of the two populations; if the populations are also symmetric, the test will be a test of means. In any event the Mann-Whitney test is particularly sensitive to differences in central tendency.

20.2 Wilcoxon's Matched-Pairs Signed-Ranks Test

Wilcoxon is credited with developing the most popular distribution-free test for independent groups, which I referred to as the Mann-Whitney test to avoid confusion and because of their work on it. He also developed the most popular test for matched groups (or paired scores). This test is the distribution-free analogue of the t test for related samples. It tests the null hypothesis that two related (matched) samples were drawn either from identical populations or from symmetric populations with the same mean. More specifically it tests the null hypothesis that the distribution of difference scores (in the population) is symmetric about zero. This is the same hypothesis tested by the corresponding t test when that test's normality assumption is met.

Wilcoxon's matched-pairs signed-ranks test
A nonparametric test for comparing the central tendency of two matched (related) samples.

The logic behind **Wilcoxon's matched-pairs signed-ranks test** is straightforward and can be illustrated with a simple example. Assume that we want to test the often stated hypothesis that a long-range program of running will reduce blood pressure. To test this hypothesis, we measure the blood pressure of a number of subjects, ask them to engage in a systematic program of running for six weeks, and again test their blood pressure at the end of that period. Our dependent variable will be the change in blood pressure over the six-week interval. If running does reduce blood pressure, we would expect most of the subjects to show a lower reading the second time and thus a positive pre-post difference. We also would expect that blood pressures that actually went up (those with a negative pre-post difference) would be only slightly higher. On the other hand, if running is worthless as a method of controlling blood pressure, then we would expect about one-half of the difference scores to be positive and one-half to be negative, with the positive differences about as large as the negative ones. In other words if H_0 is really true, we would no longer expect most changes to be in the predicted direction with only small changes in the unpredicted direction.

As is illustrated in the following numerical example, in carrying out the Wilcoxon matched-pairs signed-ranks test we first calculate the difference score for each pair of measurements. We then rank all difference scores without regard to the sign of the difference, give the algebraic sign of the differences to the ranks themselves, and finally sum the positive and negative ranks separately. The test statistic (T) is taken as the smaller of the absolute values (i.e., regardless of sign) of the two sums and evaluated against Table D.7 in the Appendices. (It is important to note that in calculating T we attach algebraic signs to the ranks only for convenience. We could just as easily, for example, circle those ranks that went with improvement and underline those that went with deterioration. We are merely trying to differentiate between the two cases.)

Assume that the study previously described produced the following data on systolic blood pressure before and after the six-week training session:

Before	130	170	125	170	130	130	145	160
After	120	163	120	135	143	136	144	120
Difference (B − A)	10	7	5	35	− 13	− 6	1	40
Rank of difference (sign ignored)	5	4	2	7	6	3	1	8
Signed rank	5	4	2	7	−6	−3	1	8

$T+ = \Sigma$ (positive ranks) $= 27$
$T- = \Sigma$ (negative ranks) $= -9$

The first two rows contain the subjects' blood pressures as measured before and after a six-week program of running. The third row contains the difference scores, obtained by subtracting the "after" score from the "before." Notice that only two subjects showed a negative change, that is, increased blood pressure. Because these difference scores don't appear to reflect a population distribution anywhere near normal, we have chosen to use a distribution-free test. In the fourth row all the difference scores have been ranked without regard to the direction of the change. In the fifth row the appropriate sign has been appended to the ranks to discriminate those whose blood pressure decreased from those whose blood pressure increased. At the bottom of the table we see the sum of the positive and negative ranks ($T+$ and $T-$). Because T is defined as the smaller absolute value of $T+$ and $T-$, $T = 9$.

To evaluate T, we refer to Table D.7, a portion of which is shown in Table 20.3. The format of this table is somewhat different from that of the other tables we have seen. The easiest way to understand what the entries in the table represent is by way of an analogy. Suppose that to test the fairness of a coin you were going to flip it eight times and reject the null hypothesis, at $\alpha = .05$ (one-tailed), if there were too few heads. Out of eight flips of a coin there is no set of outcomes that has a probability of exactly .05 under H_0. The probability of one or fewer heads is .0352, and the probability of two or fewer heads is .1445. Thus if we want to work at $\alpha = .05$, we can either reject for one or fewer heads, in which case the probability of a Type I error is actually .0352 (less than .05), or we can reject for two or fewer heads, in which case the probability of a Type I error is actually .1445 (much greater than .05). The same kind of problem arises with T because it is a discrete distribution.

Table 20.3

Critical Lower-Tail Values of T and Their Associated Probabilities (Abbreviated Version of Table D.7)

		Nominal Alpha (One-Tailed)						
		.05		**.025**		**.01**		**.005**	
n		**T**	**α**	**T**	**α**	**T**	**α**	**T**	**α**
5		0	.0313						
		1	.0625						
6		2	.0469	0	.0156				
		3	.0781	1	.0313				
7		3	.0391	2	.0234	0	.0078		
		4	.0547	3	.0391	1	.0156		
8		5	.0391	**3**	**.0195**	1	.0078	0	.0039
		6	.0547	**4**	**.0273**	2	.0117	1	.0078
9		8	.0488	5	.0195	3	.0098	1	.0039
		9	.0645	6	.0273	4	.0137	2	.0059
10		10	.0420	8	.0244	5	.0098	3	.0049
		11	.0527	9	.0322	6	.0137	4	.0068
11		13	.0415	10	.0210	7	.0093	5	.0049
		14	.0508	11	.0269	8	.0122	6	.0068
		⋮	⋮	⋮	⋮	⋮	⋮	⋮	⋮

In Table D.7 we find that for a one-tailed test at $\alpha = .025$ (or a two-tailed test at $\alpha = .05$) with $n = 8$ the entries are 3 .0195 and 4 .0273. This tells us that if we want to work at a (one-tailed) $\alpha = .025$, we can reject H_0 either for $T \le 3$ (in which case α actually equals .0195) or for $T \le 4$ (in which case the true value of α is .0273). Because we want a two-tailed test, the probabilities should be doubled to 3 .0390 and 4 .0546. We obtained a T value of 9, so we would not reject H_0, whichever cutoff we choose. We will conclude, therefore, that we cannot reject the null hypothesis that a short (six-week) period of daily running has no effect on blood pressure. It is going to take a lot more than six weeks to make up for a lifetime of dissipated habits.

Ties

Ties can occur in the data in two different ways. One way would be for a subject to have the same before and after scores, leading to a difference score of zero, which has no sign. In that case we normally eliminate that subject from consideration and reduce the sample size accordingly, although this leads to some bias in the data.

We could have tied difference scores that lead to tied rankings. If both tied scores have the same sign, we can break the tie in any way we want (or assign tied ranks) without affecting the final outcome. If the scores have opposite signs, we normally assign tied ranks and proceed as usual.

The Normal Approximation

When the sample size is larger than 50, which is the limit for Table D.7, a normal approximation is available to evaluate T. For larger sample sizes we know that the sampling distribution is approximately normally distributed with

$$\text{Mean} = \frac{n(n + 1)}{4}$$

and

$$\text{Standard error} = \sqrt{\frac{n(n + 1)(2n + 1)}{24}}$$

Thus we can calculate z as

$$z = \frac{T - \dfrac{n(n + 1)}{4}}{\sqrt{\dfrac{n(n + 1)(2n + 1)}{24}}}$$

and evaluate z using Table D.10. The procedure is directly analogous to that used with the Mann-Whitney test and will not be repeated here.

20.3 Kruskal-Wallis One-way Analysis of Variance

Kruskal-Wallis one-way analysis of variance
A nonparametric test analogous to a standard one-way analysis of variance.

The **Kruskal-Wallis one-way analysis of variance** is a direct generalization of the Mann-Whitney test to the case in which we have three or more independent groups. As such it is the distribution-free analogue of the one-way analysis of variance discussed in Chapter 16. It tests the hypothesis that all samples were drawn from identical populations and is particularly sensitive to differences in central tendency.

To perform the Kruskal-Wallis test we simply rank all scores without regard to group membership and then compute the sum of the ranks for each group. The sums are denoted by R_j. If the null hypothesis is true, we would expect the R_js to be more or less equal (aside from differences due to the size of the samples). A measure of the degree to which the R_js differ from one another is provided by

$$H = \frac{12}{N(N + 1)} \sum \frac{R_j^2}{n_j} - 3(N + 1)$$

where

n_j = the number of observations in the jth group

R_j = the sum of the ranks in the jth group

$N = \Sigma n_j$ = total sample size

and the summation is taken over all k groups. H is then evaluated against the χ^2 distribution on $k - 1$ df.

For an example assume that the data in Table 20.4 represent the number of simple arithmetic problems (out of 85) solved (correctly or incorrectly) in one hour by subjects given a depressant drug, a stimulant drug, or a placebo. Notice that in the Depressant group three of the subjects were too depressed to do much of anything and in the Stimulant group three of the subjects ran up against the limit of 85 available problems. These data are decidedly nonnormal, and we will convert the data to ranks and use the Kruskal-Wallis test. The calculations are shown in the lower part of the table. The obtained value of H is 10.36, which can be treated as a χ^2 on $3 - 1 = 2$ df. The critical value of $\chi^2_{.05}(2)$ is found in Table D.1 in the Appendices to be 5.99. Because $10.36 > 5.99$, we can reject H_0 and conclude that the three drugs lead to different rates of performance. (Like other chi-square tests, this test rejects H_0 for *large* values of H. It is nonetheless a distribution-free test.)

Table 20.4

Kruskal-Wallis Test Applied to Data on Problem Solving

Depressant		Stimulant		Placebo	
Score	**Rank**	**Score**	**Rank**	**Score**	**Rank**
55	9	73	15	61	11
0	1.5	85	18	54	8
1	3	51	7	80	16
0	1.5	63	12	47	5
50	6	85	18		
60	10	85	18		
44	4	66	13		
		69	14		
R_j	35		115		40

$$H = \frac{12}{N(N+1)} \sum_{j=1}^{k} \frac{R_j^2}{n_j} - 3(N+1)$$

$$= \frac{12}{19(20)} \left(\frac{35^2}{7} + \frac{115^2}{8} + \frac{40^2}{4} \right) - 3(19+1)$$

$$= \frac{12}{380}(2228.125) - 60 = 70.36 - 60 = 10.36$$

$$\chi^2_{.05} = 5.99$$

20.4 Friedman's Rank Test for *k* Correlated Samples

Friedman's rank test for *k* correlated samples
A nonparametric test analogous to a standard one-way repeated-measures analysis of variance.

The last test to be discussed in this chapter is the distribution-free analogue of the one-way repeated-measures analysis of variance, **Friedman's rank test for *k* correlated samples**. It was developed by the well-known economist Milton Friedman—in the days before he was a well-known economist. This test is closely related to a standard repeated-measures analysis of variance applied to ranks instead of raw scores. It is a test on the null hypothesis that the scores for each treatment were drawn from identical populations, and it is especially sensitive to population differences in central tendency.

Assume that we want to test the hypothesis that the judged quality of a lecture is related to the number of visual aids used. The experimenter obtains 17 people who frequently give lectures to local business groups on a variety of topics. Each lecturer delivers the same lecture to three different, but equivalent, audiences: once with no visual aids, once with a few transparencies to illustrate major points, and once with transparencies and flip charts to illustrate every point to be made. At the end of each lecture the audience is asked to rate the lecture on a 75-point scale, and the mean rating across all members of the audience is taken as the dependent variable. Because the same lecturers serve under all three visual aid conditions, we would expect the data to be correlated. Terrible lecturers are terrible no matter how many visual aids they use. Hypothetical data are presented in Table 20.5, in which a higher score represents a more favorable rating. The ranking of the raw scores *within each lecturer* are shown in parentheses.

If the null hypothesis is true, we would expect the rankings to be randomly distributed within each lecturer. Thus one lecturer might do best with no vi-

Table 20.5

Hypothetical Data on Rated Quality of Lectures

| | | Number of Visual Aids | |
Lecturer	None	Few	Many
1	50 (1)	58 (3)	54 (2)
2	32 (2)	37 (3)	25 (1)
3	60 (1)	70 (3)	63 (2)
4	58 (2)	60 (3)	55 (1)
5	41 (1)	66 (3)	59 (2)
6	36 (2)	40 (3)	28 (1)
7	26 (3)	25 (2)	20 (1)
8	49 (1)	60 (3)	50 (2)
9	72 (1)	73 (2)	75 (3)
10	49 (2)	54 (3)	42 (1)
11	52 (2)	57 (3)	47 (1)
12	36 (2)	42 (3)	29 (1)
13	37 (3)	34 (2)	31 (1)
14	58 (3)	50 (1)	56 (2)
15	39 (1)	48 (3)	44 (2)
16	25 (2)	29 (3)	18 (1)
17	51 (1)	63 (2)	68 (3)
	30	45	27

$$\chi_F^2 = \frac{12}{Nk(k+1)} \sum_{j=1}^{k} R_j^2 - 3N(k+1)$$

$$= \frac{12}{(17)(3)(4)}(30^2 + 45^2 + 27^2) - 3(17)(4)$$

$$= \frac{12}{204}(3654) - 204$$

$$= 214.94 - 204 = 10.94$$

sual aids, another might do best with many aids, and so on. If this were the case, the sum of the rankings in each condition (column) would be approximately equal. On the other hand, if a few visual aids were to lead to the most popular lecture, then most lecturers would have their highest rating under that condition, and the sum of the rankings for the three conditions would be decidedly unequal.

To apply Friedman's test we rank the raw scores for each lecturer separately and then sum the rankings for each condition. We then evaluate the variability of the sums by computing

$$\chi_F^2 = \frac{12}{Nk(k+1)} \sum R_j^2 - 3N(k+1)$$

where

R_j = the sum of the ranks for the jth condition

N = the number of subjects (lecturers)

k = the number of (visual aid) conditions

and the summation is taken over all k conditions. This value of χ^2 can be evaluated with respect to the standard χ^2 distribution on $k - 1$ df.

For the data in Table 20.5 χ_F^2 = 10.94 on 2 df. Because $\chi_{.05}^2(2)$ = 5.99, we will reject H_0 and conclude that the judged quality of a lecture differs as a function of the degree to which visual aids are included. The data would suggest that some visual aids are helpful, but that too many of them can detract from what the lecturer is saying. (*Note:* The null hypothesis we have just tested says nothing about differences among subjects [lecturers], and in fact subject differences are completely eliminated by the ranking procedure.)

20.5 Summary

This chapter summarized briefly a set of procedures that require far fewer restrictive assumptions concerning the populations from which our data have been sampled. We first examined the Mann-Whitney test, which is the distribution-free analogue of the independent sample t test. To perform the test we simply ranked the data and asked if the distribution of ranks resembled the distribution we would expect if the null hypothesis were true. The same general logic applies to the Wilcoxon matched-pairs signed-ranks test, which is the distribution-free test corresponding to the matched-sample t test. We then discussed two distribution-free tests that are analogous to an analysis of variance on independent measures (the Kruskal-Wallis one-way analysis of variance) and repeated measures (Friedman's rank test for k correlated samples). Although it is important to be familiar with these four tests simply because they are commonly used, the advantages we gain by limiting our assumptions may not be worth the loss in power that often accompanies the use of distribution-free tests. Whatever one's stand on this question, the general principle remains that the overriding concern in the use and interpretation of any statistical procedure is not statistical sophistication but common sense.

Some important terms in this chapter are:

- Parametric tests
- Nonparametric tests (distribution-free tests)
- Rank-randomization tests
- Mann-Whitney test
- Wilcoxon's matched-pairs signed-ranks test
- Kruskal-Wallis one-way analysis of variance
- Friedman's rank test for k correlated samples

20.6 Exercises

20.1 McConaughy (1980) has argued that younger children organize stories in terms of simple descriptive ("and then . . .") models, whereas older children incorporate causal statements and social inferences. Suppose we asked two groups of children differing in age to summarize a story they just read. We then counted the number of statements in the summary that can be classed as inferences. The data are:

Younger Children	Older Children
0	4
1	7
0	6
3	4
2	8
5	7
2	

(a) Analyze these data using the two-tailed rank-sum test.

(b) What would you conclude?

20.2 Kapp, Frysinger, Gallagher, and Hazelton (1979) have demonstrated that lesions in the amygdala can reduce certain responses commonly associated with fear (e.g., *decreases* in heart rate). If fear is really reduced by the lesion, it should be more difficult to train an avoidance response in those animals because the aversiveness of the stimulus will consequently be reduced. Assume two groups of rabbits: one group has lesions in the amygdala, and the other is an untreated control group. The following data represent the number of trials to learn an avoidance response for each animal.

Group with Lesions	Control Group
15	9
14	4
15	9
8	10
7	6
22	6
36	4

(*continued*)

19	5
14	9
18	
17	

(a) Analyze the data using the Mann-Whitney test (two-tailed).

(b) What would you conclude?

20.3 Repeat the analysis in Exercise 20.2 using the normal approximation.

20.4 Repeat the analysis in Exercise 20.2 using the appropriate one-tailed test.

20.5 Nurcombe and Fitzhenry-Coor (1979) have argued that training in diagnostic techniques should lead a clinician to generate and test more hypotheses in coming to a decision about a case. Suppose we take 10 psychiatric residents who are just beginning their residency and use them as subjects. We ask them to watch a videotape of an interview and to record their thoughts on the case every few minutes. We then count the number of hypotheses each resident includes in his or her written remarks. The experiment is repeated with the same residents at the end of the residency with a comparable videotape. The data are:

Subject									
1	2	3	4	5	6	7	8	9	10
Before 8	4	2	2	4	8	3	1	3	9
After 7	9	3	6	3	10	6	7	8	7

(a) Analyze the data using Wilcoxon's matched-pairs signed-ranks test.

(b) What would you conclude?

20.6 Referring to Exercise 20.5,

(a) Repeat the analysis using the normal approximation.

(b) How well do the two answers agree? Why don't they agree exactly?

20.7 It has been argued that first-born children tend to be more independent than later-born children. Suppose we develop a 25-point scale of independence and rate each of 20 first-born children and their second-born siblings using our scale. We do this when both siblings are adults, thus eliminating obvious age effects. The data on independence are as follows (a higher score means that the person is more independent):

Sibling Pair	First-born	Second-born
1	12	10
2	18	12
3	13	15
4	17	13
5	8	9
6	15	12
7	16	13
8	5	8
9	8	10
10	12	8
11	13	8
12	5	9
13	14	8
14	20	10
15	19	14
16	17	11
17	2	7
18	5	7
19	15	13
20	18	12

(a) Analyze the data using Wilcoxon's matched-pairs signed-ranks test.

(b) What would you conclude?

20.8 Rerun the analysis in Exercise 20.7 using the normal approximation.

20.9 The results in Exercise 20.7 are not quite as clear-cut as we might like. Plot the differences as a function of the first-born's score. What does this figure suggest?

20.10 What is the difference between the null hypothesis tested by the Mann-Whitney test and the corresponding *t* test?

20.11 What is the difference between the null hypothesis tested by Wilcoxon's matched-pairs signed-ranks test and the corresponding *t* test?

20.12 One of the arguments in favor of distribution-free tests is that they are more appropriate for ordinal scale data. (This issue was addressed earlier in the book in a different context.) Give a reason why this argument is not a good one.

20.13 Why is rejection of the null hypothesis using a *t* test a more specific statement than rejection of the null hypothesis using the appropriate distribution-free test?

20.14 Three rival professors teaching English 1 all claim the honor of having the best students. To settle the issue eight students are randomly drawn from each class and given the same exam. The exams are graded by a neutral professor who does not know from which class the students came. The data are:

Professor A	Professor B	Professor C
82	55	65
71	88	54
56	85	66
58	83	68
63	71	72
64	70	78
62	68	65
53	72	73

Run the appropriate test and draw the appropriate conclusions.

20.15 A psychologist operating a group home for delinquent adolescents needs to show that the home is successful at reducing delinquency. He samples 10 adolescents living at home who have been identified by the police as having problems, 10 similar adolescents living in foster homes, and 10 adolescents living in the group home. As an indicator variable he uses truancy (number of days truant in the past semester), which is readily obtained from school records. On the basis of the following data, draw the appropriate conclusions:

Natural Home	Foster Home	Group Home
15	16	10
18	14	13
19	20	14
14	22	11
5	19	7
8	5	3
12	17	4
13	18	18
7	12	2

20.16 As an alternative method of evaluating a group home, suppose we take 12 adolescents who have been declared delinquent. We take the number of days truant during each of three time periods: (1) the month before they are placed in the home, (2) the month they live in the home, and (3) the month after they leave the home. The data are as follows:

Adolescent	Before	During	After
1	10	5	8
2	12	8	7
3	12	13	10
4	19	10	12
5	5	10	8

(*continued*)

6	13	8	7
7	20	16	12
8	8	4	5
9	12	14	9
10	10	3	5
11	8	3	3
12	18	16	2

Apply Friedman's test. What do you conclude?

20.17 What advantage does the study described in Exercise 20.16 have over the study described in Exercise 20.15?

20.18 It would be possible to apply Friedman's test to the data in Exercise 20.5. What would we lose if we did?

20.19 For the data in Exercise 20.5 we could say that three out of 10 residents used fewer hypotheses the second time and seven used more. We could test this with χ^2. How would this differ from Friedman's test applied to those data?

20.20 The history of statistical hypothesis testing really began with a tea-tasting experiment (Fisher, 1935), so it seems fitting for this book to end with one. The owner of a small tearoom doesn't think people really can tell the difference between the first cup made with a given tea bag and the second and third cups made with the same bag (which is why it is still a *small* tearoom). He chooses eight different brands of tea bags, makes three cups of tea with each, and then has a group of customers rate each cup on a 20-point scale (without knowing which cup is which). The data are shown here, with higher ratings indicating better tea:

Tea Brands	Cup		
	First	**Second**	**Third**
1	8	3	2
2	15	14	4
3	16	17	12
4	7	5	4
5	9	3	6
6	8	9	4
7	10	3	4
8	12	10	2

Using Friedman's test, draw the appropriate conclusions.

21

CHOOSING THE APPROPRIATE ANALYSIS

$\mathbf{M}$ost of this book has been concerned with presenting and explaining procedures commonly used to describe and analyze experimental data. As important as it is for you to know *how to* apply those procedures, it is equally important for you to know *when to* apply them. One of the greatest difficulties students face when presented with real data is to know which of the many procedures they have learned is applicable to that set of data.

In Chapter 1 I presented a brief discussion of the tree diagram found on the inside front cover of this book. That diagram is designed to help you consider the relevant issues involved in selecting a statistical test (the issues of the type of data, the question of relationships versus differences, the number of groups, and whether variables are independent or dependent). The tree diagram is largely self-explanatory, and it is worth your time to go over it and make sure you understand the distinctions it makes. At the same time it is difficult to use something like that diagram effectively unless you have had practice in doing so. The exercises in this chapter are designed to give you that practice.

The exercises and examples in this chapter cite research studies drawn from the published literature. Each study is an actual one that resulted in data that someone had to analyze. Your task is to identify the appropriate statistical procedure to be used in each case. In some cases several procedures could be properly applied, and in other cases there may be room for disagreement over just what procedure would be best. In some cases the appropriate procedure may simply be the calculation of one or more descriptive statistics, whereas in others—the majority—some sort of hypothesis testing is called for. You should assume that the assumptions required by the standard parametric tests have been met unless you are told otherwise. For some of the examples I have noted what the experimenter found. This is simply for your interest and is not intended to be part of the question.

In selecting these examples I have occasionally simplified the actual experiment in minor ways, usually by omitting either independent or dependent variables. I have tried not to change the nature of the experiment in any important way. Should you be interested in following up any of these studies, they are all listed in the references. If you would like even more practice, the summaries of studies found in *Psychological Abstracts* or on *Pysch Lit* are excellent sources of examples.

I have supplied my answers to most of these examples in the answer section at the end of the book. As I said, there occasionally is room for disagreement over the appropriate analysis. My approach may differ from that of the original experimenter, who would have had a better grasp of the data. If your answer differs from mine, be sure you understand why I gave the answer I did and consider whether yours is just a different way of answering the same question, whether it answers an entirely different question, or whether you have failed to take something into account.

Figure 21.1 is a copy of the decision tree that is on the inside cover of this book. The tree provides a framework for choosing among various alternatives and should make your task somewhat easier.

21.1 Exercises and Examples

21.1 Berndt, Schwartz, and Kaiser (1983) were concerned with whether ten different psychological scales for the assessment of depression are suitable for use with adolescents and young adults. They specifically wanted to know whether subjects or clients could understand the questions. Using standard readability formulae, they computed readability scores for each of the ten depression inventories. What statistical procedures would they most likely use?

21.2 Bahrick and Hall (1991) compared individuals who had and had not taken college-level mathematics 50 years previously on their knowledge of high school algebra. The two groups had not differed in their original algebra grades in high school, and subjects did not differ in their

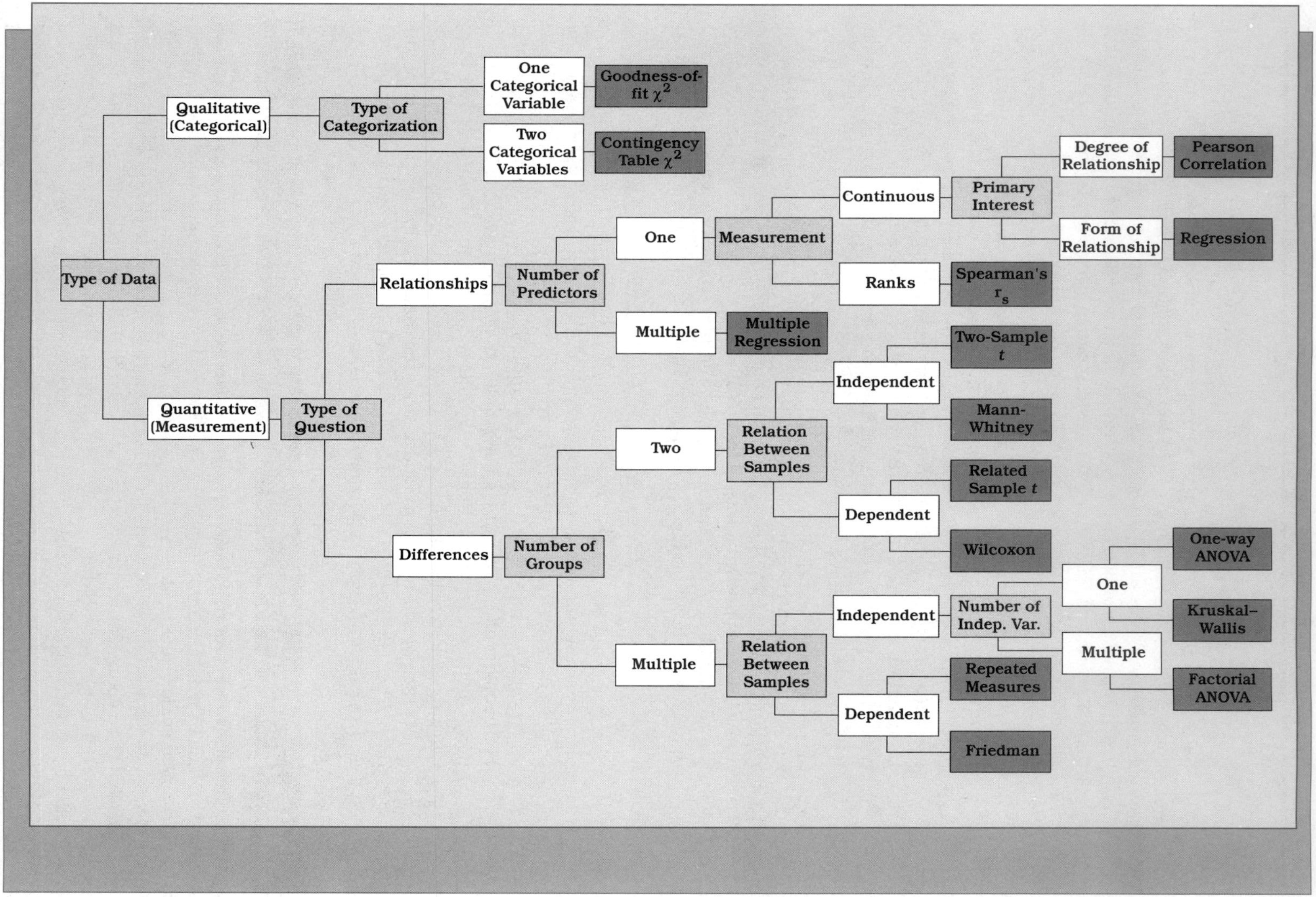

Figure 21.1 Decision Tree

use of algebra during the intervening period. (*Note:* The group who did take college-level mathematics retained significantly more of their knowledge of algebra.) *Pearson R*

21.3 Harper and Wacker (1983) examined the relationship between scores on the Denver Developmental Screening Test and scores on individually administered intellectual measures for 555 three- to four-year-old children. How would they best assess these relationships? *Independent*

21.4 Do people pay any attention to the pictures included in introductory psychology textbooks? Goldstein, Bailis, and Chance (1983) presented 47 subjects with a large number of pictures and asked them to pick out the ones they recognized. Many of the pictures were taken from the introductory psychology textbook the students were using. The experimenters also presented the same pictures to 56 students who were using a different text. For each subject they recorded the percentage of pictures correctly identified. In addition, they asked subjects in the first group to indicate the degree to which they used textbook pictures in general as study aids. How would you analyze the data on recognition and the data on reported use of pictures?

21.5 Franklin, Janoff-Bulman, and Roberts (1990) looked at the long-term impact of divorce on college students' levels of optimism and trust. They compared students from divorced families and students from intact families. (*Note:* They found no differences on generalized trust, but children of divorced families showed less optimism about the future of their own marriages.)

21.6 Newman, Olson, Hall, and Hornak (1983) presented subjects with a series of target words to learn. Each target was accompanied by a cue word that was either strongly or weakly associated with the target (e.g., Table-Chair or Table-Round). During a recall task subjects were asked to recall the target words and were presented with a different set of cues strongly or weakly associated with the target or with no cue at all. The dependent variable was the number of target words recalled. How would you analyze these data?

21.7 In studying what is called latent spatial learning, Sutherland and Linggard (1982) taught rats to swim to a small underwater (and therefore invisible) platform from a variety of locations in a round pool of water. Some rats had never seen the pool, some previously had been placed directly on the platform in a different location in the pool, and some previously had been placed on the platform in the same location. The dependent variable was the speed with which the rats learned to swim to the platform. What is the most likely statistical analysis of these data?

21.8 Carli (1990) compared males and females on their use of language and their influence on the listener. They compared male and female speakers who spoke either tentatively or assertively. They also took into account the gender of the listener. Separate groups of speakers were used for each sex of listener, and each listener heard only one speaker. The dependent variable was the perceived influence of the speaker. (*Note:* Female speakers who spoke tentatively were more influential than assertive female speakers when speaking to men, but less influential when speaking to women. Male speakers were equally influential.)

21.9 Lundberg (1983) studied the origins of what is usually called Type A behavior.

He administered a questionnaire to 15 children aged 3 to 6 and scored the children with respect to the competitiveness, impatience/anger, and aggressiveness components of Type A behavior. Those above the median were classed as Type A, and those below the median were classed as Type B. (This is called a "median split.") He then measured heart rate and blood pressure during an emotional event. How should he analyze these data for each of the dependent variables? (*Note:* There were differences, but only in systolic blood pressure.)

21.10 Supramaniam (1983) investigated proofreading errors committed by good and poor readers on easy and difficult passages. The same subjects proofread both passages. We have not covered the computational procedures for the analysis of these data, but you should be able to describe the type of analysis needed.

21.11 Flink, Boggiano, and Barrett (1990) examined the influence of the teacher on the learning of students. Teachers were either pressured to maximize student performance or simply told to help their students learn. They were also classified into those who used controlling strategies and those who did not. The dependent variable was the performance of the students on the task to be learned. (*Note:* Pressured teachers who used controlling strategies were significantly less effective than teachers in the other conditions.)

21.12 Linn and Hodge (1982) investigated locus of control in hyperactive and control subjects. Locus of control refers to the degree to which people view positive and negative outcomes as being attributable to their own internally controlled behaviors, such as skill or hard work, or to external events, such as luck or task difficulty, over which they have no control. Sixteen hyperactive and 16 control subjects were administered the Nowicki-Strickland Locus of Control Scale and the Peabody Picture Vocabulary Test (a general intelligence test). How should they deal with the locus of control scores and of what use are the Peabody scores?

21.13 Obrzut, Hansen, and Heath (1982) classified 153 Hispanic children as poor visual processors on the basis of the Matching Familiar Figures Test (MFFT). They then assigned the children to one of three treatment groups. One group received tutoring in visual information processing, another group received small-group instruction with regular classroom materials, and the third group was a control group receiving no special treatment. The dependent variable was the child's score on a second administration of the MFFT. What analysis is appropriate?

21.14 Pliner (1982) was interested in investigating whether familiarity with a flavor leads to greater approval—the "acquired-taste" phenomenon. She had 24 undergraduates taste each of four unfamiliar tropical fruit juices 0, 5, 10, or 20 times. (For each subject she randomized which juice would be tasted how many times.) Subjects were then asked to rate the degree to which they liked the taste of the juice. What statistical procedures are suitable for analyzing these data? What test would she use if she wanted a distribution-free test? (*Note:* She found the effect that she had expected—greater familiarity led to greater approval.)

21.15 Cummings, Sciandra, Gingrass, and Davis (1991) surveyed 179 researchers who were funded by the tobacco industries Council for Tobacco Research. He found that 94% of the respondents agreed that passive smoking was harmful to the non-smoker. What should they do with these data?

21.16 Fagerström (1982) studied the effect of using nicotine gum as an adjunct to a standard program for giving up smoking. One group received the standard psychological treatment program normally employed by Fagerström's clinic. A second group received the same program but was also supplied with gum containing nicotine, which they were instructed to chew when they felt the need to smoke. Each group contained 50 subjects, and subjects were classified as abstinent or not at one month and at six months. How should he analyze his data? What problem arises from the fact that there was not a group given plain-old-candy-store gum? (*Note:* The experimental [gum] group had abstinence rates of 90% and 64% at one and six months, respectively, and the control group had rates of 60% and 45%.)

21.17 Payne (1982) asked male and female subjects to rank ten common job characteristics (e.g., salary, workload) for the characteristics' personal importance to the subject and their perceived importance to a member of the opposite sex. The data were collected from 92 subjects in 1973 and from 145 subjects in 1981. How should she analyze these data?

21.18 Cochran and Urbanczyk (1982) were concerned with the effect of the height of a room on the desired personal space of subjects. They tested 48 subjects in both a high-ceiling (10 ft) and a low-ceiling (7 ft) room. Subjects stood with their backs to a wall while a stranger approached. Subjects were told to say "stop" when the approaching stranger's nearness made them feel uncomfortable. The dependent variable was the distance at which the subject said "stop." What should the experimenters do with their data? What should they do instead if they are unwilling to use a parametric test?

(*Note:* The distance was greater with a lower ceiling, which suggests that interpersonal space is not dependent on just horizontal distance.)

21.19 Robinson, Barrett, and Skeen (1983) compared scores on a scale of locus of control for 20 unwed adolescent fathers and 20 unwed adolescent nonfathers. How could they analyze these data if they were unwilling to make parametric assumptions? (*Note:* They found no difference.)

21.20 Smith and Plant (1982) studied sex differences in job satisfaction. They first matched pairs of male and female university professors on the basis of four variables known to be related to job satisfaction (i.e., years of service, rank, highest degree, and department). They then used a paper-and-pencil measure of job satisfaction to obtain a score for each subject on five satisfaction areas—work, pay, promotion, supervision, and co-workers. What statistical procedure is appropriate for these data, treating each satisfaction area separately?

21.21 Hosch and Cooper (1982) looked at the role that being a victim rather than just a bystander had on eyewitness identification. In the control condition a confederate of the experimenter entered the experimental room with a subject, completed a few forms, and left. In another condition the confederate did the same thing, but as she was leaving she stole the experimenter's calculator. In the third condition the confederate stole the *subject's* watch, which the subject had been instructed to leave on the table. There were two dependent variables. The first was whether the subject was able to correctly identify the confederate from a set of six photographs, and the second was the subject's subjective rating on a nine-point scale of his or her confidence in the identification. The experimenter was most interested in seeing whether being a victim of a theft led to better and more confident identification than just observing a theft. How can these data be analyzed? (*Note:* The two theft conditions did not differ, and there was no relationship between accuracy and confidence.)

21.22 Bradley and Kjungja (1982) experimented with the perception of subjective triangles. When you look at three points that form a triangle, there is a subjective impression of lines connecting those points to form the contours of the triangle. Bradley and Kjungja asked subjects to view the subjective triangle while it was stationary and again while it was rotating in a circle. The subject was instructed to say whether the subjective contours were stronger while the triangle was stationary or while it was rotating. Out of 37 subjects 35 said that the contours were stronger when the triangle was rotating. How could they test whether this difference was significant (although here a formal test isn't really needed)?

21.23 Lobel, Dunkel-Schetter, and Scrimshaw (1992) examined medical risk factors, gestational age, and the mother's emotional stress as predictors of low birthweight. How could they assess the relationship between these factors and low birthweight? (*Note:* Gestational age and stress predicted birthweight but not medical risks. Women who experienced daily anxiety were most likely to delivery low-birthweight babies.)

21.24 Brown, Lewis, Brown, Horn, and Bowes (1982) investigated drug-induced amnesia as a way of throwing light on organically produced amnesia. They first presented subjects with a list of words to learn and then injected the subjects with either lorazepam (which produces amnesia) or saline. After 1.5 hours they asked all subjects to recall the words they had learned. They also asked the same subjects to learn a list after the drug had been injected and to recall it after 1.5 hours. If lorazepam interferes with the *storage* of material in memory, then only recall of the second list should be affected. If lorazepam interferes with *retrieval* rather than storage, then recall of both lists should be disrupted. What statistical test would be appropriate for analyzing these data? This is another case in which you do not know how to perform the analysis, but you should be able to describe the design. (*Note:* Recall of the list learned before the injection was unaffected, but the list studied after the administration of the drug was poorly recalled.)

21.25 Hicks and Guista (1982) asked seven subjects who habitually had less than 6.5 hours of sleep per night and nine subjects who habitually had more than 8.5 hours of sleep per night to complete the Stanford Sleepiness Scale (SSS) at two-hour intervals for 30 days. The SSS is a measure of alertness and simply requires the subject to rate his or her level of alertness by responding with a number between 1 (very alert) and 7 (struggling to stay awake). The authors actually broke the data into seven different times of day, but for purposes of this example assume that the dependent variable is each subject's mean SSS score over the 30-day period. What is the appropriate analysis of these data?

21.26 The right side of a person's face is said to resemble the whole face more than does the left side. Kennedy, Beard, and Carr (1982) asked 91 subjects to view full-face pictures of six different faces. Testing for recall was conducted one week later, when subjects were presented with pictures of 12 faces and were asked to identify the ones they had seen earlier. At testing, subjects were divided into three groups of roughly equal size. One group was presented with full-face photographs, one group saw only the right side of the face in the photograph, and one group saw only the left side. The dependent variable was the number of errors. The authors were not satisfied that the assumptions of parametric tests were met. How could they compare the three groups and how could they compare the two partial-face groups? (*Note:* Contrary to the prediction the left side turned out to be easier to recognize than the right side.)

Arithmetic Review

The following is intended as a quick refresher of some of the simple arithmetic operations you learned in high school but probably have not used since. Although some of what follows will seem so obvious that you wonder why it is there, people sometimes forget the most obvious things.

One of the things that students never seem to learn is that it is easy to figure out most of these principles for yourself. For example, if you can't remember whether

$$\frac{18.1}{28.6 + 32.7} \quad \text{can be reduced to} \quad \frac{18.1}{28.6} + \frac{18.1}{32.7}$$

(it cannot, but it is one of the foolish things that I can never keep in my head), try it out with very simple numbers. Thus,

$$\frac{2}{1 + 4} - \frac{2}{5} = 0.4$$

is obviously not the same as

$$\frac{2}{1} + \frac{2}{4} = 2.5$$

It is often quicker to check on a procedure by using small numbers than by looking it up.

Standard Symbols and Basic Information

Numerator   The thing on the top.

Denominator   The thing on the bottom.

a/b a = Numerator; b = Denominator.

+, −, ×, ÷ (or /)   Symbols for addition, subtraction, multiplication, and division. Called *operators*.

$X = Y$ X equals Y.

$X \approx Y$ or $X \simeq Y$ X approximately equal to Y.

$X \neq Y$ X unequal to Y.

$X < Y$ X less than Y. (*Hint:* The small end points at the smaller number.)

$X \leq Y$ X less than or equal to Y.

$X > Y$ X greater than Y.

$X \geq Y$ X greater than or equal to Y.

$X < Y < Z$ X less than Y less than Z (i.e., Y is between X and Z).

$X \pm Y$ X plus or minus Y.

$|X|$ Absolute value of X—ignore the sign of X.

$\dfrac{1}{X}$ The reciprocal of X.

X^2 X squared.

X^n X raised to the nth power.

$\sqrt{X} = X^{1/2}$ Square root of X.

Addition and Subtraction

$8 - 12 = -4$ To subtract a larger number from a smaller one, subtract the smaller from the larger and make the result negative.

$-8 + 12$ The order of operations is not important.
$\quad = 12 - 8 = 4$

Multiplication and Division

$2(3)(6)$ If no operator appears before a set of parentheses, hereafter denoted ( ), multiplication is implied.
$\quad = 2 \times 3 \times 6$

$2 \times 3 \times 6$ Numbers can be multiplied in any order.
$\quad = 2 \times 6 \times 3$

$\dfrac{2 \times 8}{4}$ Division can take place in any order.

$\quad = \dfrac{2}{4} \times 8$

$\quad = 2 \times \dfrac{8}{4}$

$\quad = \dfrac{16}{4} = 4$

$7 \times 3 + 6$ Multiply or divide *before* you add or subtract the result.
$\quad = 21 + 6 = 27$

$2 \times 3 = 6;$
$(-2)(-3) = 6$
$\dfrac{6}{3} = 2;$
$\dfrac{-6}{-3} = 2$

Multiplication or division of numbers with the *same* sign produces a positive answer.

$(-2)3 = -6;$
$\dfrac{-6}{3} = -2$

Multiplication or division of numbers with *opposite* signs produces a negative answer.

$(-2)(3)(-6)(-4)$
$= (-6)(24)$
$= -144$

With several numbers having different signs work in pairs to get the correct sign.

Parentheses

$2(7 - 6 + 3) =$
$2(4) = 8$
or
$2(7) + 2(-6)$
$+ 2(3) = 14 -$
$12 + 6 = 8$

When multiplying, either perform the operations inside ( ) before multiplying or multiply *each* element within the ( ) and then sum.

$2(7 - 6 + 3)^2$
$= 2(4)^2 = 2(16)$
$= 32$

When the parenthetical term is raised to a power, perform the operations inside the ( ), raise the result to the appropriate power, and then carry out the other operations.

Fractions

$\dfrac{1}{5} = 0.20$

To convert to a decimal, divide the numerator by the denominator.

$\dfrac{4}{3}$

The reciprocal of $\frac{3}{4}$. To take the reciprocal of a fraction, stand it on its head.

$3 \times \dfrac{6}{5} = \dfrac{3 \times 6}{5}$

$= \dfrac{18}{5} = 3.6$

To multiply a fraction by a whole number, multiply the numerator by that number.

$\dfrac{3}{5} \times \dfrac{6}{7} \times \dfrac{1}{2}$

$= \dfrac{3 \times 6 \times 1}{5 \times 7 \times 2}$

$= \dfrac{18}{70} = 0.26$

To multiply a series of fractions multiply numerators together and multiply denominators together.

$\dfrac{1}{3} + \dfrac{4}{3} = \dfrac{5}{3} = 1.67$

To add fractions with the *same* denominator, add the numerators and divide by the common denominator.

$\dfrac{1}{6} + \dfrac{4}{3} = \dfrac{1}{6} + \dfrac{8}{6} = \dfrac{9}{6}$

$= 1.5$

To add fractions with *different* denominators, multiply the numerator and the denominator by a constant to equate the denominators and follow the previous rule.

$\dfrac{8}{13} + \dfrac{12}{25}$

This is a more elaborate example of the same rule.

$= \left(\dfrac{25}{25} \times \dfrac{8}{13} \right)$

$+ \left(\dfrac{13}{13} \times \dfrac{12}{25} \right)$

$= \dfrac{200}{325} + \dfrac{156}{325}$

$= \dfrac{356}{325} = 1.095$

$\dfrac{8}{1/3} = 8\left(\dfrac{3}{1} \right) = 24$

To divide by a fraction, multiply by the reciprocal of that fraction.

Algebraic Operations

Most algebraic operations boil down to moving things from one side of the equation to the other. Mathematically the rule is that whatever you do to one side of the equation you must do to the other side.

Solve the following equation for X:

$3 + X = 8$

We want X on one side and the answer on the other. All we have to do is to subtract 3 from both sides to get

$3 + X - 3 = 8 - 3$

$X = 5$

If the equation had been

$X - 3 = 8$

We would have added 3 to both sides:

$X - 3 + 3 = 8 + 3$

$X = 11$

For equations involving multiplication or division we follow the same principle.

$$2X = 21$$

Dividing both sides by 2 we have

$$\frac{2X}{2} = \frac{21}{2}$$

$$X = 10.5$$

and

$$\frac{X}{7} = 13$$

$$\frac{7X}{7} = 7(13)$$

$$X = 91$$

Personally I prefer to think of things in a different, but perfectly equivalent, way. When you want to get rid of something that has been added (or subtracted) to (or from) one side of the equation, move it to the other side and reverse the sign.

$$3 + X = 12 \qquad \text{or} \qquad X - 7 = 19$$
$$X = 12 - 3 \qquad\qquad X = 19 + 7$$

When the thing you want to get rid of is in the numerator, move it to the other side and put it in the denominator.

$$7.6X - 12$$

$$X = \frac{12}{7.6}$$

When the thing you want to get rid of is in the denominator, move it to the numerator on the other side and multiply.

$$\frac{X}{8.9} = 14.6$$

$$X = 14.6(8.9)$$

Notice that with more complex expressions you must multiply (or divide) everything on the other side of the equation. Thus,

$$7.6X = 12 + 8$$

$$X = \frac{12 + 8}{7.6}$$

For complex equations just work one step at a time.

$$7.6(X + 8) = \frac{14}{7} - 5$$

First get rid of the 7.6:

$$X + 8 = \frac{14/7 - 5}{7.6}$$

Now get rid of the 8:

$$X = \frac{14/7 - 5}{7.6} - 8$$

Now clean up the messy fraction:

$$X = \frac{2 - 5}{7.6} - 8 = \frac{-3}{7.6} - 8 = -0.395 - 8 = -8.395$$

Appendix B

Symbols and Notation

Greek Letter Symbols

α Level of significance—probability of a Type I error (alpha)

β Probability of a Type II error (beta)

γ Effect size (gamma)

δ Noncentrality parameter (delta)

η^2 Eta squared

μ Population mean (mu)

μ_x Mean of the sampling distribution of the mean

ρ Population correlation coefficient (rho)

σ Population standard deviation (sigma)

σ^2 Population variance

Σ Summation notation (uppercase sigma)

ϕ Phi coefficient

χ^2 Chi-square

χ_F^2 Friedman's chi-square

ω^2 Omega squared

English Letter Symbols

a Intercept; number of levels of variable A in analysis of variance

b Slope (also called regression coefficient)

CI Confidence interval

cov_{XY} Covariance of X and Y

df Degrees of freedom

E Expected frequency; expected value

F F statistic

G Grand total—total of all the scores

GM	Grand mean
H	Kruskal-Wallis statistic
$H_0; H_1$	Null hypothesis; alternative hypothesis
MS	Mean square
MS_{error}	Mean square error
n, n_i, N_i	Number of cases in a sample
$N(0, 1)$	Read "normally distributed with $\mu = 0$, $\sigma^2 = 1$"
O	Observed frequency
p	General symbol for probability
r, r_{XY}	Pearson's correlation coefficient
r_{pb}	Point-biserial correlation coefficient
r_S	Spearman's rank-order correlation coefficient
R	Multiple correlation coefficient
s^2, s_X^2	Sample variance
s_p^2	Pooled variance
s, s_X	Sample standard deviation
s_D	Standard deviation of difference scores
$s_{\bar{D}}$	Standard error of the mean of difference scores
$s_{\bar{X}}, s_{\bar{X}_1 - \bar{X}_2}$	Standard error of the mean; Standard error of differences between means
$s_{Y - \hat{Y}}$	Standard error of estimate
SP_{XY}	Sum of products X and Y
SS_A	Sum of squares for variable A
SS_{AB}	Interaction sum of squares
SS_{error}	Error sum of squares
SS_Y	Sum of squares for variable Y
$SS_{\hat{Y}}$	Sum of squares of predicted values of Y
$SS_{Y - \hat{Y}}$	Error sum of squares $= SS_{error}$
t	Student's t statistic
$t_{0.5}$	Critical value of t
T	Wilcoxon's matched-pairs signed-ranks statistic
T_j	Total for group j

T_{A_i} Total for the ith level of variable A

W_s, W_s' Mann-Whitney statistic

$\bar{X}, \bar{X}_i$ Sample mean

$\bar{X}_h$ Harmonic mean

$\hat{Y}, \hat{Y}_i$ Predicted value of Y

z Normal deviate (also called standard score)

Dataset

Howell and Huessy (1985) reported on a study of 386 children who had and had not exhibited during childhood symptoms of attention deficit disorder (ADD), previously known as hyperkinesis or minimal brain dysfunction. In 1965 teachers of all second-grade school children in a number of schools in northwestern Vermont were asked to complete a questionnaire for each of their students dealing with behaviors commonly associated with ADD. Questionnaires on these same children were again completed when they were in the fourth and fifth grades and, for purposes of this dataset only, those three scores were averaged to produce a score labeled ADDSC. The higher the score, the more ADD-like behaviors the child exhibited. At the end of ninth grade and again at the end of twelfth grade, information on the performances of these children was obtained from school records. Some of these variables are presented in the accompanying table for a sample of 88 of these students. These data offer the opportunity to examine questions about whether later behavior can be predicted from earlier behavior and to examine academically related variables and their interrelationships. The data are referred to in many of the exercises at the end of each chapter. A description of each variable follows:

ADDSC The average of the three ADD-like behavior scores obtained in elementary school

SEX 1 = male; 2 = female

REPEAT 1 = repeated at least one grade; 0 = did not repeat a grade

IQ IQ obtained from a group-administered IQ test

ENGL Level of English in ninth grade: 1 = college prep; 2 = general; 3 = remedial

ENGG Grade in English in ninth grade: 4 = A; 3 = B; etc.

GPA Grade point average in ninth grade

SOCPROB Social problems in ninth grade: 1 = yes; 0 = no

DROPOUT 1 = dropped out before completing high school; 0 = did not drop out

ADDSC	SEX	REPEAT	IQ	ENGL	ENGG	GPA	SOCPROB	DROPOUT
45	1	0	111	2	3	2.60	0	0
50	1	0	102	2	3	2.75	0	0
49	1	0	108	2	4	4.00	0	0
55	1	0	109	2	2	2.25	0	0
39	1	0	118	2	3	3.00	0	0
68	1	1	79	2	2	1.67	0	1
69	1	1	88	2	2	2.25	1	1
56	1	0	102	2	4	3.40	0	0
58	1	0	105	3	1	1.33	0	0
48	1	0	92	2	4	3.50	0	0
34	1	0	131	2	4	3.75	0	0
50	2	0	104	1	3	2.67	0	0
85	1	0	83	2	3	2.75	1	0
49	1	0	84	2	2	2.00	0	0
51	1	0	85	2	3	2.75	0	0
53	1	0	110	2	2	2.50	0	0
36	2	0	121	1	4	3.55	0	0
62	2	0	120	2	3	2.75	0	0
46	2	0	100	2	4	3.50	0	0
50	2	0	94	2	2	2.75	1	1
47	2	0	89	1	2	3.00	0	0
50	2	0	93	2	4	3.25	0	0
44	2	0	128	2	4	3.30	0	0
50	2	0	84	2	3	2.75	0	0
29	2	0	127	1	4	3.75	0	0
49	2	0	106	2	3	2.75	0	0
26	1	0	137	2	3	3.00	0	0
85	1	1	82	3	2	1.75	1	1
53	1	0	106	2	3	2.75	1	0
53	1	0	109	2	2	1.33	0	0
72	1	0	91	2	2	0.67	0	0
35	1	0	111	2	2	2.25	0	0
42	1	0	105	2	2	1.75	0	0
37	1	0	118	2	4	3.25	0	0
46	1	0	103	3	2	1.75	0	0
48	1	0	101	1	3	3.00	0	0
46	1	0	101	3	3	3.00	0	0
49	1	1	95	2	3	3.00	0	0
65	1	1	108	2	3	3.25	0	0
52	1	0	95	3	3	2.25	1	0
75	1	1	98	2	1	1.00	0	1
58	1	0	82	2	3	2.50	0	1
43	2	0	100	1	3	3.00	0	0
60	2	0	100	2	3	2.40	0	0

ADDSC	SEX	REPEAT	IQ	ENGL	ENGG	GPA	SOCPROB	DROPOUT
43	1	0	107	1	2	2.00	0	0
51	1	0	95	2	2	2.75	0	0
70	1	1	97	2	3	2.67	1	1
69	1	1	93	2	2	2.00	0	0
65	1	1	81	1	2	2.00	0	0
63	2	0	89	2	2	1.67	0	0
44	2	0	111	2	4	3.00	0	0
61	2	1	95	2	1	1.50	0	1
40	2	0	106	2	4	3.75	0	0
62	2	0	83	3	1	0.67	0	0
59	1	0	81	2	2	1.50	0	0
47	2	0	115	1	4	4.00	0	0
50	2	0	112	2	3	3.00	0	0
50	2	0	92	2	3	2.33	0	0
65	2	0	85	2	2	1.75	0	0
54	2	0	95	3	2	3.00	0	0
44	2	0	115	2	4	3.75	0	0
66	2	0	91	2	4	2.67	1	1
34	2	0	107	1	4	3.50	0	0
74	2	0	102	2	0	0.67	0	0
57	2	1	86	3	3	2.25	0	0
60	2	0	96	1	3	3.00	1	0
36	2	0	114	2	3	3.50	0	0
50	1	0	105	2	2	1.75	0	0
60	1	0	82	2	1	1.00	0	0
45	1	0	120	2	3	3.00	0	0
55	1	0	88	2	1	1.00	0	1
44	1	0	90	1	3	2.50	0	0
57	2	0	85	2	3	2.50	0	0
33	2	0	106	1	4	3.75	0	0
30	2	0	109	1	4	3.50	0	0
64	1	0	75	3	2	1.00	1	0
49	1	1	91	2	3	2.25	0	0
76	1	0	96	2	2	1.00	0	0
40	1	0	108	2	3	2.50	0	0
48	1	0	86	2	3	2.75	0	0
65	1	0	98	2	2	0.75	0	0
50	1	0	99	2	2	1.30	0	0
70	1	0	95	2	1	1.25	0	0
78	1	0	88	3	3	1.50	0	0
44	1	0	111	2	2	3.00	0	0
48	1	0	103	2	1	2.00	0	0
52	1	0	107	2	2	2.00	0	0
40	1	0	118	2	2	2.50	0	0

Statistical Tables

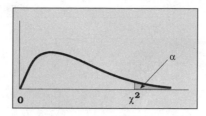

Table D.1   Upper Percentage Points of the χ^2 Distribution (Source: The entries in this table were computed by the author.)

df	.995	.990	.975	.950	.900	.750	.500	.250	.100	.050	.025	.010	.005
1	0.00	0.00	0.00	0.00	0.02	0.10	0.45	1.32	2.71	3.84	5.02	6.63	7.88
2	0.01	0.02	0.05	0.10	0.21	0.58	1.39	2.77	4.61	5.99	7.38	9.21	10.60
3	0.07	0.11	0.22	0.35	0.58	1.21	2.37	4.11	6.25	7.82	9.35	11.35	12.84
4	0.21	0.30	0.48	0.71	1.06	1.92	3.36	5.39	7.78	9.49	11.14	13.28	14.86
5	0.41	0.55	0.83	1.15	1.61	2.67	4.35	6.63	9.24	11.07	12.83	15.09	16.75
6	0.68	0.87	1.24	1.64	2.20	3.45	5.35	7.84	10.64	12.59	14.45	16.81	18.55
7	0.99	1.24	1.69	2.17	2.83	4.25	6.35	9.04	12.02	14.07	16.01	18.48	20.28
8	1.34	1.65	2.18	2.73	3.49	5.07	7.34	10.22	13.36	15.51	17.54	20.09	21.96
9	1.73	2.09	2.70	3.33	4.17	5.90	8.34	11.39	14.68	16.92	19.02	21.66	23.59
10	2.15	2.56	3.25	3.94	4.87	6.74	9.34	12.55	15.99	18.31	20.48	23.21	25.19
11	2.60	3.05	3.82	4.57	5.58	7.58	10.34	13.70	17.28	19.68	21.92	24.72	26.75
12	3.07	3.57	4.40	5.23	6.30	8.44	11.34	14.85	18.55	21.03	23.34	26.21	28.30
13	3.56	4.11	5.01	5.89	7.04	9.30	12.34	15.98	19.81	22.36	24.74	27.69	29.82
14	4.07	4.66	5.63	6.57	7.79	10.17	13.34	17.12	21.06	23.69	26.12	29.14	31.31
15	4.60	5.23	6.26	7.26	8.55	11.04	14.34	18.25	22.31	25.00	27.49	30.58	32.80
16	5.14	5.81	6.91	7.96	9.31	11.91	15.34	19.37	23.54	26.30	28.85	32.00	34.27
17	5.70	6.41	7.56	8.67	10.09	12.79	16.34	20.49	24.77	27.59	30.19	33.41	35.72
18	6.26	7.01	8.23	9.39	10.86	13.68	17.34	21.60	25.99	28.87	31.53	34.81	37.15
19	6.84	7.63	8.91	10.12	11.65	14.56	18.34	22.72	27.20	30.14	32.85	36.19	38.58
20	7.43	8.26	9.59	10.85	12.44	15.45	19.34	23.83	28.41	31.41	34.17	37.56	40.00
21	8.03	8.90	10.28	11.59	13.24	16.34	20.34	24.93	29.62	32.67	35.48	38.93	41.40
22	8.64	9.54	10.98	12.34	14.04	17.24	21.34	26.04	30.81	33.93	36.78	40.29	42.80
23	9.26	10.19	11.69	13.09	14.85	18.14	22.34	27.14	32.01	35.17	38.08	41.64	44.18
24	9.88	10.86	12.40	13.85	15.66	19.04	23.34	28.24	33.20	36.42	39.37	42.98	45.56
25	10.52	11.52	13.12	14.61	16.47	19.94	24.34	29.34	34.38	37.65	40.65	44.32	46.93
26	11.16	12.20	13.84	15.38	17.29	20.84	25.34	30.43	35.56	38.89	41.92	45.64	48.29
27	11.80	12.88	14.57	16.15	18.11	21.75	26.34	31.53	36.74	40.11	43.20	46.96	49.64
28	12.46	13.56	15.31	16.93	18.94	22.66	27.34	32.62	37.92	41.34	44.46	48.28	50.99
29	13.12	14.26	16.05	17.71	19.77	23.57	28.34	33.71	39.09	42.56	45.72	49.59	52.34
30	13.78	14.95	16.79	18.49	20.60	24.48	29.34	34.80	40.26	43.77	46.98	50.89	53.67
40	20.67	22.14	24.42	26.51	29.06	33.67	39.34	45.61	51.80	55.75	59.34	63.71	66.80
50	27.96	29.68	32.35	34.76	37.69	42.95	49.34	56.33	63.16	67.50	71.42	76.17	79.52
60	35.50	37.46	40.47	43.19	46.46	52.30	59.34	66.98	74.39	79.08	83.30	88.40	91.98
70	43.25	45.42	48.75	51.74	55.33	61.70	69.34	77.57	85.52	90.53	95.03	100.44	104.24
80	51.14	53.52	57.15	60.39	64.28	71.15	79.34	88.13	96.57	101.88	106.63	112.34	116.35
90	59.17	61.74	65.64	69.13	73.29	80.63	89.33	98.65	107.56	113.14	118.14	124.13	128.32
100	67.30	70.05	74.22	77.93	82.36	90.14	99.33	109.14	118.49	124.34	129.56	135.82	140.19

			Two-Tailed Tests		
Table D.2	*df*	***p* = .10**	***p* = .05**	***p* = .025**	***p* = .01**
Significant Values	3	0.805	0.878	0.924	0.959
of the Correlation	4	0.729	0.811	0.868	0.917
Coefficient	5	0.669	0.755	0.817	0.875
(Source: The	6	0.622	0.707	0.771	0.834
entries in this table	7	0.582	0.666	0.732	0.798
were computed by	8	0.549	0.632	0.697	0.765
the author.)	9	0.521	0.602	0.667	0.735
	10	0.498	0.576	0.640	0.708
	11	0.476	0.553	0.616	0.684
	12	0.458	0.533	0.594	0.588
	13	0.441	0.514	0.575	0.641
	14	0.426	0.497	0.557	0.623
	15	0.412	0.482	0.541	0.605
	16	0.400	0.468	0.526	0.590
	17	0.389	0.455	0.512	0.575
	18	0.379	0.444	0.499	0.562
	19	0.369	0.433	0.487	0.549
	20	0.360	0.423	0.476	0.537
	21	0.351	0.413	0.466	0.526
	22	0.344	0.404	0.456	0.515
	23	0.337	0.396	0.447	0.505
	24	0.330	0.388	0.439	0.496
	25	0.323	0.381	0.431	0.487
	26	0.317	0.374	0.423	0.478
	27	0.311	0.367	0.415	0.471
	28	0.306	0.361	0.409	0.463
	29	0.301	0.355	0.402	0.456
	30	0.296	0.349	0.396	0.449
	40	0.257	0.304	0.345	0.393
	50	0.231	0.273	0.311	0.354
	60	0.211	0.250	0.285	0.325
	120	0.150	0.178	0.203	0.232
	200	0.116	0.138	0.158	0.181
	500	0.073	0.088	0.100	0.115
	1000	0.052	0.062	0.071	0.081

5.94   2-36

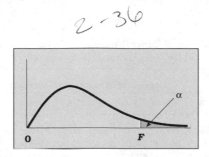

Table D.3   Critical Values of the *F* Distribution   Alpha = .05 (Source: The entries in this table were computed by the author.)

							Degrees of Freedom for Numerator									
	1	**2**	**3**	**4**	**5**	**6**	**7**	**8**	**9**	**10**	**15**	**20**	**25**	**30**	**40**	**50**
1	161.4	199.5	215.8	224.8	230.0	233.8	236.5	238.6	240.1	242.1	245.2	248.4	248.9	250.5	250.8	252.6
2	18.51	19.00	19.16	19.25	19.30	19.33	19.35	19.37	19.38	19.40	19.43	19.44	19.46	19.47	19.48	19.48
3	10.13	9.55	9.28	9.12	9.01	8.94	8.89	8.85	8.81	8.79	8.70	8.66	8.63	8.62	8.59	8.58
4	7.71	6.94	6.59	6.39	6.26	6.16	6.09	6.04	6.00	5.96	5.86	5.80	5.77	5.75	5.72	5.70
5	6.61	5.79	5.41	5.19	5.05	4.95	4.88	4.82	4.77	4.74	4.62	4.56	4.52	4.50	4.46	4.44
6	5.99	5.14	4.76	4.53	4.39	4.28	4.21	4.15	4.10	4.06	3.94	3.87	3.83	3.81	3.77	3.75
7	5.59	4.74	4.35	4.12	3.97	3.87	3.79	3.73	3.68	3.64	3.51	3.44	3.40	3.38	3.34	3.32
8	5.32	4.46	4.07	3.84	3.69	3.58	3.50	3.44	3.39	3.35	3.22	3.15	3.11	3.08	3.04	3.02
9	5.12	4.26	3.86	3.63	3.48	3.37	3.29	3.23	3.18	3.14	3.01	2.94	2.89	2.86	2.83	2.80
10	4.96	4.10	3.71	3.48	3.33	3.22	3.14	3.07	3.02	2.98	2.85	2.77	2.73	2.70	2.66	2.64
11	4.84	3.98	3.59	3.36	3.20	3.09	3.01	2.95	2.90	2.85	2.72	2.65	2.60	2.57	2.53	2.51
12	4.75	3.89	3.49	3.26	3.11	3.00	2.91	2.85	2.80	2.75	2.62	2.54	2.50	2.47	2.43	2.40
13	4.67	3.81	3.41	3.18	3.03	2.92	2.83	2.77	2.71	2.67	2.53	2.46	2.41	2.38	2.34	2.31
14	4.60	3.74	3.34	3.11	2.96	2.85	2.76	2.70	2.65	2.60	2.46	2.39	2.34	2.31	2.27	2.24
15	4.54	3.68	3.29	3.06	2.90	2.79	2.71	2.64	2.59	2.54	2.40	2.33	2.28	2.25	2.20	2.18
16	4.49	3.63	3.24	3.01	2.85	2.74	2.66	2.59	2.54	2.49	2.35	2.28	2.23	2.19	2.15	2.12
17	4.45	3.59	3.20	2.96	2.81	2.70	2.61	2.55	2.49	2.45	2.31	2.23	2.18	2.15	2.10	2.08
18	4.41	3.55	3.16	2.93	2.77	2.66	2.58	2.51	2.46	2.41	2.27	2.19	2.14	2.11	2.06	2.04
19	4.38	3.52	3.13	2.90	2.74	2.63	2.54	2.48	2.42	2.38	2.23	2.16	2.11	2.07	2.03	2.00
20	4.35	3.49	3.10	2.87	2.71	2.60	2.51	2.45	2.39	2.35	2.20	2.12	2.07	2.04	1.99	1.97
22	4.30	3.44	3.05	2.82	2.66	2.55	2.46	2.40	2.34	2.30	2.15	2.07	2.02	1.98	1.94	1.91
24	4.26	3.40	3.01	2.78	2.62	2.51	2.42	2.36	2.30	2.25	2.11	2.03	1.97	1.94	1.89	1.86
26	4.23	3.37	2.98	2.74	2.59	2.47	2.39	2.32	2.27	2.22	2.07	1.99	1.94	1.90	1.85	1.82
28	4.20	3.34	2.95	2.71	2.56	2.45	2.36	2.29	2.24	2.19	2.04	1.96	1.91	1.87	1.82	1.79
30	4.17	3.32	2.92	2.69	2.53	2.42	2.33	2.27	2.21	2.16	2.01	1.93	1.88	1.84	1.79	1.76
40	4.08	3.23	2.84	2.61	2.45	2.34	2.25	2.18	2.12	2.08	1.92	1.84	1.78	1.74	1.69	1.66
50	4.03	3.18	2.79	2.56	2.40	2.29	2.20	2.13	2.07	2.03	1.87	1.78	1.73	1.69	1.63	1.60
60	4.00	3.15	2.76	2.53	2.37	2.25	2.17	2.10	2.04	1.99	1.84	1.75	1.69	1.65	1.59	1.56
120	3.92	3.07	2.68	2.45	2.29	2.18	2.09	2.02	1.96	1.91	1.75	1.66	1.60	1.55	1.50	1.46
200	3.89	3.04	2.65	2.42	2.26	2.14	2.06	1.98	1.93	1.88	1.72	1.62	1.56	1.52	1.46	1.41
500	3.86	3.01	2.62	2.39	2.23	2.12	2.03	1.96	1.90	1.85	1.69	1.59	1.53	1.48	1.42	1.38
1000	3.85	3.01	2.61	2.38	2.22	2.11	2.02	1.95	1.89	1.84	1.68	1.58	1.52	1.47	1.41	1.36

(Degrees of Freedom for Denominator)

3.26

Table D.4   Critical Values of the *F* Distribution   Alpha = .01   (Source: The entries in this table were computed by the author.)

	Degrees of Freedom for Numerator																
	1	**2**	**3**	**4**	**5**	**6**	**7**	**8**	**9**	**10**	**15**	**20**	**25**	**30**	**40**	**50**
1	4048	4993	5377	5577	5668	5924	5992	6096	6132	6168	6079	6168	6214	6355	6168	6213
2	98.50	99.01	99.15	99.23	99.30	99.33	99.35	99.39	99.40	99.43	99.38	99.48	99.43	99.37	99.44	99.59
3	34.12	30.82	29.46	28.71	28.24	27.91	27.67	27.49	27.34	27.23	26.87	26.69	26.58	26.51	26.41	26.36
4	21.20	18.00	16.69	15.98	15.52	15.21	14.98	14.80	14.66	14.55	14.20	14.02	13.91	13.84	13.75	13.69
5	16.26	13.27	12.06	11.39	10.97	10.67	10.46	10.29	10.16	10.05	9.72	9.55	9.45	9.38	9.29	9.24
6	13.75	10.92	9.78	9.15	8.75	8.47	8.26	8.10	7.98	7.87	7.56	7.40	7.30	7.23	7.14	7.09
7	12.25	9.55	8.45	7.85	7.46	7.19	6.99	6.84	6.72	6.62	6.31	6.16	6.06	5.99	5.91	5.86
8	11.26	8.65	7.59	7.01	6.63	6.37	6.18	6.03	5.91	5.81	5.52	5.36	5.26	5.20	5.12	5.07
9	10.56	8.02	6.99	6.42	6.06	5.80	5.61	5.47	5.35	5.26	4.96	4.81	4.71	4.65	4.57	4.52
10	10.04	7.56	6.55	5.99	5.64	5.39	5.20	5.06	4.94	4.85	4.56	4.41	4.31	4.25	4.17	4.12
11	9.65	7.21	6.22	5.67	5.32	5.07	4.89	4.74	4.63	4.54	4.25	4.10	4.01	3.94	3.86	3.81
12	9.33	6.93	5.95	5.41	5.06	4.82	4.64	4.50	4.39	4.30	4.01	3.86	3.76	3.70	3.62	3.57
13	9.07	6.70	5.74	5.21	4.86	4.62	4.44	4.30	4.19	4.10	3.82	3.66	3.57	3.51	3.43	3.38
14	8.86	6.51	5.56	5.04	4.69	4.46	4.28	4.14	4.03	3.94	3.66	3.51	3.41	3.35	3.27	3.22
15	8.68	6.36	5.42	4.89	4.56	4.32	4.14	4.00	3.89	3.80	3.52	3.37	3.28	3.21	3.13	3.08
16	8.53	6.23	5.29	4.77	4.44	4.20	4.03	3.89	3.78	3.69	3.41	3.26	3.16	3.10	3.02	2.97
17	8.40	6.11	5.18	4.67	4.34	4.10	3.93	3.79	3.68	3.59	3.31	3.16	3.07	3.00	2.92	2.87
18	8.29	6.01	5.09	4.58	4.25	4.01	3.84	3.71	3.60	3.51	3.23	3.08	2.98	2.92	2.84	2.78
19	8.18	5.93	5.01	4.50	4.17	3.94	3.77	3.63	3.52	3.43	3.15	3.00	2.91	2.84	2.76	2.71
20	8.10	5.85	4.94	4.43	4.10	3.87	3.70	3.56	3.46	3.37	3.09	2.94	2.84	2.78	2.69	2.64
22	7.95	5.72	4.82	4.31	3.99	3.76	3.59	3.45	3.35	3.26	2.98	2.83	2.73	2.67	2.58	2.53
24	7.82	5.61	4.72	4.22	3.90	3.67	3.50	3.36	3.26	3.17	2.89	2.74	2.64	2.58	2.49	2.44
26	7.72	5.53	4.64	4.14	3.82	3.59	3.42	3.29	3.18	3.09	2.81	2.66	2.57	2.50	2.42	2.36
28	7.64	5.45	4.57	4.07	3.75	3.53	3.36	3.23	3.12	3.03	2.75	2.60	2.51	2.44	2.35	2.30
30	7.56	5.39	4.51	4.02	3.70	3.47	3.30	3.17	3.07	2.98	2.70	2.55	2.45	2.39	2.30	2.25
40	7.31	5.18	4.31	3.83	3.51	3.29	3.12	2.99	2.89	2.80	2.52	2.37	2.27	2.20	2.11	2.06
50	7.17	5.06	4.20	3.72	3.41	3.19	3.02	2.89	2.78	2.70	2.42	2.27	2.17	2.10	2.01	1.95
60	7.08	4.98	4.13	3.65	3.34	3.12	2.95	2.82	2.72	2.63	2.35	2.20	2.10	2.03	1.94	1.88
120	6.85	4.79	3.95	3.48	3.17	2.96	2.79	2.66	2.56	2.47	2.19	2.03	1.93	1.86	1.76	1.70
200	6.76	4.71	3.88	3.41	3.11	2.89	2.73	2.60	2.50	2.41	2.13	1.97	1.87	1.79	1.69	1.63
500	6.69	4.65	3.82	3.36	3.05	2.84	2.68	2.55	2.44	2.36	2.07	1.92	1.81	1.74	1.63	1.57
1000	6.67	4.63	3.80	3.34	3.04	2.82	2.66	2.53	2.43	2.34	2.06	1.90	1.79	1.72	1.61	1.54

Degrees of Freedom for Denominator (row labels)

Table D.5	δ	Alpha for Two-Tailed Test			
		.10	.05	.02	.01
Power as a	1.00	0.26	0.17	0.09	0.06
Function of δ and	1.10	0.29	0.20	0.11	0.07
Significance Level	1.20	0.33	0.22	0.13	0.08
(α) (Source: The	1.30	0.37	0.26	0.15	0.10
entries in this table	1.40	0.40	0.29	0.18	0.12
were computed by	1.50	0.44	0.32	0.20	0.14
the author.)	1.60	0.48	0.36	0.23	0.17
	1.70	0.52	0.40	0.27	0.19
	1.80	0.56	0.44	0.30	0.22
	1.90	0.60	0.48	0.34	0.25
	2.00	0.64	0.52	0.37	0.28
	2.10	0.68	0.56	0.41	0.32
	2.20	0.71	0.60	0.45	0.35
	2.30	0.74	0.63	0.49	0.39
	2.40	0.78	0.67	0.53	0.43
	2.50	0.80	0.71	0.57	0.47
	2.60	0.83	0.74	0.61	0.51
	2.70	0.85	0.77	0.65	0.55
	2.80	0.88	0.80	0.68	0.59
	2.90	0.90	0.83	0.72	0.63
	3.00	0.91	0.85	0.75	0.66
	3.10	0.93	0.87	0.78	0.70
	3.20	0.94	0.89	0.81	0.73
	3.30	0.95	0.91	0.84	0.77
	3.40	0.96	0.93	0.86	0.80
	3.50	0.97	0.94	0.88	0.82
	3.60	0.98	0.95	0.90	0.85
	3.70	0.98	0.96	0.92	0.87
	3.80	0.98	0.97	0.93	0.89
	3.90	0.99	0.97	0.94	0.91
	4.00	0.99	0.98	0.95	0.92
	4.10	0.99	0.98	0.96	0.94
	4.20	...	0.99	0.97	0.95
	4.30	...	0.99	0.98	0.96
	4.40	...	0.99	0.98	0.97
	4.50	...	0.99	0.99	0.97
	4.60	...	...	0.99	0.98
	4.70	...	...	0.99	0.98
	4.80	...	...	0.99	0.99
	4.90	...	...	...	0.99
	5.00	...	...	...	0.99

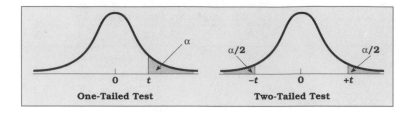

One-Tailed Test   Two-Tailed Test

Table D.6   Percentage Points of the *t* Distribution (Source: The entries in this table were computed by the author.)

df	Level of Significance for One-Tailed Test								
	.25	.20	.15	.10	.05	.025	.01	.005	.0005
	Level of Significance for Two-Tailed Test								
	.50	.40	.30	.20	.10	.05	.02	.01	.001
1	1.000	1.376	1.963	3.078	6.314	12.706	31.821	63.657	63.662
2	0.816	1.061	1.386	1.886	2.920	4.303	6.965	9.925	31.599
3	0.765	0.978	1.250	1.638	2.353	3.182	4.541	5.841	12.924
4	0.741	0.941	1.190	1.533	2.132	2.776	3.747	4.604	8.610
5	0.727	0.920	1.156	1.476	2.015	2.571	3.365	4.032	6.869
6	0.718	0.906	1.134	1.440	1.943	2.447	3.143	3.707	5.959
7	0.711	0.896	1.119	1.415	1.895	2.365	2.998	3.499	5.408
8	0.706	0.889	1.108	1.397	1.860	2.306	2.896	3.355	5.041
9	0.703	0.883	1.100	1.383	1.833	2.262	2.821	3.250	4.781
10	0.700	0.879	1.093	1.372	1.812	2.228	2.764	3.169	4.587
11	0.697	0.876	1.088	1.363	1.796	2.201	2.718	3.106	4.437
12	0.695	0.873	1.083	1.356	1.782	2.179	2.681	3.055	4.318
13	0.694	0.870	1.079	1.350	1.771	2.160	2.650	3.012	4.221
14	0.692	0.868	1.076	1.345	1.761	2.145	2.624	2.977	4.140
15	0.691	0.866	1.074	1.341	1.753	2.131	2.602	2.947	4.073
16	0.690	0.865	1.071	1.337	1.746	2.120	2.583	2.921	4.015
17	0.689	0.863	1.069	1.333	1.740	2.110	2.567	2.898	3.965
18	0.688	0.862	1.067	1.330	1.734	2.101	2.552	2.878	3.922
19	0.688	0.861	1.066	1.328	1.729	2.093	2.539	2.861	3.883
20	0.687	0.860	1.064	1.325	1.725	2.086	2.528	2.845	3.850
21	0.686	0.859	1.063	1.323	1.721	2.080	2.518	2.831	3.819
22	0.686	0.858	1.061	1.321	1.717	2.074	2.508	2.819	3.792
23	0.685	0.858	1.060	1.319	1.714	2.069	2.500	2.807	3.768
24	0.685	0.857	1.059	1.318	1.711	2.064	2.492	2.797	3.745
25	0.684	0.856	1.058	1.316	1.708	2.060	2.485	2.787	3.725
26	0.684	0.856	1.058	1.315	1.706	2.056	2.479	2.779	3.707
27	0.684	0.855	1.057	1.314	1.703	2.052	2.473	2.771	3.690
28	0.683	0.855	1.056	1.313	1.701	2.048	2.467	2.763	3.674
29	0.683	0.854	1.055	1.311	1.699	2.045	2.462	2.756	3.659
30	0.683	0.854	1.055	1.310	1.697	2.042	2.457	2.750	3.646
40	0.681	0.851	1.050	1.303	1.684	2.021	2.423	2.704	3.551
50	0.679	0.849	1.047	1.299	1.676	2.009	2.403	2.678	3.496
100	0.677	0.845	1.042	1.290	1.660	1.984	2.364	2.626	3.390
∞	0.674	0.842	1.036	1.282	1.645	1.960	2.326	2.576	3.291

Table D.7 Critical Lower-Tail Values of T (and Their Associated Probabilities) for Wilcoxon's Matched-Pairs Signed-Ranks Test (Source: The entries in this table were computed by the author.)

	Nominal Alpha (One-Tailed)						Nominal Alpha (One-Tailed)			
	.05	**.025**	**.01**	**.005**		**.05**	**.025**	**.01**	**.005**
n	T α	T α	T α	T α	**n**	T α	T α	T α	T α
5	0 .0313				**28**	130 .0496	116 .0239	101 .0096	91 .0048
	1 .0625					131 .0521	117 .0252	102 .0102	92 .0051
6	2 .0469	0 .0156			**29**	140 .0482	126 .0240	110 .0095	100 .0049
	3 .0781	1 .0313				141 .0504	127 .0253	111 .0101	101 .0053
7	3 .0391	2 .0234	0 .0078		**30**	151 .0481	137 .0249	120 .0098	109 .0050
	4 .0547	3 .0391	1 .0156			152 .0502	138 .0261	121 .0104	110 .0053
8	5 .0391	3 .0195	1 .0078	0 .0039	**31**	163 .0491	147 .0239	130 .0099	118 .0049
	6 .0547	4 .0273	2 .0117	1 .0078		164 .0512	148 .0251	131 .0105	119 .0052
9	8 .0488	5 .0195	3 .0098	1 .0039	**32**	175 .0492	159 .0249	140 .0097	128 .0050
	9 .0645	6 .0273	4 .0137	2 .0059		176 .0512	160 .0260	141 .0103	129 .0053
10	10 .0420	8 .0244	5 .0098	3 .0049	**33**	187 .0485	170 .0242	151 .0099	138 .0049
	11 .0527	9 .0322	6 .0137	4 .0068		188 .0503	171 .0253	152 .0104	139 .0052
11	13 .0415	10 .0210	7 .0093	5 .0049	**34**	200 .0488	182 .0242	162 .0098	148 .0048
	14 .0508	11 .0269	8 .0122	6 .0068		201 .0506	183 .0252	163 .0103	149 .0051
12	17 .0461	13 .0212	9 .0081	7 .0046	**35**	213 .0484	195 .0247	173 .0096	159 .0048
	18 .0549	14 .0261	10 .0105	8 .0061		214 .0501	196 .0257	174 .0100	160 .0051
13	21 .0471	17 .0239	12 .0085	9 .0040	**36**	227 .0489	208 .0248	185 .0096	171 .0050
	22 .0549	18 .0287	13 .0107	10 .0052		228 .0505	209 .0258	186 .0100	172 .0052
14	25 .0453	21 .0247	15 .0083	12 .0043	**37**	241 .0487	221 .0245	198 .0099	182 .0048
	26 .0520	22 .0290	16 .0101	13 .0054		242 .0503	222 .0254	199 .0103	183 .0050
15	30 .0473	25 .0240	19 .0090	15 .0042	**38**	256 .0493	235 .0247	211 .0099	194 .0048
	31 .0535	26 .0277	20 .0108	16 .0051		257 .0509	236 .0256	212 .0104	195 .0050
16	35 .0467	29 .0222	23 .0091	19 .0046	**39**	271 .0492	249 .0246	224 .0099	207 .0049
	36 .0523	30 .0253	24 .0107	20 .0055		272 .0507	250 .0254	225 .0103	208 .0051
17	41 .0492	34 .0224	27 .0087	23 .0047	**40**	286 .0486	264 .0249	238 .0100	220 .0049
	42 .0544	35 .0253	28 .0101	24 .0055		287 .0500	265 .0257	239 .0104	221 .0051
18	47 .0494	40 .0241	32 .0091	27 .0045	**41**	302 .0488	279 .0248	252 .0100	233 .0048
	48 .0542	41 .0269	33 .0104	28 .0052		303 .0501	280 .0256	253 .0103	234 .0050
19	53 .0478	46 .0247	37 .0090	32 .0047	**42**	319 .0496	294 .0245	266 .0098	247 .0049
	54 .0521	47 .0273	38 .0102	33 .0054		320 .0509	295 .0252	267 .0102	248 .0051
20	60 .0487	52 .0242	43 .0096	37 .0047	**43**	336 .0498	310 .0245	281 .0098	261 .0048
	61 .0527	53 .0266	44 .0107	38 .0053		337 .0511	311 .0252	282 .0102	262 .0050
21	67 .0479	58 .0230	49 .0097	42 .0045	**44**	353 .0495	327 .0250	296 .0097	276 .0049
	68 .0516	59 .0251	50 .0108	43 .0051		354 .0507	328 .0257	297 .0101	277 .0051
22	75 .0492	65 .0231	55 .0095	48 .0046	**45**	371 .0498	343 .0244	312 .0098	291 .0049
	76 .0527	66 .0250	56 .0104	49 .0052		372 .0510	344 .0251	313 .0101	292 .0051
23	83 .0490	73 .0242	62 .0098	54 .0046	**46**	389 .0497	361 .0249	328 .0098	307 .0050
	84 .0523	74 .0261	63 .0107	55 .0051		390 .0508	362 .0256	329 .0101	308 .0052
24	91 .0475	81 .0245	69 .0097	61 .0048	**47**	407 .0490	378 .0245	345 .0099	322 .0048
	92 .0505	82 .0263	70 .0106	62 .0053		408 .0501	379 .0251	346 .0102	323 .0050
25	100 .0479	89 .0241	76 .0094	68 .0048	**48**	426 .0490	396 .0244	362 .0099	339 .0050
	101 .0507	90 .0258	77 .0101	69 .0053		427 .0500	397 .0251	363 .0102	340 .0051
26	110 .0497	98 .0247	84 .0095	75 .0047	**49**	446 .0495	415 .0247	379 .0098	355 .0049
	111 .0524	99 .0263	85 .0102	76 .0051		447 .0505	416 .0253	380 .0100	356 .0050
27	119 .0477	107 .0246	92 .0093	83 .0048	**50**	466 .0495	434 .0247	397 .0098	373 .0050
	120 .0502	108 .0260	93 .0100	84 .0052		467 .0506	435 .0253	398 .0101	374 .0051

Table D.8 Critical Lower-Tail Values of W_s for the Mann-Whitney Test for Two Independent Samples ($N_1 \leq N_2$)

(Source: Table 1 in L. R. Verdooren, Extended tables of critical values for Wilcoxon's test statistic, *Biometrika*, 1963, **50,** 177–186, with permission of the author and editor.)

$n_1 = 1$

n_2	0.001	0.005	0.010	0.025	0.05	0.10	$2\overline{W}$
2							4
3							5
4							6
5							7
6							8
7							9
8						⋮	10
9						1	11
10						1	12
11						1	13
12						1	14
13						1	15
14						1	16
15						1	17
16						1	18
17						1	19
18					⋮	1	20
19					1	2	21
20					1	2	22
21					1	2	23
22					1	2	24
23					1	2	25
24					1	2	26
25	⋮	⋮	⋮	⋮	1	2	27

$n_1 = 2$

0.001	0.005	0.010	0.025	0.05	0.10	$2\overline{W}$	n_2
					⋮	10	2
					3	12	3
				⋮	3	14	4
				3	4	16	5
				3	4	18	6
			⋮	3	4	20	7
			3	4	5	22	8
			3	4	5	24	9
			3	4	6	26	10
			3	4	6	28	11
		⋮	4	5	7	30	12
		3	4	5	7	32	13
		3	4	6	8	34	14
		3	4	6	8	36	15
		3	4	6	8	38	16
		3	5	6	9	40	17
	⋮	3	5	7	9	42	18
	3	4	5	7	10	44	19
	3	4	5	7	10	46	20
	3	4	6	8	11	48	21
	3	4	6	8	11	50	22
	3	4	6	8	12	52	23
	3	4	6	9	12	54	24
⋮	3	4	6	9	12	56	25

$n_1 = 3$

n_2	0.001	0.005	0.010	0.025	0.05	0.10	$2\overline{W}$
3					6	7	21
4				⋮	6	7	24
5				6	7	8	27
6			⋮	7	8	9	30
7			6	7	8	10	33
8		⋮	6	8	9	11	36
9		6	7	8	10	11	39
10		6	7	9	10	12	42
11		6	7	9	11	13	45
12		7	8	10	11	14	48
13		7	8	10	12	15	51
14		7	8	11	13	16	54
15		8	9	11	13	16	57
16	⋮	8	9	12	14	17	60
17	6	8	10	12	15	18	63
18	6	8	10	13	15	19	66
19	6	9	10	13	16	20	69
20	6	9	11	14	17	21	72
21	7	9	11	14	17	21	75
22	7	10	12	15	18	22	78
23	7	10	12	15	19	23	81
24	7	10	12	16	19	24	84
25	7	11	13	16	20	25	87

$n_1 = 4$

0.001	0.005	0.010	0.025	0.05	0.10	$2\overline{W}$	n_2
		⋮	10	11	13	36	4
	⋮	10	11	12	14	40	5
	10	11	12	13	15	44	6
	10	11	13	14	16	48	7
	11	12	14	15	17	52	8
⋮	11	13	14	16	19	56	9
10	12	13	15	17	20	60	10
10	12	14	16	18	21	64	11
10	13	15	17	19	22	68	12
11	13	15	18	20	23	72	13
11	14	16	19	21	25	76	14
11	15	17	20	22	26	80	15
12	15	17	21	24	27	84	16
12	16	18	21	25	28	88	17
13	16	19	22	26	30	92	18
13	17	19	23	27	31	96	19
13	18	20	24	28	32	100	20
14	18	21	25	29	33	104	21
14	19	21	26	30	35	108	22
14	19	22	27	31	36	112	23
15	20	23	27	32	38	116	24
15	20	23	28	33	38	120	25

Table D.8 Continued

$n_1 = 5$ and $n_1 = 6$

n_2	0.001	0.005	0.010	0.025	0.05	0.10	$2\bar{W}$	0.001	0.005	0.010	0.025	0.05	0.10	$2\bar{W}$	n_2
5		15	16	17	19	20	55								
6		16	17	18	20	22	60	...	23	24	26	28	30	78	6
7	...	16	18	20	21	23	65	21	24	25	27	29	32	84	7
8	15	17	19	21	23	25	70	22	25	27	29	31	34	90	8
9	16	18	20	22	24	27	75	23	26	28	31	33	36	96	9
10	16	19	21	23	26	28	80	24	27	29	32	35	38	102	10
11	17	20	22	24	27	30	85	25	28	30	34	37	40	108	11
12	17	21	23	26	28	32	90	25	30	32	35	38	42	114	12
13	18	22	24	27	30	33	95	26	31	33	37	40	44	120	13
14	18	22	25	28	31	35	100	27	32	34	38	42	46	126	14
15	19	23	26	29	33	37	105	28	33	36	40	44	48	132	15
16	20	24	27	30	34	38	110	29	34	37	42	46	50	138	16
17	20	25	28	32	35	40	115	30	36	39	43	47	52	144	17
18	21	26	29	33	37	42	120	31	37	40	45	49	55	150	18
19	22	27	30	34	38	43	125	32	38	41	46	51	57	156	19
20	22	28	31	35	40	45	130	33	39	43	48	53	59	162	20
21	23	29	32	37	41	47	135	33	40	44	50	55	61	168	21
22	23	29	33	38	43	48	140	34	42	45	51	57	63	174	22
23	24	30	34	39	44	50	145	35	43	47	53	58	65	180	23
24	25	31	35	40	45	51	150	36	44	48	54	60	67	186	24
25	25	32	36	42	47	53	155	37	45	50	56	62	69	192	25

$n_1 = 7$ and $n_1 = 8$

n_2	0.001	0.005	0.010	0.025	0.05	0.10	$2\bar{W}$	0.001	0.005	0.010	0.025	0.05	0.10	$2\bar{W}$	n_2
7	29	32	34	36	39	41	105								
8	30	34	35	38	41	44	112	40	43	45	49	51	55	136	8
9	31	35	37	40	43	46	119	41	45	47	51	54	58	144	9
10	33	37	39	42	45	49	126	42	47	49	53	56	60	152	10
11	34	38	40	44	47	51	133	44	49	51	55	59	63	160	11
12	35	40	42	46	49	54	140	45	51	53	58	62	66	168	12
13	36	41	44	48	52	56	147	47	53	56	60	64	69	176	13
14	37	43	45	50	54	59	154	48	54	58	62	67	72	184	14
15	38	44	47	52	56	61	161	50	56	60	65	69	75	192	15
16	39	46	49	54	58	64	168	51	58	62	67	72	78	200	16
17	41	47	51	56	61	66	175	53	60	64	70	75	81	208	17
18	42	49	52	58	63	69	182	54	62	66	72	77	84	216	18
19	43	50	54	60	65	71	189	56	64	68	74	80	87	224	19
20	44	52	56	62	67	74	196	57	66	70	77	83	90	232	20
21	46	53	58	64	69	76	203	59	68	72	79	85	92	240	21
22	47	55	59	66	72	79	210	60	70	74	81	88	95	248	22
23	48	57	61	68	74	81	217	62	71	76	84	90	98	256	23
24	49	58	63	70	76	84	224	64	73	78	86	93	101	264	24
25	50	60	64	72	78	86	231	65	75	81	89	96	104	272	25

$n_1 = 9$ and $n_1 = 10$

n_2	0.001	0.005	0.010	0.025	0.05	0.10	$2\bar{W}$	0.001	0.005	0.010	0.025	0.05	0.10	$2\bar{W}$	n_2
9	52	56	59	62	66	70	171								
10	53	58	61	65	69	73	180	65	71	74	78	82	87	210	10
11	55	61	63	68	72	76	189	67	73	77	81	86	91	220	11
12	57	63	66	71	75	80	198	69	76	79	84	89	94	230	12

continued

Table D.8   Continued

			$n_1 = 9$								$n_1 = 10$					
n_2	0.001	0.005	0.010	0.025	0.05	0.10	$2\overline{W}$	0.001	0.005	0.010	0.025	0.05	0.10	$2\overline{W}$	n_2
13	59	65	68	73	78	83	207	72	79	82	88	92	98	240	13
14	60	67	71	76	81	86	216	74	81	85	91	96	102	250	14
15	62	69	73	79	84	90	225	76	84	88	94	99	106	260	15
16	64	72	76	82	87	93	234	78	86	91	97	103	109	270	16
17	66	74	78	84	90	97	243	80	89	93	100	106	113	280	17
18	68	76	81	87	93	100	252	82	92	96	103	110	117	290	18
19	70	78	83	90	96	103	261	84	94	99	107	113	121	300	19
20	71	81	85	93	99	107	270	87	97	102	110	117	125	310	20
21	73	83	88	95	102	110	279	89	99	105	113	120	128	320	21
22	75	85	90	98	105	113	288	91	102	108	116	123	132	330	22
23	77	88	93	101	108	117	297	93	105	110	119	127	136	340	23
24	79	90	95	104	111	120	306	95	107	113	122	130	140	350	24
25	81	92	98	107	114	123	315	98	110	116	126	134	144	360	25

			$n_1 = 11$								$n_1 = 12$					
n_2	0.001	0.005	0.010	0.025	0.05	0.10	$2\overline{W}$	0.001	0.005	0.010	0.025	0.05	0.10	$2\overline{W}$	n_2
11	81	87	91	96	100	106	253								11
12	83	90	94	99	104	110	264	98	105	109	115	120	127	300	12
13	86	93	97	103	108	114	275	101	109	113	119	125	131	312	13
14	88	96	100	106	112	118	286	103	112	116	123	129	136	324	14
15	90	99	103	110	116	123	297	106	115	120	127	133	141	336	15
16	93	102	107	113	120	127	308	109	119	124	131	138	145	348	16
17	95	105	110	117	123	131	319	112	122	127	135	142	150	360	17
18	98	108	113	121	127	135	330	115	125	131	139	146	155	372	18
19	100	111	116	124	131	139	341	118	129	134	143	150	159	384	19
20	103	114	119	128	135	144	352	120	132	138	147	155	164	396	20
21	106	117	123	131	139	148	363	123	136	142	151	159	169	408	21
22	108	120	126	135	143	152	374	126	139	145	155	163	173	420	22
23	111	123	129	139	147	156	385	129	142	149	159	168	178	432	23
24	113	126	132	142	151	161	396	132	146	153	163	172	183	444	24
25	116	129	136	146	155	165	407	135	149	156	167	176	187	456	25

			$n_1 = 13$								$n_1 = 14$					
n_2	0.001	0.005	0.010	0.025	0.05	0.10	$2\overline{W}$	0.001	0.005	0.010	0.025	0.05	0.10	$2\overline{W}$	n_2
13	117	125	130	136	142	149	351								13
14	120	129	134	141	147	154	364	137	147	152	160	166	174	406	14
15	123	133	138	145	152	159	377	141	151	156	164	171	179	420	15
16	126	136	142	150	156	165	390	144	155	161	169	176	185	434	16
17	129	140	146	154	161	170	403	148	159	165	174	182	190	448	17
18	133	144	150	158	166	175	416	151	163	170	179	187	196	462	18
19	136	148	154	163	171	180	429	155	168	174	183	192	202	476	19
20	139	151	158	167	175	185	442	159	172	178	188	197	207	490	20
21	142	155	162	171	180	190	455	162	176	183	193	202	213	504	21
22	145	159	166	176	185	195	468	166	180	187	198	207	218	518	22
23	149	163	170	180	189	200	481	169	184	192	203	212	224	532	23
24	152	166	174	185	194	205	494	173	188	196	207	218	229	546	24
25	155	170	178	189	199	211	507	177	192	200	212	223	235	560	25

Table D.8 Continued

n_2				$n_1 = 15$								$n_1 = 16$			
	0.001	0.005	0.010	0.025	0.05	0.10	$2\overline{W}$	0.001	0.005	0.010	0.025	0.05	0.10	$2\overline{W}$	n_2
15	160	171	176	184	192	200	465								
16	163	175	181	190	197	206	480	184	196	202	211	219	229	528	16
17	167	180	186	195	203	212	495	188	201	207	217	225	235	544	17
18	171	184	190	200	208	218	510	192	206	212	222	231	242	560	18
19	175	189	195	205	214	224	525	196	210	218	228	237	248	576	19
20	179	193	200	210	220	230	540	201	215	223	234	243	255	592	20
21	183	198	205	216	225	236	555	205	220	228	239	249	261	608	21
22	187	202	210	221	231	242	570	209	225	233	245	255	267	624	22
23	191	207	214	226	236	248	585	214	230	238	251	261	274	640	23
24	195	211	219	231	242	254	600	218	235	244	256	267	280	656	24
25	199	216	224	237	248	260	615	222	240	249	262	273	287	672	25

n_2				$n_1 = 17$								$n_1 = 18$			
	0.001	0.005	0.010	0.025	0.05	0.10	$2\overline{W}$	0.001	0.005	0.010	0.025	0.05	0.10	$2\overline{W}$	n_2
17	210	223	230	240	249	259	595								
18	214	228	235	246	255	266	612	237	252	259	270	280	291	666	18
19	219	234	241	252	262	273	629	242	258	265	277	287	299	684	19
20	223	239	246	258	268	280	646	247	263	271	283	294	306	702	20
21	228	244	252	264	274	287	663	252	269	277	290	301	313	720	21
22	233	249	258	270	281	294	680	257	275	283	296	307	321	738	22
23	238	255	263	276	287	300	697	262	280	289	303	314	328	756	23
24	242	260	269	282	294	307	714	267	286	295	309	321	335	774	24
25	247	265	275	288	300	314	731	273	292	301	316	328	343	792	25

n_2				$n_1 = 19$								$n_1 = 20$			
	0.001	0.005	0.010	0.025	0.05	0.10	$2\overline{W}$	0.001	0.005	0.010	0.025	0.05	0.10	$2\overline{W}$	n_2
19	267	283	291	303	313	325	741								
20	272	289	297	309	320	333	760	298	315	324	337	348	361	820	20
21	277	295	303	316	328	341	779	304	322	331	344	356	370	840	21
22	283	301	310	323	335	349	798	309	328	337	351	364	378	860	22
23	288	307	316	330	342	357	817	315	335	344	359	371	386	880	23
24	294	313	323	337	350	364	836	321	341	351	366	379	394	900	24
25	299	319	329	344	357	372	855	327	348	358	373	387	403	920	25

n_2				$n_1 = 21$								$n_1 = 22$			
	0.001	0.005	0.010	0.025	0.05	0.10	$2\overline{W}$	0.001	0.005	0.010	0.025	0.05	0.10	$2\overline{W}$	n_2
21	331	349	359	373	385	399	903								
22	337	356	366	381	393	408	924	365	386	396	411	424	439	990	22
23	343	363	373	388	401	417	945	372	393	403	419	432	448	1012	23
24	349	370	381	396	410	425	966	379	400	411	427	441	457	1034	24
25	356	377	388	404	418	434	987	385	408	419	435	450	467	1056	25

n_2				$n_1 = 23$								$n_1 = 24$			
	0.001	0.005	0.010	0.025	0.05	0.10	$2\overline{W}$	0.001	0.005	0.010	0.025	0.05	0.10	$2\overline{W}$	n_2
23	402	424	434	451	465	481	1081								
24	409	431	443	459	474	491	1104	440	464	475	492	507	525	1176	24
25	416	439	451	468	483	500	1127	448	472	484	501	517	535	1200	25

n_2				$n_1 = 25$				
	0.001	0.005	0.010	0.025	0.05	0.10	$2\overline{W}$	
25	480	505	517	536	552	570	1275	

Table D.9   **Table of Uniform Random Numbers** (Source: The entries in this table were computed by the author.)

68204	38787	73304	44886	92836	43877	61049	49249	66105
61010	78345	75444	91680	33003	24128	97817	77562	62045
04604	93468	78459	27541	19672	14220	25102	42021	19252
36021	25507	64060	72923	58848	10374	63102	41534	92884
28129	43470	94097	16753	56425	75299	93688	75569	52067
09406	06584	46324	13981	06449	42604	13372	69040	95955
86423	81835	64226	20398	65772	91052	73496	14451	95967
13249	58525	81893	32894	68627	75644	45848	61511	90232
75454	17352	56548	39618	86705	50783	48388	82047	14660
06260	46176	99237	69874	84180	32005	66130	18055	99748
38507	92795	80672	00102	22980	69115	95653	05231	94996
03917	26795	59832	19014	96206	45413	76624	71219	65855
17927	32368	08177	31236	45401	26731	92256	99530	43998
26811	88937	37187	39762	29942	40091	65731	95955	23368
18480	28160	81908	30456	22462	15677	55642	67383	86884
37589	91842	76351	90585	45588	42858	37806	67969	50621
79903	34187	26952	75820	96335	90281	04269	85202	94965
46155	30200	75000	28570	47516	06744	72193	01258	85047
60916	73212	15853	28398	04721	69363	47071	65568	88519
34419	82840	88235	61966	86517	23966	45764	42177	17269
08692	26667	12941	14813	30815	26633	68184	80721	80505
92851	44185	90848	18341	77915	00177	64014	35490	02937
97909	07280	72167	10002	27374	92880	60055	94168	30742
28437	22027	07739	30905	33151	73567	82960	50104	67005
48165	28174	17909	11230	00929	54604	32435	54120	85199
99891	30913	06315	30201	72073	39589	62868	66339	15850
98022	13010	67970	99203	12536	88149	44387	20250	50798
91292	54688	47029	38970	77880	77295	11887	17628	93802
89081	34643	12988	12971	87742	57720	24438	64088	49496
32527	74239	20056	46668	94561	70111	92537	83562	11306
01870	21584	48574	09871	74453	24812	45770	95667	52377
84011	87542	96564	64256	64653	90025	61613	94168	83254
01568	29682	67489	62984	51901	30716	24513	46678	67991
40360	19206	40321	16004	64481	16130	03904	15811	19369
09392	39926	79590	23991	82492	13032	67337	54322	06058
77323	20500	52466	33008	84211	26357	79006	41178	35169
47590	01007	65376	18189	84040	39476	25383	45398	64917
29321	65783	71403	32894	32627	39067	47985	51485	27415
09530	05358	58722	31912	73356	65884	12883	36242	29646
65612	06843	72233	73352	66600	23237	71759	76881	19652
40355	85067	40788	40148	46099	48056	27858	58365	30202
24963	49571	82377	08687	73448	95484	15155	41780	71951
87273	44050	71961	48464	84084	65225	62846	11634	04853
31643	44756	12493	09024	74204	69949	67842	36141	08477
58326	55342	31419	80776	64028	59957	52969	71997	71477
02327	00460	39178	09511	92688	88585	99257	98752	39623
19377	49122	60591	79773	66289	89650	49298	13499	53623
95046	30203	47493	74395	45213	66739	45097	91670	62152
65013	71958	48360	70885	60313	44241	18740	05705	07488
86032	89018	97117	35656	20401	86438	87250	04717	67726
11799	15777	11548	45918	45706	88554	75315	70233	72575
17843	64809	00390	11980	66129	07197	36712	55062	61191
42770	65397	45010	06463	86242	06361	14293	36343	97628
02410	96933	57864	93197	88227	57139	66382	95768	60660
70939	20457	62468	68698	74875	61111	59083	09152	93625
85616	15100	26242	28677	74655	05679	56676	67224	75318
85515	33174	05496	78789	81297	73985	82120	94070	20529

Table D.9   Continued

73466	06254	88113	98367	22018	99372	70171	52705	61202
72255	50729	05681	37216	09363	02385	93098	09502	92589
08121	48330	86725	52922	90349	81934	14849	68005	06791
94005	85164	22994	58921	85943	67506	79730	85382	61568
09108	52299	25991	00940	22493	60987	93573	79469	97147
85687	31723	67907	55306	71748	85048	17690	04784	98470
26190	02164	95889	89712	89795	73001	82210	39357	23867
34208	07539	60907	60693	01965	43492	46688	28891	23410
13032	78798	21733	35703	71707	11931	93513	78339	74754
16801	05582	47975	25046	59220	08275	67901	94954	36662
88735	91500	41654	97225	61188	24527	35220	99794	56097
82127	17594	94217	55324	06134	25207	26758	08687	06929
29284	42271	45833	19481	56972	99042	45304	39832	40188
56300	60964	13751	72385	91180	42371	55924	95783	33096
33132	33229	39955	16779	99286	23392	24255	90856	60004
65296	94444	32091	90681	95823	73091	92912	85979	30232
11069	52931	26381	71830	50467	47783	25223	81796	97745
06720	69637	99670	58392	57943	75965	14740	74814	75598
62719	14295	16605	13146	36992	50560	50121	90278	98283
95556	36672	87202	92730	81961	38894	61358	44519	71529
12490	12304	28804	42772	27104	35518	67361	84159	52442
29865	28847	70904	96638	54226	44701	67589	27352	81078
74486	63507	92193	65022	09583	43615	59910	05301	69347
01878	56351	68618	84432	30948	65180	75446	95963	75619
65405	25720	09364	51333	03752	65756	51967	92469	47296
31711	35173	45290	49326	50368	63829	05640	26675	27367
41028	50367	01904	68068	02324	58723	96333	77032	47878
76916	55336	48767	76915	79711	05182	70489	10244	45078
16404	93068	91519	85895	34872	24701	60932	91141	33252
06776	51133	76482	14812	19777	19614	51100	52943	04068
76818	05839	26058	80972	43337	24203	72345	37967	88138
16916	64028	38968	02783	63049	12261	89587	88988	88834
33696	41621	16648	11837	08094	38217	32919	16625	91567
00143	56431	90537	95332	29879	29363	48055	86410	10594
15932	59628	00086	74633	81208	05470	56385	23601	70545
86111	14530	39958	36155	60613	73849	74842	31030	30448
46218	36313	62063	59326	93522	48983	50335	30178	42755
84153	32199	77166	63912	07984	55369	56520	14633	00252
81439	35471	29742	57110	13710	21351	29816	32783	69004
92339	82043	80136	97269	28858	03036	01304	51363	40412
78421	33809	92792	96106	95191	43514	08320	25690	76117
44265	86707	80637	44879	81457	06781	11411	88804	62551
89430	51314	76126	62672	31815	12947	76533	19761	93373
36462	19901	02919	29311	31275	83593	34933	95758	63944
55996	59605	51680	27755	06077	12797	67082	12536	64069
69338	43838	06320	63988	16549	27931	27270	94711	47834
40276	17751	72508	23027	70257	42812	87319	09160	02913
67834	93014	07816	93085	14552	10115	87740	44125	51227

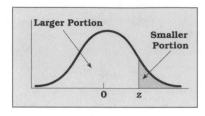

Table D.10   The Normal Distribution (z) (Source: The entries in this table were computed by the author.)

z	Mean to z	Larger Portion	Smaller Portion	z	Mean to z	Larger Portion	Smaller Portion
.00	0.0000	0.5000	0.5000	.40	0.1554	0.6554	0.3446
.01	0.0040	0.5040	0.4960	.41	0.1591	0.6591	0.3409
.02	0.0080	0.5080	0.4920	.42	0.1628	0.6628	0.3372
.03	0.0120	0.5120	0.4880	.43	0.1664	0.6664	0.3336
.04	0.0160	0.5160	0.4840	.44	0.1700	0.6700	0.3300
.05	0.0199	0.5199	0.4801	.45	0.1736	0.6736	0.3264
.06	0.0239	0.5239	0.4761	.46	0.1772	0.6772	0.3228
.07	0.0279	0.5279	0.4721	.47	0.1808	0.6808	0.3192
.08	0.0319	0.5319	0.4681	.48	0.1844	0.6844	0.3156
.09	0.0359	0.5359	0.4641	.49	0.1879	0.6879	0.3121
.10	0.0398	0.5398	0.4602	.50	0.1915	0.6915	0.3085
.11	0.0438	0.5438	0.4562	.51	0.1950	0.6950	0.3050
.12	0.0478	0.5478	0.4522	.52	0.1985	0.6985	0.3015
.13	0.0517	0.5517	0.4483	.53	0.2019	0.7019	0.2981
.14	0.0557	0.5557	0.4443	.54	0.2054	0.7054	0.2946
.15	0.0596	0.5596	0.4404	.55	0.2088	0.7088	0.2912
.16	0.0636	0.5636	0.4364	.56	0.2123	0.7123	0.2877
.17	0.0675	0.5675	0.4325	.57	0.2157	0.7157	0.2843
.18	0.0714	0.5714	0.4286	.58	0.2190	0.7190	0.2810
.19	0.0753	0.5753	0.4247	.59	0.2224	0.7224	0.2776
.20	0.0793	0.5793	0.4207	.60	0.2257	0.7257	0.2743
.21	0.0832	0.5832	0.4168	.61	0.2291	0.7291	0.2709
.22	0.0871	0.5871	0.4129	.62	0.2324	0.7324	0.2676
.23	0.0910	0.5910	0.4090	.63	0.2357	0.7357	0.2643
.24	0.0948	0.5948	0.4052	.64	0.2389	0.7389	0.2611
.25	0.0987	0.5987	0.4013	.65	0.2422	0.7422	0.2578
.26	0.1026	0.6026	0.3974	.66	0.2454	0.7454	0.2546
.27	0.1064	0.6064	0.3936	.67	0.2486	0.7486	0.2514
.28	0.1103	0.6103	0.3897	.68	0.2517	0.7517	0.2483
.29	0.1141	0.6141	0.3859	.69	0.2549	0.7549	0.2451
.30	0.1179	0.6179	0.3821	.70	0.2580	0.7580	0.2420
.31	0.1217	0.6217	0.3783	.71	0.2611	0.7611	0.2389
.32	0.1255	0.6255	0.3745	.72	0.2642	0.7642	0.2358
.33	0.1293	0.6293	0.3707	.73	0.2673	0.7673	0.2327
.34	0.1331	0.6331	0.3669	.74	0.2704	0.7704	0.2296
.35	0.1368	0.6368	0.3632	.75	0.2734	0.7734	0.2266
.36	0.1406	0.6406	0.3594	.76	0.2764	0.7764	0.2236
.37	0.1443	0.6443	0.3557	.77	0.2794	0.7794	0.2206
.38	0.1480	0.6480	0.3520	.78	0.2823	0.7823	0.2177
.39	0.1517	0.6517	0.3483	.79	0.2852	0.7852	0.2148

Table D.10   Continued

z	Mean to z	Larger Portion	Smaller Portion	z	Mean to z	Larger Portion	Smaller Portion
.80	0.2881	0.7881	0.2119	1.29	0.4015	0.9015	0.0985
.81	0.2910	0.7910	0.2090	1.30	0.4032	0.9032	0.0968
.82	0.2939	0.7939	0.2061	1.31	0.4049	0.9049	0.0951
.83	0.2967	0.7967	0.2033	1.32	0.4066	0.9066	0.0934
.84	0.2995	0.7995	0.2005	1.33	0.4082	0.9082	0.0918
.85	0.3023	0.8023	0.1977	1.34	0.4099	0.9099	0.0901
.86	0.3051	0.8051	0.1949	1.35	0.4115	0.9115	0.0885
.87	0.3078	0.8078	0.1922	1.36	0.4131	0.9131	0.0869
.88	0.3106	0.8106	0.1894	1.37	0.4147	0.9147	0.0853
.89	0.3133	0.8133	0.1867	1.38	0.4162	0.9162	0.0838
.90	0.3159	0.8159	0.1841	1.39	0.4177	0.9177	0.0823
.91	0.3186	0.8186	0.1814	1.40	0.4192	0.9192	0.0808
.92	0.3212	0.8212	0.1788	1.41	0.4207	0.9207	0.0793
.93	0.3238	0.8238	0.1762	1.42	0.4222	0.9222	0.0778
.94	0.3264	0.8264	0.1736	1.43	0.4236	0.9236	0.0764
.95	0.3289	0.8289	0.1711	1.44	0.4251	0.9251	0.0749
.96	0.3315	0.8315	0.1685	1.45	0.4265	0.9265	0.0735
.97	0.3340	0.8340	0.1660	1.46	0.4279	0.9279	0.0721
.98	0.3365	0.8365	0.1635	1.47	0.4292	0.9292	0.0708
.99	0.3389	0.8389	0.1611	1.48	0.4306	0.9306	0.0694
1.00	0.3413	0.8413	0.1587	1.49	0.4319	0.9319	0.0681
1.01	0.3438	0.8438	0.1562	1.50	0.4332	0.9332	0.0668
1.02	0.3461	0.8461	0.1539	1.51	0.4345	0.9345	0.0655
1.03	0.3485	0.8485	0.1515	1.52	0.4357	0.9357	0.0643
1.04	0.3508	0.8508	0.1492	1.53	0.4370	0.9370	0.0630
1.05	0.3531	0.8531	0.1469	1.54	0.4382	0.9382	0.0618
1.06	0.3554	0.8554	0.1446	1.55	0.4394	0.9394	0.0606
1.07	0.3577	0.8577	0.1423	1.56	0.4406	0.9406	0.0594
1.08	0.3599	0.8599	0.1401	1.57	0.4418	0.9418	0.0582
1.09	0.3621	0.8621	0.1379	1.58	0.4429	0.9429	0.0571
1.10	0.3643	0.8643	0.1357	1.59	0.4441	0.9441	0.0559
1.11	0.3665	0.8665	0.1335	1.60	0.4452	0.9452	0.0548
1.12	0.3686	0.8686	0.1314	1.61	0.4463	0.9463	0.0537
1.13	0.3708	0.8708	0.1292	1.62	0.4474	0.9474	0.0526
1.14	0.3729	0.8729	0.1271	1.63	0.4484	0.9484	0.0516
1.15	0.3749	0.8749	0.1251	1.64	0.4495	0.9495	0.0505
1.16	0.3770	0.8770	0.1230	1.65	0.4505	0.9505	0.0495
1.17	0.3790	0.8790	0.1210	1.66	0.4515	0.9515	0.0485
1.18	0.3810	0.8810	0.1190	1.67	0.4525	0.9525	0.0475
1.19	0.3830	0.8830	0.1170	1.68	0.4535	0.9535	0.0465
1.20	0.3849	0.8849	0.1151	1.69	0.4545	0.9545	0.0455
1.21	0.3869	0.8869	0.1131	1.70	0.4554	0.9554	0.0446
1.22	0.3888	0.8888	0.1112	1.71	0.4564	0.9564	0.0436
1.23	0.3907	0.8907	0.1093	1.72	0.4573	0.9573	0.0427
1.24	0.3925	0.8925	0.1075	1.73	0.4582	0.9582	0.0418
1.25	0.3944	0.8944	0.1056	1.74	0.4591	0.9591	0.0409
1.26	0.3962	0.8962	0.1038	1.75	0.4599	0.9599	0.0401
1.27	0.3980	0.8980	0.1020	1.76	0.4608	0.9608	0.0392
1.28	0.3997	0.8997	0.1003	1.77	0.4616	0.9616	0.0384

continued

Table D.10   Continued

z	Mean to z	Larger Portion	Smaller Portion	z	Mean to z	Larger Portion	Smaller Portion
1.78	0.4625	0.9625	0.0375	2.28	0.4887	0.9887	0.0113
1.79	0.4633	0.9633	0.0367	2.29	0.4890	0.9890	0.0110
1.80	0.4641	0.9641	0.0359	2.30	0.4893	0.9893	0.0107
1.81	0.4649	0.9649	0.0351	2.31	0.4896	0.9896	0.0104
1.82	0.4656	0.9656	0.0344	2.32	0.4898	0.9898	0.0102
1.83	0.4664	0.9664	0.0336	2.33	0.4901	0.9901	0.0099
1.84	0.4671	0.9671	0.0329	2.34	0.4904	0.9904	0.0096
1.85	0.4678	0.9678	0.0322	2.35	0.4906	0.9906	0.0094
1.86	0.4686	0.9686	0.0314	2.36	0.4909	0.9909	0.0091
1.87	0.4693	0.9693	0.0307	2.37	0.4911	0.9911	0.0089
1.88	0.4699	0.9699	0.0301	2.38	0.4913	0.9913	0.0087
1.89	0.4706	0.9706	0.0294	2.39	0.4916	0.9916	0.0084
1.90	0.4713	0.9713	0.0287	2.40	0.4918	0.9918	0.0082
1.91	0.4719	0.9719	0.0281	2.41	0.4920	0.9920	0.0080
1.92	0.4726	0.9726	0.0274	2.42	0.4922	0.9922	0.0078
1.93	0.4732	0.9732	0.0268	2.43	0.4925	0.9925	0.0075
1.94	0.4738	0.9738	0.0262	2.44	0.4927	0.9927	0.0073
1.95	0.4744	0.9744	0.0256	2.45	0.4929	0.9929	0.0071
1.96	0.4750	0.9750	0.0250	2.46	0.4931	0.9931	0.0069
1.97	0.4756	0.9756	0.0244	2.47	0.4932	0.9932	0.0068
1.98	0.4761	0.9761	0.0239	2.48	0.4934	0.9934	0.0066
1.99	0.4767	0.9767	0.0233	2.49	0.4936	0.9936	0.0064
2.00	0.4772	0.9772	0.0228	2.50	0.4938	0.9938	0.0062
2.01	0.4778	0.9778	0.0222	2.51	0.4940	0.9940	0.0060
2.02	0.4783	0.9783	0.0217	2.52	0.4941	0.9941	0.0059
2.03	0.4788	0.9788	0.0212	2.53	0.4943	0.9943	0.0057
2.04	0.4793	0.9793	0.0207	2.54	0.4945	0.9945	0.0055
2.05	0.4798	0.9798	0.0202	2.55	0.4946	0.9946	0.0054
2.06	0.4803	0.9803	0.0197	2.56	0.4948	0.9948	0.0052
2.07	0.4808	0.9808	0.0192	2.57	0.4949	0.9949	0.0051
2.08	0.4812	0.9812	0.0188	2.58	0.4951	0.9951	0.0049
2.09	0.4817	0.9817	0.0183	2.59	0.4952	0.9952	0.0048
2.10	0.4821	0.9821	0.0179	2.60	0.4953	0.9953	0.0047
2.11	0.4826	0.9826	0.0174	2.61	0.4955	0.9955	0.0045
2.12	0.4830	0.9830	0.0170	2.62	0.4956	0.9956	0.0044
2.13	0.4834	0.9834	0.0166	2.63	0.4957	0.9957	0.0043
2.14	0.4838	0.9838	0.0162	2.64	0.4959	0.9959	0.0041
2.15	0.4842	0.9842	0.0158	2.65	0.4960	0.9960	0.0040
2.16	0.4846	0.9846	0.0154	2.66	0.4961	0.9961	0.0039
2.17	0.4850	0.9850	0.0150	2.67	0.4962	0.9962	0.0038
2.18	0.4854	0.9854	0.0146	2.68	0.4963	0.9963	0.0037
2.19	0.4857	0.9857	0.0143	2.69	0.4964	0.9964	0.0036
2.20	0.4861	0.9861	0.0139	2.70	0.4965	0.9965	0.0035
2.21	0.4864	0.9864	0.0136	2.71	0.4966	0.9966	0.0034
2.22	0.4868	0.9868	0.0132	2.72	0.4967	0.9967	0.0033
2.23	0.4871	0.9871	0.0129	2.73	0.4968	0.9968	0.0032
2.24	0.4875	0.9875	0.0125	2.74	0.4969	0.9969	0.0031
2.25	0.4878	0.9878	0.0122	2.75	0.4970	0.9970	0.0030
2.26	0.4881	0.9881	0.0119	2.76	0.4971	0.9971	0.0029
2.27	0.4884	0.9884	0.0116	2.77	0.4972	0.9972	0.0028

Table D.10 Continued

z	Mean to z	Larger Portion	Smaller Portion	z	Mean to z	Larger Portion	Smaller Portion
2.78	0.4973	0.9973	0.0027	2.94	0.4984	0.9984	0.0016
2.79	0.4974	0.9974	0.0026	2.95	0.4984	0.9984	0.0016
2.80	0.4974	0.9974	0.0026	2.96	0.4985	0.9985	0.0015
2.81	0.4975	0.9975	0.0025	2.97	0.4985	0.9985	0.0015
2.82	0.4976	0.9976	0.0024	2.98	0.4986	0.9986	0.0014
2.83	0.4977	0.9977	0.0023	2.99	0.4986	0.9986	0.0014
2.84	0.4977	0.9977	0.0023	3.00	0.4987	0.9987	0.0013
2.85	0.4978	0.9978	0.0022	:	:	:	:
2.86	0.4979	0.9979	0.0021	3.25	0.4994	0.9994	0.0006
2.87	0.4979	0.9979	0.0021	:	:	:	:
2.88	0.4980	0.9980	0.0020	3.50	0.4998	0.9998	0.0002
2.89	0.4981	0.9981	0.0019	:	:	:	:
2.90	0.4981	0.9981	0.0019	3.75	0.4999	0.9999	0.0001
2.91	0.4982	0.9982	0.0018	:	:	:	:
2.92	0.4982	0.9982	0.0018	4.00	0.5000	1.0000	0.0000
2.93	0.4983	0.9983	0.0017				

References

Achenbach, T. M. (1991). *Integrative guide for the 1991 CBCL/4–18, YSR, and TRF profiles.* Burlington, VT: University of Vermont Department of Psychiatry.

Achenbach, T. M., Howell, C. T., Aoki, M. F., & Rauh, V. A. (1993). Nine-year outcome of the Vermont Intervention Program for low birthweight infants. *Pediatrics, 91,* 45–55.

Bahrick, H. P., & Hall, L. K. (1991). Lifetime maintenance of high school mathematics content. *Journal of Experimental Psychology: General, 120,* 20–33.

Berndt, D. J., Schwartz, S., & Kaiser, C. F. (1983). Readability of self-report depression inventories. *Journal of Consulting and Clinical Psychology, 51,* 627–628.

Blanchard, E. B., Theobald, D. E., Williamson, D. A., Silver, B. V., & Brown, D. A. (1978). Temperature biofeedback in the treatment of migraine headaches. *Archives of General Psychiatry, 35,* 581–588.

Bradley, D. R., & Kjungja, L. (1982). Animated subjective contours. *Perception and Psychophysics, 32,* 393–395.

Bradley, J. V. (1963, March). *Studies in research methodology: IV. A sampling study of the Central Limit Theorem and the robustness of one-sample parametric tests.* AMRL Technical Documentary Report 63–29, 650th Aerospace Medical Research Laboratories, Wright-Patterson Air Force Base, OH.

Bradley, J. V. (1968). *Distribution-free statistical tests.* Englewood Cliffs, NJ: Prentice Hall.

Brown, J., Lewis, V., Brown, M., Horn, G., & Bowes, J. B. (1982). A comparison between transient amnesias induced by two drugs (diazepam and lorazepam) and amnesia of organic origin. *Neuropsychologia, 20,* 55–70.

Camilli, G., & Hopkins, K. D. (1978). Applicability of chi-square to 2×2 contingency tables with small expected frequencies. *Psychological Bulletin, 85,* 163–167.

Campbell, A., Converse, P. E., & Rodgers, W. L. (1976). *The quality of American life.* New York: Russell Sage Foundation.

Carli, L. L. (1990). Gender, language, and influence. *Journal of Personality and Social Psychology, 59,* 941–951.

Clark, K. B., & Clark, M. K. (1939). The development of consciousness of self in the emergence of racial identification in Negro pre-school children. *Journal of Social Psychology, 10,* 591–599.

Cochran, C. D., & Urbanczyk, S. (1982). The effect of availability of vertical space on personal space. *Journal of Psychology, 111,* 137–140.

Cochrane, A. I., St. Leger, A. S., & Moore F. (1978). Health service "input" and mortality "output" in developed countries. *Journal of Epidemiology and Community Health, 32,* 200–205.

Cohen, J. (1988). *Statistical power analysis for the behavioral sciences* (2nd ed.). Hillsdale, NJ: Lawrence Erlbaum, Associates.

Cohen, J. (1992). A power primer. *Psychological Bulletin, 112,* 155–159.

Cohen, S., Kaplan, J. R., Cunnick, J. E., Manuck, S. B., & Rabin, B. S. (1992). Chronic social stress, affiliation, and cellular immune response in nonhuman primates. *Psychological Science, 3,* 301–304.

Compas, B. E., Worsham, N. S., Grant, K., Mireault, G., Howell, D. C., & Malcarne, V. L. (1993). When mom or dad has cancer: I. Symptoms of depression and anxiety in cancer patients, spouses, and children. Unpublished manuscript.

Conti, L., & Musty, R. E. (1984). The effects of delta-9-tetrahydrocannabinol injections to the nucleus accumbens on the locomotor activity of rats. In S. Aquell et al. (Eds.), *The cannabinoids: Chemical, pharmacologic, and therapeutic aspects.* New York: Academic Press.

Craik, F. I. M., & Lockhart, R. S. (1972). Levels of processing: A framework for memory research. *Journal of Verbal Learning and Verbal Behavior, 11,* 671–684.

Cummings, K. M., Sciandra, R., Gingrass, A., & Davis, R. (1991). What scientists funded by the tobacco industry believe about the hazards of smoking. *The American Journal of Public Health, 81,* 894–896.

Dabbs, J. M., Jr., & Morris, R. (1990). Testosterone, social class, and antisocial behavior in a sample of 4462 men. *Psychological Science, 1,* 209–211.

Darley, J. M., and Latané, B. (1968). Bystander intervention in emergencies: Diffusion of responsibility. *Journal of Personality and Social Psychology, 8,* 377–383.

Doob, A. N., & Gross, A. E. (1968). Status of frustrator as an inhibitor of horn-honking responses. *Journal of Social Psychology, 76,* 213–218.

Eron, L. D., Huesmann, L. R., Lefkowitz, M. M., & Walden, L. O. (1972). Does television violence cause aggression? *American Psychologist, 27,* 253–263.

Eysenck, M. W. (1974). Age differences in incidental learning. *Developmental Psychology, 10,* 936–941.

Fagerström, K. (1982). A comparison of psychological and pharmacological treatment of smoking cessation. *Journal of Behavioral Medicine, 5,* 343–351.

Fisher, R. A. (1935). *The design of experiments.* Edinburgh: Oliver & Boyd.

Flink, C., Boggiano, A. K., & Barrett, M. (1990). Controlling teaching strategies: Undermining children's self-determination and performance. *Journal of Personality and Social Psychology, 59,* 916–924.

Franklin, K. M., Janoff-Bulman, R., & Roberts, J. E. (1990). Long-term impact of parental divorce on optimism and trust: Changes in general assumptions or narrow beliefs? *Journal of Personality and Social Psychology, 59,* 743–755.

Geller, E. S., Witmer, J. F., & Orebaugh, A. L. (1976). Instructions as a determinant of paper disposal behaviors. *Environment and Behavior, 8,* 417–439.

Goldstein, A. G., Bailis, K., & Chance, J. E. (1983). Do students remember pictures in psychology textbooks? *Teaching of Psychology, 10,* 23–26.

Greenhouse, S. W., & Geisser, S. (1959). On methods in the analysis of profile data. *Psychometrika, 24,* 95–112.

Gross, J. S. (1985). Weight modification and eating disorders in adolescent boys and girls. Unpublished Ph.D. dissertation, University of Vermont, Burlington.

Harper, D., & Wacker, D. P. (1983). The efficiency of the Denver Developmental Screening Test with rural disadvantaged preschool children. *Journal of Pediatric Psychology, 8,* 273–283.

Hays, W. L. (1981). *Statistics* (3rd ed.). New York: Holt, Rinehart and Winston.

Hicks, R. A., & Guista, M. (1982). The energy level of habitual long and short sleepers. *Bulletin of the Psychonomic Society, 19,* 131–132.

Hindley, C. B., Filliozat, A. M., Klackenberg, G., Nicolet-Meister, D., & Sand, E. A. (1966). Differences in age of walking for five European longitudinal samples. *Human Biology, 38,* 364–379.

Holmes, T. H., & Rahe, R. H. (1967). The social readjustment rating scale. *Journal of Psychosomatic Research, 11,* 213.

Holway, A. H., & Boring, E. G. (1940). The moon illusion and the angle of regard. *American Journal of Psychology, 53,* 509–516.

Hosch, H. M., & Cooper, D. S. (1982). Victimization as a determinant of eyewitness accuracy. *Journal of Applied Psychology, 67,* 649–652.

Howell, D. C. (1992). *Statistical methods for Psychology.* (3rd ed.). Belmont, CA: Duxbury Press.

Howell, D. C., & Huessy, H. R. (1985). A fifteen year follow-up of a behavioral history of Attention Deficit Disorder (ADD). *Pediatrics, 76,* 185–190.

Hraba, J., & Grant, G. (1970). Black is beautiful: A re-examination of racial preference and identification. *Journal of Personality and Social Psychology, 16,* 398–402.

Huff, D. (1954). *How to lie with statistics.* New York: W. W. Norton.

Hunt, J. M. (1941). The effects of infant feeding frustration upon adult hoarding behavior. *Journal of Abnormal and Social Psychology, 36,* 338–360.

Huynh, H., & Feldt, L. S. (1976). Estimation of the Box correction for degrees of freedom for sample data in the randomized block and split plot designs. *Journal of Educational Statistics, 1,* 69–82.

Jackson, J. M., & Padgett, V. R. (1982). With a little help from my friend: Social loafing and the Lennon-McCartney songs. *Personality and Social Psychology Bulletin, 8,* 672–677.

Kapp, B., Frysinger, R., Gallagher, M., & Hazelton, J. (1979). Amygdala central nucleus lesions: Effects on heart rate conditioning in the rabbit. *Physiology and Behavior, 23,* 1109–1117.

Kaufman, L., & Rock, I. (1962). The moon illusion, I. *Science, 136,* 953–961.

Kennedy, D., Beard, D., & Carr, W. J. (1982). Differential recognition of the left vs. right side of human faces. *Bulletin of the Psychonomic Society, 20,* 72–73.

Knehr-McDonald, P. (1984). Carelessness: Its relationship to cognitive style and problem-solving strategies. Unpublished Ph.D. dissertation, University of Vermont, Burlington.

Langlois, J. H. & Roggman, L. A. (1990). Attractive faces are only average. *Psychological Science, 1,* 115–121.

Latané, B., & Dabbs, J. M., Jr. (1975). Sex, group size, and helping in three cities. *Sociometry, 38,* 180–194.

Linn, R. T., & Hodge, G. K. (1982). Locus of control in childhood hyperactivity. *Journal of Consulting and Clinical Psychology, 50,* 592–593.

Lobel, M., Dunkel-Schetter, C., & Scrimshaw, C. M. (1992). Prenatal maternal stress and prematurity: A prospective study of disadvantaged women. *Health Psychology, 11, 32.*

Lord, F. M. (1953). On the statistical treatment of football numbers. *American Psychologist, 8,* 750–751.

Lundberg, U. (1983). Note on Type A behavior and cardiovascular responses to challenge in 3–6 year old children. *Journal of Psychosomatic Research, 27,* 39–42.

Malcarne, V., Compas, B. E., Epping, J., & Howell, D. C. (1993). Cognitive factors in adjustment to cancer: Attributions of self-blame and perceptions of control. Unpublished manuscript.

McConaughy, S. H. (1980). Cognitive structures for reading comprehension: Judging the relative importance of ideas in short stories. Unpublished Ph.D. dissertation, University of Vermont, Burlington.

Mireault, G. C. (1990). Parent death in childhood, perceived vulnerability, and adult depression and anxiety. Unpublished M.A. thesis, University of Vermont.

Neter, J., & Wasserman, W. (1974). *Applied linear statistical models.* Homewood, IL: Richard D. Irwin.

Newman, S. E., Olson, M. A., Hall, A. D., & Hornak, R. (1983). Effects of encoding and retrieval contexts on recall. *Bulletin of the Psychonomic Society, 21,* 4–6.

Nurcombe, B., & Fitzhenry-Coor, I. (1979, October). Decision making in the mental health interview: I. An introduction to an education and research program [Paper delivered at the Conference on Problem Solving in Medicine]. Smuggler's Notch, VT.

Nurcombe, B., Howell, D. C., Rauh, V. A., Teti, D. M., Ruoff, P., & Brennan, J. (1984). An intervention program for mothers of low-birthweight infants: Preliminary results. *Journal of the American Academy of Child Psychiatry, 23,* 319–325.

Obrzut, J. E., Hansen, R. L., & Heath, C. P. (1982). The effectiveness of visual information processing training with Hispanic children. *Journal of General Psychology, 107,* 165–174.

Overall, J. E., & Klett, C. J. (1972). *Applied multivariate analysis.* New York: McGraw-Hill.

Payne, S. L. (1982). Job-orientation stereotyping: Is it changing? *Journal of Psychology, 111,* 51–55.

Pliner, P. (1982). The effects of mere exposure on liking for edible substances. *Appetite, 3,* 283–290.

Pugh, M. D. (1983). Contributory fault and rape conviction: Loglinear models for blaming the victim. *Social Psychology Quarterly, 46,* 233–242.

Reynolds, C. R., & Richmond, B. O. (1978). What I think and feel: A revised measure of children's manifest anxiety. *Journal of Abnormal Child Psychology, 6,* 271–280.

Robinson, B. E., Barrett, R. L., & Skeen, P. (1983). Locus of control of unwed adolescent fathers versus adolescent nonfathers. *Perceptual and Motor Skills, 56,* 397–398.

Rogers, R. W., & Prentice-Dunn, S. (1981). Deindividuation and anger-mediated aggression: Unmasking regressive racism. *Journal of Personality and Social Psychology, 41,* 63–73.

Ryan, T., Joiner, B., & Ryan, B. (1985). *Minitab student handbook.* Boston: Duxbury Press.

Saint-Exupery, A. de. (1943). *The Little Prince.* Tr. by K. Woods. New York: Harcourt Brace.

Sgro, J. A., & Weinstock, S. (1963). Effects of delay on subsequent running under immediate reinforcement. *Journal of Experimental Psychology, 66,* 260–263.

Siegel, S. (1975). Evidence from rats that morphine tolerance is a learned response. *Journal of Comparative and Physiological Psychology, 80,* 498–506.

Smith, D. B., & Plant, W. T. (1982). Sex differences in job satisfaction of university professors. *Journal of Applied Psychology, 67,* 249–251.

Spilich, G. J., June, L., & Renner, J. (1992). Cigarette smoking and cognitive performance. *British Journal of Addiction, 87,* 1313–1326.

St. Leger, A. S., Cochrane, A. L., & Moore, F. (1978). The anomaly that wouldn't go away. *Lancet, ii,* 1153.

Sternberg, S. (1966). High speed scanning in human memory. *Science, 153,* 652–654.

Sternglass, E. J., & Bell, S. (1983). Fallout and SAT scores: Evidence for cognitive damage during early infancy. *Phi Delta Kappan, 64,* 539–549.

Stevens, S. S. (1951). Mathematics, measurement, and psychophysics. In S. S. Stevens (Ed.), *Handbook of experimental psychology.* New York: John Wiley.

Supramaniam, S. (1983). Proofreading errors in good and poor readers. *Journal of Experimental Child Psychology, 36,* 68–80.

Sutherland, R. J., & Linggard, R. (1982). Being there: A novel demonstration of latent spatial learning in the rat. *Behavioral and Neural Biology, 36,* 103–107.

Tolman, E. C., Ritchie, B. F., & Kalish, D. (1946). Studies in spatial learning: I. Orientation and the short cut. *Journal of Experimental Psychology, 36,* 13–24.

Tufte, E. R. (1983). *The visual display of quantitative information.* Cheshire, CT: Graphics Press.

Tukey, J. W. (1977). *Exploratory data analysis.* Reading, MA: Addison-Wesley.

U.S. Department of Commerce. (1977). Social indicators, 1976. Washington, D.C.: U.S. Government Printing Office.

U.S. Department of Justice, Bureau of Justice Statistics. (1983). *Prisoners in 1982.* Bulletin NCJ-87933. Washington, D.C.: U.S. Government Printing Office.

Velleman, P., & Hoaglin, D. (1981). *Applications, basics, and computing of exploratory data analysis.* Boston: Duxbury Press.

Verdooren, L. R. (1963). Extended tables of critical values for Wilcoxon's test statistic. *Biometrika, 50,* 177–186.

Vermont Department of Health. (1982). *1981 annual report of vital statistics in Vermont.* Burlington, VT.

Visintainer, M. A., Volpicelli, J. R., & Seligman, M. E. P. (1982). Tumor rejection in rats after inescapable or escapable shock. *Science, 216,* 437–439.

Wagner, B. M., Compas, B. E., & Howell, D. C. (1988). Daily and major life events: A test of an integrative model of psychosocial stress. *American Journal of Community Psychology, 61,* 189–205.

Wainer, H. (1984). How to display data badly. *American Statistician, 38,* 137–147.

Welkowitz, J., Ewen, R., & Cohen, J. (1991). *Introductory statistics for the behavioral sciences (4th ed.).* New York: Academic Press.

Winer, B. J. (1971). *Statistical principles in experimental design (2nd ed.).* New York: McGraw-Hill.

Younger, M. S. (1985). *A first course in linear regression.* Boston: Duxbury Press.

Zuckerman, M., Hodgins, H. S., Zuckerman, A., & Rosenthal, R. (1993). Contemporary issues in the analysis of data. *Psychological Science, 4,* 49–53.

Answers to Selected Exercises

CHAPTER 1

1.3 People who have trouble stopping smoking report being more likely to light a cigarette at a party than when they are when going for a walk.

1.4 The student body would be considered a population when the interest is in being able to make statements about the opinions and the behavior of the university's own students. The entire student body of a university would be considered a sample when the interest is in drawing inferences about all university students in the country.

1.5 It would be a nonrandom sample because not every student in the population has an equal chance of being included in the sample.

1.6 Not all residents of the city are listed in the phone book. Transients, poor people, and especially women and children are underrepresented.

1.8 Average, mean, median, range.

1.9 The mean caloric intake of Americans living on Social Security could be of considerable importance.

1.10 Is the mean weight of a group of 30-year-old women who dieted consistently as teenagers different from the mean weight of a sample of 30-year-old nondieters matched on weight as teenagers?

1.12 Measurement data:
  (a) Nearness-of-approach to a fear-arousing stimulus
  (b) Heart rate during rapid eye movement (REM) sleep
  (c) Score on the Beck Depression Inventory

1.13 A personality construct of authoritarianism could be measured either as a relatively continuous variable (e.g., number of authoritarian items endorsed) or as a three-point classification of authoritarian, neutral, or laissez-faire.

1.14 **(a)** We could be interested in the relationship between cognitive development as measured at age 2 and again at age 18—do subjects who do well at 2 also do well at 18?
  (b) We could be interested in the relationship between the number of times a sub-ject rehearsed a list of irregular French verbs and the number of verbs correctly used on a later test.

1.15 **(a)** Do parents who receive counseling on adolescent problems respond more appropriatcly toward their children than parents who do not receive counseling?
  (b) Do science majors perform better in a course on logic than do social science majors?

1.16 We could add a group that is receiving morphine for the first time. Comparisons against this group would show that we can produce morphine tolerance in the first place.

CHAPTER 2

2.1 **(a)** nominal—hair color
  (b) ordinal—social dominance ordering among a group of children
  (c) interval—the set of dates on which subjects complete an assigned task
  (d) ratio—the number of homework problems completed correctly for an assignment

2.3 It is a poor measure of learning unless we assume that the animal who suddenly went to sleep had forgotten all it ever knew about the task, which is not very likely.

2.4 Speed is probably a much better index of motivation than of learning.

2.5 **(a)** independent variables—good versus poor readers; male versus female
  (b) dependent variables—reading speed; score on a measure of anxiety

2.6 The experiment examined the difference in response to morphine (dependent variable) in novel or familiar contexts (independent variable).

2.8 **(a)** pass-fail on a test item
  (b) number of items correct on a five-item test
  (c) number of convictions for DWI

2.9 **(a)** 9, 10, and 8; **(b)** 77; **(c)** $\Sigma_{i=1}^{10} X$

2.11 **(a)** 5,929,657; **(b)** 7.7; **(c)** average (mean)

2.13 **(a)** 460; **(b)** 4389; **(c)** 2.344

2.14   **(a)** $\Sigma(X + Y) = (10 + 9) + (8 + 9) + \ldots + (7 + 2) = 134 = 77 + 57 = \Sigma X + \Sigma Y$
   (b) $\Sigma XY = 460$; $\Sigma X\Sigma Y = 4389$
   (c) $\Sigma CX = \Sigma 3X = 3(10) + 3(8) + \ldots 3(7) = 231 = 3(77) = C\Sigma X$
   (d) $\Sigma X^2 = 657$; $(\Sigma X)^2 = 5929$

CHAPTER 3

3.1   **(b)**   unimodal and positively skewed

3.3   The problem with making a stem-and-leaf display of the data in Exercise 3.1 is that almost all the values fall on only two leaves if we use the usual 10's digits for stems. The problem is not much better if we double the number of stems. Instead, use the units digits for stems and add a catchall category for high or low values.

3.4   **(a)**   The scores for adults appear to be noticeably smaller.

3.8   It would be bimodal with one peak at 0 and another peak at about one pack (20) per day.

3.11   **(a)**   Mexico has very many young people and very few old people, while Spain has a more even distribution.
   (b)   The difference between males and females is more pronounced at each age in Spain.
   (c)   You can see the high infant mortality rate in Mexico.

3.12   We use HI and LO categories to keep the stem-and-leaf display from straggling off at the ends.

3.15   The figures support the hypothesis that people process information sequentially rather than simultaneously.

3.17   The individual observations all came from the same subject and in that sense are not independent. However, if there is no pattern of improvement or decrement over the course of the experiment, it is probably safe to treat them as if they were independent.

3.18   When these animals lived in stable groups, differences in affiliation made little difference with respect to immunity. When the animals lived in unstable groups, however, affiliation played an important role.

CHAPTER 4

4.1   mode = 18; median = 18; mean = 18.9

4.3   Adults say "and then . . ." about half as often as do children.

4.5   The mean falls above the median.

4.6   1   9   10   15   15

4.7   mean = 21.33; median = 21.

4.11   ADDSC: mean = 52.60, median = 50, mode = 50
GPA: mean = 2.46, median = 2.635, mode = 3.00

4.12   The numerical codes for the levels of SEX and ENGL are arbitrary. The (mean $-$ 1) for SEX would be the proportion of subjects who were female.

4.13   The mode does not depend on the relationships among the points on the scale, whereas the mean and the median do depend on such relationships.

CHAPTER 5

5.1   range = 30; variance = 20.214; s = 4.496

5.3   The two standard deviations are roughly the same, although the range for children is about twice the range for adults.

5.5   The interval $X + 2s_X = 3.39\text{---}17.01$ includes 96% of the scores.

5.8   2.381, 3.809, 1.428, 3.809, 2.857, 4.286, 4.286, 3.333

5.9 -0.893, 0.536, -1.845, 0.536, -0.417, 1.012, 1.012, 0.060

5.14   **(a)**   variance = 0.894; standard deviation = 0.946
   (b)   In computing the GPA we average over four or five courses and can thus balance out an extreme grade in one course with more moderate grades in others.

5.15   The range would not be affected. The standard deviation and the variance would be reduced because we have added a score that does not deviate from the mean.

5.18   Although we usually draw only one sample from the population, we would like to know that the statistics we calculate from that sample are like the statistics we would calculate if we had drawn a different random sample.

5.19   We want an unbiased statistic because we want one that is a fair estimate of the corresponding population parameter, that is, one that does not differ systematically from that population parameter.

5.21   The vertical bars lie at those points that cut off the minimum, the lowest 10%, the lowest

25%, the 50% point, the lowest 75%, the lowest 90%, and the maximum scores. The diamond marks out the mean and a region around the mean that we will later identify as the 95% confidence interval. (The mean is at the tallest point of the diamond.)

CHAPTER 6

6.2 For $X = 2.5$, $z = -0.92$, 18% of the distribution lies below $X = 2.5$.
For $X = 6.2$, $z = 1.35$, 91% of the distribution lies below $X = 6.2$.
For $X = 9$, $z = 3.07$, 99.9% of the distribution lies below $X = 9$.

6.3 **(a)** 68%; **(b)** 50%; **(c)** 84%

6.4 **(a)** $964.875 \leq X \leq 985.125$
(b) $X = 985.125$
(c) $945.6 \leq X \leq 1004.4$

6.5 $z = (950 - 975)/15 = -1.67$; only 4.75% of the time would we expect a count as low as 950, given what we know about the distribution.

6.6 **(b)** 15.87%; **(c)** 30.85%

6.7 The answers to parts (a) and (b) of Exercise 6.6 will be equal when the two distributions have the same standard deviation.

6.8 $z = -1.28$; $X = \bar{X} - 1.28(30) = 111.6$

6.10 **(b)** $z = (62 - 44)/7 = 2.57$. Only 0.51% of the time would we expect to find a result as large as this if the student is conscientiously sampling from a distribution with a mean of 44 and a standard deviation of 7. I suspect that he made up his data.

6.11 Multiply the raw scores by 10/7 to raise the standard deviation to 10. Then add 11.43 points to each new score to bring the mean up to 80.

6.12 **(b)** I suggested that she take the set of scores and empirically (i.e., by counting) determine the point that has 10% of the scores below it. Normal approximations are useful only when you are working with a distribution that is at least roughly normal.

6.13 $z = (600 - 489)/126 = 0.88$; therefore, 81% of the scores fall below this, so 600 represents the 81st percentile.

6.16 The choice of the reference group determines the answer you receive.

6.18 $z = 2.05$; $(X - 50)/10 = 2.05$; $X = 70.5$

CHAPTER 7

7.1 Analytic. A mouse in a maze who is responding at random has a probability of .50 of turning left at a choice point.
Relative frequency. A mouse who has turned left on 700 of the last 1000 trials has a probability of .70 of turning left this time (assuming no trend in the data over trials).
Subjective. "I would give this experiment about a 70% chance of coming up with useful results."

7.2 **(a)** $1/1000 = .001$; **(b)** $2/1000 = .002$; **(c)** $3/1000 = .003$

7.3 **(a)** $1/9 = .111$; **(b)** $(2/10) \times (1/9) = .022$ **(c)** $(1/10) \times (2/9) = .022$; **(d)** .044

7.4 **(b) (c)**, and part of **(d)**

7.5 **(a)**

7.8 $(2/24) \times (3/24) = 6/576 = .010$

7.10 If the difference is reliable (a concept we discuss in Chapter 8), it suggests that the message and the behavior are not independent events.

7.11 the probability that you are 20 years old

7.12 the classification of the visual spectrum into about seven colors

7.14 $10/1000 = .01$

7.15 **(a)** $10/200 = .05$; **(b)** $p = .00$

7.16 $z = (50 - 52.602)/12.422 = -0.21$; $p(z \leq -0.21) = .58$.

7.19 Compare the probability of dropping out of school, ignoring the ADDSC scores, with the conditional probability of dropping out of school *given that* ADDSC in elementary school exceeded some value (e.g., 66).

CHAPTER 8

8.1 I set up the null hypothesis that last night's game was actually an NHL hockey game. On the basis of that hypothesis I expected that each team would earn somewhere between 0 and 6 points. I then looked at the actual points and concluded that they were way out of line with what I would expect if this were an NHL hockey game. I therefore rejected the null hypothesis.

8.2 **(b)** No
(c) I set up the null hypothesis that I was charged correctly. Therefore, I would expect to receive about $1.00 in change,

give or take a quarter or so. The change that I received was in line with that expectation; therefore, I have no basis for rejecting H_0.

8.3 concluding that I had been shortchanged when in fact I had not

8.5 The critical value would be that amount of change below which I would decide that I had been shortchanged. The rejection region would be all amounts of change less than the critical value, that is, all amounts that would lead to rejection of H_0.

8.7 $z = (490 - 650)/50 = -3.2$. The probability that a student drawn at random from those properly admitted would have a GRE score as low as 490 is .0007. I suspect that the fact that his mother was a member of the board of trustees played a role in his admission.

8.8 We are not looking at a random sample of all students who took the GREs. We are looking at a selected sample of high-scoring students.

8.10 I would draw a very large number of samples. For each sample I would calculate the mode, the range, and their ratio (M). I would then plot the resulting values of M.

8.11 M is called a test statistic.

8.13 The alternative hypothesis is that this student was sampled from a population of students whose mean is not equal to 650.

8.14 Sampling error is variability in a statistic from sample to sample that depends on which observations happened to be included in the sample.

8.16 If α were to decrease, β would increase and power would decrease.

CHAPTER 9

9.2 $r = .62$

9.3 $r = .35$

9.7 **(a)** 4.67, 3.33, -4.67

9.8 $r = .99, .71, -.99$; three possible ways: 2 8 6 4, 6 4 2 8, and 6 2 8 4

9.9 **(b)** $r = .74$

9.10 The correlation between I-131 and Verbal = $-.2408$. The correlation between I-131 and Math = $-.5501$. No. The large correlation is with Math SAT and not with Verbal, as reported.

9.13 In computing correlations each data point (state) counts equally, but because some data

points are based on very small numbers of students, these states are overrepresented in the correlations.

9.18 $r_S = .80$

9.20 Yes. The coefficient (r) would still tell you how well a straight line fits, even if you think that a curved line would fit better. Often the fit of a straight line is sufficiently good for our purposes.

9.21 When we say that a correlation coefficient is reliable, we mean that if we drew repeated samples from the same population the correlation coefficients for those samples would be of the same general magnitude. Correlations based on small samples are often unreliable because unusual data points can have an important influence on the correlation coefficient.

CHAPTER 10

10.1 $\hat{Y} = 0.069X + 3.53$

10.2 $s_{Y-\hat{Y}} = 0.5805$

10.3 The incidence of birthweight < 2500 grams would be 8.36.

10.5 $\hat{Y} = 0.475X + 43.16$

10.7 $\hat{Y} = 109.13$

10.10 $\hat{Y} = 1.05X + 17.33$

10.11 A one-unit difference in the SAT Verbal score is associated with a 1.05 difference in the predicted SAT Math score. The intercept has no interpretable meaning. A Verbal score of 0 is not even a legitimate value.

10.14 $\hat{Y} = -0.0426X + 4.699$

10.16 The best estimate of starting salary for faculty is $28,000. For every additional year of service, salary increases by $900 on average. For administrative staff the best estimate of starting salary is $18,000, but every year of additional service increases the salary by an average of $1500. They will be approximately equal after 16.67 years of service.

CHAPTER 11

11.1 **(a)** As the mean temperature increases by 1 degree, the assessed quality of life decreases by 0.01 point. As mean income and per capita expenditures on social services increase by a single unit, the quality of life is judged to increase by 0.05 and 0.003 unit, respectively. The judged quality of life is expected to decrease by 0.01 unit for a one-unit increase in population density. There is no interpretable meaning to the intercept.

(b) 4.92

(c) 3.72

11.2 **(a)** Yes. $F(4,70) = 16.57, p = .000$

(b) $\hat{Y} = 1.66926 + 0.60516*Respon - 0.33399*Numsup + 0.48552*Envir + 0.07023*Yrs$

(c) $R = .6974$

11.3 The only variable to make a significant contribution to predicting Satisfaction is Years of Service.

11.4 Respon and Numsup are fairly highly correlated with other predictors, but Envir, and especially Yrs, are not.

11.5 Years of Service is largely independent of the other predictors, so it brings information to the equation that other predictors do not share. This is not the case with Responsibility.

CHAPTER 12

12.6 **(a)** $z = 3.86; p(z \geq +3.86) = .0002$. We would reject the null hypothesis that these scores were drawn from a population with a mean of 100.

(b) You would not reject the null hypothesis if you had been using a one-tailed test that $\mu < 500$.

(c) Either North Dakota's students greatly outscore the average American student or the mean of the population of students taking the exam is not 500.

12.7 It is not a random sample. In addition we have no definition of what is meant by "a terrible state" nor whether SAT scores measure it.

12.9 The sample sizes are considerably different.

12.10 $t = 2.18$ on 5700 df. We can reject H_0.

12.12 No, because we want to reject H_0 whenever $\mu \neq 500$. We cannot wait until we see the data and then decide which tail to use.

12.13 In this case it is not an important finding because the difference is so small. Even if $\mu = 503$ instead of 500, it makes no particular difference to anyone—it hardly qualifies as a sign of major improvement in GRE scores, especially because it is based on a selected sample.

12.14 $t = -1.47$. We cannot reject H_0.

12.16 $512.3 \leq \mu \leq 537.7$

12.18 In Exercise 10.16 we knew σ but not s and could solve for confidence limits using the population standard deviation. In Exercise 10.17 we knew s, although nothing was said about σ, and we solved for the confidence limits using s. In both cases the critical value of t or z was $+1.96$, but only because there were so many df for t (5700).

12.19 $\bar{X} = 101.82, s = 12.68, t = 0.82$ on 32 df. We will not reject H_0.

12.21 First we need to take a table of random numbers with a known variance. We would then draw many samples of five scores each. For each sample we would calculate the sample variance. When we had obtained several thousand sample variances, we would plot their frequency distribution.

CHAPTER 13

13.1 $t = 2.23$ on 14 df. Reject H_0 and conclude that physical guidance has reduced the amount of assistance required.

13.2 The physical guidance condition came second for all subjects, and improvement may reflect just the passage of time or delayed effects of imitation.

13.4 $0.068 \leq \mu \leq 3.666$

13.5 $t = 0.45$. We cannot reject H_0.

13.7 The data in Exercise 13.5 suggest that the program was not successful. The data in Exercise 13.6 on the other hand would suggest that it may have been successful for some of the smokers but led other smokers to smoke even more. These two effects largely cancel each other out in the combined data.

13.9 $t = 1.39$ on 19 df. Do not reject H_0.

13.10 To answer this, we need to know the critical value of t, which in turn requires knowing df, which requires knowing N. But we can use 2.00 as a critical value as a rough approximation. Then the required $N = [(2.00 \times 2.870)/0.333]^2 = 298$.

13.12 As the correlation between the two variables increases, the t will increase as well.

CHAPTER 14

14.1 $t = 1.44$ on 28 df. Do not reject H_0.

14.2 There is quite a substantial variance within each group.

14.3 By measuring the same subject under both

conditions (as in Chapter 13), we were able to eliminate subject-to-subject variability.

14.4 $t = 1.60$ on 16 df. Do not reject H_0.

14.6 $t = 4.54$ on 16 df. Reject H_0.

14.8 The differential dropout rate may be very important. Only half as many people were able to complete Program A as completed Program B.

14.9 $t = 0.59$ on 15 df. Do not reject H_0.

14.10 $-3.03 \leq (\mu_1 - \mu_2) \leq 5.34$

14.13 $t = 3.77$ on 86 df. Reject H_0.

14.14 The ADDSC score can be used to create groups who later turn out to differ on GPA. In other words ADDSC is a predictor of ninth-grade performance.

14.15 $t = -2.36$ on 8 df. Reject H_0.

14.17 If the two sample sizes are equal, the pooled and unpooled estimates would be the same.

14.19 Perfectly legitimate and reasonable transformations of data can produce different results. It is important to consider seriously the nature of the dependent variable before deciding on a measure to use.

CHAPTER 15

15.1 **(a)** 0.25; **(b)** 2.50; **(c)** 0.71

15.3 $N = 98, 125, 169$

15.4 Power = .965

15.6 **(a)** $N = 15.21 \approx 16$; **(b)** $N = 31.36 \approx 32$

15.8 Power = .31

15.10 **(a)** Power = .22
(b) $t = -1.19$
(c) t is numerically equal to δ although t is calculated from statistics and δ is calculated from parameters.

15.11 The first one. Because he found a significant difference with an experiment having relatively little power, he must have been examining a fairly large effect.

15.14 He should use the Dropout group. (You can let σ be any value as long as it is the same for both calculations. Then calculate δ for each situation.)

15.15

Effect Size	γ	One-Sample t	Two-Sample t
Small	.20	289	1156
Medium	.50	47	186
Large	.80	19	74

15.17 not if the assumptions underlying the test are met

15.18 Power would be equal to the probability of a Type II error when $\mu_1 = \mu \pm 1.645\sigma$.

CHAPTER 16

16.1

Source	df	SS	MS	F
Groups	2	2100.000	1050.000	40.13*
Error	15	392.500	26.167	
Total	17	2492.500		

*$p < .05$

16.2 $t = 1.69$: not significant; $t = 6.77$: reject H_0.

16.4 **(a)**

Source	df	SS	MS	F
Groups	3	655.143	218.381	10.78*
Error	24	486.286	20.262	
Total	27	1141.429		

*$p < .05$

(b)

Source	df	SS	MS	F
Groups	1	51.572	51.572	1.23 n.s.
Error	26	1089.857	41.918	
Total	27	1141.429		

n.s. = not significant
This question examines differences due to Location, ignoring the effect of Brand.

16.6 **(a)**

Source	df	SS	MS	F
Groups	1	1.260	1.260	0.87 n.s.
Error	10	14.532	1.453	
Total	11	15.792		

n.s. = not significant

(b) t (unpooled) $= -0.883 = \sqrt{0.780}$
(c) t (pooled) $= -0.931 = \sqrt{0.867}$
(d) the pooled t

16.7 $\eta^2 = 0.196$; $\omega^2 = 0.087$

16.8 (a)

Source	df	SS	MS	F
Groups	2	826.867	413.433	9.64*
Error	27	1157.662	42.877	
Total	29	1984.529		

*p < .05

16.10 Group 1 versus Group 2: $t = 2.77$; reject H_0. Group 1 versus Group 3: $t = -1.57$; do not reject H_0.

16.11 I have somewhat more faith because it is a significant result produced by a less powerful experiment.

16.14

Source	df	SS	MS	F
Groups	2	22.500	11.250	22.74*
Error	85	42.059	0.495	
Total	87	64.559		

*p < .05

16.15 $\eta^2 = 0.35$; $\omega^2 = 0.33$

16.18 Group 1 versus Group 2: $F = 2.856$; do not reject H_0. Group 2 versus Group 3: $F = 45.874$; reject H_0. In each case the critical value of F is 7.36.

16.21

Source	df	SS	MS	F
Groups	2	2.178	1.089	0.05 n.s.
Error	42	894.133	21.289	
Total	44	896.311		

n.s. = not significant

16.24

Source	df	SS	MS	F
Groups	2	437.644	218.822	9.26*
Error	42	992.667	23.635	
Total	44	1430.311		

*p < .05

CHAPTER 17

17.1

Source	df	SS	MS	F
Pay	1	3.828	3.828	10.43*
Sex	1	0.078	0.078	<1
Pay × Sex	1	3.403	3.403	9.27*
Error	16	5.875	0.367	
Total	19	13.184		

*p < .05

17.2

Source	df	SS	MS	F
Parity	1	28.9	28.9	6.08*
Weight	1	14.4	14.4	3.03*
P × W	1	0.1	0.1	<1 n.s.
Error	36	171.0	4.75	
Total	39	214.4		

*p < .05; n.s. = not significant

17.3 no, because 50% of the population of primiparous mothers do not give birth to LBW infants

17.4 $F = 1.78$; not significant

17.7 $t = 3.03$ on 36 df; $t = 3.00$ on 36 df; both are significant.

17.10

Source	df	SS	MS	F
Brand	1	567.000	567.000	27.98*
Location	1	51.571	51.571	2.55 n.s.
Brand × Location	1	36.571	36.571	1.80 n.s.
Error	24	486.286	20.260	
Total	27	1141.429		

*p < .05; n.s. = not significant

There is a significant effect for Brand but not for Location or the Interaction.

17.11 The Location effect in the one-way and the Location effect in the two-way have the same df, SS, and MS. However, the F is different because when we combine the groups into larger groups we inflated the error term. (*Note:* The one-way on four groups and the 2 × 2 produce the same error term.)

17.12 $\eta^2_{Educ} = .10; \omega^2_{Educ} = .09$
$\eta^2_{Group} = .19; \omega^2_{Group} = .15$
$\eta^2_{E \times G} = .03; \omega^2_{E \times G} = .00$

17.18

Source	df	SS	MS	F
Group	2	354.548	177.274	1.64
Task	2	28661.526	14330.763	132.895*
Group × Task	4	2728.652	682.163	6.326*
Error	126	13587.200	107.835	
Total	134	45331.926		

*$p < .05$

In this particular case the interaction is of more interest than the main effects. The interaction shows us that in the pattern recognition task, which requires low levels of information processing, there are no differences between groups (we saw this in Exercise 16.21). But in the comprehension (Exercise 16.22) and driving simulation (Exercise 16.24) tasks, which require greater levels of processing, subjects in the Active Smoker group perform much more poorly than subjects in the other two groups.

CHAPTER 18 *Repeated Measures.*

18.1

Source	df	SS	MS	F
Subjects	7	189,666.67		
Sessions	2	1808.33	904.165	3.66 n.s.
Error	14	3458.33	247.024	
Total	23	194,933.33		

n.s. = not significant

There is no significant difference among the session totals.

18.3

Source	df	SS	MS	F
Subjects	9	60.000		
Time	2	27.467	13.735	5.03*
Error	18	49.200	2.733	
Total	29	136.667		

*$p < .05$

There were significant changes in self-sufficiency over the course of the experiment.

18.4 Comparison of Baseline with Training: $t = -2.98$; reject H_0; performance improved with training. Comparison of Baseline with Follow-up: $t = -0.54$; do not reject H_0; after a Follow-up period, performance was not significantly better than it was during Baseline.

18.10 $F = 0.1536$; $t = -0.3919 = \sqrt{F}$

CHAPTER 19

19.1 $\chi^2 = 11.33$ on 2 df. Reject H_0 and conclude that students do not enroll at random.

19.2 We cannot tell if students chose different sections because of the instructor or because of the times at which the sections are taught— Instructor and Time are confounded. We would at least have to offer the sections at the same time.

19.3 $\chi^2 = 2.4$ on 4 df. We cannot reject the H_0 that my daughter's sorting behavior is in line with my theory.

19.4 It generalizes only to the population of data that could be generated by my daughter. In other words we have only a sample of *her* behavior. We do not have a random sample of the behavior of people in general.

19.5 $\chi^2 = 29.35$ on 1 df. We can reject the H_0 that the children chose dolls at random (at least with respect to color).

19.7 $\chi^2 = 34.18$ on 1 df. Reject the H_0 and conclude that the distribution of choices between black and white dolls was different in the two studies. Choice is not independent of Study. We are no longer asking whether one color of doll is preferred over the other color, but whether the pattern of preference is constant across studies. In analysis of variance terms we are dealing with an interaction.

19.10 $\chi^2 = 5.38$ on 1 df. Reject H_0 and conclude that achievement level during high school varies as a function of performance during elementary school.

19.15 $\chi^2 = 0.658$. Do not reject H_0.

19.16 As sample sizes increase, with the same percentages in the cells, the power of the test increases.

19.18 Although there may be no significant differences between the percentages, the fact that 45% of the students feel that the course needs major improvements is an important result.

19.21 $\chi^2 = 11.95$. Reject H_0 and conclude that accuracy varies by rank. In fact students numerically outperformed all other groups.

curacy varies by rank. In fact students numerically outperformed all other groups.

CHAPTER 20

20.1 (a) $W_S = 23$; $W_{.025} = 27$

(b) I would reject H_0 and conclude that older children include more inferences in their summaries.

20.2 (a) $W_S = 53$; $W_{.025} = 68$

(b) Reject H_0 and conclude that subjects in the Lesion group take longer to learn the task, as the theory predicted.

20.3 $z = -3.15$; reject H_0.

20.5 (a) $T = 8.5$; $T_{.025} = 8$. Do not reject H_0.

(b) We cannot conclude that we have evidence supporting the hypothesis that there is a reliable increase in hypothesis generation and testing over time. (Here is a case in which alternative methods of breaking ties could lead to different conclusions.)

20.8 $z = -2.20$, which agrees with our earlier conclusion.

20.9 The difference between the pairs is heavily dependent on the score for the firstborn.

20.11 The Wilcoxon matched-pairs signed-ranks test tests the null hypothesis that paired scores were drawn from identical populations or from symmetric populations with the same mean (and median). The corresponding t test tests the null hypothesis that the paired scores were drawn from populations with the same mean and assumes normality.

20.12 The nature of the scale is important for the interpretation of the results but not for the choice of a statistical test on the actual numbers.

20.14 $H = 5.124$. Do not reject H_0.

20.16 $\chi^2 = 9.042$. Reject H_0—the truancy rate improved.

20.17 It eliminates the influence of individual differences (differences in overall level of truancy from one person to another).

20.20 $\chi^2 = 9.00$. We can reject the null hypothesis and conclude that people don't like tea made with used tea bags.

CHAPTER 21

21.1 This study involves straight descriptive statistics, probably including boxplots of readability scores for items on each test.

21.3 They would use Pearson's r to correlate Denver test scores and scores on individually administered intellectual measures. The question might be taken to imply that some children's scores were based on one measure of intelligence and the rest of the children's scores were based on a different measure. In this case you could sort the children into groups based on the measure used and compute correlations for each group.

21.4 They could run a t test for two independent groups to compare the two groups. They could then obtain the correlation between the percent correct score and the reported level of use of study aids. (You should recall that with two groups a t test and a one-way analysis of variance are equivalent tests.)

21.6 This is a 2×3 analysis of variance (Type of Cue during Learning × Type of Cue during Recall).

21.7 This is a one-way analysis of variance with three groups. They could also use protected t tests to compare individual groups if necessary.

21.9 He should run three separate t tests for two independent groups.

21.10 This is a more complex repeated-measures analysis of variance than the one we considered in Chapter 18. It is a 2×2 factorial design with Good Readers versus Poor Readers and Easy Passages versus Difficult Passages as the factors. Readers is a between-subject variable (different people are in the two groups) and Passages is a within-subject variable (each Reader read both kinds of Passages).

21.12 They should compare the two groups on locus of control scores, and maybe on Peabody scores, using t tests for independent samples. They could also correlate Nowicki-Strickland and Peabody using Pearson's r.

21.13 They could use a one-way analysis of variance on the MFFT score for the second administration. They should probably also run it on the scores for the first administration to check the experimental hypothesis that the groups started out together. (A more complex repeated-measures design also would be suitable [see Exercise 21.7], but I'd be inclined to stick with the two one-way analyses because of their ease of interpretation.)

21.14 This is a simple repeated-measures analysis of variance. The corresponding distribution-

(b) We don't know whether the nicotine in the gum had any effect. It might be that having any kind of gum to chew was the controlling factor.

21.17 She could first find the mean rank assigned to each of the 10 characteristics (for each sex, target, and year; for self and opposite sex). Because the raw data were originally ranks, I probably would be inclined to rank the mean values. She could then calculate Spearman's r's between males and females for each year or between respondent within each year. The correlations would be obtained across the 10 pairs of scores (one pair per characteristic).

21.18 They should use a t test for two related samples. If they don't want to use a parametric test, they should use the Wilcoxon matched-pairs signed-ranks test.

21.19 They should use a Mann-Whitney test.

21.20 They should use a t test for related samples—the samples are related because Smith and Plant formed matched pairs.

21.21 They should begin with a 2×3 chi-square test for the contingency table formed by Group Membership and Correct versus Incorrect identification. They could then follow this up with a one-way analysis of variance on confidence scores. Assuming that the F is significant, they could follow this up with a protected t test, comparing the two "theft" conditions.

21.22 This is a situation for a chi-square goodness-of-fit test.

21.24 This is another complex repeated-measures analysis of variance. The comparison of recall of the two lists (one learned before administration of the drug and the other learned after) is a repeated measurement because the same subjects are involved. The comparison of the drug-versus-saline groups is a between-subjects effect because the groups involve different subjects.

21.25 This is a t test for two independent groups.

21.26 They could use the Kruskal-Wallis test to compare the three groups and, if that was significant, use the Mann-Whitney test the way they would otherwise have used a protected t test.

Index

Power

Effect Size (One Sample)	$\gamma = (\mu_1 - \mu_0)/\sigma$
Effect Size (Two Sample)	$\gamma = (\mu_1 - \mu_2)/\sigma$
Effect Size (Correlation)	$\gamma = \rho_1 - \rho_0$
Delta (One-Sample t)	$\delta = \gamma \sqrt{N}$
Delta (Two-Sample t)	$\delta = \gamma \sqrt{\dfrac{N}{2}}$
Delta (Correlation)	$\delta = \gamma \sqrt{N - 1}$

Correlation and Regression

Sums of Squares
$$SS_X = \Sigma X^2 - \frac{(\Sigma X)^2}{N}$$

Sum of Products
$$SP_{XY} = \Sigma XY - \frac{\Sigma X \Sigma Y}{N}$$

Covariance
$$\text{cov}_{XY} = \frac{\Sigma XY - \dfrac{\Sigma X \Sigma Y}{N}}{N - 1} = \frac{SP_{XY}}{N - 1}$$

Correlation (Pearson)
$$r = \frac{\text{cov}_{XY}}{s_X s_Y} = \frac{SP_{XY}}{\sqrt{SS_X SS_Y}}$$
$$= \frac{N \Sigma XY - \Sigma X \Sigma Y}{\sqrt{[N \Sigma X^2 - (\Sigma X)^2][N \Sigma Y^2 - (\Sigma Y)^2]}}$$

Slope
$$b = \frac{\text{cov}_{XY}}{s_X^2} = \frac{SP_{XY}}{SS_X}$$

Intercept
$$a = \frac{\Sigma Y - b \Sigma X}{N} = \bar{Y} - b\bar{X}$$

Standard Error of Estimate
$$s_{Y-\hat{Y}} = \sqrt{\frac{\Sigma (Y - \hat{Y})^2}{N - 2}} = \sqrt{\frac{SS_{error}}{N - 2}}$$
$$= s_Y \sqrt{(1 - r^2) \frac{N - 1}{N - 2}}$$

SS_Y
$$\Sigma Y^2 - \frac{(\Sigma Y)^2}{N}$$

$SS_{\hat{Y}}$
$$\Sigma \hat{Y}^2 - \frac{(\Sigma \hat{Y})^2}{N}$$

$SS_{Y-\hat{Y}}$
$$SS_Y - SS_{\hat{Y}} = SS_{error}$$

SS_{error}
$$SS_Y(1 - r^2)$$